Human Resource Management in a Business Context

JOHN KEW AND JOHN STREDWICK

The Chartered Institute of Personnel and Development is the leading
publisher of books and reports for personnel and training professionals,
students, and all those concerned with the effective management and
development of people at work. For details of all our titles, please contact
the publishing department:
tel: 020 8612 6204
e-mail: publish@cipd.co.uk
The catalogue of all CIPD titles can be viewed on the CIPD website:
www.cipd.co.uk/bookstore

Human Resource Management in a Business Context

JOHN KEW AND JOHN STREDWICK

Chartered Institute of Personnel and Development

Published by the Chartered Institute of Personnel and Development,
151, The Broadway, London, SW19 1JQ

This edition first published 2010
© Chartered Institute of Personnel and Development, 2010

Typeset by Fakenham Photosetting Ltd, Norfolk
Printed in Spain by Graphycems

British Library Cataloguing in Publication Data
A catalogue of this publication is available from the British Library

ISBN 978 1 84398 252 4

The views expressed in this publication are the authors' own and may not necessarily
reflect those of the CIPD.

Chartered Institute of Personnel and Development,
CIPD House, 151, The Broadway, London, SW19 1JQ

Tel: 020 8612 6200

E-mail: cipd@cipd.co.uk Website: www.cipd.co.uk

Incorporated by Royal Charter. Registered Charity No. 1079797

Contents

Preface

It has been accepted for many years that human resource management (HRM) does not operate in a vacuum. To be effective, it needs to be deeply embedded in the business environment of the organisation. The organisation's business strategy should both react to changes in the environment and identify future changes that provide opportunities for operational success in a harshly competitive world, and it is essential that HR contributes to this.

The worldwide interest in business theory and practice continues to grow at an extraordinary pace, fuelled by the burgeoning power and influence of Far Eastern economies and especially by the growth of China. An understanding of the business environment continues to be vital for all business and HR students who wish to gain a fuller understanding of both the context in which business decisions are taken and the major influences underpinning those decisions. As the context becomes more turbulent and unpredictable, the more important it becomes to grasp the complexity of the many issues presented and the strategic options that can be followed.

Human Resource Managment in a Business Context includes:

- up-to-date information on crucial political, economic and legal areas, including the European Union, international institutions and regulatory developments. Wide coverage is given to the causes and implications of the recent world financial crisis and the swiftly changing demographic patterns

- a chapter dealing with the internal business environment that identifies a variety of management issues and evaluates the forces shaping the HRM agenda in response to these issues, including a debate on the best-practice/best-fit debate.

This publication follows closely the new CIPD module HRM in Context, but is suitable for students at all levels whose syllabus includes a module in business environment, as it covers all the standard subjects normally included in such modules. The emphasis is very much on developing the knowledge and understanding of students, while the main aim has been to make the text accessible and encourage students to follow up key issues by linking the text with up-to-date cases, activities and associated reading.

The distinctive feature of this book is the large number of practical activities and case studies which apply the theory to real-life situations. A large number of case studies are included, and there is a seminar activity for each chapter, as well as a number of self-assessment questions.

A summary of the book's contents is as follows:

Chapter 1

This chapter sets the scene for the whole book by considering the interaction between the environment, the organisation, HR and strategy. We explore models of environmental analysis, models of organisational design, and models of HR strategy.

Chapter 2

Chapter 2 begins by summarising the development of management theory and examining the issues involved in management power, authority and legitimacy. This is followed by an examination of the contemporary analysis of HR models and roles and the key issues facing HR practitioners. Specific consideration is given to the role of HR in areas such as quality assurance and customer care.

Chapter 3

This chapter begins with an analysis of supply and demand, followed by a consideration of market structures, including Michael Porter's Five Forces model. We then move on to the application of microeconomic theory, the working of the labour market, and a consideration of changes in the industrial and employment structure of the UK.

Chapter 4

In this chapter we analyse the evolution of government policy in social, economic and industrial fields, and the impact of government policy on organisations. As developments in the UK are heavily influenced by the actions of the EU, we are concerned with both UK and EU policy. We start with formal legislative procedures in the UK and the EU, and then go on to consider informal influences on the evolution of policy. We then explore recent developments in policy in the UK.

Chapter 5

Chapter 5 examines a wide range of legal and regulatory aspects, starting with an essential summary of the UK legal system and the way that the regulation has developed in the fields of employment, health and safety, consumer and commercial law. The impact of regulation on particular sectors is discussed and the direction of regulation is debated, especially in relation to regulation of the financial sector.

Chapter 6

Since the end of the Second World War, the world economy has become more and more integrated. Partly this has been a deliberate, planned development. The International Monetary Fund, the World Bank and the General Agreement on Tariffs and Trade were set up to regulate the world economy, and to ensure that the world did not suffer from a recurrence of the Great Depression of the 1930s.

The European Economic Community, the predecessor of the EU, was set up partly to ensure that France and Germany could never again go to war with each other. Other developments were only made possible as a result of technological developments in communication and transport which enabled the growth of globalisation. We examine the impact of the EU and globalisation on HR practice in the UK.

Chapter 7

Chapter 7 summarises the startling changes in demography in recent years both in the UK and worldwide, discussing the major implications of an ageing population in the advanced economies and a still rapidly rising population growth in the developing countries. There is a debate about the natural flow of migrants from one grouping to the other. The influence on markets for goods and services and the challenges and opportunities in the employment field are considered in detail, together with government initiatives in key areas, such as pensions and migration. This is followed by a focus on the major social trends and attitudes alongside the changing social structure. The causes of major social problems, such as the increase in criminal behaviour, are debated and the implications for employment and labour markets are examined. How organisations can react to the changes and the options available are considered.

Chapter 8

This chapter presents an analysis on technological change and its substantial influence on the business environment, especially in the fields of information and communication technology. The opportunities in the labour markets that technology offers, such as teleworking and online recruitment, are discussed together with the benefits and difficulties associated with such techniques. The reasons why there is considerable resistance to technology in certain quarters are examined.

Chapter 9

This chapter examines the nature of ethics, and different approaches which can be taken to ethical problems. It discusses professional and business ethics, stakeholder theory, values and codes of ethics. The second half of the chapter analyses corporate governance, corporate social responsibility (CSR) and sustainability, the role of businesses, HR and the government in promoting CSR, and the extent of compatibility between CSR and profit.

Chapter 10

This chapter analyses the nature of strategic management and identifies different models of strategy. It looks at the stages of strategic decision-making – analysis, choice and implementation – and explores the interactions between HR and strategy. The last part of the chapter concentrates on the nature and practice of change management.

Chapter 11

This final chapter applies the themes explored earlier in the book to a series of activities based within one organisation: the National Health Service. The NHS has been chosen because it is large, complex, subject to a great number of pressures, and familiar – and important – to us all.

We would like to acknowledge the help and encouragement we have received from colleagues and friends in writing this new text. A special word of thanks goes to Rod Smith, a long-standing colleague at Bedfordshire University, for his contribution to Chapter 2. Continuing thanks are extended to our families for their encouragement, support and forbearance over an extended period.

Human Resource Management in Context

The content of this CIPD module is covered as follows:

Number	Learning outcome	*Human Resource Management in a Business Context* chapters
Understand, analyse and critically evaluate:		
1	Contemporary organisations and their principal environments	**Chapter 1 – Human Resource Management in Context** **Chapter 9 – Ethics, Social Responsibility and Sustainability**
2	The managerial and business environment within which HR professionals work	**Chapter 2 – The Managerial Context of Human Resources**
3	How organisational and HR strategies are shaped by and developed in response to internal and external environmental factors	**Chapter 10 – Strategic Management**
4	The market and competitive environments of organisations and how organisational leaders and the HR function respond to them	**Chapter 3 – The Competitive Environment** **Chapter 4 – Government Policy**
5	Globalisation and international forces and how they shape and impact on organisational and HR strategies and HR practices	**Chapter 6 – The World Economy**
6	Demographic, social and technological trends and how they shape and impact on organisational and HR strategies and HR practices	**Chapter 7 – Demographic and Social Trends** **Chapter 8 – Technology**
7	Government policy and legal regulation and how these shape and impact on organisational and HR strategies and HR practices	**Chapter 4 – Government Policy** **Chapter 5 – Regulation**

Walkthrough of textbook features and online resources

LEARNING OUTCOMES

When you have completed this chapter you should be able to:

- understand the essential features of the UK legal system, including the sources and types of law and the courts system, including tribunals
- analyse the significance of existing and new regulation for particular sectors and organisations and discuss the type and nature of responses to the regulation
- identify the nature of regulation in respect of contract, consumer and competition law and the implications for stakeholders to whom the law applies

LEARNING OUTCOMES

At the beginning of each chapter a bulleted set of learning outcomes summarises what you can expect to learn from the chapter, helping you to track your learning.

ACTIVITY 8.3 COMPETITIVE ADVANTAGE

It is evident that some forms of technological development provide organisations with a competitive advantage. One example is the invention by the St Helens glassmaker Pilkingtons of the float glass process in the 1950s. This brought huge competitive advantages in both the quality of the sheet glass and the productivity levels. Apple's marketing of iTunes, where it is impossible for songs bought to be played on competitor's equipment, allowed Apple to capture 80 per cent of the US and UK market in the first two years and gave it huge bargaining power with the major record companies.

Think of a further three examples of this process and explain why such an advantage was gained in this way.

REFLECTIVE ACTIVITIES

Questions and activities throughout the text encourage you to reflect on what you have learnt and to apply your knowledge and skills in practice.

CASE STUDY 6.5 RETAIL GLOBALISATION IN THAILAND

Retailers in the developed world are increasingly facing saturated markets. Companies like Tesco and Wal-Mart already dominate their home markets, and prospects for further growth are limited. An obvious solution is to expand overseas.

However, retailing is much less globalised than other major industries. Of the world's top 250 retailers in 2006, 104 have no international operations at all. The most globalised retailer, the French supermarket Tesco and Boots in Thailand provide some clues.

To most people in the West, Thailand is little more than an exotic holiday location, but it is actually a significant player on the world stage, and is one of the 20 biggest world economies. Its population is 64 million, and its GDP per head (on a purchasing power parity basis) is slightly higher than that of Brazil or Turkey. The Thai economy on a purchasing power parity basis is one-third

CASE STUDIES

A number of case studies from different sectors and countries will help you to place the concepts discussed into a real-life context.

KEY LEARNING POINTS

- Three main approaches can be taken to ethics, and these lead to a larger number of ethical guidelines. The most commonly used of these are the golden rule, the disclosure rule and the intuition ethic.
- All managers face ethical dilemmas on a daily basis in their work; professionals have an ethical responsibility both to their organisation and to impartial professional integrity.
- There is a considerable argument over whether a separate business ethic exists.
- Stakeholder theory holds that organisations have responsibilities to a wide range of stakeholders.

- the organisation's culture, do not guarantee ethical behaviour.
- Corporate governance is concerned with issues of conflict of interest and accountability.
- CSR is the way in which an organisation expresses its values through its behaviour towards stakeholders.
- Sustainability or sustainable development is concerned with safeguarding the environment for future generations. Risk management is an important element of a sustainability strategy.
- HR and the government have key roles to play in promoting CSR and sustainability.

KEY LEARNING POINTS

At the end of each chapter, the key learning points are designed to consolidate your learning.

QUESTIONS

1. In what ways does technology offer improved marketing opportunities?

2. Name five difficulties associated with the employment of teleworkers.

3. Provide four examples of how technology helps HR administration and management become more efficient.

6. Provide four examples of how technology can provide difficulties in the employment setting, as well as benefits.

7. What are the four main cycles of K-waves?

8. Give four examples of the use of technology in the recruitment and selection process.

QUESTIONS

These review questions are aimed at reinforcing what you have learnt in the chapter.

EXPLORE FURTHER

Further Reading

Books on the EU tend to be dry and fact-ridden, but two which are relatively readable are:

- Nugent, N. (2006) *The Government and Politics of the European Union*. 6th ed. Basingstoke: Palgrave Macmillan.

- Cini, M. (ed.) (2007) *European Union Politics*. 2nd ed. Oxford: OUP.

Globalisation:

- Micklethwait, J. and wooldridge, A. (2000) *A Future Perfect: The Challenge and Hidden Promise of*

Truth about Globalisation. London: Abacus.

- Stiglitz, J. (2003) *Globalization and its Discontents*. London: Penguin. (Fiercely critical of the role of the IMF.)

For both the EU and globalisation, the way to keep up to date is read good quality newspapers regularly. The same general advice applies as in Chapter 2 – make sure you attain a balance of left- and right-wing views.

Websites

The BBC news website (www.bbc.

EXPLORE FURTHER

Explore further boxes contain suggestions for further reading and useful websites, encouraging you to delve further into areas of particular interest.

SEMINAR ACTIVITY

ECONOMIC DEVELOPMENT IN INDIA AND CHINA

Between 1985 and 1995, GNP growth in the developing world averaged 6 per cent a year, more than twice that of the developed world (World Bank 2000). This suggests that the developing world will soon catch up with the developed world. Unfortunately, this hopeful forecast ignores two key factors. One is the rapid rate of population growth in the developing world. When this is stripped out and growth converted to GNP per head, the growth rate per head in the developing world falls to 3.8 per cent, while that of the developed world falls to 2.1 per cent.

Secondly, the developing country figures are distorted by the outstanding success of the two most populous countries, India and China. In the period 1985–95, India's GNP per head

10 per cent or more in China, and 8 per cent in India.

China's success has been particularly remarkable. It took England 58 years to double its GDP after 1780, the US 47 years from 1839, Japan 34 years from 1885, and South Korea 11 years from 1966 (Meredith 2007). It took China nine years from 1978. It then doubled again by 1996, and doubled yet again by 2006 (Hutton 2007).

Why have India and China done so well? To some extent both countries are returning to their historic position in the world economy. At the time of the Roman Empire, China had 26 per cent of the world's economy, and India 33 per cent. Even by 1820, China had 33 per cent, India 16 per cent (compared with western Europe at 24 per cent, and the US at 2 per cent) (Smith 2007a). It was only in the nineteenth century that the Indian and Chinese economies collapsed. China's GDP per head in

SEMINAR ACTIVITIES

Each chapter ends with a longer activity, suitable for use in seminars, with questions.

ONLINE RESOURCES FOR TUTORS

Visit **www.cipd.co.uk/tss**

- Lecturer's Guide – practical advice on teaching the HRM in Context module using this text

- PowerPoint slides – build and deliver your course around these ready-made lectures, ensuring complete coverage of the module

- Additional case studies – for you to use with students in seminars or lectures

CHAPTER 1

Human Resource Management in Context

LEARNING OUTCOMES

By the end of this chapter, you should be able to understand, explain and critically evaluate:

- the distinction between the general and the task environment
- the relationships between the environment, organisations and strategy
- the STEEPLE model of environmental analysis
- the difference between placid, dynamic and turbulent environments, and their impact on organisations
- the identification of key environmental factors
- the use of SWOT analysis
- models of organisational structure – bureaucracy, divisionalisation, matrix organisations, networks and virtual organisations
- the use and limitations of strategic alliances
- the advantages and disadvantages of HR outsourcing and shared service centres
- connections between the environment, strategy, organisational design and HR
- the E-V-R congruence model
- links between competitive strategy models and HR practices
- the Miles and Snow classification of environmental responses, and its impact on HR practices
- stakeholder analysis.

INTRODUCTION

This chapter sets the scene for the whole book – the interaction between the environment, the organisation, HR and strategy. We will explore models of environmental analysis, organisational design and HR strategy.

VIETNAM AND IRAQ

In the early 1960s, the US intervened in the civil war in Vietnam. The North Vietnamese, under the political leadership of Ho Chi Minh and the military leadership of Vo Nguyen Giap, had driven the French colonial government out of Vietnam in the 1950s, and the country had been divided in two: North Vietnam, under communist control; and South Vietnam, with a pro-western government. The Northerners and their South Vietnamese communist allies, the Vietcong, had started a guerrilla civil war in the south against the South Vietnamese government.

The Americans had overwhelming military superiority, and won every pitched battle between the two sides, including the North's biggest attack, the Tet Offensive in 1968, when Vietcong soldiers infiltrated the South Vietnamese capital, Saigon, and even penetrated the US embassy.

Even so, in the end it was the North Vietnamese and the Vietcong who won the war. The Americans lost over 50,000 dead (compared with more than a million Vietnamese dead), and in 1975 they finally pulled out of Saigon. The next day, 30 April 1975, the North Vietnamese army took the presidential palace in Saigon, and the unified communist republic of Vietnam was born.

Why did the Americans lose? Firstly, The North Vietnamese understood that ultimately the war was political, not military. If they could pin down the Americans for long enough, public opinion in the US would turn against the war and the loss of American life, and political pressure at home would force the Americans to pull out. Ho Chi Minh also had a clear aim: to unify Vietnam under the communist banner. The Americans did not. Were they supporting the South Vietnamese government, fighting the Vietcong, seeking to defeat North Vietnam, or to stop the advance of world communism? An example of their ambivalence was the decision not to invade North Vietnam with a ground force, but instead to bomb the country, including its capital, Hanoi.

Secondly, the Americans had no clear strategy for fighting a guerilla war. Their strategy was based on their overwhelming advantage in firepower, but this was of little use when every Vietnamese citizen was a potential guerrilla fighter. Typical was the way the Americans could do nothing to prevent the infiltration of fighters and equipment into Saigon in 1968. The 'overkill' approach used by the Americans also caused hundreds of thousands of civilian casualties, which helped to turn public opinion in the US, and throughout the West, against the war.

In 2003, a US-led coalition invaded Iraq. In 1990, Iraq, under Saddam Hussein, had invaded and occupied its neighbour Kuwait. A massive widely based but US-led coalition had expelled him from Kuwait in a brilliant military campaign. This operation had clear limited objectives – to liberate Kuwait – and commanded a high level of world support. The 2003 war was different. This time, the Americans had much less world support, did not have the clear endorsement of the United Nations, and were unable to make it clear to the world exactly why the invasion was happening. Was it to depose Saddam Hussein (regime change)? Was it because Saddam was alleged (incorrectly) to possess chemical and biological weapons (the so-called 'weapons of mass destruction')? Was it to protect ethnic and religious elements in the Iraqi population who had been persecuted by Saddam – the Kurds in the north, and the Shia in the south? Was it to fight world terrorism and in particular Al Qaida? Was it a desire on the part of the US president, George Bush Jr, to complete the job his father, George Bush Sr, had started as president in 1991? Or, as many observers cynically suggested, was it to seize control of Iraq's huge reserves of oil?

The Americans believed that they would be welcomed as liberators, and for a brief period there was relief among many Iraqis at the overthrow of Saddam, particularly among the Kurds, but also to some extent among the Shia in the British-occupied southern part of the country. However, the Americans had underestimated the underlying religious and political divisions in the country. Iraq was an artificial country, created after the First World War from the wreckage of the Turkish empire. The Shia had close links with their co-religionists in Iran, while the Kurds had much more in common with the Kurdish minority in eastern Turkey than with the rest of Iraq.

Although the Shia formed the majority in the country, the Saddam government had been dominated by the minority Sunni, who were strong in Baghdad and central Iraq. The Sunni population was generally hostile to the Americans because they had overthrown Saddam, and they quickly started a guerrilla campaign against the Americans. The Shia sought revenge on the Sunni, while Al Qaida, who had previously had no influence in Iraq, took advantage of the chaos to move into the country.

The Americans were again involved in a guerrilla war, just as in Vietnam, and again they reacted in a heavy-handed fashion, launching punitive operations against guerrilla-controlled towns, and making little effort to reconstruct the country or to win hearts and minds. American casualties rose into the thousands, and Iraqi casualties into the hundreds of thousands.

Again, just as in Vietnam, the war was increasingly unpopular in the US, and the guerrillas realised that in order to win, all they had to do was to outlast the Americans. In 2009, the US announced that its troops would cease to play a combat role, although 150,000 US troops remained in the country.

What has an account of wars in Vietnam and Iraq got to do with business? What lessons can we learn from the wars that are relevant to business environment and strategy? A surprising amount.

- The need for clear objectives. If a business does not know what it wants to achieve, any amount of strategic planning is irrelevant. There is a clear contrast between the totally clear objectives of Ho Chi Minh and Vo Nguyen Giap, and the confused objectives of the Americans in both Vietnam and Iraq.

- An understanding of the environment. The guerrillas in both Iraq and Vietnam were totally at ease in their local environments. The Americans, on the other hand, did not understand the motivation of their enemies in Vietnam, or the complex political environment in Iraq. The Vietnamese also understood and exploited the political environment in the US.

- Understand the competition. The Americans did not understand the strengths and motivations of their enemies in either Vietnam or Iraq.

- An understanding of one's own resources. The Vietnamese made the most of their limited military resources, while the Americans were hamstrung when the enemy in both Vietnam and Iraq neutralised their key resource: their overwhelming firepower.

- The importance of organisational structure. The difference in structure is epitomised by Robert McNamara, the US Secretary of Defense in the mid-1960s, and one of the main architects of US strategy in Vietnam (Jackson

2009). As a young man, McNamara was involved in planning the US bombing offensive on Germany, an example of detailed logistical planning. After 1945 he rose to be president of the Ford Motor Company. Ford was a classic huge, bureaucratic, hierarchical US corporation which had given its name to a scientific approach to organisational structure ('Fordism'). The US army under McNamara in Vietnam was equally rigid and bureaucratic. In contrast, the Vietcong was organised on a highly flexible cell basis, and thus able to react much more quickly to changing tactical situations.

- The importance of HR. The North Vietnamese and Vietcong were highly motivated. The US army, on the other hand, was largely a conscript army, most of whom did not want to be in Vietnam. To make matters worse, there were extensive exemptions from conscription (the draft), which made those who could not avoid the draft even more bitter about their fate. The alienation of the rank and file US soldier expressed itself in a contempt for the Vietnamese, and also in occasional atrocities against civilians.

- The importance of values and culture. The communist beliefs of the Vietnamese gave them a motivation and a will to win that the Americans could not match. At a tactical level, the gung-ho, macho culture of the US Marine Corps made them ideal for spearheading the invasion of Iraq, but totally unsuitable for any campaign to win hearts and minds.

- The importance of stakeholders. Businesses, like countries, have external stakeholders – third parties who can affect their actions. In Iraq, the key external stakeholders were Iran, with considerable influence over the Iraqi Shia, and Turkey, the sworn enemy of the Kurds. In addition, a key stakeholder was US public opinion, which eventually turned strongly against both wars. The views of stakeholders must be taken into account in strategic management.

- The importance of an exit strategy. Businesses, like armies, need to know how to abandon a strategy at minimum cost. The Americans in Vietnam were forced to make a humiliating exit, while they have been heavily criticised over Iraq for their seeming failure to have a clear exit strategy.

All these themes will be explored later in this book.

HRM IN CONTEXT

The theme of this chapter, and indeed of the book as a whole, is the interaction between human resource management (HRM), the environment and the organisation. The theoretical underpinning for this approach is the best-fit or contingency model of HR strategy, particularly associated in the UK with John Purcell (Boxall and Purcell 2008). This model argues that there is no one model of HR strategy which suits all circumstances. Instead, different strategies are appropriate in different environmental and organisational settings.

You should bear in mind that the best-fit model is not the only model of HR strategy. Other models include the best practice model, which argues that there is one approach to HR strategy; the high performance workplace model, which is suitable in nearly all organisational and environmental settings; and the resource-based model, which argues that resources, particularly human capital and core competencies, are much more important for HR strategy than the environment. All these models are explored in much more depth in Chapter 10.

The next section will explore in more detail the relationships between the environment, the organisation and HR strategy.

THE ENVIRONMENT, ORGANISATIONS AND STRATEGY

WHAT IS THE ENVIRONMENT?

At its simplest, the environment is anything outside an organisation which may affect an organisation's present or future activities. Thus the environment is situational – it is unique to each organisation. As a result, we must always bear in mind the interaction between a particular organisation and its particular environment.

It is useful to think of the environment on two levels. One is the general environment (also known as the societal environment, the far environment or the macro environment). The other is the task environment (or the specific environment, the near environment or the micro environment).

Forces in the general environment have a major impact at the level of the industry. These forces include national culture, including historical background, ideologies and values; scientific and technological developments; the level of education; legal and political processes; demographic factors; available resources, the international environment; and the general economic, social and industrial structure of the country.

The task environment covers the forces relevant to an individual organisation within an industry. These include customers, suppliers, competitors, regulators, the local labour market and specific technologies.

The distinction between general and task environments is not a static one. Elements in the general environment are continually breaking through to the task environment and impacting on individual organisations.

A different but complementary approach is to see the organisation as an open system, which interacts in two main ways with its task environment. It takes in resources from the environment, converts them into goods and/or services, and returns outputs to the environment in order to satisfy some need (see figure 1.1).

In order to function effectively in such a system, the organisation must fully understand both its input and its output environments.

A more complex variation is to add a third element – that of regulations which control the conversion process. The three elements (inputs, outputs and

Figure 1.1 A systems model of the organisation and its environment

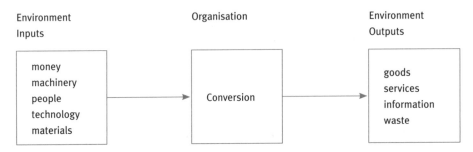

regulations) provide the organisation with both opportunities and constraints. All three elements are also subject to the influences of the general environment.

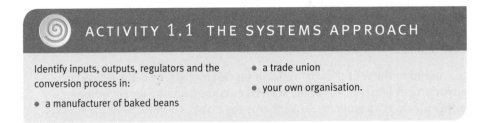

ACTIVITY 1.1 THE SYSTEMS APPROACH

Identify inputs, outputs, regulators and the conversion process in:

- a manufacturer of baked beans

- a trade union

- your own organisation.

ORGANISATIONS AND STRATEGY

The simple systems model used above takes us only so far. It treats the organisation as a 'black box' and does not analyse what goes on inside the organisation. We now have to build further elements into our model: HR, strategy and organisational structure.

In case study 1.1 (Vietnam and Iraq), we identified that the environment has an impact on HR. The political environment in the US, where the country was only 20 years away from the Second World War, led the US to rely on a conscript rather than a volunteer army to fight the Vietnam War. At the same time, HR had an impact on the environment – the alienation created by the draft affected the way in which the rank and file soldiers fought the war.

This gives us a two-way model of the relationship between the environment and HR (see figure 1.2).

Figure 1.2 The environment and HR

The next stage is to distinguish between HR strategy and HR practice. In figure 1.3 we assume that HR practice flows from HR strategy.

Figure 1.3 HR strategy and HR practice

The next stage is to put HR strategy in the context of the organisation's overall strategy. In figure 1.4 we see HR strategy as an integral part of overall strategy.

Figure 1.4 HR strategy and overall strategy

Finally, we need to add the organisation.

The great organisational theorist of the 1960s, Alfred Chandler, argued that 'structure follows strategy' (Chandler 1962). A more nuanced approach would suggest that there is a two-way flow between strategy and organisational structure and, similarly, that there is a two-way relationship between the environment and both structure and strategy, although the stronger flow would be between environment to structure and strategy, rather than the other way around.

An example of strategy following structure was discussed in the *Harvard Business Review* (Slywotsky and Nadler 2004). The French producer of industrial gases, Air Liquide, was producing gases in small plants at customers' factories. An unrelated company reorganisation suddenly gave the on-site teams involved greater autonomy. They seized the new opportunities, developing new lines of business which now make up 25 per cent of Air Liquide's revenue, compared to 7 per cent previously.

Figure 1.5 The environment, strategy and structure

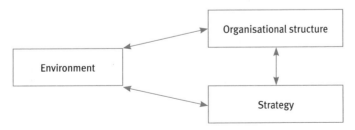

Putting everything together, we arrive at the following comprehensive model:

Figure 1.6 The comprehensive model

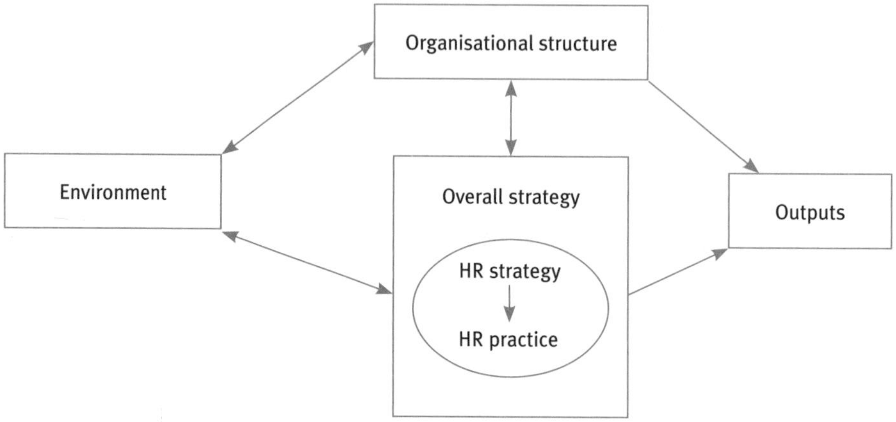

ANALYSING THE ENVIRONMENT

Most organisations will not have problems in analysing their task environment. They know who their customers, suppliers, competitors, etc are. Analysing the general environment is rather more complex. The first step will probably be to brainstorm a list of various environmental factors which seem to impact on the organisation. This is a start, but to progress further it will be necessary to classify these influences.

One widely used tool for classification is PEST analysis and its derivatives. PEST analysis breaks down environmental influences into four categories:

Political/Legal   Taxation policy, European Union directives, trade regulations, geopolitical factors like the 'war on terror', government stability, employment law, contract law, competition law, etc.

Economic   Business cycles, economic growth, interest rates, supply and demand factors, competition factors, public spending, money supply, inflation, unemployment, disposable income.

Socio-cultural   Demographic trends, income distribution, social mobility, lifestyle, attitudes to work and leisure, levels of education.

Technological   Research and development, new inventions or innovations, speed of technology transfer, rates of obsolescence, development of systems.

PEST analysis was widely used during the 1980s and early 1990s. By the mid-1990s, it was becoming more common to talk of PESTLE analysis. Political and Legal were split from each other, and an extra factor, Environment, was added. This reflected a growing awareness of environmental factors, and the first concerns about global warming.

By the early 2000s, PESTLE had evolved into STEEPLE, with the addition of Ethics reflecting the development of concern for corporate social responsibility and business ethics.

The classification currently used is thus:

S   Social
T   Technological
E   Economic
E   Environmental
P   Political
L   Legal
E   Ethical

The STEEPLE model forms the structure of this book. We will be examining each of the STEEPLE elements in turn (although not in this order), and we will conclude by bringing everything together in an analysis of strategy formation.

The next stage in a STEEPLE analysis is to identify what impact each identified factor would have on the organisation.

WHY DO WE NEED TO UNDERSTAND AND MANAGE THE ENVIRONMENT?

Organisations have a choice in how they manage their relationships with their environment. They can sit back and wait for the environment to change, without attempting to predict its behaviour, and then react to changes as they happen. Here they are being reactive – constantly firefighting immediate problems. Or they can identify and foresee changes in the environment, and plan their responses before these changes happen. They are being proactive – planning for the future. A few organisations are in the fortunate position of being able to go even further and manage the environment in their own interests: at different times since 1900, Ford, IBM, Sony, McDonald's and Microsoft have done this.

The nature of the environment is also significant. Some organisations have static or placid environments, where it is reasonable to suppose that the future will be a continuation of the past. For example, this was true of many UK nationalised industries before privatisation. An organisation in this happy situation can afford to limit its analysis of its environment to past history. However, such an organisation is likely to be caught totally unawares if the nature of its environment does change rapidly. For example, many airlines in continental Europe were either owned by, or heavily protected by, their home governments. This cosy relationship was totally disrupted by the events of 11 September 2001, with the resultant rapid collapse of two national airlines – Swissair and Sabena – whilst to add insult to injury, American Airlines received massive subsidies from the US government.

Other organisations face turbulent environments, either because the environment is dynamic or in a state of rapid change, for example the pharmaceutical industry or the defence industry; or because the environment is complex, and thus difficult to analyse, for example a multinational company with interests in many countries or industries. Turbulent environments are uncertain.

Igor Ansoff (1987) argued that the extent to which an environment is turbulent depends on:

- changeability of the market environment
- speed of change
- intensity of competition
- fertility of technology
- discrimination by customers
- pressure from government and influence groups.

In order to cope with a turbulent environment, the organisation must be aggressively ready to change.

 VIDEO BLUES – A TURBULENT ENVIRONMENT

CASE STUDY 1.2

On 18 June 2007 the BBC2 business programme *Working Lunch* highlighted the plight of Peter Citrine, owner of a video rental store on the Wirral. His turnover had fallen by 70 per cent over the previous five years, even though several rival stores in his area had gone out of business. He was not alone. In June 2007, the rental chain Global DVD, with 47 stores, went into liquidation, following the third largest retail group, Apollo Video Film Hire, which failed in April 2007, with the closure of 100 stores. In five years, the number of stores nationally had halved to less than 1,000.

The retail video rental market has been the victim of a whole series of hammer blows from changes in its turbulent environment.

- Nobody rents or buys videos any more. The VHS format has been totally superseded by DVD, which means that store owners have had to replace a lot of worthless VHS stock.

- DVDs are one of many markets in which supermarkets fight their price wars. The typical price of a DVD in a supermarket is £11, while some DVDs are imported from Jersey and sold for as little as £3.93, virtually the same as a rental fee. Since 2000, DVD sales have grown from 16 million to 227 million a year, while rentals have fallen from 200 million to 116 million.

- Small stores like Peter Citrine's are hit by the dual pricing policy of the major film studios. DVDs for rental are charged a much higher price – £25 rather than the £11 in a supermarket. This is permitted under the EU's Rental Rights Directive of 1992.

- Until 2002, video stores benefited from a rental window of up to a year, during which the only sales allowed were to rental stores. This gave the rental stores the opportunity to recoup the higher price that they were charged before they faced competition from supermarkets. In 2002, Warner Home Video abolished the rental window, but still kept its dual pricing, and was followed by other suppliers.

- The structure of the industry has changed. The Amazon model of orders placed over the Internet being met centrally from a enormous backlist of titles has been applied to the DVD market, by Amazon itself, by Blockbuster, and, most successfully, by Lovefilm. Lovefilm has 400,000 subscribers, who in 2006 rented two million DVDs each month, 20 per cent of the UK market. The company owns 1.5 million DVDs, covering 75,000 titles, far more than a local store could stock. Through analysis of orders and customer feedback, it has a huge database of customers' rentals and preferences.

- The online rental sector also has a different pricing structure. Customers pay a monthly fee, typically £9.99 a month, for which they can rent one DVD at a time, and up to £14.99 for three DVDs at a time. Orders are placed over the Internet and delivered by post. There are no limits on the total number that can be rented each month and no late fees. The online suppliers also have the opportunity to earn more revenue by including junk mail in the post with the DVDs.

- As broadband speeds improve, it becomes easier to download films over the Internet. In May 2007 Tiscali started to offer legal downloads, charging between 99p and £3.49.

- DVD rentals are also being hit by social changes. With the proliferation of TV channels, many showing films, available via satellite or Freeview, competition for the DVD rental industry is constantly increasing. The market is also being hit by the increasing range and sophistication of games consoles.

In April 2007, Choices, the second biggest rental chain, issued a profits warning, and its CEO, Anthony Skitt, said that it was unlikely that any retail video/DVD rental stores would survive the next five years.

If the environment facing an organisation is dynamic, the organisation will need to have procedures for anticipating future environmental changes, and contingency plans for dealing with a range of possible changes. This involves the technique known as scenario building. This increases managerial awareness by examining 'what-if' situations – if x happens, what will its impact be on us, and what can we do about it? The technique was first developed by Shell in the early 1970s, when it correctly forecast the 1973 oil crisis and so was ready to deal with it. Schwartz (2003) argues that although most scenarios will be wrong, the mere fact of having been through the scenario-building process will make managers more able to cope with change.

 WILD GARDENS

CASE STUDY 1.3

In the mid-1990s, British Airways carried out a scenario-planning exercise for 2005. Two scenarios were developed. One (called Wild Gardens) predicted:

1. rapid growth in Asia

2. a US recession

3. EU enlargement into eastern Europe

4. no single currency

5. a Tory election win in 1997

6. an EU–US open skies agreement, which would partially open up European routes to US competition, and vice versa.

They were right on three of the six (numbers 1, 3 and 6), partially right on one (number 2) and wrong on the other two. However, what is more important is what they didn't foresee – the two most traumatic events to hit world aviation for many years, namely 9/11 and the Iraq war.

In organisation with a complex environment may need to break down the complexity, so that environmental analysis is decentralised to product groups or countries within the organisation.

The most difficult situation of all, of course, is where the environment is both dynamic and complex. Here the organisation may have to recognise that it cannot predict its environment, and what is important is to foster a culture in the organisation that welcomes, and is able to cope with, radical change. The organisation must learn to live with chaos. One definition of a learning organisation is an organisation which has developed systematic procedures to ensure that it can learn from its environment.

 ACTIVITY 1.2 TURBULENT ENVIRONMENTS

In what ways have the environments of local authorities become more turbulent in recent years?

ANALYSING THE ENVIRONMENT

Johnson, Scholes and Whittington (2004) propose a five-stage model in analysing the environment, as follows:

Stage 1   Audit of environmental influences
Stage 2   Assessment of nature of the environment
Stage 3   Identification of key environmental factors
Stage 4   Identification of the competitive position
Stage 5   Identification of the principal opportunities and threats

Stage 1 involves the preparation of a STEEPLE analysis. Stage 2 builds on the placid/dynamic/turbulent classification of environments discussed above. Stage 3 involves a more sophisticated analysis which may include:

● Identifying a smaller number of key environmental influences. For example, for the NHS these might be demographic trends (ageing population), technological developments in health care and implementation of government policy (public–private partnerships).

● Identifying long-term drivers of change. For example, the increasing globalisation of markets for some products, eg consumer electronics, cars and pharmaceuticals.

The key principle here is that not all environmental influences are equally important. The analysis in Stage 3 involves identifying those that are most important.

Stage 4 (identifying the organisation's competitive position) will be considered in Chapter 3, using techniques such as Porter's Five Forces (Porter 1980).

Stage 5 (identifying principal opportunities and threats) involves another well-known technique, SWOT analysis.

SWOT stands for:

S   Strengths
W   Weaknesses
O   Opportunities
T   Threats

Strengths and weaknesses are inward-looking, and particularly concerned with the resources of the organisation. Opportunities and threats are outward-looking and involve the analysis of environmental factors. The organisation should ensure that its strengths (or core competencies) are appropriate ones to exploit opportunities or to counter threats.

Both opportunities and threats can be analysed using matrices. Opportunities can be assessed according to their attractiveness and the organisation's probability of success.

Figure 1.7 An attractiveness/probability of success matrix

		Probability of success	
		High	Low
Attractiveness	High	1	2
	Low	3	4

Opportunities in cell 1 offer the greatest scope, and organisations should concentrate on these. Cell 4 represents opportunities which in practice can be ignored. Cells 2 and 3 may be worth investigating further.

Threats can be assessed on the basis of their seriousness and their probability of occurrence.

Figure 1.8 An impact/probability of success matrix

		Impact	
		High	Low
Probability of occurrence	High	1	2
	Low	3	4

A threat which has a high probability of happening, and is likely to have a considerable impact on the organisation (cell 1) will be a key factor which must be a driver of the organisation's strategy, and for which detailed contingency plans must be prepared. At the other extreme (cell 4), a threat which has little likelihood of happening, and little impact if it does happen, can be largely ignored. The threats in cells 2 and 3 should be carefully monitored in case they become critical.

It should be remembered that opportunities and threats are rarely mutually exclusive. Many factors can be both – indeed, the Chinese characters for 'threat' and 'opportunity' are identical (Nathan 2000). For example, the technological development of EFTPOS (electronic funds transfer at point of sale) money transfer systems (using debit and credit cards) can be a threat to small retailers, as their use by rivals may give the latter a competitive edge, as well as an opportunity to make the shop less attractive to thieves as less money is likely to be left in tills.

 ACTIVITY 1.3 THE HOSPITAL

How would you classify the following factors on a probability/seriousness matrix for a hospital trust? What contingency planning should the trust make?

a. a serious accident on the local railway line, causing scores of deaths and injuries

b. an ageing local population

c. a leakage of radioactive material at a nuclear power station 200 miles away downwind.

SWOT AND STRATEGY

Weihrich (1982) argues that SWOT is misnamed. He suggests renaming it TOWS. His argument is that SWOT implies that strengths and weaknesses come first, but that this is mistaken. The only logical starting point for analysis is with opportunities and threats. They are outside the organisation, largely beyond its control, and must be managed using the organisation's strengths and weaknesses. He thus argues that SWOT should be used as a contingency model.

Four combinations of opportunities, threats, strengths and weaknesses are possible, and each suggests a possible strategy.

● Strengths–opportunities (maxi–maxi). The organisation should pursue strategies which make most use of its strengths to capitalise on opportunities.

● Strengths–threats (maxi–mini). The organisation should use its strengths to minimise or neutralise threats.

● Weaknesses–opportunities (mini–maxi). Make the most of any new opportunities to overcome weaknesses.

- Weaknesses–threats (mini–mini). This combination calls for a defensive strategy to minimise internal weaknesses and avoid external threats.

CRITICISMS OF SWOT

As an analytical technique, SWOT has many strengths. It is simple, easy to understand and (at least at a superficial level) easy to use, and it does encourage managers to think about both the internal and external aspects of their business.

However, it does have a number of weaknesses. It runs the risk of being subjective, particularly if it is carried out primarily by one person. It encourages generalisations. It has a tendency to be backwards rather than forward-looking, and it often leads to a feeling of 'So what?' when faced with a long list of factors.

In order to be a useful tool, SWOT (or TOWS) must be used intelligently.

- Don't give it as a job to one person. It is an ideal technique for use in a focus group, which could usefully include customers and suppliers as well as internal managers.

- Use the probability/attractiveness and probability/seriousness matrices discussed earlier to identify which opportunities and threats are most important.

- Identify why they are important.

- Be specific. For example, don't just list 'overseas expansion' as an opportunity. Identify which markets represent the best opportunity, and why; eg 'opportunities for expansion in France, because the major producers of our product in France are very weak'.

- Similarly, identify why weaknesses are important. You may think something is a weakness, but this is only so if it affects your competitiveness. For example, you may identify 'authoritarian management style' as a weakness, but if this does not affect your competitiveness, it is not really a weakness.

- Don't put down the same factor as both an opportunity and a threat. Decide which is more important. For example, earlier we looked at the impact of EFTPOS on small retailers. On balance, this is clearly an opportunity rather than a threat, because it provides the chance to give a better service to customers.

In essence, SWOT is a simple framework and a potentially valuable tool which is often badly used by managers as an alternative to undertaking the grind of detailed internal and external analysis.

MODELS OF ORGANISATIONAL STRUCTURE

In this section we concentrate on the organisation, and examine different models of organisational structure and their attendant strengths and weaknesses.

Formalisation of the bureaucratic form of organisation dates back to the sociologist Max Weber's work on government departments in the 1890s (Weber 1964). The form reached its peak in the US of the 1950s and 1960s.

Weber identified three central principles of bureaucratic organisation:

- specialisation
- hierarchy
- impersonal rationality.

Specialisation

Labour tasks are highly divided, and workers are recruited with specific skills to carry out specific roles. Tasks are functionally separated, and organised into rigid departments ('smokestack management'). Movement from department to department would be unusual. Some departments, such as production, would carry out the core tasks of the organisation, while others, such as finance or HR, would provide technical or physical support for the core activities. This was identified by Fayol as the distinction between line and staff activities (Fayol 1916/1949). Parallels with Frederick Taylor's minute definition of tasks and Henry Ford's Model T production line should be obvious (Taylor 1947).

Hierarchy

Along with a rigid definition of tasks came a rigid definition of power and authority. The result was a hierarchical structure, with only those higher in the organisational hierarchy able to give instructions to those lower down. Promotion up the hierarchy was possible on the basis of either merit or seniority.

Impersonal rationality

In a bureaucracy, power belonged to the office, not to the office-holder. Power was based on rules, which provided precedents for action. Behaviour was rational, based on logical principles, not on individual whim or prejudice. Remember that it was not long before Weber that reforms were enacted in the UK to eliminate corruption and nepotism in the civil service and the army. Impersonal rationality at least in theory made corruption and nepotism impossible. Impersonal rules also form the basis for our present-day anti-discrimination legislation – the right to be judged on your own merit, not on your sex, gender, skin colour, nationality, religion, disability or sexual orientation.

As a form of organisation, bureaucracy had many strengths:

- It provided predictable and secure career paths for those who worked in them – the civil service 'job for life'.
- Rules provided a number of protections. They guaranteed fair treatment within the rules, and avoided the arbitrary exercise of power, and they protected civil liberties because everyone was subject to the rules.

However, there were also weaknesses:

- The rules could become so complex that the worker or the client of the organisation could feel helpless, confused and trapped. See, for example, Franz Kafka's *The Trial* (Kafka 1956) or the labyrinthine regulations surrounding present-day tax credits.

- Minute definition and sub-division of tasks could produce an alienated workforce, particularly as the hierarchical structure did not easily permit worker empowerment.

- Rigid adherence to rules could produce a 'jobsworth' mentality – 'No, you can't do X, it's not in the rules' (Clegg, Kornberger and Pitsis 2008). Perhaps most crucially, its very rigidity, which is in some ways its greatest strength, is also its greatest weakness. A pure bureaucracy can only operate successfully in a placid environment, and it becomes progressively less able to cope effectively as the environment becomes more turbulent.

Despite the weaknesses of the model, there are still strong bureaucratic elements in virtually all organisational forms today.

DIVISIONALISATION OR M-FORM

This is a development of the bureaucratic organisation. As the organisation becomes larger, it becomes more difficult to manage everything from the centre. As a result, some decision-making is decentralised. The divisionalised organisation sets up a number of separate product, market or geographic divisions, each responsible for operational decisions, which will usually include production, marketing and some elements of HR (although US companies are more reluctant to delegate HR to divisions). Each division will thus be a mini-bureaucracy, competing against the other divisions. Strategic decisions will be taken at headquarters, including, crucially, investment decisions and allocation of capital, and setting and monitoring of targets (Boxall and Purcell 2008).

Divisionalisation was effectively invented by Alfred Sloan at General Motors in the 1920s. Here the motive was not so much to give more autonomy to operating divisions – Chevrolet, Buck or Cadillac – but to centralise authority over subsidiaries which had previously been independent businesses (Hales 2001). The divisional structure is particularly common among multinational corporations, with divisions usually organised on a country or regional basis.

The divisional form is more flexible than pure bureaucracy, but as noted above, there is a tendency for the divisions themselves to become highly bureaucratised, which then limits their flexibility. There is also a tendency for US or UK divisional organisations to impose mainly short-term targets on their operating divisions – in contrast to the longer-term goals favoured by the Japanese.

A more extreme form of divisionalisation operates through strategic business units (SBUs). The typical SBU is smaller than the classic division, and based on a niche product, service or unit. Specialist services, like IT or training, will often themselves be supplied by SBUs, which are profit centres in their own right. These may not just provide services within the organisation, but compete for outside business. An extreme example of this was the internal market in the BBC under John Birt in the 1990s. Here, under a programme called Producer Choice, programme makers were given budgets which they could spend either on in-house facilities or on external contractors. If the in-house facilities could not attract enough work, they were closed (Hales 2001). The intention was to increase efficiency, but the internal market process was so expensive that any benefits were more than cancelled out. Producer Choice was abandoned by the next Director-General of the BBC, Greg Dyke.

GENERAL MOTORS, DIVISIONALISATION AND CHAPTER 11

CASE STUDY 1.4

On 1 June 2009, General Motors (GM) filed for Chapter 11 bankruptcy, the third biggest bankruptcy ever, after Lehman Brothers and WorldCom, and the biggest industrial bankruptcy. A month before, the third-biggest US car maker, Chrysler, had also gone into bankruptcy (Clark 2009a). Was GM's failure, which followed losses of US $81 billion over the previous four years, purely the result of the credit crunch, or were more deep-seated factors at play, and did they have anything to do with the way the company was structured?

In the 1950s, Charles Wilson, the then head of GM, declared, 'For years I thought that what was good for our country was good for General Motors, and vice versa' (Noyes 2009), while the management guru Peter Drucker said that it was General Motors who 'won the war for America' (Chakrabortty 2009). At its peak in 1955, GM's share of the US market was 54 per cent – now it is 19 per cent and falling, and GM has been overtaken by Toyota as the world's biggest car maker.

General Motors was founded in 1908 in Flint, Michigan, when William Durant acquired the Buick Motor Company, still one of the core GM brands. By 1909, he had also bought Oldsmobile and Cadillac, as well as four other brands. The pattern for GM's strategy had already been set – growth through acquisition, a stark contrast to Henry Ford's strategy of organic growth. In

the 1920s, the company moved into Europe, acquiring Vauxhall in 1923 and Opel in 1929 (Wearden 2009).

By the late 1920s, GM was under the control of the legendary management pioneer Alfred Sloan, much admired by Peter Drucker, who pulled together the sprawling GM empire, and divisionalised its organisational structure. Each division targeted a social market niche – Chevrolet the entry-level blue-collar worker, Pontiac the sporty market, Buick established professionals, and Cadillac top professionals. Each division introduced a new model every year, with the emphasis on styling rather than engineering (DesJardins 2007).

The strategy was successful. Ford, which stuck with its organic growth and its centralised bureaucratic organisational structure, was soon overtaken, and by 1954 GM had made its 50 millionth car. However, life became more difficult in the 1960s, as competition from Europe increased, while after 1973, GM, and the whole American car industry, was hit by the aftermath of the oil crisis. Suddenly, big, over-styled US gas guzzlers were yesterday's cars, and the future lay with smaller, more economical and better quality Japanese models. GM tried hard to introduce Japanese production methods and culture, but the fit with the traditional GM culture was too hard to achieve.

By the 1980s GM was making losses. Market share shrank, and the CEO at the time, Roger Smith, made tens of thousands of redundancies. Smith was recently ranked 13th in a list of worst American CEOs of all time. Redundancies and loss of market share continued through the 1990s and 2000s. GM did try to escape from the spiral of decline. It formed a joint venture with Toyota in the 1980s, called NUMMI, in order to learn more about Japanese techniques, and it simplified its organisational structure, concentrating its car models into two divisions, Midsize and Luxury Car Group, and Small Car Group (Grant 2008 p188) but it was already too late. By 2005, GM was making US losses of US $1 billion, and was crippled by falling market share, an unpopular product mix, rising raw material prices, and the deadweight cost of US health insurance, which amounted to $1,500 per car (Worthington and Britton 2006). The collapse in 2009 had become inevitable. The last symbolic touch came in August 2009, when Toyota announced that the NUMMI plant was to close, the first plant closure in Toyota's history, and the end of its 25-year partnership with GM (McCurry 2009).

So what went wrong? Why did GM go bust, while its nearest rivals, Ford and Toyota, survived relatively unscathed?

- Ford's bureaucratic and centralised organisational culture ensured that it could share parts between models, and Ford was also famous, or notorious, for its savage cost controls. Toyota was probably the most efficient of the Japanese car companies, brilliant at both lean production and quality management, and famous for its flexibility and its innovation. GM had the advantages of neither. The duplication of facilities through its divisional structure cost money, and it did not exploit cost-saving opportunities to the same extent as its rivals. Chrysler suffered from the same disadvantages, and was also crippled by its failed merger with Daimler.

- Compared with its main rivals, GM was too US-centric. The UN agency UNCTAD produces a Transnationality Index, which measures the extent of globalisation of a company through three ratios: foreign sales as a percentage of total sales; foreign assets as a percentage of total assets; and foreign employment as a percentage of total employment. Aggregating these three figures gives the firm's Transnationality Index. In 2002, for Ford this was 47.7 per cent, for Toyota 45.7 per cent, but for GM only 27.9 per cent (Worthington and Britton 2006, p396). GM was thus much more dependent on the US market, while its rivals could spread their risks worldwide.

GM's period in bankruptcy was short. Unlike UK or European bankruptcy, US Chapter 11 bankruptcy is more of a technical device. It gives a corporation time to recover while shielding it from its creditors. A deal was quickly reached, and GM's bankruptcy lasted only 40 days. The new GM was radically different from the old one. In future it would focus on only four brands – Chevrolet, Cadillac, Buick and GMC. Its blue-collar workforce would fall from 113,000 in 2006 to 38,000 in 2011. The number of US plants would fall from 47 to 31, and top management would be cut by 35 per cent. More radical still, the US government now owns 60.8 per cent of GM, the Canadian government 11.7 per cent, and a union-controlled pension fund 17.5 per cent. Creditors of the old company get 10 per cent, and the old shareholders get nothing (Clark 2009b).

THE MATRIX ORGANISATION

The matrix model of organisation was first developed in the US aerospace industry in the 1960s. Here the organisation is involved in a series of short or medium-term projects, each of which has a finite life. Each project requires the services of a number of specialists, drawn from functional departments. Who is going to control these functional specialists – their departmental manager or the project manager? The solution offered in a matrix organisation is that he or she will be answerable to both the departmental and the project manager.

Figure 1.9 A matrix organisational structure

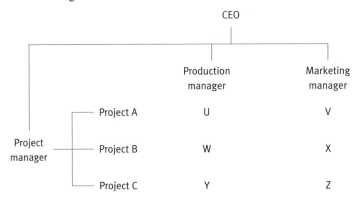

Production specialist U will report to his functional manager, the production manager, but while he is working on project A, he will be answerable to the project manager in charge of project A. He will also be working on project A alongside his colleague from marketing, V.

The matrix structure has a number of advantages:

- communication within the organisation is improved, and as a result decisions can be made more speedily and effectively
- use of human and capital resources becomes more flexible
- the use of project teams increases motivation, job satisfaction and personal development.

However, there can also be disadvantages:

- As each individual is answerable to at least two bosses, there can be problems of loyalty, and feelings of insecurity.
- Power struggles are likely over decision-making and the allocation of resources between the functional and project managers.
- Although communication and decision-making should be improved, decisions may be more difficult to make as decision-making authority is diffused.
- The structure is particularly threatening to functional managers, who can see their power base eroded.

THE NETWORK ORGANISATION OR N-FORM

The network organisation is a less formal version of the matrix organisation. The aim is to build up networks and connections between different parts of the organisation in order to break down rigid departmental smokestacks, and to ensure the faster diffusion of ideas throughout the organisation.

This can be done in several ways. Unilever, for example, works hard to build up lateral relationships between managers in different divisions. Career development is carefully planned on a multiple spiral, with managers progressing between functions, divisions and countries (Boxall and Purcell 2008, p264).

Another approach is to use network managers, with several roles:

- boundary-spanners between levels and functions
- initiators of networks
- co-ordinators of information transfer
- conveyors of corporate vision downwards and advocates of decentralised initiatives upwards (Child 2005, p255).

A third approach is to use communities of practice. These are informal networks of people with common interests within an organisation (and often pulling in people from outside the organisation). Often run on the Internet or a company intranet, they enable quick informal communication of information and knowledge. All students know that you learn at least as much from your fellow students as from formal tuition, and communities of practice operate on the same principle of social learning (Clegg, Kornberger and Pitsis 2008). CIPD professional communities (a form of community of practice) had 88,480 participants on 20 August 2009, taking part in 12,310 discussions (www.cipd.co.uk/communities [accessed on 17 April 2010]).

One key element in ensuring the success of any N-form organisation is culture. As Whittington and Mayer (2000) said, 'N form works best with Eastern appreciation of the tacit, the embedded and the ambiguous, rather than the explicit, tightly specified knowledge systems of the West.'

Networks can operate outside as well as inside the organisation. Hansen and Von Oetringer (2001) identified the concept of the T-shaped manager, with the vertical part of the T representing the manager's role within the organisation, and the horizontal part of the T representing the role of networking outside the organisation.

VIRTUAL ORGANISATIONS

In a virtual organisation, physical assets – buildings, machinery, etc – are replaced by computer networks. Warner and Witzel (2003) identify six characteristics of virtual organisations:

- *Lack of physical structure.* They have fewer physical assets, and ultimately might exist solely in cyberspace.
- *Reliance on communications technology.* Virtual organisations use communication networks supported by the Internet.
- *Mobile work.* Members of teams no longer have to be in physical contact. They

can work anywhere, and communicate through information and computing technology (ICT).

- *Hybrid forms.* Some virtual organisations are brought together for short-term projects, like producing a film or a book. Others are longer term, like a virtual supply chain.

- *Boundaryless and inclusive.* Virtual organisations often closely involve suppliers (through partnership sourcing) or customers (through customer relationship management). The fashion accessories company Topsy Tail, for example, had revenues of US $80 million in 1998, but only three employees. It outsources everything, and never touches its product (Child 2005).

- *Flexible and responsive.*

Perhaps the best example of a virtual organisation is Dell Computer Corporation. The key to Dell's business model is its direct sales strategy, which relies on demand pull. A computer is only produced against a firm customer order. The company therefore has no finished goods inventory or warehouses. It operates with half the staff and one-tenth the inventory of its competitors. On average it carries six days' work in progress stock, all held against firm orders. In 2000, 50 per cent of orders were received online (Gillespie 2000). The ordering system permits the customer to write their own specification (mass customisation). In theory, each computer sold is unique. When Dell receives an order, it sends electronic orders for components to its suppliers worldwide. These components are then assembled in a Dell factory and despatched direct to the customer. In some cases the process is totally virtual – for example, when Dell receives an order for a computer monitor, it is despatched direct to the customer from a supplier like Sony (Child 2005).

STRATEGIC ALLIANCES

Strategic alliances are any medium- to long-term co-operative relationships between firms which involve joint working. They can variously be called alliances, partnerships or joint ventures. They have become increasingly common. Between 1996 and 2001, US companies formed 57,000 alliances (Dyer, Kale and Singh 2004). The average US corporation manages more than 30 alliances, while many have several hundred. By 2001, they already accounted for up to 15 per cent of the market value of the typical US company. However, it has been estimated that 60 per cent have been outright failures (Parkhe 2001).

Alliances can take many legal and contractual forms. These are illustrated and discussed in Child (2005, pp223–225). Contractor and Lorange (1998) identify six main objectives for alliances:

- reduction of risk
- achievement of economies of scale
- technology exchange
- countering competition

- overcoming government trade or investment barriers
- vertical quasi-integration advantages – linking the complementary contributions of partners in a value chain.

Dussauge and Garrette (1999) identified six different types, three between non-competing firms, and three between competing forms.

Non-competing:

- International expansion joint ventures. Until the late 1990s, western firms seeking to invest in China could only do so through a joint venture with a local firm.
- Vertical partnerships between firms at different stages in the same value chain. For example, Intel and Hewlett-Packard set up a join venture to develop a new microprocessor.
- Cross-industry agreements: American Airlines and SNCF (French Railways) set up a joint venture to develop a computerised railway ticketing system.

Competing:

- Shared supply alliances. These are common in the car industry.
- Quasi-concentration alliances, designed to counter competition. An example is Airbus Industrie, formed between competing European aircraft manufacturers to counter the threat from Boeing.
- Complementary alliances, designed to reduce risk and achieve synergy. These are common in the pharmaceutical industry. For example, in 1996, Pfizer used its superior marketing expertise to collaborate in the marketing of Lipitor, a cholesterol-reducing drug developed by a rival company, Warner-Lambert. By 1999. Lipitor had achieved sales of US $3 billion a year (Dyer, Kale and Singh 2004).

Why do so many alliances fail? Many reasons have been put forward:

- *Communication problems.* A US–UK joint venture had to appear before a crucial British government hearing. The US firm asked the UK firm to 'table' several key points at the meeting. To the horror of the Americans, the British firm brought up these very issues at the hearing, leading to disaster. The Americans had forgotten that 'to table' in UK English means to 'place on the table', whereas in US English it means 'hide under the table'.
- *Culture clashes.* In the 1990s, Siemens, Toshiba and IBM were working together to develop a new memory chip. Siemens representatives were horrified when the Toshiba scientists appeared to go to sleep in meetings – a common practice among Japanese when the discussion does not directly concern them. The Japanese found it difficult to work in mixed-nationality groups speaking English. The Americans felt the Germans planned too much and the Japanese would not take decisions (Parkhe 2001).
- *Diverging strategic directions.* Alliances which might have made perfect strategic sense at the time may diverge over time.

- *Failure to protect strategic knowledge.* In the early 1980s, Macintosh used Microsoft to develop software applications for the Apple Mac. As a result, Microsoft acquired crucial knowledge about Apple's mouse-based graphical user interface, which it then used to develop the Windows operating system. Eventually Apple brought an unsuccessful lawsuit against Microsoft to try to protect its intellectual property (Norman 2001).

- *Uneven benefits.* In 2001, Coca-Cola and Procter & Gamble formed a US $4 billion joint venture that would control more than 40 brands contributed by the parent companies. However, the markets felt that P&G would get more out of the alliance than Coke. P&G's share price immediately rose 2 per cent, while Coca-Cola's fell 6 per cent. Predictably, the alliance lasted only six months (Dyer, Kale and Singh 2004). The same thing may well happen with the Internet search technology joint venture announced by Microsoft and Yahoo! in July 2009, intended as a defensive alliance against the market leader, Google. Here the share price disparity has been even more marked. Microsoft shares rose 2 per cent, while Yahoo! shares fell 15 per cent. Both sides moved fast to defend the alliance. Steve Ballmer, CEO of Microsoft, described the Yahoo! share price fall as 'sort of unbelievable', while Tim Morse, chief finance office at Yahoo!, said, 'It's a perfect fit for our strategy' (Waters and Menn 2009). Watch this space.

- *Exit problems.* Daimler-Benz had a long-standing alliance with ABB called Adtranz. The alliance had been losing money, and after Daimler-Benz merged with Chrysler, an ex-Chrysler executive suggested putting it into liquidation. The Daimler reaction was horror – 'You don't understand. This is Europe. Bankruptcy is not good over here.' Eventually ABB was bought out. In another example, Suzuki wanted to make redundancies at a joint venture in Spain. The result was riots outside the Japanese embassy in Madrid (Inkpen and Ross 2001).

 SUCCESSFUL PARTNERSHIPS – GALANZ

CASE STUDY 1.5

Guangdong Galanz is the global leader in microwave manufacture, producing over 18 million units in 2004, 40 per cent of the global market. It is one of the largest home appliance manufacturers in China, employing 20,000 people and with 2004 revenues exceeding US $1 billion.

This is a far cry from the first incarnation of the company, as the Guizhou Down Product Factory, a township enterprise set up by Qingde Leung in 1978, when the Chinese government set up its first Special Enterprise Zones in Guangdong in southern China. The company washed and processed goose feathers for clothing companies

such as Yves St Laurent. By 1992, the company had sales of US $19 million, and ranked in the top 100 village and township enterprises in China.

However, Leung was worried that intense competition would kill the textiles business, and he took the momentous decision to diversify into microwaves, at that time a luxury item in China. He changed the name of the company to the Galanz Group of Guangdong, recruited experts from a radio factory in Shanghai, and licensed microwave technology from Toshiba. In 1993, the company produced a trial run of 10,000 microwaves, and persuaded the

Shanghai No 1 Department Store to stock them.

In 1994 Chinese government policy changed, and township enterprises were required to sell two-thirds of each enterprise to management. The result was a broad base of middle managers with a stake in the company's success.

Galanz was faced with fierce competition from the market leader SMC. However, ironically, SMC was crippled by its partnership agreement with the huge American white goods manufacturer Whirlpool. Whirlpool put in its own management team, and required that all major decisions were cleared first through regional headquarters in Hong Kong and ultimately through corporate headquarters in Michigan. By 1995 Galanz had a 25 per cent share of the Chinese market, surpassing SMC, and by 1998 this had grown to half the market. Clearly further growth in the domestic market would be difficult.

In 1997, one result of the Asian financial crisis was that South Korean microwave manufacturers, including Samsung and LG, were accused of dumping microwaves on the European market. European manufacturers felt that they were unable to compete.

In a novel deal, Galanz offered to make their microwaves in China for half the European cost. European manufacturers shipped their whole production lines to Guangdong, where they could take advantage of Galanz's lower labour costs and efficient supply chain. The microwaves would then be exported back to Europe to be sold under the European companies' brand names. Galanz also secured permission from its partners to use their facilities to produce Galanz branded goods in China. Galanz signed up 200 European partners, and its microwave production grew from one million in 1996 to 12 million in 2001.

The deal was a win–win. The European partners obtained product at a much lower cost than they could have produced themselves, while Galanz was able to expand and become a global presence without having to make heavy capital investments itself.

(Source: Sull 2005.)

A FAILED ALLIANCE STRATEGY – SWISSAIR

CASE STUDY 1.6

In the 1990s, Swissair was one of the most successful and respected airlines in the world, noted for its high quality, which permitted it to charge high prices. In 1998 it made a profit of SFr 400 million (around £200 million). Yet by 2000, the company was losing SFr 2.9 billion, and in October 2001 it went into receivership.

What went wrong? The immediate cause of the collapse was the world crisis in the airline industry following the terrorist attacks on 11 September 2001, but a more fundamental cause was Swissair's failed alliance strategy.

Until the late 1980s, the European airline industry was dominated by national carriers with effective monopolies in their home markets. This kept competition low, and prices and profits high. However, the first steps towards the liberalisation of the world airline industry came in 1988. This represented a threat to Swissair, with its small home market. In 1993, talks (code named Alcazar) were opened between Swissair, SAS (Scandinavian Airlines), KLM (the Netherlands) and Austrian Airlines. A new company was proposed, with Swissair, SAS and KLM each holding 30 per cent, and Austrian 10 per cent. However, Swiss public opinion was hostile to the idea of Swissair losing its name, and the talks broke down.

In 1994, Swissair hired McKinsey to develop a new strategy. Three options were put forward:

● *Go it alone.* Given the small size of the Swiss home market, this was not seen as viable.

● *Develop a new business alliance (in effect a repeat of the Alacazar strategy).* This was seen as high risk, but the most politically acceptable.

● *Ally with one of the large European airlines (BA, Lufthansa or Air France).* This was seen as the safest option, but politically unacceptable, as Swissair would inevitably be a very junior partner.

As a first step, in 1994 Swissair acquired a 49.5 per cent stake in the Belgian airline Sabena, which had only made a profit once in its 75-year history. Meanwhile, the world aviation industry was changing rapidly. In 1996, BA, American Airlines, Cathay Pacific and Qantas formed a new global alliance called Oneworld. Two other alliances followed – Skyteam, led by Air France; and Star, including United Airlines, Lufthansa and SAS.

Swissair decided to go for a strategy of forming a fourth alliance. It acquired minority stakes in the Polish airline LOT, the French company Air Littoral, the Italian airlines Air Europe and Volare, and South African Airways (SAA), in addition to its existing holding in Sabena and Austrian Airlines. None of the partners, with the possible exception of SAA, was known as a strong airline.

Swissair already had long-standing alliance relationships with Delta and Singapore Airlines, both strong companies. However, Delta decided to join Skyteam in 1999, while Singapore Airlines joined Star. In 2000, an aggressive attempt to increase Swissair's stake in Austrian Airlines led to that airline also defecting to Star. Meanwhile, the European market was increasingly being penetrated by the low-cost airlines Ryanair and EasyJet. The latter set up a hub in Geneva, directly threatening Swissair on its home ground.

By mid-July 2001, Swissair had debts of SFr 7.8 billion, six times the value of its equity, and its share price was one-fifth of its peak in 1998. Given this weakness, 9/11 was merely the last straw. Both Swissair and its partner Sabena were doomed.

The main lesson of this case – if you have weaknesses yourself, don't ally with partners who are even weaker.

(Source: Ruigrok 2004.)

 CASE STUDY 1.7

PARTNERSHIP FAILURE – THE HATFIELD TRAIN CRASH

In the mid-1990s, Britain's rail system was privatised. A single company, British Rail, was replaced with a network of partnerships as the rail system was fragmented. Railtrack was made responsible for operating, developing and maintaining the physical track network, but did not operate trains. This was done by train operating companies (TOC), which obtained medium-term contracts from the government to operate particular lines.

They then paid access charges to Railtrack for use of the track. Tensions inevitably built up between Railtrack and the operating companies. Railtrack needed access to the track to carry out maintenance, but this prevented the operating companies from running trains. There were several high-profile rows over the West Coast Main Line, when Christmas maintenance over-ran, causing vociferous complaints from the TOC, Richard Branson's Virgin.

In addition Railtrack took the decision not to carry out its own maintenance, as British Rail had. Instead, maintenance was outsourced to seven main contractors, who in turn outsourced particular aspects to 2,000 sub-contractors. This meant that Railtrack was dependent on sub-contractors over whom they had no control. Maintenance policy was also changed from planned replacement to replacement when required.

On 17 October 2000, a serious accident happened on the East Coast Main Line at Hatfield, when a rail broke under the wheels of a GNER express from London to Leeds. Four people died and 70 were injured.

Any fatal rail crash is a tragedy, but subsequent investigations proved that the accident was a disaster waiting to happen, and that it was directly attributable to the breakdown in the relationships between the various players involved in the post-privatisation railway system.

In the winter of 1999, a routine inspection by Balfour Beatty, the main contractor, spotted cracks in a rail near Hatfield, and recommended that the rail should be ground to get rid of the cracks. This would be carried out by a sub-contractor, Serco. Before this could be done, Balfour Beatty recommended that the rail should be replaced – by another sub-contractor, Jarvis. In March 2000, Railtrack agreed that the rail should be replaced as a 'priority #1', which meant that the work should be completed within a month.

The replacement was booked to be done on 19 March, but before this could be done, replacement rails had to be delivered to the site. However, the train delivering the new rails – owned by Railtrack and manned by Jarvis – was late, and the rails could not be dropped. The replacement slot was lost. After three more attempts, the rails were finally delivered at the end of April 2000.

Four months then passed while Railtrack attempted to negotiate a rail replacement date with Jarvis that was also acceptable to the TOC, GNER. Eventually a date was set for the last week of November – a year after the original problem was spotted. Meanwhile, Railtrack was still worried about the deteriorating state of the rail, and ordered it to be reground by Serco. This was done in September, though some experts think that the rail was already so damaged that regrinding may have made the problem worse.

Before the rails could be replaced, the Hatfield accident happened. As a result of the accident, crippling speed restrictions were placed on the whole railway network – a classic example of the stable door being shut after the horse has bolted. As an indirect result of the crash, Railtrack was taken into administration by the government in October 2001, and replaced by the not-for-profit organisation Network Rail, which speedily brought its major engineering maintenance contracts back in-house.

The lessons for partnerships: the key need to agree on priorities (in this case, that passenger safety is paramount), and the crucial role of communication. It may also be significant that the partnerships in the rail industry were in effect imposed by the government as part of rail privatisation, rather than being voluntary.

(Sources: Child 2005, Jowit 2001.)

HR OUTSOURCING

Case study 1.7 illustrates how outsourcing can be a key element of a partnership strategy. One popular candidate for outsourcing is HR. HR outsourcing can cover a wide spectrum of activities, from a small business using a local personnel freelancer to handle its HR on a part-time basis, to a joint venture formed between a multinational company and an HR services company to handle all of the former's HR function. Here we are more concerned with the latter end of the spectrum, where control over significant elements of the outsourcer's HR function is outsourced to a partner organisation.

A 2009 CIPD survey found that 29 per cent of organisations sampled were using HR outsourcing, with 64 per cent increasing their use of outsourcing in the previous five years, and only 11 per cent reducing it (CIPD 2009). The top drivers for HR outsourcing were access to skills and knowledge not available within the organisation (71 per cent), improving quality (64 per cent), and cost reduction (61 per cent). Outsourcers seem to have achieved these objectives. Ninety-one per cent claimed to have accessed knowledge and skills, 83 per cent to have improved quality, and 90 per cent to have reduced costs.

The most common functions to have been outsourced were legal, payroll, pensions, training and recruitment. Least likely to have been outsourced were resource planning, appraisal, strategy and policy. There seems to be a clear trend to outsource operational parts of the HR function, and to keep more strategic elements in-house.

Also interesting are reasons given for not using HR outsourcing, even when the organisation involved outsources other significant functions. The three most commonly given reasons for not outsourcing HR were:

- effective, well-resourced HR team within the organisation (52 per cent)
- remain unconvinced of the benefits of HR outsourcing (35 per cent)
- already use effective shared-service model (24 per cent).

Shared-service centres are a common alternative to HR outsourcing and are discussed below.

In practice, HR outsourcing does not always go smoothly. BP, for example, was the first major company to sign a large HR outsourcing deal, with Exult in 1998. Exult was taken over by Hewitt in 2004, and the deal started to run into trouble. By 2006, Hewitt was losing US $166 million, citing problems in HR outsourcing, while BP took back expatriate administration in-house, and also gave two years' notice that it intended to end the contract with Hewitt. However, in February 2009, it signed a new contract, extending the scope of the contract worldwide (rather than just the UK and US), but taking most aspects of recruitment back in-house (Pickard 2009).

Cable & Wireless went further. In 2006, it announced that it was not renewing its five-year contract with Accenture. The main reason given was that Cable & Wireless had drastically downsized following the dot-com crash in 2001, from 57,000 staff to 14,000, and as a result could more easily do its own HR in-house. However, Ian Muir, the international HR director, admitted that some valuable tacit knowledge had been lost through outsourcing (Pickard 2006).

An alternative to HR outsourcing is a shared-service centre. This involves the use of a call centre to give HR advice to line managers and, often, individual employees (Marchington and Wilkinson 2008). Three models are common:

- an in-house function
- an in-house function which also offers services on the open market to other organisations seeking to outsource their HR
- a specialist unit offering HR services for a number of employers in a network. This model is common among schools and in the NHS. An NHS example is discussed by Marchington and Wilkinson (pp197–198).

 ACTIVITY 1.4 MANAGING AN HR OUTSOURCING CONTRACT

You are responsible for managing an HR outsourcing contract in your organisation. What steps do you need to take to ensure that this contract is managed effectively?

 ACTIVITY 1.5 SEMCO

Semco is a Brazilian manufacturing company based in São Paulo and owned by Ricardo Semler. It is run like no other company. Its basic rule is that there are no rules.

- Workers make decisions.
- Management sets its own salaries and bonuses.
- Everyone has access to the company books.
- Shop-floor workers set their own productivity targets and work flexi-time.
- Workers negotiate with management the level of profit-sharing, and then decide among themselves how it is allocated.
- Before anyone is hired or promoted to a management position, they are interviewed, evaluated and approved by all the people who will work for them.
- Every six months, Semco managers are appraised by all their subordinates, and the results are published for all to see.
- Workers have the option of taking 75 per cent of their basic pay, and receiving a supplement taking it up to 125 per cent, but only if the company has a good year.

- Workers are encouraged to set up their own satellite companies to supply Semco.
- When a job opening occurs, a Semco employee who meets 70 per cent of its requirements is given preference over an outsider.
- Semco doesn't have an organisation chart. Only the respect of the led creates a leader.
- Ricardo Semler takes two months' holiday a year, leaves no contact number, and does not himself contact the company. When he had a serious car accident in 2005, spending months in intensive care with a broken neck, the company maintained its 25 per cent plus growth rate, and ran seamlessly without him.
- The guiding rule on everything is common sense.

Semco is one of Latin America's fastest-growing companies, acknowledged to be the best in Brazil to work for, and has a waiting list of thousands of applicants waiting to join it.

Would you feel comfortable working for Semco?

(Sources: Semler 1993, Fisher 2005.)

CONNECTIONS BETWEEN THE ENVIRONMENT, STRATEGY, ORGANISATIONAL DESIGN AND HR

In this section, we will examine three models: Thompson's model of E-V-R congruence, Porter's model of competitive strategy, as developed by Schuler and Jackson, and Miles and Snow's model of strategic configurations, as developed by Delery and Doty.

E-V-R CONGRUENCE

Thompson (2005) developed the concept of E-V-R congruence as a measure of how well an organisation is attuned to its environment. It develops the idea of SWOT analysis to incorporate values. In his model, E represents the environment (the opportunities and threats elements of a SWOT analysis), while R represents resources and V represents values, both of which are traditionally subsumed within the strengths and weaknesses elements of a SWOT. To Thompson, resources are physical, while values represent the human strengths and weaknesses of the organisation, specifically its leadership and culture, as well as the underlying values which it holds.

More important than the basic idea of E-V-R is the concept of congruence. An organisation will achieve congruence when its environment, resources and values are mutually reinforcing. Its strategic position will be strong. A congruent organisation is illustrated below.

Figure 1.10 The congruent organisation

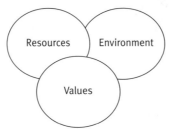

Thompson then identifies types of organisations where the three elements are not congruent.

Figure 1.11 The unconsciously competent organisation

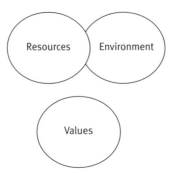

Here the values of the organisation are out of line with its environment and resources, but because environment and resources are aligned, the organisation still works, at least on a superficial level. This type of organisation is likely to be complacent, and runs the risk of serious trouble if its environment and resources start to drift out of line. The strategic imperative here is for a change in leadership style and a redefinition of values and culture.

Figure 1.12 The consciously incompetent organisation

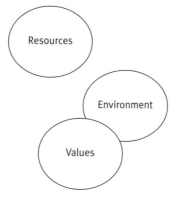

Here the organisation is aware that there is a resource mismatch, but tends to see it as a series of short-term problems. The organisation will tend to be reactive and to fight fires, while unable to take a long-term strategic view of resources.

Figure 1.13 Strategic drift

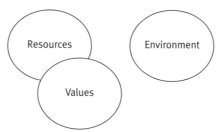

Here the organisation has lost touch with its environment, perhaps because of complacency, or of a failure to scan the environment effectively. It must either find a way to change its environment, or to bring its resources and values back in line with changes in the environment.

Figure 1.14 The lost organisation

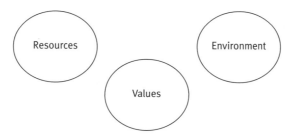

Unless this organisation takes swift and drastic action to reachieve congruence, in the long run it is doomed.

THE NATIONAL TRUST AND E-V-R

CASE STUDY 1.8

The National Trust (NT) has as its core aim to 'look after special places, for ever, for everyone'. It is the largest private landowner in Britain, owning 640,000 acres, mostly rented out to tenants on commercial terms. It also owns 600 miles of Britain's coastlines, guaranteeing free public access to the coast, and around 300 houses and gardens, which are open free to members, and at a small charge to others. In 2005–06, there were 13.7 million visits to NT properties, of which 2.9 million, or around 20 per cent, were paying visits, while the rest were visits by members (National Trust 2006).

Clearly the NT estate is a hugely valuable asset, which on an open market valuation would be worth billions of pounds. However, remember the words 'for ever' in the core purpose. The Trust is legally prohibited from selling property, and the result is that in many ways the estate must be seen as a liability rather than an asset, which must be maintained at ever-growing expense (Legg 2005).

More conventional physical resources include NT gift shops at most sites, and also extensive catering facilities (which earned £25 million in 2005–06, twice as much as admissions).

A key resource of the Trust is its membership. This has increased from 152,000 in 1971 to 3.4 million in 2006. Over the same period income has risen from £2.4 million to £337 million (Clover 2003). The Trust makes a healthy surplus of around £20 million a year, or about 6 per cent of turnover. In addition, the NT has 6,000 staff, many of them highly qualified in conservation, property management or gardening, and tens of thousands of active volunteers.

However, the membership is overwhelmingly white, middle-aged and middle class, with little penetration in the inner cities, and it is thought that most members join solely to get free access to Trust properties. The activists – the volunteers – who to visitors are the public face of the NT, are older and more middle class than the membership and are seen by many as representatives of the 'green welly' country set.

By the 1990s, the NT, though growing rapidly, was seen as increasingly out of touch – reactionary, elitist and part of the Establishment, not interested in promoting social inclusion. Operation Neptune, a populist campaign begun in the 1960s to improve access to the coastline, had run out of steam.

Just as it was out of touch with modern urban society, the NT also antagonised many of its country-based members by getting involved in the hunting dispute. In 1997 it banned stag hunting on its property, and was split over fox hunting, with each side accusing the other of dirty tricks. Part of the problem was the Trust's system of governance. It was controlled by a 52-member council, mostly nominated by interest groups like the RSPB and the Open Space Society, which met only four times a year. The council was widely seen as a self-perpetuating old-boy network (Houlder 2003). The system also gave great power to the chairman, who controlled proxy votes which he could use at his discretion. The pro-hunting lobby complained that the proxy voting system was frequently used against them.

A turning point came with the appointment of a new director-general, Fiona Reynolds, in 2001. She had previously headed the Cabinet Office's womens' unit, was close to New Labour, and talked of shedding the Trust's 'remote and elitist' image. She appointed Lord Blakenham, sometime chairman of the *Financial Times* and the RSPB, to review the NT's system of governance.

Blakenham reported in April 2003. He recommended that in future the governing body should be a 12-member board of trustees (effectively a board of directors). The council would remain and would in effect become a supervisory board on the German model. The proxy voting system should be replaced by postal voting. The board of trustees formally took control in 2005. The Blakenham report seems to have turned the tide. The national ban on fox hunting has also helped, defusing the main internal bone of contention. Reynolds has increased the educational role of the Trust, expanded family memberships, bringing younger people into membership, and has spearheaded a move into the inner cities, preserving back-to-back working-class houses in Birmingham, and John Lennon and Paul McCartney's boyhood homes in Liverpool (Proby 2005).

How does the NT rate in terms of E-V-R convergence? In the late 1990s the organisation was at best unconsciously competent. Its values were clearly out of line with resources and environment. At worst, it was at severe risk of becoming a lost organisation, with resources and environment slipping apart. Reynolds' leadership since 2001 seems to have pulled the NT back into congruence, with environment, resources and values back in line.

There are still tensions, of course. When the NT outsourced its membership administration, the result in the short term was chaos. In 2005, the Trust ran into trouble when it imposed charges at its car parks on the South Downs, seemingly in contradiction to the free-access principles of Operation Neptune (Payne 2005), and again when it decided to split up one of the Lake District hill farms which it had inherited from the author Beatrix Potter (Page 2005). There are also possibly worrying signs in the NT's own annual report. Visitor ratings for customer service (67 per cent) and for a 'very enjoyable visit' (62 per cent) are both low and below target.

In 2007, the NT published a new strategy document, covering the period to 2012 and beyond. This demonstrates an extension of the new thinking in the Trust. The key future role of the Trust was to be an environmental education group, engaging with government and society in a quest to find ways of tacking climate change. Fiona Reynolds stressed that this represented a return to the original aims of the Trust's founders, which emphasised social philanthropy and mutual benefit. As Reynolds said, 'This is going back to our roots. We are a cause. It's a profound moment of recognition' (Vidal 2007). Whether she can carry the more diehard and reactionary elements among the Trust's volunteers is another issue.

COMPETITIVE STRATEGY AND HR PRACTICES – PORTER, SCHULER AND JACKSON

Michael Porter argued in *Competitive Advantage: Creating and Sustaining Superior Performance* that firms need to choose between three fundamental approaches to gaining competitive advantage:

- cost reduction
- quality enhancement
- innovation.

The HR implications of these strategies were examined by Schuler and Jackson (1987). Firms pursuing a cost reduction strategy concentrate on tight controls, minimisation of overheads and economies of scale. The emphasis is on quantity rather than quality. They will pursue cost reduction through increased use of part-time and temporary employees; outsourcing (including offshoring to low-wage countries); low wages (at or close to minimum wage levels); minimal levels of training and development; explicit job descriptions that allow little room for ambiguity; narrowly defined career paths; and short-term, results-oriented performance appraisals. There is usually little employee involvement, and unions are likely to be discouraged.

An extreme example of a cost reduction strategy is that pursued by some gangmasters, who sometimes employ illegal immigrant labour at below minimum wage levels, and with little or no consideration for health and safety. After the Morecambe Bay tragedy in 2004, when 23 illegal Chinese immigrant cockle-pickers were drowned, the Gangmasters Licensing Authority was set up to regulate employment in agriculture, fishing (including cockle picking) and food processing, but in 2009 Oxfam reported that gangmasters had subsequently moved into the less regulated construction, hospitality and care sectors, where there were still reports of workers being paid as little as £50 for a 49-hour week (Oxfam 2009).

Firms pursuing a quality enhancement strategy are likely to be much more attractive to work for. Their employment practices are very close to the high commitment HR model, emphasising sophisticated methods of recruitment and selection, and extensive and long-term training and development. There will typically be high levels of employee involvement and empowerment; a high degree of job security; competitive pay; and a concern for work–life balance. Unions are common, and there is likely to be a partnership approach to industrial relations. HR has a key role in supporting the organisation's culture. Quality-enhancing firms are also likely to be concerned with the HR practices at their suppliers. It is vital to the success of the quality-enhancement strategy that suppliers buy into it. A classic example is the Japanese-owned segment of the car industry.

With an innovation strategy, people are managed in order to work *differently* (unlike either the cost reduction strategy, where they are encouraged to work *harder*, or the quality strategy, where they are encouraged to work *smarter*). The emphasis is on informality, flexibility and problem solving. The HR implications are:

- an emphasis on creativity
- long-term focus
- high level of co-operative, interdependent behaviour
- moderate degree of concern for both quality and quantity
- a high degree of risk-taking
- personal and self-development, rather than employer-directed training and development

- a high degree of ambiguity and unpredictability
- an emphasis on individuality, with little demand for unions
- an emphasis on profit-sharing, rather than high wages.

A classic example of long-term successful implementation of an innovation strategy is the American company 3M, which is discussed in case study 1.9.

 INNOVATION AND SIX SIGMA AT 3M

CASE STUDY 1.9

One of the most innovative companies over the past 80 years has been 3M – an abrasives manufacturer that broke its own mould by inventing masking tape in 1925, and which has carried on developing highly innovative new products ever since, from the audio tape to Post-it sticky notes. Its latest new idea is Post-it Picture Paper, which marries the Post-it technology to photographic paper, allowing users to print out pictures from their computer straight on to Post-its.

How does 3M do it? The secret is bottom-up innovation. Someone in the labs, or manufacturing or marketing, comes up with a new idea. When he has convinced his supervisor that he's on to something interesting, he will be set up with a small budget and told to get on with it. Harry Heltzer, who developed the idea that became Scotchlite for adhesive reflective road marking, and later reflective signs, eventually went on to become president of 3M (Grant 2008).

To facilitate the innovation process, 3M has had a long-running policy which permits all research or marketing employees to spend up to 15 per cent of their (and the company's) time on their own projects. In addition, the company operates two career ladders, which make it possible for a technical person to move as high as vice-president without having to take on a managerial role. The result: for years 3M was number one on Boston Consulting Group's Most Innovative Companies list, and it was praised in Collins and Porras' best-seller *Built to Last* in 1994.

Larry Wendling, 3M's vice-president of corporate research, identified 'The Seven Habits of Highly Successful Corporations':

- From the chief executive down, the company must be committed to innovation.
- The corporate culture must be actively maintained.
- Innovation is impossible without a broad base of technology – 3M is a leader in 42 different technologies.
- Networking, both formal and informal. The scientists themselves run an annual symposium for all 9,700 research and development personnel, where ideas and ongoing projects are shared.
- Set individual expectations and reward employees for outstanding work. Hundreds of employees – selected by their peers – are honoured for scientific achievement every year.
- Quantify efforts. 3M carefully tracks its spending to see whether its research and development money is spent wisely.
- Research must be tied to the customer.

(Arndt 2006.)

However, in the late 1990s the dream started to go sour. At a company which has prided itself on earning one-third of its revenue from products invented in the previous five years, the proportion had fallen to a quarter, and by the late 1990s, the company's share price was stagnating.

In 2000, 3M appointed James McNerney as its new CEO. McNerney was the first outsider ever to head the 100-year old company. He came from General Electric, where he had been a disciple of the legendary Jack Welch. His mission: to bring discipline to 3M. He sacked 8,000 workers (11 per cent of the total) and imported GE's Six Sigma programme, a world-renowned statistical quality control technique. The basis of Six Sigma was to reduce variability, and so lower cost. The two main Six Sigma tools are DMAIC (define, measure, analyse, improve, control), and, more critical for 3M, Design for Six Sigma (or DFSS), which aimed to systemise the new product development process. DFSS stressed constant review and quick results. The result was that incremental improvement took precedence over blue-sky research. Traditionally, 3M had allowed researchers years to tinker with new ideas. The consensus within the company was that a new product like Post-it would have been impossible under a Six Sigma regime.

The results of the McNerney regime were predictable. The share price shot up, and so did short-term profits, but innovation stagnated. From number 1 on the Most Innovative Companies list in 2004, 3M fell to second in 2005, third in 2006 and seventh in 2007.

In 2005, McNerney left to head Boeing, and was succeeded by George Buckley, a scientist who quietly proceeded to reverse many of his predecessor's reforms. He said, 'Perhaps one of the mistakes we made as a company – it's one of the dangers of Six Sigma – is that when you value sameness more than you value creativity, I think you potentially undermine the heart and soul of a company like 3M' (Hindo 2007). He has exempted the research scientists from DFSS, and increased the research and development budget by 20 per cent. As one 3M executive said, 'We feel we can dream again.'

MILES AND SNOW AND EMPLOYMENT SYSTEMS

Miles and Snow (1978) suggest four main ways in which organisations can cope with and manage their environments. These involve an interaction between the organisation's strategy, its culture and its environment. They can be:

Defenders   They operate in generally placid environments. They do not actively search for new opportunities, but concentrate on maximising the efficiency of their existing operations. They are very vulnerable to a sudden shift in their environment.

Prospectors   They are attracted to turbulent environments. They are constantly experimenting with novel responses to the environment. They thrive on change and uncertainty, but pay little attention to efficiency. They are decentralised and promote creativity and innovation. They are thus vulnerable if the environment settles down.

Analysers   They are successful poachers. They watch competitors for new ideas and adopt the successful ones. Their approach to the environment is therefore second-hand, and they let the prospectors make the mistakes. They are seeking at the same time to maintain their shares in existing markets, and to exploit new opportunities. They can be seen as a hybrid between defenders and prospectors. A classic example of the analyser strategy is the video recorder war. Sony pioneered the industry with the Betamax format, but was eventually defeated by Matsushita and its VHS format.

Reactors   They make adjustments to their strategy when forced to do so by environmental pressures. Unlike the defenders, they are prepared to change, but they are even more market followers than the analysers. They are not prepared for change, and do little planning. Miles and Snow see this strategy (or lack of it) as basically a failure mode.

Organisations must recognise that a strategy which suited them very well in the past may no longer be appropriate if the nature of the environment which faces them has changed. For example, big national airlines, which were highly bureaucratic and cost-efficient, were highly successful in the tightly regulated environments of the 1960s and 1970s, but were hit hard by more agile budget airlines (Southwest in the US, Ryanair and EasyJet in the UK) as the airline market was deregulated and became more turbulent.

In appropriate types of environment, each of the defender, prospector and analyser strategies can be successful, but the reactor strategy is unlikely to be successful in the long term.

Many later scholars have tested the validity of Miles and Snow's model, and generally have confirmed their findings. For example:

- Shortell and Zajac (1990) found that defenders are the first type of organisation to adopt new production technologies; analysers the first to adopt new management systems; and prospectors the first to develop new products.

- Gimenez (1999) found that among Brazilian small and medium enterprises, reactors were the least successful in terms of increasing their turnovers.

- Peng, Tan and Tong (2004) found that in China, state-owned firms followed defender strategies; privately owned firms prospector strategies; and foreign owned forms analyser strategies.

Delery and Doty (1996) extended Miles and Snow's analysis, and looked at the degree of fit between the organisational models and HR systems. They concentrated on the defender and prospector models (they see the analyser model as a middle-of-the-road system, with elements of both defender and prospector).

They argued that the defender organisation concentrated on efficiency, on producing existing products in a better way, rather than developing new ones, and that this could be best supported by what they described as an internal employment system, which stressed:

- internal career opportunities and recruitment, with well-defined career ladders

- extensive formal training, with a high level of socialisation within the organisation
- behaviour-based appraisal, largely used for developmental purposes
- transparent pay structures based on hierarchy and seniority. Little profit-sharing
- employment security
- a high degree of employee participation, with unions likely to be recognised
- highly defined jobs
- a well-established HR function, with considerable influence.

The prospector organisation constantly searches for new products and markets. The emphasis is on being new rather than being efficient. This is best supported by what they call a market-type employment system, which stresses:

- hiring from outside rather than developing insiders, with little use of career ladders
- little formal training, and only based on short-term needs
- results-based appraisals, with little tolerance for failure
- incentive-based pay systems
- very little employment security
- little employment voice, with unions tolerated at best
- loose and flexible job definitions
- limited role for HR.

A defender organisation is thus likely to attract someone looking for a long-term career, but not for excitement, while working for a prospector organisation is likely to be a lot more stimulating, but much more short-term (see also Marchington and Wilkinson 2008, pp152–153).

Delery and Doly attempted to test their hypotheses empirically through an analysis of the US banking industry, but their findings were not particularly strong. They only examined one role within the banks, that of loan officer. They obtained questionnaire results from 216 banks, but only a minority of these fitted either the market or the internal employment models. Two-thirds were middle of the road in their employment policies. They found that banks that implemented a prospector strategy 'reaped higher return from more results-oriented appraisals and lower levels of employee participation than did banks that relied on a defender strategy' (p826). However, although the theory suggested that internal career paths were more consistent with a defender strategy, their empirical research found the opposite. In general, they found that in the banking industry, 'the closer a bank's employment system resembled the market-type system, the higher its performance' (p827).

ACTIVITY 1.6 MECHANISTIC AND ORGANIC ORGANISATIONS

Mary Jo Hatch (1997) distinguishes between mechanistic and organic organisations. Mechanistic organisations specialise in routine activities with strictly demarcated lines of authority and responsibility. Tasks are highly specialised. Organic organisations have less specialisation. They are less formalised and hierarchical than mechanistic organisations, and use lateral communication.

Question: What parallels can you see between the analyses of Hatch and Miles and Snow?

ACTIVITY 1.7 HENRY MINTZBERG'S ORGANISATIONAL HYPOTHESES

Henry Mintzberg has put forward a number of hypotheses about how situational factors affect the structure and functioning of organisations:

- The older the organisation, the more formalised its behaviour.

- The larger the organisation, the more formalised its behaviour.

- The larger the organisation, the more elaborate its structure.

- The more dynamic an organisation's environment, the more organic its structure.

- The more complex an organisation's environment, the more centralised its structure.

- The more diversified an organisation's markets, the greater the propensity to split into market-based units or divisions.

- Extreme hostility in the environment drives any organisation to centralise its structure temporarily.

(Source: Mintzberg 1998.)

From your knowledge of your own organisation, or any other organisations with which you are familiar, how far do you think these hypotheses are valid?

STAKEHOLDERS

One point of interaction between organisations and the environment comes through stakeholders. Stakeholders are 'those individuals or groups who depend on the organisation to fulfil their own goals and on whom, in turn, the organisation depends' (Johnson and Scholes 1997). Stakeholders can be inside the organisation, eg shareholders or employees; or outside, eg customers or suppliers. In some cases, the relationship is legal, as with statutory regulatory bodies or lenders; or moral, as with the local community; or a mixture of the two, as with employees (to meet the requirements of the contract of employment and to respect legal employment rights (legal), and to fulfil the expectations of the psychological contract (moral)). In the case of the public sector, there are no shareholders, but a wide range of client stakeholders.

Note that the CIPD has a narrower definition of a stakeholder. It includes only those parties who have a legal or financial relationship with the organisation. All others are defined as 'other interested parties' – the CIPD specifically mentions the media and the local community (CIPD 2003). However, this narrow definition ignores the moral and ethical dimensions of stakeholder theory. For example, a local community may have no legal claim on a company that routinely but legally pollutes its environment, but few would deny its moral claim on the company.

Stakeholder theory states that organisations have responsibilities to a wide range of stakeholders. This can be contrasted with the stockholder theory of corporate governance, which states that the organisation's only responsibility is to its shareholders (stockholders in America). Stockholder theory has been defended from several different angles. One is the agency approach associated with Milton Friedman. He argues that managers are legally the agents of the organisation's owners (its shareholders), and under agency law are thus legally obliged to serve only their interests, as long as they keep within the law. Another is the logical argument put forward by John Argenti (1993), who argues that it is logically impossible for an organisation to pursue multiple objectives, ie it cannot simultaneously serve the interests of a range of stakeholders. In times of prosperity, the organisation might be able to deal out rewards in such a way as to keep all the stakeholders quiet, but in hard times, shareholders will take priority, if only because, in the last resort, shareholders can sack the board of directors.

 OXFORD BUS COMPANY

CASE STUDY 1.10

The Oxford Bus Company, a subsidiary of the transport group Go-Ahead, has a stakeholder board. This consists of representatives of customers; a local pressure group representative, nominated by the National Federation of Bus Users; and the Transport Strategy Officer of a local NHS trust, representing large employers; as well as company employees and managers.

The board meets quarterly to discuss company performance and other matters of concern. Although purely advisory, it has been involved in vehicle design, ticketing and customer care issues. In future the company intends that one meeting a year will be held as an open meeting, to which members of the public will be invited. (Weldon 2003.)

Not all stakeholders are equal. Some are much more important to the organisation than others. The relative importance of stakeholders can be analysed using stakeholder mapping (Johnson and Scholes 1997, pp197–203). Stakeholder mapping classifies stakeholders by the power which they have over the organisation, and the degree of interest which they have in it. These can be plotted on a two-by-two matrix.

Figure 1.15 Stakeholder matrix

Level of interest

	Low	High
Low **Power**	A Don't bother	B Inform
High	C Satisfy	D Crucial

Stakeholders of type A can effectively be ignored. They are not interested in the organisation, and have little power to affect it anyway. Conversely, type D are critical, and their interests must be taken into account at all times. Type B are interested in the organisation, but do not have the power to affect it significantly. They need to be kept informed, particularly as they may in turn be able to influence other stakeholders. Type C are passive stakeholders. They have great potential to influence the organisation, but at present little interest in doing so. They need to be kept quiet, so that they do not suddenly take an adverse interest in the organisation and shift into type D.

The implication is that stakeholders have to be actively managed. They can be crucial in mobilising support for the organisation or, if things go badly, they can cripple it.

 ACTIVITY 1.8 EDEXCEL

Edexcel is one of three major examination boards in England, Wales and Northern Ireland. It awards 1.5 million qualifications a year, which include GCSEs, A levels, BTEC qualifications, NVQs and GNVQs. Its annual turnover is £112 million. The other major examination boards are AQA (turnover £128 million) and OCR (turnover £77 million).

Edexcel was formed in 1996 as a result of a government-inspired merger between BTEC, a quango (quasi-autonomous non-governmental organisation) that specialised in vocational qualifications, and the University of London Examinations and Assessment Council, owned by London University, which specialised in

GCSE and A level qualifications. At this stage Edexcel had charitable status.

Edexcel and the other exam boards are answerable to the Qualifications and Curriculum Authority (QCA), the regulator for the industry, and ultimately to the Department for Children, Schools and Families (previously the Department for Education and Skills).

Running an examination board is a high-risk activity. GCSE and A level results are issued in a blaze of publicity each summer, and any mistakes made by the exam boards are picked up by the media in a blaze of adverse publicity. Exam boards always seem to get the blame, even for things which are not their own fault.

An extreme example occurred in the summer of 2002. Edexcel had already endured a wave of bad publicity in the winter of 2001–02, which culminated in a threat by the Education Secretary, Estelle Morris, to strip Edexcel of its licence, condemnation by Number 10 as 'sloppy' and 'unacceptable', and a public apology by Edexcel's chief executive John Kerr. Then in the summer of 2002, there was a row over late changing of grade boundaries for A levels, which led to many A level grades having to be changed, and hundreds of university places being put at risk. Ironically, Edexcel was not at fault – the main culprit was OCR – but all the exam boards suffered from the resulting media storm. The chairman of QCA, Sir William Stubbs, was sacked, and eventually the Education Secretary herself resigned.

In 2003, Edexcel was taken over by the media giant Pearson, a FTSE 100 company with wide interests, including the *Financial Times*, and the publisher Pearson Education. Pearson already had interests in examination systems overseas, and saw it as its aim to 'globalise the marking process'. It is investing heavily in order to computerise the examination system, including online testing and marking.

Ken Boston, the new chairman of QCA, said at the time of the takeover, 'I see no reason why we should blanch at private sector companies.' However, other commentators were less complacent. Martin Ward, deputy general secretary of the Secondary Heads Association (since renamed the Association of School and College Leaders), said, 'the entry of a commercial organisation ... has the potential for less accountability', while Ted Wragg, emeritus professor of education at Exeter University, said, 'I feel alarmed about the future ... People want to feel that an examination board is focused on standards, not profit.'

(Sources: Lewis 2002 and Curtis 2004.)

Questions:

1. Identify and map the stakeholders (including 'other interested parties') of Edexcel as at the summer of 2004.

2. Do you think that the public service role of Edexcel is incompatible with its private ownership?

KEY LEARNING POINTS

- The general environment consists of factors which impact at an industry-wide level, while the task environment is primarily concerned with the immediate environment, which impacts on an individual organisation within an industry.

- Organisations can be seen as open systems which interact with their environments.

- The STEEPLE model lists and classifies the major general environmental factors which impact on organisations.

- The main point of STEEPLE analysis is to identify key environmental drivers.

- Opportunities and threats to the organisation can be classified according to probability of success and attractiveness; and probability of occurrence and impact respectively.

- There are a wide range of different organisational structures, including bureaucracy, divisionalisation, matrix, network and virtual.

- Strategic alliances are of growing importance.

- Links can be identified between Porter's cost reduction, quality and innovation strategies, and HR strategy and practice.

- Miles and Snow have identified four different ways in which organisations react to their environments, and these can be shown to have connections to HR practice.

- Stakeholder theory states that organisations have responsibilities to a wide range of stakeholders.

QUESTIONS

1. What do you think are the main differences between the general and the task environments?

2. What do you understand by the best-fit model of HR?

3. Why did Weihrich suggest that SWOT analysis should be renamed TOWS analysis?

4. Give examples where structure follows strategy.

5. What do you think are the main strengths and weaknesses of the bureaucratic form of organisation?

6. Can you see any disadvantages of the network form of organisation?

7. Why can strategic alliances fail?

8. Do you agree with the proposition that HR outsourcing is most suitable for very small or very large organisations?

9. What HR practices are particularly suitable for an organisation following a quality enhancement strategy?

10. What HR practices are particularly suitable for a defender organisation?

EXPLORE FURTHER

FURTHER READING

Mick Marchington and Adrian Wilkinson's book, *Human Resource Management at Work* (2008, 4th ed), covers much of the material discussed in this chapter, particularly in Part 1 in general, and Chapter 4.

WEBSITES

A key website to assist your study is the CIPD site (www.cipd.co.uk). If you are not a member of the CIPD, you will only be able to access part of the site, but you will have access to the latest HR news, and to factsheets on a range of HR topics. If you are a member, you will have access to a much wider variety of materials, including the library, company profiles, Employment Law at Work, and, most usefully, online journals. CIPD provides direct access to about 350 journals, including *The Economist*, the *Harvard Business Review* and *HR Magazine*, and also gives you entry to the EBSCO database, which provides access to 3,000 journals, including all the leading HRM and HRD journals, as well as the American equivalent of *The Economist*, *BusinessWeek*. The CIPD members' site also gives you access to the archive of *People Management*.

SEMINAR ACTIVITY

ACTIVITY HOLIDAYS

The holiday industry

The holiday industry is in a state of flux. The mainstay of the industry, the foreign package holiday – two weeks in the sun, with everything (flight, accommodation, food, transfers and so on) provided by the tour operator – is in slow decline. In the 1980s, package holidays had 60 per cent of the market, but in 2005 this had fallen to 45 per cent (*Daily Telegraph* 2006). In 2001 20.6 million package holidays were sold, and this had fallen to 19 million in 2006.

Looking more closely at market segments, the bottom of the package holiday market is relatively stable, although not very profitable. The top end is growing rapidly and has better profit margins. The segment which is really coming under pressure is the mainstream mid-market sector, which is in the most rapid decline, and where the competition is fiercest, with wafer-thin margins.

The package holiday market as a whole is coming under increasing threat from the short break market, built around the budget airlines, particularly Ryanair and EasyJet. Increasingly, people take a number of short, often city-based, breaks, booking both their flight and their accommodation through the Internet. The other major growth area is the specialist package holiday segment, loosely described as activity holidays, about which more later.

At the same time as the traditional package holiday was declining, the method of selling them has been changing. In 1999, 61 per cent of package holidays were booked through a high street travel agent, but by 2003 this had fallen to 49 per cent. At the same time, the number of bookings made either direct with a tour operator or through the Internet rose.

The trend is even more stark when we look at all holidays, rather than just package holidays. In 2004, travel agents and the Internet each shared one-third of bookings, with the other third shared between family and friends and direct booking with a tour operator (*Marketing* 2004).

Until 2007, there were four major players in the UK overseas travel industry. All are vertically integrated, operating retail travel agents as well as tour operations and an airline. The market leader, Thomson, is owned by the German company TUI, while Thomas Cook is also German-owned. First Choice and the weakest company, My Travel, are UK public limited companies.

Different companies have adopted different strategies to cope with changes in the market. Thomson has concentrated on marketing different segments of its packages, rather than the complete traditional package holiday. If the customer wants to buy just a flight, or just accommodation, that is fine with Thomson. First Choice has gone for market segmentation. It is concentrating on two major segments: the bottom of the package market, and the much more upmarket specialist (particularly activity) segment. In early 2007, it put its mainstream package operations up for sale, with both My Travel and Thomas Cook expressing interest. However, these two companies decided to merge instead, leaving My Travel out in the cold. In response, in the spring of 2007, First Choice and Thomson/TUI agreed to merge.

The activity holiday market

An activity holiday is broadly defined as a holiday in which some form of physical exertion is the main reason for the holiday. It covers a wide range of activities, including skiing, boating, golf, walking, cycling, fishing and birdwatching, as well as multi-activity holidays.

Unlike mainstream package holidays, activity holidays are growing rapidly. Twenty-four per cent of the population claim to have taken an overseas activity holiday in the past five years, and a further 20 per cent say they are likely to in the future. Numbers of holidays sold (including UK holidays) are expected almost to double between 2001 and 2010, from around five million a year to around 10 million, with the value of holidays sold also doubling from around £4.5 billion to around £9 billion or around 17 per cent of all holidays (Keynote 2006). At an average cost of nearly £1,000, activity holidays are also significantly more expensive than other packages, and much more profitable. In 2006 the operating profit of First Choice's activity holiday division made up half of all group profits (First Choice 2007).

This seminar activity will concentrate on two types of activity holiday: walking/trekking and multi-activity. Walking holidays are the most popular activity holiday, with 10 per cent of the population claiming to have taken a walking holiday in the past five years, while 9.5 per cent claim to have taken a multi-activity holiday.

However, the consumer profiles for the two types of holiday are different. Walking holidays are almost exactly split between male and female, and are more popular with the ABC1 social groups (broadly the middle class), people who live in the south, the Midlands and Wales, and single people. People are more likely to take a walking holiday as they get older, with penetration among the 45–54 age group (11.4 per cent) and 55–64 (10.8 per cent) higher than the penetration for the population as a whole (10 per cent). Multi-activity holidays are favoured by men (70 per cent) and the under-35s, but again have a bias towards ABC1s, the south and the single. Perhaps people who enjoy activity holidays when they are young switch towards walking holidays as they get older.

Companies

This activity will look at five companies in the walking/multi-activity segments of the market. Two (Exodus and Waymark) are owned by First Choice, one (Explore) is owned by the holiday group Holidaybreak plc, and two by member organisations (HF Holidays by the Holiday Fellowship and Ramblers Holidays by the Ramblers Association).

Exodus

Exodus is one of two leading companies in the 'soft adventure' sector. It provides walking/trekking holidays combined with sightseeing, white-water rafting, sailing and other activities. Founded in 1973, it was taken over by First Choice in 2002. The number of bookings is unknown, but is believed to be in the region of 30,000 a year. Most holidays are outside Europe, including many in exotic locations, operated in liaison with indigenous specialist companies and guides.

Waymark

Waymark is a small specialist walking company with around 4,500 bookings a year,

but a loyal clientele. Like Exodus, it was taken over by First Choice in 2002, with the remit to grow volumes and margins. In 2004, its managing director Stuart Montgomery admitted that clients 'have a problem' with being part of First Choice (although First Choice ownership is very much played down in the Waymark advertising material) (*Travel Weekly* 2004). Most holidays are in Europe, often using local agents. In 2006–07 Exodus and Waymark started to cross-promote each other.

Explore Worldwide

Founded in 1981, Explore uses a similar business model to Exodus. The average price of holidays is around £1,000. Holidays are usually offered on a bed and breakfast basis, with extensive use of local agents to guide tours. Explore was taken over by Holidaybreak in 2000, and forms about half of Holidaybreak's Adventure Travel division. The division had a turnover of £76 million in 2006, and operating profit of £5.6 million (Holidaybreak 2007). The average Explore client is in their early 40s. About 30,000 holidays are sold each year, and 45 per cent are repeat bookings. Like Exodus, most bookings are made direct, but the company also sells through local travel agents in Australia, Canada and the US.

HF Holidays

This is the oldest of the companies surveyed, and also the biggest. Founded in 1913 and owned by the Holiday Fellowship, it has over 50,000 guests, over half of whom are in the UK. The company runs 17 country house hotels. It is noted for its 'English House party style of warm hospitality' (HF Holidays 2007) and has a very high degree of client loyalty. It claims that at least 80 per cent of customers come back again the following year. It explicitly aims at the 'grey' market, and has the oldest client base of the companies surveyed.

Ramblers Holidays

Ramblers Holidays was founded by the Ramblers Association in 1946, and covenants its net profits to a charitable trust which supports environmental projects. Originally purely a walking company, in recent years it has expanded the proportion of sightseeing on many of its holidays, and also runs a range of holidays concentrating on birds or flowers. More than half of holidays are in Europe, but the proportion of long-haul (and more expensive) holidays has been increasing. In 2006 it introduced 'cruise and walk' holidays. It recently acquired Countrywide Holidays to increase its UK holiday coverage, and also offers a range of holidays aimed at the under-40s. Holidays are led by a volunteer leader from the UK, but on long-haul holidays, a local agency or guide is also used. In 2001 17,000 holidays were sold, and in 2004 turnover was £14 million, giving a pre-tax profit of £1.1 million. Details are not available of the average age of clients, but from personal experience this seems to be mid-50s.

Questions

1. Compile a STEEPLE analysis for the activity holiday industry.

2. Compile a SWOT analysis for Ramblers Holidays.

3. On long-haul holidays, Ramblers Holidays always uses a UK-based leader, directly employed by Ramblers, as well as a local guide, employed by their local partner organisation. Explore sometimes only uses a local guide. What do you think are the HR implications of this difference in policy?

4. How far do you feel that a tour operator like Ramblers or Explore is a virtual organisation?

5. What do you think has been the impact on Ramblers of the implementation of legislation against age discrimination? What about the impact on Club 18–30?

CHAPTER 2

The Managerial Context of Human Resources

LEARNING OUTCOMES

When you have completed this chapter you should be able to:

- summarise the main theories of management, both traditional and contemporary

- explain the difference between power and influence and assess their suitability to a variety of management situations

- use and integrate conflict-handling styles including methods of operating repair situations

- identify the determinants of an effective customer care regime

- explain the difference between the group dynamics and the open systems approaches to managing change and integrate this knowledge into your 'toolbox' of skills for effective change management

- contrast the four stages of quality management and put forward proposals to implement each stage successfully

- reflect on the ability of HR to improve organisational performance

- explore the various models of HR, identifying which is appropriate for differing employment contexts

- evaluate and interpret the various approaches to change management

- in all the above areas, to identify the role of HR to contribute towards successful prevention and resolution of identified problems.

INTRODUCTION

Much of the context of this book concerns the effect and influences of the external environment on the role and function of HR. This chapter deals with the effects *internal* to the organisation together with a brief resume of the roles that HR can play in meeting organisational needs. It starts by providing a summary of the theoretical approach to management, both classical and contemporary; the nature of power and conflict in organisations is then analysed. This is followed by an analysis of how different roles and structures of HR can adjust to and provide effective service to managerial requirements. Finally an examination is made of the specific HR contribution to organisational change, quality assurance and customer care.

THEORIES OF MANAGEMENT

RATIONAL GOAL MODELS

These were the earliest models set out by three principal theorists in the early twentieth century. Frederick Taylor (1947) carried out his research on manufacturing management at the Ford Motor Company while Max Weber's (1925) models of bureaucracy emerged from 30 years studying large complex organisations, especially those under government control.

Their key findings relating to operating organisations effectively overlapped to a large degree, for example:

- Rationality and scientific methods should be used to study work and experiment with human activity. Staff, for example, should be selected on merit judged by a rational selection process.

- Jobs should be fractionised with extensive division of labour to allow individual employees to become highly specialised in jobs which were easy to learn.

- Systems and procedures of management (both in the factory and in the office) should clearly be written down with instructions as to how they should be followed.

- There should be separation of those that plan the work (set out in a clearly ranked managerial hierarchy) and those that actually carry the work out.

- It must be recognised that employees will tend towards economic self-interest in the way that they approach the work situation.

The third theorist, Henri Fayol (1947), concentrated on the art of management, identifying core management tasks (such as planning, organisation of work, control and co-ordination) and setting out principles of effective management that can apply in all organisations. These included:

- unity of command, with orders coming from one source only, and clarity of organisation structure

- consistency of purpose, usually associated with centralised control (although he did recognise there were some circumstances where decentralisation could be appropriate)

- a widespread sense of order with a place for everything (supplies, plant and machinery, clean working conditions), including fixed times for breaks and a well-understood organisation chart

- the operation of 'equity', where management operated not just within the law but within the spirit of the law, treating employees both fairly and kindly

- long-term employment at all levels leading to a sense of order and stability, rather than a constant change of personnel.

In their day, these three theories represented a great step forward and often proved highly successful in practice, such as Taylor's changes in work practices at Bethlehem Steel where, in one example, he reduced the number of workers needed in physical labour from 500 to 140, and the huge increase in productivity his ideas brought at Ford through the implementation of piecework and other motivational schemes. Aspects of all three writers have some resonance today for HR practitioners who support equitable and rational selection processes, and clear communication of management procedures from mission statements to fair sick pay schemes.

However, the overall approaches of so-called 'rational goal models' have major defects in the light of changes in changes in society in the late twentieth century and the start of the twenty-first century:

- The main context of the studies on which these models were based has been very large organisations with dominant positions in their sectors who wish to enhance their dominance and eliminate potential competitors. The growth of regulatory environments, which began in the early part of the twentieth century in America, but which became much more developed from the 1970s, aimed to prevent monopolisation and create healthy competition. There have been many examples of governments legislating to break up organisations with dominant positions, through privatisation of monopolist utilities or through industrial reorganisation. There are therefore fewer organisations to whom the theories immediately apply.

- Establishing a prescribed system of work makes it much more difficult to react to changes in the marketplace. For example, the rapid technological changes in information and computing technology (ICT) and telecommunications have condemned companies who lack nimbleness in a quickly changing competitive environment to decline and often complete disappearance. Examples here are GEC-Marconi in the UK and Nortel in Canada.

- The lack of employee empowerment and the discouragement of flexibility had negative effects on employee commitment, innovation and engagement.

HUMAN RELATIONS MODELS

Although the needs of the employee at work had been considered by early psychologists, the field of human relations study grew through the disquiet felt by some researchers of the work organisation in large industrial organisations in the 1920s and its effect upon employees. The leading exponent here was Elton Mayo (1933) who carried out a series of experiments at the Hawthorne works consisting of measuring productivity and employee satisfaction when changing the physical environment and work systems of the employees.

The results indicated that productivity rose every time changes were made, even if these appeared to be negative such as reducing the light sources and cutting down on rest breaks. The experiments demonstrated that favourable social relations and situations were a much greater influence on performance than physical conditions. Taylorism's claim of overriding employee economic self-interest was rejected. Expressions of encouragement worked better than management coercion and the influence of the peer group was high, emphasising the importance of informal groups within the workplace. It was recognised, therefore, that the group dynamics and social make-up of an organisation were extremely important forces in determining a successful organisation. From this stemmed growing awareness of the concepts of participation, greater trust, team-working and openness – concepts that were supported by the growing personnel profession.

The practical implications of these two schools of thought (rational goals and human relations) were radically different and for much of the latter half of the twentieth century caused confusion among management as to which should be implemented in practice. Towards the end of the century, a number of theories were put forward to synthesise existing theories and to produce more practical advice regarding the conflict.

CONTEMPORARY MANAGEMENT THEORIES

Contingency theory

In simple terms, this theory states that there is no best practice in management and that using rational goal concepts can work in one environment and human relations concepts in another (Fielder 1967). What came to be regarded as much more influential was a two-pronged process. Firstly, the organisation's design and its subsystems (including its working processes and employee relations) must fit with its environment. So the Weber-style bureaucratic design matched with the Tayloristic style of management control may work in a prison or a nuclear power station where systems of control are absolutely vital, but a human relations style is much more appropriate in an advertising agency where creativity and new ideas are paramount. Secondly, the quality and style of leadership are key to the successful implementation of the systems of management in place.

The contingency theory allows for predicting the characteristics of the appropriate situations for effectiveness. Three situational components determine the favourableness or situational control:

- group atmosphere, ie the degree of mutual trust, respect and confidence between the leader and the subordinates
- task structure, ie the extent to which group tasks are clear and structured
- leader position power, ie the power inherent in the leader's position itself.

When there is a good leader–member relationship, a highly structured task and high leader position power, the situation is considered a favourable situation.

Chaos and complexity theories

For many years, mathematicians and scientists had been finding that not all of nature's phenomena can be explained simply. For example, Edward Lorenz, a meteorologist from the Massachusetts Institute of Technology (MIT), was experimenting with computational models of the atmosphere and, in the process of his experimentation, he discovered one of chaos theory's fundamental principles – the Butterfly Effect. The Butterfly Effect is named for its assertion that a butterfly flapping its wings in Tokyo can impact on weather patterns in Chicago. More scientifically, the Butterfly Effect proves that forces governing weather formation are unstable.

Chaos theory was adapted to management theory by Peters (1987) to identify that events can be rarely controlled, especially in a global economy. Chaos theory posits that systems naturally become more complex and, as they do so, they become more volatile and must expend more energy to maintain that complexity and therefore need a bigger structure to maintain stability. This trend continues until the system breaks down completely. It takes an effective management system to identify what is happening and try to prevent it. This theory has received additional credence from the recent credit crunch where the complexity of financial instruments created by hedge funds and merchant banks arising principally from collateralisation of the US mortgage market created a bubble effect which eventually collapsed. The lack of a competent management system which allowed this to happen existed both in the banks – where top management did not understand the financial instruments – and in the regulatory system, which was both slow to act and badly structured (see Chapter **5**)

Complexity is an interdisciplinary field which has emerged from the work of scientists associated with the Santa Fe Institute in the US, such as Murray Gell-Mann, Stuart Kauffman and John Holland, and also scientists based in Europe, such as Ilya Prigogine and Brian Goodwin. Complexity theories lead us to view organisations as complex evolving systems which exist on the edge of order and chaos. It challenges the notion of striving for equilibrium and suggests instead that systems survive and thrive when they are pushed away from equilibrium.

A number of managing innovations are commonly associated with working effectively within a complex environment. This is shown in case study 2.1.

 INTEGRATING COMPLEXITY THEORY AT HUMBERSIDE TRAINING AND EDUCATION COUNCIL (TEC)

CASE STUDY 2.1

Training and Enterprise Councils were established by the government to promote local economic development. Within its region, a TEC would seek to ensure a programme of appropriate training for business and encourage organisations to take advantage of the training opportunities made available. In 1998, Humberside TEC had 150 staff and a budget of £30 million.

For some time, its chief executive, Peter Fryer, had been studying complex adaptive systems and their implications for employing organisations, and he made a conscious decision to explore how the principles of complexity theory could be integrated into the running of the TEC. Using this perspective, he took out of the organisation many of the traditional approaches to management, such as rules, hierarchy charts, budgets, appraisals, job descriptions and, importantly, those posts relating to checking and supervising.

In their place, he introduced a culture which treated all its staff as responsible adults and who were trusted to act in the best interests of the business. Within these parameters, staff were free to take whatever decisions they felt were appropriate. The purpose of this approach was to recognise that the real business of the organisation took place at the interface between the staff member and the client or stakeholder. Therefore, the more staff who were available at this interface and were able to take decisions on behalf of the TEC, the better the standards of service would become. As employees developed a sense of ownership of their contribution to the TEC, it became more effective and efficient, as was demonstrated by various independent benchmarking studies. The approach also encouraged employees to be more creative, to feel a valued part of the organisation and consequently to work smarter.

The effect of this was to disperse the leadership throughout the organisation with the chief executive taking up a 'holding' style of leadership. This style entailed:

- helping determine the broad framework of the organisation and communicating it so that employees knew the parameters within which they were free to take decisions

- identifying and feeding back both the internal and external emergent patterns in the environment.

This created the space within which possibilities could be explored by all employees, and risks taken and mistakes made and built on by recognising the new opportunities which were not previously apparent. It also nurtured the culture of self-responsibility and accountability.

Examples of the practical implications are as follows:

- *Learn continuously* – the TEC as a system needed to respond to its environment; learning was seen as integral to the job and mistakes were valued as learning opportunities. The only form that all employees were required to complete each month (to be passed to the managing director) was one which asked what people had learned. This communicated the message that learning was highly valued.

- *Make processes ongoing* – the TEC was a self-organising system in which learning, planning and evaluating were an ongoing process. Structures should follow, not lead, and systems and processes should be based on the best people in the organisation rather than the one or two people who might abuse the system. Many TEC policies were changed to trust people to use their judgement and take responsibility. For example, the expenses policy stated that any reasonable expenses incurred on TEC business will be reimbursed.

- One of the TEC's most powerful interventions was the formation of a steering group comprising people from the HR team and IT team. The aim of this group was to implement IT in a way that encouraged and increased learning. There was the realisation within the TEC that IT could be implemented in a number of ways on a continuum from controlling to empowering, and it therefore seemed important to challenge assumptions about IT. These two groups of people differed quite markedly in their language and assumptions and priorities. The steering group gave them a common agenda and frequent opportunities to work together.

- Another example of creating space for *collaborative learning* was the process of developing and introducing 360-degree appraisal. This was undertaken by a group of volunteers who approached the task as an action research project. Every member of the group both contributed to the development and also piloted the system on themselves. The resulting system was a paperless appraisal system in which the appraisee was responsible for his/her own appraisal. Appraisal was moving away from being a tool to 'know' or 'measure' employees and thus to better govern them (Townely 1996), towards being a vehicle for learning which was in the hands of the job-holder.

To help staff cope with this new freedom and responsibility, a substantial self-development support programme was introduced which emphasised the development of thinking, learning skills and self-confidence.

An important part of this approach was the annual stakeholder study, which was conducted independently through face-to-face interviews with a representative group of over 70 stakeholders. The study looked at both the progress towards meeting the aims of the TEC and also how well it was living its stated values. The report was published each year in an unabridged version, however critical it was, and formed the basis of the following year's TEC plans in an open and responsive fashion.

Some years later, the TECs were replaced by Learning and Skills Councils and Peter Fryer, before his departure, said:

> This approach to running the TEC has been incredibly successful in terms of levels of customer service and staff satisfaction. We have started to extend this style of leadership to all those in the community that interact with the TEC, through approaches such as contracting for outcomes. However, a word of caution; no matter how many times I tell this story and no matter how many caveats I put on it, it always sounds as though we knew where we were going and that we had some grand plan for becoming a learning organisation. But we didn't, and for those of you who have experienced complexity you will know that we couldn't have, because complexity just doesn't work that way.

(Sources: University of Hull Business School 2007, Storr 2009.)

POWER, POLITICS AND THE SEARCH FOR MANAGERIAL LEGITIMACY

INTRODUCTION

Power is the ability to do something; the capacity for producing an effect. The possession and exercise of power is, clearly, an essential aspect of management. Managers usually have to achieve results in situations where there are a number of forces both for and against the aims they are pursuing and/or the manner in which they are being pursued. Consequently, an understanding of the nature of power, and skill in its acquisition and use, are important attributes of effective managers.

The political nature of organisations is increasingly recognised by managers, and the need for such recognition is well expressed by Burns (quoted in Pugh et al 1971, pp46–47):

> For a proper understanding of organisational functioning, it is necessary to conceive of organisations as the simultaneous working of at least three

social systems. The first of these is the formal authority system derived from the aims of the organisation, its technology and its attempt to cope with its environment. This is the overt system in terms of which all discussion about decision making normally takes place. But organisations are also cooperative systems of people who have career aspirations and a career structure, and who compete for advancement. Thus decisions taken within the overt structure inevitably affect the differential career prospects of the members, who will therefore evaluate them in terms of the career structure as well as the formal system, and will react accordingly. This leads to a third system of relationships which is part of an organisation – its political system. Every organisation is the scene of political activity in which individuals and departments compete and cooperate for power. Again all decisions in the overt system are evaluated for their relative impact on the power structure as well as for their contribution to the achievements of the organisation.

Political activity within organisations is often regarded as inappropriate behaviour. On the other hand, organisations of all kinds actively promote the development of leadership that is regarded as a key quality in managers. And yet, leadership has to do with the exercise of power and influence; it is the process of influencing others, and the use of power is one means by which leaders gain the support of those they lead.

POWER AND INFLUENCE

MacMillan (1978) draws a useful distinction between power and influence. He defines influence as the capacity to control and modify the perceptions of others whereas power is defined as the capacity to restructure actual situations. Power and influence, in combination, determine political capability. MacMillan defines politics as the process that takes place when one or more 'actors' attempt to structure a situation so that their individual goals are promoted. An actor can be an individual, a group, an organisation or a nation.

In relation to their own staff, with whom, in the main, they would not be in competition, effective managers will normally use their influencing skills, rather than overt power, to persuade staff of the merits of proposed courses of action. The exercise of influence and power can be considered in terms of a continuum in which a manager may move from, for example, a neutral style to more overt use of power. The following illustrates, in very simple terms, such a progression.

- 'This is something for your unit, Bill.' – neutral drawing of attention.
- 'This is the situation and I suggest you do so and so …' – reference to the needs of the situation.
- 'As your superior I am telling you to do this.' – influence sought by reference to formal authority.
- 'I'm moving you on to another section.' – the manager has demonstrated his/ her power to restructure the actual situation.

Effective managers seldom need to move to the 'power' end of this continuum with their own staff and colleagues.

In other circumstances, however, overt use of power may be the more important factor in achieving desired results. For example, if several competing developers are bidding for the same plot of building land the successful bidder will be the one who has the necessary purchasing power to outbid the rivals. In such circumstances power rather than influence is the dominant element in determining the political capabilities of the parties involved.

Thus, the exercise of power and influence has an internal and an external dimension.

BUSINESS AS A POLITICAL INSTITUTION

In discussing business as a political institution Drucker (1981) points to the development, in a pluralist society, of all institutions as political institutions defined by their 'constituencies'. This makes it essential, in Drucker's view, for managers to think politically. He elaborates on this as follows:

> In a political system there are far too many constituencies to optimise. One must try to determine the one area in which optimisation is required but in all other areas – their number in a political system is always large – one tries to satisfice, that is, to find a solution in which enough of the constituencies can acquiesce. One tries to find a solution that will not create opposition, rather than one that would generate support. Satisficing is what politicians mean when they talk of an 'acceptable compromise'. Not for nothing is politics known as 'the art of the possible', rather than the art of the desirable.

It is through the exercise of power and influence, then, that individuals and groups seek to persuade, induce or coerce others into following certain courses of action.

Power does not function in isolation. It provides a base, a springboard from which to act, but there are a number of preconditions that need to be satisfied before its potential can be realised. Fundamentally, power involves the ownership or control of resources, and the influence of such resources is governed by the degree of dependence that others have on them and the extent to which alternative resources are available.

Changes in the organisation, such as new technology, mergers and redundancies, can reduce the power of some parts of the organisation and increase the power of others. So, power relationships can change, and these changes are dependent upon changes in the environment in which the organisation operates. The parallels with evolutionary psychology are unmistakable. In summary, organisations are collections of linked coalitions whose relative power determines the decisions taken in the organisation relative to the environment facing the organisation.

INDICATORS OF POWER

Johnson and Scholes (1988), drawing on Pfeffer (1981), suggest that power may be assessed by looking for indications of it. They identify the following four factors as useful power indicators:

- *Status of individual or group.* This may be indicated by position within the organisation, salary levels and reputation within and/or outside the organisation.

- *Claim on resources.* The proportion of the organisation's resources claimed by a group can be a useful indicator of the group's power. If, in addition, the increase or decrease of this proportion is known this will indicate a parallel increase or decrease in the group's power. A comparison with the claim on resources of similar groups in other organisations can give a further indication of the relative power base of the individual or group concerned.

- *Representation in powerful positions.* The functional areas of an organisation that are represented or not represented at board level provide a useful indicator of the influence of different functions on the major decisions of the organisation. The relative power of accounting, engineering or marketing, for example, may be the result of the functional origins of the organisation's founders or key decision-makers, and will inevitably affect the strategic orientation of the organisation.

- *Symbols of power.* These are very varied and will be displayed both by those with formal power and by those whose power is derived from more informal sources. The demonstration of easy access to senior people, for example, can be an indicator of power.

 ACTIVITY 2.1 POWER IN YOUR DEPARTMENT

What indicators of power do you notice in your department or division of your organisation? Is it a high-status department or division? Is this confirmed by the indicators? Record your analysis and reflections in your self-development diary.

SOURCES OF MANAGEMENT LEGITIMACY

Morgan (1986) has identified the following power bases within the organisation as being among the most important sources of management power:

- The formal authority exercised by the owner/manager.

- Authority set out under legislation. This covers a very wide area including duty of care to employees, where employers can enforce health and safety rules, obligations under old master–servant common law which still apply (such as manager's right to enforce confidentiality of critical details – production methods, list of customers, etc) and duties to shareholders under public limited companies legislation.

- Authority as established by the formal organisation chart.

- Delegated authority, such as authority to spend under delegated budgets or instigate capital expenditure within prescribed limits.

- Authority through possessing vital knowledge or skills. For example, HR practitioners may possess authority because of their skills in negotiating or their ability to win tribunals. IT staff may be the only employees able to fully understand aspects of the company's networking system. Research and development staff may have crucial knowledge of patented inventions. Certain production and maintenance staff may be the only employees who know how to carry out major alterations on vital production equipment.

- Political power (or connection power) can be exercised through the development of networks, both inside the organisation (inter-divisional networks) or external (customers, suppliers, lobbying, legal).

- Charismatic power, usually exercised at the top, is the simple, but rare ability to convince all they met that they know the correct answers and should be listened to.

- Reward power is that power exercised by managers who have the authority to give rewards that are valued by employees – bonuses, salary increases, benefits or other forms of recognition.

- Crisis power is the ability to manage under considerable uncertainty, such as prevails constantly in money markets or where instant decisions by those confident enough to grasp the opportunity are unquestioned.

- Countervailing power can be operated by specialists who can step in to oppose policies because of their unique knowledge or authority. For example, the regulators, such as OFT, can step in to halt a merger, or the tax authority can question dubious financial transactions. Internally, auditors can do the same (but rarely do), but accountants can attempt to prevent excess spending or the HR manager to prevent an instant unfair dismissal. In the 1970s in the UK, the greatest countervailing power was exercised by the trade unions and this still applies today in isolated areas, such as the London Underground.

 ACTIVITY 2.2 SOURCES OF POWER

What are the sources of power in your department or division of your organisation? How has this changed over time? Are the sources becoming more important? Or less? Record your analysis and reflections in your self-development diary.

POWER ACTIVITIES

We saw earlier that there is always competition for limited resources, and that individuals have to create political strategies in order to pursue personal goals. This pursuit will inevitably involve political action with others which will itself involve some assessment of their power bases.

Hunt (1979) recommends acquiring the expertise likely to be required by the organisation ahead of others, rather than joining a department whose status and influence appear to be in decline, and assessing and adopting the values, attitudes and behaviour of those with power. He suggests that managers should get results that are regarded as important by those who hold power and establish social contacts with powerful individuals.

In a similar vein, Schein (quoted by Dixon 1978) identifies a range of tactics typically used by managers in pursuing their objectives. The following are examples of these behaviours:

- *Presenting a conservative image.* According to Schein, enthusiasm can be interpreted as threatening behaviour in some organisations. He suggests that important proposals should be phrased as nothing more than modest adjustments to the status quo. He argues that many controversial projects have started in a small way – perhaps as pilot schemes – and are then linked to some existing non-controversial programme. Radical changes can then be viewed as a normal development of current activities.

- *Strike while the iron is hot.* Schein suggests that a manager should capitalise immediately on any success by bringing forward another project he/she wishes to progress.

- *Instituting research.* Some projects are likely to face stiff opposition. Emotional subjects such as equal opportunities fall into this category. Research can provide hard data which conservative colleagues will find much more difficult to argue against. Schein quotes the way in which such data are typically presented: 'Well, here's the evidence. I don't necessarily believe all of it but we can't just ignore it, can we?'

- Schein claims that these are all legitimate activities if they help the manager achieve his/her objectives. However, this sounds suspiciously like the ends justifying the means, and we each have our own views about that. It is difficult to generalise about what is acceptable behaviour in any particular situation, and we each have to reconcile conflicting pressures in coming to terms with the situation.

HANDLING CONFLICT

INTRODUCTION

Handling conflict is concerned with managing the differences between individuals and groups of individuals. In business, as in all activities, conflict is inevitable as the needs and objectives of business stakeholders vary. Examples of conflict are:

- between the organisation and employees (and their unions) over the size of the pay increase or allowances

- between the organisation and its suppliers over terms and conditions of the suppliers' contracts on price, quality and delivery schedules

- between the organisation and its shareholders over the amount of profit to be distributed as dividends
- between line management and HR over the control and operation of the performance management system
- between the production department and quality assurance (QA) over the interpretation of the operation of the QA system.

Other examples can involve conflicts with customers, with banks and the tax office.

Conflict can come about because of the need to change the way the organisation operates. It also has to be recognised that much of the conflict arises from a competitive environment. In both of these cases, it can be the general viewpoint that one side has to win and the other to lose. For example, the current conflict between Google and the newspaper industry is seen by the newspaper industry as one that will only be resolved with one of them gaining so much power over the other that one side will be fatally wounded (probably the newspaper industry).

One of the signs of a well-managed organisation is the ability to resolve conflicts peacefully and amicably while ensuring that participants do not badly lose face.

CONFLICT-HANDLING STYLE

A number of conflict style inventories have been in active use since the 1960s. Most of them are based on the Managerial Grid Model developed by Blake and Mouton (1964). This model uses two axes: 'Concern for people' is plotted along the vertical axis and 'Concern for task' along the horizontal axis. Each axis has a numerical scale of one to nine. These axes interact so as to diagram five different styles of management. This grid posits the interaction of task versus relationship and shows that according to how people value these, there are five basic ways of interacting with others.

Figure 2.1 Conflict-handling style (based on Blake and Mouton)

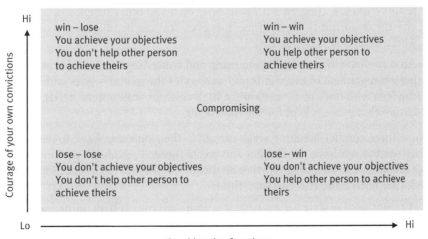

(Adapted from Thomas 1976.)

In the model shown in figure 2.1, the two axes are:

- courage of your own convictions
- consideration for others.

So, to be assertive, you need high courage of your own convictions and high consideration of others.

Courage of your own convictions

This refers to your ability to set an objective and pursue it. It implies single-mindedness – and sometimes bloody-mindedness and ruthlessness. We can usefully think of the idea of having a bottom line to help us understand this concept. A bottom line is the line we will not move beyond, even under pressure. We will walk away rather than retreat. For example, imagine that you are a union negotiator dealing with the HR director of a company for the annual pay review. This director offers you his sixth final offer. What do you do? You reject it, of course, and wait for his seventh final offer. Clearly he doesn't have a bottom line and so he will continue to retreat.

Consideration for others

This means trying to understand the objectives of the other person. In doing so, it may be possible to satisfy one's one objectives – meet your bottom line – and meet theirs at the same time. This is the cherished win–win position.

Combinations of these two dimensions give us the following five styles:

- A *confrontational* (aggressive) style of conflict-handling – involving, for example, demanding apologies from others and redress of perceived 'wrongs' – tends to be adopted by people who are high in concern for their own needs and low in concern for others' needs.

- An *avoidance* style – which means refusing to acknowledge that a problem exists, while reducing interaction with the other person(s) as far as possible – results from low concern with both one's own and other people's needs. It does give the opportunity to gain time, however, and can be utilised in a situation where neutrality is important.

- An *accommodation* style – apologising and conceding the issue to the other person regardless of the 'rights and wrongs' of the matter – goes with a low concern with one's own needs and a high concern with others' needs. It does ensure that peace is kept for the time being.

These three conflict-handling styles are all, in their different ways, undesirable. They tend to reinforce the conflict and create more ill feeling, to prolong it below the surface, or to encourage further aggression in others. The remaining two styles are both more effective than these:

- A *compromising* style is next best; this approach means bargaining, explicitly or implicitly, with the other person until a compromise is reached. Though this is often a reasonable approach, there is the well-known danger that the actual compromise agreed on will be 'the worst of all worlds' and only be a temporary solution.

- A *collaborative (assertive)* style, then, is the optimal choice. It treats the need to repair the relationship as a problem that the parties need to solve together. More guidance on how to implement this style is given below.

Collaborative style

- Aggressiveness and submissiveness (avoiding and accommodating) get you nowhere. Don't use them.

- Ensure that you jointly identify what differences exist and analyse the cause of those differences.

- Be honest and relevant, and stick to facts, not personalities.

- Consider the alternative solutions and work through the implications together, seeing which alternative is closest to each side.

- Each side should know its bottom line and stick to it. That bottom line should be honestly expressed so there is no misunderstanding.

- It is usually wiser to have an adjournment when a sticking point is reached to allow reflection from both sides and enable the points made to sink in. In most circumstances, a return to the meeting brings new ideas for a solution.

- When a solution is agreed, ensure there is no misunderstanding by going over it again and making sure it is correctly recorded.

- Ensure agreement is reached on how the preferred solution is implemented (although a certain vagueness in places is allowable – without this, no European Union agreement would ever be made).

This type of collaborative bargaining is often called 'integrated bargaining' and the solution reached is often win–win. The opposite confrontational approach, is called 'distributive bargaining'; this is where a win–lose result emerges.

REPAIR TECHNIQUES

Edgar Schein (1980) is one authority on organisational behaviour who has looked at the question of how to repair relationships after breakdown. It is clear from his discussion that the main requirement, as so often in face-to-face work, is to come to terms with your own psychological blockages. Being afraid that unpleasant events will be repeated often prevents people from starting to build bridges. For instance, you may be afraid that when you make an overture – a friendly or helpful remark – to someone else, they will snub you. Alternatively, you may find it easier to blame others than to work out how to renegotiate your relationship with them. These are some suggestions for overcoming one's own psychological barriers to bridge-building:

- Look for new elements in the situation that you may not have noticed before: for one thing, the other people in the situation may have changed in significant ways. Other people tend to be more flexible and adaptive than our assumptions about them allow; our impressions become straitjackets or self-fulfilling prophecies. The confrontation itself is likely to have affected them in some way: often, it is true, people become more rigid after such an experience, but some may wish to change even if they lack the skills to do so.

- Look to superordinate goals around which a new set of relationships can be built. If you needed to keep in touch with this person before, you still need to even though you have quarrelled.

- Force yourself to see what happened from the other person's point of view. A friend or sympathetic colleague can often help to make this process less painful than it would otherwise be.

- A colleague who is a good listener can also be very helpful if your blockage is emotional (eg hurt or anger). Talking it through, if necessary over and over, blunts the edges of emotions which otherwise may prevent you being skilled in handling the repair interaction. Allowing some time to pass also helps in this because emotions tend to recede over time.

When you have handled yourself, you are ready to deal with the situation, using, as recommended above, a collaborative approach. To succeed you should:

- Set up a meeting that is explicitly for the purpose of making the repair. This approach, which can be thought of as confronting the problem, is more likely to succeed than either evading it or attempting to build bridges in the course of other business. The best way to set up the meeting is to telephone the person with whom your relationship has broken down – or intercept them in the corridor – and say something on the lines of 'Look, Andrew, do you think we should get together to sort out why we are at loggerheads like this? I do, because it's affecting my work, and making me miserable. I very much dislike being on bad terms with colleagues.' You may need to persist to get agreement to the meeting, but usually you can get it in the end, because the other party is aware that it is unreasonable to refuse. It is important not to be dragged into discussing the cause of the dispute itself at this stage, because your objective is to get agreement to the meeting, this agreement itself being the first stage in the bridge-building process. An intermediary may be used to set up the meeting if someone really suitable is available, but this is less satisfactory because it reduces the amount of repair achieved by this first overture.

- In the meeting, allow the other person to express their negative emotions about what has happened, while keeping close control on your own. If you detect that they are in the grip of emotion that is not being expressed at the start, encourage them to bring it into the open. This may be painful for you, but is an essential first step in the bridge-building process. Make it clear that you are listening to and understanding what they say, though you do not necessarily accept that they are right.

- Make it clear that you do not intend the repair process to lead to further loss of face for either party.

- Treat the repair as a problem to solve jointly rather than a self-abasement: your objective is to reach agreement on a new basis for the relationship, but your offer is not unconditional. You are trying to explore differences creatively and locate some common ground, but you do need to protect yourself from any attempt by the other person to exploit your overture, perhaps to gain, unfairly, the point on which you differed before. If their position was unjustified before, it remains so now, even if you do want to apologise for having lost your temper. You will need to be articulate and assertive to clarify what you are and are not conceding.

ACTIVITY 2.3 REPAIRS

Think of a situation that needs repair. Using the techniques described in this section, start this process. Record your reflections over time in your self-development diary as you try to make this repair.

Actively reflecting on how to improve situations involving conflict is an excellent way of planning how to retrieve the situation. You should find that doing this exercise will make you more effective and confident.

FORCES SHAPING HRM AT WORK

In the course of this book we are examining the ways in which the external influences the role of HR in practical terms. You will see many examples in each of the forthcoming chapters but here are some brief extracts:

- *Social* – how demographic changes influence the need for HR to engage in initiatives such as flexible working and to widen the pool of recruitment.

- *Technological* – how technological developments have provided scope for new ways of working, eg in call centres and distance working/teleworking.

- *Economic* – how economic cycles influence both the internal and external labour market and how HR needs to move swiftly to anticipate and utilise such changes.

- *Environmental* – how the growing international emphasis on environmental issues provides opportunities for HR to lead in areas such as engagement with the community and secondments.

- *Political* – how developments in Europe have influenced the migratory pattern and employment regulation, with the associated need for HR to ensure advantages are gained from such changes.

- *Legal* – HR needs to respond to changes in the UK regulatory climate through ensuring organisations understand fully the implications of such changes and implement appropriate policies and procedures.

- *Ecological* – the growing support for socially responsible organisations provides the opportunity for HR to take the lead in areas such as ethical behaviour codes towards employees, customers, the community and in business transactions.

We have already seen the responses that HR make to the some of the internal effects, such as organisational structure, power, conflict and change. The remainder of the chapter deals with the way that HR can be structured and the effect it can have on the efficiency of the organisation.

MODELS AND ROLES OF THE HR FUNCTION

Given that HR can make a contribution to organisational performance and that there is a healthy debate how this can be effected, the next question relates to the models and roles of the HR function that can effectively and cost-efficiently organise this contribution.

This next section, therefore, briefly examines the changing employment relationships before setting out the various models and roles of the HR function as examined by the last 30 years of research.

THE HR EQUATION — MODELS OF THE EMPLOYMENT CONTRACT

The traditional employment contract was simple. In return for a wage or salary, the employee carried out the work indicated to the required standards. However, a subsidiary, unwritten contract has also been present in most employment contracts that is more difficult to pin down and often deals with unexpected and unforeseeable changes in the nature of the work concerned. This is often referred to as the 'psychological contract', first explained by Schein (1980) and discussed by many writers since (Herriot 1998, Conway and Briner 2005). This form of contract deals with the expectations that employees and employers have of their relationship, especially how each expects to be treated by the other.

In the traditional form, the format was for the employer to offer a secure and dependable income, a degree of job security, a safe environment and a possible opportunity for advancement while the employee carried out the work indicated in the contract, followed the prescribed rules and standards and showed long-term loyalty. Although this contract never applied to large numbers of employees (temporary, low-paid and unskilled) and varied considerably by sector of employment, for the good majority to whom it applied, it reflected a dependable, foreseeable environment.

Since around the early 1980s, however, there has been a recognisable change in the nature of this contract which reflects the rapidly changing employment market and the unpredictability and volatility of the organisational context. This has lead to a restating of the psychological contract. Employment for life is not the expected norm (police, prison and fire services excepted). There has developed a growing intensification of work in many sectors where employees are expected to work much longer hours and take on much more varied and flexible responsibilities beyond their apparent contractual duties ('going beyond contract'). In return, employers offer the opportunity to gain experience, learn extra skills and competencies and, in many cases, additional variable pay and bonuses. This has been identified as a change from a relational contract to a transactional contract, moving from an emotional commitment to one that can be regarded as a simple economic exchange (Taylor 2008).

In theory, this change in the psychological contract should have led to much lower levels of job satisfaction and equally low degrees of satisfaction with the state of the psychological contract. However, research by Guest and Conway (2002) in the late 1990s and early 2000s found evidence to the contrary. In general, employees have expressed a reasonable (if varied) degree of satisfaction both with their jobs and with their psychological contract. This may have been because, over the period 1995–2008, the UK enjoyed a steady period of economic growth with a healthy labour market, which meant that most employees unhappy with their employment could move on if they chose to do so, rather than remaining dissatisfied.

With a tight labour market and a shortage of key skills, employers have reacted by attempting to be much more attractive to key employees by setting out to develop an employer brand and becoming an 'employer of choice'. This has been achieved not just by increasing the salary rates but also by improving employees' work–life balance, entering into extensive recognition initiatives which regularly support special employee achievements in the workplace and by introducing attractive benefits, such as flexible hours, the ability to work at home and systems of flexible benefits.

MODELS OF THE HR FUNCTION

There are a number of examples of models illustrating the varying roles and styles for the operation of HR departments and practitioners; three are outlined below.

Legge

Karen Legge (1978) identified three types of HR practitioners ('personnel' in those days) who were seeking to develop their power within the organisation:

- The *conformist innovator* works with the conventional organisational objectives and identifies with them, coming up with initiatives that help the organisation achieve those objectives through cost-saving, productivity increases and reducing conflict.

- The *deviant innovator*, on the other hand, stands somewhat aside from the conventional organisation aims and adopts an independent professional stance. The initiatives they recommend tend to be unconventional and their adoption will depend on their individual status and conviction, with the results somewhat unpredictable. Subject areas here could, today, involve proposals on work–life balance, empowerment or knowledge management. Their innovative ideas, which may face considerable opposition, can provide results which lead to the organisation obtaining clear competitive advantages.

- The *problem-solver* adopts a more conventional role, one that looks to provide day-to-day assistance to the line management.

Storey

Storey's (1992) analysis set up a grid which contrasts on one axis how far the work undertaken is strategic or merely tactical and, on the other axis, the degree to which the HR manager intervenes in the management process. This is shown in figure 2.2 and discussed below.

Figure 2.2 HR interventions

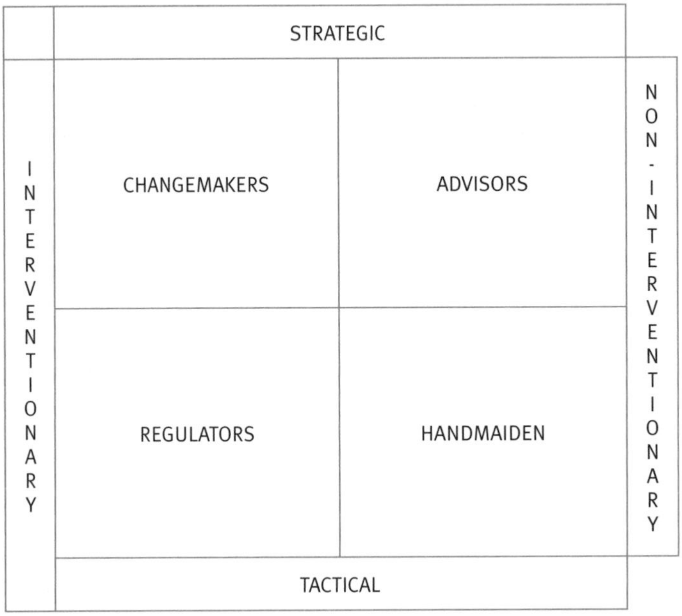

	STRATEGIC		
I N T E R V E N T I O N A R Y	CHANGEMAKERS	ADVISORS	N O N - I N T E R V E N T I O N A R Y
	REGULATORS	HANDMAIDEN	
	TACTICAL		

(Adapted from Storey 1992.)

Working clockwise:

- HR specialists who fall into the *advisor* category are those who focus on strategic issues but are not themselves responsible for carrying out the actions they recommend.

- *Handmaidens* are those who also have little part in implementing policy but operate only at a tactical level, dealing with administration and the provision of welfare, training and basic recruitment.

- *Regulators* are, again, involved only in tactical issues but they are more interventionary, trying to ensure that HR policy is carried out properly in co-operation with line managers.

- The *changemakers*, on the other hand, are both strategic and interventionary, concerned less with administration and more with the broader view of people management in their organisations. A changemaker is expected to assess the organisation's needs, reach appropriate conclusions and then drive the required changes to completion. This is regarded, Storey indicates, as the proper role for an effective and senior HR specialist.

Ulrich

Ulrich (1998) followed a similar tack, but developed the model so that the x axis measures the degree to which the HR practitioner manages the process and, on the other hand, manages the people involved, as shown in figure 2.3 and discussed below.

Figure 2.3 Role of HR

(Adapted from Ulrich 1998, Ulrich and Brockbank 2005.)

- The *administrative/functional expert* manages the processes on a day-to-day basis, ensuring that policies on, for example, grievances, discipline, equal opportunities and incentive arrangements work effectively. This is not a role to be derided because it is generally vital to the organisation's smooth running. Recognition, however, does not come easily from this role as it is only really noticed when things go wrong. These activities have, in recent years, been prime candidates for outsourcing or into some form of shared services system (see Chapter 1).

- The *employee advocate/champion* acts as a voice for employees on a day-to-day basis, working for an improvement in their position, their contribution and their engagement with the organisation. This role is intended, by improving their engagement, to improve their overall performance. In Ulrich's 2005 revised version, the role is strengthened with an additional dimension of *human capital developer*, who works to develop employees as assets through extending their skills and developing their career.

- The *change agent* works from a strategic viewpoint attempting to ensure that employees go along with business changes, making sure that visions and values are translated into action and reality.

- The *business partner* works with line management to ensure board strategy is developed and put into effect, identifying areas where action is required and instituting remedial initiatives. Line managers use them as consultants to debate issues in their area, such as salary and incentive issues and difficult disciplinary cases.

The concept of the business partner has found substantial support in recent years, adopted by a huge range of companies. It is interpreted in different ways but the central precept is of close relationships with business units, helping to solve practical problems and delivering real value to the organisation. Three examples are shown in case study 2.2.

CASE STUDY 2.2

BUSINESS PARTNERS AT ELIOR GROUP, GENERAL MOTORS AND PRUDENTIAL INSURANCE

Elior, a 5,400-employee European contract catering group, introduced business partnering in 2008 which provided benefits for both HR and business managers. HR professionals gained insights into business concerns while business managers appreciated the importance of a more scientific approach to people issues. Senior HR specialists could spend more time on strategic issues, such as succession planning and performance management, while line management gained a much greater control over performance management. A key difficulty in setting up the scheme was a lack of formal meetings for exchanging views and understanding between business partners where good practice could be exchanged.

In 2003, Vauxhall Motors at Ellesmere Port (part of General Motors) reorganised its HR departments with HR staff either outsourced to specialist or routine roles or assigned to a business-focused role. The latter staff were trained to understand all aspects of the business and given a desk in the unit's open-plan offices next to the car production lines. They engage in day-to-day operations, such as assisting managers

in performance management, identifying training needs, coaching and discussing the facts and figures about people in their unit, their promotions, potential, disabilities and concerns. The main purpose is to develop close relationships with line managers and helping to solve business issues through their knowledge of people management.

At Prudential Insurance, the HR business partner works in a business unit as a consultant, drawing down help from centres of excellence, while a service centre deals with HR administration issues. As an example, one partner works in the marketing and innovation function running the people management side of a major change initiative to improve how to deal with customer complaints. Having worked out with the unit manager what needs to be achieved, the partner pulls together an HR team for the project, uses the recommendations of the specialist HR group and co-ordinates the delivery of the project. This needs skills in relationship-building and a good understanding of the business.

(Sources: Hennessy 2009, Pickard 2004.)

A survey by Roffey Park in 2009 found that 58 per cent of respondents judged the change to a business partner system to be successful while only 10 per cent found it unsuccessful. It was most likely to become successful where the organisational culture had a higher level of sociability, with high scores for focusing on people, building relationships and a concern for colleagues, and where there was also a good degree of solidarity (a strong focus on working together to deliver shared objectives) (Griffin et al 2009).

Purcell and Ahlstrand (1994) have taken a different approach, setting out the nine core activities that HR departments should engage in to become fully influential in an organisation. They believe these to be applicable to most, but not all, medium-to-large organisations, but it will depend on the nature of the business and the way the organisation is directed. Some are indisputable, such as HR planning and developing essential HR policies; others are more debatable:

- *Corporate culture and communications.* Organisations are bound together internally not just by common ownership or by everything being included on the balance sheet. Culture – 'the ways we do things around here' – is difficult to define but easy to identify, especially when it is articulated well and often. It is normally up to the chief executive to set out or redefine the principal aspects, philosophy, set of values and the essential style of management, but it is HR that must be responsible for championing and disseminating these cultural aspects around the organisation in an effective fashion.

- *HR planning in strategic management.* Developing an HR plan, which emerges from the strategic plan, is the second core activity. This is clearly a core activity but one where the link is not always made as tightly as it should be.

- *Essential policy formulation and monitoring.* Established policies and procedures remain an essential feature of an effective organisation and policies regarding the way people should act and be treated are no exception. Standards need to be set and monitored for compliance. The recognised difficulty here is striking the happy medium between a rigid bureaucratic set of procedures that deals with every eventuality but restricts innovation and empowerment and a set of vague guidelines that has many interpretations and is largely ignored.

- *'Cabinet office' services.* This is a more unusual observation and based on the need for the chief executive to have advice from a trusted senior subordinate who is not linked to a major department such as finance or sales, which would be liable to defend their own territory and not be regarded as independent. The advice would be principally concerning the implications for staff in general and succession planning for senior executives, but would also include cultural development issues and some specific investigations set in place through issues raised by non-executive directors. This is a considerable source of power and influence for HR and emerged from their personal relationship, not from their specific position.

- *Senior management development and career planning.* This is another undisputed, important role, even when longer-term planning is more difficult to undertake. It is linked with the succession planning process and with the need to develop managers with wide experience so there is flexibility in place for strategic moves into new or existing market places.

- *External advocacy – internal advice.* As HR develops a close relationship with the chief executive, its 'cabinet' responsibilities may stretch to representing the organisation in the corridors of power. This is not just on local matters such as trade association committees, but some political lobbying on crucial issues such as government legislation or interpretation of European directives. 'Internal advice' means feeding matters such as this back to the executives in the organisation.

- *Information co-ordination.* This involves helping large organisations to co-ordinate necessary information across the group on pay, bargaining and general personnel statistics, such as headcount, turnover and absenteeism.

- *Internal consultancy and mediation services.* Included in this role are aspects of organisational design and learning. The introduction of competencies would be an example here.

- *HR for small units.* An extension of the internal consultancy to part of the larger group that has little or no HR presence.

Purcell and Ahlstrand recognise that this list does not indicate a comprehensive attention to all HR matters. Training, health and safety, recruitment and pay issues do not come to the fore on their own. In fact (p113):

> Our research shows that the role and authority of corporate personnel departments is becoming more ambiguous and uncertain ... Much of the activity identified ... places a premium on political and interpersonal skills and 'corridor power'. In this situation, the authority of corporate human resources staff comes more from their own expertise and style than from a clearly defined role and function. It has often been noted that human resource managers need to be adept at handling ambiguity.

In Chapter 10, the role of HR in improving organisational performance is examined further.

HR AND LEADERSHIP STYLES

The role of developing leadership skills is sometimes downplayed in UK writing but it is very strong in American versions of successful HRM ambitions. Rucci (1997) has set out six key requirements for HR departments to add value to the organisation and ensure its own survival:

- *Create change* – HR should move away from the control, standardisation and compliance model and encourage the development of an organisational capability of flexibility, speed and risk-taking. This will mean eliminating unnecessary rules and giving greater emphasis to individual judgment and accountability for line managers.

- *Develop principled leaders* – top executives who ground themselves in a base of moral or ethical principles are few and far between, but it is they who lead organisations to sustained long-term success. HR needs to set in motion systems to develop such talent, especially leaders who have the courage of their conviction and an unwillingness to compromise on ethical issues.

- *Promote economic literacy* – too much specialisation has led to many managers not having the breadth of outlook to understand the 'big picture' within the organisation. HR should give more emphasis to ensuring managers learn all the skills and knowledge so they can contribute advice on big policy decisions.

- *Centre on the customer* – HR should help to create boundary-less organisations where the customer's viewpoint seriously influences policy decisions and ensure that customer-directed activity is central in performance reviews, promotion criteria and reward decisions.

- *Maximise services/minimise staff* – HR needs to focus on its internal customers, identifying where it adds value and driving down its costs.

- *Steward the values* – HR's role should not just be the organisation's conscience or the 'values police'. It should ensure that the values are understood and ensure that the progress is monitored and measured by embedding them in all HR activities – selection, training, performance management and reward.

These prescriptions reflect the nature of HR programmes entered into by progressive and successful companies. An example in practice is set out in case study 2.3.

 HR STRATEGIES AND ACTIONS AT AEHN

CASE STUDY 2.3

In the late 1990s, AEHN, an American acute care hospital, was faced by what it regarded as a tumultuous and unpredictable period in its history, and the new CEO undertook to transform it from one that was largely stable and complacent to one that was 'nimble, agile and change-hardy' or it may not have survived. Alongside a number of strategic changes in direction, five key HR initiatives were set in motion:

- *Achieving contextual clarity* – AEHN went to great lengths to be quite sure that employees at all levels understood the CEO's new vision for the organisation, the progress towards achieving that vision and the links between their individual and collective actions to raise organisational performance. Although using conventional methods, the messages were delivered in a

fairly intense way with bulletin boards refurbished with a constant flow of relevant stories and reports, banners saying 'Are you ready for change? Are your skills ahead of the game?' and a steady flow of short courses and meetings to illuminate the organisation's progress for all to understand. Workshops included subjects such as 'survival tactics in times of change'.

- *Embedding core values* – central to the culture change process, embedding and sustaining the set of core values became the fundamental driving force for the HR initiatives. Taken up by the top team after a year's debate, they were cascaded through the organisation with references woven into all forms of communication and into HR practices. For example, the selection process was revised to add an assessment of applicants' core values by means of situational interviewing, and the performance management scheme was heavily revamped to focus on behavioural manifestations of the values.

- *Enriching work* – a number of work redesign experiments were started to encourage much greater flexibility and empowerment. A new position, patient care associate, was created to administer tests, take blood and do other duties that previously had been carried out by specialists; staff moved much more around units to fill gaps and to broaden perspectives and encourage social networks; self-managed teams were created to provide 'seamless, patient-focused care'.

- *Promoting personal growth* – employees were encouraged to take responsibility for their personal growth to help them perform better and be prepared for promotions. This was helped by the introduction of 360-degree feedback which generated more convincing

reasons for personal development and change. Alongside this, there was an agreed policy of zero tolerance of employees who failed to pursue required self-development.

- *Providing commensurate returns* – Not a great deal could be done on substantially improving salaries so the programme concentrated on non-financial benefits. The work enrichment was one important step and the 'Recognise, Appreciate, Celebrate' initiative as another. Staff received 'pat on the back notices' and a 'celebration of a risk taken award' (given for a good effort irrespective of result).

These initiatives were business-based and fitted together well so employees were able to understand both why the changes were necessary and also to see them as a coherent set which would benefit the patients, the staff and the organisation.

(Source: Shafer et al 2001.)

RESOURCE-BASED VIEW OF THE ORGANISATION

Alongside these investigations, theories have been developed regarding the uniquely valuable nature of HR because it contributes a collection of assets (skills, competencies, experience) that are much more difficult to imitate or replicate than conventional assets such as land or capital. This is associated with the resource-based view (RBV) of the organisation where competitive advantage is associated with four key attributes: value, rarity, a lack of substitutes and difficult to imitate:

- *Value* – looking at employees of football teams, for example, the very skilled ones are certainly seen to be extremely valuable, and some senior executives transfer to new organisations with an upfront payment. The cost of replacing employees who leave organisations is often high, especially if they are experienced and seen by customers as important. As explained by Boxall and Purcell (2003, p83):

> [organisations] … can never entirely capture what individual … [employees] … know. Some of what we know – including many of our best skills – cannot be reduced to writing or to formulas. When we leave the firm, we take this knowledge with us. When whole teams leave … the effects can be devastating.

- *Rarity* is associated with value as there will always be a labour group which is in short supply, eg IT staff in the 1980s and 1990s, nurses and teachers in the early 2000s, and plumbers most of the time. Organisations that have a steady supply of skills that are in short supply elsewhere will have a competitive advantage.

- It is possible to *substitute for labour*, eg through automated call centres and production lines, but those organisations that possess skilled employees where such substitution is impossible (most service organisations, consultancies, etc) should be able to gain an advantage. It has been argued that the UK's competitive advantage has been maintained because of our very large service sector whereas Germany's large manufacturing sector has been constantly chipped away by international competition and automation.

- Similarly, it is *difficult to imitate* the skilled work of employees. Cheaper versions of services can be available (eg self-service in restaurants) but the market for high-quality service by skilled employees is normally in a state of constant growth.

Having recognised the importance of people as a resource, it provides encouragement to employers to identify and then improve the quality of their 'human capital'. In terms of identification, the CIPD (Brown 2003) proposed a framework so organisations could report on the way they:

- acquire and retain staff, explaining how the firm sources its supply, the composition of the workforce in terms of diversity and employment relationships and its retention policies

- develop staff, including details of skill levels and development strategies

- motivate, involve and communicate with employees

- account for the value created by employees including how they manage the bank of employee knowledge and the methods of determining team and individual performance.

CUSTOMER CARE

Customers are the lifeblood of any organisation. If they do not receive satisfactory and even pleasurable experiences then they will go elsewhere. The purpose of customer care, therefore, is to ensure that customers' needs and expectations are met or exceeded so that they remain committed to that organisation. An American survey by Infoquest (2002) found that a totally satisfied customer contribute 17 times as much revenue to a company as a dissatisfied customer, but a totally dissatisfied customer decreases revenue by a factor of 30. So with twice as many satisfied customers as dissatisfied, a business will still be doing little better than standing still. Other surveys have shown that a one per cent increase in customer satisfaction translates into a three per cent market value increase and that companies with more highly regarded customer care systems increase their sales per annum twice as fast as organisations where customer care is poorly regarded (Fraterman 2009).

STRATEGIC APPROACH TO CUSTOMER CARE

Driving an effective customer care approach through the organisation requires a strategy that incorporates all aspects of the company's operations. Marketing must find out what products and services will meet customer needs, and design and development departments must produce them in ways that provide sufficient choice and at acceptable prices. Production must produce goods that have very high quality levels backed up by guarantees that will satisfy customers. Distribution must ensure they are available for customers within acceptable deadlines. Even more important, employees throughout the organisation must buy in to the concept that customers must be treated fairly, speedily and with consideration to detail. Without the thorough commitment by staff and the built-in desire to 'go the extra mile', then gaps will develop in the process through which customers will fall, so any strategic plan will have the employees at its centre.

The strategic plan will need to establish a set of standards and measures which will identify critical success factors in customer service. These will include:

- *Measures of immediate customer dissatisfaction*, such as volume and value of goods returned within the seven days or a month, number of service contracts cancelled within seven days and number of time-limited contracts which are not renewed.

- *Number and type of customer complaints*, identified by product and sales area.

- *Metrics associated with surveys of customer satisfaction*. Many organisations ask customers to respond immediately after buying goods or services. For example, the national double glazing companies usually provide customers with a short questionnaire to fill in when the products are installed relating to their sales and installation experience. Others companies will circulate questionnaires to a selection of customers on service contracts on a periodic basis.

- *Measures of on-time production and delivery* compared to contracted times.

- *Quality and speed of response* to customer contact in terms of sales achieved, problem-solving and returning customers.

- *Specific metrics on call-handling* for call centres.

- *Metrics from mystery shoppers*. Although the implementation of mystery shopping schemes was first regarded with suspicion by employees, there has been remarkable acceptance of the process, especially as most reporting systems do not identify specific employees but measure the general milieu of customer relations.

CUSTOMER CARE — THE EMPLOYEE DIMENSION

To thoroughly involve employees, the following areas need to be included in any customer care training programme:

- *Training employees in products and services*, so that all employees, not just sales teams, can be in a position to deal with customers' needs.

- *Specific training for sales staff*, especially retail staff to ensure that sales made benefit both the organisation and the customer. Customers need to leave the sales environment feeling confident that they have not been persuaded to purchase by clever sales techniques. This may lead to a short-term sales increase but ultimately will lead to poor customer relations and, in the worse cases, litigation. An important issue here is the danger of mis-selling. The Office of Fair Trading (OFT) has carried out two major investigations in this area. The first, in the 1990s, was into pensions mis-selling and the second, in 2003, into the selling of extended warranties. In the first case, heavy fines were imposed on a number of companies involved and, in the second, the OFT imposed a number of conditions under which the financial service could be sold, both to ensure customers received better protection in the future.

- *A clear understanding of the standards established* in customer care and the processes operated. This is not always straightforward. Although guidelines are usually established in, say, when and how contracts can be changed or cancelled, it may be necessary to go outside of these guidelines as a means to solve difficult problems. The authority for such action used to be restricted to senior management, but some companies with sophisticated customer care systems have delegated authority to low levels to allow problems to be solved swiftly. They have found that this often wins back customers who do not have to wait to talk to a manager and whose anxiety or anger over the issue is quickly assuaged.

- *Specific training for service staff* in areas where the quality of service is the essential feature of the sale, such as in hotel and catering operations and in-flight service. The switch to call-centre handling of sales and service operation since the mid-1990s has meant that specialised staff training is required in dealing with customers over the phone, although anecdotal experience leads most people to doubt that such training has taken place in many cases. In recent years, the specialised customer care in the NHS has been the subject of comprehensive training, although results, again, still appear to be mixed.

- *Training in communication and problem-solving*. The development of the competency frameworks in organisations where emphasis is placed on the necessary enhancement of skills in communication and problem-solving is closely related to customer care and not just restricted to immediate customer-facing staff. The ability to identify where contracts have gone wrong (problem-solving) and for staff to effectively communicate with each other to ensure problems are immediately solved, and preventing them happening again is crucial to the process of improving customer care.

- *Providing incentives for efficient customer care*. There is a growing trend for incentives schemes to contain a strong element of measuring and rewarding customer care performance, rather than simply using output or quantity measures. Often this change has been made because, under previous schemes, employees have acted to raise output at all costs without considering the consequences of poor quality, delivery times or unacceptable service quality. Examples here include the Sainsbury's store-based team incentive, which is wholly based on the Customer Satisfaction Index (CSI) (IRS 2003); the DaimlerChrysler Aftersales Managers scheme*, where CSI scores represent 20 per cent of the managers' bonuses; and AOS Heating, a small plumbing firm based in Cheshunt, where the plumbers' bonuses are entirely based on the customer ratings*.

● *Recognition of employee action.* As an additional reward for demonstrating the required employee behaviours, many organisations have instituted a formal system of recognition for excellent customer care. For example, Claridge's Hotel in London has a 'Pot of Gold' recognition scheme where an employee who has demonstrated 'service perfection' in the course of a day's work (a core value in the organisation) can be nominated by a fellow employee to take part in a lucky dip from a pot of gold envelopes in the HR director's office. The reward can vary from an extra day of holiday, or a facial treatment in the hotel's spa to an all-expenses paid night in the hotel's top suite, which would normally cost over £4,000 (IRS 2004).

*author's research

The aim of an integrated policy is to develop a customer care culture within the organisation where employees put the requirements of the customer first and behave in line with this belief.

Although customer care has developed primarily in the private sector as an essential way of improving the brand and enhancing profits, there have been a number of initiatives in the public sector, as shown in case study 2.4 concerning the MoD outsourced housing contract.

 CUSTOMER CARE AT THE MOD HOUSING PRIME CONTRACT

CASE STUDY 2.4

MODern Housing Solutions (MHS) is a dedicated venture company between Enterprise plc and Carillion plc constructed specifically to deliver the Housing Prime Contract, valued at £700 million over seven years, which maintains 43,000 units for service families' accommodation in England and Wales.

Service re-enlistment rates have been found to be highly correlated to service families' satisfaction with living accommodation, so ensuring families have decent, habitable and stress-free accommodation, regardless of rank, is vital to the future HR plans for the defence forces. In previous years, the reputation for quality maintenance has not always been high, both in terms of work

carried out and, in particular, the level of response. A key initiative in this contract has been the development of a dedicated customer care centre incorporating a 24-hour freephone help desk.

The customer care centre, which needed the highest level of security accreditation, was established in Liverpool with state-of-the-art telephony equipment which received, on average, 7,000 calls per week. According to Enterprise, after two years of operation, the service level has been running consistently above KPI requirements (such as 95 per cent of calls answered within two minutes) with customer satisfaction rates showing substantial improvements.

However, the National Audit Office showed a mixed view of customer satisfaction. When the new contract began in 2006, there was a higher than expected level of demand for repairs, which the help desk and other systems could not cope with. Many families remain dissatisfied with the service, in particular with the understanding shown by help-desk operators of the nature of the maintenance problems. Survey respondents reported that only 42 per cent of problems were rectified at the first visit and, in cases where the respondent felt the help desk had not understood their problem, it fell to 13 per cent. However, families were generally satisfied with the manner in which the work was carried out and confirmed that there had been an upward trend in the contractor's performance against key performance indicators.

(Sources: Enterprise 2009, National Audit Office 2009.)

QUALITY MANAGEMENT

THE IMPORTANCE OF QUALITY MANAGEMENT

Quality management has moved on a long way from the traditional view that a quality product just meets the technical specification and that customers have to accept and pay for the product or the service if the company can show it has met that specification. Today, the successful companies are those that aim to produce products and services that exceed customers' expectations and succeed in that aim. Meeting the specification is just one step on the road to high quality.

In many industries, quality failures can be catastrophic. The failure to prevent fire spreading was one (among other) quality faults that caused the deaths of 189 people in the Piper Alpha North Sea oil rig disaster in 1989; the failure in signalling quality was a major cause of the Paddington rail crash in 1999, killing 30 people and, worldwide, other, larger disasters at Bhopal in India (Union Carbide) and Chernobyl caused multiple deaths and untold misery for thousands.

Quality remains a subjective subject. Organisations whose entire business is geared to producing products and services at the highest possible level (eg Ferrari, the Ritz Hotel and Cartier) will not be so concerned with cutting costs, only with ensuring nothing ever goes wrong. Other organisations, such as McDonald's or Tesco, will seek to provide good value (generally meaning cheap) products and services associated with a pleasant experience with the costs being firmly under control. Both examples concern organisations that are totally focused on quality. Slack et al (2007) call the first example the 'transcendent' approach and the second, the 'value-based' approach.

HIERARCHY OF QUALITY MANAGEMENT

It is possible to identify five developments in quality systems as shown in figure 2.4.

Figure 2.4 Quality management analysis

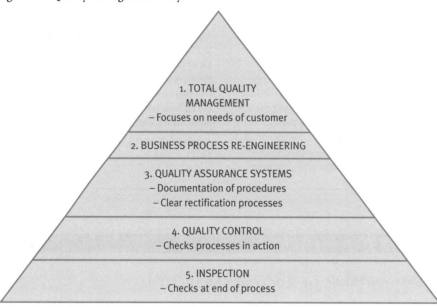

1. TOTAL QUALITY
MANAGEMENT
– Focuses on needs of customer

2. BUSINESS PROCESS RE-ENGINEERING

3. QUALITY ASSURANCE SYSTEMS
– Documentation of procedures
– Clear rectification processes

4. QUALITY CONTROL
– Checks processes in action

5. INSPECTION
– Checks at end of process

Level 5 – Inspection

Inspection systems have been in place for centuries, with records available of the inspection that took place during the building of the Egyptian pyramids more than 4,000 years ago. Inspection is generally an after-the-event activity concerned with identifying faults, removing defective items from the process and either reworking or scrapping them. Without inspection, faulty goods would proceed to the retailer and eventually the customer, where rejection would take place. Solving the problem at that stage would be much more costly and damage the company's reputation.

Inspection systems, however, have their difficulties:

- Having an inspector at the end of each process is expensive in labour costs and the work can be extremely tedious (although it is possible to replace human inspection with automated processes).

- Inspection may remove the immediate problem, but it does not always attack the symptom of the problems.

- Operatives may not be too concerned with the quality of their work, knowing that an inspector will pick up any faults in the process. Inspection is linked closely with Tayloristic principles of fractionalising work, which presents the inherent difficulties of reducing the value of the work and, hence, the operative's regard for it.

Level 4 – Quality control

Quality control (QC) is a step up from inspection in that it relies on more scientific and statistical data in examining quality issues. This makes use of sampling techniques, relating both to the inputs (eg supplies, materials) and the outputs at different stages in the manufacturing process. Statistical results are compared to predictive charts and control limits. An obvious example of its use is in the water industry where water is sampled and tested for numerous hazards before it is released into the water supply. The operations are normally controlled by a quality department which consists of training and qualified personnel. The benefit of quality control is that the problems are identified at an early stage in a thorough, scientific way. For example, the sampling of braking components before they are released to the assembly line will prevent problems later in terms of both cost and time, eg having to reject full braking units.

Difficulties still remain, however, especially the separation of quality management from the manufacturing process and the difficulties in ensuring that samples are representative.

Level 3 – Quality assurance systems

Quality assurance (QA) systems are quality systems that are subject to external verification. The most comprehensive and well known are the ISO 9000 series (International Standards, launched in 1987) and European Foundation for Quality Management standards (EFQM, launched in 1999), which have both built on less complex systems from the 1960s. They were initially introduced in industries where failure of the products would cause severe problems, including loss of life – such as guided weapons and the aircraft industry – as a response to customers (especially governments) demanding complete assurance on the quality of the product.

At the heart of these standards is the initiating by the organisation of a comprehensive system of quality management throughout the organisation. This includes comprehensive identification of the correct manufacturing methods (no short cuts allowed by employees!), methods of identifying customer satisfaction, and full recording of all data and training of all employees concerned. The QA systems can apply to all organisations (manufacturing, service, government and not-for-profit). Systems need to be agreed with the external agencies, which will make periodic unscheduled visits to ensure the quality processes are being followed. If there are gaps found by the external agencies, then the accreditation can be withdrawn.

There is no doubt that quality assurance accreditation has improved the overall quality in organisations. This has occurred both because of the comprehensive approach required and the discipline imposed throughout the organisation, and also because all employees do become aware of the catastrophic effect that the removal of the accreditation would have on the organisation's reputation and act accordingly. The system encourages a regular rethink of processes and acting to meet feedback from customers. The accreditation can also be used in marketing. Increasingly, large government and private contracts are only offered to organisations that have the appropriate accreditation.

Criticism of the QA systems essentially concern the bureaucratic approach required. For example, every time a new process or material is introduced, this has to be reported to the accrediting body. The external verification procedures are also seen as draconian at times. The processes are costly. Too much emphasis is placed on following the Quality Manual, rather than using a sensible and flexible approach. As the Manual constantly changes, some employees find it difficult to keep up with the changes. Finally, from an employee viewpoint, QA accreditation can be seen as an management imposition and employees may do no more than they have to, ie following the rules (Hill 1991).

Level 2 – Business process re-engineering

Business process re-engineering (BPR) is the process of systematically examining every stage of production or service to ensure that value is added for the benefit of the customer at each stage of the value chain. It has arisen chiefly from the work of Porter (1985) and Hammer and Champy (1993) whose emphasis on getting ahead of the competition laid a strong emphasis on building quality into the product or service through a radical rethink of every process. In practice, this has meant speeding up decision-making, becoming much more responsive to the customer, allowing new ideas to shape internal processes and empowering employees.

This process incorporates many of the facets of QA accreditation (if fact, they can operate side by side) but there is a much greater emphasis on employees taking hold of quality issues themselves. In a number of radical solutions, such as at Vauxhall in Luton, employees agreed to the elimination of all inspection jobs because the attention they subsequently gave to quality made inspection redundant (Stredwick 1997).

However, in the process of reducing bureaucracy and becoming more flexible, it has also led to de-layering management, reducing the number of employees (except in customer-facing areas) and, evidence indicates, placing more stress on employees at all levels. Although shown to be effective in many cases in improving quality, it is much criticised for its top-down and secretive approach, which leads to cost saving at the expense of employees.

Level 1 – Total quality management

Total quality management (TQM) is a strategic approach to quality that incorporates most, if not all, of the facets described at the lower levels. It attempts to take the best of the QA systems and BPR and incorporate them into a model of best practice. It therefore expresses itself as culturally based and has a big emphasis on employee involvement. The key ideas were introduced to Japan by the Americans as the occupying force immediately after the Second World War as part of the process of resuscitating their manufacturing industry (Needle 2004). The main initiators of the concept were Deming (1986) and Juran (1988).

In organisational terms, it integrates the company systems with those of suppliers and, in a business-to-business environment, major customers as well. For example, the 'just in time' system operating with suppliers will be integrated with supply sample testing and production schedules. Strong attempts are made to eliminate all costs associated with control and failure, and an emphasis is put on 'right first time' and 'right every time'.

There are the following associations with employee involvement:

- Key values, such as customer awareness, teamworking and continuous improvement, are cascaded down the organisation through training, performance management and regular communication.

- TQM statements regularly emphasise teamworking, creative thinking and empowerment.

- Initiatives on improving quality are encouraged through concepts such as quality circles and recognition schemes. All of these initiatives support teams to work together to achieve improved quality. These are especially focused on preventing problems, rather than solving them.

- An important aspect of training includes multi-skilling, so employees understand the quality requirements on a number of jobs, enabling them to cover for absence, vacancies and where sections have any additional pressures. This is in response to research which has indicated that, to nobody's surprise, poor quality is associated with lack of employee expertise.

- Another training aspect is better understanding of statistical and recording methods so employees comprehend what is actually happening in their department.

- Communication is enhanced with regular feedback on quality performance and employee recognition awards.

An effectively run TQM system will produce better benefits than the other systems set out in figure 2.4 on their own. Despite this, not all TQM systems have been an unqualified success. Difficulties faced have included the following:

- Employees still regard TQM as a form of management control which can work to stultify individual initiative and increase the stress faced by employees, especially where quality standards are not met.

- TQM is associated with a high-trust environment, especially where serious attempts at empowerment are made. Therefore, when employees make suggestions that are not taken up, or where they are blamed for not implementing initiatives effectively, it can reduce that degree of trust and lead to cynicism.

- The whole TQM approach can be seen as a marketing device, unassociated with the reality of the situation.

- It can also remain a high-cost bureaucratic process, by its very nature.

THEORIES OF MANAGEMENT OF CHANGE

There are essentially two main groups of theories that underpin models of change management. They all have their respective benefits and they focus in principle on individuals, group and organisational-wide issues.

These two groups represent the major schools of thought concerning change management theory. They are:

- the individual perspective school
- the group dynamics school.

THE INDIVIDUAL PERSPECTIVE SCHOOL

This, as its name suggests, focuses on the individual as the principal unit of change. There are two major camps within the school: the behaviourists and the gestalt-field psychologists.

The behaviourists believe behaviour is the result of an individual's interaction with their environment. They advocate that behaviour is learned, that the individual is a passive recipient of external and objective data, and that individuals respond to the manipulation of reward-enforcing stimuli. Behaviour that is rewarded will tend to be repeated. The behaviourist approach is very close to that of the classical school of management, which presented humans as cogs in a machine responding to external stimuli.

The gestalt-field psychologists believe that an individual's behaviour is the product of their environment and their own reason. They claim that learning is a process of gaining or changing insights, outlooks, expectations or thought patterns. The group takes into account not only the individual's behaviours or actions, but also the responses that these elicit.

In applying these theories to change, the behaviourists seek to achieve change by modifying the external stimuli acting upon the individual, while the proponents of the gestalt-field theory seek to help individuals of organisations change their understanding of themselves. In turn this leads to changes in behaviour. In simple terms, behaviourism is a 'carrot and stick' approach to achieving change. For example, systems of rewards and sanctions are very visible in sales environments such as call centres and recruitment agencies.

Both of these approaches have had some influence in management of change, and have many of the characteristics of the human relations school of management, largely brought about through the work of Maslow (1943), which stresses the need for both internal and external stimuli in order to influence human behaviour. The human relations school, in understanding the role of the individual, also draws attention to the roles of social groups in organisations, as does the group dynamics school.

Pavlov and his dogs

Pavlov, a Russian psychologist, is possibly the most well-known behaviourist. In a famous experiment, Pavlov used a group of dogs. He rang a bell and then immediately produced food for the dogs. After a time, the dogs began to associate the ringing of the bell with the provision of food, and began to salivate when they heard it. Once this stage had been reached, Pavlov rang the bell but did not provide food. The dogs still salivated on hearing the bell. Their behaviour had been changed.

Kurt Lewin and field theory

Kurt Lewin (1958) is a major figure in change management. He made major contributions in the areas of force field analysis (a method of identifying and measuring resistance to change), group dynamics, organisational development, action research and gestalt-field psychology.

Hall and Lindzey (1978, p386) summarised the central features of Lewin's force-field theory as follows:

> Behaviour is a function of the field that exists at the time the behaviour occurs. Analysis begins with the situation as a whole from which are differentiated the component parts, and the concrete person in a concrete situation can represented mathematically.

It is not only in the area of organisations that you see the application of these theories. Until the end of the 1980s, the therapy regime in mental hospitals used the 'carrot and stick' approach of the behaviourists. Since then, mental health therapy has adopted a development approach, more representative of the gestalt-field approach.

A detailed critique of Lewin's force field theory is set out in Chapter 10.

THE GROUP DYNAMICS SCHOOL

Group dynamics is the field of study within the social sciences that focuses on the nature of groups. In management, they are called teams, but the terms are interchangeable. The main theme of the school is that the influence of the group or team may become very strong indeed and overwhelm the individual's actions and tendencies. Thus the group may well change the behaviour of the individual. This, effectively, also forms the basis of group therapy. There is particular interest in group dynamics at the moment because of the rise of online interaction made possible by the Internet.

Since the late 1970s in the UK, there has been great interest in teambuilding, which can involve a variety of activities from departmental away days (structured days spent away from the workplace) to full-blown outward-bound activity sessions run by ex-military types. The Leadership Trust in the UK is an excellent example of this.

The chief proponents of group dynamics are discussed below.

Kurt Lewin is commonly identified as the founder of the movement to study groups scientifically. He coined the term 'group dynamics' to describe the way groups and individuals act and react to changing circumstances.

William Schutz (1966) looked at interpersonal relations from the perspective of three dimensions: inclusion, control, and affection (now called openness). This became the basis for a theory of group behaviour that sees groups as resolving issues in each of these stages in order to be able to develop to the next stage. Conversely, a group may also devolve to an earlier stage if unable to resolve outstanding issues in a particular stage. Schutz developed a psychometric instrument – Fundamental Interpersonal Relations Orientation (FIRO) – to incorporate these ideas.

Wilfred Bion (1961) studied group dynamics from a psychoanalytic perspective. Many of his findings were reported in his published books, especially *Experiences in Groups*. The Tavistock Institute has further developed and applied the theory and practices developed by Bion.

Bruce Tuckman (1965) proposed the four-stage model called Tuckman's Stages for a group. Tuckman's model states that the ideal group decision-making process should occur in four stages:

- *forming* – being polite to others and pretending to get on with them
- *storming* – dropping the pretence of politeness and focusing on the issues even if emotions rise
- *norming* – getting used to each other and developing trust and productivity
- *performing* – working in a group to a common goal on a highly efficient and co-operative basis.

Later, Tuckman added an 'ending' stage, recognising that the work of a group may come to an end and the group disband.

It should be noted that this model refers to the overall pattern of the group, but of course individuals within a group work in different ways. If distrust persists, a group may never even get to the norming stage.

The school's primary emphasis is on bringing about organisational change through teams and work groups rather than individuals. Lewin suggested that the rationale behind this is that because people in organisations work in groups, individual behaviours must be modified or changed in the light of the prevailing group practice and norms.

He went on to suggest that group behaviour is an intricate set of symbolic interactions and facets, which not only affect group structure, but also modify individual behaviour. He argued that individual behaviour is a function of the group environment.

To enable change, according to the group dynamics school, the focus must be at group level and should concentrate on influencing and changing the group's norms, roles and values. Therefore, it is useless to concentrate on the behaviour of individuals (French and Bell 1984). In this context, norms are the rules or standards that define what people should do; roles are patterns of behaviour that individuals are expected to conform to; and values are the ideas and beliefs that individuals hold about what is right and wrong.

The group dynamics school has proved to be very influential in developing the theory and practice of change management. Mullins (1989) remarked 'that this can be seen by the very fact it is now usual for organisations to view themselves as comprising groups and teams, rather than merely a collection of individuals'.

French and Bell (1984) pointed out:

> The most important single group of interventions in OD (organisational development) are team building activities, the goals of which are the improved and increased effectiveness of various teams within the organisation. The team building meeting has the goal of improving team effectiveness through better management of task demands, relationship demands and group processes. The team analyses its way of doing things and attempts to develop strategies to improve its operation.

Here, norms, roles and values are examined, challenged and changed. Despite the emphasis many place on groups within organisations, others argue that the correct change-management approach should be one that focuses on the organisation as a whole.

MANAGING INDIVIDUAL CHANGE

The DREC model – how individuals cope with change

Elisabeth Kübler-Ross (1969) was a psychiatrist and the author of the groundbreaking book *On Death and Dying*, where she first discussed what is now known as the Kübler-Ross model.

She proposed the now-famous Five Stages of Grief as a pattern of phases, most or all of which people tend to go through, in sequence, after being faced with the tragedy of their own impending death. The five stages, in sequential order, are: denial, anger, bargaining, depression and acceptance. The five stages have since been adopted by many as applying to the survivors of bereavement and, subsequently, to survivors of all change situations.

The Kübler-Ross model has become known in management circles as The Coping Cycle. In this section, we will use an adapted version of this model, known as DREC (denial, resistance, exploration and commitment). The model is shown graphically in figure 2.5 below.

Figure 2.5 The DREC model

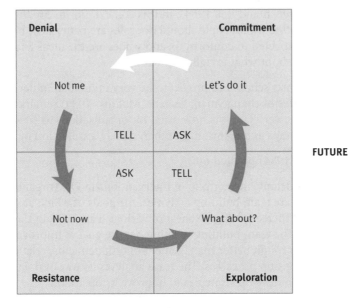

The stages of the cycle are as follows:

- *Denial.* Initially, the individual concerned will refuse to accept that the change affects him/her. The immediate response is to say 'Not me!' At this stage of the cycle, the individual is still firmly attached to the past and the change is seen as something external. The best response is to give specific instructions to the individual; to tell him/her what to do next.

- *Resistance.* After a period of time, the individual will accept that the change will take place, but not now. The individual is still attached to the past, but not as strongly as before, and is beginning to internalise the need for change. The correct response to this is to ask the individual what they are going to do next.

- *Exploration.* By this stage, the individual has accepted the need for change, and is beginning to explore options. They are now looking to the future and everything seems possible. But there are dangers. The individual will wish to experiment with everything, become overloaded and achieve nothing. Focus is needed and this is provided by telling the individual to choose their focus.

- *Commitment.* At this stage, the individual is fully committed to the change, has internalised it, has a clear focus and gets on with it. Individuals clearly face towards the future. They have internalised the change, and need no telling – just asking to learn what they will do next.

There is one more danger: it takes time for individuals to work through the cycle. They cannot be hurried. Any attempts to rush them through the cycle may result in a cosmetic change from denial to commitment, but when individuals experience pressure or failure, they revert back to denial. When this happens, it is known as the Tarzan swing, because it represents Tarzan making two giant swings in quick succession.

HR: THE CHANGE AGENT

Earlier in this chapter, the various models of HR were identified, and most of them emphasised that HR has a key role as a change agent, especially the Ulrich model. There are numerous areas when this role can be played, such as:

- Helping the organisation to adjust to changes in the external environment, both in the immediate term with legislative changes and in the longer term, such as changes in ethical behaviour and in advancing corporate social responsibility (see Chapter 9).

- Leading negotiating teams in persuading unions to change working practices and to become more flexible and efficient to meet the changing competitive environment.

- Involvement with mergers and acquisitions where, in this most sensitive area, changes may need to be taken quickly, and perhaps painfully, in the employee area, and survivors need to be quickly turned round to ensure they contribute to the long-term benefit of the merged organisation.

- Initiating changes in the organisation's culture, such as introducing a new behavioural environment or an enhanced competency framework.

- Introducing innovations in reward, such as greater emphasis on performance-oriented rewards, and moving away from job- or service-related payments. Here, the creation of a robust and fair performance management system becomes crucial and this involves a substantial change programme for management and employees to ensure it works appropriately.

- Organising research into the degree of employee engagement through employee surveys and producing proposals aiming to increase the engagement metrics.

- Working with the board and consultants to create and develop an employee brand, using the defined organisational culture and building up an integrated system of recruitment and selection; learning and development; employee relations; and reward and recognition to enhance that brand.

A further review of the role of HR in change is found in Chapter 10.

KEY LEARNING POINTS

Throughout this chapter, the implications for HR practitioners have been emphasised. In short, HR practitioners need to:

- understand the management systems and identity the power structure so they are able to use their influence selectively and effectively to improve organisational performance

- be regarded as an expert in handling conflict so that people issues can be addressed fully and appropriately and resolved in the interests of the great majority of stakeholders

- be aware of the options available for the structure of the HR function and be able to recommend the option that is most appropriate for the organisational context

- use their influence to improve employee understanding of the importance of systems of customer care and quality assurance, and ensure that employees respond accordingly

- act in the best interests of the organisation in facilitating organisational change, ensuring that employees willingly support the required changes.

QUESTIONS

1. What did Fayol consider to be the main principles of effective management?

2. What is the "Butterfly effect?"

3. According to MacMillan, what is the distinction between power and influence?

4. What is 'satisficing' according to Drucker?

5. What are the benefits of operating a "Business Partner" HR system?

6. Identify the main important sources of management power according to Morgan.

7. What are the crucial differences between a collaborative management style and an avoidance style?

8. Contrast the role of the business partner with that of an administrative expert in the Ulrich 1998 analysis.

9. What are the four key attributes of HR that are associated with the resource-based view of the organisation according to Boxall and Purcell?

10. Identify the main stages in the DREC model relating to change.

EXPLORE FURTHER

This chapter covers a very wide range of subjects so the list of additional reading can be extensive. You will find a long list for this chapter in the Bibliography section but here is an additional short selection.

Theories of management

Cole, G. (2010) *Management Theory and Practice*, 6th edition. London: Thomson.

Mintzberg, H. (2009) *Managing*. Harlow: FT/Prentice Hall.

Power in organisations

Jermier, J., Knights, D. and Nord, W. (1994) *Resistance and Power in Organisations*. London: Routledge.

Pfeffer, J. (1992) *Managing with Power*. Boston MA: Harvard Business School Press.

Handling conflict

Rahim, A. (2001) *Managing Conflict in Organisations*. Westport CT: Quorum Books.

Nicotera, A. (1995) *Conflict and Organisations*. New York: State University of New York.

Models of the HR function

Marchington, M. and Wilkinson, A. (2008) *Human Resource Management at Work*. London: CIPD.

Daniels, K. (ed) (2008) *Strategic Human Resource Management*. London: CIPD.

Customer care

Johns, T. (1994) *Perfect Customer Care*. London: Arrow Books.

Cook, S. (2008) *Customer Care Excellence*, 5th edition. London: Kogan Page.

Quality management

Mauch, P. (2009) *Quality Management: theory and practice*. London: CRC Press.

Besterfield, D. et al (2003) *Total Quality Management*. New Jersey: Prentice Hall.

Management of change

Hughes, M. (2006) *Change Management*, 9th edition. London: CIPD.

SEMINAR ACTIVITY

GESTALT-FIELD EXERCISES

Introduction

These are a series of exercises that you, as a student, can use to manage your own change. They are based on exercises used by life coaches, but they employ standard techniques such as critical incident techniques and gestalt. Students can work on these individually and then compare their results in small groups to aid the learning process. The group's most interesting examples can be shared with the whole class.

Rules for winning

This is an essential system to enable you to build on what you already do well, so that you can do even better. It uses the critical incident technique.

1. Recall a time when you succeeded in achieving something.

2. How did you manage to achieve the successful result? Write down your answers to the following questions:

   - What worked for you?

   - What can you learn about yourself from these results?

- What got in the way?

- What can you learn from that? (positive responses only)

- How will you overcome that difficulty next time?

Rules for winning are personal to each individual, and help you to identify positively how you as an individual overcome a given situation and achieve required objectives.

Golden moments

This uses ideas from gestalt psychology. Fundamentally, it asks you what you are feeling, seeing, sensing – but *not* thinking – in given situations.

- Identify your bottom line, ie the line you will not move beyond. It could be such things as trying to right injustice where you see it, not being treated as a doormat, standing up to unreasonable fellow students you share a flat with, etc.

- Think of times when you exemplified your bottom line.

- List times in your life when you achieved your objective. What did it feel like? (These last two experiences are the golden moments.)

These moments are personal to you and help you to affirm positively that you can achieve your objectives and stick to your bottom line.

The lifeline

Graph the highs and lows of your life on the chart below.

Label the highs and lows with life events, such as changing schools, a new job, father dying, and so on. For the purposes of the exercise, we are interested in the business-related highs and lows of the lifeline, and the messages these send to us.

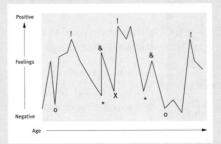

Code the business-related highs and lows of the lifeline in this way:

!   I took a great risk.

*   I played it safe.

o   Someone else made a major decision I thought should be mine.

+   I made one of my best decisions.

x   I felt I had no control.

&   I was in control.

What does this now tell you about yourself?

CHAPTER 3

The Competitive Environment

LEARNING OUTCOMES

By the end of this chapter, you should be able to understand, explain and critically evaluate:

- the fundamental economic problem of scarcity and choice, and the ways in which this problem is tackled by market and mixed economies

- determinants of supply and demand

- the main types of market structure, including perfect and monopolistic competition, monopoly and oligopoly, and their implications for price and output

- Michael Porter's Five Forces model of competitive structure

- portfolio approaches to SBU analysis, including the Boston Matrix

- the working of the labour market: wage determination and employment levels; perfect competition; and monopsony models of the labour market

- changes in the industrial and employment structure in the UK

- the feminisation of the workforce

- the growth of flexible forms of organisation

- the nature and importance of the psychological contract

- work–life balance

- the future of the workplace

- the changing nature and role of trade unions

- HR responses to changes in the competitive environment.

INTRODUCTION

This chapter begins with an analysis of supply and demand, followed by a consideration of market structures, including Michael Porter's Five Forces model. We then move on to the application of microeconomic theory; the workings of the labour market; and a consideration of changes in the industrial and employment structure of the UK.

ECONOMIC SYSTEMS

Different types of societies have organised their economies in different ways, but all have to produce answers to the same questions, whatever their economic system.

 ACTIVITY 3.1 SCARCITY AND CHOICE

Economists often say that economics is about scarcity and choice. What do you think they mean by this? What problems are caused by the conflict of scarcity and choice?

Three main models have emerged:

- the command economy
- the market economy
- the mixed economy.

Of these we will consider the market and mixed economies in some depth. The pure command economy we can dismiss quite quickly, as it no longer exists in any real sense, except perhaps in North Korea. Here all economic decisions are made by the state, or rather by a central planning authority acting on the state's behalf, which decides what will be produced, by whom and how it will be distributed. However, a command mentality was powerful in Western economies at least until the 1970s. In the UK, large sectors of the economy were controlled by the state through nationalised industries.

Nor was the private sector much different. The 1960s and 1970s were the heyday of detailed quantitative corporate planning, which in many companies bore a close resemblance to the Soviet Union's Five Year Plans. A classic example was General Electric. When Jack Welch took over as CEO in 1981, he inherited what the US Defense Department described as 'the World's most effective strategic planning system'. Welch promptly dismantled the whole elaborate planning system, and in its place brought in systematic decentralisation of decision-making (Kay 2003, pp96–97).

THE MARKET ECONOMY

Here economic decisions are taken on the basis of prices. There are no central planners, and decisions are taken by millions of individual consumers and producers. Producers produce only what they can sell to consumers; workers sell their services to producers and receive income, which they use to buy goods and services from the producers. In the last resort it is thus the consumers who decide what is produced (consumer sovereignty), and the economy is a closed two-player system.

Figure 3.1 Flows in the market economy

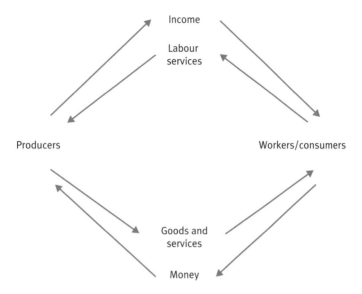

Our core economic problems are thus answered as follows:

- *What is going to be produced?* Anything which consumers are prepared to buy (demand, in the jargon).

- *How is it going to be produced?* In the most efficient way. If a producer is not efficient, he/she will be driven out of business by an efficient one.

- *Who is going to get it?* Anyone who is prepared to pay for it.

MIXED ECONOMIES

In practice all economies are mixed to a greater or lesser extent. Command elements commonly include:

- a framework of law: the law of contract, company law, etc

- publicly provided social goods, eg defence, police, education, welfare and health

- publicly owned industries, eg BBC in the UK, Amtrak in the US, Électricité de France in France

- state regulation of the level of economic activity

- control of economic behaviour, eg employment law, anti-trust law, anti-discrimination law, etc

- often, the use of taxation to redistribute income as well as to raise revenue for public services.

Throughout the rest of this chapter, we will be analysing the working of the mixed economy, with particular reference to the UK.

MARKETS IN THE NHS

CASE STUDY 3.1

In an article in the *Guardian*, a Sheffield GP, Paul Hodgkin (2007), discusses the different types of market operating in the NHS:

- *The market economy*. This is the model which underpins the concept of patient choice, where informed consumers choose between different providers, thus driving up quality. Unfortunately, there are at least two snags. Firstly, in the public sector, markets are zero-sum. As spending is capped, more spent on one procedure means less on another. Secondly, consumers (patients) are not informed, and they are not attempting to 'buy' a desirable good. No one in their right mind would positively desire a major operation! The patient is by definition anxious, and frequently not in a fit state to make an informed decision.

- *The barter economy*. This most clearly operates between the NHS and social services. Partnerships here are only possible given local give and take and mutual obligations, eg 'Do me a favour today with patient X, and next month I'll do the same for you'.

- *The centrally planned economy*. Evidence-based medicine; treatment dictated by the National Institute for Health and Clinical Excellence; targets; star ratings; inspections; and so on.

- *The gift economy*. This has always existed throughout the public sector, and is part of the public service ethos, ie giving more than is strictly required under contract, for the good of the patient. Hodgkin sees this as being eroded in the NHS, as new contracts become much more restrictive and time-based. A classic example of the gift economy which Hodgkin does not mention was identified in the NHS many decades ago – the totally free and voluntary UK blood donor scheme.

MARKET STRUCTURES

Economists classify market structures by the number of firms within the market (and to a lesser extent the number of purchasers).

The main classifications are:

- perfect competition
- monopolistic competition
- monopoly
- oligopoly.

There are also two other less commonly found forms:

- monopsony
- bilateral monopoly.

Perfect competition

This is a market where no one producer has an advantage over any other producer. There are many producers, none of whom has a sufficient share of the market to be able to influence the market price. They are known as price takers. Similarly, there are a large number of buyers, who are also price takers. The price in the market is set by supply and demand.

Demand measures the amount of the good or service which buyers are willing to buy at a given price (NB not the amount they need: demand is based on willingness to pay). Broadly speaking, the lower the price the greater the quantity which buyers will demand. This enables us to plot a demand curve – in practice plotted as a straight line:

Figure 3.2 A typical demand curve

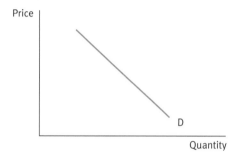

If the price rises, the quantity which buyers are prepared to buy will fall. This is known as a fall in quantity demanded. On the other hand, some external event may mean that buyers are prepared to buy more of the product at all prices – perhaps their incomes have increased. This is known as a rise in demand, and is illustrated on our diagram by a shift of the demand curve to the right. Similarly, a fall in demand is shown by a shift of the curve to the left.

Figure 3.3 An increase in demand

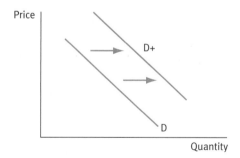

The same principles apply to supply. Broadly speaking, the quantity of a good which producers are prepared to supply is higher, the higher the price, producing a supply curve. Again, a movement along this line is known as a change in quantity supplied; a shift of the curve to the right or left is known as an increase or decrease in supply.

Figure 3.4 The supply curve

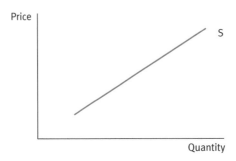

Figure 3.5 shows what happens if we put together the supply curve and the demand curve. There is one unique combination of price and quantity where the two lines intersect (point E). This sets the price that will be charged in that market, and the quantity which will be bought and sold, and crucially, this is an outcome which is equally acceptable to both buyers and sellers.

Figure 3.5 Supply, demand and equilibrium

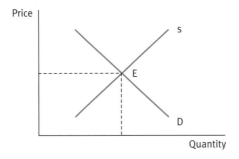

ACTIVITY 3.2 OIL PRICES

In 1973, Opec quadrupled the world price of oil overnight. The result was a severe bout of 'stagflation' for the world economy – simultaneous rising inflation and unemployment. In 1990–91, the oil price again rose rapidly in the build-up to the first Gulf War. However, after the war, oil prices quickly fell back, and by the late 1990s were at their lowest level for many years. In 1993, oil prices again rose rapidly in the build-up to the second Gulf War, but this time, after a brief fall in the immediate aftermath of the war, they have continued to rise, and on 2 January 2008 reached US $100 a barrel, five times their low in the late 1990s. Despite this,

world inflation has stayed relatively low, and economic growth has stayed high. Oil prices eventually peaked at around US $150 a barrel, before collapsing after the onset of the world recession in mid-2008. After falling to around US $35 they then recovered to stabilise at around US $70 in mid-2009, and have gone up dramatically since.

Questions:

1. Why have oil prices been so high from the war in 2003 to mid-2008?

2. Why did the increase in the price of oil after 2003 not lead to stagflation, as in the mid-1970s?

EASYJET AND DYNAMIC PRICING

CASE STUDY 3.2

The classic way to price a product is to charge each consumer exactly the same price. Tesco and Sainsbury's do not haggle with their customers – a price is published and the customer takes it or leaves it. However, supermarkets do reduce prices as goods approach their sell-by date, or where perishable goods are unlikely to keep until the next day. This is an example of dynamic pricing or yield management – if the alternative is to throw the good away, any price for it is better than nothing.

A much more sophisticated use of the dynamic pricing model is common in the airline industry. Taking advantage of its computerised reservations system, and the deregulation of airlines in the US in the late 1970s, American Airlines (AA) introduced dynamic pricing in the early 1980s, charging different customers different fares, depending on when they booked their flight. This is much easier to administer online than in the physical market, as the costs involved in changing prices are much lower. AA is alleged to make up to US $500 million a year through its dynamic pricing system. It changes half a million prices each day – an enormous number, as it only carries 50,000 passengers a day (McAfee and te Velde 2005). The model is widely used by the low-cost airlines in the UK, and has been copied by full-cost carriers like British Airways. The result is that theoretically each passenger on a particular flight might have paid a different fare, although they are all consuming the same product: a flight from A to B.

The economic theory underlying dynamic pricing is price discrimination – the idea that different consumers will place a different value on the same product, and that if possible the seller will strive to extract as much of this value as possible from each customer (Weiss and Mehrotra 2001).

The classic model for dynamic airline pricing is that the price will start low for a flight which is several weeks or even months ahead. This will attract the tourist or leisure market, where customers are not prepared to pay a premium price, but are prepared to book some time ahead of the flight. As the date of the flight approaches, the price will rise, attracting business travellers, who are less price-sensitive, and who may well have to fly at relatively short notice. As the date of the flight approaches, the price will fall if there are still large number of seats unsold, or will rise if the plane is nearly full.

To test the model, I plotted the prices charged by EasyJet on flight 211 from London Stansted to Glasgow, departing on 3 July 2007 at 11.25 am. I checked the price being charged on the EasyJet website once a day from 3 June 2007 until the day of take-off on 3 July (EasyJet 2007).

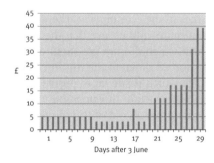

The results confirmed the classic model. The price on 3 June was £4.99, and remained at this level until 13 June, when EasyJet started its summer sale and the price fell to £2.99. It stayed at that price until 20 June, when it rose to £7.99, but it was back to £2.99 over the next two days. It then started a steady rise – £7.99 on 23 June, £11.99 on 24 June, and £16.99 on 27 June. The price remained at £16.99 until 1 July, when it rose to £30.99, and then to £38.99 on 2 and 3 July.

The product sold in a perfectly competitive market is assumed to be identical; thus there is no reason to favour one seller over another on grounds of quality or special features or service. It is also assumed that all players in the market are extremely well informed, and capable of reacting very quickly to any changes. There is thus no point in advertising – all products are identical and buyers know them to be identical. Buyers will react very quickly to any change in price, while sellers will very rapidly copy any innovation introduced by one of their rivals. Entry to the market is also completely free – anyone can enter or leave the market at any time.

Because of the nature of the market, there is no incentive for any one seller to cut his price; remember, he can sell as much as he likes at the current market price. Conversely, if he raises his price even a fraction above the market level, he will sell nothing, because there is no incentive for his customers to stay loyal.

Economists freely admit that perfect competition is extremely unlikely to exist in the real world – its assumptions are too restrictive. Why spend so much space describing it, you may ask. The reason is that it is a classic example of an economic model. It is a stylised attempt to explain behaviour, rather than a prescription for managers who want to make sound decisions. Models simplify the real world, and cut it down to its bare essentials, and on the basis of these bare essentials they make logical predictions. Thus the essence of the perfect competition model is to say that if the real world was like this, certain predictions would logically follow from it.

One consequence of the model is that it would lead to an efficient use of resources in the economy. Market forces would push production costs down to the minimum, and ensure that the most efficient production methods are used. Any firm which did not use them would be forced out of business. Profits would also be forced down to the minimum level required to keep firms in business. Any firm which made more profits than the minimum in the short term would be unable to sustain this position in the long term. Unfortunately, this also writes economic progress out of the model. There is no incentive to innovate or develop new products, because any advantage will be immediately wiped out through perfect knowledge.

It is also possible to apply the perfect competition model to labour markets. The lower the wage, the higher the number of workers demanded by employers, while the higher the wage, the greater the incentive to work in that industry. The only difference is that people's labour services are being sold, rather than, say, apples. Again, the result will be a market equilibrium: exactly the number of workers who are prepared to work for the equilibrium wage will be employed. The labour market will be examined in more detail later in this chapter.

Monopolistic competition

Rather more likely is that many firms will compete in a market, but each will sell a slightly different product. This type of market is classified as monopolistic competition. As the product is differentiated, the firms in the market have slightly more freedom in setting their prices. They can decide to charge a slightly higher price and sell a slightly lower volume of goods, and vice versa. To a small extent they are price makers. They can build up customer loyalty, and loyal customers will be prepared to pay a higher price for what they perceive as higher quality, or a closer match with their precise requirements, either in the product itself, or in the services which surround its delivery. Each firm is thus seeking to obtain a mini monopoly for its product.

Note that a real difference in product is not necessary; what is required is that consumers perceive there to be a difference. Firms in monopolistic competition frequently advertise in order to differentiate their product, while firms in perfect competition do not, as they can sell all they wish anyway.

Monopoly

Theoretically, a firm has a monopoly if it is the only firm supplying a market, ie it has 100 per cent of the market. This is very rare in practice, particularly if one defines a market widely. The Post Office has a monopoly in the UK for delivery of letters of a certain weight, but we also need to include close substitutes for letters in our definition of this market. Once we do this, it is clear that the Post Office faces competition in information transfer from a host of organisations and services, including e-mail, faxes and courier services. Virtually the only organisation with anything approaching a worldwide monopoly is Microsoft, whose operating systems have about 90 per cent of the PC market. Even here, in practice the monopoly is weakened by software piracy, with some estimates saying that half of all software in the UK is illegally copied.

In practice economists tend to define monopoly functionally: a firm is in a monopoly position if it is able to control the market price of the product it produces. This depends on the size of the firm relative to that of other firms in the industry. If firms in the industry tend to be large, the market leader may need to have perhaps half the market in order to dominate, but in an industry characterised by very small firms, 20 per cent of the market may be enough.

Because it has some control over price, a monopoly can manipulate the price and the quantity which it produces in order to maximise its own profit. Thus price will tend to be higher and quantity produced lower than in a competitive market. This does not necessarily mean that a monopoly will make an excessive profit. If no one wants to buy the product sold by the monopoly, there will be no excessive profit. Being the only producer of horse-drawn hansom cabs is not the best short cut to a fortune!

However, monopoly does have a tendency to excess profit, as well as other disadvantages. It encourages inefficiency in management and production, as there is no competition to force efficiency, and, most crucially, monopoly leads to a misallocation of resources in the economy as a whole. This would tend to suggest that monopoly will not be in best interests of consumers, and therefore should be at worst controlled, at best banned. This is broadly the approach taken by anti-trust legislation in the US.

In practice things are not so simple. Often monopolists can gain significant cost advantages (economies of scale) purely because they are big, and the end result might be both higher profits for the monopolist and a lower price for the consumer. As we will see later, this argument is put forward by supermarkets in the UK. The natural monopoly argument also has been put forward to oppose the break-up of British Rail at privatisation. Similarly, it may be judged desirable for a company to have a monopoly in the UK market if the result is that it is big enough to compete efficiently on the world market. As a an example, the Monopolies Commission in the 1970s and 1980s was prepared to tolerate both British Airways' dominant position in the UK market and its takeover of competitors like British Caledonian and Dan-Air.

There is also a view that monopolies and monopoly profits may well be a necessary part of the competitive process (Schumpeter 1950). Entrepreneurs are continually trying to exploit new opportunities. If they do so, they will achieve a temporary monopoly. Unless this monopoly arises from the sole ownership of a resource for which there is no substitute, the monopoly will be temporary because other firms will recognise the opportunity and enter the market, or they will devise substitute products. Schumpeter called this process 'creative destruction'.

Profits may thus be true monopoly profits, based on ability to restrict entry to the industry; windfall profits, based on short-term fluctuations in the environment and which in different circumstances could be windfall losses; and entrepreneurial profits, based on superior foresight or management, exploiting opportunities which were open to all. This view is supported by the law on patents. Anyone may invent a new process or product, but the reward for doing so is to be granted a temporary monopoly by the state, in return for the entrepreneurial risk and research-and-development expenses which have been incurred. Patent protection is the driving force behind industries like pharmaceuticals.

Following this view, the key element in assessing monopoly power is not market share but barriers to entry. This has led to the development of the concept of contestable markets (Lipsey and Chrystal 1999). Markets are contestable if entry is easy, entrants can compete on equal terms with incumbents, and they are not deterred by the threat of retaliatory price cutting by incumbents. The threat of entry to the market can be as effective as actual entry.

Oligopoly

An oligopoly exists when a few large producers control a market between them. The number of firms may vary between two (a duopoly) and about a dozen, and the products can be homogeneous or diversified. Oligopolies are also known as complex monopolies, and it is the latter term which is used by the UK competition authorities. In all cases, the firms in the industry are interdependent. The performance of each firm depends not only on its own actions, but also on the actions of the other firms in the industry. Thus, for example, before an oligopoly takes the decision to raise its prices, it must decide whether the other firms are likely to follow, or to keep its prices down and aggressively push to increase its market share.

Oligopoly is extremely common in the UK. Indeed, think of any major consumer good or service, and it will almost certainly be supplied by oligopoly firms: cars, petrol, banks, cigarettes, soap powder, instant coffee, chocolate, baked beans, etc.

One way of measuring oligopoly is by calculation of the five-firm concentration ratio. This is simply the share of the market in percentage terms held by the five largest firms. The higher this figure, the higher the degree of oligopoly.

Table 3.1 UK concentration ratios 1990

Industry	Concentration ratio (%)
Tobacco	99.3
Motor vehicles	87.7
Ice-cream and sweets	58.8
Pharmaceuticals	55.8
Toys and sports goods	24.7
Leather goods	12.4

(Source: Central Statistical Office 1992.)

Remember that these figures only cover UK producers. As a result of globalisation, all manufacturers are subject to increasing international competition, and only in tobacco and pharmaceuticals of the industries listed above can the UK be considered world class. Real oligopoly power is higher in services, where there is less chance of competition from imports. The five-firm ratio in food retailing in 2003 was 75 per cent, and this has become a four-firm ratio since the takeover of firm number four (Safeway) by Morrisons (number five). In the case of food production and retailing we have a bilateral oligopoly. Many branded goods are produced by oligopolies, and then sold through oligopolies.

Firms in an oligopoly market have a choice between a number of broad types of behaviour:

Collusion

One possible outcome is that the firms in the industry join together and collectively behave as if they were a monopolist. They can then collectively exploit any monopoly profits which are available. Unfortunately, from the point of view of potential cartel members, in most countries cartels and other forms of collusive behaviour are illegal. Cartels also tend to be unstable. They must have some mechanism for dividing up production and market quotas among their members, and this is fraught with difficulty. There is also a great temptation for individual members to cheat on their quotas. The cartel may be undercut by new producers, or new substitutes may be developed.

Price war

An opposite possibility may be a price war, with the aim of driving the competition out of business, and eventually emerging with a single-firm monopoly, which can then be exploited. The enormous risk, of course, is that you might lose, and yourself be forced out of business. In nearly all cases, the stakes are simply too high, and the risks too great. Indeed, in many cases it is only the market leader that can afford the risk of a price war, and it is the market leader that has the least need of one. In practice, most apparent price wars are extremely limited, and are used by the market leader as a sharp shock to the rest of the industry to stay in line. There are also risks in winning a price war. Driving a weak competitor out of business may just create a vacuum which can be filled by a much more formidable rival. A parallel would be the decision taken by the US to disband the Iraqi army after victory in the Iraq war in 2003. This left a military and political power vacuum which was quickly filled by sectarian militia groups and by Al Qaida.

Non-price competition

Rather than risk an all-out price war, firms will frequently engage in non-price competition, ie compete on everything except price. This might include competitions, quality, individual features, BOGOF (buy one get one free – for a limited period), etc. The aim is not to drive the competition out of business, but to gain a marginal increase in market share. All participants understand the rules of the game, and know very well that the war is limited, not total. Another possible form of non-price competition is complexity. In the old days, there was one mortgage rate, charged by all mortgage lenders on all mortgages. Now there is a multiplicity of mortgage types, each with its own terms and conditions, with the result that it is almost impossible to compare rates. The same thing has happened with utility pricing.

 ## OLIGOPOLY AND THE CUT-PRICE AIRLINE INDUSTRY

CASE STUDY 3.3

The cut-price airline industry has developed in the UK since the mid-1990s, on the lines pioneered in the US by Southwest Airlines. It is based on providing a no-frills service at low cost. It is dominated by two firms, Ryanair and EasyJet, who between them control half the total European low-cost market. Both Ryanair and EasyJet are constantly engaged in sniping at each other, with each claiming that it has the lowest fares, and that the other is inefficient, incompetent or worse. There appears to be every sign of a constant price war, with both companies sometimes in effect offering free flights, and offers of twice the fare back if a customer can find the same flight cheaper elsewhere. However, appearances can be deceptive. Until 2003, the main target of Ryanair's knocking copy was its bête noire, the Irish state airline Aer Lingus (which it unsuccessfully tried to take over in 2007), while EasyJet's prime target was British Airways, and particularly its low-cost subsidiary, Go. Neither has the serious intention of driving the other out of business. Direct competition between them (in the sense of flights to and from the same airport) is limited. On a strict definition, Ryanair and EasyJet are direct competitors on only one route, London Stansted to Rome Ciampino. As a result, the 'price guarantee' is almost meaningless. The price war is aimed much more at deterring new entrants to the industry (Ryanair and EasyJet have each taken over one of their main competitors: Buzz in the case of Ryanair and Go in the case of EasyJet), and to squeeze better terms out of airports who gain from a big throughput of passengers.

Price leadership

Here one firm within the industry is regarded unofficially as the price leader. If the leader changes its prices, the other firms in the industry are likely to follow suit. In order to be legal, it is essential that there is no collusion between the firms.

Monopsony and bilateral monopoly

Monopsony is a market form where there is a monopoly buyer. Normally the monopsonist is the government or one of its agencies. For example, for all practical purposes the NHS is a monopsony buyer of pharmaceuticals in the UK. If we have a market where a monopoly is selling to a monopsony, we have a bilateral monopoly. This applies where the NHS buys a particular patented drug from one pharmaceutical company. Monopsony will be important in our later discussion of the labour market (as well as the buyer version of oligopoly, known as oligopsony).

COMPETITIVE STRUCTURE

MICHAEL PORTER'S FIVE FORCES MODEL

The economic theory of market structure, distinguishing perfect and monopolistic competition, monopoly and oligopoly, provides a powerful but inevitably simplified model. The real industrial world is much more complex. One important model which attempts to match this complexity is Michael Porter's Five Forces model of competitive rivalry (Porter 1980).

According to the model, the structure of competition in an industry can be described in terms of five major forces. These are:

- the threat of entry of new firms
- the power of buyers
- the power of suppliers
- the threat of substitutes
- the intensity of rivalry among existing forms.

Each of the five forces is itself determined by a number of different factors.

When the five forces are completely analysed, this determines how attractive the industry is to firms within it, and those who might wish to enter it.

Unlike economic models, the value of this model lies not in its predictive ability, but in the way in which it provides a checklist whereby particular firms can clearly analyse and define their own position in relation to their own industry. It is a tool which can be used as the first stage of strategic analysis.

The threat of entry

The threat of entry of new firms to an industry depends on the extent of barriers to entry. These include:

- economies of scale
- capital requirements
- access to distribution channels
- absolute cost advantages
- expected retaliation
- government policy
- differentiation
- switching costs for buyers.

The power of buyers

Buyer power will depend on:

- concentration of buyers
- alternative sources of supply
- component cost as a percentage of total cost
- possibility of backward integration.

Power relationships between buyers and suppliers can be changed as a result of deliberate strategic decisions. For example, car manufacturers since the 1980s have followed a deliberate strategy of reducing the number of their suppliers. Suppliers have gained bigger orders and greater security, but at the cost of strict adherence to quality and 'just in time' (JIT) requirements.

The power of sellers

Seller power will depend on:

- number of suppliers
- switching costs
- brand power
- possibility of forward integration
- dependence on customer.

Threat of substitutes

The threat of substitution can take many forms. There could be technological substitution of one product for another – the fax for the letter, then the e-mail for the fax. In the last resort all goods are substitutes for each other, because they are all competing for consumer spending. This is particularly true of non-essential goods, where there is the ultimate substitute of doing without.

Key questions that need to be addressed are:

- relative price and performance of substitutes
- switching costs
- buyers' willingness to substitute.

Competitive rivalry

Competitive rivalry is to some extent a function of the other factors. However, there are other special factors:

- industry growth
- high fixed costs
- volatile demand
- product differentiation
- extra capacity in large increments
- balance of firms
- high exit barriers.

Bear in mind when using Five Forces that it is an analytical technique, which can tell you where you are now, probably why you are there, but not how to get where you want to get. There is also a danger in carrying out more and more detailed analysis – paralysis by analysis!

CRITICISMS OF FIVE FORCES

It must be remembered that Porter takes an economist's approach to his analysis. As a result, his model is over-simplified, and makes some basic assumptions. In particular, it is a static analysis. It assumes that change will be slow, and that as a result, the firm can take a planned approach to strategy once it has carried out its Five Forces analysis. This view is challenged by more recent writers on strategic management, who advocate a much more experimental emergent approach to strategic management (see Chapter 10).

There are also some serious gaps in the Five Forces analysis. It ignores the influence of government, and of regulation, which restricts the freedom of organisations to act as they might like. It is very much a private sector model, and so much less relevant to the public or not-for-profit sectors. It also assumes that competition is a zero-sum game – if one organisation wins, then another must lose. However, it does not take account of co-operation-based strategies like strategic alliances or joint ventures (Lynch 2006). Sumantra Ghoshal (2000) has developed this point. He argues that an excessive preoccupation with competition and market forces, by stressing efficiency at the cost of effectiveness will discourage innovation.

The Five Forces analysis was a product of its time. Porter was writing before the economy was transformed by mass computerisation and the Internet. In a comprehensive critique of Five Forces, Larry Downes (1997) identified three new forces which had to be taken into account:

- *Digitalisation* – The development of the Internet means that all players now have instant access to enormous amounts of information. As a result, change has become much more rapid than in the late 1970s, and the environment much more unpredictable.

- *Globalisation* – Businesses now operate on a global scale, and customers, using the Internet, can shop around and compare prices on a global scale. A Five Forces analysis must now take account of global as well as of national trends.

- *Deregulation* – In the UK, the US and the EU, many industries have been radically deregulated since Porter wrote about the Five Forces. Again, the effect is to make the environment more dynamic, complex and unpredictable.

Remember, though, that just as Porter was a product of his time, so was Downes. He was writing in 1997, approaching the peak of the dot-com boom. Since the dot-com crash in 2000, views on the future of the Internet have become perhaps less gung-ho than in 1997.

PORTFOLIO ANALYSIS

In the 1970s and early 1980s, strategic emphasis was on organisations building up a balanced portfolio of activities, or strategic business units (SBUs). Several techniques were developed to assist with analysis of portfolios of SBUs.

BOSTON MATRIX

This technique was developed in the 1970s by the Boston Consulting Group, and plots SBUs according to their rate of market growth and their market share.

Market growth rate is arbitrarily divided into high growth and low growth, ranging between 0 and 20 per cent per annum. Market share is assessed as share relative to that of the largest competitor, with a high of 10 times the nearest rival, and a low of one-tenth. SBUs are plotted on the matrix, with their precise position within a cell depending on their exact market share and market growth rate.

The significance of the Boston Matrix is that an SBU's position on the matrix has an impact in its profits and its cash flow. One of the main selling points of the technique is the colourful names attached to the various cells (Joyce and Woods 1996):

Figure 3.6 The Boston Matrix

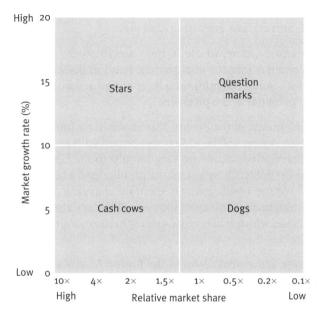

Dogs:
: They have a weak market share in a low-growth market. They generate a very low profit or even a loss, and also may well have negative cash flow.

Stars:
: They have a high market share in a high-growth market. Production will be at relatively low cost because of economies of scale, and profits are likely to be sound. However, because the market is growing rapidly, heavy investment will be needed to sustain market share. Cash flow is therefore likely to be at best neutral.

Question marks:
: They have a low market share in a high-growth market. This means that like the stars they need heavy investment, but as they are not the market leader they cannot fully exploit economies of scale.

Cash cows:
: They have high market share in a low-growth mature market. In the short and medium term this is an ideal position. Because the product is a market leader, it will be low cost, and it does not need heavy investment to cope with market growth. It is therefore likely to produce both profits and positive cash flow.

Two further types have also been identified off the bottom of the matrix. These are war horses (high market share and negative growth – a cash cow on its last legs) and dodos (low market share and negative growth – dead dogs!).

The strategic implications are that an organisation should aim for a balanced portfolio of SBUs, which should include products which can evolve through the sequence of question mark > star > cash cow. Some organisations, particularly at the height of the popularity of conglomerates in the 1980s, became extremely successful by identifying and exploiting cash cows.

One such was Hanson Group, whose strategy was to purchase cash cow products or companies (Imperial Tobacco in cigarettes; London Brick in bricks; Ever Ready in batteries), put in the minimum level of new investment, and exploit the cash-generating potential of the products.

The ideal types identified in the Boston Matrix also have implications for HR practice. The dog business will be mainly concerned with redundancy and redeployment. Star businesses are growing rapidly, so the HR priorities are recruitment and flexibility. Question marks ideally should be converted into stars, which will require a willingness to embrace change, and an emphasis on training and development. Cash cows focus on efficiency and effectiveness, and on customer service, which will require an emphasis on training, motivation and reward.

There are, however, some weaknesses in the Boston Matrix approach. One is that there is no clear-cut way to define markets. If the market is defined too narrowly, the organisation will overstate its market strength, and so tend to ignore 'over the horizon' competitors, who may be quietly building up their strength in a related market. Possibly more serious is that the matrix ignores any synergy factors. Synergy is defined as the way in which the whole organisation is greater than the sum of its parts. SBUs are not totally self-contained – they often provide each other with benefits, such as sharing production processes or distribution channels, or being part of a balanced catalogue of products. As a result, if an organisation decides to kill off a dog product, this may have adverse impacts on its other products. A final weakness is that it assumes a simple relationship between market leadership and profitability. This ignores the way in which many organisations have prospered in the long term by exploiting small niche markets. Despite these weaknesses, however, the Boston Matrix has been used successfully by a number of companies (Walker 1990).

 ACTIVITY 3.3 KILLING THE DOG

The board at Gamma Manufacturing was deeply divided. Under discussion was Product X, which had been a source of argument within the company for years past. The finance director wanted Product X dropped. He argued that it had absorbed considerable development funds over the years, but had never fulfilled its original promise. It tied up valuable production capacity in the factory, and wasted a lot of management time. 'It's a dog,' he said. 'We should put it out of its misery now.'

The marketing director disagreed. She argued that a lot of time, energy and money had been put into the product, and it would be a shame to waste all this just at the point when it might be about to take off. She also made the point that it filled a hole in the product mix. With some customers, it was important to be able to offer a complete product line, including Product X. 'If we haven't got X, I can name at least two big customers who will go straight to the competition,' she said.

Question: If you were the managing director, how would you evaluate the arguments put forward by the finance and marketing directors?

THE WORKING OF THE LABOUR MARKET

The same supply and demand analysis which we discussed earlier in relation to goods can be applied to labour, although, as we will see, there are some important differences.

DEMAND FOR LABOUR

Demand for labour is a derived demand. No employer will demand workers purely because he/she enjoys employing them. They are demanded because the output which they will produce is valuable to the employer. Demand for labour is thus derived from the demand for the goods or services which they produce.

To understand the demand for labour, we have to consider the law of diminishing returns. This states that marginal output (the addition to total output resulting from the employment of one more worker) will fall as more and more units of labour are combined with a fixed quantity of other factors of production (land and capital). A typical situation is illustrated in the following table.

Table 3.2 Diminishing returns to scale

Labour input (workers)	Total output (units)	Marginal physical product (units)	Price of product (£)	Marginal revenue (£)	Wage rate (£)
1	8	8	10	80	70
2	17	9	10	90	70
3	25	8	10	80	70
4	32	7	10	70	70
5	38	6	10	60	70
6	43	5	10	50	70
7	47	4	10	40	70

At a wage rate of £70, it is just worth employing the fourth worker, but not the fifth, because this would lose the firm £10. If the wage rate rises to £80, it is only worth employing three workers, while if it falls to £60, it becomes worth employing five workers. Plotting this on a graph gives us the familiar downward-sloping demand curve. Demand thus equals marginal revenue product.

Figure 3.7 The demand curve for labour

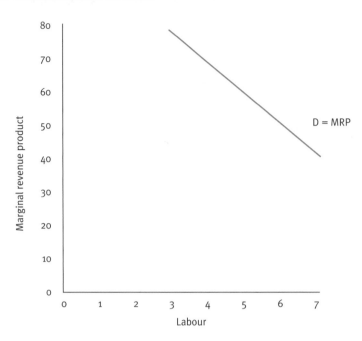

The demand (D) curve for labour can shift to the left or right if the marginal revenue product (MRP) of a given quantity of labour changes. The curve will shift to the right (an increase in demand for labour) if either marginal physical product increases (a rise in productivity per worker) or the price of the product increases.

THE SUPPLY OF LABOUR

As wage rates rise, the average worker is prepared to work more hours per week. The extra money earned, and the purchases of goods and services which it represents, is more attractive than extra hours spent in bed. Workers substitute work for leisure as wages increase. However, beyond a point, high wages do not tempt a worker to put more hours in. It is more attractive to work fewer hours and spend more time on leisure. This is known as the income effect. At high levels of income, the positive substitution effect of a wage increase is more than offset by the negative income effect. The result is an individual supply curve like that in figure 3.8.

Figure 3.8 The supply curve for an individual worker

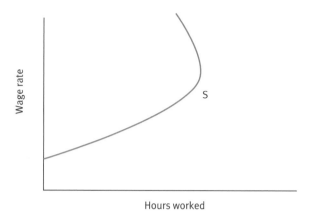

Figure 3.9 Supply of labour to a firm in perfect competition

The supply of labour to a firm depends on assumptions we make about the type of labour market facing the firm. If we assume that the labour market is perfectly competitive, there are many firms hiring many individual workers. In these conditions, an individual firm can hire an extra worker at the existing wage rate. In other words, the supply curve for labour facing that firm is perfectly elastic, as shown in figure 3.9.

Figure 3.9 Supply of labour to a firm in perfect competition

However, things are very different if we assume that the employing firm has some monopoly power (ie that it is a monopsonist, or a monopoly purchaser). The supply curve facing this firm will be upward-sloping, which means that to employ more workers, it needs to offer a higher wage. The cost of employing an extra worker (the marginal cost) (MC) will be higher than the wage rate the firm has to pay the extra worker. This is because it has to pay the higher wage to all its other employees as well. This is illustrated in table 3.3 and figure 3.10.

Table 3.3 Labour costs facing a monopsonist employer

Units of labour supplied	Cost per unit (£)	Total cost (£)	Marginal cost (£)
0		0	
			20
1	20	20	
			60
2	40	80	
			100
3	60	180	
			140
4	80	320	

Figure 3.10 Supply curve and marginal cost curve of labour facing a monopsonist employer

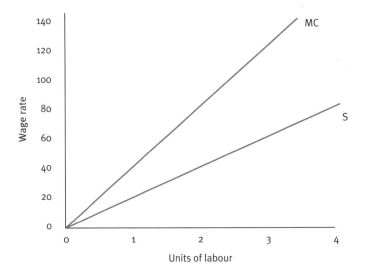

WAGE DETERMINATION

Putting together our demand and supply models helps us explain how wages are determined.

Firstly, assume that there is a perfectly competitive market for labour. Supply and demand would be as follows:

Figure 3.11 Employment and wage rates, perfectly competitive market

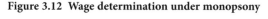

The wage rate, W, is set by the industry as a whole. The firm will employ OA workers at this wage rate.

As you would expect, the situation with a monopsony employer is more complex. Here the number of workers who will be employed is dependent on the firm's marginal cost curve (MC), not its demand curve.

Figure 3.12 Wage determination under monopsony

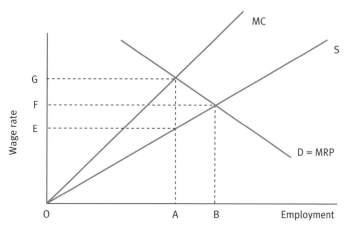

A monopsonist will only recruit labour if the marginal revenue product of that labour is equal to its marginal cost (ie point OA). However, it does not have to pay a wage OG. The wage rate depends on the supply curve, not the MC curve. It will therefore pay only OE.

If the market were perfectly competitive, OB workers would be employed, and they would be paid a wage OF. A monopsonist drives down both wages and employment compared with a perfectly competitive market.

Wage determination with trade unions

The aim of a trade union in a labour market is to increase the bargaining power of labour. Rather than being an individual selling his/her labour to a monopoly employer, the union member becomes a part of a monopoly supplier of labour.

What the union does is to fix a minimum price for labour. The result is to kink the supply curve for labour, as shown in figure 3.13.

Figure 3.13 Trade unions in a competitive market

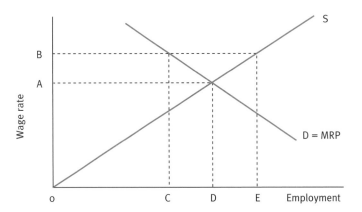

Here the union has set a floor for wages at OB. At this wage, the firm will employ OC workers. If there had been no union, the wage rate would have been lower, but employment would have been higher, at OD. At wage rate OB, OF workers would have chosen to work, but only OC can do so. As a result, there will be unemployment equal to CD.

The situation is totally different if the labour market is monopsonistic, as shown in figure 3.14.

Figure 3.14 Trade unions in a monopsonistic market

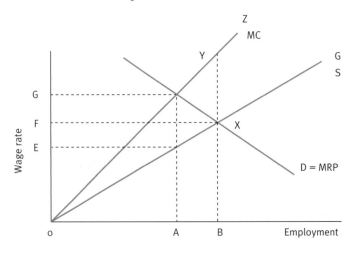

The union sets a floor wage of OF. The result is that the supply curve is now FXG, while the marginal cost curve is FXYZ. Thus not only is the wage rate higher (at OF rather than OE), but the level of employment has also increased, from OA to OB – the total opposite of the perfect competition case. Workers are better off and more are employed, and the only loser is the employer, who will lose some of his/her monopoly profits.

It can be argued that unions are not only good for workers, they are also good for employers. This is because unions can exert discipline over their members. If an employer wishes to introduce change, and it is not unionised, it will need to negotiate individually with all workers, which will be expensive and potentially disruptive. On the other hand, if it can persuade the union to support the change, its introduction will be much easier. This is the reasoning which underpins the TUC's New Unionism project, and the moves towards social partnership, which are discussed below.

For an extensive discussion of wage determination see Anderson (2006), or for a more scholarly approach, Manning (2003).

THE IMPACT OF THE NATIONAL MINIMUM WAGE

CASE STUDY 3.4

The national minimum wage (NMW) was one of the major labour market reforms of the first New Labour government, introduced in April 1999 at a rate of £3.60 an hour. The rate is set annually by the Low Pay Commission, an independent body with three employer representatives, three workers and three independents.

Successive increases have seen it rise to £5.80 in October 2009. This represents an increase of over 60 per cent in nominal terms, and over 30 per cent in real terms (after adjusting for changes in the retail price index (RPI)). The NMW has risen faster than average earnings. Between 1999 and 2007 it rose from 47 to 52 per cent of median earnings. The increase in 2009 is minimal (only 7p an hour) but this has to be set against a fall in the RPI and a very small increase in average earnings.

It is clear that the NMW has had an impact on wages. When it was first introduced, it raised the pay of between 5 and 6 per cent of workers (1.2 to 1.3 million workers) by about 15 per cent on average. The effect was much more marked for women, 8.5 per

cent of whom gained in 1999, compared with 3.2 per cent of men.

The effect on employment is much less clear-cut. As we found earlier in relation to trade unions, there are two conflicting theoretical perspectives. Just like a trade union, the NMW sets a floor to wages. One perspective is the classical (perfect competition) model, which argues that the result will be a fall in employment. The other is the monopsony (imperfect competition) model, which argues that employment will increase, as a result of a squeeze on employers' profits.

The former view was taken by the Conservative Party in the 1990s. In 1991, the then Employment Secretary, Michael Howard, argued that a minimum wage would cost two million jobs. This would be caused both by the classical theory model, and by a knock-on effect, where higher-paid workers demanded compensation in order to maintain their wage differential over the low-paid, which would have the effect of increasing inflation and interest rates in the economy as a whole. The monopsonist view was taken by the Labour Party, following a long socialist tradition dating back to the first call for a minimum wage by the Fabian Society in 1906.

In practice the effect of the NMW on employment has been complex:

- In some cases, the monopsonist model has applied, and both wages and employment have risen.

- In other cases, marginal firms have gone out of business as a result of the NMW, leading to a fall in employment.

- In cases where there is a large number of small employers, such as the care-home sector, the market approximates more to the perfect competition than to the monopsony model, and there has been a small fall in employment.

- In some cases the NMW has led to an increase in training, aimed at increasing the productivity of workers to compensate for the higher wage.

- There has also been some evasion of the NMW. One study suggested that 20 per cent of workers who should have been paid at the minimum wage were actually paid below it in 2000.

The above effects seem to broadly cancel each other out, and the overall impact on employment has been minimal. As a result, there is now a political consensus on the NMW, and in the 2005 general election, the Conservative Party pledged to keep it.

Finally, the NMW has to be put in a wider context. Firstly, it is part of a wider package of welfare-to-work measures introduced by Labour, including the Working Families Tax Credit. Secondly, many of the poorest householders do not benefit from the NMW because they have no one in employment: pensioners, the disabled, many single parents, etc.

(Sources: Metcalf 2007, Draca and Dickens 2005.)

CASE STUDY 3.5

WAGE SUBSIDIES – ARE THEY AN EFFECTIVE WAY TO SAVE JOBS?

Are wage subsidies an effective way of saving jobs during a recession? The Welsh Assembly says yes, and so do Germany, France, Italy and Spain, but many labour economists and the UK government say no.

In November 2008, the Welsh Assembly agreed a wage subsidy scheme called ProAct, which came into force in January 2009. The scheme pays a subsidy of £4,000 per worker to firms on short-time working, of which half goes towards training, and half is a wage subsidy. By August 2009, the scheme had paid out to 90 employers and safeguarded over 5,500 jobs. The scheme costs £48 million of which £30 million comes from the EU's European Social Fund and £18 million from the Welsh Assembly. There is a much bigger scheme in Germany, costing €6 billion. By August 2009,

Germany had already officially moved out of recession, while Wales was the only region of the UK where unemployment was falling. There is no direct evidence that either of these happy outcomes is a direct result of wage subsidies, but the coincidence may be suggestive.

A larger-scale scheme for the UK as a whole has been proposed by the TUC and the Federation for Small Businesses (FSB). They propose a scheme costing £3.3 billion a year, based on paying 600,000 workers 60 per cent of median wages for up to six months. They estimate that the gross cost would be offset by savings of £1.2 billion in reduced unemployment benefit and £850 million in increased income tax receipts, giving a net cost of £1.25 billion.

The schemes sound ideal, so why would

anyone oppose them? The main argument made against wage subsidies is the deadweight cost or moral hazard argument that subsidies would be paid to firms which would not have laid off workers anyway, putting public money in their pockets with no social return. One survey estimated that deadweight spending on wage subsidies in Ireland in the early 2000s had been between 40 and 80 per cent, and in Belgium in the late 1990s between 46 and 62 per cent. The TUC/FSB proposal suggested that moral hazard could be overcome by making access to the scheme contingent on long-term business viability and genuine need, as assessed and agreed by union, employer and government representatives.

There is also some evidence that employers are lukewarm towards the idea of work subsidies. The spring 2009 CIPD *Labour Market Outlook* (CIPD 2009a) survey found that only 28 per cent of employers would

pursue a short-time working subsidy, while 29 per cent would not. Two in five were 'don't knows'.

UK government policy has concentrated on getting the unemployed back to work, rather than on preserving existing jobs. There are three schemes:

- government-funded apprenticeships
- government-funded internships for graduates
- a recruitment and training subsidy of £2,500 to recruit the long-term unemployed.

In addition, the CIPD has called for a six-month work placement subsidy of £1,250 for the young unemployed.

(Sources: Connecting Industry 2009, Bailey 2009, CIPD 2009a, p1, *People Management* 2009a, Girma et al 2007.)

 ACTIVITY 3.4 THE LEMON

In 1970 the economist Akerlof discussed the case of the used-car market as an example of imperfect information. In the used-car market, sellers have much better information than buyers. In particular, sellers know whether there is something wrong with the car they selling – whether it is a lemon. Because the buyer knows that some cars being sold are lemons, but not which ones, the price in the market will be an average of the values of good cars and lemons. If a particular car is a good one, the buyer will get a better deal than the seller. The opposite happens with a lemon. As a result, owners of lemons will be willing to sell, but owners of good cars won't. As a result, the proportion of lemons in the market will increase, the more suspicious buyers will be, and the more prices will be pushed down. The whole used-car market will spiral downwards.

It is in the interests of potential sellers of good cars to do something to improve information in the market, and so to get better prices. There are many ways of doing this. One is to offer warranties on used cars, as is done by Ford through its dealers, for example. Another is to encourage buyers to get the car checked by an independent third party, like the AA.

From the point of view of the buyer, it is essential to know the reputation of the seller. Large, established main dealers of the major car brands are likely to have a better reputation than the back-street garage or cars sold through small ads in newspapers.

The lemon problem is really a modern application of Gresham's law, which dates from the 16th century. This law – 'bad money drives out good' – was established by Sir Thomas Gresham, treasurer to Queen

Elizabeth I. Governments at the time were
notorious for debasing the currency, ie mixing
cheaper material into the gold and silver
used to make coins. The government made a
profit on this, as the coins cost less to make
than their face value. If you had two coins,
one of which you knew to be good (of full
gold content), and the other to be debased,
you would hoard the good one, and spend
the bad one – bad money drives out good.
Unfortunately, everyone else would know
that only bad coins would stay in circulation,
and as a result prices would go up. Gresham

advised Elizabeth to avoid inflation by
resisting the temptation to debase the
currency.

Questions:

1. Do you think the lemon model is relevant to
   wage determination?

2. Find out how eBay, the online auction site,
   gets round the problem that buyers know
   very little about the reputation of sellers on
   the site.

TRENDS IN EMPLOYMENT

CHANGES IN THE INDUSTRIAL STRUCTURE

In 1951, manufacturing accounted for a third of the gross domestic product
(GDP) and nearly 40 per cent of employment. By 2001 employment in
manufacturing had fallen to 14 per cent of the workforce, although as the size of
the workforce had increased considerably, the number working in manufacturing
had only fallen from 8.7 to 3.7 million. Part of the reason for this fall was the
shift of manufacturing jobs to eastern Europe and the Far East, a consequence of
globalisation. Another reason was peculiar to the UK – the chronic overvaluation
of the pound since the late 1970s, which made UK manufacturing uncompetitive,
and triggered recessions in the early 1980s and early 1990s. The trend continues:
before the recession of 2008 there was much talk of an over-strong pound and
a two-speed economy – booming services and recessionary manufacturing. By
2008, the number of manufacturing jobs was down to 2.8 million (10 per cent
of the workforce), a fall of nearly a million in seven years (Clancy 2009). Where
manufacturing has survived, the nature of work within it has changed, from
skilled and semi-skilled manual work to much more knowledge-based and less
manual work.

The fall in mining and quarrying has been even more marked, from 880,000
workers in 1951 to 76,000 in 2001 (Philpott 2002). The share of public services
in GDP has fallen markedly since the early 1950s, although employment has
remained more or less constant at around five million. Falls in privatised public
corporations and the armed forces have been matched by growths in education
and the NHS. Services of all kinds have boomed, and have grown from about half
of employment in 1966 to 83 per cent in 2008 (Clancy 2009).

There have also been changes in the occupational level of the workforce. The
share of manual workers in the workforce fell from 64 per cent in 1952 to 38
per cent in 1991, with the biggest proportionate fall among unskilled manual
workers, whose percentage has fallen by nearly two-thirds. Skilled manual

workers fell from 25 per cent of the workforce in 1951 to 12 per cent in 2001, while the managerial professional and technical workforce has risen from 12 per cent in 1951 to nearly 40 per cent in 2001, and relatively poorly paid service sector jobs have also increased.

The above trends are typical of most of western Europe, although the proportion of workers in manufacturing is higher in Germany and Italy, and the proportion working in services higher in the Netherlands (Gallie 2000).

REDUNDANCY AND THE RECESSION

Costs of redundancy

Redundancies are a fact of life in a recession, such as that experienced in the UK in 2008–09. The CIPD *Labour Market Outlook* for summer 2009 showed that redundancy intentions among employers peaked in spring 2009. The *Outlook's* net employment intentions figure – the difference between the proportion of employers who expect to increase their staff numbers and those who expect to decrease them – has been negative since winter 2008–09, when it was a net minus nine. This rose to a peak of minus 19 in spring 2009, but fell back to minus 10 in summer 2009, with 34 per cent expecting to decrease their staff numbers (CIPD 2009b, p2).

Within the figures there has been a dramatic shift between sectors. The net employment figure for the private sector has improved between spring and summer 2009 from minus 30 to minus two, while for the public sector it has worsened just as dramatically, from minus three to minus 28. Thirteen per cent of public sector organisations expect to reduce their workforce by more than 10 per cent. Optimism in the voluntary and not-for-profit sector has also worsened, with 30 per cent expecting to make redundancies.

As unemployment is a lagging indicator (it is slow to rise in a recession, but continues to rise after a recession is technically over), it is likely that redundancies will continue on a significant scale through 2010.

In the February 2009 edition of *Impact*, the CIPD research journal, John Philpott (2009a, p1) discussed the cost of redundancy. Although redundancies can sometimes be inevitable, employers should always remember that there are significant costs associated with them.

Philpott gives a formula for calculating the cost of redundancy as:

$$CR = nR + xH + xT + ny(H+T) + Wz(P-n)$$

Where

CR = total cost of redundancy
n   = number of people made redundant
R   = redundancy payments
x   = number of people subsequently hired
H   = hiring costs

T   = training/induction costs
y   = percentage quitting post-redundancy
W   = average monthly staff salary
z   = percentage reduction in output per worker caused by lower morale
P   = number of people employed prior to redundancies

Redundancy payments (R): Any employee made redundant after two years' service is entitled to statutory redundancy pay. Many employers pay more. The average redundancy payment in autumn 2008 was £10,575.

Hiring costs (H): After the recession ends, it is likely that new workers will have to be hired. The average cost of recruitment in 2008 was £4,667.

Training costs (T): New hires will have to be trained, at an average 2008 cost of £1,133.

Survivor syndrome:

- $Wz(P-n)$. There is likely to be a decline in morale among those left employed (survivors). The CIPD *Employee Outlook: Job Seeking in a Recession* (CIPD 2009c, p3) found that seven out of 10 employees whose organisations had made redundancies reported a fall in morale, while 27 per cent said they were personally less motivated in their jobs. On the other hand, half of employees feel under increased pressure to perform after redundancies. The formula calculated the cost of a fall in morale by multiplying the reduction in output of survivors (z), by their average earnings (w).

- Increased turnover as a result of redundancies: $(ny)(H+T)$. This measures the cost of additional hiring and training costs if turnover increases as a result of redundancies. However, this effect may be small during a recession, when there are few other jobs to go to, although turnover may shoot up once the recession is over and alternative jobs become available. A CIPD survey in August 2009 found that 22 per cent were so unhappy with the way that redundancies had been handled that they were planning to change jobs as soon as the labour market improved (Churchard 2009a).

If we ignore survivor syndrome costs as being indirect and very difficult to quantify, we are still left with an average figure per redundancy (on CIPD figures) of between £10,575 (where redundant workers are not subsequently replaced) and £16,375 (where rehires need training). Put another way, it costs roughly six months' wages (at the average wage) to make a worker redundant.

Alternatives to redundancy

Most employers have some idea that redundancies cost money, and most also feel a sense of responsibility to minimise suffering to their workforce. Hence a search for alternatives to redundancy discussed by John Philpott in a follow-up to his *Impact* article quoted above (Philpott 2009a).

One possibility is to use voluntary rather than compulsory redundancy. This has the advantage that it is likely to be more atttractive to employees, and so may marginally reduce survivor syndrome costs, but its direct costs are the same as compulsory redundancy, and there is the added disadvantage that as the employer does not choose who is made redundant, the organisation might inadvertently lose key workers. Much the same is true of early retirement, where there is again a loss of control, as well as additional pension costs.

Philpott identifies six common alternatives to redundancy, and their rate of use by employers. These are set out in table 3.4 and discussed below.

Table 3.4 Usage of main alternatives to redundancy 2009

	(%)
Recruitment freeze	50
Termination of temporary contracts	44
Flexible working	19
Cutting bonuses	17
Short-time working	15
Cutting pay	7

Recruitment freeze

This reduces the headcount through natural wastage, and has the advantage of being cheap, but like voluntary redundancy, the wrong people may be leaving. The recruitment freeze may need to be combined with redeployment to ensure that key tasks are covered.

Termination of temporary contracts

This is attractive, as temporary workers can be terminated without redundancy pay, but the effect for the temporary worker is the same as a redundancy: he/she is out of a job.

Flexible working

This may be desirable in its own right, but is not usually an alternative on its own to redundancy.

Cutting bonuses

This is usually simple and straightforward, as there is rarely a contractual right to a bonus. However, by definition, it is only possible if a bonus is already being paid.

Short-time working

A number of possibilities are available here:

- Lay-offs – Here the worker is told to stay at home for a specified period of time, during which time they are likely to be unpaid, or paid at a reduced rate.

If the lay-off is without pay, employers are required to pay statutory guarantee pay of £21.50 a day for a maximum of five days in a three-month period (DirectGov 2010).

- Short-time working – Here hours are reduced (for example a four-day week), usually with a commensurate pay reduction.
- Sabbaticals – this is in effect a form of lay-off, where employees are offered an extended period of (usually) unpaid leave while retaining all their employment rights.

Unless there is a specific right written into the contract of employment, all of the above are dependent on the agreement of the employee. If they are introduced without agreement, this is breach of contract.

Cutting pay

Again, cutting pay will need to be agreed. However, it is cost-effective. If one reckons that a redundancy costs half a year's pay, a 5 per cent pay cut for 10 workers is the equivalent of one redundancy, and can be sold to the workforce as a fair way of spreading the pain, particularly if managers take a bigger pay cut than workers.

One interesting proposal has been put forward by the CBI. Known as Alternative to Redundancy (ATR), this would involve a six-month delay to redundancy, during which time the employee would not work, but would receive an ATR allowance worth twice the rate of jobseekers' allowance, half paid by the government and half by the employer (Churchard 2009b).

Philpott calculates the savings from the various alternatives to redundancy. He finds a recruitment freeze and terminating temporary workers to be the most cost-effective. Other measures save less than redundancy, but they have the advantages of retaining talent, and of having less impact on survivor morale.

 ACTIVITY 3.5 ALTERNATIVES TO REDUNDANCY

A. Xilinx

Xilinx is a medium-sized US semiconductor company with about 2,600 employees. In 2001, it was hit hard by the collapse of the dot-com boom, with its revenues falling by 50 per cent in six months. Other firms in the industry reacted by introducing redundancy programmes, but the Xilinx management wanted to avoid this if possible. They understood the cyclical nature of the industry, and the need to hold on to skilled staff ready for the upturn.

In 2001, they implemented a programme of pay cuts, ranging from zero for the lowest-paid workers to 20 per cent for the CEO, and a two-week shutdown. Employees were given the choice of taking the shutdown without pay, using paid leave entitlement or 'borrowing' future leave entitlement if they had not accrued enough leave to cover the shutdown. The CEO announced that lay-offs would only be considered as a last resort.

As the market continued to deteriorate, employees agreed to take an additional

7.5 per cent pay cut, with the choice of taking stock options in lieu of pay. However, the events of 9/11 then hit the industry, and even further measures were needed. After extensive consultations throughout the company, two additional programmes were agreed:

- voluntary redundancy and early retirement, taken up by 82 employees

- a one-year sabbatical leave, with two months' pay, an education bonus of US $10,000, and/or a bonus of US $10,000 for working as an executive on loan to a local non-profit organisation. The employee could return with no loss of benefits, seniority or stock options. This was taken up by 41 employees.

In 2002, the market recovered, and the pay cuts were restored. By 2003, Xilinx had increased its market share from 30 to 52 per cent, and it was making profits which exceeded that of its three major competitors combined (Cascio and Wynn 2004).

B. Honda and British Airways

Both Honda and British Airways were hard hit by the 2009 recession, and both took imaginative measures to cope. Honda decided that it had to reduce production at its Swindon car factory from a planned 218,000 vehicles to 113,000, which in effect made half its 4,700 staff surplus to requirements. The first step was a voluntary redundancy programme, taken up by 1,300 workers.

However, the company still felt that it had 490 more workers than it needed, but it did not want to lose them as they would be needed when the economy picked up in 2010. Two major programmes were agreed with the union, Unite. One was a four-month shutdown, ending in June 2009. Staff received full pay

for the first two months of the shutdown and 60 per cent for the second two months. The second was a pay cut, of 3 per cent for employees, and 5 per cent for managers, for 10 months from June 2009 to April 2010, with six extra days of paid leave. In Japan, pay cuts of 10 and 15 per cent respectively had been agreed. The pay cut was agreed to by 89 per cent of Honda employees, and the Unite regional officer Jim D'Avila said, 'In true solidarity the workers at Honda are standing together during difficult times to protect hundreds of jobs.' In addition, some of the surplus workers were found jobs in Honda's nearby suppliers (Pidd 2009, Stewart 2009, Churchard 2009c).

In June 2009, British Airways was reported as asking staff to work for free for one month. Willy Walsh, the CEO, set an example by foregoing his pay for July, a total of £61,000. However, there were media reports that undue pressure was being put on workers to agree to the proposal, and cabin crew and ground staff were reported to be considering industrial action. BA then widened the proposal to a range of options including unpaid leave and a temporary switch to part-time work as well as unpaid work, while making it clear that employees who took up the unpaid work option would still receive allowances and shift pay.

In the end the take-up for the company's proposals was small. Total take-up was 8,000, or 20 per cent of the company's workforce, while the unpaid work option was only accepted by 800 workers, or 2 per cent (*People Management* 2009b, Churchard 2009d, McCarthy 2009.)

Question: Why do you think the programmes at Xilinx and Honda were successful, while that at BA was a relative failure?

THE FEMINISATION OF THE WORKFORCE

Male participation rates (the proportion of the population of working age who are in employment) have fallen steadily since 1951 (and indeed since 1911). They were 88 per cent in 1951 and had fallen to 71 per cent in 1998 (Gallie 2000). The fall is explained by early retirement, and greater levels of sickness incapacity. However, by 2008, this had risen to 78 per cent, mainly because of an increased participation rate among the over-50s (Kent 2009). Female rates over the same period have risen from 33 to 70 per cent in 2008. As a result the share of women in the labour force has risen from 30 to 48 per cent. All of the gain in female employment has come about as a result of an increased participation on the labour force of married women. The single women participation rate has fallen from 73 per cent in 1991 to 64 per cent in 1991, while the married women participation rate has risen from 22 to 53 per cent. It is difficult to remember that in the early 1950s women in occupations like the civil service were routinely expected to resign when they married! The overall percentage working part-time has risen from 23.6 per cent in 1992, to 25.5 per cent in 2008. This increase has been driven by men, who are more likely to work part-time in 2008 than in 1992, while women are less likely to do so. Overall, 42 per cent of women in employment were working part-time, compared with 11.6 per cent of men (Kent 2009).

Women are under-represented in the higher professions, management, administration and manual work, while they are over-represented in the lower professionals clerical work, sales, personal service and as technicians (primarily education and the NHS).

Why has the workforce become feminised? Giddens (2006) puts forward three main reasons.

Demographic trends

The birth rate has declined, and women are having children at a later age. As a result, they work for longer before they have children. As families are smaller, it is easier for them to return to work after having children. Domestic housework has also become much less labour-intensive, and men are at last tending to take a greater share of it. Women spend nearly three hours a day on housework, but men spend one hour 40 minutes.

Financial pressures

Single mothers often have little choice but to work, and increasingly this is being encouraged by the workings of the welfare support system. Even two-parent families often find they need two incomes to maintain their desired standard of living.

Personal fulfilment

The women's movement in the 1960s and 1970s increased women's self-esteem, and a desire among women for more independence.

A fourth reason could be that women workers are particularly attractive to employers, because they are much more likely to want to work part-time. In 2004, there were 5.2 million women in the UK in part-time employment, as against only 1.2 million men. Part-time workers are much more flexible than full-time ones, and this gives a considerable advantage to employers.

The reasons for women taking part-time work in 2004 were identified as follows.

Table 3.5 Reasons for women to seek part-time work

Reason	(%)
In education or training	3
Disabled	2
Caring for children or other family member	36
Found no full-time job	7
Did not want full-time job	19
Other	34

(Source: Manning and Petrolongo 2005.)

WORK ORGANISATION

THE FLEXIBLE ORGANISATION

The idea of the flexible firm was first identified by Atkinson (1984), and the concept was refined by Handy (1991). Atkinson identified four types of flexibility:

- *Numerical flexibility* – achieved by altering working hours or altering the number of workers employed through part-time working, etc.
- *Functional flexibility* – achieved by training workers to perform a wider range of tasks (multiskilling) and breaking down barriers to deploying workers on different tasks (demarcation).
- *Distancing* – replacing employees with sub-contractors.
- *Pay flexibility* – switching from centralised collective bargaining and rigid pay scales to individually negotiated pay and benefits.

With the development of the Internet, it is possible to add a fifth type, geographical flexibility, as many workers can now work from home, with considerable control over exactly when and how they work.

The result is a segmentation of the workforce into core and peripheral workers. Core workers are those key workers who are central to the organisation's main functions. They will be long-term employees, possibly with guaranteed employment, and highly trained. They will be committed to the organisation, and the organisation will be committed to them. Peripheral workers will be those performing non-core services, often as sub-contractors. They will be hired and fired as required, and will serve as a buffer protecting the core workforce from fluctuations.

Handy developed the core–peripheral concept into his Shamrock concept. This type of organisation has three interlocking leaves consisting of three distinct groups of workers who are treated differently and have different expectations: specialist core workers; a contractual fringe, who may or may not work exclusively for the organisation, and who are paid a fee based on results rather than a wage based on time taken; and a flexible workforce, who are likely to be employed on a temporary or casual basis.

Remember, however, that what Atkinson and Handy are discussing is a theoretical model of organisations. Although many organisations have moved towards this kind of structure, many have not. As with other new management techniques, British management tends to be conservative and reluctant to adopt new ideas (Marchington and Wilkinson 2008).

ACTIVITY 3.6 THE CHALLENGES OF FLEXIBLE WORKING

What problems are posed by the movement towards more flexible ways of working?

THE PSYCHOLOGICAL CONTRACT

All employees have a legal contract of employment, but for the employee this is usually presented as a 'take it or leave it' situation, ie he/she has to accept it or leave. The psychological contract is different. It is implicit rather than explicit, individual rather than collective, tacit rather than written (although elements of it may be incorporated into a social partnership agreement with a trade union) (CIPD 2003, p1). There are dangers in making it too explicit, as organisational and environmental changes may make it impossible to deliver on an explicit contract (Briner and Conway 2001). It can be defined as 'the perceptions of the two parties … of their mutual obligations towards each other' (Guest and Conway 2002). By its very nature, the psychological contract is dependent on trust between the employer and the employee.

One view of the psychological contract is that it has changed from an 'employment security' contract to an 'employability' contract. This reflects the shift from the monolithic to the flexible organisation which was discussed above. Under the employment security contract, the employee offered time and loyalty in return for security of employment and the possibility of promotion (Kimberly and Craig 2001). As redundancy and downsizing became more common, employers could no longer guarantee their side of the bargain, and gradually it was replaced by the employability contract: employees would still offer time and loyalty, but in return the employer would ensure that they received the work experience and training that would enable them to get another job elsewhere. This has been described as the 'new deal' at work and as producing a 'free agent' mentality among workers.

If this model is correct (and there is some doubt about this – the 'old' psychological contract often still exists, and where it has gone, it has not necessarily been replaced by an employability contract), loyalty may not be enough to keep the free agent employee on board. The organisation may have to offer more, including possibly empowerment. If workers are to be trusted, they expect trust back from the organisation.

Rousseau (2004) distinguished between relational contracts, based on give and take and on trust in the employer; and transactional contracts, which are more short-term in approach and concentrate on pay and conditions. The CIPD (2005) points to a suggestion that there has been a shift in recent years from relational to transactional, as trust in employers has declined, but refutes this, saying that employee commitment is broadly stable.

Other implications of the new psychological contract suggested by the CIPD include:

- *Process fairness* – employers need to put in processes which ensure that employees see the way in which decisions are made as being fair.
- *Communications* – communication mechanisms have to be set up to ensure that employers are aware of the employee 'voice' (this is reflected in the EU Information and Consultation Directive).
- *Management style* – employees expect to know what is going on; management style needs to change from 'top-down' to 'bottom-up'.
- *Managing expectations* – managers must be seen to be fair, honest and open.
- *Measuring employee attitudes* – managers need to know what their employees are thinking.

The employability and free agent approaches in many ways put a lot of pressure on employees. They are forced to take responsibility for their own future in a way which, while attractive to many, does not suit everyone. Many people want security rather than opportunity. Those who really crave opportunity may well have shifted to self-employment already (the self-employment rate in the UK is currently around 12 per cent of the workforce; Philpott 2009b). Increasingly employers have to offer something else as part of their side of the psychological contract. This is work–life balance, which we discuss in the next section.

WORK–LIFE BALANCE

Changes in social structure have increased pressure on people in work:

- In the 1950s and even into the 1960s, women routinely gave up work on marriage, and so were at home to care for children. People married young, and had children young, with most people having completed their families by the age of 30. At the time when children were dependent, many parents also had an extended family to draw on and relatively young grandparents, who probably lived nearby.
- In the 1990s and 2000s, over half of all married women were in work, whether or not they had children, and families had come to expect and need two incomes. The age of marriage had risen, and many women had not had their first child by 30. The extended family had broken down, and by the time the

family needed support, grandparents were too old, did not live locally, and increasingly needed care themselves.

- The increase in the rate of marriage breakdown meant that greater numbers of single parents with children, particularly women, needed to work to support their families, but had no external support networks to draw on. In 1991, 20 per cent of dependent children lived in single-parent families.

- Millions of women in their fifties have to care for an elderly dependent parent.

- An increased desire on the part of employers as well as employees for a more flexible workforce.

An Institute of Management survey in 2001 highlighted the extent of the problem (*Professional Manager* 2001):

- 46 per cent of female managers have children

- 26 per cent care for others such as elderly parents

- 27 per cent cite family commitments as a career barrier (up from 17 per cent in 1992).

In 2003, 9 per cent of males and 33 per cent of females had at some time given up work to care for somebody (*Social Trends* 2004).

In addition, people without caring responsibilities also feel that they are entitled to a life outside work. One in five people take work home almost every day, and one in 10 work more than 48 hours a week (CIPD 2003).

There are some legal requirements on employers to meet the needs of their employees for work–life balance. These are mainly concerned with the right to time off to cope with one-off situations or emergencies, and full details are given in the CIPD Factsheet, 'Work-life balance' (CIPD 2003). In addition, from 2003, (under the Employment Act 2002), employees with children under the age of six (18 if disabled) can request a change in their hours, time or place or work. The employer must consider such a request, and can refuse it, but only after following a detailed procedure and basing their decision on specified business grounds. This was extended in 2007 to employees with children under 17, as a result of the Work and Families Act 2006 (CIPD 2009d, p5).

Although only parents of young children have the right to request flexible working, any other employee can ask for flexible arrangements, and many employers have granted this. Figures for 2003 showed that 18 per cent of men and 27 per cent of women working full time have some kind of flexible working arrangements, but the most common arrangements as follows:

Table 3.6 The most common flexible working arrangements

	Males (%)	Females (%)	All (%)
Flexible working hours	9.7	14.9	11.6
Annualised hours	4.9	5.1	5.0
4.5-day week	1.8	1.1	1.5
Term-time work	1.2	5.8	2.9

There are similar patterns for part-time workers, with flexible working hours and term-time working being the most used options. Twenty-six per cent of males and 47 per cent of females had changed their hours or working arrangements to look after someone.

 ## ACTIVITY 3.7 WORK–LIFE BALANCE

- Our discussion above has been in terms of flexible working hours or time off. What other family-friendly arrangements could employers offer?

- What business case could you put to your employers to persuade them to adopt family-friendly policies?

- Among your workforce are two workers: Anne, who is a single parent with a daughter aged four, who has asked to work school hours only; and Peter, who is the sole family carer for his elderly mother, who has Alzheimer's disease. He has asked to work a 30-hour week, instead of the normal 35, and to leave work one hour early, in order to get home before his daytime carer leaves. What response would you make to each worker?

THE INTERNAL LABOUR MARKET

Many organisations have sought to bypass the external labour market by operating their own internal labour market. This was based on permanent employment contracts with a high level of job security, career progression from low-skilled to high-skilled jobs, and internal training. The prime example of such an internal labour market is the classic Japanese manufacturing firm, with its job-for-life culture and promotion based on seniority, but similar practices were followed in many sectors in the UK, including local government, the Post Office, banks and insurance companies.

The approach was the product of a benign external environment, characterised by full employment, which made recruitment of new staff difficult; steady economic growth, which lessened the need for downsizing; and strong trade unions, which provided resistance to downsizing and lay-offs. However, the increasing turbulence in the external environment produced by new technology, globalisation, severe recessions in the early 1980s, early 1990s and late 2000s, and government measures to make labour markets more flexible and to weaken trade union power have put pressure on the internal labour market. Downsizing has killed the concept of a job for life, and organisations have become flatter, which makes it more difficult to climb a clearly defined career ladder. Opportunities for promotion have lessened, and the jump in skills involved in promotion has increased. Increasingly, new workers are recruited on temporary and/or agency contracts, rather than on permanent contracts. Where the internal labour market model has survived, it has so primarily through a core and periphery model, where internal market features were confined to the core.

Grimshaw et al (2001) examined the erosion of the internal labour market in five organisations, drawn from banking, local government, the NHS, retailing and telecoms. They found a range of responses, suggesting that there is no one best way, but rather 'different routes to partial failure' (Hyman 1987, p30). They examined the four major features of the internal labour market model:

- *Recruitment into a permanent job.* Both the bank and the telecoms company had mainly expanded through the use of call centres, overwhelmingly staffed by agency workers. In the other three organisations, recruitment was still mainly through permanent non-agency contracts, although the retailer met peaks in demand through temporary staff.

- *Career progression from low-skilled to high-skilled.* In the classic model, work at one level prepared a worker for the next level in the ladder. In all the case study organisations, except possibly the NHS trust, de-layering had broken the promotion ladder. In the retail organisation, 95 per cent of staff were general assistants, and the rest were managers, with little movement between the two. The same was true at the banking and telecoms call centres

- *Protection against lay-offs.* The bank and the council had no compulsory redundancy policies, which meant that staff could be redeployed if necessary, while through their extensive use of agency staff both the bank and the telcoms company could ensure that lay-offs were restricted to agency staff.

- *On-the-job training.* Traditional employer-led training had declined, with a growth in individualised, employee-led training, concentrating on generic rather than on specific job-related skills. This is linked with an increasing emphasis on employability, clearly expressed by the training and development manager at the bank: 'We owe staff a duty to make them employable outside the organisation.'

Employment security is seen as a key element of the internal labour market model, and also of the high-commitment HRM model. The European Commission has developed the concept of 'flexicurity' – 'an integrated strategy to enhance, at the same time, flexibility and security in the labour market'. It stresses that security includes not just maintaining one's job, but also enhancing one's employability (European Commission 2007 quoted in Marchington and Wilkinson 2008). The trends in unemployment during the 2008–09 recession suggest that employers may belatedly have to learn some of the lessons of the internal labour market model – although the decline in GDP has been much more severe than in the earlier recessions of the early 1980s and early 1990s, the rise in unemployment has been much less (at least half a million less than expected).

THE FUTURE OF THE WORKPLACE

Moynach and Worsley (2001) put forward three possible scenarios for the future development of the workplace by 2020. They identify two key variables:

- The degree to which organisations must adapt to their workers, and conversely the degree to which workers must adapt to organisations. Tight labour markets will shift power to workers, while more intense competition in the product market will shift power to organisations.

- The stability of networks. Will employers favour stable networks that allow them to retain knowledge in the organisation, or will rapid change lead to virtual teams which change so frequently that long-term relationships between their members become unsustainable?

On the basis of these two variables, Moynach and Worsley identify three possible scenarios for 2020, discussed below.

Fragile communities – workers forced to adapt, but networks stable

Individualised contracts are widespread, and workers are contracted to perform specific tasks and paid by results, but skills shortages encourage employers to retain knowledge workers. However, this model is unstable, because competitive pressures are forcing rapid change, which puts pressure on networks.

Stable communities – organisations adapt, and networks are stable

Competitive pressures are lessened as organisations merge or collaborate, and organisations must adapt to the needs of their workers through measures such as work–life balance. However, this may not be viable because of the pressures of globalisation.

Disposable communities – workers forced to adapt, and networks are fragile

Labour is seen as a commodity, and employers tap into a global pool of skilled labour. Knowledge is stored electronically, so there is no pressure to retain workers as the corporate memory of the organisation. Workers are insecure and stressed, and may respond to this by opting out of the labour market, through downshifting or self-employment. In the long run, this may make the model self-defeating.

All three of the models are plausible, but all three contain the seeds of their own destruction. The result may be a labour market that oscillates between them.

TRADE UNIONS

So far in this section on work organisation we have concentrated on the position of individuals. We conclude by analysing the collective: the role and position of trade unions.

Trade union membership peaked in 1979, at more than 13 million. Since then it has nearly halved, to around 7.5 million in the late 1990s. It has since stabilised, helped by legislation on union recognition in 1999. The nature of trade union membership has also changed. Union density (the proportion of workers who are union members) has fallen from 54 per cent in 1979 to 29 per cent in 2003, but for women it has only fallen from 37 to 29 per cent.

Density is also affected by age. Density among the over-50s is 33 per cent, while for the age group 25–34 it is 25 per cent (*Social Trends* 2004). Density among full-time workers is 32 per cent; but among part-time workers only 21 per cent.

Density among professional and associate professional workers and personal service workers is higher than among manual workers. Density in the public sector is 60 per cent, while in the private sector it is only 20 per cent.

In 1979 the typical union member was a male manual worker in heavy industry, eg a miner or a steel worker. By 2003, the typical union member was a female teacher or NHS worker.

Many reasons have been put forward for the decline in union membership. These include:

- the decline of traditional highly unionised sectors of industry
- the anti-trade union legislation of the Conservative governments between 1979 and 1997
- the recessions of the early 1980 and 1990s
- the growth of a flexible workforce, which is more difficult to unionise
- the growth of pay review bodies in the public sector
- the spread of performance-related pay and individualised HRM systems
- the fall in the size of firms
- defeat in highly publicised set-piece disputes like the 1980s miners' strike.

The response of the trade unions, led by the TUC, was to change their orientation. The traditional perspective taken by unions was a pluralist one – that management and unions have some common aims, but many more conflicting aims, within the employment relationship. Collective bargaining was seen as managing the balance between the interests of management and workers, and would frequently be adversarial. Many individual union leaders took a more radical Marxist perspective, and saw the management–labour relationship as an exploitative one.

In the early 1990s, unions in America had developed a different approach, known as New Unionism, based much more on a co-operative relationship, recognising that management and unions have basic agreement in wanting the employment relationship to work more smoothly, and that both sides benefit from a high-wage, high-productivity environment. New Unionism also recognised that the approach of union members and potential members is an instrumental one – they want a union to protect their individual interests. They buy union membership like they buy a foreign holiday – they want value for their money.

In 1996, the TUC adopted New Unionism. The emphasis in future was to be on developing social partnerships with willing employers, and on stressing casework for individual members (Barber 1998). To further New Unionism, the TUC set up an academy in 1998 to train union representatives. The typical academy student was female and from an ethnic minority.

SOCIAL PARTNERSHIP AT VERTEX

CASE STUDY 3.6

Vertex is an outsourced services company, part of United Utilities, formed in 1996 when North West Water merged with North West Electricity. In five years, it has moved from collective bargaining to union derecognition to non-union consultation to collective bargaining based on partnership.

The head of employee relations, Tony Stark, said, 'I'd had a bellyful of trade unions after working in the car industry and the docks in Liverpool.' However, he was to lead negotiations with Unison which led to partnership. Even when the union was derecognised, union officials were elected on to the company-wide employee consultation forum, and proved constructive partners.

After the passing of the Employee Relations Act 1999, Unison applied for a ballot on

recognition. Rather than fight the request, Vertex set up a working party with the union, which produced agreement on recognition and social partnership. The company and the union put in a successful bid to the DTI's Partnership Fund, which aims to make organisations aware of best practice in partnership. This funded six months of workshops, facilitated by Ruskin College.

The partnership has produced tangible results, including a pay progression agreement, which has helped the company to achieve a retention rate much higher than that prevalent in the call centre industry. The partnership has also helped the company to win contracts with the public sector (Walsh 2001).

New legislation introduced by the Labour government supported the new approach. Under the Employment Relations Act 1999, all workers have the right to be accompanied by a fellow worker or union official to disciplinary proceedings. The Employment Act 2002 set out the statutory rights of union learning representatives, who have a key role in helping to promote learning and development within organisations which recognise unions (CIPD 2004, p1).

Perhaps most important, the 1999 Act introduced a statutory right to union recognition through ballot, as long as 50 per cent of workers vote in favour of recognition, and at least 40 per cent of those eligible to vote are in favour. This ensures that a small minority of the workforce cannot force through recognition.

ACTIVITY 3.8 UNION RECOGNITION

What do you think are the advantages and disadvantages to employers of recognising trade unions?

HR RESPONSES TO CHANGES IN THE COMPETITIVE ENVIRONMENT

We illustrate this section with a case study which demonstrates where environmental change had to be met with HR responses.

TALENT MANAGEMENT

The CIPD (2009e, p6) defines 'talent' as 'those individuals who can make a difference to organisational performance, either through their immediate contribution or in the longer-term by demonstrating the highest levels of potential', while talent management (TM) is 'the systematic attraction, identification, development, engagement, retention and deployment of those individuals who are of particular value to an organisation'. Capelli (2008) has a simpler definition of TM: 'a matter of anticipating the need for human capital and then setting out a plan to meet it'.

Capelli argues that TM, at least in the US, is in a mess. One approach is to do nothing internally, and to rely on hiring in talent from outside as needed. This poaching model is dependent on someone else developing the talent, and is ultimately self-defeating. The alternative approach harks back to the heyday of detailed quantitative strategic planning in the 1950s, when the environment was much more stable and benign. The problem with this approach is that all plans fail in a turbulent environment, and the organisation will end up with either a surplus or a deficit of talent. A deficit is not so serious, as the shortfall can always be met by hiring in. A surplus means that talented and qualified individuals have no role to perform. An example he quotes is that of Unilever India, which found itself with 1,400 well-trained managers in 2004, 27 per cent up on 2000, despite the fact that its demand for managers had fallen after the 2001 recession.

Capelli's approach is to apply the just-in-time principles of supply chain management to TM:

- Aim to undershoot in internal talent development, and to buy-in any shortfall.
- Break up development programmes into smaller segments. Rather than recruiting graduates once a year, for example,

plan for two intakes instead. Break down a development programme into smaller modules, so that needs can be reassessed at the end of each module. Concentrate on general management rather than functional skills in the early modules.

- Share the cost of development with trainees. Common in the UK, this is apparently rarer in the US.
- Keep in touch with leavers. Deloitte, for example, informs former employees of important developments in the firm.
- Involve the employee in TM. Rather than relying on detailed succession plans, throw promotion posts open to internal competition.

In a 2009 report, 'Fighting back through talent innovation' (McCartney 2009), the CIPD identified a number of strategies organisations can use to manage their talent through the recession:

- *Build up the employer brand*. This will make it easier to acquire talent when the economy turns.
- *Acquire talent from other organisations.* Some organisations are making talented individuals redundant, making more talent available on the market. Both Tesco and Standard Chartered are actively recruiting talent.
- *Keep talent warm for the future.* Interest potential future recruits in the company, even if there are no vacancies at present.
- *Increase your focus on talent performance, engagement and retention.* It is vital that talented employees are fully engaged and motivated.
- *Review the effectiveness of current TM programmes.*
- *Maximise any available funding opportunities.* Management is not the only type of talent. A flow of skilled workers is also vital. The government has

increased funding for apprenticeships, and this has been exploited by the Borough of Tower Hamlets and National Express.

- *Encourage line managers to be less risk-averse and provide support for stretch assignments*. Recruitment freezes force line managers to make better use of internal talent.

- *Ask for innovative suggestions from talent pools*. The talent is there – make best use of it.

- *Experiential-based learning*. On-the-job learning need not be expensive, and can give a quick pay-off.

- *Set up a leadership exchange group and partner with other organisations*. TM across firms on a partnership basis can provide a wider range of experiences, eg the secondment of managers to a charity, for example.

- *Build a sense of community*. People in talent pools progress faster if they can learn, share ideas and network with each other, and if they know this is actively encouraged by the organisation.

KEY LEARNING POINTS

- The fundamental economic problem is how to reconcile scarcity and choice. Market and mixed economies tackle these problems in slightly different ways.

- Market economies are underpinned by the concepts of supply and demand, and their interaction to create equilibrium.

- Perfect competition is an unrealistic but ideal model. Other models of the market are measured by their deviation from perfect competition.

- Performance in oligopoly markets depends on an interaction between the firms operating in the market.

- Porter's Five Forces model is a powerful way of analysing the competitive forces operating in an industry.

- The perfect competition and monopsony models are alternative ways of explaining the working of the labour market.

- Since the 1970s, manufacturing has declined rapidly in the UK, along with a growth in employment in services. This has helped to lead to an increasing feminisation of the UK workforce. Globalisation and computerisation have also led to the growth of flexible forms of work organisation.

- The labour force in the UK has increasingly been feminised, although inequality of opportunity between men and women still persists.

- The psychological contract has evolved from an emphasis on job security to employability and to work–life balance.

- Trade union membership in the UK has almost halved as a result of changes in social and industrial structure. The response of the unions has been to develop the concept of New Unionism.

1. What would you say are the differences between a pure command economy and an economy with a command mentality?

2. What do you understand by the concept of dynamic pricing?

3. What are the differences between oligopoly and monopolistic competition?

4. Why is non-price competition a favoured strategy in an oligopolistic market?

5. What are the Five Forces identified by Porter in his model?

6. What criticisms have been made of the Five Forces model?

7. Why might a firm decide not to drop a 'dog' product, as identified in the Boston Matrix?

8. How well do you think that the perfect competition model of the labour market explains wages and employment?

9. Under what circumstances can trade union activity increase both wages and employment?

10. Why do you think that the share of manufacturing in the UK's GDP has fallen?

EXPLORE FURTHER

Further Reading

The theoretical background to this chapter is covered in any good economics textbook, such as Lipsey and Chrystal's *Principles of Economics*, or Alain Anderson's *Economics*. Each edition of *Impact*, the CIPD's quarterly update in policy and research (available through the CIPD website) has an article by John Philpott, the CIPD's chief economist, on some aspect of the labour market.

Websites

As a manager you need to be able to apply the theory to contemporary examples and situations. The best way to do this is to make sure that you regularly read *The Economist*, and at least one of the quality broadsheet newspapers – preferably two, one broadly liberal, like the *Guardian* or the *Independent*, and one broadly conservative, like the *Times* or the *Daily Telegraph*. The *Financial Times* is also very useful, and easier to read than you might think. All of these have their own websites, on which you can access their archives, but only the *Guardian* website (www.guardian.co.uk), which also includes the *Observer*, has free access to its archive. You can access *The Economist* via the CIPD website. Most local libraries provide free access to the Thomson newspaper website, which includes all the newspapers mentioned above.

SUPERMARKETS: AN OLIGOPOLISTIC INDUSTRY

Introduction

The supermarket industry has come a long way since the 1970s, when the industry was fragmented, with a large number of supermarket groups mostly operating small stores, and over 100,000 independent grocery outlets of various types. Economies of scale were low, with deliveries being made direct by wholesalers or manufacturers to individual stores. Supermarkets were in town centres, and most people shopped regularly several times a week.

By the late 1970s, two leaders had emerged from the pack: Sainsbury's and Tesco. Sainsbury's was a private family company until 1973. It was concentrated in London and the south-east, with a mainly middle-class clientele. Tesco was a much younger company, founded by Jack (later Lord) Cohen, who was responsible for the notorious slogan 'pile 'em high, sell 'em cheap'. In the late 1970s, Tesco began the slow and at times painful move upmarket that has continued ever since. The two firms were neck and neck in the market until 1995, when Tesco took the lead for the first time.

Tesco is now way out in front, with a market share of 30.4 per cent in 2006 (Competition Commission 2007). Sainsbury's, with 15.9 per cent, is neck and neck with Asda (16.5 per cent), which was a northern-based also-ran until it was taken over by the biggest grocer in the world, Wal-Mart of the US, in June 1999. In fourth place is Morrisons, which again was a long-established northern chain which came from nowhere to take over the struggling but larger Safeway group in 2004. It had 10.3 per cent of the market in 2006, but is having trouble in digesting its prey. Its market share was significantly higher immediately after the takeover.

Between 2000 and 2006, total supermarket grocery sales rose by 26 per cent in real terms, although there was a small fall in the total number of stores. Supermarkets had increased their share of grocery sales over this period from 67 to 72 per cent. Convenience stores held their market share at 20 per cent, while other grocery outlets, including specialist grocery stores, fell from 13 to 8 per cent (Competition Commission 2007).

Superstores

In the late 1970s, the UK supermarket groups started to adopt the French concept of hypermarkets, huge out-of-town stores. In the UK they became known as superstores. A superstore was defined as a store with at least 25,000 square feet of selling space, at least 20 check-outs and selling at least 16,000 lines. Superstores yielded very high economies of scale. They were supplied from huge centralised depots, which minimised distribution costs, and the huge superstore buildings were very cheap to maintain. Increasingly the big groups used new technology to improve efficiency and lower costs.

By the mid-1990s, the explosive growth period of superstores was over. Most of the best sites had gone, and the government was tightening up the planning controls on new development. The response of the supermarkets, particularly Tesco, was fourfold:

- Extended opening hours. Many of the larger stores are now open 24 hours a day, and only close (very reluctantly) on Christmas Day.

- A move into e-commerce, with grocery deliveries co-ordinated from the local store.

- A move back into town centres. Tesco started to develop its Tesco Metro chain, and Sainsbury's started Sainsbury's Central. Both aimed particularly at lunchtime and commuter shoppers, selling a more restricted range of convenience goods.

- Introduction of new services, like pharmacies, film processing and in some cases dry-cleaning.

Diversification

Another growth route for the supermarkets was diversification. Both Tesco and Sainsbury's accelerated their movement into the convenience-store market through takeovers. Tesco took over T&S Stores in 2004, acquiring 850 stores, and Sainsbury's took over Jacksons Stores (110 stores) (Wheatcroft 2004). Even the Co-op got into the act, taking over Alldays, doubling its number of convenience stores to over 2,300. At the end of 2006, Tesco owned 1,150 convenience stores, and Sainsbury's 287, together making up 3 per cent of the national convenience stores total (Competition Commission 2007). The big groups also moved heavily into non-food sales, which now make up more than 10 per cent of their total sales (Hiscott 2004). One pound in every eight spent in the UK goes to Tesco. It sells more DVDs than HMV and more shampoo than Boots (Purvis 2004). In the summer of 2004, it was reported that Asda had become the UK's biggest clothing retailer, overtaking Marks & Spencer. Sainsbury's for a long time owned the DIY store Homebase.

Diversification has also been global, particularly by Tesco. It has moved into France, Hungary, Poland and Thailand, and is poised to move into China. It was thus excellently positioned to exploit the expansion of EU membership into central Europe in May 2004. Sainsbury's has made less good strategic decisions by opting for expansion in the US, a saturated market. Asda has gone the other way. It has been expanded into by Wal-Mart, with its huge purchasing power, which gives Asda a bigger influence on the market than its market share would suggest.

Price wars

Supermarkets are notorious for their price wars. These are launched by all the groups at regular intervals with a fanfare of publicity. The reaction of customers to price wars tends, probably rightly, to be cynical. Market research in the summer of 1993, during a particularly intense period of price-cutting, showed that more than half of shoppers regarded price cuts as gimmicks; 20 per cent said they took no notice; and only 22 per cent believed they were genuine. Price cuts always tend to be concentrated on known-value items (KVIs) – the 200 or so items like tea, butter and coffee where customers remember prices. The great bulk of the 20,000 lines stocked by the average superstore are not affected by price cuts. The 1993–94 price war would have saved on average 1.5p on an £100 shopping trolley. Remember also that in the main it is not the supermarkets that pay for the price cuts – it is the suppliers.

All the major supermarkets engage in below-cost selling (selling goods below their cost price), representing up to 3 per cent of total revenue. Below-cost selling is concentrated on dry groceries, alcohol, CDs, DVDs and books. The Competition Commission does not think that below-cost selling is part of a predatory policy aimed at excluding rivals, but does think that it could unintentionally harm smaller grocery retailers and specialist stores. If it leads to these shops exiting the market, this could harm consumers (Competition Commission 2007).

After an investigation of the industry, the Office of Fair Trading in 2002 brought in a 'voluntary' code of practice governing how supermarkets treat their suppliers, particularly farmers. A review of the working of the Code of Practice in 2005 found that on the whole the supermarkets had complied with its terms (Competition Commission 2007).

Competition

In the mid-1990s, supermarkets appeared for the first time to be facing serious new competition. This came from the entry into the market of discount stores from the continent, particularly Aldi, Lidl and Netto, which had been very successful in Germany and the Netherlands. They stocked a very limited range, mainly of tertiary brands (brands which no one had ever heard of), and at rock-bottom prices. Although much feared at the time, they seem only to have affected the bottom end of the market, particularly Kwik Save.

Supermarkets and the recession

Like the rest of the economy, supermarkets were hard hit by the recession that started in 2008, which coincided with a spike in food price inflation to 13 per cent. The first impact was a significant trading down by consumers. In the summer of 2008, the 'hard discounter' Aldi was achieving annual sales growth of 17 per cent, with a 25 per cent increase in footfall, and a 17 per cent increase in customers from the ABC1 social groups. By Christmas 2008, Aldi's growth rate was up to 25 per cent. By contrast, Tesco's year-on-year growth, at 4.6 per cent, was below the market average of 6.2 per cent (Finch 2009a). The other big losers were the upmarket Waitrose and Marks & Spencer.

By the summer of 2009, the big retailers had recovered their nerve, and were hitting back hard against the hard discounters. Tesco launched its own 'discounter' range, and rebranded itself as 'Britain's biggest discounter'. Asda went for a 'round pound' promotion, selling hundreds of goods for £1. Sainsbury's went for 'switch and save', showing the saving in switching from branded products to its own brands, while its advertising frontman, Jamie Oliver, showed how to 'feed a family for a fiver'. Even Waitrose launched a new budget range called Essentials, which now accounts for 15 per cent of its turnover.

The result was that the explosive growth of the hard discounters was stopped in its tracks. In the year to July 2009, Aldi's sales were up 8.3 per cent, but this was beaten by Morrison at 9.5 per cent, and virtually equalled by Asda, Sainsbury's and Waitrose. The only group unable to show a strong comeback was the market leader, Tesco, with growth of just 4.5 per cent. The result was a fall in its market share, down from a peak of 32 per cent to just 30.6 per cent (Finch 2009b). In August 2009, it announced that it was doubling the value of Clubcard reward scheme, from 1 to 2 per cent, in effect a further price cut of 1 per cent on all purchases (Thomas 2009).

The other significant change to the structure of the market was the demise of Somerfield, taken over by the Co-op in March 2009. The Competition Commission required more than 100 former Somerfield stores to be sold off, of which 22 were bought by Waitrose. The new Co-op has a market share of around 7 per cent, putting it firmly in fifth place, well ahead of Waitrose and Aldi (*Retail Week* 2009).

Questions

1. Why do you think the competition authorities allowed Tesco to take over T&S Stores, even though Tesco had a market share over the 25 per cent, which would make it a monopoly under UK law?

2. In what ways does the behaviour of the supermarkets fit with the theory of oligopoly?

3. Carry out a Five Forces analysis of the UK supermarket industry.

4. Tesco has a full-time equivalent UK workforce of 194,000. How can such a huge organisation keep track of its talent?

5. Why would a large supermarket chain be interested in local pay bargaining? Why would the union (USDAW) be opposed to this?

CHAPTER 4

Government Policy

By the end of this chapter, you should be able to understand, explain and critically evaluate:

- the legislative process in the UK and the EU
- informal influences on policy formation, including the role of political parties and pressure groups
- the key components of the UK economy
- the key objectives of UK economic policy
- the tools of economic policy including fiscal, monetary, competitiveness and exchange rate policy
- techniques for managing interest rates in the UK, and their impact on inflation and economic growth
- the causes and impact of the credit crunch of 2008–09
- public ownership, privatisation, private finance initiatives and public–private partnerships
- the voluntary sector
- public interest companies
- factors which influence productivity and competitiveness
- skills policy in the UK
- recruitment, retention and workforce planning issues in the public sector.

INTRODUCTION

In this chapter we will analyse the evolution of government policy in social, economic and industrial fields, and the impact of government policy on organisations. As developments in the UK are heavily influenced by the actions of the EU, we will be concerned with both UK and EU policy. We start with formal legislative procedures in the UK and the EU, and then go on to consider informal influences on the evolution of policy. We then explore recent developments in policy in the UK.

THE LEGISLATIVE PROCESS IN THE UK AND THE EU

THE UK

Most legislation originates in government departments and is directly sponsored by the government. Some legislation, particularly on matters of conscience, starts as a private member's bill. Most of these fail. Normally they only pass with substantial cross-party support, and support – or at worst neutrality – from the government. Indeed, frequently the purpose of a private member's bill is not actually to pass a new law, but to bring public attention to an issue which is important to an individual MP and those pressure groups that support him/her. In this section, we are only going to look at government bills.

At least for bills published relatively early in the life of a parliament, the general subject matter of the bill will appear in the governing party's election manifesto, eg, 'We intend to bring in legislation to put right the long-standing grievances concerning ...'

The next (optional) stage is a Green Paper. This is a consultative document setting out the case for the forthcoming legislation, and the pros and cons of various approaches to legislation. This does not commit the government to anything, but forms a basis for discussion with interested parties and pressure groups. After consultation on the Green Paper, the government may choose to:

- follow it up with a White Paper
- go straight to legislation
- drop the proposal.

A White Paper firms up on the proposal, but again does not commit the government on detail. A lengthy period of consultation may then follow.

The parliamentary session normally starts in November, with the Queen's Speech, where the Queen sets out the programme of legislation for the coming year: 'My government intends to introduce legislation on ...' The government will then publish a bill, drafted by specialist parliamentary lawyers. The bill then goes through a number of formal stages:

- First reading – a formal presentation of the bill to the Commons.
- Second reading – a full debate on the principles of the bill rather than the details.
- Committee stage – the bill is then scrutinised in detail by a standing committee of the Commons, consisting of between 15 and 20 MPs, with a government majority. The bill will be debated and voted on clause by clause, and some provisions may be amended.
- Report stage – the amended bill goes back to the full Commons, where the government has an opportunity to reverse any amendments forced on it at the committee stage.
- Third reading – this is formal, and not usually debated.

- The bill then goes to the House of Lords, and repeats the same stages as in the Commons. The Lords can amend the bill or reject it. If they reject it, this delays the bill for one parliamentary session. Having passed through the Lords, the bill goes back to the Commons, which can reject any amendments made by the Lords.

- Royal assent – the Queen then agrees to the bill, which becomes an act. In theory the Queen could reject the bill, but this has not been done for 300 years.

As a legal document, every word of an act matters, and it is subject to interpretation by the courts.

THE EU

This is very different from the process in the UK. Initial proposals for legislation are drawn up by the European Commission, and must be based on one of the EU treaties (Rome, Maastricht, Amsterdam, Nice, etc). Each treaty has to be unanimously ratified by the member states. By contrast, in the UK the government has a free hand to legislate on anything that it chooses (including leaving the EU).

At this stage, the proposal is known as a draft framework law or a draft directive. The draft then goes out for consultation to the Council of Ministers, the European Parliament, and the social partners (the two employers' bodies Unice and CEEP, and the trade union body ETUC). The Commission then revises its proposals, which are then formally presented to the Council of Ministers, which will take a decision on unanimity or qualified majority voting, depending on the nature of the legislation. The European Parliament has the right to debate and to comment on the proposed directive, but until the Lisbon Treaty was adopted, no right to amend or reject it. Under the Lisbon Treaty the European Parliament will have the right to reject or amend the proposal, but only by a majority of more than half of all MEPs (not just those who vote).

The law will be adopted if

- both the Parliament and the Council of Ministers approve it (by either unanimity or qualified majority, depending on the type of legislation)

- the Council of Ministers approves the Parliament's amendments (if the Commission opposes an amendment, it must be approved by a unanimous vote of the Council of Ministers).

The directive then has to be implemented by member states, ie EU directives become law in the UK through a UK act of parliament. At the end of 2003, there were about 2,500 EU directives, and the compliance rate by member states ranged between 96 and 99 per cent (Mulvey 2003).

ACTIVITY 4.1 UK AND EU LEGISLATION

What are the differences in passing legislation between the UK and the EU? Which system do you think is more democratic?

INFORMAL INFLUENCES ON POLICY

Political parties

Traditionally the electoral system in the UK has ensured a predominantly two-party electoral system (plus regional and/or nationalist parties representing Scotland, Wales and Northern Ireland): a broadly right-wing party in favour of maintaining the status quo (the Tories in the early nineteenth century, the Conservatives from the late nineteenth century onwards), and a broadly left-wing party in favour of change (the Whigs in the early nineteenth century, the Liberals in the late nineteenth century, Labour from the 1920s). The two wings broadly represented different class interests – the right wing the 'haves' who resisted change (the ruling class, and later the middle class), and the left wing the 'have-nots', those seeking change (the working class). Thus ideology and social class were seen as underpinning the UK party system. In activity 4.2 you will explore how far this is still true.

The influence of members of political parties, even MPs, over government policy-making is small, and probably getting smaller. MPs are subject to party discipline, and although they can and do vote against their own government on occasions, every MP knows that if he votes to bring down his own government, his party career will be finished. Even massive revolts are unlikely to change government policy, as can be shown by the Labour revolt on university fees, and on the Iraq war, where even the resignation of a leading cabinet member, Robin Cook, had no influence on policy.

Party conferences can pass resolutions critical of government policy, but governments have never had to take much notice of these. Policy is nowadays decided much more by focus groups and think-tanks. MPs do have the power to force an election for the post of party leader, and when the Conservatives ousted Margaret Thatcher and replaced her with John Major, the decision was taken solely by Conservative MPs. However, the Conservative Party, like the Labour Party, now elects its leader through a complicated electoral college system, where MPs, peers, MEPS and party members all have a weighted vote.

ACTIVITY 4.2 POLITICAL PARTIES

1. What arguments would you put forward if asked to support the argument that ideology and class no longer underpin the present party system?

2. David Farnham (1999) argues that there are two crucial differences between a political party and a pressure group:

   - Parties try to win political control to use political power. Pressure groups seek to influence political decisions, not to get in a position where they can make those decisions themselves.

   - The political programmes of parties are broad-based, while pressure groups tend to concentrate on a single issue.

Given the above, would you say that the UK Independence Party (UKIP), which won many seats in the EU elections in 2009, is a political party or a pressure group? What about the Scottish National Party?

 EASYCOUNCIL AND JOHN LEWIS COUNCIL

CASE STUDY 4.1

With a General Election looming in 2010, it is always difficult to predict what the opposition would do if it came to power. However, in the case of the Conservative Party, we do have some evidence coming from local government, which is overwhelmingly controlled by the Conservatives. Hammersmith and Fulham, for example, is raising the rents for its social housing to market levels, and has suggested an end to the 'tenure for life' held by social housing tenants. Essex has suggested that social security benefits should be set and administered locally.

The most radical changes are coming from Barnet council in north London, which includes Margaret Thatcher's old constituency of Finchley. The council has consciously modelled itself on the low-cost airlines EasyJet and Ryanair. The key to the low-cost airline business model is that you get what you pay for. The *Guardian* quotes the example of a Ryanair flight from Stansted to Perugia where the fare is £2.99, but once you add in online booking (£5 – cheaper than checking in at the airport), taxes, priority booking and two bags of luggage, the cost rises to £69.26. Ryanair argues that this extends customer choice, as customers choose

the level of service they need, and pay accordingly.

Barnet is extending this model to local authority services. It is proposing a charge for 'jumping the queue' on planning applications. Recipients of adult social care will be given a personal budget, which they can spend how they wish, including perhaps a weekend in Eastbourne, rather than the council saying 'you need help with shopping, cleaning and meals on wheels' whether the clients wanted that package or not.

Another controversial proposal is to remove live-in wardens from sheltered housing and to replace them with mobile (and outsourced) wardens who can be summoned through alarm buttons. As the leader of Barnet council says, 'It is surprising how able even so-called vulnerable people are. Helping people help themselves, that's the new Conservatism.' A council document, 'Future Shape', says the goals of the proposed reforms are 'facilitating self-help through behaviour change' and 'more services delivered by organisations other than the council'. Outsourcing services such as street cleaning, parking, planning and residential care is expected to save up to £15 million a year.

The programmes of councils such as Barnet present a dilemma for the Conservative leadership. David Cameron has worked hard to change the image of the Tories as the 'nasty party', but at the same time, there would be considerable attraction for a Conservative government in having cuts administered locally, where they are less visible to the general public. Hammersmith and Fulham's 3 per cent reduction in council tax has received more attention outside the borough than its spending cuts. Indeed, the shadow Chancellor, George Osborne, said in a major speech in September 2009 that a Conservative government will have 'much to learn from Conservative local councils'.

Charges for jumping the queue on NHS waiting lists, perhaps?

Labour has hit back with a John Lewis council proposal – to run Lambeth council in London as a co-operative. Suggestions include:

- an 'active citizens dividend', whereby those involved in community organisations would get a council tax rebate
- turning local services like primary schools into citizen-led mutuals
- turning council housing estates into co-operatives.

(Sources: Mulholland 2009, Travers 2009, Burgess 2009, Booth 2009a, Booth 2009b, Booth 2009c, Stratton 2010.)

Pressure groups

A pressure group is 'any group in society which, through political action, seeks to achieve changes which it regards as desirable or to prevent changes which it regards as undesirable' (Forman and Baldwin 1999, p128). They can broadly be classified into two main types:

- interest or sectional groups
- attitude or cause groups.

Interest groups are those pressure groups which have a common interest, and they exist to promote the interests of that group. Classic examples are trade unions and employers' associations, but interest groups also include bodies such as the Royal British Legion and the Automobile Association (AA), the last of which started as a members' organisation but later became a public company, and later still was acquired by a private equity group.

Attitude groups are those pressure groups whose members have attitudes or beliefs rather than material interests, and they seek to advance particular causes. Examples include the National Trust, Oxfam, Greenpeace, Liberty and the RSPB. Some pressure groups appear to be hybrids. The Countryside Alliance, for example, would see itself as an attitude group, while its opponents would see it as an interest group.

Pressure groups have a number of important functions:

- *Intermediaries between the government and the public.* The prime role of a pressure group is obviously to apply pressure on the government (or sometimes on other political bodies like the EU, the International Monetary Fund or a foreign government). They channel and express public opinion on key issues. Some pressure groups use professional lobbying organisations to put forward their point of view to decision-makers. American gaming interests are alleged to have spent £100 million in 2004 in support of the Gambling Bill which would introduce Las Vegas-style 'super-casinos' to the UK (Mathiason 2004). For a detailed analysis of the tactics used by the lobbyists in this case, see Hencke (2004).

- *Opponents and critics of government policy.* Party discipline prevents governing party MPs from opposing government policy, while criticism from opposition parties tends to be ignored because everyone expects the Opposition to oppose. Pressure groups can provide detailed and (hopefully) constructive criticism of policy. Indeed, on some occasions pressure groups in effect write government policy for it.

- *Agents of government.* This is controversial. Increasingly, pressure groups which themselves provide services, particularly charities, receive government grants towards providing those services, which some feel may compromise their independence.

- *Publicists to promote an interest or defend a standpoint.*

 ACTIVITY 4.3 A QUESTION OF INFLUENCE

Make a list of the ways in which pressure groups can influence the government.

THE GOVERNMENT AND THE ECONOMY

SOME KEY DEFINITIONS

Before we can examine ways in which the government can manage the economy, we need to define some key concepts.

Gross domestic product

The most common method of measuring the output of an economy is gross domestic product (GDP). This is the measure of the country's total annual output of goods and services. This is not the same as the sum of the outputs of all organisations in the economy, as this would involve double counting. For example, sales of cans of baked beans made by a supermarket are counted, but not sales of the tinplate for the cans made by a steelworks. When calculating GDP:

- indirect taxes and subsidies (like VAT) are normally ignored
- exports are included, because they form part of the output of the UK
- imports are excluded, because although they are consumed in the UK, they are part of the output of other countries.

An important distinction to make is between GDP and the standard of living or quality of life. Governments are concerned to achieve economic growth, defined as an increase in GDP over time. Individuals are much more concerned with their own standard of living.

 ### ACTIVITY 4.4 STANDARD OF LIVING

How might an individual's standard of living increase without there being an increase in GDP?

Business cycles

The economy tends to move in a series of ups and downs in the short term, although the long-term trend is for the size of GDP to grow. These fluctuations, over a five-to-10-year period, are known as the business cycle. Governments attempt to dampen the effects of these cycles, but have not succeeded in abolishing them entirely. The top of a cycle is known as a peak, the bottom as a trough. In the period between a peak and a trough, economic growth may merely slow down, as in the period 2001–03 following the terrorist attacks of 11 September 2001, or GDP may actually fall. If GDP falls for two consecutive quarters, this is technically known as a recession, as the UK experienced in 1973–75, 1979–81, 1990–92 and 2008–09. If a recession is both deep and long-lasting, it is known as a depression, as with the Great Depression of 1929–33 following the Wall Street Crash.

Unemployment

Unemployment is a surprisingly complex concept which has significant social as well as economic consequences. It is not even simple to define unemployment. A person can only be unemployed if he/she is out of work and seeking work. But what about someone who is:

- working part-time but would rather work full-time?
- apparently seeking work, but has totally unrealistic expectations about the sort of job which he/she could obtain?

There are two main ways of measuring unemployment:

- to count those people who are claiming unemployment benefit (the claimant count). This means that those who do not have work, and are seeking work, but who do not qualify for benefit, are excluded. On the other hand, some people who are not genuinely seeking work may be included
- to carry out a survey and ask people whether they are employed or unemployed. This is carried out through the Labour Force Survey, using internationally agreed definitions provided by the International Labour Organisation (ILO). Here someone is classified as unemployed if they are:
  - out of work
  - have been seeking work within the last four years
  - available to start work within two weeks.

The ILO method is now the government's preferred measure, but both are regularly published in the UK. The ILO figure comes out higher than the claimant-count measure, mainly because it includes large numbers of women who are ineligible for unemployment benefit.

Inflation

Inflation is a general rise in the level of prices. In the UK it is measured in three ways:

- *RPI – the retail price index.* This is calculated by measuring monthly changes in the price of a basket of goods which is meant to represent the spending pattern of the average family. This is the measure used to assess yearly increases in pensions and other state benefits.

- *RPIX – the RPI excluding mortgage interest.* Until November 2003 this was the government's preferred target measure, as it represents the underlying rate of inflation in the economy (mortgage interest rates depend on the general level of interest rates, set by the Bank of England).

- *CPI – the consumer price index.* This is the agreed measure of inflation used through the European Union, and was adopted as the official inflation target in the UK in November 2003 (when it was known as the harmonised index of consumer prices – inevitably called hiccup!).

Balance of payments

The balance of payments is a measure of flows of money into and out of the UK economy. It is extremely complex as it has a number of different components. The most commonly used elements are:

- The balance of trade – this measures imports and exports of goods.

- The balance of payments on current account – this measures imports and exports of goods and services.

ECONOMIC OBJECTIVES

All governments, whatever their political complexion, are basically trying to achieve four main economic objectives:

- *Economic growth.* Since the 1990s this has increased by an average of around 2–2.5 per cent with some periods of falling GDP, and others when the growth rate in the short term has gone as high as 4 per cent.

- *Full employment.* This does not mean that nobody is unemployed, but that there are in theory jobs available for those seeking them, at current wage rates. In practice, this means that full employment is achieved if the number out of work is matched by the number of unfilled vacancies.

- *Stable prices (or low inflation).* Again there is some dispute about the optimum level of inflation, but most economists would agree that it is around the Labour government's target of 2.5 per cent on the RPIX index in the late 1990s (restated as 2 per cent on the CPI index in November 2003).

- *Equilibrium in the balance of payments* – ie that the value of goods and services exported should roughly equal the value imported. This has deteriorated in recent years, with the trade deficit expected to be around £82 billion in 2009, although this is offset to some extent by a strong surplus on the balance on services.

The New Labour government since 1997 has been more successful than most governments, at least until 2007, achieving full success on economic growth and inflation, and considerable success on full employment. The only blot on its record is a worsening balance of payments.

In addition, governments will have policies on other economic objectives. These might include:

- *Redistribution of income* – this is seen as a social objective in its own right, but its prime economic function is as a means to achieve economic growth.

- *Exchange rates* – the exchange value of the pound is seen as a political virility symbol, but it is primarily important as a means of managing the balance of payments. UK entry to the euro is of course a long-running contentious political issue.

- *The level of taxation and the level of government spending* – both in terms of their absolute level in the economy and of the balance between them.

- *Interest rates* – these are seen either as a means of controlling inflation or of managing growth.

- *Money supply* – in the 1980s this was considered an objective in its own right, but is now seen as a means of achieving other objectives.

- *Privatisation (or nationalisation).* Linked with this is more general regulation or deregulation of the economy.

As you will see from the above list, economics is not value-free. Managing the economy inevitably has strong political and social, as well as economic, elements.

THE TOOLS OF GOVERNMENT POLICY

A range of tools is available to the government in its objective of managing the economy.

Fiscal policy

This involves a manipulation of the level of taxation and/or government spending. The theory underpinning this was established by the economist John Maynard Keynes in the 1930s. If there is a persistent level of unemployment in the economy, he argued, this is fundamentally due to a lack of demand. In order to increase demand in the economy, the government can inject demand into it, either by increasing its own spending, which will directly lead to a higher demand for goods and services, or by cutting taxation, which will put more money into the hands of consumers, and so enable them to demand more goods and services. However, changes in taxation or public spending are subject to long time-lags before they take effect, and increasingly Chancellors of the Exchequer have not seen fiscal policy as an appropriate tool for short-term management of the economy. Instead, they have taken the view that the level of spending and taxation are much more issues of political rather than demand management policy. Gordon Brown has expressed this in his Golden Rule, which states that over an economic cycle, the government should aim for a balanced budget, ie the revenue raised through taxation should equal the amount spent on current goods and services. This policy does allow for some flexibility, ie for expenditure to exceed taxation during the trough phase of the cycle, as long as this is balanced by a surplus at the peak. However, the Golden Rule, and its accompanying more general policy, Prudence, were torn up when the full impact of the credit crunch became apparent in the autumn of 2008.

Monetary policy

Monetary policy was strongly in vogue during the 1980s, at the height of the power of Margaret Thatcher, and under the influence of the American economist Milton Friedman, who argued a direct causal link between the supply of money and the level of inflation. Policies were therefore implemented directly to control the supply of money. However, as the leading monetarist economist Sir Alan Budd, who was chief economic adviser to the Treasury between 1991 and 1997, says, 'I hope I can say without offending anyone that the experiment in seeking to control inflation by setting quantitative monetary targets did not match the hopes of its most enthusiastic supporters (among whom I am willing to count myself)' (Keegan 2004a). One of the main problems was not the existence of the link between money supply and inflation, but the difficulty in producing a watertight definition of money at a time of great technological change, including the explosive growth in the use of credit cards (which enable people to spend money they do not possess, and which does not exist until they spend it).

Monetary policy is now much simpler. It consists of control over interest rates, set by the independent Bank of England. The way in which this works will be explored in considerable detail below.

Competitiveness (supply-side) policy

Policy here is linked to the concept of NAIRU (or non-accelerating inflation rate of unemployment), ie the rate of unemployment which ensures a stable level of inflation. If the economy can be made more competitive, the rate of NAIRU should fall, and the economy will be able to operate at lower levels of inflation and unemployment. This involves deregulating the markets for both goods and services and for labour, through policies including privatisation and rigorous control of monopolies and cartels. It also involves a concerted drive to increase the rate of growth of productivity in the economy, by encouraging investment in research and development, and in the enhancement of worker skills. Again, this policy will be examined in depth below.

Exchange rate policy

It is possible to manipulate the exchange rate in order to achieve economic objectives. For example, if an exchange rate is set at a level below that justified by market forces, the currency will be undervalued. This will stimulate exports, which will be artificially lowered in price, and discourage imports, which will be artificially highly priced. An overvalued currency will have the opposite result. However, there are two major snags with this.

Manipulation of the exchange rate is only seriously possible if the exchange rate is fixed. However, since the 1970s, most currencies have floated, ie been subject to market forces. Even in a fixed exchange rate system, it is very difficult in the long term to maintain an exchange rate markedly different from that implied by market forces.

The other key issue in exchange rate policy is of course the euro. Should the UK join, or not? At the moment, the UK has an opt-out from the economic and monetary union (EMU), and thus from the euro. However, the UK is qualified to join EMU if it chooses. In 1997, the Chancellor of the Exchequer postponed a decision on entry, saying that the UK would only consider joining only if five economic tests were met, and if a referendum voted in favour.

Public opinion in the UK appears to be heavily against euro entry, and entry is opposed by the Conservative Party and by significant elements in industry. In the last resort, any decision on entry is likely to be political rather than economic. Labour may be in favour in principle, but will only hold a referendum if it is sure it will win. Most voters will probably make their decision on gut feeling, rather than the detail of the economic arguments. To no one's surprise, the government decided in 2003 that the five tests had not been met, and as a result, any decision in favour of entry has been postponed indefinitely.

 INFLATION AND INTEREST RATES

CASE STUDY 4.2

The impact of inflation

We have already defined inflation as a general increase in the level of prices in the economy, measured in various ways: RPI, RPIX or CPI. In the last resort this is caused by excess demand in the economy, ie when the amount of goods and services which people want to buy is greater than the productive potential of the economy ('too much money chasing too few goods'). The generally accepted view is that inflation is harmful, and it follows from this that low inflation is beneficial, for the following reasons.

- *Increased price competitiveness for UK goods.* The important factor here is relative inflation: in order for UK goods to be competitive, UK inflation must be rising at a slower rate than that of our international competitors. Of course, if UK inflation is very rapid, it is likely that the value of the pound will fall, but this itself could generate further inflation, as import prices will rise.

- *Distribution of income will be less distorted.* High inflation benefits borrowers, particularly those with outstanding mortgages, which fall in value in real terms as the value of their houses tends to rise. In addition, the gap in money terms between wage settlements obtained by strong unions as compared with weak ones tends to be greater in times of rapid inflation.

- *Reduced uncertainty.* The more rapid the rate of inflation, and particularly the more variable it is, the more unpredictable the environment becomes for business and individuals. As a result, investment will be discouraged, as firms do not want to take risks, and the result could be falling output and rising unemployment.

- *High inflation means high nominal interest rates.* This puts pressure on the cashflows of borrowers if their main source of income is interrupted, for example by unemployment.

 ACTIVITY 4.5 DEFLATION

If the effects of high inflation are adverse, would it be better to have falling prices (deflation), as in 2008–09?

THE LINK BETWEEN UNEMPLOYMENT AND INFLATION

Professor A W H Phillips (1958) identified that over the previous 100 years there had been an inverse relationship between the rate of change of money wages and the level of unemployment. In the short term this intuitively makes sense. If unemployment is low, workers can demand higher wages, and vice versa. As wage inflation is a very important component of general inflation, it could thus be argued that there was an inverse relationship between unemployment and inflation – if unemployment rose, inflation would fall, and vice versa. This implied that governments could in principle choose the trade-off between inflation and unemployment which best suited their overall objectives.

Unfortunately, almost as soon as Phillips identified the relationship, it ceased to apply. Throughout the 1970s, both inflation and unemployment rose steeply at the same time, giving rise to a phenomenon known as stagflation. Gradually over the 1980s, inflation was squeezed out of the system through strict control of the money supply, but only at the cost of continuing high levels of unemployment. Since 1992, unemployment has fallen considerably, while inflation has stabilised at the 2–3 per cent level.

Clearly the simple concept of the Phillips curve no longer applies, but it has been replaced by the concept of NAIRU. This is the level of unemployment at which inflation will be stable. NAIRU appears to have been about 7–8 per cent in the 1970s, but to have fallen to around 3–4 per cent (on the ILO measure) by the early 2000s. One prime objective of governments is to continue to improve the trade-off between inflation and unemployment by lowering the level of NAIRU. This can be done through making the labour market more competitive.

However, as the Bank of England (2004, p1) says, 'The level of the NAIRU cannot

be determined with any precision for the purposes of setting monetary policy
… It is easier to construct plausible estimates after the event – ie once we have
observed inflation – rather than in anticipation of it.' NAIRU appears to be much
lower in the UK and US, with largely deregulated labour markets, than in the
eurozone, where labour markets are much more heavily regulated. Of course,
there is a political and social, as well as an economic trade-off here – which is
preferable, a higher risk of unemployment in the eurozone, or the higher level of
benefits which accompany unemployment there?

INTEREST RATES

An interest rate is simply the price of money. However, unfortunately, the real
world is more complicated. As an individual, you are almost certainly paying
and receiving several different rates of interest – on your bank current account,
on your building society account, your internet savings account, your mortgage,
your credit card, your hire purchase agreement. Ultimately these come back to
one rate, the official rate set by the Bank of England, and at which it will lend
money to the banks and other financial institutions. This is set monthly by the
Bank's Monetary Policy Committee.

If this official rate changes, the banks and building societies will change the rates
for their own savers and borrowers. Equally importantly, an increase in interest
rates affects expectations. If interest rates start to rise after a period when they
have been static or falling, the expectation is that they will continue to rise in the
near future. The Bank of England used this to great effect in 2004, when it made a
series of quarter-point increases in interest rates, none of which was particularly
serious on its own, but which had a big effect on expectations. A series of
aggressive interest-rate cuts in 2008–09 signalled the seriousness of the credit
crunch crisis.

INTEREST RATES AND DEMAND

When interest rates are changed, demand can be affected in a number of ways.

Spending and saving

An increase in interest rates makes saving more attractive and spending less
attractive. Consumer spending is likely to fall. At the same time industrial
investment will fall, as the margin between what an investment costs and the
profit which it will produce becomes narrower.

Cashflow

Higher interest rates mean higher mortgage rates (normally paid monthly) and
higher rates of interest on savings (normally paid annually). The short-term effect
on the cashflow of individuals is likely to be negative, reducing demand.

Asset prices

A change in interest rates affects the price of stocks and shares. If interest rates go up, the price of stocks and shares tends to fall, as it becomes more attractive to hold cash. There will be a similar effect on house prices. An increase in interest rates thus marginally reduces individuals' wealth, again making them more reluctant to spend.

Exchange rates

At the same time, the exchange rate is likely to rise marginally, as it becomes more attractive to hold pounds rather than other currencies. This makes export prices higher, which again reduces demand. At the same time, import prices become cheaper, which immediately reduces inflation (Bank of England 2004a).

An increase in interest rates thus clearly reduces demand in the economy, which will lower the rate of inflation. However, as with everything in economics, this is subject to time lags. Some effects are almost immediate, such as the impact on the exchange rate; some take a matter of weeks, such as the impact on mortgage and savings rates; while others are long term, like the wealth effect of falling share prices. The Bank of England calculates that it takes up to two years for the full impact to work through the economy. In making its interest rate decisions, the Bank of England thus has to make estimates of the level of inflation two years hence. This produces the apparently perverse result that the Bank can sometimes cut interest rates at a time when current inflation is above target, or vice versa.

CENTRAL BANKS AND INTEREST RATES

The Bank of England

The Bank of England has been involved in setting interest rates for many years, and this system was formalised in the mid-1990s when interest rates were set at a monthly meeting between the Chancellor, Kenneth Clarke, and the governor of the bank, Eddie George. However, in the last resort, the decision was the Chancellor's. This was changed in the first act of the incoming Labour government in May 1997. To great surprise, Gordon Brown announced the granting of operational independence to the bank. In future, interest rate decisions would be taken monthly by the Monetary Policy Committee, chaired by the governor, which consists of both bank and government nominees (a total of nine members).

Interest rate decisions were to be taken in line with the government's inflation target, initially set as 2.5 per cent on RPIX, subject to a margin of plus or minus 1 per cent. The target was thus a symmetrical one, unlike the previous Conservative target, which was 2.5 per cent or less.

Under the Bank of England Act 1998, the Bank's remit was to:

- maintain price stability
- subject to that, to support the economic policy of the government, including its objectives for growth and employment.

In its remit for the Monetary Policy Committee, this was interpreted as (Bank of England 2003):

> The Government's central economic policy objective is to achieve high and stable levels of growth and employment. Price stability is a precondition for these high and stable levels of growth and employment, which will in turn help to create the conditions for price stability on a sustainable basis.

In December 2003, the target inflation rate was changed to 2 per cent on CPI, again plus or minus 1 per cent. This was a slightly looser target, as 2 per cent on CPI roughly equates to 3 per cent on RPIX.

If inflation moved away from target by more than one percentage point in either direction, the governor was required to send an open letter to the Chancellor, setting out:

- the reasons why inflation has missed the target
- what the Bank is doing about it
- the time span for remedial action
- how the remedial action meets the government's monetary policy objectives.

It is a measure of the success of the policy that such a letter was only required once before the impact of the world recession, when inflation became much more volatile.

The European Central Bank

The European Central Bank (ECB) was set up in 1998, to manage the EMU, including setting interest rates for the eurozone. Interest rates are fixed on a monthly basis by the governing council, which consists of the executive board of the ECB, six members appointed by the eurozone countries, headed by the president of the ECB, the Dutchman Wim Duisenberg, plus the governors of the 12 central banks of the euro area.

The ECB is totally independent, and sets its own inflation target. The prime objective of the ECB is to maintain price stability, originally defined as 2 per cent or less on CPI. On 2003, this was slightly but significantly modified to 'close to 2 per cent over the medium term' (*Guardian* 2003a). This was slightly less deflationary. The objective was modified again in 2004, when the ECB said that, 'without prejudice to the objective of price stability', the eurosystem will also 'support the general economic policies in the Community', including, 'a high level of employment', and, 'sustainable and non-inflationary growth' (ECB 2004).

The Federal Reserve

The central bank of the US is the Federal Reserve, headed until recently by the octogenarian Alan Greenspan, and currently headed by Ben Bernanke. It has no specific inflation target, but its remit is laid down by the Federal Reserve Act as to 'promote effectively the goals of maximum employment, stable prices and moderate long-term interest rates' (Federal Reserve 2004). Interest rates are set monthly by the Federal Open Market Committee.

THE CREDIT CRUNCH CRISIS OF 2008–09

In October 2008, the world financial system came within a whisker of complete meltdown. In September 2008, the US government had decided to allow the investment bank Lehman Brothers to go bust, and in October the UK government nationalised Royal Bank of Scotland (RBS) and Bradford & Bingley, and forced Halifax Bank of Scotland (HBOS) into a shotgun takeover by Lloyds, funded by government money. Also in October, the US government nationalised the massive insurance group AIG. Meltdown was avoided, but the world moved rapidly into recession, with an almost complete shutdown of bank lending and rapidly rising unemployment.

What went wrong? The seeds of the crisis were sown with the terrorist attacks of 11 September 2001. The US economy was already slowing before the attacks, and Alan Greenspan, the head of the US Federal Reserve, felt that decisive monetary action was needed to avoid outright recession. He quickly slashed US interest rates to an unprecedented 1 per cent, and the Bank of England and the European Central Bank followed, although not to the same extent. US interest rates were held at this low level for several years.

With hindsight, it is clear that Greenspan went too far, too fast. The economic impact of 9/11 proved to be short-lived, and by 2004, the US economy was back in boom. In normal circumstances, such a loose monetary policy would have rapidly let to a rise in inflation, but retail prices in the US, the UK and the eurozone were kept down by the boom in cheap imports from China. Instead, inflationary pressures built up on asset prices, particularly house prices.

Mortgage lenders in the US started an aggressive lending programme, buoyed by the expectation that house prices would continue rising indefinitely. Many specialised in lending to so-called 'ninja' borrowers – no income, no job, no assets – in the so-called sub-prime market. In the UK the ex-building society Northern Rock followed a similar policy, lending on mortgages of 125 per cent of the value of a property, financed by its own borrowing from the wholesale money markets. The money markets themselves became contaminated. In order to spread their risk, the US mortgage lenders packaged up their mortgages (a process known as securitisation), into so-called collateralised debt obligations (CDOs) – a package of mortgages sold as a bond to other institutions. By 2007, CDOs in the US were valued at US $1.3 trillion, and this was only the tip of an enormous syndicated debt iceberg worth US $14 trillion, 7 per cent of total US GDP. The securitised bundles were so complex that an individual bank found it almost impossible to assess the risk it was running.

Like any pyramid scheme, the whole thing only worked as long as house prices continued to rise. Unfortunately, as US interest rates began to rise again, the ninja borrowers were no longer able to meet their mortgage obligations. US house prices peaked in summer 2006, and fell 25 per cent over the next year.

The first victim of the crisis was Northern Rock, which failed in September 2007, and was eventually nationalised by the UK government. In March 2008, the US government rescued the investment bank Bear Stearns, and in July it rescued the two major US mortgage providers, Fannie Mae and Freddie Mac. As explained above, the crisis then reached its peak between September and October 2008.

An underlying contributory factor was the very loose supervision of financial institutions in the UK, and to a lesser extent in the US. As Vince Cable (2009, p13) points out, the Financial Services Authority 'to the end remained supportive of Northern Rock's business model.'

The result of the bank crashes was that inter-bank lending totally dried up, as no bank could be sure how safe its fellow bank was. This was passed on to customers, who found it increasingly difficult to obtain loans. Many totally viable companies with temporary cashflow needs were forced into bankruptcy. Spending dried up, unemployment rose and the economy spiralled downwards, rapidly moving into recession (two successive quarters of negative GDP). Mervyn King, the governor of the Bank of England, described this bank behaviour as 'individually understandable but collectively suicidal' (Cable 2009, p57).

The UK government's reaction to the crisis was swift and decisive. HBOS and RBS were bailed out to the tune of £35 billion, VAT was cut from 17.5 to 15 per cent, interest rates quickly slashed to 0.5 per cent, and a fiscal expansion package worth 1 per cent of GDP introduced. The Bank of England also undertook a programme of quantitative easing, in effect printing more money. All these policies were generally applauded, except by the Conservative opposition, quickly followed by the US and endorsed by the G20. However, each policy had risks:

- The bail-out of the banks risked moral hazard, where in effect the banks were shielded from the effects of their folly.

- The VAT cut was widely seen as minimal and unlikely to stimulate spending.

- If interest rates were held down for too long, there was a risk that inflationary pressures could build up in the long term. The same was true of the quantitative easing. However, as Keynes said, 'in the long run we are all dead'.

- The fiscal stimulus, coupled with the bail-out of the banks and a natural fall in tax receipts and rise in government spending due to unemployment, ran the risk of driving the government deficit to unacceptable levels. However, as the government pointed out, the UK deficit before the crisis was on the low side compared with the rest of the G7, and even after all the extra spending would still be relatively low by historical standards.

For a concise and relatively impartial account of the crisis, see the Liberal Democrat shadow chancellor, Vince Cable's, book *The Storm: the world economic crisis and what it means* (2009).

ACTIVITY 4.6 GORDON BROWN AND THE RECESSION

The Conservative Party blames Gordon Brown for the recession in the UK in 2008–09. Is this fair?

PUBLIC OWNERSHIP, PRIVATISATION AND PFI/PPP

PUBLIC OWNERSHIP

When most people think of public ownership, they think of the nationalisations of the Labour government in the late 1940s. But public ownership goes back a lot further than that. The beginnings of a state system of welfare came with the Elizabethan Poor Law in the sixteenth century. The Post Office dates back to the seventeenth century, and developed telegraph services in the nineteenth (the percursor of British Telecom). The Metropolitan Police was founded in 1829, while a primitive system of policing through parish constables goes back hundreds of years before that. A state system of education dates from 1870, and in the 1840s Gladstone gave the state reserve powers to nationalise the railways if necessary. In the late nineteenth century, gas, electricity and water services were developed by local authorities ('municipal socialism').

During the First World War, the state obtained a controlling interest in what later became BP; in 1919 the Forestry Commission was set up to manage Britain's woodlands; and the BBC came into public ownership in the 1920s.

These early examples illustrate some of the driving forces behind public ownership:

- to ensure adequate coverage of services (Post Office, Poor Law, schools)
- to safeguard interests vital to the state (BP, Forestry Commission, BBC)
- to control natural monopolies (police).

The nationalisations of the 1940s added a further motive: a socialist desire to control the 'commanding heights' of the economy in the interests of the state. But even here things were not entirely straightforward. When the Bank of England was nationalised in 1946, it had been effectively under total state control for at least 100 years. The nationalisations of water, gas and electricity involved taking over municipally owned companies rather than private ones. The railways were in private hands, but had been subject to compulsory amalgamations in the 1920s. The NHS took over Poor Law hospitals, by this time under local authority control, as well as charity hospitals. The truly socialist aspect of the NHS was the concept of services free at the point of use, rather than ownership. Perhaps the only truly socialist nationalisation was the National Coal Board, which took over from the widely hated coal owners. Generally, the force behind the 1940s nationalisation could be seen equally as a desire to exercise effective centralised planning (Kay 2003).

The nationalised industries had a mixed record of performance, but suffered from a number of systemic flaws:

- John Kay has argued that in order for any type of organisation to operate efficiently and effectively, it must be subject to 'disciplined pluralism'. Because there was no requirement to make a profit, there was little pressure to achieve greater efficiency, ie no discipline. And because the nationalised industries were monopolies, there was also no pluralism (Kay, quoted in Palmås 2005).

- Although day-to-day management was given to the public corporations that controlled the industry, there was a great temptation for governments of all persuasions to interfere, and government also strictly controlled the level of investment. Nationalised industries thus tended to be used as an instrument of macroeconomic policy, with their investment levels moved up or down depending on the state of unemployment or inflation.

- Nationalised industries were at their height in an era before most businesses – public or private – gave much attention to customer service. As a result, allied with the strength of trade unions, nationalised industries tended to be run in the interests of staff rather than the customer – television in the 1970s loved to expose 'jobsworths' in the nationalised industries and local government. On the other hand, public sector staff did tend to share a public service ethos, which in the case of the railways, for example, led to a high emphasis on safety, and a determination to 'muddle through'. Thus trains kept running during the terrible winter of 1963 in a way which in many cases they failed to do during the floods of 2007.

PRIVATISATION

The Thatcher/Major governments between 1979 and 1997 embarked on an extensive programme of privatisation, starting with British Telecom in 1982 and ending with British Rail in 1996. Most of the big privatisations were public offers of shares to the general public, while others, like the National Freight Corporation and National Bus, were trade sales.

The arguments for privatisation were partly financial and partly political. Privatisation raised very large sums of money for the Treasury, and so permitted tax cuts (memorably criticised by Harold Macmillan as 'selling the family silver'). It also reduced the role of the state (a key element in Thatcherism), which hopefully would give managers more autonomy to manage efficiently. By making the privatised businesses leaner and meaner, they would be better able to compete effectively in a globalised economy. Privatisation was also intended to stimulate personal share ownership. To ensure that the privatised companies did not exploit their monopoly positions, they were subject to detailed regulatory controls, particularly overpricing, which were intended to force efficiency.

However, just as with nationalisation, flaws in the model gradually become apparent. Firstly, there is no evidence that personal share ownership was significantly expanded. The small investors who bought shares in the privatised companies usually have no other equity investments.

In most cases, prices to the consumer have been reduced, but it is impossible to say whether this is the result of privatisation. In the case of BT, for example, privatisation coincided with a period of rapid technological advance and globalisation in telecommunications. It appears more likely that it is intense competition which has transformed BT rather than privatisation. Privatised industries which are not subject to competition, like water and railways, have been much less successful.

There is also the problem that once an industry is privatised, the state loses effective control over it. One way to try to alleviate this was the system of golden shares – a single share, held by the state, which gave it veto powers over the ownership of the privatised company. For example, the state retained a golden share in the airport operator BAA, which capped a single shareholding at 15 per cent. In other words, the state could veto any takeover of BAA. This was declared illegal by the European Court of Justice in 2003, as it was against EU rules on free movement of capital (Osborn 2003). The hostile takeover of BAA by the Spanish company Ferrovial duly followed in 2006. Other privatised industries which did not have a golden share, such as water and electricity distribution, are now effectively in the hands of French and German companies, including the state-owned Électricité de France. Surely if a key part of the economy is to be in public hands, those hands should be British rather than French!

A fourth problem is what happens when a privatised company fails. By definition, the services provided by a privatised company are vital, and it is important that there is continuity in their supply. An example of where this happened, Railtrack, is discussed below.

Finally, although often regarded with amused contempt, the nationalised industries had a fund of goodwill from the public. When things went wrong, as with train crashes under British Rail, these tended to be regarded as acts of God rather than the fault of the company. The privatised companies have not been successful at building up a similar fund of goodwill. Thus the drought in Yorkshire in 1996 was widely, if unfairly, seen as the fault of the (privatised) Yorkshire Water (Kay 2002).

THE PUBLIC AND VOLUNTARY SECTORS

Broadly speaking, four types of organisation operate in the UK today: businesses, which produce goods and services with the aim of making a profit; the public sector, which supplies goods and services which cannot be supplied at a profit; public goods, where the whole of society benefits from a service such as public health, whether they pay for it or not; and natural monopolies. The voluntary sector meets the needs of its members (clubs, mutual organisations or professions), its clients (charities), or campaigns on issues (Greenpeace, RSPB).

Unfortunately, these distinctions are not as watertight as they were 30 years ago. Some public goods and natural monopolies are now supplied by privatised businesses; the private and voluntary sectors provide some services, such as refuse collection and welfare services, on behalf of the public sector. Many public sector and voluntary bodies have commercial arms (like BBC Enterprises and CIPD Enterprises) which operate in competition with the private sector. One organisation, Railtrack, has changed in a five-year period from being part of a nationalised industry (British Rail), to being a privately owned company on privatisation, and then to a non-profit-making trust (Network Rail) when Railtrack collapsed in 2001.

A growing trend is social enterprise. Social enterprises are profit-making, but plough their profits back into society, rather than paying dividends to shareholders. Examples include Jamie Oliver's Fifteen restaurants, the *Big Issue* and Divine Chocolate. There are 62,000 social enterprises in the UK, with a combined turnover of £27 billion (Harding 2004, Lucas 2009).

The four sectors also have more similarities than differences in how they are managed. They all:

- spend money
- need income to carry out their activities
- produce a product or service
- have consumers of their good or service (whether or not the consumers directly pay for this)
- need people to staff their operations
- use the same range of management services, eg accounting, IT, personnel, etc.

This all suggests a convergence. This view would be supported by the former Prime Minister, Tony Blair. His Third Way philosophy argues that what is important is not ownership (public or private), but how efficiently services are delivered, along with accountability.

Lawton and Rose (1994) distinguish four different cultures which they see as prevalent in the public sector:

- *Political culture.* Particularly prevalent in local government, where council officers are in almost day-to-day contact with the politicians to whom they are answerable. Also true in the sense that the whole of the public sector is ultimately politically directed.

- *Legal culture.* Public bodies are only permitted to do what is specifically allowed to them by statute. Any other action is ultra vires (beyond their powers), and is subject to judicial review. Private sector companies are in theory limited in their activities by their Memorandum and Articles of Association, but the control is much less strict.

- *Administrative culture.* Concerned with rules, roles and authority – the 1960s and 1970s caricature of the local authority 'jobsworth'.

- *Market culture.* Where public sector organisations are exposed to the market through competitive tendering, best value, contracting out, internal markets, etc.

They argue that the last of these, the market culture, is becoming predominant, and that as a result, running the public sector is becoming much more an issue of management, and much less an issue of administration.

The distinction between the sectors is becoming more and more blurred:

- Many local authority services which may previously have been free are now charged for, and often contracted out to the private sector (leisure centres, for example). This has involved the development and application of legal systems such as TUPE.

- Much of the long-term finance for the public sector is now provided by the public sector, through the private finance initiative and public–private partnerships. The biggest of these is London Underground, where train services continue to be provided by the public sector, but where all the maintenance of and investment in improving the lines is carried out by three private sector consortia.

- There is a growing realisation that the private sector, almost as much as the public sector, operates in a political environment, and that the activities of the private sector are heavily constrained by the legal environment.

- The government is keen to increase the involvement of the voluntary sector in the delivery of public services, partly to move the debate away from a head-to-head clash between the public and private sectors (Ward 2000). Not-for-profit trusts are the government's preferred option for failing public services. They can borrow private cash without this counting as public borrowing, and they can also reinvest any surpluses into service improvement (Weaver 2001).

 MANAGING VOLUNTEERS

CASE STUDY 4.3

One major issue for the voluntary sector is how to manage staff, both paid and volunteers. Paid staff are likely to have a high commitment to the objectives of the organisation, and thus likely to be prepared to work for less than the current market wage, but in return want a high degree of autonomy. The psychological contract is highly important, and any move by management to alter the contract will lead to resentment, and perhaps staff moving to other organisations.

The issue is even more crucial with volunteers. By definition, volunteers can move to other organisations at any time. Volunteers want autonomy, the ability to put their knowledge and skills to best use, and a sense of being valued. They do not

want to be seen as having a lower status compared with paid staff, and they do not want to be over-regulated.

Moreton (2006) suggests that the ideal management style for managing volunteers is the Team Management style on the Blake and Mouton Management Grid (1964) (see Chapter 2). This has a high concern for production combined with a high concern for people. It is characterised by work accomplishment through committed people, and interdependence through a common stake in organisation purposes that leads to relationships of trust and respect.

All organisations need some degree of bureaucratic management systems, if only to conform with the law and regulation, but

Moreton recommends that these should be disguised so that volunteers are as far as possible unaware of them. He quotes the analogy of the swan, which appears graceful to the onlooker, but is actually paddling furiously under the surface.

This case study is based on material kindly supplied by Stephen Moreton of the charity Attend, which is gratefully acknowledged.

 SOCIAL PARTNERSHIP IN THE IRISH REPUBLIC

CASE STUDY 4.4

One method of managing a national economy, which has been used by different countries at different times and with differing degrees of success – including the UK in the 1970s – is social partnership. One of the most successful and long-lasting experiments with social partnership was in the Irish Republic.

In the mid-1980s, the Irish economy was in severe trouble. The initial boost from EU membership in 1973 had worn off, unemployment was at 15 per cent, the national debt ratio was 115 per cent, and inflation was over 5 per cent. The future seemed to be one of continued decline, with emigration continuing to take the best of Ireland's young people out of the country (House and McGrath 2004, Mac Cormaic 2008).

Over the next 20 years Irish economy and society was transformed. Economic growth peaked at an annual rate of 11.5 per cent in 2000 – as good as China's – and GDP grew by six times between 1985 and 2001 – the best performance in the Organisation for Economic Co-operation and Development (OECD). Unemployment fell to 4.3 per cent in 2002. Social change was also evident. Female participation in the workforce grew from traditionally very low levels to near the EU average. National population rose for the first time in 150 years, with Irish emigrants returning, and an inflow from the rest of the world. The 'Celtic Tiger' was born (House and McGrath 2004).

Many reasons have been put forward for the 'Irish Miracle': support from EU

regional policy; low interest rates resulting from the EMU and the launch of the euro; a favourable tax structure; incentives to attract multinational investment; strong education and training programmes – but one key factor has been the successive social partnership agreements since 1987.

Membership of the EU led to a growing interest in Ireland in continental forms of social capitalism, as practised in Scandinavia, Holland and Germany, and a moving away from Anglo-Saxon models of capitalism. One institution in Ireland which supported this social capitalist approach was the advisory National Economic and Social assembly, first set up in 1973, and consisting of representatives from government, business, the unions, farmers and the community. In 1986, it put forward a Strategy for Development, which led directly to the first social partnership agreement, the Programme for National Recovery, in 1987. This set annual pay awards of 2.5 per cent over three years, tax cuts of £225 million and a commitment to build a fair, inclusive society with better public services. Over successive three-year agreements, membership of the social partners was widened to include environmental groups, and the scope of the agreements widened to cover areas such as housing, transport, urban planning, lifelong learning and welfare benefits.

All sides gained from the programme. In return for wage restraint, labour received commitments on social benefits and tax reduction, as well as an accepted role in decision-making. Business gained from the assurance of moderate wage increases and a stable business-planning and investment climate. Political agreement on the programmes gave a stability to Irish politics through successive coalition governments.

However, by the mid-2000s the Irish economy was coming under severe pressure. The housing market was out of control, inflationary pressures were mounting and social inequality was growing. As a result, Ireland was one of the most severely affected countries when the world recession hit in 2008. Unemployment soared to 12 per cent, and GDP went into steep decline. The reaction of the Irish government, a left–right coalition of Fianna Fail and the Greens, differed from that of the rest of the OECD. Rather than opting for a Keynesian programme of public spending, Ireland brought in a series of deflationary budgets, culminating in December 2009.

These cut public sector pay, child benefit and unemployment benefit, and put up prescription charges.

The result was the effective collapse of social partnership. The General Secretary of the Irish Congress of Trade Unions, said the policy, 'puts very deep blue water between this government and the majority of Irish people', while the leader of the Irish Labour party described it as, 'viciously anti-family, fundamentally unfair and socially divisive'. Even the Irish police were threatening strike action (Elliott 2010).

What does this tell us about social partnership? The policy undoubtedly played a part in the Irish miracle, but distinguishing its impact from that of other factors is very difficult. Was its collapse inevitable? Probably yes, given the policies adopted by the Irish government in 2008–09. (See also CIPD (Ireland) 2009.)

PUBLIC INTEREST COMPANIES

The advent to power of the New Labour government in 1997 revived interest in a third way of delivering public services, which was neither a nationalised industry nor a privatised company. This was the public interest company (PIC). These had three main characteristics

- they do not normally have shareholders
- they are independent from the state
- they deliver a public service.

Legally the PIC is normally a company limited by guarantee. A typical PIC was a housing association, providing and managing social housing.

As Maltby (2003) points out, it has always been an oversimplification to see a simple dichotomy between privatised companies and nationalised industries. In fact, there is a continuum of types. Going from pure public sector to pure private sector, we have:

- nationalised industries
- public plcs, where a company operates as though it is in the private sector, but is wholly owned by the state. A good example is the Post Office
- PICs
- public–private partnerships, including private finance initiative contracts (see below)

- regulated private companies – typically privatised companies
- private companies – ordinary plcs.

PICs appealed to New Labour for two main reasons:

- they represented a third way between nationalisation (socialism) and privatisation (capitalism)
- they provided an opportunity to give formal influence to stakeholders.

As Palmås (2005) argued, PICs combined the management freedom, efficiency and innovativeness of the traditional plc, the public interest ethos of the public sector, and the stakeholder governance of mutuals and the voluntary sector.

Dwr Cymru Welsh Water is a leading example. Originally privatised, it has been owned and managed by Glas Cymru as a PIC since 2001. All financial surpluses are reinvested for the benefit of customers, and since 2001 it has returned £98 million to customers as 'customer dividends'. It has also reduced its level of borrowing from 91 per cent to 75 per cent, so lowering its level of risk (Article 13 and CBI 2007).

An opportunity to experiment with the PIC model on a large scale came with the collapse of Railtrack in 2001. Railtrack had been set up as a result of rail privatisation in 1996, with responsibility for running the rail infrastructure (train services were provided by TOCs such as Virgin or GNER, which rented track use from Railtrack).

At first, Railtrack was very successful in financial terms, mainly because it laid off 65 per cent of its staff and outsourced most of its maintenance. It was then hit by a series of accidents, culminating in the Hatfield crash of 2000, caused by a broken rail. In response to public pressure, Railtrack was forced to impose drastic speed restrictions on the network while rails were checked. As a result, Railtrack's profits were shattered, leading to a £534 million loss in 2001. However, Railtrack then paid out a dividend of £137 million.

Railtrack's fortunes continued to decline, and in October 2001, the company was put into administration. By this time its share price had dropped from a peak of £17 to 280p. Eventually, in the spring of 2002, the government effectively bought Railtrack at a price of 250p a share, and handed its management to a new PIC, Network Rail (Palmås 2005).

Network Rail's governance was in the hands of a large group of individuals representing major stakeholders, including 30 drawn from companies already heavily involved in rail, including Amey, Jarvis and London Underground; 34 public members drawn from a range of organisations ranging from Eurotunnel to the National Farmers Union; and 51 individual members selected by a membership panel, and who were mostly drawn from 'the great and the good' who frequently appeared on the boards of quangos (*Guardian* 2003b).

The government argued that the members of Network Rail represented a fair cross-section of those with an interest in the railways, but it could be argued that too many represented vested interests. It is also unclear exactly what influence the members have on the operation of Network Rail. There is an argument that Network Rail is effectively answerable to no one. In these circumstances, argues Jeremy Warner (2003), 'the engineers are taking over', and 'all [they] want is a shiny new train set'. However, because Network Rail did not have to distribute profit to shareholders, it was unlikely to be so obsessed on the short term as Railtrack.

THE PRIVATE FINANCE INITIATIVE AND PUBLIC–PRIVATE PARTNERSHIPS

Public–private partnership (PPP) refers to any financial collaboration between the public and private sectors. For example, in the 1980s, local authorities were forced to put many of their services out for tender to the private sector under the Compulsory Competitive Tendering system. The result today is that the council dustman has virtually disappeared. Instead, they are employed by private waste disposal companies, although their job is still to collect people's rubbish.

Other examples include the use by schools of private security companies, or the way in which the BBC uses private production companies to produce many of its TV programmes. Some PPPs are really public–voluntary partnerships, eg the transfer of local authority social housing to housing corporations since 1989 (Ward 2000).

The private finance initiative (PFI) is a specialised type of PPP. Set up by Norman Lamont in 1992 after the UK was forced out of the EU Exchange Rate Mechanism, it was seen as a way simultaneously to stimulate the economy and to hold down public spending. Say the NHS wants to build a new hospital. Under the old system, the capital cost of the hospital was financed by the state, and so public borrowing increased. Under PFI, the private sector provides the cash, which is repaid with interest once the new hospital opens. The NHS (and the government) avoids a high capital payment upfront, but it is committed to monthly payments for the next 25–30 years, which will amount to much more than the hospital would have cost in the first place. Deals will include penalty clauses if the terms of the contract are not met, eg if the heating system fails. The private sector company will gain a guaranteed flow of income for 25–30 years, but takes the risk if there are cost over-runs.

Many PFI deals went much further. Not only would the contractor in effect lease the hospital to the NHS, but the contract also included the provision of ancillary hospital services, typically catering, cleaning and security. This included the transfer of NHS jobs to the private sector, where they were subject to the EU Transfer of Undertakings (TUPE) regulations.

When New Labour came to power in 1997, it was at first thought that the days of PFI were numbered. Instead, the system was expanded. The opportunity for Gordon Brown to keep public sector capital spending off the public sector borrowing requirement was too good to miss. However, Labour did bring in some safeguards. The system of compulsory competitive tendering for local authorities was changed to best value, where the local authority could continue to provide services in-house if it could establish that it provided as good value as outsourcing. PFI was also stopped for small projects, where the cost of the tendering process outweighed any financial savings, and for IT projects, where many contracts had proved expensive failures. It was also stressed that PFI could only be used where it did not come at the expense of employees' terms and conditions.

Several possible models for PFI/PPP were identified by the Institute for Public Policy Research in 2001. These were:

- *Public sector default* – the public sector provides all services, broadly the position for police and fire services.

- *Private sector rescue* – the private sector acts as provider of last resort only if the public sector is seen to be underperforming, eg some failing local education authorities have been taken over by the private sector.

- *Level playing field* – equal treatment between different organisations seeking to deliver public services – broadly the position with local authority best value.

- *Public sector rescue* – the public sector acts as provider of last resort only if the private sector is seen to be underperforming, eg the replacement of Railtrack by Network Rail.

- *Private sector default* – the private sector provides all services, eg the building and operation of new prisons.

The Treasury stressed that one of the main benefits of PFI was that it transferred risk to the private sector. The public authority received the certainty that specified services would be delivered at the cost at which they were contracted. In 2006 the Treasury estimated that PFI would total 10–15 per cent of total investment in public services, and in the five-year pipeline were 200 projects worth £26 billion.

In 2003, Tony Blair seemed to herald a big expansion of PPP into clinical services in the NHS. He said, 'We are anxious to ensure that this is the start of opening up the whole of the NHS supply system so that we end up with a situation where the state is the enabler, it is the regulator, but it is not always the provider' (Carvel 2003).

Treasury research in 2006 also established that on the whole the public sector was satisfied with the results of PFI:

- 79 per cent said service standards are delivered always or almost always

- overall performance of 96 per cent of projects was at least satisfactory

- 70 per cent of public sector mangers believe relationships with private sector partners are good or very good.

Only 20 per cent of PFI projects are late, compared with 70 per cent of non-PFI contracts, while 20 per cent are over budget, compared with 73 per cent of non-PFI projects (Treasury 2006).

However, there are many criticisms of PFI:

- They lock the public sector into contracts that are too long. It is very difficult to forecast demand for facilities as far ahead as 30 years. Schools, for example, are frequently surplus to requirements long before 30 years because of changes in local population. Government NHS policy is to shift significant portions of the work of hospitals into the community. This again puts in doubt 30-year contracts (Batty and Weaver 2006).

- A PFI contract may deliver on time, but this does not take into account the length of time required to finalise contracts – frequently a matter of years. The contracting process itself is also extremely expensive, and the contracts often too restrictive. The process also creates a 'contract culture', with endless arguments over exactly what the contract does and does not require.

- PFI threatens the public sector ethos. For example, when cleaners in hospitals were employed by the NHS, they were driven by a desire to produce the best possible service for the patients. When the same people are employed by the private sector under PFI, they are ultimately contract- and profit-driven – they are not permitted to go beyond the terms of the contract, because this will cost their employer money.

- Many PFI companies are moving into areas well away from their core expertise. The leading firms involved in educational administration are Jarvis and Atkins, both primarily civil engineering specialists, and VT Education, the service arm of defence and shipbuilding firm Vosper Thornycroft. In a Fabian report, Colin Crouch argued that the main expertise of these companies lies in their experience in lobbying and negotiating large contracts with the government (Woodward 2003).

- PFI drains public services of current spending power. At the end of 2006, £8 billion worth of NHS hospital PFI schemes were operational or under construction in England. On these, the NHS would have to pay £37 billion in debt payments over the next 30 years. It is estimated that 50 per cent of NHS trusts with major PFI schemes are in financial difficulties, much higher than the average across the NHS. Some, like South Tees and Queen Elizabeth Woolwich, both in substantial deficit, are paying 20 per cent of their turnover to PFI partners (Hellowell 2006). In the case of Queen Elizabeth, the PFI deal cost £9 million a year more than an equivalent hospital built with money borrowed directly from the government (Batty and Weaver 2006).

- In practice, risk is not completely transferred to the PFI partner. In 2004, the PFI contractor Jarvis was in severe financial difficulty following its involvement in the Potters Bar train crash, where it was responsible for track maintenance. At the time Jarvis was responsible for 14 PFI projects, all of which ground to a halt as the City sorted out a rescue package for Jarvis. Part of the problem appeared to be that Jarvis had been 'lowballing' – bidding too low in order to secure bargain-basement PFI contracts, and then running into trouble when unexpected problems appeared. At the very least, Jarvis's failure led to delays and waste for its public sector partners; at worst, contracts would have to be renegotiated with another partner, leading to higher costs than originally budgeted (Hirst 2005).

COMPETITIVENESS

In the 1970s, the UK was widely seen as a failed economy. It was subject to wide fluctuations in economic performance, and suffered from high inflation and unemployment. Taxation was high, the economy was heavily regulated, and trade unions were widely seen as too powerful. Some of these shortcomings were tackled by the Thatcher governments between 1979 and 1991, which lowered taxation, cut back on regulation and attacked the power of the trade unions. The result was an increase in the efficiency of the economy, although this was largely a function of the contraction of manufacturing. The manufacturers which survived were inevitably more efficient than those which had failed.

However, the impetus behind the reforms of the Thatcher governments was as much political as economic. Policy changed with the advent of the Major government in 1991. This was much less ideological. Policies were to be followed because they were effective, rather than because they were politically correct.

This approach was continued by New Labour in 1997, with an almost seamless transition from Ken Clarke to Gordon Brown as Chancellor of the Exchequer. Competitiveness became the watchword, and pragmatism the policy. The aim was to reform the British economy so that it could compete with the best in the world.

PRODUCTIVITY

Competitiveness has a large number of facets, from a tightening of anti-trust legislation to the promotion of a higher skills base in the UK, and stabilisation of macroeconomic policy. What ties them all together is the concept of productivity. This is a measure of how much the economy is producing per worker employed. This is dependent on both the efficiency of the worker and on the hours worked, so a better measure is probably output per worker hour.

In 2002, productivity measured by output per worker was 39 per cent below the US, 15 per cent below France and 7 per cent below Germany. However, France and Germany work fewer hours than the UK, and the US works more, so on the better measure (output per worker hour), the UK is 26 per cent behind the US, 24 per cent behind France and 11 per cent behind Germany. This is known as the productivity gap (Philpott 2002).

The 2002 figures represented a considerable improvement on the position in 1991, when the UK was 35 per cent behind France on output per worker hour, and 30 per cent behind Germany (Daneshkhu 2007a). The improvement continued after 2002, and by 2007, the UK was 18 per cent behind the US and 20 per cent behind France, although the gap with Germany had widened slightly, to 31 per cent (Daneskhu 2007b). Between 1995 and 2006, UK labour productivity growth was 2.1 per cent per annum, France's 1.9 per cent, Germany's 1.7 per cent, and Italy's 0.4 per cent (Giles 2007).

Since the 1950s, the underlying rate of growth of productivity in the UK has been around 2 per cent. Government policy is to try to increase this underlying rate, with a wide range of detailed polices put forward in two White Papers, 'Building the Knowledge Driven Economy' in 1998, and 'Opportunity for All in a World of Change' in 2001. Success in doing so would increase the UK's long-term rate of economic growth, and would also lower NAIRU, allowing the UK economy to control inflation at a lower level of unemployment (Philpott 2002). A similar programme was launched by the EU at the Lisbon Summit in 2000 (European Union 2004), which set the objective of becoming the most competitive, dynamic, knowledge-based economy in the world by 2010. Its detailed proposals included creating an environment which was conducive to business start-ups, a fully operational internal market, education and training suitable for a knowledge society, and a raising of the EU employment rate from 61 per cent in 2000 to 70 per cent in 2010, thereby creating 20 million new jobs. Of these, five million had been created by 2003 (Philpott 2003).

In 2004, a group appointed by the EU, under the chairmanship of the former Dutch Prime Minister, Wim Kok, reported on progress (Hutton 2004). It proposed:

- EU members should spend 3 per cent of GDP on research and development (the UK at present spends 1.9 per cent)
- there should be a European Research Council supporting centres of scientific excellence
- degrees and qualifications should be mutually recognised, in order that researchers can develop career paths within the EU rather than joining the brain drain to the US
- there should be an EU-wide patent law.

However, in 2005, the *Economist* pointed to slow progress towards the Lisbon targets, and blamed this on the failure of Germany, France and Italy to open up their economies to competition, citing their opposition to the EU Services Directive, intended to liberalise cross-border trade in services.

An increase in productivity depends on changes in a number of factors. These include:

- *Capital investment.* The more modern the equipment with which people work, the more efficient they will be. Historically, investment in the UK has been low, and increases in productivity have come more through the shutdown of the most inefficient plant rather than the building of new plant. A telling comparison with the US is that while the UK produces the same volume of manufacturing output with half the capacity of the 1970s, the US produces twice the output with the same capacity.

- *Economic stability.* One key factor which deters investment is economic instability. Investors need to be convinced that there will be a consistent demand for what they produce, and that inflation will be stable. Here the UK has made great advances over the last decade. De Grauwe (2001) has argued that a comprehensive and reliable welfare state is also necessary, although this does not seem to be required in the US.

- *Research and development (R&D)*. The UK is excellent at scientific research but much less good at the applied R&D needed to convert this into practical products and processes. It is significant that the UK's only world-class industry, pharmaceuticals, is the heaviest investor in R&D.

- *IT and the Internet*. During the dot-com boom of the late 1990s, the Internet was seen as the Holy Grail of productivity, and some US economists put forward the concept of a New Economic Paradigm, where the business cycle was abolished, and growth would continue indefinitely. This rosy view was shaken by the dot-com crash in early 2000, and shattered by 11 September 2001. Of the dot-com companies, virtually only Amazon, eBay and a few business-to-business companies are profitable.

- *Restrictive practices*. Restrictive practices by the trade unions were tackled by the Thatcher governments, so the main concern is restrictive practices by industry. The UK has anti-trust laws (covered in more detail in Chapter 5), but they are much less tough than in the US. One change here has been to make participation in price-fixing activities a criminal offence, subject to imprisonment – a measure in force in the US since 1890 (Lennan 2001).

- *Management*. The quality of management in the UK is widely perceived as being poor, despite the spread of management qualifications such as the MBA. As with the whole of UK industry, there are some very good examples of management practice, but a very long tail of poor performers. The average standard needs to be raised to be nearer the best. Two main failings are a short-termist approach, which discourages long-term investment and development, and a failure to introduce modern management practices such as Just in Time (JIT) and continuous improvement. Many sectors of industry still experience high levels of stress and alienation, and many managers refuse to consider a partnership approach with their workers.

- *Infrastructure*. The UK has the most congested roads in the EU. This adds to business costs and makes the operation of techniques such as JIT more difficult.

- *Flexibility*. Industry must become more flexible in order to optimise its use of resources. This involves being:
  - *Numerically flexible*. Working time must adjust to meet customer demand: 'the 24/7 society'. This involves the use of techniques such as annual hours.
  - *Functionally flexible*. Skills levels must be improved, and these skills fully utilised.
  - *Occupationally flexible*. Workers must become multi-skilled.
  - *Wage flexible*. Reward must be used as an incentive to higher productivity.
  - *Mindset flexible*. Diversity must be encouraged in order to tap all available talent, and organisations must be family-friendly in order to encourage diversity. (Philpott 2002, Merrick 2001, Briner 2001.)

- *Education*. A key element is the need to develop workforce skills. The UK has a higher proportion of low-skilled workers than other comparable economies. A whole series of initiatives have been introduced, ranging from NVQs to TECs, ILAs to LSCs. The result has been an alphabet soup, without a great deal of impact on the skills base. As usual, the UK pattern is one of excellence at the top, with very effective degree-level provision, a gap in the middle, where technician-level skills are poorly developed, and a long tail of functional illiteracy and innumeracy. However, it is becoming clear that workforce development is a dual responsibility, with the government responsible for developing the basic skills of numeracy, literacy and IT (as stressed in the Tomlinson Report on the reform of 14–19 education in October 2004), and industry being responsible for the development of workplace-specific skills.

The best that can be said at present about the effectiveness of competitiveness policy is that the UK is holding its own and not falling further behind its main competitors. Short-term gains are unlikely, and these policies should be seen as essentially long term.

In 2003, Michael Porter and Christian Ketels carried out a study for the DTI on the UK's competitiveness. Their conclusions were rather more optimistic. They said that successive governments have 'fundamentally changed the macroeconomic, and, more importantly, the microeconomic context for competition'. They identified what they saw as the strengths of the UK business environment: its openness to international trade and investment, its very low regulatory barriers to national-level competition, and its sophisticated capital markets; but also identified weaknesses, particularly a deteriorating physical infrastructure, skills deficits, and low levels of R&D and innovation despite a strong science base. The challenge for the future was to manage the transition from an economy based on low cost to one based on unique value and innovation.

However, the Porter report has been criticised for its emphasis on economic issues at the expense of behavioural ones. For example, US-owned firms in the UK have higher productivity than UK-owned ones. Andrew Pettigrew of the University of Warwick points out that the most obvious explanation for this lies in the 'varying abilities of managers to perceive, incorporate or even change [environmental] conditions' (Caulkin 2003).

It is also important to remember that productivity per head is not the only driver of economic growth. As William Keegan pointed out in October 2004 (Keegan 2004b), superior economic growth in the US is largely caused by factors such as:

- a growing labour force, driven by high rates of immigration. This tends to lower the average age of the workforce, and also forces a high rate of investment to keep pace with the demand created by a growing population
- long hours and short holidays
- generally expansionary macroeconomic policies.

SKILLS POLICY

In 2006, Lord Leitch identified the skills weaknesses of the UK. He discovered that only 85 per cent of adults had basic literacy skills, and 79 per cent basic numeracy. Only 69 per cent of adults had gained at least a level 2 qualification (equivalent to five GCSEs at A*–C grade), and 29 per cent had a higher education qualification (level 4 or above). In order to be in the top 25 per cent of OECD countries by 2020, these figures would have to be considerably improved:

- basic literacy up from 85 to 95 per cent

- basic numeracy up from 79 to 95 per cent

- level 2 qualifications up from 69 to 90 per cent

- level 4 qualifications up from 29 to 40 per cent

- apprenticeships to reach 500,000 a year in England.

The Leitch proposals were accepted in full by the government in July 2007 (DIUS 2007), and the government also set out intermediate targets.

By 2011:

- 89 per cent of adults to achieve basic literacy, and 81 per cent basic numeracy

- 79 per cent of adults qualified to level 2

- 56 per cent of adults qualified to level 3 (two A level equivalent).

By 2014:

- 36 per cent of adults qualified to level 4.

The Leitch Review stressed that the emphasis in the skills strategy should be on adults, as 70 per cent of the 2020 workforce was already beyond the compulsory education age in 2006.

As significant as the targets were the mechanisms by which Leitch felt they should be achieved. He stressed a demand-led approach, with employers and workers given funding to commission their own training. In the case of employers,

funding would be channelled through the Train to Gain programme, which was forecast to rise from £440 million in 2007–08 to £900 million in 2010–11. Funding for individual training would come through a new scheme of Skills Accounts.

The Leitch proposals were broadly approved by interest groups. The TUC (2008) welcomed the proposal to create a statutory right to workplace training to level 2, but questioned the emphasis on an employer-led approach. It felt that a social partnership approach between both employers and employees would be more appropriate, and that greater emphasis should be placed on the role of union learning representatives. It also questioned whether employers would actually take up their responsibility to lead on training. The CBI (2005) welcomed the employer-led approach, and stressed the cost of low skills to business. Low basic skills cost a typical SME with 50 employees £165,000 a year, and the cost to the whole UK economy was £10 billion a year.

The CIPD (2008) pointed out that the government should not put all its efforts into improving basic and low skills. They stressed that the productivity gain from boosting basic skills is only 1 per cent, whereas higher-level skills would boost productivity by 4.4 per cent. The Conservative Party (2008) has attacked the emphasis on Train to Gain, which it regards as wasteful and bureaucratic.

The skills strategy produced some early successes. Between 2001 and 2007, the percentage of establishments with any staff who were not fully proficient fell from 23 per cent to 15 per cent, while the percentage of staff not fully competent fell from 9 to 6 per cent. The number of vacancies caused by lack of skills fell from 25 per cent in 2005 to 21 per cent in 2007. The National Employers Skills Survey 2007 identified the main causes of skills gaps as lack of experience/newly recruited (68 per cent), staff lack motivation (28 per cent), failure to train and develop staff (20 per cent), and inability of the workforce to keep up with change (19 per cent) (LSC 2008).

INVESTORS IN PEOPLE

CASE STUDY 4.6

Investors in People (IIP) was introduced in October 1991. It is one of the key competitiveness-promoting initiatives which has been truly non-political, enthusiastically backed by both the Major and the Blair governments. By 2001, 25,000 organisations had qualified for the standard, employing 24 per cent of the UK workforce.

Research carried out for IIP suggests that 73 per cent of organisations awarded the standard more than 12 months previously felt that it had increased their productivity. However, there is a counter view, put forward by Scott Taylor of the Open University, that IIP frequently has little impact on performance (Brown 2001), and this is supported by research from the Institute of Directors, where only 15 per cent of 275 company directors felt that IIP had increased profitability, and a quarter thought it had increased productivity (Nelson 2001).

Arguments in support of Taylor's contention could include:

- Some organisations see IIP as a marketing exercise. The standard is treated as 'just another badge on the wall' rather than a development tool.

- Achievement and maintenance of the standard involves considerable amounts of management and worker time. These have to be offset before there can be any overall improvement in productivity.

- There is considerable emphasis on measurement of outputs. There is a risk that too much emphasis may be put on the targets rather than the processes. To many people, the present government seems obsessed with targets, which can cause distortions. In a recent case, patients waiting for accident and emergency assessment were held in ambulances outside an A&E department, because there is a target for maximum waiting times in A&E, but the clock does not start ticking until the patient actually enters the building (Bowcott 2004)!

- More generally, IIP can only succeed where it is seen not as a box-ticking exercise, but as a fundamental change in values and attitudes. As with similar initiatives such as Total Quality Management, a belief in the virtues of development must be internalised in the organisation and become an integral part of its culture. Many organisations of course do this, and it is clear that in many cases IIP has been a total success.

HR ISSUES IN THE PUBLIC SECTOR

The final section of this chapter, on HR issues in the public sector, consists of a case study, on recruitment of social workers, and an activity, on labour force planning in education.

BABY P AND THE RECRUITMENT OF SOCIAL WORKERS

Child-protection social work must be one of the most stressful jobs imaginable. Not only are interactions with difficult, evasive and often violent or abusive clients emotionally draining, but social workers know they are constantly walking a tightrope. If they make a mistake and, at worst, a child for whom they are responsible dies, they will be vilified by the tabloid press as murderers, while if they err on the side of caution, and take children too readily into care, they will be condemned by the same tabloid press as callous family-breakers. In addition, social work, like teaching, the police and the NHS, is a victim of the government's target culture for the public services, which has resulted in an increase in time-consuming bureaucracy (Hudson 2009, Kirkpatrick and Ackroyd 2003).

As a result, the level of unfilled posts in local authority social services departments is high. The national average for social work vacancies in June 2009 was 12 per cent, while some authorities had much greater problems: Sandwell, in the West Midlands, had a vacancy rate of 39 per cent; Waltham Forest in East London 34.9 per cent; Hounslow in West London 31 per cent; and Essex county 28.1 per cent (Bowcott 2009a). There is also some concern over the quality of social workers. Like teaching and nursing, social work is an all-graduate profession, with qualification through a bachelor's degree in social work or a postgraduate qualification. A Commons committee found that since 2003–04, the failure rate of students is only 2.62 per cent, much lower than for other degree courses. The entry level of students is also lower than average. In 2006–07, nearly half the students admitted to social work degree courses had fewer than 240 points, which is the equivalent of three C grades at A level (Newman 2009). The social work qualification is a generic one. There are no specialist degrees in child protection.

Already suffering from severe recruitment problems, social work was then hit by the Baby P case. Baby P (Peter) was born in Haringey, north London in March 2006. In December 2006, he was placed on the Haringey child protection register for physical abuse and neglect. Despite extensive contacts with social services, the NHS and the police, it was decided in July 2007 that the case did not meet the legal threshold for care proceedings. On 3 August 2007, Peter was taken to hospital, but pronounced dead on arrival. In November 2008, his mother, stepmother and a lodger were found guilty of causing his death.

A review by Lord Laming declared Haringey's child protection services to be exceptionally inadequate. The council leader and cabinet member for children and young people resigned. The director of children's services was summarily dismissed on the direct instructions of Ed Balls, the children's secretary. Later, Haringey dismissed a social worker and three managers. A hospital consultant who examined Peter just before his death but found no cause for concern was suspended, as was Peter's GP, who had seen him 14 times before his death. No action was taken against any of the police involved in the case (Batty 2009).

In May 2009, Ed Balls announced a series of measures designed to improve recruitment and retention. These included:

- a recruitment campaign designed to attract 500 social workers who had left the profession to rejoin it, supported by refresher training

- sponsoring 200 university places to encourage 'the highest achieving graduates, from any disciplines' to take social work conversion courses

- improvement of supervision for newly qualified social workers in their first post

- a new master's degree in social work
- advanced social work status. At present the only progression route for social workers is to go into management. As with teaching, the proposal would provide for a practitioner progression route, as well as a managerial one
- simplification of the Integrated Children's System software system for recording social workers' interactions with children and families.

Balls said he expected these initiatives to cost £58 million (Carvel 2009).

Other measures which emerged later included:

- a national social work college, to give support, leadership and enhanced status to the profession (Brindle 2009)
- an advertising campaign to raise the

image of social workers by highlighting success stories, featuring, among others, the Oscar-nominated actor Samantha Morton, who was herself in care as a child (Samuel 2009)
- Haringey has recruited 22 social workers from the US and Canada, after failing to recruit in the UK (Bowcott 2009b).

The government has so far refused to implement two of Lord Laming's key recommendations:

- ring-fencing of spending on child protection
- specialist undergraduate programmes in child protection (Carvel 2009).

Nothing, of course, has been done about what one commentator described as the 'vicious reporting' of the tabloids (Sawford 2009).

ACTIVITY 4.7 TEACHERS AND WORKFORCE PLANNING

Intuitively you would think it would be easy to plan the supply of teachers. After all, you know how many children are born each year and where they are born, because all births have to be registered. Then you just project four years ahead (for primary schools) and 11 years (for secondaries), and you know how many children will be entering each level of school in each year. Adding up the years gives you a total school population. Divide this by your planned pupil–teacher ratio, and you know exactly how many teachers you need in each year.

Unfortunately, of course, it doesn't work like that. Over the period 1946–2001, there was a shortage of teachers (an excess demand) for all but 10 years, reaching a peak of 80,000 in the early 1990s. There was a surplus (excess supply) for 10 years from the mid-1970s to the mid-1980s, peaking at about 15,000 (Dolton 2005).

Question: Why is it so difficult to plan the supply of teachers?

- Legislation in the UK is normally initiated by the government, whereas in the EU it is initiated by the Commission. The role of parliament is much greater in the UK than in the EU.

- Political parties and their members have some influence on policy formation, but this influence is tending to decrease.

- Pressure groups are of two main types: interest or sectional groups; and attitude or cause groups. They have considerable influence both on the evolution of government policy and on its implementation.

- There are crucial differences between gross domestic product and standard of living or quality of life.

- All governments, of whatever political colour, are striving to achieve economic growth, full employment, stable prices and equilibrium on the balance of payments.

- Policy instruments available to governments include fiscal policy, monetary policy, competitiveness policy and exchange rate policy.

- Interest rates in the UK are set by the Bank of England, subject to an inflation target set by the government.

- The inflation target in the UK is symmetrical, and therefore less restrictive than that of the European Central Bank.

- A drive to increase productivity and competitiveness is a key aim of both UK and EU economic policy, but does not lead to quick results.

- Despite their very different political systems, both India and China have been very effective at stimulating economic growth.

1. What is the difference between a Green Paper and a White Paper?

2. Through what stages does a bill pass in the UK before it becomes an act?

3. What are the differences between an interest and an attitude pressure group?

4. What are the differences between RPI, RPIX and CPI? Which do you think is the best measure of inflation?

5. What are the five tests on whether the UK should join the euro?

6. What were the main causes of the credit crunch recession of 2008–09?

7. What is a public interest company?

8. What is the difference between PFI and PPP?

9. What major competitiveness weaknesses of the UK economy were identified by Michael Porter?

10. What were the main recommendations of the Leitch Report?

EXPLORE FURTHER

Further Reading

For the underlying economic theory, see Lipsey and Chrystal. John Philpott, the CIPD's chief economist, produces an occasional series for the CIPD entitled *Perspectives*, which is invaluable.

Websites

For the evolution and application of policy, the Bank of England (www.bankofengland.co.uk) and the Department of Business, Innovation and Skills (www.bis.gov.uk) websites are useful. For current political party policy, you should access the main party websites (www.labour.org.uk, www.conservatives.com, www.libdems.org.uk); and for the reaction from the major political interest groups, see the TUC (www.tuc.org.uk), CBI (www.cbi.org.uk) and CIPD (www.cipd.co.uk) websites.

SEMINAR ACTIVITY

ECONOMIC DEVELOPMENT IN INDIA AND CHINA

Between 1985 and 1995, GNP growth in the developing world averaged 6 per cent a year, more than twice that of the developed world (World Bank 2000). This suggests that the developing world will soon catch up with the developed world. Unfortunately, this hopeful forecast ignores two key factors. One is the rapid rate of population growth in the developing world. When this is stripped out and growth converted to GNP per head, the growth rate per head in the developing world falls to 3.8 per cent, while that of the developed world falls to 2.1 per cent.

Secondly, the developing country figures are distorted by the outstanding success of the two most populous countries, India and China, In the period 1985–95, India's GNP per head rose by 3.2 per cent a year, and China's by an impressive (although possibly unreliable) 8.3 per cent a year. Stripping out India and China from the figures, the rest of the developing world actually had a GNP per head which fell by nearly 1 per cent a year. Since the 1990s, growth in both countries has accelerated, to 10 per cent or more in China, and 8 per cent in India.

China's success has been particularly remarkable. It took England 58 years to double its GDP after 1780, the US 47 years from 1839, Japan 34 years from 1885, and South Korea 11 years from 1966 (Meredith 2007). It took China nine years from 1978. It then doubled again by 1996, and doubled yet again by 2006 (Hutton 2007).

Why have India and China done so well? To some extent both countries are returning to their historic position in the world economy. At the time of the Roman Empire, China had 26 per cent of the world's economy, and India 33 per cent. Even by 1820, China had 33 per cent, India 16 per cent (compared with western Europe at 24 per cent, and the US at 2 per cent) (Smith 2007a). It was only in the nineteenth century that the Indian and Chinese economies collapsed. China's GDP per head in 1950 was only three-quarters of its 1820 value. By the early 1970s, China's share of world output was only 5 per cent, and India's 3 per cent, compared to western Europe's 26 per cent and the US and Canada's 25 per cent.

India and China have some distinct similarities in their economies. Both had their Year

Zero in the 1940s, when their political and economic status was transformed – India's by independence in 1947, China's by the victory of Mao and the communists in 1949. Both have huge populations, and a dominant agricultural sector, employing more than half of the population. Both went through the same sequence of economic development, of emphasis on heavy industry and a planned economy, followed by agricultural reform, followed by export-led growth, with greater emphasis on the market (Goyal and Jha 2004).

The main difference comes in their political systems. China has been a unitary state since the time of the first emperor (he of the terracotta warriors) in the second century BC. Throughout most of its history, India has been a cultural rather than a political entity, and has only been a single state under foreign conquerors, from the Mughals in the fifteenth and sixteenth centuries to the British in the eighteenth to twentieth centuries. China is a one-party state with power centralised in the Communist Party; India is a multi-party democracy. China is relatively homogeneous racially, with few religious or racial minorities, except for Muslims in the far west, while India is a heterogeneous state both racially and religiously, with a very large Muslim minority population (India has a bigger Muslim population than Pakistan), and significant numbers of Sikhs, Buddhists and Christians.

Both initially made economic mistakes, but both laid the foundations for their future success immediately after their respective Year Zeros. Mao took over a state where illiteracy was rife, with a male illiteracy rate of 70 per cent, and female illiteracy up to 99 per cent in rural areas (Hutton 2007, p76). Mao immediately instituted a crash programme of primary education, and by the mid-1990s adult literacy was up to 80 per cent. It is forecast that by 2025 there will be more English speakers in China than there are native English speakers in the rest of the world (Smith 2007a, p100). China's economic policy was eccentric and destructive until the 1970s. The Great Leap Forward between 1958 and 1961 tried to industrialise China through village communes, which predictably proved to be a

failure, while the whole Chinese economy was torn apart by the Cultural Revolution between 1966 and 1976.

India after independence went for a moderate socialist economy similar to that constructed in the UK in the 1940s, with extensive nationalisation of key industries, and also, following the ideas of Gandhi, opted for economic self-sufficiency (autarky). Small industries were encouraged, and tariff barriers were high. The economy was also highly bureaucratic (known as the Permit Raj), and this discouraged entrepreneurialism. However, many small to medium-sized firms prospered under this benign and protectionist regime, and India developed skills in small-scale manufacture.

The first prime minister of India, Pandit Nehru, was also, like Mao, committed to education. His legacy was the foundation of a group of seven Indian Institutes of Technology (IITs), founded in 1947. Although small, these were excellent, rated in 2005 as the third best institutions of technology in the world, behind only MIT and the California Institute of Technology. Graduates from the IITs were later to develop the Indian software industry, as well as much of Silicon Valley.

China's switch to a high-growth economy began in 1978, when the veteran communist Deng Xiaoping came to power. Deng realised that results were more important than ideology. One of his sayings is: 'It doesn't matter whether a cat is black or white as long as it catches mice.' Deng dismantled the rural communes, giving land back to the peasants, which immediately led to a rise in agricultural output. He ensured that state enterprises were run by managers rather than party bureaucrats, and he set up Special Economic Zones, tax-free enclaves which welcomed foreign investment, initially from the Chinese diaspora in Hong King, Singapore and Taiwan, but later from the West, particularly the US. He cut tariffs on imports, and launched a huge programme of infrastructure investment, with tens of thousands of miles of motorway and dozens of new international airports being built.

The combination of good infrastructure and

plentiful, cheap but well-educated labour proved irresistible to foreign investors. By 2008, China produced two-thirds of the world's photocopiers, shoes, toys and microwaves, half the DVD players, digital cameras and textiles, a third of the desktop computers, and a quarter of mobile phones and TVs (Jacques 2009). China's manufactured exports have boomed, although there has been some criticism that the result is that goods are 'made in China', but not 'made by China' (Hutton 2007, p114). There are very few major Chinese-owned companies, and none which are truly world-class. However, the success of Chinese companies like Galanz (see case study 1.5) suggests that this will soon change.

Potentially the Chinese economy was at severe risk from the onset of world recession in 2008, because one of the first manifestations of the recession was a collapse in world trade. This hit China hard, as its economy was crucially dependent on exports of manufactured goods, particularly to the US. However, the Chinese government took quick and decisive action, putting a large fiscal stimulus into the economy, and switching production to the home market.

For over 40 years, India bumbled along, with some economic growth, but not sufficient to cut rural poverty significantly (what JK Galbraith described as 'functioning anarchy' (Smith 2007a, p172)). Despite the success of the IITs, illiteracy, especially in rural areas, remained high, and India was also held back by its caste structure. Since independence, discrimination against *dalits* (untouchables) has been illegal, but in practice persisted. Only 20 per cent of rural residents are *dalits*, but they make up 38 per cent of the very poor. A further 11 per cent are *adavasis* (members of tribal groups), but they are even poorer, making up 48 per cent of the very poor (Meredith 2007, p119).

India's point of change came in 1991, when the country faced a financial crisis. This led to reforms introduced by Manmohan Singh, the finance minister, and now (2010) Prime Minister of India. He liberalised external trade and deregulated the domestic economy,

copying Deng's concept of Special Economic Zones. The growth rate accelerated, reaching 8 per cent by 2000. India built on its strength in small and medium-sized manufacturing, backed by highly skilled craftsmen.

Whereas China was the country of choice for mass production, India concentrated on short, highly specialised production runs. More important, India latched on to the boom in new technology in the 1990s. Not only did it scoop the market in call centres and business process outsourcing, by the 2000s taking a 48 per cent share of the world market (Smith 2007a, p132), but it also developed a world-class software industry, centred on the southern city of Bangalore, where Infosys and Wipro are world class and rapidly growing software companies.

The software for Apple's highly successful iPod was developed in India (and the product assembled in China) (Meredith 2007, p102) Services now account for more than half of India's GDP (Rudiger 2008). Older industry also started to flourish, led by the long-established conglomerate Tata, which now owns Corus (formerly British Steel) as well as a range of western companies including Tetley Tea. It subsequently bought Jaguar and Land Rover from Ford in 2008 for US $2.3 billion. In 2007, India became the world's 12th largest economy (De Vita 2009). India seems to have weathered the world recession without too much damage, and expects economic growth soon to return to the pre-credit crunch figure of 9 per cent.

India also had great institutional strength: the English language, a vibrant democracy, a free press, and universal acceptance of the rule of law. Hutton sees these soft attributes as key. However, like China, India has weaknesses. Its literacy rate lags well behind China, and its physical infrastructure is very weak. Its roads, with a few exceptions, are appalling, and anyone who has experienced Agra airport will know that the same can be said for most of its airports.

Each of the 28 Indian states has its own border controls and regulations. Smith (2007a, p164) describes a lorry journey from

Kolkata (Calcutta) to Mumbai (Bombay), a distance of 2,150 kilometres, which took eight days, including 32 hours waiting at border tollbooths. However, the latest Five Year Plan (2007–12) has earmarked US $500 billion for infrastructure improvement.

Like China, India also suffers from endemic corruption. In 2007, Andrew Wileman described an attempt to transport a bull elephant from Kerala to Bangalore in order to take part in a Hindu ceremony at one of the IT companies, Aditi. The 300-mile journey involved the payment of £250 in bribes at every state border to and from Bangalore, because 'elephant transportation papers were not in order'. He also tells the story of the auto-rickshaws in Delhi. Apparently there are 500,000 of these, but only 100,000 official licences. The other 400,000 stay in business by paying regular 'fines' to the traffic police (Wileman 2007).

As a democracy, India is relatively slow to take decisions, and to make major shifts in policy. On the other hand, decisions in India have democratic legitimacy. China can take quick decisions, and tends to be better at taking long-term decisions, as its government is not answerable to an electorate, while decisions in India are shorter-term, and geared to the electoral cycle. As a result, China was better placed to make long-term investments in its education and health programmes, and to steamroll through its infrastructure improvements. Despite its centralised political system, China has been very effective at decentralising economic decision-making. It has given a great deal of economic autonomy to the growth areas of Shanghai, Quangdong and Hong Kong.

China has also been more effective at opening its economy to the West and at encouraging foreign direct investment through a stable exchange rate and low real interest rates. India has gained through the widespread use of English in its higher education system, which has led to the outsourcing of large numbers of service jobs from the West. China has tended to gain from the outsourcing of manufacturing rather than service jobs. This has led to a big increase in Chinese exports, particularly to the US and Japan.

Both countries clearly have economic systems which are highly effective at generating economic growth. As an authoritarian state, China has been able to be more single-minded in its pursuit of growth, and as a result has achieved a higher rate of growth. However, there are costs in the Chinese system. As the development economist Amartya Sen has pointed out, no democratic country has experienced a devastating famine, whereas authoritarian states like China have (Steele 2001).

It appears that a combination of authoritarian political control and a decentralised market-run economic system seems to be highly effective at producing economic growth, but with accompanying costs such as loss of freedom, economic inequality and social disruption.

However, it is possible to overhype the success of China (Hilton 2004). It took until 1993 before China's exports were back at the level they reached in 1928 (before the Japanese invasion), and despite its vast population, China's GDP in 2000 was only a quarter that of Japan. The dash for growth has also caused enormous environmental degradation. China has 16 of the world's 20 most polluted cities.

Question

1. Which do you think is more likely to sustain its economic growth in the long term, India or China?

There are three excellent books, all published in 2007, which provide background material for this seminar activity. Two are journalistic accounts of the economic rise of India and China. David Smith's (2007b) *The Dragon and the Elephant: China, India and the new world order*, examines the issues from a UK perspective. Robyn Meredith's *The Elephant and the Dragon: the rise of India and China and what it means for all of us*, covers much the same ground from a US perspective. Will Hutton's *The Writing on the Wall* takes a more analytical approach, concentrating on China, and is as much a critique of the West as it is of China. A further book, published in 2009, is Martin Jacques' *When China Rules the World*, which takes a mainly cultural perspective on the rise of China.

CHAPTER 5

Regulation

LEARNING OUTCOMES

When you have completed this chapter you should be able to:

- understand the essential features of the UK legal system, including the sources and types of law and the courts system, including tribunals

- analyse the significance of existing and new regulation for particular sectors and organisations, and discuss the type and nature of responses to the regulation

- identify the nature of regulation in respect of contract, consumer and competition law, and the implications for stakeholders to whom the law applies

- critically evaluate the range of employment legislation and the ways that it influences the labour market and management policy and practice in organisations.

INTRODUCTION

The rule of law that applies in democratic societies is one of the key features that differentiate democracy from dictatorship and tyranny. Legal decisions cannot be taken capriciously or for small special interest groups, but for the long-term benefit of society as a whole. Laws, as determined by elected parliament and interpreted by the independent judiciary, are fundamental to a well-governed and stable society.

The last time that this was tested was in March 1984 when Arthur Scargill led the National Union of Mineworkers into a national strike to try to improve working conditions in the mines and to prevent a massive programme of pit closures. He dismissed the legislation passed two years earlier requiring a ballot before strike action could go ahead, taking the view that 'bad laws should be ignored', just as the trade union movement had successfully done in 1972 against earlier Tory trade union legislation. In a defining moment of the Thatcher administration, the government brought the full force of the establishment – police, army, public opinion – to restore the rule of law, supporting the concept that laws passed in a proper democratic process must be obeyed by individuals and organisations. The view was widely promulgated that 'societies where the rule of law can be flouted with impunity cannot survive', and it was the almost unanimous support of this view across the UK that ultimately sealed the miners' fate.

The legal system, then, is at the heart of a democratic society. It sets out the rules within which people and organisations live and do business with each other; it reflects the current views on morality held by the majority of its citizens; it defines the punishments for breaking these rules; and it establishes the nature of the contracts between the individual, the organisation and the state whereby the state is paid (through taxation) to protect the interests of all parties in a fair and impartial way. It allows everybody to plan their lives with the fair certainty of foreseeing what actions and behaviour are allowed and what is forbidden.

This chapter provides a general introduction to the structure of UK law; details some of the specific legislation that sets out a level playing field for business and the consumer; indicates the main protection for employees in the workplace; examines how law regulates particular sectors and labour markets; and suggests ways that employers can respond to new legislation. Law is a complex subject and organisations and individuals regularly call on experts to advise them, so the outline provided in this chapter is primarily to raise awareness of the legal framework together with a good number of working examples.

LEGAL CONTOURS

LEGAL CONCEPTS

There is a clear division of authority between the judiciary and the executive, a factor that distinguishes true democracy from a dictatorship. Judges are independent and, once appointed, cannot be dismissed, except in extreme cases such as where they are convicted of corruption or another serious offence. If they take decisions that the government does not like (and this is happening more regularly with the increased use of judicial review) then the government simply has to accept their decisions.

Precedent requires courts to follow decisions laid down in earlier cases where the facts are broadly similar. To give an example, in decisions made on unfair dismissal claims soon after the Industrial Relations Act was passed in 1972, higher courts confirmed the circumstances under which an employee could claim constructive dismissal, including the need for the individual to immediately resign and leave the employment once the incident had occurred. If a claim reaches a tribunal today and the claimant delayed by a few weeks in leaving the employment after the incident occurred, then the tribunal would be required to follow the precedent and throw out the claim.

When lawyers are advising on a case, then, they need to be well read not just in the law itself, but in the way it has been interpreted by the courts as shown in the precedents involved. They need to read the *obiter dicta*, which are the judge's recorded comments justifying their decisions. Faced by precedents which indicate that a case would be unsuccessful, a lawyer would either advise their client to withdraw or would try their best to argue that the facts of the case were significantly different so the precedent did not apply.

That is not to say that precedents cannot be changed. One of the duties of the Court of Appeal is to examine precedents argued before them and judge whether such precedents are out of date for changing social times or preserve a system which is clearly unfair. In such cases, it may decide precedents need to be altered at the margins or be completely reversed. A well-known example of reversal was the *Walker v Northumberland County Council* case (see case study 5.1).

 CHANGING A PRECEDENT

CASE STUDY 5.1

In *Walker v Northumberland County Council* [1995] IRLR 35 John Walker was a social work manager who returned to work having had a mental breakdown brought on through an excessive workload. He requested a reduction in his duties and additional resources to allow him to cope with his responsibilities and serve the community. His employer did very little to help him and he subsequently suffered a further extended breakdown which ended his career. Prior to this case, the precedent had been that the employer had a clear duty of care in respect of preventing foreseeable physical illness, but not mental illness brought on by stress. The Court of Appeal confirmed that this duty of care should be extended to foreseeable mental illness because there was no logical reason why it should be excluded from the scope of the Health and Safety at Work Act 1974. Walker was awarded £175,000 in damages and this decision established a change in precedent. Consequently, employers have had to give much more careful consideration to issue of foreseeable stress and subsequent mental illness among their staff.

In serious criminal cases (and surprisingly, civil cases for libel or slander), the final decision is made by a jury: one is judged by one's peers. In jury trials, even the judge's advice can be overturned in the belief that it is a matter of whose word can be trusted, and a jury of 12 people is the best way to test this.

TYPES OF LAW

The law is divided into two main divisions.

Civil law

The ground rules dealing with relationships between individuals and between an individual and an organisation are laid down under civil law. Where one side believes that the law has been broken, they will take the case up in the civil courts and aim to have the wrong righted and/or obtain compensation. The main areas under which civil cases are brought are breach of contract (where it is claimed that one party has broken the terms of a legally enforceable contract) and torts, which are civil wrongs independent of contract, such as negligence, nuisance or defamation (see case study 5.2).

EXAMPLE OF A TORT

CASE STUDY 5.2

Your next-door neighbour has allowed a tree to grow so large that parts are overhanging your small garden and taking away most of your light. You have asked him politely to take some action but nothing happens. You therefore bring a case claiming nuisance. Before the case comes to court, a gale brings down a large branch which smashes your fence and greenhouse. You therefore add a further claim for negligence to the case.

The remedies you can obtain are:

- Compensation (damages) – but only to the extent of your proven losses, plus costs you have expended.

- Specific performance – where the court instructs the plaintiff to carry out an action (see case study 5.3).

- Injunction – where the court instructs the plaintiff to *not* carry out an action, such as demolishing a listed building.

 SPECIFIC PERFORMANCE

CASE STUDY 5.3

You have successfully bid for an original painting at an auction but you learn subsequently that the owner has decided to withdraw the painting for sale. You believe you have a valid contract and you successfully ask the court to instruct the owner to complete the contract and deliver the painting to you. You have set your heart on obtaining that unique painting and no alternative or compensation would satisfy you.

Criminal law

Here offences (crimes) which society believes need punishing are defined. The court case is a result of a police investigation and a case brought by the Crown Prosecution Service. Very occasionally, a private prosecution takes place, such as by the parents of the murdered teenager Stephen Lawrence in the 1990s. In general, however, these have a very low success rate and can be stopped by the Attorney General if they are not regarded as in the public interest.

Cases are divided into indictable offences, generally serious crimes where conviction can result in imprisonment, eg murder, rape, serious fraud; and summary offences, which are less serious and where conviction brings a fine, eg parking, petty theft.

ACTIVITY 5.1 CORPORATE MANSLAUGHTER CASE

In February 2010, Cotswold Geotechnical Holdings was charged with gross negligence manslaughter over the death of a geologist. He was taking small samples from a development site when the pit he was working in collapsed, killing him.

Look up the Corporate Manslaughter Act 2007 and trace the outcome of this case, which was the first brought under this recent legislation. The outcome will indicate under what other circumstances an organisation can commit a criminal offence.

FROM WHERE DOES THE LAW ORIGINATE?

We are so used to a flood of new legislation (statute law, as explained in Chapter 4), emerging from parliament each year that it is a common fallacy to believe that this process is the only source of law. However, there are two other main sources.

Common law

Up until the nineteenth century, most law was 'common', meaning that it had come into effect through judges recognising custom and practice (and common sense) and had been spread around the country by judges on their circuits. These decisions made up the precedents. In most areas today, common law decisions have been incorporated into statute, but there are a number of fundamental common law concepts that remain, such as those relating to the law of contract and employee rights (see later in this chapter). There are also remain some more isolated specific rights under common law, such as those grazing rights held by New Forest commoners.

Codes of practice

Although not technically law, formal codes have a strong influence on decisions taken by the courts. For example, an organisation facing a tribunal claim for unfair dismissal that has not followed closely the ACAS Code on Disciplinary and Grievance Procedures is less likely to make a successful defence. Similarly, an employer facing an equal pay claim should ensure that the Equality and Human Rights Commission's Code on Equal Pay has been incorporated into its procedures.

It should also be noted that much of the statute law originates from the EU whose legislative processes were also set out in Chapter 4.

COURTS SYSTEM

In figure 5.1, the courts system for England and Wales is set out (Scotland has had its own somewhat different system for more than 500 years). Courts are distinguished through their regulation of civil or criminal law and whether they are courts of first instance or whether they hear appeals, or both.

Figure 5.1 Court system in England and Wales

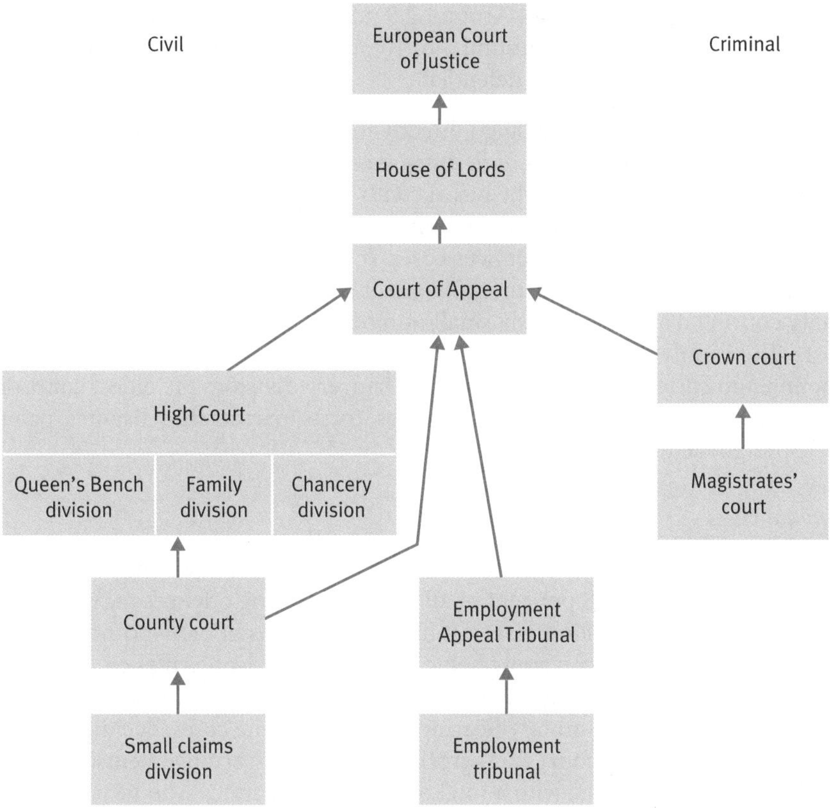

Note: the tribunal route indicates the process for employment law only.

Civil cases

Claims start in the county court or, if the amount at issue is less than £5,000, the small claims division. Speed, accessibility and informality are the keynotes here with representation frowned upon, and costs normally limited to the value of the summons. The judge acts alone as the arbitrator. It provides an opportunity for businesses and individuals to claim small debts and for torts to be examined and resolved. One day it may be resolving the overhanging tree dispute, the next, dealing with a claim from an ex-employee for unpaid overtime. There are around 200 county courts situated in cities and market towns with judges still working within circuits to try to ensure a degree of consistency, although small claims courts are overseen by a registrar.

In the county courts, actions for less than £15,000 are heard together with some others up to £50,000 by agreement with the parties, depending on their complexity (although this can vary depending on the nature of the claim).

Additional subject areas at the county courts, apart from contract and tort cases, include probate disputes, bankruptcy, undefended divorces, consumer credit issues and some land questions. Around 2.5 million summons a year are taken out at county courts but only around 5 to 10 per cent arrive in court and an even smaller percentage are actually defended.

Summons valued at over £50,000 go directly to the High Court. This has three divisions which deal with cases of first instance and appeals from lesser courts. The Queen's Bench division is the busiest with jurisdiction over high-value contract and tort cases, and a special commercial court dealing with banking, insurance and other financial services cases. It also has an admiralty court to hear cases involving ships and aircraft while it also hears some appeals from the county court and a comparatively small number of criminal appeals from crown courts. The Family division handles matrimonial cases, including wardship, adoption and custody claims. Finally, the Chancery division, the oldest court of all, has jurisdiction over high-value tax cases, trusts, partnership disputes, patent and copyright actions and land disputes.

Criminal cases

The magistrates' courts manage most of the criminal cases, presiding over the outcome of around 98 per cent of all crime. Motoring offences make up around half of it (two million cases). It handles all forms of petty crime with the maximum penalty it can apply being a six-month prison sentence, although few prison sentences are awarded. It has special arrangements to handle juvenile cases and it acts as a preliminary hearing in serious crime cases, deciding on 'committing' to a crown court and agreeing bail/custody arrangements. There are 400 magistrates' courts, with a total of 30,000 magistrates who hear the cases. They are a mixture of stipendiary (paid) officials and unpaid appointees. Stipendiary magistrates can sit alone. It is possible for those accused at a magistrates' court to decide to be heard in front of a jury at a crown court, usually in the hope that juries convict less often than hardened magistrates. Appeals (there are few) go generally to the crown court.

There are close to 70 crown courts, the most famous being the Central Criminal Court (Old Bailey). Cases are heard by juries, although the judge has a strong influence through control of the proceedings, interventions to clarify issues and the summing up. From 2010, a number of serious cases may be heard by a judge sitting alone when jury tampering may be a serious threat.

Higher courts

The Court of Appeal hears both criminal and civil court appeals, with three to five judges in attendance and a majority decision prevailing, with each judge's reasons published. Their judgments are extremely influential, much used to clarify the law and to set the ultimate precedent. Cases are sometimes referred to this court when new evidence has come to light that casts doubt on the validity of criminal convictions, cases that may have been held as long as 20 years or more ago. The appeal to the House of Lords can only be on a legal issue and the decision is final, except where the case comes under European law, where much of employment law resides. If so, the case is heard by the European Court of Justice, which gives a ruling and then refers the case back to the UK court for implementation.

Tribunals

The most well-known tribunals are those in employment areas, such as unfair dismissal and sex, race and disability discrimination. However, there are numerous tribunals set up by statute in other areas. There are rent tribunals, set up to help protect tenants from unscrupulous landlords; social security appeal tribunals, to provide an opportunity for citizens to questions decisions made about their right to benefits, such as unemployment and sickness; and various tribunals related to appeals over taxation. They all have the same intention, ie to provide a formal yet accessible process for the aggrieved citizen to have their cases heard fairly, impartially and thoroughly by persons not involved in the original decision. The accessibility comes about through, firstly, some discouragement of legal representation, as with the small claims court, by generally not awarding costs, and secondly, by ensuring that help in the initial stages is provided by the tribunals themselves and by volunteer bodies such as the Citizen's Advice Bureau.

In the employment area, the tribunals are bound by rules of evidence and precedent, but the three member tribunals are allowed to operate a much more informal and inquisitive approach than the higher courts. Appeals to the Employment Appeal Tribunal and subsequent appeals to higher courts can only be on the basis of law.

Ombudsmen

A final grouping of quasi-legal intent are the sets of ombudsmen, set up by legislation to investigate complaints of maladministration, mostly in the public arena. There are a number of commissioners (ombudsmen) in areas such as local government, the National Health Service and parliament whose reports have no precise legal standing but put pressure on the bodies concerned to rectify mistakes and improve their services. An example of the cases they deal with is set out in case study 5.4.

CASE STUDY 5.4

PARLIAMENTARY OMBUDSMAN REPORT ON PENSION LOSSES

Between 1997 and 2005, 400 private sector pension schemes were closed with outstanding deficits. The main reason for the closures was the demise of the company or its financial inability to continue contributing to the scheme. The outcome was that 85,000 employees, ex-employees and pensioners did not receive the pensions they had been promised under the scheme. Some, indeed, lost all of their pension entitlement.

In 2005, the Parliamentary Ombudsman was asked to investigate the Department for Work and Pension's (DWP) role in encouraging employees in this debacle. In March 2006, Commissioner Ann Abraham reported that the DWP had been guilty of maladministration. Its official guidance to employees was 'inaccurate, incomplete, unclear and inconsistent'. Much of the criticism was directed at government information leaflets which gave a misleading impression of the security of the schemes. They had not given sufficient warnings of the possibility of scheme closures and loss of pension rights.

The government responded by dismissing the report, pointing out that employees did not rely exclusively on these leaflets as a basis for their financial decisions. The minister declared that the government could not take on the heavy financial responsibility for the failure of private pension schemes. The government was not obliged under legislation to take any further action and would not do so.

Pension campaigners then took the matter to the High Court and, in 2007, obtained a decision that the government had wrongly rejected the Ombudsman's findings. It confirmed that the DWP had committed maladministration in its advice on the schemes.

This put additional pressure on the government, who were forced, in April 2007, to make concessions in terms of compensation to many of those who lost out. The government agreed to cover 80 per cent of the losses at a cost of around £2 billion.

LAW OF CONTRACT

Contracts are at the heart of all business and employment activity, and the common law governing their operation goes back further in time than most other law. For centuries, judges interpreted the law in a way that reflected the laissez-faire approach to all business, with the state interfering very little and people in business and employment left alone to run their affairs. This was partly to preserve the inequality of the 'master and servant' relationship and partly because most business contracts were on a relatively equal basis. To buy a pair of shoes, a customer went to the local cobbler and negotiated a price on a fairly equal basis. However, this was to change by the mid-nineteenth century as the Industrial Revolution and the development of capitalism had created large enterprises in commerce and industry which produced many unequal bargaining situations. In the next section, we shall see how the state has intervened over the last 100 years by introducing legislation to establish a more balanced situation.

The essence of a contract is to provide a legally binding format to a set of mutual promises. In general, the contract involves one party providing goods or a service and the other paying for them, and a typical organisation will have scores of contracts with suppliers, customers, service providers, intermediaries, staff and contractors. These contracts do not have to be in writing to be legally binding (apart from those related to land), although for clarity and certainty most of them are confirmed in this way. However, any informal changes that both parties agree to, even if not confirmed in writing, will supersede those written into the contract, as long as one side can produce compelling evidence that such an informal arrangement took place.

Interestingly, there are some very important contracts where the parties have agreed that they are not legally binding. These are agreements between employers and trade unions where, by tradition, both sides reserve the right to go back on the deals they make should they choose to do so. This is an interesting reflection on the trust between the parties under British employment relations.

There are six main elements in any contract.

Offer and unconditional acceptance

For each contract, the offer must state all the terms, be communicated effectively and be clear and unambiguous. It is different from what is known as an 'invitation to treat'. When shops first started putting prices in their shop windows, the courts were asked to intervene to distinguish between what appeared to be a legal 'offer' and what was merely an invitation to people to come into the shop and start negotiating. They decided that the prices marked on goods in the shop window or in advertisements are not 'offers' (or even 'special offers') and a potential customer cannot go into the shop and demand the legal right to buy the goods at the prices shown. It needs the shopkeeper's acceptance to make this a contract.

Acceptance must be unconditional and within the stipulated (or reasonable) time. An offer can be withdrawn at any time prior to acceptance. If the acceptance stipulates conditions, then this becomes a counter-offer. If both parties act as if they are working under an agreement, then a contract is deemed to have been agreed.

An area that still provides some difficulties with the courts is that of standard terms and conditions. One business will ask for tenders for providing goods (an invitation to treat). Another company will respond, making an offer on documentation which has its standard terms and conditions of trading printed on the back. The first company then accepts the offer on documentation with its own standard terms and conditions on the back. If the terms differ, it could be held to be a counter-offer, of course. If there is a dispute over some small detail which differs between the companies, the courts have tended to decide that the last set of documentation applies, but will be influenced by the actions of the parties and any evidence that can be offered to support the view that a particular term applied. It still does lead to problems, however, which are regularly resolved by an arbitration service.

Genuine agreement

Each party must have the same understanding of what makes up the contract and there must be no misrepresentation – this is genuine agreement. For example, if a car seller knowingly indicates a mileage that is not genuine, then the contract will be void and the buyer can claim damages. What often needs to be clarified is what were 'representations' (eg 'I think this is a most reliable motor') and what were actual terms of the contract (eg 'the tyres are three months old'). A buyer acting on representations has no redress. Contracts must not be entered into under duress or undue influence, including drink or drugs. If this is the case, the contracts can be voided.

Capacity to contract

The parties must have the capacity to contract – so minors are excluded, except for necessities (such as sweets and bus journeys!) but not for larger items. The same applies to those of an unsound mind. An interesting area is that it can be assumed that employees of an organisation who appear to have the authority to contract do in fact have this authority. This is to avoid the situation where an organisation can go back on a contract they subsequently decide is not in their favour.

Intention to create legal relations

There must be an intention to create legal relations. In general, legal relations between close relatives are rarely upheld by the courts, unless there is clear evidence to the contrary. The opposite applies to all business relationships where the presumption is that there is an intention present.

Legal purposes

The contract must be for legal purposes, so a contract is void if, for example, payment is made as cash in hand where National Insurance should be paid or any contracts set up which are purely to evade taxation.

Consideration

There must be consideration; this is normally money, although it can be any right or benefit which can be held to be of monetary value either currently or in the future. Contracts of barter are legal (ie international contracts of grain in exchange for oil). Without consideration, as in an agreement to paint the house of a friend for nothing, there can be no enforceable contract. In the voluntary world, this still provides some problems, of course. The payment must refer to the future and not to some past payments or obligations. Finally, the payment does not have to be adequate, fair or reasonable – that is up to the parties concerned.

A contract of employment arises directly out of contract law. A job must be offered and unconditionally accepted; there must be genuine agreement with no misunderstanding of the essential terms and conditions, such as the need to work night shifts or the type of company car; the contract must be legal, with no illegal activities such as cash-in-hand payments; there must be consideration (a wage or salary), as voluntary work is not enforceable and only those over 13 can have an employment contract and there are strict regulations relating to the employment of those under 18. Interestingly, the courts recognise the employment of wives and husbands as long as there is clear evidence of a contract existing.

There are more details on employment law on pages 199 to 206.

REGULATING BUSINESS AND PROTECTING THE CONSUMER

On a hot summer's day in 1930, a bottle of ginger beer was bought at the end of a walk by a young man for his lady friend. She gratefully drank up but, in finishing the opaque bottle, the remains of a decomposed snail appeared and, not surprisingly, she became very ill. On recovering, she wanted recompense for her unhappy experience, but she could not sue the shopkeeper because she had no contract with him, nor could she sue her boyfriend because there was no consideration – the bottle was a gift. Nor did she have a contract with the manufacturer. However, a lengthy legal case was commenced which, two years later, appeared at the House of Lords (*Donaghue v Stevenson* [1932] AC 562) where the landmark decision was reached that manufacturers can be guilty of the tort of negligence.

Prior to the case, caveat emptor ('let the buyer beware') applied in all consumer purchases, but *Donaghue v Stevenson* established that manufacturers have a duty of care to their customers not to be negligent and to avoid any acts or omissions which can be reasonably foreseen to kill, injure the consumer or member of the public, or to damage property. Subsequent cases have clarified guidelines, such as drug manufacturers having a greater duty of care than newspaper publishers because the consequences of faulty goods are far more serious.

Donaghue v Stevenson was an important case and the outcome was a distinct improvement in the degree of protection for consumers. By the late 1960s, however, governments started to take a more supportive view for the consumer. There were a number of reasons for this:

- the growth of huge multinational corporations made it much more difficult for the view to be held that a contract was made between equal partners

- mergers and acquisitions were growing to the stage that some companies had control of substantial sectors of the marketplace and could dictate terms

- the growth in practice of large organisations inserting 'small print' into contracts where special conditions were inserted and liabilities excluded to the detriment even of the observant consumer

- pressure had developed from consumer organisations, such as *Which?* magazine, which helped develop consumer awareness of shady practices, and politicians appreciated they needed to take notice of this pressure

- Britain decided to join the EU in the early 1970s and some legislation was required to bring the UK in line with European law

- trading practices were changing in line with technological and monetary developments and there were gaps in the law in these areas.

The legislation can be divided into the macro area, which controls and enhances competition generally, and the micro area, where specific unfair business practices are made illegal.

CONTROLLING AND ENHANCING COMPETITION

Fair Trading Act 1973

It was considered essential that a watchdog with wide powers of investigation should exist to champion the consumer interest and provide independent advice to the government. The Office of Fair Trading (OFT) took this role, and its powers have been increased with subsequent legislation, including the Competition Act 1998 and the Enterprise Act 2002. The Director-General of Fair Trading has responsibility to investigate commercial activities which may appear to be against the interests of consumers and advise the government if it believes action is necessary. The scope of activities investigated is wide, covering all sectors, businesses large and small, and dealing with contract terms, selling methods, packaging and promotion. Although its powers have limits, the fact that an investigation can take place and that it can seek orders from the government to stop certain activities are, in practice, strong deterrents and have often changed the way business is carried out. In its early days, it investigated pyramid selling and ensured its abolition.

Restrictive Trade Practices Act 1976 / Competition Act 1998

This legislation was passed to prevent the use of monopoly power either by individual companies or groups of companies colluding. A restrictive practice is defined as collusion on prices, terms of supply, manufacturing processes and any activity that is likely to have the effect of restricting, distorting or preventing competition. The OFT has the right to enter premises and demand documents and to enforce restrictions on movement or destruction of evidence. If an organisation refuses to co-operate, then it can penalised to the extent of 10 per cent of turnover.

When a restrictive practice is found to exist, it can only be successfully justified by the argument that it:

- protects the public from injury
- is a counterweight to another monopoly (such as in negotiations with the Royal Mail)
- provides extensive benefits to exports.

Examples of investigations in recent years include extended warranties (see case study 5.5); operation of small pharmacies and the major chains; private dentistry; consumer IT services; and estate agencies. It has also investigated some business methods, including doorstop selling and public sector procurement. A number of investigations were carried out in the 1980s and 1990s regarding price-fixing by colluding cement companies (see Chapter 3 for a discussion of the economic aspects of collusion) which eventually resulted in the cartel being broken up and cement prices substantially reduced.

COMPETITION COMMISSION REPORT ON EXTENDED WARRANTIES

CASE STUDY 5.5

In 2003, the Competition Commission carried out an investigation into the £500 million market in extended warranties (chiefly for electrical goods), following on from a referral from the OFT. It found that the bulk of warranties were purchased at the point of sale of the goods and could add 50 per cent to the price of the product and were generally poor value. Bad practice reported included:

- sales staff emphasising the risk of product failure

- customers being told that independent repairs were difficult to obtain and were expensive

- the consumer not being encouraged to shop around.

It was also reported that self-regulation had not worked and that the large electrical retailers were exploiting their monopoly situation to the detriment of consumers.

(Source: Competition Commission 2003.)

The OFT reports to the government, which can decide to refer the matter to the Competition Commission either for a decision or, in the case of an impending merger where the organisation will have 25 per cent or more of the market, a fuller enquiry to decide if the merger is in the public interest and under what terms the merger would be allowed to progress. Full-scale investigations by the Commission in recent years have included one into the position of Nestlé (where it found it did not have excessive monopolistic power on coffee prices); video games (where it recommended the abolition of licence controls); and UK car prices (where it found that the exclusive dealership system operated against the public interest).

Investigations of potential wrong-doing, or the threat of referral to the OFT or the Competition Commission, have a huge impact on organisations and their future planning of possible mergers. A raid on premises by the OFT can cause the company's share price to drop 10 per cent and many mergers have been decided by the policy of the Competition Commission.

A direct effect on the resourcing aspect of HRM is shown in case study 5.6.

COLLUSION BY RECRUITMENT AGENCIES

CASE STUDY 5.6

In 2009, six recruiting agencies were fined £40 million by the OFT for operating a cartel that fixed fees and boycotted a rival. The biggest company involved, Hays, was fined £30 million, equivalent to more than 2 per cent of its turnover. The agencies, acting together as the Construction Recruitment Forum, met five times over two years to fix prices to allow higher profits. At the same

time, they organised an effective boycott of contracts where a competitor, Parc (which was not part of the cartel), was offering cheaper rates. Two other companies which participated in the cartel were offered immunity in return for providing evidence against the six companies (Mathiason 2009).

ACTIVITY 5.2 DOORSTEP SELLING

The OFT carried out a survey of doorstep selling in response to complaints from the Citizen's Advice Bureau. Its report in 2004 recommended that legislation needs to be updated to combat the psychological tactics employed by many salespeople.

The study into the practice of selling goods and services on the doorstep and in the home, worth at least £2.4 billion a year, found that a range of sales tactics and influencing techniques can lead consumers to make inappropriate purchases which they later regret. This highlights a gap in consumer protection. The current legislation gives consumers who are cold-called a seven-day period in which to cancel a contract. This protection does not apply to consumers who asked for the visit.

Buying in the home provides a unique setting for a business transaction – salespeople effectively have a captive audience. Nearly 40 per cent of consumers have bought goods or services in the home. While 70 per cent of those were satisfied, a significant minority of 30 per cent experienced problems: at least 15,000 complaints a year are made to trading standards departments regarding doorstep sales. Most respondents to the OFT's consumer survey said they felt buying in the home was more pressurised than other settings.

The OFT recommended that the government should extend the legislation to give cancellation rights to solicited visits as well as unsolicited visits. The OFT will also run a consumer education campaign in conjunction with interested groups to raise awareness of consumers' rights and alert them to the psychological techniques used and how to combat them.

Look up the OFT's website and examine two more of its recent investigations, including the remit to the OFT, the decisions it has made and the justification for those decisions.

CONSUMER PROTECTION

Economic theory would argue that rational behaviour by consumers makes their protection unnecessary. Poor-performing products would not survive and consumers simply walk away from poor service. To a large extent that it is true, but the consumer is not always in a position to behave rationally. They may not have sufficient information about the product (hence the need for product description on the label), they may not have a choice of products if an uncontrolled monopoly exists, and they may not be able to challenge a large and unscrupulous supplier. So a whole raft of legislation has been passed in recent years covering all business–consumer relationships and attempting to tighten up legal loopholes. Much of the legislation encoded the common law in place and then extended it. Here is a brief summary of the key features.

Trade Descriptions Act 1968 / Consumer Protection Act 1987

These two acts protect against traders who deliberately give false descriptions of the price, quality and nature of service. These are criminal offences and can result in fines and even imprisonment for repeated offences. The acts are policed by local government Trading Standards officials, who, incidentally, also assist the OFT in gathering information. Examples of cases include:

- advertisements showing massive price reductions when the prices had only been increased the day before (regulations now state that goods must have been sold at the pre-reduction price for 28 continuous days during the previous six months)
- cars being advertised with 'one previous owner', which was a leasing company that had leased the car out for long periods to five different drivers
- prices being advertised but no indication that VAT is to be added.

 MISLEADING REDUCTIONS

CASE STUDY 5.7

MFI was fined £18,000 in 1993 by magistrates in Enfield, north London, for giving out false information on nine counts. They advertised 'massive reductions' and '30 per cent off' furniture suites when, in fact, the prices had been the same for the previous six months, with a number of suites actually having gone up in price at the time of advertising.

The Consumer Protection Act also places strict (but not absolute) liability on suppliers for damage and death/injury caused by defects in their products. There is no need to prove negligence or a contractual relationship, but there is a defence that the state of scientific and technical knowledge at the time the product was supplied was not sufficiently advanced for the defect to be recognised (the 'state of the act' defence).

Unfair Contract Terms Act 1977

Introduced to prevent 'small print' removing consumers' rights, generally without their knowledge, this act has two parts. Firstly, the seller cannot remove the liability for death or injury through negligence under any circumstances. Secondly, a trader cannot enforce a contract term that the courts hold to be unfair. For example, a coach company advertised a tour by luxury coach with videos, toilet, etc, but added in its small print that it reserved the right to substitute a coach of inferior quality. The courts held this to be unfair as it gave too much leeway to the coach company and most customers would not have picked up this particular item among the small print. The claimant was awarded compensation. Most decisions in this area are now dealt with by the OFT through an informal undertaking agreed with the company, and a 2007 example of this is set out in case study 5.8.

CASE STUDY 5.8

UNFAIR CONTRACT TERMS — CARPETRIGHT PLC

Carpetright had a series of clauses in its contracts which the OFT considered unfair. These included:

- all delivery dates were not legally binding
- time was not an essence of the contract
- the fitter, not the company, was responsible for any liability arising from the work carried out
- exclusion of liability if the consumer did not inform the company of the nature of the existing floor surface
- right to charge for cancellation of order without limit.

After consultations between the two parties, these were removed or altered by the company.

(Source: OFT website 2007.)

A number of well-publicised cases and the constant vigilance of consumer societies and other pressure groups have resulted in much greater honesty in communicating the real (and generally reasonable) contract terms by suppliers since this act was passed.

Sale of Goods Act 1979 / Supply of Goods and Services Act 1982

These acts enable dissatisfied customers to take civil action against the supplier. The acts require that:

- goods and services must match the description
- they must be of merchantable quality – in appearance, finish and durability
- they must be fit for the purpose
- services provided must be carried out with reasonable skill and within a reasonable time.

As the Sale of Goods Act has been interpreted, the issue of reasonableness is key. A very cheap pair of canvas shoes is fit for the purpose if they last six months, while a pair of expensive, handmade leathers would not be fit if they wore out after four years' light wear. In essence, it has been for the court to decide what are the bounds of reasonableness, and we shall see this again in the field of employment law.

If the product fails to meet the tests under the act, the consumer has the remedy of the right to their money back, or to receive a credit note, or for the goods to be replaced free of charge, or the consumer can take the goods at a reduced price.

Consumer Credit Act 1974

Introduced following the boom in hire purchase and credit agreements in the 1960s and 1970s, which led to high-pressure selling, especially in people's homes, and high rates of interest. The act took two main directions. Firstly, it aimed to clean up the industry by enforcing licensing of lenders for all credit activities, including credit cards. The licensing involves an inspection regime and a requirement for effective staff training and proper funding of the business.

The second direction was to ensure that contracts were not oppressive. All credit contracts and all contracts signed outside of business premises have a seven-day 'cooling-off' period where the consumer can cancel without loss to either party. The terms of the credit can be altered by the courts if they regard the rate of interest as excessive. The consumer has the right to full details of the agreement before signing, including the annual rate of charge (calculated by means of the current OFT formula), the full cost of the loan, the debtor's right to pay the loan off early and the terms under which they would do so. The act does not apply to loans over an upper limit (currently £25,000) and only applies to consumer credit, not corporate credit.

Additional EU-wide consumer protection has been introduced for ordering on the Web (Electronic Commerce Regulations 2002) and mail order (Consumer Protection (Distance Selling) Regulations 2000).

On pages 208 to 218 we will look in more detail at the effect these laws and additional regulations have in specific sectors and industries.

EMPLOYMENT LAW

The regulation of employment relationships has changed out of all recognition over the last 40 years. Originating from the individual master–servant contract, the fundamental inequality of the parties to the relationship became clear by the mid-nineteenth century and a political party (the Labour Party) was set up essentially with the aim to rectify these inequalities through legislation by establishing employee rights and removing legal restraints on collective bargaining. It was clear that there was a major difference between a conflict over an employment contract that could lead to unemployment and abject poverty, and buying a pair of shoes. Moreover, the evidence of misuse of employer power was widespread.

Although much progress was made in these areas in the early twentieth century, especially in the collective bargaining field, the stimulus to enacting more radical and extensive employee protection has come from the EU. At the same time, the political consensus in recent times has been that the rights granted to trade unions in the collective bargaining field went too far and they were reined in by Conservative governments between 1980 and 1992.

SOURCES OF THE EMPLOYMENT CONTRACT

The terms of an employment contract come from a surprising number of sources. It is not just the express terms, which are those specifically included in the contract (usually set out in the offer letter) such as salary, notice and holiday entitlement. Other sources are of equal importance:

- There are a number of implied terms, originating from common law. These include the duty of the employee to co-operate with the employer in such areas as reasonable changes to the job, exercising due care in looking after the employer's goods and property, and showing loyalty (eg by not disclosing confidential information). The employer also has duties, such as to exercise due care over the employees' health, safety and well-being (see pages 214–218), to provide work, indemnify the employee if he/she incurs loss, expense or liability in carrying out the employer's instruction, and to pay wages on time and correctly.

- Many contracts incorporate collective terms, negotiated between the employer(s) and union(s) either at a local or national level. These may deal with issues such as overtime payment, holidays and disciplinary procedures.

- Contract terms are also incorporated through the Employee Handbook, which sets out the employer's rules and policies to which the employee must sign up.

- Many more unwritten contract terms reflect employment laws covering employee rights and benefits (see pages 204–205).

An additional complication is that the contract terms do not need to be written down. Rules relating to, eg, employees swapping shifts, which have operated informally for some years (ie through custom and practice) with the full knowledge of management, become part of the contract. In claims for unfair dismissal, the tribunal is very keen to establish whether terms written into contracts are those that actually operate in practice. For example, if an employee is dismissed for fighting (as clearly laid out in the Employee Handbook) but it comes to light that the last two occasions when a similar incident occurred, the employees were merely warned, then the tribunal can take the view that custom and practice is that dismissal is not the normal punishment under the contract.

That is not to say contractual terms cannot be changed by either party. An individual employee can request changes to his/her holiday arrangements that are different from the standard contractual terms. Or changes can be negotiated on a collective basis, usually through unions but sometimes through a works council. An employer can change shift arrangements and introduce different work practices and systems. In doing so, they should consult with the workforce, be able to justify the changes for business reasons and ensure they are published widely. They do not need to get every individual's signed agreement to the changes. An employee who continues to work under the changes has deemed to have accepted the changed contract.

A further complication is differentiating between the normal employee contract (the contract of service) and the contract for the self-employed, who work under a contract for services. The legal implications are great in that a different tax regime applies (hence considerable interest by HMRC in this area) and the self-employed have none of the rights and benefits detailed below. Legal tussles have occurred in areas such as commission-only salespeople and those providing occasional but regular services, such as consultants. Although a complex area, the courts examine the degree of control and the nature of exclusivity of contract, which can sometimes overcome the apparent clarity of the payment and tax arrangements.

Under the Employment Rights Act 1996, employers are required to give to each new employee within two months a statement of certain contract terms under 16 headings, which includes details such as the date that continuous employment started, hours of work and holiday entitlement. This is called the principal statement but, to repeat, it is not the actual contract of employment.

EMPLOYEE RIGHTS

The bulk of employment law since the 1970s has been enacted to improve the minimum level of benefits for employees and to protect them from potential employer abuse. There was some earlier legislation in this area, such as the prohibition of child labour and the nine-hour working day in the coal mines from the nineteenth century, but the recent legislation has taken the process much further and allowed employees to benefit extensively from the changes.

Employee protection has been enhanced in the following areas.

Protection from discrimination

Since the 1970s, groups seen as vulnerable in the employment field because of well-evidenced discrimination, harassment and bullying, have been given legal protection. The various acts make it unlawful to discriminate on the grounds of sex, ethnic origin, disability, age, religion or sexual orientation. Discrimination has taken three forms.

Direct discrimination

An instance here would be to advertise for a Girl Friday or to use different criteria for selection for promotion. In the case of race discrimination, it may relate to an employer indicating to a recruitment agency that they do not want black casual workers; or an employer may turn down a deaf or partially sighted applicant specifically because of this disability. In each case, an individual or group is treated less favourably than another on the grounds of sex, race or disability. The employer has no defence even if they genuinely believe what they are doing is right. The motives are irrelevant.

Indirect discrimination

This occurs where the employer treats all applicants or employees the same but a practice, condition or policy adversely affects, for example, one sex or race more than another, or if it affects the disabled more than the able-bodied, or the elderly more than the young. The way it normally adversely affects that group is because the proportion of people from a particular group able to meet the condition or policy is considerably smaller. Moreover, the employer cannot objectively justify the practice, policy or condition. If the employer cannot convince the tribunal that the defence is genuine and substantial, then the employer will lose the case. Tribunal cases have included:

- the requirement to restrict applicants geographically by residence to a specific area, which discriminated against ethnic minorities, whose representation in that area was slight
- recruiting only through word of mouth in an employment site dominated by white males
- promoting internally when the workforce is unbalanced.

The Equal Pay Act 1970 prohibits discrimination in pay and benefits between men and women, where work is 'like' or rated as similar under a job evaluation scheme. In addition, an employee can claim that their work is of 'equal value' to that of another employee of the opposite sex.

Harassment and bullying

Described as 'unwanted behaviour which a person finds intimidating, upsetting, embarrassing, humiliating or offensive', the courts have increasingly punished harassment and bullying, using both the concept of an employer's duty of care and discrimination legislation, supported by the EU Equal Treatment Directive (amended in 2000). This reflects the changing social attitudes in society where a predominately male, white culture in workplaces – where power may be exercised over staff in a vulnerable position – is no longer acceptable in a modern state. It has been accepted by the courts that the judgment as to whether behaviour is acceptable or not comes from the subject(s) of the harassment. There can be additional compensation awarded for 'loss of feelings'.

No service requirement is necessary in any area of discrimination. Protection applies from day one of employment.

Protection from unfair dismissal

Since 1972, employees with one year's service have been protected from arbitrary and unfair dismissal. To successfully defend a claim, the employer has to show that they have a justifiable reason (usually based on poor performance, conduct or redundancy) and that they have carried out the dismissal using the correct procedures. If they fail, the tribunal awards compensation up to a maximum of £65,300 (2010), and, occasionally, can order the employer to reinstate the employee.

ACAS has provided codes of practice in dealing with dismissal and redundancies which organisations need to observe to defend claims successfully. For example, where the offences are deemed to be misdemeanours (timekeeping, attendance, poor performance, etc) warnings are required, whereas with gross misconduct (theft, violence, etc) instant dismissal is permitted. Employees' rights, including that of a fair hearing, having a colleague to help support their case and a fair appeal procedure, must be observed.

The same protection is also afforded against dismissal due to pregnancy or for being a union activist (see case study 5.9).

 DISMISSAL BECAUSE OF PREGNANCY

CASE STUDY 5.9

In *Hildreth v Perdu* (2007) UKEAT 0533/06, Hildreth, a finance manager, endured a campaign of harassment, intimidation, embarrassment and verbal abuse by the company owners after she had told them she was pregnant. They indicated strongly that they would not want to continue to employ her in a pregnant state. Her position had become so difficult that she resigned and successfully claimed constructive dismissal, receiving £8,000 in compensation.

Protection from working excessive hours

Arising from a EU directive, and essentially a health and safety measure, the Working Time Regulations 1998 have had a controversial history. They have established that employees cannot be forced to work in excess of 48 hours a week, averaged over 17 weeks. Employees should have 11 consecutive hours of rest in any 24-hour period and a 24-hour rest in every seven-day period, plus a 20-minute break if the shift exceeds six hours. The regulations also insist on the provision of 27 days' holiday.

The controversial aspect is that employers and employees can agree to opt out of the regulations so that they often apply as a voluntary measure. How voluntary they are and whether the opt-out should remain is discussed later.

Protection when being transferred

The Transfer of Undertakings (Protection of Employment) Regulations 1981 (known as TUPE) were introduced as a result of the EU Acquired Rights Directive. The philosophy here is that employees need to be protected when their organisation is sold to or merged with another organisation, or they are outsourced with their work. Prior to these regulations, employees' terms could be fundamentally and unilaterally altered, with the employees having the choice to accept or leave.

Under the TUPE regulations, all employment terms and conditions are protected (except pensions) and prior service is recognised. This does not stop the new employer having the right to change terms at a later date, but this right is limited by statute. Full consultation must take place with the employees being transferred.

Protection of deductions from pay

Under the Employment Rights Act 1996, employees have the right to an itemised pay statement, and deductions can only be made with prior authorisation from the employee in writing.

Benefits

A summary of the minimum benefits introduced through legislation is set out in table 5.1.

Table 5.1 Employee benefits introduced through legislation

Minimum benefit	Legislation	Summary of key details
Minimum wage	National Minimum Wage Act 1998	Provides low minimum (£5.80 for employees aged 22 and over in 2010); includes bonuses and tips with lower rates for employees under 22. Aims to eradicate exploitative pay in vulnerable sectors, such as homeworkers and hospitality.
Holidays	Working Time (Amendment) Regulations 2007	Minimum entitlement, including public holidays, is 28 days.
Maternity pay	Employment Rights Act 1996 amended by Employment Act 2002	Payable by employers for 39 weeks. Six months' qualifying period paid at 90 per cent of average earnings for six weeks, then £125 per week (2010) for remaining 23 weeks.
Ante-natal care	As above	Right to paid time off during working hours for all ante-natal care and treatment.
Maternity leave	As above	On top of paid maternity leave, an additional 26 weeks' unpaid maternity leave can be taken, with the right to the same job back upon return (see case study 5.10)
Paternity leave and pay	Employment Act 2002	Six months' qualifying period. Applicable to father of child, mother's husband or partner, who is expected to have some responsibility for upbringing of child. Paid for two weeks at £125 per week (2010). Government plan to allow sharing of maternity/paternity leave in 2011.
Adoption leave	Employment Act 2002	One of the parents can take up to 26 weeks' unpaid leave when an adoption takes place. Six months' qualifying service.
Parental leave	Maternity and Parental Leave Regulations 1999	Parents with children under five (or disabled children under 18) can take up to 13 weeks' unpaid leave with the right to return to the same job. One-year qualifying service.

Minimum benefit	Legislation	Summary of key details
Time off for dependants	Employment Rights Act 1996	Reasonable unpaid time can be taken off to provide assistance when a dependant dies, falls ill, gives birth or is injured/assaulted, or when any school problems arise or there is disruption to existing care arrangements. It is not applicable simply to provide normal care on a regular basis and only applies for an immediate crisis. In *Qua v John Ford Morrison Solicitors* [2003] IRLR 184, the EAT confirmed a fair dismissal when Qua took 17 different days to look after her child who had medical problems.
Flexible working	Employment Act 2002/ Employment Rights Act 1996/Work and Families Act 2006	Provides the right of a parent of a child under six years (18 if disabled) to apply for change in working arrangements, including to work flexibly in order to care for the child. Employer can refuse on the basis of burden of additional costs; detrimental effect on ability to meet customer demand or quality of service; and disruption of staff/department. Six months' qualifying period. These rights also cover employees responsible for caring for adults.
Time off for public duties	Employment Rights Act 1996	Reasonable unpaid time can be taken off relating to work as a member of a local authority, health authority or similar.
Time off for trade union duties	Trade Union and Labour Relations (Consolidation) Act 1992	Officials of independent trade unions have right to time off with pay during working hours to carry out reasonable and relevant trade union duties and to undertake training, as specified by the ACAS code of practice.
Statutory sick pay (SSP)	Social Security Contributions and Benefits Act 1992/Statutory Sick Pay Act 1994	Employers are responsible for payment of SSP for up to 28 weeks of sickness/injury in any single period of entitlement.
Redundancy consultation, time off and pay	Trade Union and Labour Relations (Consolidation) Act 1992	Consultation with employees/representatives must take place 90 days before redundancies take effect if 100 or more employees are redundant (30 days if between 20 and 99 employees) and adequate information must be provided by employer. Redundancy pay entitlement at one week's pay (1.5 weeks at age 41 and over, 0.5 from 18 to 21) for each year of service, up to 20 years. The maximum week's pay is £380 (2009). Reasonable time off with pay must be given to look for alternative work.
Time off for study	Employee Study and Training (Procedural Requirements) Regulations 2010	Employees with 26 weeks' service have the right to request time off to train or study. There is no requirement for employers to agree with the request or to give time off with pay, or pay for the training itself.

Notes

- These benefits are correct at the time of writing but are subject to amendment both in terms of the pay arrangements and in other details.

- These are minimum benefits and employers can (and do) improve them by granting pay where there is no entitlement under the legislation, increasing the rates or enhancing the terms and conditions.

RIGHT TO RETURN TO SAME JOB

CASE STUDY 5.10

In *Blundell v St Andrew's Catholic Primary School* UKEAT/0329/06, Blundell, a primary school teacher, was allocated a different class on her return from maternity leave. She claimed she should have returned to teach the same class in the same room. The EAT held her job was to teach at the school, not to teach the same class. The terms and conditions of the job gave the school head discretion in allocating staff, and although staff could indicate a preference, they could not insist on a particular class. The school also pointed out that staff were rotated to different classes and the change in Blundell's class was due to this rotation. But the school lost on its procedure. They did not consult her because she was away on maternity leave (all other staff were consulted), and this was held to be sex discrimination.

REGULATION OF CONTRACTS THROUGH COLLECTIVE BARGAINING

In the nineteenth century, government legislation was put in place to stamp out the infant trade unions, which were attempting to interfere with the employment contract. Over the last 200 years, as explained in Chapter 3, the pendulum has swung, firstly to provide a legal framework for union immunity so union activities are protected in tort, and then back the other way under Thatcherite reforms, where tight restrictions on this immunity were introduced to protect employers from arbitrary union power.

Under a variety of acts in the period 1980–1995, legal immunity is only available for unions in leading their members to break their contracts through strikes or other industrial actions when they:

- have a secret ballot before action is taken (with strict requirements as to notifying the employer, how the ballot should be carried out and who is entitled to vote)

- only take action against their own employer (so-called secondary action against suppliers or customers is not protected)

- carrying out picketing only at their own place of work and in very small numbers (to prevent the dangerous and oppressive mass picketing which took place during the 1984 miners' strike)

- do not insist on a 'closed shop' – employees can join or not join a union as they wish

- ensure they elect their full-time officials on a regular basis under strict governance and follow their own rules on disciplining and expelling members.

Since the 1997 election of a Labour government, the pendulum has somewhat swung back towards improving the regulation of relationships with the workforce, chiefly through organised labour. Firstly, the statutory recognition procedures in the Employment Relations Act 1999 have served to support union members who wish to formally negotiate in the workplace (see activity 5.3). Secondly, the European-initiated Information and Consultation of Employees Regulations 2004 gave rights to employees to be informed and consulted about the business for whom they work. Thirdly, the requirement for proper grievance and disciplinary procedures to be in place and operating fairly in all organisations was set out in the Employment Act 2008.

This conferred discretionary powers on employment tribunals to adjust awards by up to 25 per cent if parties fail unreasonably to comply with a relevant code of practice.

Not all attempts at legislation in this field obtain the desired result. For example, the main intention behind the Employment Act 2002 (Dispute Resolution) Regulations 2004 (predecessor of the Employment Act 2008), was to cut down on tribunal claims by encouraging employers to set up and follow appropriate procedures and insisting that employees exercised their rights to hearing and appeals under such procedures. Either side would be penalised when they did not follow procedures. However, after three years of operations, the number of unfair dismissal claims actually increased, chiefly due to the number of disputes over the nature and operation of such internal procedures and the legal wrangles associated with the disputes. Cases have taken longer to settle and the whole process was reviewed in 2007, leading to the regulations being abandoned.

 ACTIVITY 5.3 UNION RECOGNITION

An application was made to the Central Arbitration Committee (CAC) in 2009 by GMB union for the right to carry out a recognition ballot for manual staff at Canal Engineering. The employer had responded to the request by stating that an agreement already existed with Unite, another trade union, and that a staff council carried out the role that the union recognition claim would try to meet. When CAC investigated this issue, it found that the previous union agreement had expired in 2006. The union claimed that 26 out of the 34 employees were already members. CAC carried out an independent survey and found that 23 out of 39 employees were in the proposed bargaining unit and that the staff council was ineffective. It therefore approved the union right for recognition for bargaining purposes.

Look up the website for CAC (www.cac.gov. uk) and examine a further two of the decisions that they have taken recently, including the parties involved, the background to the dispute over recognition and the justification for the decision.

IMPLICATIONS OF REGULATION

Earlier in this chapter, the roles of the OFT and Competition Commission in disseminating, regulating and enforcing commercial and consumer legislation were set out. Additional industry-specific regulation has been put in place over the last 20 years, and this section will examine the operation of a selection of these regulators and their implications in the fields of privatised utilities, financial services, communications and areas of the public sector.

INDUSTRY REGULATORS – PRIVATISED UTILITIES

During the period 1980–1995, public utilities in the UK were privatised in what is now seen as a momentous and generally successful business revolution. The Labour Party ideology of nationalisation of key industries, which led to coal, steel, gas, electricity, railways and many others coming under state control in the post-war period until 1976, was replaced by the free-trade and competition philosophy, promulgated by Milton Friedman (1970). It had become clear that the philosophy of moving towards a centrally controlled interventionist state operation, which had operated for the previous 20 years in western economies, had failed to produce the economic success that had been promised. Managers in state-controlled industries complained of constant ministerial interference, starvation of investment and regular changes in strategic direction. At its peak, almost 10 per cent of GDP came under government control. By 2002, after privatisation, this had been reduced to only 1 per cent.

Detailed studies (Martin and Parker 1997, Electricity Association 1998) have shown that since privatisation labour productivity has risen at an average of 15 per cent, service provision has improved substantially, and prices have generally fallen, especially in telecommunications and electricity.

In Chapter 3, you will have read about the issues associated with the privatisation of state monopolies. The model for privatisation was essentially one of attempting to break up state monopolies, introducing a variety of methods to stimulate competition and to keep a measure of control through regulation in the interests of the consumer. Unbundling has involved separating out the potentially competitive areas (eg electricity generation, telecommunication value-added services) from the monopoly part (eg transmission and distribution grids, telephone lines to homes). This picture has been repeated across Europe with only a handful of mostly Scandinavian governments owning the state telecommunications company, reinforced by EU directives requiring member states to establish independent regulatory agencies to provide a 'level playing field' for potential competitors (Pollack 1997, Curwen 1997). This policy has continued with EU accession states having to sign up to privatisation of their main utilities.

Regulators

In each privatised sector in the UK, a regulator has been appointed to oversee the operation of the business for the benefit of the consumer (business and private) and to try to ensure that privatisation actually works in practice. The main responsibilities of the regulator are to:

- set out the pricing model (with or without agreement from the participants)
- establish and monitor service standards
- encourage the working of a competitive market
- ensure stable sources of supply (in the case of products such as gas and electricity)
- prevent the exercise of any remnant of monopolistic power
- ensure the industry meets social and environmental responsibilities.

The regulator is appointed by the government but is independent of government control. Each industry has been faced by a specific business context and the model of regulation has constantly been changed as the nature of the competitive challenges within each sector has altered. For example, one of the major issues in the telecommunication industry has been the role of the dominant provider, BT, which originally controlled landlines into most of UK homes. The challenge was to encourage competition to this control, achieved mainly through the development of cable and mobile phone systems; complex agreements allowing other companies access to the landlines to provide alternative services; and through acting as a mediator in resolving disputes between the parties, such as the dispute in 2004 over Number Translation Services discounts. The telecommunications industry has, in fact, moved from one monopoly provider in 1984 (BT) to over 75 providers in 2007, while the degree of competition in the power industry has extended so far that 2.6 million customers switched their electricity supply in the first six months of 2007. In 2004, industry regulator Ofgem fined Powergen £700,000 after the company stopped more than 20,000 domestic customers from switching to new gas/electricity contracts.

In another sector, the policy of the water industry regulator Ofwat has changed over recent years. At the time of privatising in the early 1990s, the water industry was allowed to make a substantial increase to fund the considerable investment required to transform sewage treatment, reduce effluent discharge and thereby improve water quality around the UK coastline. However, in 2009, the regulator drafted a new five-year pricing regime which required water companies to cut prices by 0.2 per cent per year and increase capital expenditure. Since the draft publication, a number of water companies have called a halt to capital projects which has lead to redundancies among engineering companies supplying the water industry (Waples 2009). Despite this pressure, the final decision by Ofwat in November 2009 confirmed tight price controls.

In terms of its policing role, Ofwat fined United Utilities £8.5 million in 2007 for breaching rules governing trading arrangements with associated companies, and threatened to revoke their licence.

The ability to set pricing models (unsuccessfully challenged in the courts in the mid-1990s by the gas industry) and to discipline players in the industry has given the regulator substantial power over operating companies. However, the need for establishing a fair pricing model has been reduced in recent years as more sophisticated markets have been introduced into gas and electricity (see above), allowing more providers to enter the market and create more competition, while natural competition has developed in the telecommunications industry.

INDUSTRY REGULATION – FINANCIAL SERVICES AND COMMUNICATIONS

A second strand of regulation covers two industries that the state regards as needing special forms of regulation: financial services and communication. These are industries which, generally, have not been government-owned (apart from the BBC and BT), but where there is a strong public interest. This interest is not just to preserve or encourage competition but to inspire confidence in the financial or communication systems, regulate ethical behaviour and to act as a watchdog over technical developments.

Ofcom

Ofcom, set up in 2003, covers activities previous controlled by, among others, the Broadcasting Standards Commission, Radio Authority, Oftel and the Independent Television Commission. It has a duty to 'balance the promotion of choice and competition with the duty to foster plurality, informed citizenship, protect viewers, listeners and customers and promote cultural diversity' (Ofcom 2010). Its activities include the following:

- Competition policy:
  - reform of public service broadcasting, the effects of digital television on the BBC's channel provision and the regular licence review
  - policy on awarding of radio and ITV licences
  - policy on television advertising under a single terrestrial commercial provider (ITV)
  - advising the government on foreign takeover of major communication players, such as national newspapers.

- Protecting small players – producing codes on the ability of independent programme producers to retain their programming rights.

- Technology reviews – advising on the digital switchover between 2007 and 2012.

- Protecting public morals – advising on television programme content in terms of sex and violence.

Financial Services Authority

Regulating financial markets has, in recent years, been a key part of government economic activity. Understanding that confidence is at the heart of a country's financial system, and fearful of the meltdown that could occur should this confidence suddenly evaporate, governments have established systems of financial supervision to try to avoid rogue activities. Much of this authority has been delegated to the Bank of England, but a good part of the detailed supervision, investigation and enforcement has gradually been taken up by the Financial Services Authority (FSA) whose main aims are set out in figure 5.2.

Figure 5.2 Aims of FSA

Securing the right degree of protection for consumers	Vetting firms and individuals trading in specific areas, such as financial advisers and credit providers, for honesty, competence and financial soundness. Monitoring how these standards are met in practice. When problems arise, investigation takes place and, if appropriate, disciplinary action or prosecution results.
Promoting public understanding of the financial system	Communications and publicity to try to ensure that the consumer is more knowledgeable and can manage their financial affairs more effectively.
Maintaining confidence in the UK financial system	Supervising exchanges, settlement houses and market infrastructure providers (IT, etc), conducting market surveillance and monitoring transactions.
Helping to reduce financial crime	Investigating cases that may involve money laundering, fraud and dishonesty and criminal market misconduct such as insider trading.

The FSA certainly has teeth. Examples of disciplinary action from the FSA website in 2009 include:

- Fining Barclays Capital Securities Ltd and Barclays Bank Plc (Barclays) £2.45 million for failing to provide accurate transaction reports to the FSA and for serious weaknesses in systems and controls in relation to transaction reporting.

- Fining Christopher Davies, director of Newquay Investment Services (2004) Limited, an independent financial advisor based in Cornwall, £17,500 for not disclosing to the FSA important information about an adviser Davies had employed at Newquay. This led to an unacceptable risk of customers being recommended unsuitable mortgages. After Newquay had applied to the FSA last year for the adviser to be confirmed as an approved person, Davies became aware that the adviser's previous employer had suspended the adviser because of concerns about his business methods and ethics including apparently inflating income figures in mortgage applications. Davies raised these concerns with the adviser and concluded that the adviser had lied to him about why he had left his previous employment. Davies then failed to disclose this significantly adverse information to the FSA.

- Banning Newcastle Home Loans from carrying out regulated mortgage activities, together with its directors who have been heavily fined, the maximum being £85,000. The directors knowingly submitted mortgage applications to a lender containing false information resulting in the lender unsuspectingly advancing sums which were higher than the purchase price of the property. Northumbria police have subsequently arrested four of the directors.

As a direct result of the financial crisis of 2007–10, the FSA issued a Code of Practice on Remuneration Practices in August 2009 which applied to 26 large financial institutions (banks, building societies and investment firms). This code aims to discourage the payment of large cash bonuses for short-term gains, which has been considered as one of the major causes of the recent crisis as this encouraged substantial risk-taking.

The essential features of the code were:

- bonuses should be based on employees' long-term contributions to minimise the impact of volatility on awards
- profits should determine bonus pools, which should be adjusted to reflect current and future risk profiles
- a proportion of bonuses should be deferred to reflect the long-term aspects of financial performance
- firms should be able to explain how individual pay awards have been calculated
- the practice of agreeing 'guaranteed bonuses' for new employees should be discouraged and limited to a period of one year only.

This code has been criticised by commentators on a number of counts:

- It is only a code and therefore non-binding, except on those organisations where the UK government has a majority holding. Although the affected companies have signed up to the code, no action can be taken for any subsequent evasions. 'Toothless' is a word that has been often used.
- The FSA has retreated from its original position on the deferment of bonuses. It previously was an important 'principle' but has been converted to 'good practice' in the final version.
- Restriction on bonuses will affect the long-term position of the City of London as the top performers will move to unregulated companies in places such as the Gulf or Hong Kong. In 2009, there were a number of anecdotal examples of this occurring.

This issue is an important example of the difficulty of applying regulation in a global economy. Without international agreement, organisations and individuals will migrate to those countries which have the most amenable forms of regulation.

A further difficulty in the financial sector has been the allocation of regulatory responsibility. The responsibilities of the FSA can overlap with those of the Bank of England and the Treasury. In the Northern Rock crisis of 2007–08 much of the problem has been put down to the confusion between these three regulatory bodies. Despite these criticisms, the government has found it difficult to change the system without reaching some form of agreement in the EU and across the world (Dey and Smith 2009).

REGULATION AND THE PUBLIC SECTOR

The Audit Commission carries out a different form of regulation in the public sector. It is a true 'watchdog', carrying out investigations into the operations of local authorities, health services and government departments. It principally examines issues of efficiency and ethical behaviour, endeavouring to establish realisable targets, examples of best practice and to shame poor performers into change by publicising their faults. Although it has no executive power to change an organisation's policies or practices, the government takes note of its findings when it takes decisions over funding, especially with local authorities. It has had a degree of success in leading public organisations to carefully examine their methods of operation and benchmark their performance against similar bodies.

REGULATION AND OTHER SECTORS

Although most sectors operate without a specific regulator, they are touched by regulation in a number of ways:

- their practices may be investigated by the OFT and Competition Commission, such as the doorstep selling example above
- a planned merger or takeover can be referred to the Competition Commission to decide if it breaches the monopolies guidelines, such as was threatened in the 2003 battle over Safeway plc.
- their detailed operations can be constrained by UK or European law in areas such as labelling and packaging, information to consumers or environmental regulations
- planning laws have become increasingly intrusive, such as the government policy in 2000 to reject any further out-of-town shopping developments, including supermarkets, because of their effect on traffic growth and decline of the local high street.

CODES OF PRACTICE

Each of the regulators is authorised to produce codes of practices. Ofgem, for example, has produced a code of practice for the action that should be taken when a provider proposes to cut off a consumer's gas or electricity supply, and Ofcom has a Code of Advertising Practice. They do not in themselves have a force of law but they have strong influence on business behaviour. They help to raise standards throughout the industry, stopping organisations from indulging in dubious practices which, although not illegal, give the industry a bad name. Many organisations are happy to accept and influence the production of a code rather than having a legal restrictions imposed on them.

ACTIVITY 5.4 BENEFITS OF REGULATORY SYSTEM

What are the benefits of a regulatory system as opposed to a state-controlled system?

HEALTH AND SAFETY REGULATION

The protection of employees in the workplace has been extended in recent years by a substantial collection of legislation emanating from both Europe and the UK. Regulation of health and safety in the UK is very extensive with over 100 current pieces of legislation. Although there has been a steady decline in the number of deaths and serious accidents over the last decades, over 200 people are killed in accidents at work each year, including nearly 100 members of the public. Not only is this a huge waste of HR but it is very costly for the economy. The main aim of the regulation, therefore, is to reduce the number of accidents and resultant ill health and to ensure that a safety-conscious culture becomes widespread so that business can operate more efficiently.

Role of HR in health and safety

In the majority of organisations where separate HR departments exist, they either have responsibility for health, safety and welfare issues in that organisation or they play a major part in those activities. The main activities are outlined below.

Formulating policies and procedures

This activity is more than a formality required by law. It is essential that new employees understand how safety works within an organisation, and the policies and procedures will set out how the safety responsibilities are structured, and the requirements from each employee. Specific references to areas (such as responsibility for checking lifting gear, or guards) should be clearly spelt out. The document should give a statement of management intent as to how safety issues will be treated in the workplace. Detailed procedures should be set out for dealing with emergencies, safety training, information arising from the investigations under the Control of Substances Hazardous to Health Act 1988 (COSHH), and procedures should be set out for all departments where hazards have been identified. HR should ensure that such documents are logical, readable and have been circulated correctly.

Monitoring policies and procedures

At regular intervals, all procedures need examining to see if they need updating to take account of new processes, materials and layouts. By attending management and safety meetings, HR can ensure such necessary revisions can be identified and put into place.

Advising management and employees on safety legislation

The defining legislation is the Health and Safety at Work Act 1974, but HR practitioners should be aware of other legislation dealing, for example, with control of substances hazardous to health, reporting of diseases and dangerous occurrences (1995) and those relating to manual handling and display screens. New regulations continue to emerge, especially from Europe, with different levels of importance and implementation dates.

Designing, providing and recording health and safety training

Systematic training is essential if procedures are to operate properly. It should start with induction training to ensure that employees who are involved in any hazardous operation have instruction in key areas before they set foot on the work site. Safety instruction should be incorporated into any new processes or where new materials are introduced on to site. There is a legal requirement to recognise safety representatives and they have the right for time off for training.

Assisting in risk assessments

It is a legal duty for employers to assess and record health and safety risks for all of their operations. Much of this work involves attempting to balance the nature of the risks, their seriousness in terms of likely danger to employees and the cost of implementing protection from these risks.

Identifying and dealing with occupational stress

Stress has become one of the most serious health issues of recent years. A survey by the HSE (2006) estimated that stress cost nearly £10 billion per year in the UK, over 2 per cent of GDP, close to £400 per employee per year. The number of work-related stress cases reaching the courts rose to 6,428 in 2003 (Palmer and Quinn 2004). 12.8 million working days were lost to stress, anxiety and depression in 2004–05 (Yarker and Lewis 2007). Employees aged between 34 and 44 suffer the most, while the problems worsen the longer they stay in the same job.

The causes of occupational stress are numerous. They are associated with perceptions of job insecurity, increase in work intensity, aggressive management styles, lack of effective workplace communication, overt or insidious bullying and harassment, faulty selection for promotion or transfer, and lack of guidance and training (Cartwright and Cooper 1997). Employees may be exposed to situations which they find uncomfortable, such as continually dealing with customers, excessive computer work, repetitive or fragmented work, or having to make regular public presentations. Probably the most common cause, however, is the constant fear of organisational change through restructuring, takeovers, mergers or business process re-engineering. A lack of control over their work, their environment or their career progression can also be stressful (Rick et al 1997).

When a work environment containing these cultural aspects is added to personal problems, such as divorce or separation, ill or dying relatives, difficult housing conditions and financial problems, then it is not surprising that the employer will be faced with a good proportion of employees with stress-related problems.

Stress is manifested not only in high absence levels. Fatigue, increases in infections, backache and digestive illnesses are commonly found. Irritation, hostility, anxiety and a state of panic can arise in the workplace with knock-on effects on working practices and relationships between employees. The end result may be that the employee is 'burnt out', unable to cope with pressures that previously had been regarded as challenging and stimulating. Employees may also turn to palliatives, such as alcohol or drugs.

The employer who neglects the problem of occupational stress may face legal action. The first legal breakthrough for an employee was John Walker, a social work manager with Northumberland County Council who, having had a mental breakdown arising from his occupation, returned to his job but received no positive assistance from his employer to help him to cope successfully. (As set out on page 184.)

Successive cases have included a primary school head who won £100,000 after suffering two nervous breakdowns allegedly caused by stress brought on from bullying and harassment, and an out-of-court settlement reached in 1998 between an NHS trust and the bereaved spouse of an employee who committed suicide. In a later case, Birmingham City Council admitted liability for personal injury caused by stress where they moved a 39-year-old senior draughtsman to the post of a neighbourhood housing officer without sufficient training. The nature of the work was so different and the interpersonal demands so great that she suffered long periods of ill health leading to early retirement on medical grounds. She was awarded £67,000 (Miller 1999).

Greater clarification as to the employer's responsibility in the case of psychiatric injury resulting from exposure to unacceptable levels of stress was given by the Court of Appeal in 2002 (*Sutherland v Hatton* [2002] IRLR 263). The court held that an employer was entitled to assume that an employee was able to withstand the normal pressures of the job and to take what the employee said about her own health at face value. It was only if there were indications that would lead a reasonable employer to realise that there was a problem that a duty to take action would arise. In terms of whether the injury to health was foreseeable, factors that should be taken into account include whether:

- the workload was abnormally heavy
- the work was particularly intellectually or emotionally demanding
- the demands were greater compared to similar employees.

If the only way of making the employee safe was to dismiss him/her, then there would be no breach of duty by letting the employee continue if he/she was willing to do so (IRS 2002).

An organisation's responsibilities for stress reduction was shown in stark outline in 2008 when the HSE issued an improvement notice to United Lincolnshire NHS Hospitals Trust for 'failing to identify the potential risks to the health and safety of its employees from exposure to work-related stress'. The issue in this case was the complete lack of a work-related stress policy and a risk assessment (Scott 2009).

All of these cases show that employers need to carefully consider the way that the work demands affect their employees and ensure that they investigate each case, taking appropriate action to ameliorate potentially health-damaging situations (Earnshaw and Cooper 1996). A further consideration is the level of employees' expectations of welfare provision. A sympathetic and caring employer will make special provision for the personal and individual needs of employees. Finally, an CIPD study (Tehrani 2002) has shown that employers who have some form of 'wellness' programmes incurred annual employment costs of between £1,335 and £2,910 less per employee than employers who did not.

 ## ACTIVITY 5.5 STRESS

You have been brought in as a consultant to carry out a review of the level of stress in an organisation. Having investigated safety and welfare statistics, and carried out an employee attitude survey, you report on the following indicators of stress:

- The absenteeism levels had risen from 6 per cent to 9 per cent over the last three years, of which 3 per cent was reported as being caused by stress-related illnesses.

- The number of staff on long-term sick had increased from eight to 14, with six incidents of stress or other mental problems.

- The level of reported accidents had doubled from 12 to 24 over the same period.

- There had been three incidents of violence inside the site, two alcohol-induced. Five employees had been dismissed as a result, two of whom took claims to employment tribunals.

- The staff attitude survey showed that over 70 per cent considered that they worked excess hours, which caused stress 'occasionally' or 'regularly'.

- 20 per cent of staff found that their relationships with their managers were 'poor' or 'very poor'.

- 30 per cent believed that urgent improvements in their physical environment were required.

What advice would you give to the employer to alleviate the causes of stress in this organisation?

Helping create a healthy working environment.

All the research indicates that a healthy workforce will be a successful and higher-performing one, so being proactive in introducing and encouraging initiatives to support health programmes can make a substantial difference to organisational performance, as shown in case study 5.11.

IMPROVING EMPLOYEE HEALTH AT KIMBERLY-CLARK

Kimberly-Clark, which makes products such as Kleenex and Huggies nappies, has made cost savings of £500,000 per annum and reduced long-term staff absence from 6.8 per cent to 0.5 per cent after launching schemes in 2002 aimed at improving the health of its 174 UK staff. Under the programme, the company introduced work–life balance coaching sessions, massages for desk workers and sleep management workshops to improve employees' sleep quality. It also provided free fruit twice a week to promote healthy eating. Evidence that the scheme was producing immediate results was that, after six months, only 19 per cent said they suffered sleep problems, which was down from 68 per cent before the scheme started.

(Source: Watkins 2003.)

A test of overall success is whether a safety-conscious culture pervades the organisation. This is shown through management operating systems and procedures not just because of the legal requirements but because they see that it makes good business sense, both in terms of reducing costs arising from accidents and from establishing a caring relationship with the labour force.

TRENDS TO WATCH

Governments of all shapes – both EU and UK – find it difficult to restrain themselves from introducing legislation, so expect developments in the following areas:

- In employment law, the extension of flexible working rights in the UK beyond working parents and carers, and a resolution of the long-standing debate on the rights of what the EU calls 'atypical working', such as agency workers.
- In consumer protection, greater clarification and consistency on the roles of regulators, the OFT and the Competition Commissions, with a more consistent approach across Europe.

HOW FAR SHOULD REGULATION EXTEND?

There have been two major debates concerning the extent and development of regulation in recent years. The first covers the breadth of the regulation – the degree to which regulation should be local, national or international. The second deals with the depth of the regulation – how tightly it should apply and in what detail. We shall deal with each of these in turn.

BREADTH OF REGULATION

Governments in the West have led the way in most areas of regulation, from creating and protecting individual employment rights to enhancing consumer power and protecting the environment. However, this action has been taken at a number of levels, as shown in environmental regulation in the UK (Brooks and Weatherston 2004).

At the local level, local authorities have a number of responsibilities, including food hygiene, pest control and noise pollution. At the national level, a number of enabling laws, such as the Environmental Protection Act 1990 and the Environment Act 1995, cover a wide area of environmental control, including waste disposal and recycling requirements, mostly enforced by the Environment Agency. At the international level, the EU has taken a number of initiatives through Environment Action programmes to obtain compliance across the EU, with mixed success. Many attempts have been made by governments to agree to international environmental standards, the most well known being the Kyoto Protocol in 1997, which has mixed take-up during the twenty-first century. There have been numerous attempts subsequently to gain worldwide approval to standards of greenhouse gas emissions and systems of carbon emission trading.

The benefits of operating at different levels are:

- it involves all communities at whatever level to get involved in subjects that affect them

- without multi-level involvement, it would be difficult to get general support for regulatory action

- a combination of experimental policies can be tried out in different countries (or within countries) to see which ones can work and to identify the main problems faced

- it is recognised that international agreement is always problematic, so it is foolish to wait for a complete international solution before acting. Partial success is seen as better than no progress

- the long-term aim of organisations and countries operating and competing on a level playing field is to be applauded and has been successful in some areas, such as agreements within the World Trade Organisation.

The disadvantages of operating at different levels are:

- the raft of regulation can be very confusing for companies trying to operate within the law

- international companies may choose to locate to the less regulated environments. Most shipping companies, for example, operate with 'flags of convenience' in countries which have little enforcement on labour rights and minimum health and safety regulation. Similar action has been threatened recently by hedge funds

- there is little optimism that some countries, such as China, will accept international regulation and the slow progress in increasing the breadth of regulation allows them to continue to operate as accepted competitors without having to change their policies in fields such as ecological effects and human rights, because there is not the willpower to penalise them.

DEPTH OF REGULATION

There is much debate as to the degree of regulation that is ideal for a society. The current trend is for government to steadily increase the intensity of regulation in all fields, this being their main thrust of legislation. Occasional attempts to reverse the tide, such as Margaret Thatcher's policies on privatisation and encouraging more competition in the financial and other sectors, though having a good degree of success, can be set against the huge amount of additional legislation in recent years in enhancing labour rights, controlling financial activities, increasing planning controls and protecting the environment.

Those who doubt the benefits of additional regulation put forward the following arguments:

- Regulation discourages entrepreneurial activity and therefore restricts job creation, especially in small organisations, which have to cope with an annual raft of laws with which they have to comply, despite having few resources to judge the degree and cost of compliance necessary.

- Regulation is expensive. There are large costs involved in obtaining agreement, especially on the international front, in terms of providing incentives for poorer countries and those less willing to comply, let alone the huge costs of endless international conferences. There are similar large costs in enforcing the regulations. It has been estimated that 50,000 UK staff are employed within financial organisations to ensure compliance to regulation set out by the Bank of England and the FSA.

- Some businesses argue that regulation goes too far. In the field of employment law, for example, much lobbying continues to take place to try to ensure the UK national minimum wage is kept as low as possible, and French employers have attempted, with some success, to reverse the legislation which introduced the 35-hour working week. The rapid increase in financial regulation has been hotly opposed by many companies, although the opposition has been much quieter of late following the worldwide credit crunch of 2008–10.

KEY LEARNING POINTS

- UK law can be divided into criminal and civil law and originates chiefly from legislation emanating from the EU, the UK parliament and common law. Courts are bound by precedent.

- The last 30 years have seen a substantial increase in the volume and intensity of legislation to protect employees and consumers with increased regulation of business activity.

- The burden of this legislation has been borne by businesses, which need to adapt their operations to ensure compliance.

- A larger emphasis has been put on organisations carrying out safety audits and risk assessment to ensure accident prevention and a healthier workplace.

- Few sectors now manage to avoid a form of regulation, with a substantial presence in the privatised utilities and the financial and communications sectors, where regulators have considerable legal powers.

- Consumers are also protected through the regulation of markets to prevent the use of monopolistic powers by large organisations.

1. What are the main roles of the OFT?

2. What actions should HR practitioners take to improve health and safety?

3. Set out the main influences on governments which have led to the enhancement of consumer rights through legislation from the 1960s onwards.

4. What are the main sources of the employment contract?

5. Describe the main roles of a regulator in the utilities sector.

6. Give six examples of legislation introduced in the UK to give protection to employees.

7. Trace the path of a tribunal application through the UK/European courts.

8. What is the meaning of the expression 'precedent' under UK law?

9. What are the six main elements in any contract?

10 What are the responsibilities of an employer concerning stress in the workplace?

EXPLORE FURTHER

Further Reading

There are large numbers of legal textbooks available dealing with the English legal system. Some cover the whole picture, including criminal and civil law; others specialise in areas such as contract law, commercial law or employment law. It is worthwhile for the HR practitioner to have a general legal textbook on their shelves together with a specialist book on employment law. Current publications of the latter include:

- Lewis, D. and Sargeant, M. (2009) *Essentials of Employment Law*. London: CIPD.

- Daniels, K. (2008) *Employment Law, An Introduction*. London: CIPD.

In terms of legal issues relating to discrimination, a good source is:

- Daniels, K. and MacDonald, L. (2005) *Equality, Diversity and Discrimination*. London: CIPD.

For financial regulation, a good introductory approach is given in:

- Gray, J. and Hamilton, J. (2006) *Implementing Financial Regulation*. London: Wiley.

SEMINAR ACTIVITY

RACE DISCRIMINATION

In 2004, Mahmood Siddiqui, aged 59, was awarded £180,000 from the Royal Mail arising from a four-year campaign of racial abuse at work. He was repeatedly sworn at, bullied and called a 'Paki' by colleagues at a sorting office in Harlow, Essex. One one occasion, one of them ignited a cigarette lighter in front of him and threatened to burn him. Others daubed offensive graffiti including the messages 'Siddiqui hang him' and 'Paki scab lover'. His car was vandalised and threats were made to his wife and children.

Despite repeated complaints to his managers, the racial harassment continued with 'tacit support' from his boss. It was only some time later when a hidden camera was installed that the culprits were caught and disciplined. By then, Mr Siddiqui, the only non-white on the night shift, was suffering severe stress. Ill health forced him to retire in 2002 after 12 years' service. The tribunal commented that, 'throughout the case, the word "banter" was used. We consider this to have often been employed as a euphemism for racial abuse for which he alone was singled out.' His award consisted of £104,000 for loss of earnings, plus £20,000 for loss of interest and £8,000 legal costs together with £48,000 for personal injury and injury to feelings.

Questions

1. What action should the organisation have taken when the complaints were first made?

2. What specific steps should HR departments take to try to prevent such action occurring in their organisations?

CHAPTER 6

The World Economy

LEARNING OUTCOMES

By the end of this chapter, you should be able to understand, explain and critically evaluate:

- the role and functions of the European Union (EU) and its major institutions
- debates about the evolution of the EU (integration and enlargement)
- major international bodies that impact on the business environment of organisations (International Monetary Fund, World Bank, World Trade Organisation)
- the causes and extent of globalisation processes
- multinational and transnational organisations, and their HR systems
- major debates about the significance and desirability of globalisation
- the response of governmental organisation to globalisation processes
- the impact of globalisation on markets for goods and services
- the impact of globalisation on employment and labour markets
- management and HR styles in selected members of the G20
- Geert Hofstede's cultural dimensions.

INTRODUCTION

Should the UK hold a referendum on the Lisbon Treaty? Is globalisation good or bad for the developing world? These are the kinds of issues that will be explored in this chapter on the international economy.

Since the end of the Second World War, the world economy has become more and more integrated. Partly this has been a deliberate, planned development. The International Monetary Fund (IMF), the World Bank and the General Agreement on Tariffs and Trade were set up to regulate the world economy, and to ensure that the world did not suffer a recurrence of the Great Depression of the 1930s. The European Economic Community (EEC), the predecessor of the EU, was set up partly to ensure that France and Germany could never again go to war with each other. Other developments were only made possible as a result of technological developments in communication and transport which enabled the growth of globalisation.

THE EUROPEAN UNION

THE HISTORICAL BACKGROUND TO THE EU

The origins of the EU go back to the period just after the Second World War, when there was a strong desire in continental Europe (particularly France and West Germany) to ensure that a further war would be impossible.

The founding states of the EEC, set up by the Treaty of Rome in 1957, were France, West Germany, Italy, Belgium, the Netherlands and Luxembourg. Britain declined an invitation to join, seeing its economic interests as lying much more with the US and the Commonwealth.

The UK, Ireland and Denmark joined in 1973, Greece in 1981, Spain and Portugal in 1986, and Sweden, Austria and Finland in 1995. The former East Germany automatically joined upon German reunification in 1990. Norway twice negotiated entry, but on each occasion was rejected by a referendum. Switzerland did not apply to join, citing its long-standing policy of strict neutrality (it is not even a member of the United Nations), but it has close economic relations with the EU.

In 1976, the institution adopted the name European Community, and the Maastricht Treaty of 1992 adopted the name European Union from 1 January 1993.

Up to the end of the twentieth century, the EU was very much a Western European club. With the exception of Greece, Spain and Portugal, which had recent histories of fascist rule, all the members were long-standing stable, prosperous, democratic countries. This changed fundamentally with the next enlargement, from 15 to 25 members on 1 May 2004. This came about with the accession of five post-communist central European states (Poland, Hungary, the Czech Republic, Slovakia and Slovenia), the three Baltic states of Estonia, Latvia and Lithuania, which had previously been republics within the USSR, and two small Mediterranean islands (Malta and Cyprus). The implications of this expansion for the EU will be considered below.

THE AIMS OF THE EU

The EU has a number of general aims. These include:

- upholding peace in Europe by integrating national economies
- increasing prosperity by developing a single market
- easing inequalities between people and regions
- pooling the energies of member states for technological and industrial development
- developing an effective means of resolving political disputes
- implementing a Union-wide social policy

- implementing European Monetary Union
- assisting people of the Third World.

These aims reflect a number of different perceptions concerning the future development of the Union (Morris and Willey 1996).

Single market ('single European market')

This sees the EU in economic terms, and concentrates on removal of national restrictions which limit the free movement of labour, capital, goods and services. In effect, the EU is seen as solely a free-trade area, without a political dimension. Common political institutions should be minimal, and so should the structure of EU law, which should be limited to that necessary to ensuring that the single market functions effectively. The single market concept underpinned the early development of the European Community, and reached its fullest expression in the Single European Act 1986, which led to the setting up of the single European market in 1993. At least in theory, this ensured the free movement of labour, capital, goods and services. However, this does not fully work in practice. For example, the Schengen Agreement in 1990 eliminated internal border controls within the EU, meaning that travel within the EU was possible without a passport, but the agreement has never been implemented by the UK and Ireland.

Federalist ('United States of Europe')

Here the EU is seen as having the structure of a federal state like the US or Germany – a central, or federal government which sets the general direction of policy, and local governments (states in the US, Länder in Germany, nation states in the EU) which are responsible for the practical administration of policy. Some political mechanism is needed at the centre to preside on overall policy, but this should be kept to a minimum. The function of EU law is to settle disputes between the central authority and the member states. Central to this perspective is the concept of subsidiarity, which says that as a matter of principle, decision-making in the EU should be taken at the lowest possible level.

Integrationist ('Europe')

The aim here is ultimately a long-term shift of power from member states to EU-wide institutions. The classic example of this is Economic and Monetary Union, which led to a single currency (the euro), and to control of EU monetary policy passing from member states to the European Central Bank. Subsidiarity may still apply, but the member states would only have those powers specifically delegated to them by the central government. EU law would not only settle disputes between member states and the centre, but would also directly impinge on EU citizens.

The issue of how far to move towards the integrationist model underpins the ongoing argument about an EU constitution, which has occupied much of the EU's efforts since the Nice Summit in 2000, and is discussed in detail below.

ACTIVITY 6.1 MODELS OF THE EU

- Which of the models of EU organisation (single market, federalist, integrationist) would best describe the view of the following political parties in the UK?
  - New Labour
  - Conservative
- Liberal Democrat
- UK Independence Party.
- Why do the other members of the EU feel that true implementation of the single market also requires harmonisation of taxation, and why does the UK oppose this?

THE INSTITUTIONS OF THE EU

In this section, we examine the institutions of the EU as they were just before the massive changes made in mid-2004: the EU enlargement of May 2004, from 15 to 25 members, and the agreement on the EU Constitution, in June 2004. In later sections, we will look at the impact of the enlargement and of the Constitution, and its successor, the Lisbon Treaty.

Responsibility for achieving the aims of the EU rests with four institutions:

- the Commission
- the Council of Ministers
- the European Parliament
- the European Court of Justice.

And two auxiliary bodies:

- the European Central Bank
- the Economic and Social Committee.

The Commission

The Commission is the executive of the EU. It is responsible both for proposing policy and legislation, and for implementing policy after it has been agreed. It is completely independent of member states, even though its members are appointed by the member states.

Before the 2004 enlargement, the Commission had 20 members, two each from France, Germany, the UK, Italy and Spain, and one from each of the other member states. Each commissioner was responsible for an area of EU policy. The Commission is headed by a president, appointed by the Council of Ministers. The president is usually a powerful figure in his/her own right. The president until October 2004 was Romano Prodi, ex-prime minister of Italy, and from late 2004, Jose Manuel Durao Barroso, ex-prime minister of Portugal.

The Treaty of Nice in 2002 made provision for reform of the Commission after enlargement. Each member was to have one commissioner, a major concession by the large member states, who previously had two commissioners.

The responsibilities of the Commission are laid down by the various EU treaties (Rome, Maastricht, Amsterdam, Nice, etc). They include:

- *Initiating legislation.* The Commission tables proposals to the Council of Ministers after wide-ranging consultation with interested parties.

- *Guardian of the treaties.* The Commission has to ensure that the treaties and EU legislation are properly implemented.

- *Implementing policy.* The Commission either directly implements policy itself, or supervises programmes administered by member states under the principle of subsidiarity, which we looked at earlier.

The Commission is collectively answerable to the European Parliament, and can be removed by a vote of censure carried by a two-thirds majority – although there is no procedure for removing individual commissioners. In early 1999, after a report which criticised the then President, Jacques Santer, and several individual commissioners, and a series of debates in the European Parliament, the whole Commission resigned, and Santer was replaced by Romano Prodi.

Council of Ministers

The Council is the final decision-making body of the EU. It consists of representatives of the governments of the member states. In practice, the Council is really a series of specialist bodies, dealing with particular areas of policy, and attended by the appropriate ministers from the member states. Council meetings are attended by the president of the Commission, who has a full right to take part in discussions, but does not have a vote.

Until 1986, decisions in the Council of Ministers were taken by unanimity, which meant that each member state had an absolute veto. This was becoming unworkable, and would clearly become more so as more countries joined the EU. The Single European Act in 1986 introduced the concept of qualified majority voting (QMV), under which decisions in clearly specified areas could be taken by a majority vote. In practice, this gave the Big Four states a collective veto, but meant that they could not force a proposal through unless they obtained the support of several of the smaller states.

European Parliament

This is directly elected by all member states for five years. The most recent elections were in June 2009. Its powers are mainly budgetary. It has the final say on all 'non-compulsory' spending (any spending which is not the inevitable consequence of EU legislation, making up 25 per cent of the budget). It can also reject the budget in total, and did so in 1979 and 1984.

The Parliament has a right to debate all EU issues, and the Council can reject its views only by a unanimous vote. It cannot initiate legislation (the responsibility of the Commission), nor does it have the final say in passing law (the responsibility of the Council of Ministers), but it can reject measures which were passed by the

Council of Ministers through QMV. In October 2004, it came very close to rejecting the whole of the new Commission proposed by the new president, Jose Manuel Durao Barrosso, because of the illiberal views held by the Italian nominee. The crisis was only defused at the last minute when Barrosso withdrew his whole Commission for reconsideration, and the Italian government withdrew its nominee.

European Court of Justice

The European Court of Justice (ECJ) consists of judges appointed by the member states and rules on the interpretation and application of EU rules, and on disputes between the Commission and member states. Its decisions apply directly in the member states.

Economic and Social Committee

This is a consultative body made up of representatives of employers (the Union of Industrial and Employers' Confederations of Europe (UNICE) and the European Centre of Enterprises with Public Participation (CEEP)), trade unions (the European Trade Union Confederation (ETUC)), and special interest groups (collectively known as the 'social partners'). It must be formally consulted by the Commission on economic and social proposals.

European Central Bank

The European Central Bank (ECB) was set up in 1999 to administer Economic and Monetary Union (EMU). It has sole responsibility for setting interest rates in the eurozone. It is headed by a president appointed by the Council of Ministers, and representatives from each member of EMU (which does not include the UK).

 ACTIVITY 6.2 EU INSTITUTIONS AND POWER

- Why do you think that ultimate power in the EU lies with the Council of Ministers rather than the Commission?

- You work for a FTSE-100 company. Your company is concerned about a possible change in EU social policy that could lead to legislation in the next few years. How can your company influence forthcoming EU decisions on this change?

EU ENLARGEMENT

The enlargement of the EU from 15 to 25 members, which took place on 1 May 2004, increased the population of the EU by 74 million, ranging from 38 million in Poland to 400,000 in Malta. This enlargement was qualitatively different from any which had gone before:

- The sheer number of new entrants was larger than any before. This in itself put new strains on the EU's institutions, and increased pressure for speedy agreement on the new constitution.

- Some of the new entrants – Latvia, Lithuania and Slovakia, for example – are far poorer than any previous entrant. GDP per head of the new entrants is about 15 per cent of the old EU average.

- The largest new entrant, Poland, has a massive and under-developed agricultural sector.

- There are fears in some quarters that enlargement will release a flood of immigrants from the new to the old EU states.

- Eight of the new entrants are ex-communist, and three, the Baltic states, were once part of the USSR. Russia will inevitably feel threatened by this, particularly as an outlying part of its territory, Kaliningrad, is now completely surrounded by EU territory (Poland and Lithuania).

- One new entrant, Cyprus, is divided between an officially recognised Greek state, which is in the EU, and a non-recognised Turkish state, which is not.

- Further expansion is inevitable. Bulgaria and Romania joined in 2007. These countries are even poorer than the 2004 entrants. The accession of Croatia and Iceland is likely in the near future.

 ACTIVITY 6.3 EU ENLARGEMENT

What do you think is the likely impact of EU enlargement on your own organisation or sector?

 TURKEY AND THE EU

CASE STUDY 6.1

Turkey has been an associate member of the EU since 1963, and has sought full membership since that date. It was formally recognised as a candidate in 1999 (Lungesen 2004), and formal accession talks started in October 2005 (Akcapar and Chaibi 2006). However, accession talks were 'part-suspended' in December 2006 following a dispute about Turkish recognition of Cyprus (Tisdall 2007).

Should Turkey join the EU?

There are four requirements for new entrants to the EU, known as the Copenhagen criteria:

- Each applicant must show that it is in sympathy with the fundamental ethos of the EU by demonstrating that it practises liberty, democracy, respect for human rights and fundamental freedoms, and the rule of law.

- Each applicant must create a functioning market economy.

- Each applicant must comply with the body of EU laws and standards (the *acquis communitaire*) – which is 100,000 pages long!

- The applicant must be part of Europe.

Turkey does have a history of military coups and a dubious human rights record in relation to its treatment of its Kurdish minority, but the country argues that it meets the criteria. It is a long-standing democratic country, and since the present government came to power in 2002, it has taken a number of steps to improve its human rights record. It has abolished the death penalty, released some Kurdish activists, and started TV broadcasts in Kurdish. Few dispute that it has a functioning market economy. Only a small part of Turkey (Thrace) is technically within geographical Europe, with the rest (Anatolia) being in Asia, but Turkey has always seen itself as part of Europe. The geographical position of Turkey could be a problem, as it has frontiers with Iraq, Iran and Syria, but the former EU enlargement commissioner, Guenter Verheugen, saw this as an asset rather than a drawback: membership would demonstrate to the Middle East that the EU could work with a Muslim country (Lungesen 2004). As the Portuguese foreign minister said about the negotiations with Turkey, this was a victory for Europe and a bitter defeat for Osama Bin Laden. Turkish membership should increase Turkish prosperity and so, paradoxically, decrease rather than increase immigration from Turkey (Kirisci 2007).

There is some opposition to Turkish entry on the grounds that its 70 million predominantly Muslim population would upset the religious and cultural balance of the EU, but Turkey is a fiercely secular state, not an Islamic one, and to say that we don't want Muslims in Europe is an insult to the Muslim minorities in the UK, France, Germany and Spain. However, in April and May 2007 there was considerable unrest in Turkey over the election of a known Islamist as president, with the threat of a military coup to preserve secularism.

One argument against Turkish entry was that Turkey was too poor. However, this is difficult to support, as Turkey's GDP per head on a purchasing power parity basis is almost identical to that of Romania, which joined the EU in 2007 (CIA 2007). Another fear is an increased influx of Turkish workers into the EU, which already has three million Turkish-born workers. However, Turkey claims that by 2015 its economic growth will have reached a point where it will itself be a net importer of labour.

The strongest argument against Turkish entry is its sheer size. Its population is just smaller than that of Germany, but it is rising at 1 per cent per annum, and will soon overtake Germany. The population of the EU 27 is probably already falling. By 2050, Turkey could make up between a fifth and a quarter of the total EU population. This is of particular concern to France and Germany, which see their power base being eroded.

In surveys in 2005, 35 per cent of EU citizens supported Turkish entry, while 52 per cent opposed it. If Turkish entry were approved, Austria would hold a referendum on the issue before agreeing to ratify the accession. Only 10 per cent of Austrians support Turkish entry, which may be a historical folk memory of two sieges of Vienna by the Turkish Empire (Akcapar and Chaibi 2006).

Until recently, Turkish public opinion has been firmly in support of EU membership, but this is now waning, due to what the Turks see as the patronising approach of the EU. One Turkish commentator recently said, 'The EU is off the radar. It has confirmed Turkey's worst expectations. At present, it is an irrelevancy,' while another said, 'Europe is not ready for Turkish membership' (Tisdall 2007).

THE EU CONSTITUTION AND THE LISBON TREATY

By the late 1990s, it was clear that the EU was about to undergo a dramatic enlargement, and equally clear that the existing structure of EU institutions would not be able to cope with a greatly increased membership – hence the move towards an EU constitution to modernise the EU's structure. A first attempt at modernisation was made at the Nice Summit in 2000, but the arrangements agreed there really satisfied no one. A convention under the former French president, Giscard D'Estaing, produced a draft constitution, and eventually, after much haggling and amendment, a new constitution was agreed by the member states in June 2004.

The main points of the constitution were:

Council president

The European Council (the heads of state or government of member states) will elect a president of the Council, by qualified majority, for a term of two and a half years, renewable once. The president must be approved by the European Parliament. The idea here was to give greater continuity. At present, the presidency rotates through the member states every six months.

Foreign minister

The European Council would appoint a foreign minister, by qualified majority. That individual would speak for the EU on foreign policy. This new post effectively combines two existing posts. However, the foreign minister will not decide policy, and will only be able to speak for the EU where the European Council has decided on policy. Most importantly, foreign policy is one of the three areas (the others being defence and taxation), where each member state still has a veto.

The Commission

From November 2004, each member state will appoint one commissioner. This means that the big powers (Germany, France, UK and Italy) would lose one of their commissioners, as already agreed at Nice. However, it was agreed that by 2014 the size of the Commission will be reduced to two-thirds of the number of member states, although the precise mechanism for doing this has still to be negotiated.

Parliament

The powers of the Parliament are being significantly increased. It will have powers of 'co-decision' with the Council of Ministers for those policies requiring a decision by qualified majority. This means that the Parliament will effectively have the right to veto proposed legislation, a very real increase in power.

Qualified majority voting

There are two significant changes to the system of qualified majority voting in the Council of Ministers. Firstly, more areas will now be subject to majority voting. These include asylum and immigration policy, and cross-border crime. As we saw above, only foreign affairs, defence and taxation are still subject to veto. Secondly, the procedure of qualified majority voting will change. Gone is the system where member states had different numbers of votes. Now all will have one vote, but a qualified majority is defined as at least 55 per cent of the members of the Council, comprising at least 15 of them and representing member states comprising at least 65 per cent of the population of the Union.

Several points are of interest here:

- The constitution already made provision for some limited expansion (presumably the accession of Bulgaria and Romania). In 2004, 15 members represented 60 per cent of membership, not 55 per cent.

- By setting a population threshold, the constitution gives considerable power to the big states, particularly to Germany, which on its own represents 18 per cent of the EU's population. Together, Germany, France and either Italy or the UK would have a blocking minority.

Charter of Fundamental Rights

This sets out key 'rights, freedoms and principles'. These include the right to life and liberty, and the right to strike. This could affect existing UK industrial relations law, although the UK government believes that national laws will not be affected. This has yet to be tested by the European Court of Justice.

The fact that the member states agreed on the constitution did not mean that it immediately came into force. The constitution had to be ratified by each of the 25 member states. Along with several other states, including Spain, France, the Netherlands and Ireland, in the case of the UK this would only be after a referendum.

The key referenda were those in France and the Netherlands, held on 29 May and 1 June 2005 respectively. Both campaigns were very difficult for the national governments and the EU. France voted 54.9 per cent against, and in the Netherlands, 61.7 per cent voted against (Nugent 2006). This was sufficient to kill off the constitution. In each case, non-EU issues muddied the picture. In polls held by the Commission after the referenda, a third of Dutch people who voted against said it was because of lack of information, and 14 per cent said it was because they opposed the ruling party. A third voted against on specifically constitution-related issues – 19 per cent because of a fear of loss of national sovereignty, and 13 per cent because they felt Europe was too expensive (the Netherlands is the largest per-head contributor to the EU budget). In France, reasons for voting against were predominantly economic – either a fear of negative effects on employment (31 per cent) or that the economic situation was too weak (25 per cent). Another third thought that the constitution represented an unacceptable move towards Anglo-Saxon models of capitalism, or a weakening of the European social model (Church and Phinnemore 2006).

The constitution was renegotiated in June 2007 at the Lisbon Summit and significant changes were made (BBC 2007):

- the name constitution was dropped and replaced with 'reform treaty'
- the constitution proposal for a 'double majority' system of qualified majority voting (55 per cent of member states representing 65 per cent of the EU's population) is maintained, but to meet Polish objections that this gives too much weight to Germany, it will not be phased in until 2014–17
- the national veto will be maintained for social security and culture, as well as for defence, foreign policy and taxation
- the post of EU Council president remains, but the EU foreign minister's title is changed to 'high representative'
- the UK has obtained an opt-out from the Charter of Fundamental Rights.

Like the constitution, the Lisbon Treaty still had to be ratified. The UK government had decided that it would not hold a referendum, and the treaty was ratified by parliament. Ireland held a referendum, which voted no, but a second referendum voted yes in October 2009. Poland then ratified the Treaty, leaving only the Czech Republic refusing to ratify. Here the Treaty had been approved by parliament, but the Euro-sceptic president refused to sign the Treaty. After obtaining a last-minute opt-out from the Charter of Fundamental Rights, the Czech Republic finally signed in November 2009, completing ratification of the Treaty. The Conservative Party in Britain had pledged to hold a referendum on Lisbon if the Treaty was still unratified if and when it came to power, and this pledge was now abandoned. Instead, the party pledged to hold a referendum on any future EU treaty (Watt 2009).

 ## ACTIVITY 6.4 THE EU CONSTITUTION

The opinion polls after the announcement of agreement on the constitution suggested that there would have been a two-to-one majority against it in a UK referendum. Why do you think this is so?

EU EMPLOYMENT POLICY

Employment policy in the UK is influenced by the EU at several different levels.

EU treaties

The treaties set out the competencies of the EU. The organisation is only allowed to act in areas set out in the treaties. The various treaties, culminating in the Lisbon Treaty of December 2009, have always been committed to improvements in working conditions. National economic policies must be consistent with the

EU's broad economic guidelines, which stress a high level of employment as a major objective. Employment policy is a key element of the Lisbon Strategy on EU competitiveness agreed in 2000.

The treaties stress a commitment to improved living and working conditions with a view to harmonisation (remember that one of the key EU principles is a level playing field between member states); social protection; dialogue between management and labour; development of HR with the aim of lasting high employment; and combating exclusion. However, the treaties also stress that the EU should avoid placing excessive burdens on small and medium-sized businesses.

An important element in the Lisbon Treaty was the incorporation of the Charter of Fundamental Rights, originally agreed in 2000, but never accepted by the UK. The Charter guarantees a number of individual rights, some of which relate to employment, but as part of the treaty negotiations, the UK and Poland were granted an opt-out from the Charter, joined at the last minute by the Czech Republic.

The Lisbon Treaty also lays down how decisions must be taken on employment matters. Unanimity is required for proposals that concern social protection and social security, and protection of workers' interests on termination of the employment contract. All other employment issues are subject to co-decision, which gives a significant role to the European Parliament and ensures that no one member state can exercise a veto.

EU directives

While the treaties deal with the principles of EU employment policy, details of implementation are implemented through EU directives. HR professionals will be familiar with most of them, including collective redundancies, TUPE, discrimination, equal pay, health and safety, information and consultation, atypical workers, pregnant workers, agency workers and working time. If the requirements of an EU directive set a lower standard than that already existing in national law, member states are not allowed to reduce their level of worker protection.

Social partner agreements

EU employment policy is also made by agreements between the social partners, the European Trade Union Confederation (ETUC), representing trade unions (including the TUC), and UNICE, representing employers (including the CBI). EU-level social partner agreements include parental leave and leave for family reasons; the protection of fixed-term, part-time and teleworkers; and workplace stress. The European Commission also encourages agreements made by sectoral social partners.

For further details, see the CIPD's *EU Employment Policy* worksheet, last revised in November 2009.

THE EU AND OTHER REGIONAL BLOCS

The EU is not the only major regional trading group in the world. The North American Free Trade Agreement (NAFTA) covers the US, Canada and Mexico, while the Association of Southeast Asian Nations (ASEAN) includes the Asian Tiger states of Indonesia, Malaysia, the Philippines, Singapore and Thailand, as well as states including Vietnam and Myanmar, with China, India, Japan and Australia as dialogue partners. Both NAFTA and ASEAN are primarily free-trade-area agreements, and thus of much narrower scope than the EU.

All three encourage trade within their own area, and thus may indirectly discourage trade between the three blocs.

In 2000, the so-called Triad of the US, the EU and Japan received 71 per cent of total world inward direct investment, and was responsible for 82 per cent of outward direct investment (Williams 2007).

INTERNATIONAL FINANCIAL INSTITUTIONS

THE BRETTON WOODS CONFERENCE

In 1944, the wartime western allies held a conference at Bretton Woods in New Hampshire which was to shape the economic future of the international economy. Their prime aim was to prevent a repetition of the competitive devaluations and protectionism which had followed the Wall Street crash in 1929, and which had made the ensuing Great Depression even more severe in its impact. The idea was to impose strict controls on the ability of each country to follow beggar-my-neighbour policies, and to force international economic co-operation.

Out of Bretton Woods came three great international institutions: the International Monetary Fund (the IMF), the International Bank for Reconstruction and Development (the World Bank), and the General Agreement on Tariffs and Trade (GATT).

INTERNATIONAL MONETARY FUND

The main plank of the IMF regime was a system of fixed exchange rates, which all member countries agreed to maintain. In practice this meant that each member state fixed the value of its currency in terms of the US dollar, while the US dollar itself was linked to gold. It was recognised that members might experience problems with their balance of payments in the short term (an excess of imports over exports). In such a situation, the IMF agreed to make hard currency available to them on a short-term basis, to allow the member a breathing space to adjust its economy. Only if the balance of payments problem was long term was the member state permitted to devalue its currency. The system was financed by subscriptions from member countries, with by far the largest contribution coming from the US.

The system worked reasonably smoothly for nearly 30 years, although there were still balance-of-payments crises and occasional devaluations (most notably in the UK, France and Italy). Most lending was to developed countries, and the IMF had little involvement with the Third World. However, the world economic structure changed fundamentally in the early 1970s. Now it was the US which experienced a balance-of-payments crisis. The IMF system could not cope with this – the absolute stability of the dollar was fundamental. Eventually, President Nixon abandoned the fixed-price link between the US dollar and gold, in effect devaluing the dollar. As a result, fixed exchange rates were abandoned and have never been restored on a world level.

The floating exchange rate regime immediately removed the IMF's major role. It still carries out its role of alleviating short-term financial crises, but almost always with developing rather than developed economies – the Asian Tiger economies (Thailand, South Korea, Indonesia) in 1997, Russia in 1998, Brazil in 1999 and Argentina in 2001 – but the IMF also started to develop a wider role of encouraging structural reform in member states (often known as 'mission creep'; a typical example of an organisation broadening its original aims beyond all recognition). An early example of this was the loan to the UK in 1976, which was made conditional on the (Labour) government cutting public spending and adopting monetarist policies.

This process has now gone much further, and from the 1980s onwards the IMF has followed a policy of imposing Thatcherite, free-market neo-liberal conditions (particularly privatisation) on its support, particularly to Third World countries (Mathiason 2003):

- Tanzania was forced to charge for hospital visits and school fees
- Ecuador was forced to sell its water system to foreigners and to increase the price of cooking oil by 80 per cent
- Malawi was told to sell off its strategic reserves of maize, two years before the country was hit by famine
- Guyana was told to privatise its sugar industry
- Zambia was told to privatise its banks.

Should the IMF try to impose long-term neo-liberal reform in the Third World, rather than concentrating on lending money to countries in short-term financial difficulties?

There are three main arguments in favour of this policy:

- State-run sectors in Third World countries tend to be inefficient, corrupt devourers of resources, and they discourage foreign investment. The state may also spend wastefully and not in the best long-term interests of its population, for instance, by excess spending on arms.
- Moral hazard – the concept that because countries expect to be bailed out if they get into difficulties, they will be reckless in their behaviour, because they know they will never really be called to account for their actions. For

example, Brazil has defaulted on its debts five times, and Venezuela nine times. In essence, this is the same argument that says that insurance companies should carry out very strict checks before they pay out on policies, in order to discourage fraudulent claims.

- Short-term intervention tends by definition to treat short-term symptoms rather than the long-term illness. The only way to tackle long-term problems is through long-term reform.

There are two counter-arguments:

- While the above may be true in the long run, the short-term effect of privatisation and liberalisation is to increase poverty and inequality in the Third World.
- By concentrating on the long-term rather than the short-term, the IMF is moving into areas which should more appropriately be the responsibility of the World Bank (Stiglitz 2003).

The current consensus seems to be that the IMF should concentrate on macroeconomic factors such as budget deficits and inflation, rather than trying to micromanage the economies of clients. Charles Wyplosz, professor of economics at the Institute of International Studies in Geneva, was quoted in the *Financial Times* in May 2004 as saying, 'When firemen come to your house to put out a blaze, you would not expect them to meddle in your marriage' (Swann 2004).

Ngaire Woods (2007) suggests that the IMF:

- should be the cornerstone of global monetary co-operation
- should help countries mitigate or cushion shocks from the global economy
- must command the confidence of all its members.

WORLD BANK

Like the IMF, the World Bank was set up at Bretton Woods, and nearly all countries in the world are members. Unlike the IMF, its main role is to provide access to capital for long-term development, particularly in the Third World. It does this partly through direct lending via a number of its own agencies, some of it interest-free, and partly by leveraging investment from the private sector.

It also has a wider social remit than the IMF. It emphasises social services, the environment and gender equality as well as economic growth. However, like the IMF it has been criticised for the neo-liberal conditions which it tends to attach to its loans, and also for over-lending to relatively advanced developing countries like Brazil and particularly China, which have sufficient clout to be able to borrow to finance their development on a commercial basis. The Bank is also a key component in the so-called Washington consensus, not least because of the convention that its president is nominated by the US (Woods 2007).

One proposal that has been put forward is that the IMF and the World Bank should merge. There is clear overlap – in practice, if not in theory –

between the activities of the IMF and World Bank, although in principle their functions are distinct. A merger might therefore seem logical, and it might help to prevent mission creep. However, if the IMF had a dominant role in the merged organisation, its neo-liberal agenda might swamp the wider social and environmental principles of the World Bank.

International trade and comparative advantage

Very few countries are self-sufficient, in the sense that they produce everything which they need within their own boundaries. Ever since the Stone Age, societies have traded with each other. The most obvious reason for a country to trade is to obtain something which it is incapable of producing for itself. For example, until the discovery of North Sea oil, the UK had to import oil. However, strictly speaking this only applies to extractive industries. Anything else could be made or grown, at a price. There is nothing to stop the UK growing its own bananas in greenhouses (except common sense!). It is a much more efficient use of resources for countries to concentrate on what they are best at producing, and to import other goods. For example, if we compare the UK and the Windward Islands, the UK has an absolute advantage in the production of pharmaceuticals, while the Windwards have an absolute advantage in the production of bananas. It therefore makes sense for the UK to specialise in pharmaceuticals, and to export these to the Windwards, while the Windwards should export bananas to the UK. (As we will see later when we look at the banana war, the real world is a lot more complicated than this simple example suggests.)

Even if one country is better at producing everything than another country, international trade will still benefit both sides. Let's stretch our banana example even further. Assume that the UK is four times as efficient as the Windwards at producing pharmaceuticals, but twice as efficient at producing bananas. In this case, the UK has a comparative advantage in the production of pharmaceuticals, and the Windwards a comparative advantage in bananas. Both sides would benefit if the UK specialised in pharmaceuticals and the Windwards on bananas. The mathematics to prove this can be found in any textbook on international economics.

For comparative advantage to work, however, it is essential that there are no restrictions on trade between the countries involved, ie that there is free trade. For example, assume that the UK has a banana industry which is struggling to cope with competition from Windwards bananas, and then assume that the UK banana industry persuades the UK government to place either quotas (restrictions on quantity) or tariffs (taxation) on imports of Windwards bananas. People working in the UK banana industry would benefit, but everyone else in both economies would lose.

If you think that this example seems totally unrealistic, you are probably right, but bear in mind that Japan, for example, protects its rice growers with a 500 per cent tariff on imported rice.

ACTIVITY 6.5 IS COMPARATIVE ADVANTAGE GOOD FOR YOU?

The theory of comparative advantage suggests that everyone gains from free trade. Why then do so many countries protect their own domestic industries?

WORLD TRADE ORGANISATION

After the Second World War, the Allies set up the General Agreement on Tariffs and Trade (GATT), whose remit was to encourage free trade, and prevent the destructive protectionism that had blighted the world economy in the 1930s. Its objectives were to:

- eliminate existing trade barriers
- deter the formation of new barriers
- eliminate all forms of trade discrimination.

In 1995, GATT was absorbed into a new body, the World Trade Organisation (WTO), with wider objectives. Its membership now includes virtually the whole world, following the accession of China and Taiwan in the early 2000s. The WTO continues the process of liberalising world trade, but its powers also extend to trade in services as well as goods, and also the regulation of international property rights like patents and copyright. It also has the power to adjudicate on disputes between members, with the right to impose financial penalties.

THE BANANA WAR

CASE STUDY 6.1

The banana war was one of the most bitter trade disputes of the 1990s, and one of a number of disputes between the two dominant trading blocs, the EU and the US. The key to the dispute was the preference that the EU gave to bananas from ex-British and French colonies in Africa, the Pacific and the Caribbean (the APC countries). The EU argument was that without protection, the banana industries in these areas, particularly in the Caribbean, would collapse, devastating the local economies, and perhaps pushing producers to alternative, less desirable crops like cannabis or coca. They pointed out that the WTO had an objective to assist developing and transition economies.

The US responded that the EU action

was a gross breach of WTO rules. Three US companies – Chiquita, Dole and Del Monte – control two-thirds of world trade in bananas from their huge plantations in Central America (the APC has 4 per cent of the world market).

Legally, the US had an unanswerable case, but it weakened its moral position by imposing punitive import tariffs in 1998 on a range of EU exports to the US in retaliation, before the WTO delivered its judgment. Worse, this was announced shortly after Chiquita gave a big donation to the ruling US Democratic Party.

The WTO ruled in favour of the US, and ordered the EU to abolish its protective quotas on APC bananas by 2005. The effects on the Caribbean have been predictably devastating. Between 1993 and 2000, two-thirds of the banana growers in the Windward Islands went out of business, while exports of bananas from St Vincent and the Grenadines fell from US $120 million to US $50 million (Ryle 2002). By 2009, only 4,000 of the 24,000 Windward Island banana growers in 1993 were still in business. Between 1992 and 2007, UK banana imports almost doubled from 545,000 to 927,000, but the proportion imported from the Caribbean fell from 70 per cent to less than 30 per cent (Doward 2009).

The working of the WTO

The WTO (and its predecessor GATT) works in a series of long trade rounds, initiated at a major conference and then negotiated and implemented over a long period. The Uruguay Round in the 1990s was primarily concerned with textiles, where the developing world had a comparative advantage, but with the developed countries maintaining protection of their own textile industries. The developed western countries agreed to eliminate protection, but only over a 10-year period, with most of the concessions coming in the last year! This tends to be the pattern – the West speaks the language of free trade, is keen to impose free trade on the developing world, but drags its heels when it comes to its own concessions.

Larry Elliott in the *Guardian* in 2004 drew a telling parallel with medieval Europe, where in theory all states owed spiritual allegiance to the papacy and the universal values of the church, but in practice spent most of their time at war with each other.

THE FAILURE OF DOHA: FROM 9/11 TO THE IRAQ WAR

CASE STUDY 6.2

The Doha Round of trade negotiations was launched by the WTO in 2001 in the wake of the 9/11 terrorist attacks on New York and Washington. The negotiations were specifically designated as a 'development round', aimed at improving the economic position of developing countries, as a symbol of world solidarity against terrorism.

WTO negotiations are always difficult, as all agreements have to be unanimous. Unlike the IMF, rich countries do not have disproportionate power. Three main issues of particular interest to developing countries dominated the negotiations: special trade treatment for developing countries, supply of cheap generic medicines for poor countries, and liberalisation of agriculture (De Jonquieres 2003).

The deadlines for special trade treatment and generic medicines were missed at the end of 2002 – in the case of generic medicines the only country voting against agreement was the US.

Agricultural liberalisation was a much more crucial issue. When the first Doha meeting was called, it produced a pledge to improve market access for Third World countries, to reduce trade-distorting domestic support and to reduce export subsidies.

Reform was urgently needed. In 2001, assistance to rich-country farmers amounted to US $311 billion, compared with US $50 billion in development aid. The EU paid subsidies of US $913 a year to each EU cow, and US $8 in aid to each sub-Saharan African. Comparable figures for Japan were US $2,700 and US $1.47. The EU was the world's largest exporter of skimmed milk powder, sold at half its cost of production, and of white sugar, sold at a quarter the cost of production (Wolf 2005).

Stuart Harbinson, the WTO chairman for agriculture, proposed a package that would:

- end export subsidies in nine years
- reduce tariffs by 40–60 per cent
- cut trade-distorting farm support by 60 per cent.

It was calculated that these proposals would increase annual global income by US $100 billion, with 20 per cent of the gain going to developing countries and 80 per cent to rich countries through lower prices (De Jonquieres 2003).

The US and the Cairns Group of major agricultural exporters (including Australia and Canada) argued that the Harbinson proposals did not go far enough, while the EU and Japan claimed that they were too ambitious. India wanted to maintain its own tariffs to protect its farmers. The ACP (Africa, Caribbean and Pacific) group of developing countries sided with the EU, worried about losing their preferential access to EU markets (see case study 6.1).

The key to the negotiations was the attitude of the EU. The European Commission proposed reform of the Common Agricultural Policy (CAP), which by phasing out incentives for overproduction, and switching to support based on rural development and protection of the environment, would reduce export subsidies, but would not make EU markets more open to imports. Meanwhile France and Germany had reached an agreement to maintain spending on the CAP until 2013.

Under the terms of the negotiations, agreement was required by 31 March 2003, by which time the Iraq War had just broken out, relations between the US and France

were at an all-time low and, ironically, Doha was the military headquarters for the war.

The 31 March deadline was missed. The day after this, Franz Fischler, the EU agriculture commissioner, and Pascal Lamy, the trade commissioner, wrote an article in the *Financial Times* justifying the EU position (Fischler and Lamy 2003). They criticised the Cairns Group, arguing that they wanted nothing more than 'an unlimited right to exploit its members' undeniable comparative advantages'. They also pointed out that the EU is the largest importer of agricultural products and the main importer of food from developing countries, taking in more food imports than the US, Japan, Canada and Australia put together. Lamy is now (2010) the head of the WTO – a classic case of poacher turned gamekeeper!

Negotiations staggered on for another three years. In Geneva in August 2004, the WTO agreed that export subsidies should be abolished, but no starting date or timetable was agreed. The final breakdown came over fundamental disagreement between the EU and the US. The US argued that the EU was not offering big enough reductions in tariffs, while the EU claimed that the US was not proposing a big enough reduction in subsidies. Eventually the US decided that no deal was better than a weak deal – 'Doha lite', as the US trade representative, Susan Schwab, put it. On 24 July 2006, the Doha Round was formally suspended, with no date set for a resumption (*Economist* 2006a).

The failure of Doha highlights:

- the hypocrisy of the developed world, which is ready to impose trade liberalisation on the developing world, but not to make meaningful concessions itself
- the strength of the farm lobby in both the EU and the US, which prevented any agreement
- divisions among the developing countries and agricultural exports, with diametrically opposing stances being taken by India, the Cairns Group and the ACP.

DEBT RELIEF

One of the most pressing problems of the world economy is the crushing burden of Third World debt. The 52 most indebted countries, mostly in Africa, have debts of US $375 billion, most of it unpayable, but on which interest still has to be paid. In 1998, it cost these countries US $23.4 billion to service their debt, mostly owed to western governments, the IMF or the World Bank. In many countries, debt repayment dwarfs welfare budgets. Mauritania pays US $63 million to service its debt, but only US $51 million on education, and US $17 million on health (Madeley 2001).

Much of the debt is a product of the cold war period, when the West was keen to tie the Third World to its side, and much of the money was wasted, either going on armaments, or disappearing through corruption, by the likes of the late unlamented Presidents Amin and Mobutu.

Many arguments can be advanced for relieving at least some of this burden of debt. These range from the moral (that debt is denying the inhabitants of these countries the human rights of decent education and health); the economic (that money being spent on debt repayment is not being spent on imports from the West); and the geopolitical (that poverty and discontent create an environment conducive to terrorism).

An international campaign for debt relief was launched in 1996 by the pressure group Jubilee 2000, which has produced some results. The IMF and the World Bank have set up the Heavily Indebted Poor Countries (HIPC) initiative to administer debt relief to the 52 poorest states; the G7 promised the cancellation of US $110 billion of debt; and the UK government agreed to hold debt repayments in a trust for poverty relief, to be released when each country agreed a poverty reduction plan (Madeley 2001).

However, progress has been limited. By the end of the Jubilee 2000 campaign in December 2000, only one country – Uganda – had debt cancelled, with reductions agreed for another 21, and in line with normal IMF/World Bank policy, stringent conditions were attached.

The Jubilee 2000 campaign was followed by the Make Poverty History campaign, which seemed to have attained success at the Gleneagles conference of the G8 in July 2005, chaired by Tony Blair. This pledged to double development assistance to Africa, including debt relief and aid, to US $100 billion a year by 2010. However, in April 2007, the Africa Progress Panel (APP), set up to review progress on the pledge, headed by Kofi Annan, the former UN secretary general, reported that the G8 was only 10 per cent of the way to reaching its target. The UK, alone of the G8, has met its commitments in full, but Bob Geldof, who is also a member of the APP, singled out Germany and Italy as countries which were significantly failing to meet their commitments. At the same time the OECD reported that after one-off packages of debt relief for Iraq and Nigeria were taken into account, aid flows from the West fell for the first time in a decade in 2006 (Elliott and Connolly 2007).

However, the issue of debt relief and aid is not straightforward. Boone (2005) argues that much aid is ineffective. Countries which received large aid flows did not do better at reducing child mortality than those which received small amounts of aid. Indeed, contrary to popular belief, little aid goes to finance social reform. Only 4 per cent went to health, 12 per cent to education and 6 per cent to emergencies. Countries or regions which were most successful at reducing child mortality were Cuba, Sri Lanka and the Indian state of Kerala. These had very different political systems, but all had put a lot of effort into developing their infrastructure. As a result, aid was spent where it was needed, rather than being wasted on bureaucracy or corruption.

ACTIVITY 6.6 DEBT RELIEF

Can you put forward any arguments against either the principle or the practice of debt relief for the Third World?

GLOBALISATION

Globalisation is an emotive word. It has inspired violent demonstrations all over the world, and also vehement defence. But what is globalisation? There is no single clear definition.

First, it is useful to look at what globalisation is not (Scholte 2000):

- *Internationalisation.* The world has always been international. There were trade links between the Roman and Chinese empires, for example.
- *Free trade.* Trade was at least as free in the late nineteenth century as it is now.
- *Westernisation.* Western culture was exported to much of the world as a result of the dominance of western empires in the late nineteenth and early twentieth centuries.
- *Universalisation.* Global lifestyles and ideas are nothing new. Islam spread across half the known western world in 50 years in the sixth century, and later spread to countries as far apart as Nigeria and Indonesia.

John Gray (1995) sees its key features as free mobility of capital and free trade. Ngaire Woods (2000) sees globalisation as much wider, and political and social as well as economic. She distinguishes the following three elements.

THE EXPANSION OF MARKETS

Technological changes like the mobile phone and above all the Internet have speeded up communications to the extent that both financial and physical transactions can be carried out instantaneously, while improvements in transport permit goods to be shipped quickly and relatively cheaply anywhere in the world (think of the universal availability in the UK of asparagus from Peru and French beans from Kenya). Simultaneously, governments throughout the world have been deregulating and reducing their control over their economies, at the same time as the growth of e-commerce has started to erode their control of their tax base. The result has been the spread of transnational enterprises and global brands, leading to what Kenichi Ohmae (1990), the Japanese management guru and one of the early proponents of globalisation, called 'The Borderless World'.

The knowledge economy also creates a borderless world. Knowledge is not dependent on possession of natural resources, and can instantaneously be transmitted via the Internet. As Lester Thurow (1999) says, 'Knowledge is the new basis for wealth'; hence the outflow of call-centre and data-handling jobs from the UK to India.

THE TRANSFORMATION OF POLITICS

Free movement of capital has produced a world financial market which has the potential to swamp any single economy. At the same time, transnational issues have become of increasing importance: global warming, human rights, drugs, world poverty and immigration, terrorism, etc. Increasingly, in order to have any influence, nation states have to join together in regional groupings. The EU is the best known, but there are other important groupings like the North Atlantic Free Trade Area and ASEAN. Just as nation states are handing over power to regional groupings, they are also devolving power internally to regional entities, eg Scotland and Wales in the UK, Catalonia in Spain.

THE EMERGENCE OF NEW SOCIAL AND POLITICAL MOVEMENTS

A global (or American) culture has developed, with US corporations like McDonald's, CNN, Disney and Nike setting trends across the world. At the same time, counter-movements have developed, ranging from the anti-globalisation movement to militant Islam.

Globalisation is nothing new. It has often been argued that the golden age of globalisation was the period 1880–1914, when the world economy was regulated by the universal use of the Gold Standard, and there was almost universal free trade and free movement of capital. Indeed, this period had one element of globalisation which does not apply today: free movement of people. Not only could an individual travel without a passport, there was also free movement of labour, and very little control on international migration – this is the period when the Statue of Liberty was erected in New York. One commentator even said in 1911 that a major war was now impossible, as the world had become so interdependent (Micklethwait and Wooldridge 2000).

Two dates mark the development of modern globalisation. One is 1973, the year of the first oil crisis. The consequences of this were twofold: a realisation that the world economy was inextricably linked through its dependence on oil, and the collapse of the Bretton Woods system of fixed exchange rates, which ushered in a period when world financial markets became much more dominant.

The other key date is 1989. One factor here was the collapse of communism as a world ideology, and the triumph of the US in the cold war – what the US political scientist Francis Fukuyama called 'the end of history'. The other factor, much less noted at the time, but equally important, was the final bursting of the Japanese 'bubble economy'. Throughout the 1980s, it seems that globalisation was likely to be Japanese- rather than US-dominated. Japanese industrial techniques were sweeping the world, and most of the world's biggest corporations were Japanese. The economic collapse of Japan ensured that globalisation would be US-dominated economically, as well as politically and culturally.

DRIVERS OF GLOBALISATION

A number of drivers of globalisation have intensified in the last 20 years or so.

Technology

The most important developments here are in information and communication technology (ICT), particularly the mobile phone and the Internet. These have transformed the way in which particular industries operate. An example is the insurance industry, which traditionally was staid and conservative, but has been transformed by the application of new technology, which has led to a wave of mergers.

Cultural homogenisation

The universal availability of television, and global audiences for international sporting events like the World Cup and the Olympic Games, combined with the explosion in overseas travel, has led to a homogenisation of international culture, which permits the development of global brands. However, global brands like McDonald's still have to be responsive to local cultural differences – no traditional beef Big Macs in India, for example.

Economies of scale

Developments in manufacturing techniques have meant that the minimum efficient scale of operations in many industries has become a significant percentage of the available world market. The most extreme example is the aircraft industry, where the total world market is barely big enough to support two firms (Boeing and Airbus).

Deregulation

Deregulation has been driven by bodies such as the WTO and the EU. It reduces the costs of cross-border trade, and so promotes the development of global companies

Competition

If one firm in an industry globalises, it will gain a competitive advantage. In order to stay in touch, its competitors will also be forced to globalise (Segal-Horn 2002).

TWO GLOBAL COMPANIES

CASE STUDY 6.3

Siemens

Siemens was founded in Germany in the mid-nineteenth century, and by 1865 was already operating in the UK and Russia. In 1872 it supplied China with its first telegraph. It is now Europe's largest engineering company, operating in 190 countries. Eighty per cent of its sales, 70 per cent of its factories and 66 per cent of its workforce are outside Germany.

Its workforce in China numbers 36,000, and its annual Chinese sales €4.4 billion. Like most globalised companies, it uses low-cost countries to manufacture components. But unlike most, it also carries out a lot of its research and development abroad. For example, a tailor-made low-cost body scanner for use in poorer countries was developed and is manufactured solely in China. Customers are happy to buy the product because they know that they can trade up at a later date to a more sophisticated German-made product using the same software. The company's Medical Solutions Group is investing over €30 million in its Asia Center of Excellence in Shanghai.

In non-medical areas, the company is building 60 high-speed trains in China with its local partner Tangshan Locomotive & Rolling Stock Work, in a contract worth €670 million to Siemens. In 2005, Siemens filed over 1,000 patents in China. The company also sees India as key to its world development. It exports railway locomotives to the Middle East, but does so through India, where it employs 15,000 people.

Philips

Philips is smaller than Siemens, employing only 122,000 people in 60 countries. It has also had a much more chequered recent history. It started as a light bulb manufacturer in Holland in 1891. It then moved into X-ray machines and radio equipment. In the 1970s it entered the record business, and also expanded in electronics, including mobile phones and semiconductors.

By 2000, Philips had run into trouble. In most of its markets it was number three, four or worse, and so very vulnerable to competition. In 2001–02, it lost over €3 billion, and shed 55,000 jobs. It cut its 30 separate divisions to five – domestic appliances, lighting, medical, consumer electronics and semiconductors. This turned the company around, but downsizing continued. Philips exited the mobile phone business, and sold a majority stake in its semiconductor business to the private equity company KKR.

The company's strategy now is to develop advanced products that are well designed and easy to use. China is key to this. Philips has long had links with China. In the 1920s, it sold an X-ray machine for the personal use of the last Chinese emperor. It now has 20,000 employees in China, with production there worth €6 billion, half of which is exported. Like Siemens, it carries out research and development in China, at 15 centres employing 900 staff. The CEO, Gerard Kleisterlee, recently said (Philips 2007), 'For us, China is not just a workshop or a marketplace – it is a centre of innovation for new products and services with global applications.'

The lessons

- Globalisation leads to constant and rapid change. It makes the environment more turbulent. Both companies, but particularly Philips, are continually restructuring, developing new product ranges and dropping old ones.

- It is an old-fashioned view of globalisation to see India and China solely as low-cost manufacturing production lines. They are huge, rapidly growing and increasingly sophisticated markets in their own right. Successful globalisers design products for China, in China (and India).

ACTIVITY 6.7 WHY DO PEOPLE HATE THE WTO AND GLOBALISATION?

Throughout the West, there is deep suspicion, in many cases verging on hatred, of the progress of globalisation in general, and the activities of the WTO in particular. Why do you think this is?

MULTINATIONAL AND TRANSNATIONAL CORPORATIONS

Multinational corporations (MNCs) are companies producing or distributing goods or services in two or more countries. A transnational corporation is an MNC with more than two-thirds of its activities outside its home country. Such companies can locate different activities in parts of the world where they reap the biggest comparative advantage. Thus Rupert Murdoch's News Corporation is controlled through holding companies in the Cayman Islands, a notorious tax haven. The result is that News Corporation pays an average tax rate of 10 per cent.

In another example, the fall in the costs of air transport have led to the centralisation of the world flower industry in the Netherlands. Flowers are flown in from Kenya or India one day, sold at auction and then flown to customers in Europe or the US the next day.

The best-known example of local advantage is low labour costs. This is most obvious in low-wage industries like textiles, but a high-tech example is that of the Brazilian manufacturer of regional jet airliners, Embraer. Its employment costs in 2002 were US $26,000 per employee, as against US $63,000 in the regional jet business of its major Canadian competitor, Bombardier (Ghemawat 2003).

Rollinson (2008) suggests a more complex model. The simplest form is the domestic organisation, which supplies only its home market in its country of origin. Next in complexity is the international organisation, which serves home and overseas markets, but has a centralised headquarters in its country of origin. The multinational organisation produces goods or services in relatively autonomous overseas subsidiaries. The global organisation operates worldwide through independent overseas divisions, which are co-ordinated rather than controlled by a central headquarters. Finally, there is the transnational organisation (TNC), first described by Bartlett and Ghoshal (1991), which operates simultaneously as an international, multinational and global organisation. Specialised units could be located anywhere in the world, and are managed as a seamless network, by footloose managers with a global mindset.

In 2001, there were estimated to be 63,000 TNCs, which had 800,000 foreign affiliates, and which controlled two-thirds of world trade. Of the top 100 non-financial TNCs, 91 were based in the US, the EU or Japan (Unctad 2001). Of the companies in the 2006 Fortune Global 500 (measured by turnover), 172 were based in the EU, 114 in the US, 70 in Japan and 20 in China (Fortune 2006).

Not all industries can be globalised. Clark (2005) distinguishes four patterns of industry internationalisation, based on level of international trade in the industry's products, and degree of foreign direct investment. These are illustrated in figure 6.1 and discussed below.

Figure 6.1 Patterns of internationalisation

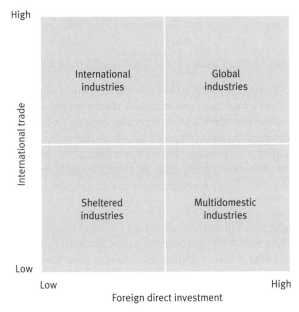

- Sheltered industries supply a domestic market, and are not attractive to foreign investment. Typical examples would be hairdressing or railways.

- Multidomestic industries supply domestic markets, but may do this in a number of countries. Typical examples would be hotels or management consulting.

- International industries supply a world market, but are tied to one country by availability of raw materials (diamond mining or agriculture) or by economies of scale (aerospace).

- Global industries have no national restrictions, and can truly be globalised, eg cars, oil, consumer electronics.

However, even global industries may still be forced to differentiate between national markets. This may be because of:

- laws and regulations. Cars must be made either left- or right-hand drive, depending on local regulations

- distribution channels may differ between national markets

- some markets are lead markets – they have a higher level of sophistication and acceptance of innovation

- differences in national culture may affect acceptability of products (Clark 2005).

Perlmutter (1969) identified three major types of multinational companies:

- *Ethnocentric.* Each local subsidiary is expected to conform to the style and culture of the parent company, regardless of local conditions. Managers here are typically expatriates from the home country. This corresponds to Rollinson's international organisation.

- *Polycentric.* Each subsidiary is allowed to manage in its own way, and to develop its own culture. For example, IBM Ireland was allowed to recognise unions, although the IBM culture is generally anti-union (Marchington and Wilkinson 2008). Managers in the local subsidiaries are likely to be nationals of that country, with few, if any, expatriates. This corresponds to Rollinson's multinational and global organisations.

- *Geocentric.* Local subsidiaries focus on worldwide objectives, making a unique contribution based on their local core competencies. Managers would be recruited on a global level, taking the best from anywhere in the world. Pucik (2007) quotes the example of ABB, where Percy Barnevik, the CEO, decided that the company needed about 500 hand-picked global managers – from a workforce of 200,000 – ready to move across countries, functions and businesses. The geocentric organisation corresponds to the transnational corporation.

 RETAIL GLOBALISATION IN THAILAND

CASE STUDY 6.4

Retailers in the developed world are increasingly facing saturated markets. Companies like Tesco and Wal-Mart already dominate their home markets, and prospects for further growth are limited. An obvious solution is to expand overseas.

However, retailing is much less globalised than other major industries. Of the world's top 250 retailers in 2006, 104 have no international operations at all. The most globalised retailer, the French supermarket group Carrefour, has stores in 29 countries (*Economist* 2006b). Turn this on its head, and Carrefour has no presence in over 80 per cent of the world's countries.

Many retailers have had spectacular failures overseas. Wal-Mart pulled out of Germany in 2006, having previously failed in Indonesia; Marks & Spencer pulled out of continental Europe in 2001; while IKEA abandoned Japan as early as the 1980s (Emmott et al 2002, *Economist* 2006b).

So what is the secret of success as a global retailer? The contrasting experiences of

Tesco and Boots in Thailand provide some clues.

To most people in the West, Thailand is little more than an exotic holiday location, but it is actually a significant player on the world stage, and is one of the 20 biggest world economies. Its population is 64 million, and its GDP per head (on a purchasing power parity basis) is slightly higher than that of Brazil or Turkey. The Thai economy on a purchasing power parity basis is one-third of the size of the UK's.

In the 1980s and 1990s, it was one of the Asian Tiger economies, which enjoyed the kind of explosive growth experienced by China today. It received a severe setback in the late 1990s (the Asian financial crisis started in Thailand in 1997), but by 2000 it was back on the growth path, and in 2003 its growth rate of GDP was 6.9 per cent. Literacy is high at well over 90 per cent, which encourages the rapid dissemination of new ideas; inflation and unemployment are low; and its capital,

Bangkok, is one of the major world conurbations (CIA 2007).

The Asian financial crisis provided an ideal opportunity for western retailers to enter Thailand. During the crisis, the Thai baht collapsed in value by 25 per cent against the dollar, making inward investment much cheaper. Among those retailers taking advantage of the opportunity were Boots and Tesco.

Boots opened its first store in Thailand in 1997, and by 2001 operated 67 stores throughout the country. The stores were very similar to those operated in the UK. Boots' own brands represented 60 per cent of the product range, while only 18 per cent, or about 400 lines, were produced in Thailand (Jitpleecheep 2002a). As most lines were imported, they were too expensive for the price-conscious Thais, even though the typical Boots Thai customer was affluent by Thai standards, with average earnings of 17,000 baht a month (about £280).

The standalone Boots operation was not a success. Between 1997 and 2001, it had accumulated losses of 700 million baht (about £11 million). In 2001 alone, it lost 388 million baht (about £6 million) on turnover of 1.5 billion baht (about £25 million) (Jitpleecheep 2002b).

Boots ceased new store openings in 2001, and decided instead to sell through dedicated sections in supermarkets. Its chosen partner was the Tops supermarket chain, operated by CRC Ahold, the Thai arm of the Dutch retailer Royal Ahold. For Boots this lowered risk, while it gave Ahold the opportunity to attract more upmarket customers (Jitpleecheep 2001). Meanwhile, Boots closed 12 non-performing stores in 2002 (Jitpleecheep 2002a). In 2002, Boots had 20 outlets in Tops stores, with a turnover of around 100 million baht (about £1.6 million) (Jitpleecheep 2002c).

Tesco took a different route. It entered Thailand in 1998 by purchasing the Thai retailer Lotus. Expansion has been rapid. In February 2007, Tesco Lotus had 366 stores open: 57 hypermarkets, 17 Value stores, 23 Talad Lotus stores, and 269 Express stores. By 2008, it expected to have up to 500 Express stores opened (Tesco Lotus 2007).

By 2006, Thailand had the third highest sales in the Tesco group (after the UK and South Korea), at just under £1 billion a year (Fletcher 2006). Group sales in Asia grew by over 60 per cent in 2006 (Datamonitor 2006). Information on profits from the Thai operation is not available, but as Tesco Lotus paid over one billion baht (about £16 million) in corporation tax in 2006, profits must be substantial.

Why has Tesco done so well in Thailand and Boots so badly? Boots seemed to have cloned a UK operation in Thailand, with little consideration for local conditions or sensibilities. Its style of operation seems to have been aimed at expatriates, tourists and wealthy cosmopolitan Thais. This could have led to a profitable niche operation, but Boots' prices were too high for a mass Thai market.

The company predominantly imported Boots' own brand products from the UK. While these had a strong reputation for quality in the UK, they were virtually unknown in Thailand. The joint venture with CRC Ahold promised access to a bigger market with lower risk, but still did not tap local Thai expertise. In short, the Boots operation was a typical example of western-centric globalisation.

The Tesco expansion was different in almost every way. It is a classic example of 'glocalisation' (Swyngedouw 2004). Throughout the process, Tesco was extremely sensitive to Thai conditions. Rather than starting with a greenfield operation like Boots, it took over Lotus, but was careful to retain the Lotus brand name and logo, which were well known in Thailand. It tailored its scale of operations by opening hypermarkets, supermarkets (Value stores) or convenience stores (Express stores) as appropriate to local demand. It even supported small 'mom and pop' competitors by selling them 'club packs' for resale (Tesco Lotus 2007).

Whereas Boots imported 82 per cent of its products, Tesco sourced 97 per cent in Thailand, and it also facilitated the export of Thai products worth over £100 million a year to Tesco UK. The company also set up a charitable foundation, Tesco for Thais, which although small scale was valuable in securing goodwill in Thailand.

Both Boots and Tesco have gained from the open-market policies espoused by the Thai prime minister Thaksin Shinawatra between 2001 and 2006. However, there are always losers in globalisation, and Thailand has been no exception. Between 1996 and 2001, the share of retail food sales in Thailand made through traditional markets fell

from 75 to 50 per cent, which has severely damaged the earnings of thousands of Thai market traders.

Before he was overthrown by a military coup late in 2006, Thaksin was seriously considering placing curbs on foreign-owned retailers and giving greater support to small shopkeepers. These policies have been taken further by the military government, and this may clip even Tesco's wings in the future (*Economist* 2007a).

This case study illustrates Perlmutter's model of globalisation. Boots' approach was an ethnocentric one, giving very little autonomy to the Thai operation, while Tesco's was polycentric, with the whole operation driven by Thais.

THE GLOBALISATION DEBATE

Aisbett (2003) identifies four main areas of concern over globalisation:

- An objection not to globalisation in principle, but to the way in which it is skewed in favour of developed countries. This is exemplified by the protectionist agricultural policies of the US and the EU.

- Loss of sovereignty, to transnational corporations and to institutions like the IMF and the WTO.

- Neo-liberal or 'Washington consensus' policies, as imposed by the IMF on debtor countries, eg privatisation, welfare cutbacks, etc.

- The rise of big corporations. Of the 100 biggest economic units in the world, 52 are corporations. They can expand or contract their activities in particular countries in order to maximise their overall profit.

However, Aisbett points out that the debate is no longer between supporters and opponents of globalisation. The anti-capitalist protest movements of the late 1990s have run out of steam, and the main arguments are now between enthusiastic and cautious globalisers. Even Oxfam has recognised that globalisation can have some benefits. A similar point is made by Jacobs (2001).

Aisbett identifies areas of agreement between the enthusiastic and cautious globalisers. These include:

- Trade is often a source of economic growth and growth is good for the poor (although the Green Party argues that local production may be more efficient (Lucas 2001).

- The US and the EU should open their markets to the developing world.

- Safety nets should be provided for the losers from globalisation, and education, health and welfare in developing countries should be safeguarded.
- Income is an inadequate measure of poverty, and social factors should be taken into consideration.
- Excessive corporate power is a problem.
- Political reform is needed in many developing countries.

There are also still important areas of difference, outlined in table 6.1 below.

Table 6.1 Alternative views on globalisation

Issue	Enthusiastic view	Cautious view
Attitudes to poverty	Globalisation in all its forms is good for the poor, and reducing poverty is what matters, even at the cost of increased inequality.	Reducing inequality is equally important, and globalisation frequently increases it.
Trade liberalisation	Trade liberalisation is always beneficial.	Totally free trade will often have adverse social or environmental side-effects. Decisions should be taken on a case-by-case basis.
Transnational corporations	Their activities should be encouraged as they provide jobs and bring in new technologies.	Big corporations destroy indigenous producers, and the net effect may be negative.
Privatisation	Government provision of essential services in developing countries is invariably corrupt and/or inefficient, and therefore these services should be privatised.	Only government provision of essential services can ensure that they are available to the poor.
Competitiveness	Opening developing economies to foreign trade and investment improves competitiveness by destroying local monopolies.	Opening developing economies to foreign trade destroys indigenous producers whether or not they were monopolies, and further increases the power of the transnational corporations.

GLOBALISATION, GROWTH AND POVERTY

The evidence appears to be indisputable that globalisation has led to higher growth in most of the developing worlds, particularly in China and East Asia. The Asian Tigers, particularly South Korea and Thailand, were early to liberalise their trade, and have experienced rapid growth. So has China following its market reforms in the 1980s, and India, where Manmohan Singh, then finance minister, now prime minister, reduced protectionism.

Wolf (2005) quotes World Bank figures from 2002 which suggest that the gains from globalisation have been widespread. In 1980s the less globalised countries had higher GDP per head than more globalised ones, while by 1997 the situation was reversed. Annual growth rates per head in the more globalised countries were 3.1 per cent, in the less globalised ones only 0.5 per cent. Further evidence came from growth of a global middle class (defined as an annual income of between US $3,650 and US $14,600 a year, at purchasing power parity and 1993 prices). In 1960, 64 per cent of the global middle class lived in high-income western countries, and only 6 per cent in Asia, the Middle East and North Africa. By 2000, only 17 per cent lived in developed countries, and 51 per cent in Asia, the Middle East and North Africa.

There is some evidence that multinationals in developing countries pay higher wages than local manufacturing employers, although the evidence is rather old, dating from 1994 (Emmott et al 2002). Multinationals in low-income countries paid an average wage of US $3,400, while local employers paid US $1,700. The ratio of 2:1 between multinational and local wages was higher than that in high-income countries, where the ratio was 1.4:1.

Strong as the evidence seems, there are some caveats. GDP per head is not the same as standard of living, and there were losers as well as winners in the globalising country. Winners tended to work in manufacturing, losers in agriculture and extractive industries (see case study 6.1). Workers in developing countries tend to be non-unionised, capital inflows are unstable, multinationals can move out very quickly, and the risk of financial crisis increases, as in Thailand in 1997 (*Economist* 2001).

There is also evidence that inequality has increased in globalising countries (Legrain 2003). As Legrain points out, globalisation is no guarantee of economic success. It won't help war-torn countries like Somalia or the Democratic Republic of Congo, it won't cure Aids (particularly after the collapse of the Doha trade round; see case study 6.2), and it won't stop crooked rulers salting money away in Switzerland (Legrain 2003). But not although not a sufficient cause for economic growth, it seems to be a necessary one.

MULTINATIONALS AND BRANDS

Are multinationals and their brands too powerful? Foreign-owned multinationals employ one worker in every five in European manufacturing, and sell one euro in every four of manufactured goods in Europe (Venables 2005). Aisbett (2003) quoted the claim that 52 of the world's largest economic units are corporations, not states. However, supporters of globalisation like Legrain (2003) dispute this. They point out that this figure compares the turnover of corporations with the GDP of states. This leads to double or triple counting in the case of corporations. The correct comparison is with company value added (after deducting the cost of inputs). On this measure, there are only two corporations in the top 50 (Wal-Mart and Exxon), and 37 in the top 100. The US economy is 200 times bigger than Wal-Mart, Japan 100 times bigger, China 20 times bigger.

Corporations are also less powerful than nation states. They cannot impose taxes or regulations, they cannot go to war, they cannot force people to buy their products, and – unlike states – they can go bust.

There are also limits to their mobility, although this tends to benefit their home country rather than the developing world. It is very rare for companies to move their headquarters from one country to another (although Ericsson did it in 1999, when it moved its corporate HQ from Sweden to London to avoid high Swedish taxes) (Legrain 2003). Nokia is happy to stay in very high-cost Finland, and Lego in Denmark. On the other hand, the 'branch factory syndrome' seems to apply. When companies downsize, it always seems to be the branch factories rather than those near the headquarters that are closed down first.

Foreign direct investment (which creates multinationals) originates predominantly from developed countries (93 per cent in 1998–2000), and also is directed to other developed countries (78 per cent). Of the foreign direct investment which goes to developing countries, the bulk goes to China (the 2005 takeover of Rover by China's Nanjing Automotive, and the 2007 takeover of Corus by India's Tata Steel are very much the exceptions – for now). Inward investment creates jobs in the host country, but can also force up wages there, which in the long run makes the host less competitive.

One clear counterweight to global corporations would be global trade unions. On 1 May 2007, the TGWU and Amicus merged to form the UK's biggest union, Unite, with two million members. Its joint general secretaries, Derek Simpson and Tony Woodley (2007), writing in the *Guardian*, said, 'The challenges presented by world capitalism … cannot be met by any union that confines its operations within one country alone.' They announced an agreement to seek a merger with the United Steel Workers of the US and Canada, to form the first transatlantic union. 'Only a worldwide organising agenda has any long-term hope of levelling the playing field.'

The high point of globalisation came in the 1990s, in the euphoria which followed the collapse of communism, and 'the end of history'. This era of full-blooded, red in tooth and claw globalisation may have already passed. The onward march of e-commerce, and the idea that the world had entered a new economic paradigm of endless economic growth, was shattered by the dot-com crash in 2000, and the collapse of giant new economy corporations like Enron and WorldCom. Just as the economic confidence of the US was shaken, its sense of political and military invulnerability was shattered by the attacks of 11 September 2001.

Coupled with the US military response to the 'War on Terror', there is a growing though implicit feeling that the War on Terror will be lost unless the West wins the hearts and minds of the Third World. Hence the criticisms from both left and right of the aggressive neo-liberal policies of the IMF and the World Bank, and the demand for a more caring approach to debt relief and aid.

At the same time there is a growing realisation that globalisation has not made the nation state redundant. The role of the nation state is to provide good governance. In an article previewing his book, *State Building*, Francis Fukuyama quotes the doyen of free-market economists, Milton Friedman, as saying that his advice to former communist countries 10 years before had been to concentrate on privatisation. Now he feels that he was wrong: 'It turns out that the rule of law is probably more basic than privatisation' (Fukuyama 2004, p4).

GLOBALISATION AND THE LABOUR MARKET

Does globalisation help or harm workers in developed countries? As always, the evidence is mixed. Legrain (2003) argued that it is very hard to separate out the impact of globalisation from the impact of higher technology. Manufacturing has been declining for many years in all developed countries, while at the same time manufacturing jobs have been outsourced to Third World countries. He suggests that most of the impact comes from technology rather than globalisation. He cites the example of Bethlehem Steel in the US, where the Sparrows Point plant in Maryland produces the same amount of steel as it did in the 1960s, but with 3,500 workers rather than 30,000. As Legrain (p37) says, 'producing more with less is what economic growth is all about'.

Legrain makes an attempt to quantify the relative effects of globalisation and technology. Between 1990 and 2000, manufacturing's share of GDP fell by around 6 per cent, while the manufacturing trade deficit worsened by only 0.4 per cent of GDP.

The impact on jobs has been disproportionately on unskilled workers. Third World countries have an abundance of unskilled workers, which suggests that it is jobs using unskilled workers which will be offshored from rich countries.

However, more recent work suggests that the impact of globalisation on rich-country workers may be greater than previously realised. Globalisation is becoming more complex. Increasingly, individual parts of production processes are being offshored, rather than the whole process. This is known as 'high resolution globalisation', 'trade in tasks' (*Economist* 2007) or 'vertical disintegration' (*International Labour Review* 2006). A good example is the Barbie Doll. The raw material (plastic and hair) comes from Taiwan and Japan. Assembly takes place in the Philippines, Indonesia and China. Moulds come from the US, as does the last coat of paint. Marketing and research and development is centred in the US.

The rich world's comparative advantage in high tech sectors is falling, as education levels in countries like China and India are rising rapidly. China and India produce as many graduate scientists and engineers as the US, EU and Japan combined (*Economist* 2006b). Increasingly, higher-skilled jobs are being offshored – in software, medical diagnostics, finance and business consulting.

These finding are supported by a 2006 CIPD report, 'Offshoring and the role of HR'. A total of 589 organisations responded to a survey, covering 2.4 million employees. Of these, 14 per cent had offshored at least one activity in the past five years, 7 per cent were currently considering it, and 4 per cent had decided against it. The most popular offshoring locations were India (53 per cent) followed by China (27 per cent) and Poland (18 per cent). A wide range of functions was offshored:

Manufacturing and production	34 per cent of those who have offshored
IT support	24 per cent
IT development	22 per cent
Call centres/customer services	22 per cent
Financial, back-office support	19 per cent
Product development	18 per cent
Accounts	16 per cent

Fifteen per cent have brought back activities that were previously outsourced. The most common motives for outsourcing were cost reduction (86 per cent), UK skills shortages (27 per cent), to improve processes (21 per cent) and involvement in a joint venture (21 per cent). The biggest disadvantages were seen as: managerial control is more difficult (48 per cent), associated job losses in the UK (44 per cent), language problems (30 per cent) and risk of disruption to supply (24 per cent).

Most interesting was the type of job lost:

Skilled	29 per cent
Semi-skilled	25 per cent
Managerial	19 per cent
Unskilled	15 per cent
Graduate	8 per cent

The report includes a case study of a telecommunications firm, which offshored 500 jobs to Delhi 2004–05. It decided to employ these staff directly, rather than to outsource the operation, because it was felt that outsourcing might compromise quality of service and managerial control. Activities offshored included transactional processing for all operational areas, including order handling; part of engineering and sales support; processing of company payments and credit control; and IT support and development.

Motives for offshoring were to reduce costs; to take advantage of skilled Indian graduates; to exploit the differences in time zone; and to take advantage of less restrictive Indian employment law.

The company employed 4,100 staff across Europe, including 1,200 in the UK. Of these a total of 400 were made compulsorily redundant, with 100 of these redundancies in the UK.

A report by McKinsey in 2003 suggested that financially offshoring was a win–win situation. They claimed that every US $1 previously spent in the US and now offshored to India creates a benefit of US $1.47. The lion's share of this – US $1.14 – went to the US in the form of cheaper services and greater export of US goods to India, while 33 cents accrued to India as new wages, extra profit and extra tax revenue (Finch 2003).

The threat of globalisation seems to be increasingly to wages, rather than jobs. Real wages in the US, Germany and Japan are all falling. The share of wages in GDP is the lowest for three decades, while profits are at all-time highs. In the US, the share of profits in GDP rose from 7 per cent in 2001 to 13 per cent in 2006 (*Economist* 2006b).

Globalisation has boosted profits in several ways. Firms have reduced their costs by offshoring, while the bargaining power of workers in developed countries has been weakened as firms can always threaten to offshore. The global capital-to-labour ratio has massively shifted against workers. In the last 20 years, China, India and the former Soviet Union have effectively joined the world market economy, doubling the world supply of workers from 1.5 billion to 3 billion. Economic theory says that this would raise the return to capital and lower that to labour, which is exactly what has happened. At the same time, incomes have become more unequal. The top 1 per cent of workers in the US now receives 16 per cent of GDP, up from 8 per cent in 1980.

The following case studies examine some of the impacts of globalisation on the UK, US and Mexican labour markets.

 THE OUTSOURCING OF CALL CENTRES

CASE STUDY 6.5

The call centre industry in the UK is large, employing 867,000 people, or 3 per cent of the workforce, in 2004 (Shah 2004). It is also a new industry, having grown from almost nothing over the past 15 years. As a result, there has been considerable concern about the steady movement of call centre jobs, predominantly in the financial services industry, to India, particularly to Mumbai and Bangalore. Opponents of globalisation see this as an example of the detrimental effect of globalisation on UK employment, while supporters see it as a positive development, lowering costs for UK industry, and so increasing national prosperity.

Both are right. The short-term effect is that the UK is losing jobs. Call centres in the UK were frequently set up in areas of high unemployment, and the loss of these jobs is disproportionately felt. On the other hand, if outsourcing increases the profits of UK companies, this should free up resources for future investment. A short-term loss must thus be set against a long-term gain.

The typical Indian call centre goes to great lengths to make its service acceptable to UK consumers. The call centres operate on UK rather than Indian time, and operators are expected to keep themselves informed about the English weather, and the latest plot twists in *EastEnders* (Warren 2007). However, there is some evidence that Indian call centres are less efficient than UK ones. One study claimed that UK operators answered 25 per cent more calls per hour, resolved 17 per cent more calls first time, and stayed with their company three times as long, although this is offset by average salaries only 12 per cent of the UK level (Clennell 2004). This would suggest that UK companies, which are more concerned with the quality of their customer service than with minimising their short-term costs, should think very seriously before they outsource to India.

The long-run future of the call centre industry in the UK must lie with developing a more sophisticated knowledge-based, value-added service. Basic information-giving services can be better performed in India or over the Internet.

THE GIANT SUCKING SOUND

CASE STUDY 6.6

The term 'the giant sucking sound' was coined by the right-wing US presidential candidate Ross Perot in 1992, and refers to what he saw as the likely adverse effects of the North American Free Trade Agreement (NAFTA) with Canada and Mexico, which was about to go into effect. Perot feared that NAFTA would result in US manufacturing jobs heading south to Mexico.

One result of the NAFTA agreement was a considerable increase in the number of *maquiladora* assembly plants in northern Mexico, assembling goods mainly for the US market – an example of the phenomenon known as nearshoring, where operations are outsourced to a near geographic neighbour. However, there is dispute about the impact of this on both the US and Mexican economies.

The *maquiladora* programme was launched by the Mexican government in the 1960s. It encouraged foreign companies to establish assembly plants along the Mexican side of the US–Mexico border. The US encouraged this development, because it felt that increased job opportunities in the border region would reduce illegal Mexican immigration to the US. These plants were allowed to import components and sub-assemblies free of duty, as long as they were re-exported. Employment in *maquiladoras* grew from 0.12 million in 1980 to 1.2 million in 2006. The sector accounts for nearly 3 per cent of Mexico's GDP, 20 per cent of its manufacturing value added, and 46 per cent of Mexican exports to the US in 2001 (GAO 2003). Four US border states (California, Arizona, New Mexico and Texas) account for 62 per cent of all US exports to Mexico. Population on the Mexican side of the border soared, by 32 per cent between 1990 and 2000. Huge twin cities (a city on each side of the border), such as San Diego–Tijuana and El Paso–Juarez, have expanded rapidly (Bergin, Geenstra and Hanson 2008).

It is difficult to estimate the effect of the *maquiladora* programme on the US, as it is hard to separate its effects from the general effects of the NAFTA agreement.

However, it has been estimated that NAFTA led to an increase of US $12 billion a year in US exports, and that this directly created 100,000 US jobs. On the other hand, it is also argued that NAFTA has resulted in some loss of well-paid US manufacturing jobs, and their replacement with lower-paid service jobs. Perhaps on balance there has been a small sucking sound of job losses, rather than Perot's giant one.

The effect on the Mexican economy is again mixed. Mexico is a proud country, with a long-running streak of anti-Americanism, and does not want to be seen as an economic colony of the US. It is clear that the *maquiladoras* have created many jobs in Mexico, but the quality of those jobs is less clear. Although wages are relatively high by Mexican standards, the cost of living is also high. Mexico has very tight labour protection laws, but these laws seem to be laxly administered in the border *maquiladora* regions. Hours are long, unions are discouraged and health and safety standards poor. The environmental impact is also adverse, with overcrowding, swamped infrastructure and the growth of shanty towns. Most workers in the maquiladoras are women, attracted from poor areas in Mexico's interior. Separated from their families, far from home, and usually living in hostels, they are easy prey for pimps, people traffickers and drug pushers (Cohen and Kennedy 2007, Aragon 2008).

The *maquiladoras* are also extremely vulnerable to competition from China. Mexican wages, although very low by US standards, are higher than Chinese wages, and the only advantage that Mexico has is its close proximity to the US. As long as international shipping rates are low, it cannot compete with China. The *maquiladoras* are also vulnerable to competition from lower-wage economies in Central America. Wages in Honduras, for example, are half those in Mexico. Between 2000 and 2002, employment in the *maquiladora* sector fell by 21 per cent and production by 30 per cent (GAO 2003).

ACTIVITY 6.8 GLOBALISATION AND YOUR ORGANISATION

What impact, if any, has globalisation had on your own organisation?

MANAGEMENT AND HR IN THE G20 — JAPAN, CHINA, INDIA AND SOUTH AFRICA

JAPAN

The best way to understand HR in Japan is through Japanese history. Until the mid-nineteenth century, Japan was a feudal society. Power was exercised through great land-owning families, the *daimyo* (equivalent to the barons in feudal England). They were answerable to (and frequently rebelled against) the hereditary military dictator, the *shogun*, who was himself answerable, at least on paper, to the figurehead emperor, who was seen as divine. Under the *daimyo* were the *samurai*, a military caste comparable to knights in medieval Europe, whose role was to serve their lord for life, sacrificing their own lives if required, and who in return received lifetime support from their lord. The whole system was based on mutual obligation. The duty of the *samurai* was reinforced by the concepts of *gambare* (will to endure) and *gaman* (stoical acceptance of hardship). Although the samurai's role was originally purely military, by the nineteenth century they also undertook many administrative roles on behalf of their lord. The rest of the population – the merchants and peasants – were of little account, and the *samurai* had the right to kill a peasant without legal redress.

The feudal system was formally abolished after the Meiji Restoration in the 1860s, when the emperor seized back power from the *shogun*, and embarked on a breakneck programme of modernisation, but the *samurai* system evolved seamlessly into the new Japan. Industrialisation was organised around huge industrial conglomerates, the *zaibatsu*, which in effect replaced the *daimyo*, while the samurai evolved into industrial managers. The zaibatsu were abolished by the Americans after 1945, but speedily re-emerged as *keiretsu*, which still dominate much of the Japanese economy – companies such as Mitsui and Mitsubishi.

Hangovers from the feudal system include:

- Lifetime employment (*nenko seido*) – male employees and managers in large corporations, particularly the *keiretsu*, stay with the same company for life, with little recruitment above entry level, and a promotion system based on seniority. Managers are predominantly generalists, who may well work in a number of specialisms during their career. There is little sense of a distinct HR progression.

- Loyalty to the company is paramount, and there is almost total identification of the employee with the company. This extends to industrial relations, where unions are organised on an enterprise basis, with much movement of executives between the company and the union.

- The culture of organisations is based on the concept of *wa* (harmony). Conflict is to be avoided wherever possible. This extends to decision-making within the organisation. New proposals are circulated throughout the organisation on formal cards (*ringi*), and each department adds its comments to the ringi. The aim is to reach mutual understanding (*nemawashi*). Decision-making is thus slow, but commitment to a decision, once taken, is strong.

- *Gambara* and *gamban* are still expected. Japanese managers work extremely long hours, and a recognised illness in Japan is *karoshi* (death through overwork).

- There is an emphasis on perfection (reflecting Japanese institutions such as the tea ceremony and calligraphy), hence the Japanese obsession with quality.

- Those outside the *nenko seido* system (workers in small companies, contract workers, women) have fewer rights and much inferior employment conditions.

The Japanese system has many strengths, but also some weaknesses. Conformity is all, and mavericks are not encouraged, as they threaten *wa*. A Japanese proverb says 'the protruding nail should be hammered down'. It is also important to remember that the *nenko seido* system only ever applied to a minority of workers. Even within the *keiretsu*, lifetime employment only applied to 'salarymen'.

The system has also come under increasing pressure since the onset of the long recession in 1990. For the first time, large companies such as Sony and Nissan have made large-scale redundancies among core workers, not just contract workers, and the *ringi* decision-making system has largely been abandoned as too slow. However, the underlying commitment to wa remains (Hales 2001).

CHINA

Management in China has been affected by two major factors: the influence of Confucianism and the influence of the communist revolution.

Confucianism stresses harmony, respect, discipline and technical competence (Jacques 2009). This is reflected in a great respect for authority, particularly authority based on seniority and/or age. Chinese organisations are highly hierarchical, with considerable distance between managers and workers (no open-plan offices), and a high degree of formality (no first names, managers addressed by their name and job title – Engineer Wu, Accountant Liu, etc) (Gamble 2003).

Chinese desire for harmony is very similar to the Japanese concept of *wa*, although the latter is derived from Buddhism rather than from Confucianism. Also important is the concept of face. Managers will see any personal reprimand or expression of disapproval as a loss of face, and a serious setback to their self-esteem, while a western manager will treat a rebuke as just one of those things, quickly forgotten.

After the revolution, the Communist Party introduced the concept of the iron rice bowl (*tie fan wan*), whereby state-owned enterprises (SOEs) (often owned by local authorities or the People's Liberation Army rather than directly by the state) were the mechanism through which welfare was delivered in China. They literally protected their workers from cradle to grave. Since the reforms introduced by Deng Xiaoping 30 years ago, the iron rice bowl has slowly rusted away. Many SOEs have gone bust, while others have evolved into joint ventures with foreign companies, or Chinese private enterprise companies like Galanz. Workers from the old SOEs have found it difficult to adjust to a more dynamic work environment, but there is an endless supply of new, young, usually female, workers from the provinces who have no preconceptions about work, but who have been brought up to respect authority and to conform.

One factor unique to China (and to the overseas Chinese) is *guanxi*, or connections. This is a system of mutual obligation, whereby a favour made must be returned. This can override loyalty to one's employer, and is second only in importance to loyalty to one's family. *Guanxi* can be used by management – doing favours for one's employees will create a reciprocal obligation – but on the other hand, it can be a danger to organisations. Vanhonacker (2004) gives the example of a Chinese sales representative for a pharmaceutical company who sells drugs on the side from local companies that compete with his foreign employer, but with which he has a *guanxi* obligation. Selling competitors' products is a way to pay back favours, fortify *guanxi* and make money.

INDIA

Three major influences have shaped the Indian approach to management: the legacy of the British, of Gandhi, and of Hindu Vedic philosophy:

- The British left a tradition of bureaucracy (the Permit Raj), which still permeates much of Indian management today.

- Gandhi left a preference for small-scale, village-based industry (symbolised by the spinning wheel), heavily protected by import tariffs and regulation. This is still seen as an ideal by many Indians, but in practice has been swept away by the economic reforms started by Manmohan Singh (see the seminar activity in Chapter 4).

- From the Hindu Vedic scriptures comes the concept of cosmic order, supported by common vision, universal brotherhood and equitable prosperity for all (Sharma and Talwar 2004). Business excellence can only be achieved through prosperity for all, or by taking care of all stakeholders. The ultimate good is the good of society, not personal wealth or self-esteem. As one of the Vedic hymns puts it: 'One should sacrifice the individual for the sale of family interest, family for the sake of village, village for the sake of nation, and abandon everything for defending higher values of life' (Sharma and Talwar 2004). Modern Indian management gurus like C K Prahalad and Rakesh Khurana stress capitalism's ethical and societal obligations (Crainer and Dearlove 2005).

The Vedic principles are clearly displayed in the philosophy of the leading Indian conglomerate Tata (although the Tata family are actually Parsees, not Hindus). The founder of the Tata group, Jamsetji Tata, said in 1868, 'In a free enterprise, the community is not just another stakeholder in business, but is in fact the very purpose of its existence' (Branzei and Nadkarni 2008).

SOUTH AFRICA

The African concept of *ubuntu* has striking similarities with the Japanese concept of wa. Ubuntu can be defined as humaneness: a sprit of caring and community, harmony and hospitality, respect and responsiveness (Mangaliso 2001).

Ubuntu stresses the collective – the family, the clan, the community – an exact parallel with the Indian Vedic approach. Kinship and teamwork are key to the concept. As in China, age is equated with wisdom. *Ubuntu* permeates decision-making in South Africa. Just as with *nemawashi* in Japan, decision-making is a slow process, considering all points of view, and the aim is to reach consensus.

One practical application of *ubuntu* comes in reactions to recession. The ubuntu approach is to share the burden in a fair way, leading to pay cuts across the board rather than lay-offs.

What do those explorations of management and HR practices in the non-western world tell us? What is striking is the similarity of approach across Japan, China, India and South Africa. Each culture stresses harmony, consensus, and community – a very different approach from the self-centred and profit-oriented approach of the West. There are clear parallels with the best practice of high-performance HRM (Marchington and Wilkinson 2008).

 ## ACTIVITY 6.9 JAGUAR LAND ROVER – A CULTURAL FOOTBALL

Few companies have been through as many different international owners as Jaguar Land Rover. Both Jaguar and Land Rover became part of British Leyland (BL) in 1968. In 1975 BL was nationalised, and in 1988 it was sold to British Aerospace (BAe). In practice Jaguar and Land Rover, along with the rest of the group, was managed by Honda under a strategic alliance with BAe. In 1994, the whole group was sold to BMW, which itself sold out to Ford in 2000. Finally, in 2008, Ford sold Jaguar and Land Rover to Tata. Land Rover has thus successively been under British (both private and public), Japanese, German, American and Indian management.

The Dutch guru Geert Hofstede has identified what he calls his cultural dimensions, which he says accurately describe national characters. His dimensions are:

Power distance (PD). The extent to which societies accept that power is and should be distributed unequally. Organisationally, high power distance will lead to hierarchical organisations with large wage differentials.

Individualism (IDV). The degree to which individuals are integrated into groups. Collectivist societies with a low individualism score will have a high level of employment security and commitment to staff.

Masculinity/femininity (M/F). Masculine societies are assertive and competitive, with high levels of organisational conflict.

Uncertainty avoidance (UA). The degree to which people feel comfortable in ambiguous situations. Low uncertainty avoidance is reflected in informal, unstructured organisations.

Long-term orientation (LTO). In organisations this will be reflected in short-term profit maximisation versus long-term growth.

Table 6.2 summarises those of Hofstede's findings which are relevant to Jaguar Land Rover:

To some extent, table 6.2 is reflected in attitudes to quality at Jaguar Land Rover. Under British management, quality was a low priority: most of the time the group was struggling for survival. Honda brought in a high priority for quality, with the emphasis placed on the 'soft' aspects – total quality management, *kaizen* (continuous improvement), quality circles, just in time – and a realisation that the pay-off from quality would be long term. BMW was also concerned with quality, with a shorter-term orientation and a more top-down approach, while Ford concentrated on 'hard' aspects of quality, such as Six Sigma. It is yet to be seen what Tata's approach will be, but evidence on Tata's management style suggests a high commitment to quality (see page 262).

It is important to bear in mind that Hofstede's approach has been heavily criticised. One key criticism is that his basic research is very old, carried out between 1967 and 1973, and originally based solely on (mainly male) employees of IBM.

What other criticisms can you make of Hofstede's approach, (a) in general, and (b) in relation to Jaguar Land Rover? (You will find Marchington and Wilkinson (2008) pp29–31 useful.)

Table 6.2 Hofstede's cultural dimensions

Country	PD	IDV	M/F	UA	LTO
UK	Low	High	Medium	Low	Low
Japan	Medium	Low	High	High	High
Germany	Low	Medium	Medium	Medium	Low
US	Low	High	Medium	Low	Low
India	High	Medium	Medium	Low	Medium

(Source: Hofstede (2009) www.geert-hofstede.com/hofstede [accessed 17 April 2010].)

- The EU's key aims have always been to maintain peace in Europe (particularly between France and Germany) and to enhance prosperity.

- Although there is general agreement on these overriding aims, there are considerable differences of opinion about the future direction of the EU, epitomised by the single market, federalist and integrationist perspectives.

- The Commission is the executive of the EU, initiating and implementing policy; the Council of Ministers is the political decision-making body; the Parliament is mainly consultative; the European Court of Justice rules on the legal interpretation of the EU treaties and legislation.

- The EU expanded from 15 to 25 members in 2004, and to 27 in 2007. This has necessitated the drafting of a new constitution, published in 2004, which eventually led to the Lisbon Treaty in 2009.

- Since the mid-1940s, the world economic system has been regulated by three major international institutions: the IMF, the World Bank and GATT (now the WTO). All have been criticised by the Left as imposing capitalist norms on the developing world.

- Multinational corporations tend to have polycentric employment patterns, while transnational corporations have geocentric employment patterns.

- Globalisation has been characterised as having three main elements: the expansion of markets, the transformation of politics and the emergence of new social and political movements. The theory of comparative advantage and international specialisation underpins the concept of globalisation. Globalisation has also become more feasible with modern developments in communications, particularly air transport and the Internet.

- Aisbett (2003) identified four main areas of concern over globalisation: an objection not to globalisation in principle but to the way in which it is skewed in favour of developed countries; loss of sovereignty to transnational corporations and to institutions like the IMF and the WTO; neo-liberal or 'Washington consensus' policies; and the rise of big corporations.

- Offshoring of jobs to developing countries increasingly affects skilled and professional jobs as well as the less skilled call centre jobs.

- The HR systems in Japan, China, India and South Africa share a desire for harmony and a regard for stakeholders.

QUESTIONS

1. What are the key elements of the single market, federalist and integrationist approaches to the EU?

2. What are the main roles of the European Parliament?

3. What are the three criteria for accession to the EU?

4. Why was there such a high level of immigration from Poland to the UK after 2004?

5. What are the main roles of the IMF, the World Bank and the WTO?

6. What are the major differences between multinational and transnational corporations?

7. What do you understand by ethnocentric, polycentirc and geocentric patterns of employment?

8. What were the main reasons for the collapse of the Doha Round?

9. In what ways does globalisation (a) help, and (b) damage the Third World?

10. What do you understand by the expressions '*wa*', 'the iron rice bowl' and '*ubuntu*'?

EXPLORE FURTHER

Further Reading

Books on the EU tend to be dry and fact-ridden, but two which are relatively readable are:

- Nugent, N. (2006) *The Government and Politics of the European Union*. 6th edition. Basingstoke: Palgrave Macmillan.

- Cini, M. (ed). (2007) *European Union Politics*. 2nd edition. Oxford: OUP.

Globalisation:

- Micklethwait, J. and Wooldridge, A. (2000) *A Future Perfect: The challenge and hidden promise of globalization*. London: Heinemann. (A readable (but positive) introduction to globalisation.)

- Wolf, M. (2005) *Why Globalization Works*. New Haven: Yale Nota Bene.

- Legrain, P. (2003) *Open World: the truth about globalisation*. London: Abacus.

- Stiglitz, J. (2003) *Globalization and its Discontents*. London: Penguin. (Fiercely critical of the role of the IMF.)

For both the EU and globalisation, the way to keep up to date is read good-quality newspapers regularly. The same general advice applies as in Chapter 2 – make sure you attain a balance of left- and right-wing views.

Websites

The BBC news website (www.bbc. co.uk) often has useful background information. For a generally anti-globalisation perspective, check out websites like Oxfam (www.oxfam. org.uk) or ActionAid (www.actionaid. org.uk).

SEMINAR ACTIVITY

POLISH PLUMBERS

On 1 May 2004, 10 new member states joined the EU. Eight of these, known as the A8, came from Central and Eastern Europe, the biggest of these being Poland, with a population of about 38.5 million. The UK already had a significant Polish minority, the descendants of the Free Poles who had fought on the Allied side in the Second World War, and who had decided not to go back to a communist Poland. The 2001 census showed that in the UK there were nearly 61,000 people who had been born in Poland, with a third of these living in London (BBC nd). With their descendants, they made up a population of Polish ancestry of about a quarter of a million.

Under the EU rules on free movement, people from the A8 countries had the right to move between other EU countries, but this did not necessarily extend to the right to work. As part of the accession arrangements, the 15 'old' EU countries had the right to impose restrictions on work for A8 citizens for up to seven years. Only Sweden allowed A8 citizens an unrestricted right to work. The UK and Ireland granted them right to work, but no right to unemployment benefit until they had worked continuously for a year.

It was forecast at the time of accession that 13,000 A8 workers a year would come to the UK. However, this has proven to be a gross underestimate. Denis MacShane (2006), who was Europe minister at the time, claimed that the original figure was based on all 15 old EU members opening their doors to A8 workers.

Although it is clear that many more A8 workers, particularly Poles, are working in the UK than originally thought, nobody really knows how many. As Poles and other A8 citizens can enter the EU without a visa, there is no way to telling how many of those who enter the country intend to work, and how many are just passing through. The Office for National Statistics carries out random interviews on arrivals to the UK, and on this basis estimates that 56,000 Poles entered the UK to work in 2005. However, the DWP says that 170,000 Poles applied for national insurance numbers in 2005 (Doward and McKenna 2007).

The other main source of information on numbers is the Worker Registration Scheme (WRS), under which A8 workers are encouraged to register. This is not compulsory, is not required for the self-employed, and costs £75. There is also no requirement to deregister if a worker leaves the UK. In May 2005, the BBC reported that 176,000 had registered by March 2005. Of these 82 per cent were aged between 18 and 34, 96 per cent were working full time and a third may have been working illegally in the UK before accession and merely regularising their position. Poland was the biggest provider, with 56 per cent of the total, followed by Lithuania with 15 per cent and Slovakia with 11 per cent (BBC 2005a). This is not surprising, as Poland had by far the biggest population of the A8 countries, with 20 per cent unemployment, wages one-sixth of those in the UK, and a well-educated population, many of whom spoke English.

By January 2007, 579,000 had registered under the WRS, of whom 63 per cent were from Poland. The anti-immigration pressure group claimed that this was an underestimate, and that the true figure was nearer 600,000, although it conceded that many of these will have left the country (Migration Watch 2007). By December 2007 the number registered had increased to 750,000 (House of Lords 2008).

Some figures are also available from the Polish end of the migration. In 2004, the year of accession, there were fewer movements of Poles out of the country than in 2003 (27.2 million compared with 38.6 million) (Iglicka 2005). However, there is no way of telling how many of these were going out of Poland to work, or, perhaps, on day trips to Germany or the Czech Republic. What may be significant, however, is that the number of those leaving by air increased by 37 per cent in 2004 to 1.89 million. Official emigration in 2004 was also lower than in 2003, and only 543 Poles officially emigrated to the UK, compared with 12,646 to Germany.

Rumours and urban myths abound of the number of Poles in the UK. There are said to be 10,000 in Slough, 15,000 in Boston, Lincolnshire and 3,000 in Crewe (Doward and McKenna 2007). According to some stories, every other plumber in the UK is now Polish, although according to WRS figures there are only about 100 registered Polish plumbers (but note that the self-employed do not have to register).

Despite the myths, most Polish and other A8 immigrants are not plumbers. Among them, 24 per cent work in distribution, hotels and restaurants, 21 per cent in manufacturing, 14 per cent in construction and a significant but unstated proportion in agriculture and food processing (House of Lords 2008).

The plain truth is nobody really has any idea how many Poles are working in Britain. It is thought that most Polish and other A8 workers come to the UK with every intention of going back to Poland, and, unlike other immigrant groups, going back is very easy and cheap – £10 on a Ryanair flight. When questioned by the Joseph Rowntree Foundation immediately after accession, only 6 per cent said they intended to stay in the UK permanently. A year later, this had risen to 29 per cent (Spencer et al 2007). In September 2007, 62 per cent of those arriving in the previous 12 months said they intended to stay for less than one year (House of Lords 2008), although the experience of other immigrant groups suggests that more will stay than initially expected to. The best estimate is probably that at any one time, there are about 200,000–250,000 Polish workers in the UK, which approximately doubles the figure of Polish descent in 2001. We will not have any really accurate figures until the 2011 census.

Questions

1. What do you think is the likely economic and social impact of the influx of Polish and other A8 workers into the UK?

2. How can trade unions respond to the issues raised by the influx of Polish workers?

CHAPTER 7

Demographic and Social Trends

LEARNING OUTCOMES

When you have completed this chapter you should be able to:

- identify the key demographic statistics in a local, national, European and international setting

- understand the important effects produced by changes in demographic influences

- reflect on how demography has major influences on businesses and government, who need to respond in a positive way

- discuss the appropriateness of responses by businesses and government to take advantage of major demographic changes

- understand the major theories of social stratification and their application to the UK setting

- evaluate the nature and extent of social mobility in the UK

- understand the reasons for the slowing rate of social mobility in the UK, and its effects

- discuss the extent and nature of inequality and poverty in the UK

- reflect on the similarities and differences between equal opportunities and diversity.

DEMOGRAPHY

INTRODUCTION

Demography looks at population: their sizes, characteristics and the way they change. It sounds like a dry and academic subject but that is far from the truth. Population changes throughout the ages have been one of the major determining factors in economic development, political activity and social change. A growth in population can lead to a number of consequences. It can lead to wars, such as when the Roman Empire constantly fought with the barbarians in order to extend its boundaries and thus secure more extensive food supplies for its growing population, or its sweeping hordes out of Mongolia and the Far East a few centuries later. It can also lead to extensive economic growth. It was only possible for the Industrial Revolution to get under way in the UK factories in the late eighteenth century with the growing supply of surplus labour from the countryside, following the enclosure movement and technological agricultural developments. Nor would the vast choice of international food and restaurants we enjoy today have happened without the post-war migratory patterns, firstly from the new Commonwealth countries, followed by young entrepreneurs from all around the world.

Rapid movements in demography have occurred in recent years. Throughout history, the human race has been young, but now that is changing. In the next 50 years, both birth rates and death rates will continue to decline so fast that populations will age dramatically. For the first time in history, there will be more older people than young people, with the average age rising from 22 in 1978 to 38 in 2050. In a growing number of countries, the population will actually start to decline. It is, indeed, likely that the world population itself will peak around the middle of the century (Wallace 2001).

These changes will change economies and working habits, revolutionise pensions and health care provision, and even alter some of the markets for goods and services.

POPULATION GROWTH

In the year 1000, world population has been estimated to be at around 300 million. It grew slowly over the next 750 years to 728 million in 1750. Over the next 250 years, there was a spectacular growth, with a doubling of population to 1,500 million by 1900 and a further doubling to three billion by 1960. It has taken only 40 years for the population to double again to six billion.

The breakdown by continent of the growth from 1800 to 2010 is shown in table 7.1.

Table 7.1 World population 1800 to 2010

millions

Year	1800	1850	1900	1950	1975	2000	2010*
Asia	635	809	947	1,402	2,395	3,683	4,111
Africa	107	111	133	224	416	784	1,026
Europe	203	276	408	547	676	729	732
Latin America and Caribbean	24	38	74	166	322	519	581
North America	7	26	82	172	243	310	345
Oceania	2	2	6	13	21	30	35
World total	972	1,262	1,650	2,524	4,073	6,055	6,829

(Source: United Nations 2009.) *Estimate

It can be seen that the growth has not been consistent across the world. Up until 1900, population increased rapidly in the developing world, but stayed relatively subdued in the poorer developing world. Since 1900, the bulk of the world population growth has been in the developing world with an astonishing tripling of population in Africa and Latin America since 1950. This has been accompanied by a rapid slowing in growth in the developed world, especially in Europe, with some countries, such as Germany, showing an absolute decline in recent years.

In the ex-communist countries, the population is already falling sharply in the Ukraine and Bulgaria and is expected to drop by over 10 per cent by 2025 in Russia, Georgia, Belarus and Romania (Lucas 2006).

In the UK, as shown in table 7.2, the spurt in population took place in the nineteenth century and has slowed considerably since 1900. Scotland's population actually declined during the 2000s. However, for the UK as a whole, there have been tentative signs of a small reversal of this trend at the end of the 2000s (see below).

The effects of the potato famine and lack of industrial development in Ireland can be seen with an actual decline in population from 1851 to 1901 where vast numbers of young people left Ireland for the England mainland, America and the colonies. In fact, Ireland has also reversed the UK trend with a considerable growth in population since 1951, reflecting a more buoyant agricultural and industrial economy arising principally from joining Europe in 1973; greater economic opportunities have also halted mass migration abroad. The increase in population since 1991, however, has slowed to 0.3 per cent per year.

Table 7.2 UK population

thousands

Year	1801	1851	1901	1951	2001	2008
England	8,305	16,764	30,515	41,159	50,035	51,446
Wales	587	1,163	2,013	2,599	2,988	2,993
Scotland	1,608	2,889	4,472	5,096	5,258	5,169
Northern Ireland	*	1,443	1,237	1,371	1,701	1,775
Total	*	22,259	38,237	50,225	59,982	61,383

(Source: National Statistical Office 2009.) *Not available

DRIVERS OF POPULATION CHANGE

Taking the world as a whole, the only two factors controlling population change are the level of the birth rate and the level of the death rate. Within any particular country or region, the migration in and out of that country or region is also an important factor.

Birth rate

The birth rate is usually expressed in terms of the number of live births per 1,000 of the population. The fertility rate is the average number of births for each woman of child-bearing age. A rate of 2.1 is required to maintain the population over an extended period of time, excluding migration.

Table 7.3 Birth statistics – UK

Year	Actual births – annual average for decade (thousands)	Fertility rate
1900s	1091	3.5
1930's	824	1.8
1950's	839	2.2
1960's	962	2.6
1970's	736	2.0
1980's	757	1.8
1990's	744	1.7
2000's	701	1.65
2008	791 (actual year)	1.96 (actual year)

(Source: Office for National Statistics 2009.)

During the twentieth century, the fertility rate peaked at 2.95 in 1964, while the lowest year for births was 1977 (657,000).

The birth rate is determined by:

- the number of women in the population who are of child-bearing age
- the proportion of this group of women who actually have children – this is called the 'fertility rate'.

It is clear from table 6.3 that there was a steady drop in the birth rate from 1900 to the early 2000s, with the exception of a baby boom in the 1960s (plus a similar shorter boom in the period 1946–49). The birth rate mirrored the fertility rate, although the latter has had greater variations.

However, the birth rate in the UK began to rise again during the early 2000s and the fertility rate also began to steadily rise. This has been due to a number of factors:

- Continuing economic affluence providing a sense of economic security that allowed family units to trade off the risks of the potential loss of income.
- The influence of government policies to encourage working mothers through a raft of measures including enhanced maternity pay and new rights to apply to work flexibly.
- The influence of an increased migrant population, especially from the Indian sub-continent, where larger families are the norm. By 2008, the number of live births had risen to 791,000, an increase of 33,000 over the previous year, with one quarter of the babies born to mothers who came from outside the

UK, most commonly from Pakistan, Poland and India; the fertility rate for this group is around 2.5.

This trend has been mainly responsible for a spurt in the UK population to over 61 million in 2008, an increase of over 400,000. Another trend is that women are having children much later in life. The mean age of women having their first baby was 23.7 in 1970, but this had increased to 28.6 in 2008. An increasing number of women are childless. One in five women in their 40s have no children compared to one in 10 in the 1940s.

Table 7.4 compares the UK with other countries, showing that its fertility rate is generally higher than the rest of Europe but lower than most developing countries.

Table 7.4 World fertility rates

	2007	Estimate 2030
UK	1.8	1.85
USA	2.1	1.85
Japan	1.3	1.72
Germany	1.3	1.69
Greece	1.3	1.57
China	1.7	1.85
Hong Kong	0.9	1.31
India	2.8	1.85
Pakistan	3.5	2.43
Brazil	2.3	1.86
Nigeria	5.4	2.95
Algeria	2.4	1.93
World	2.3	2.17

(Source: United Nations 2009.)

The suggested causes of the reduced fertility rate in the developed countries are as follows:

- Women are taking charge of their fertility. The widespread use of the contraceptive pill and other modern devices from the 1970s onwards allowed decisions to be taken on family planning, unheard of previously. Many women (and couples) have decided not to have families or to have just one child often so that two careers can be pursued. This is connected with postponing starting a family until later. Having children usually brings a savage reduction in household income as one member, usually the mother, may stop working or go part time.

- It is no longer necessary to have a large family as an insurance against obtaining care in older age. The extended family has generally declined in importance as the state has stepped in to provide or support services that have traditionally been carried out by family members.

- The cost of bringing up families has risen, especially if university costs are anticipated, so the average expenditure on children has not fallen with the birth rate – it is simply a case of each child representing a larger financial investment, despite government financial incentives.

- In the wider world, children are no longer as useful as they once were. Fewer people live on farms where children can help out and child labour, although still an area of international concern, is far less prevalent: strong attempts have been made to eradicate this practice in recent years.

About three-quarters of the African countries are presently participating in various family planning programmes. Most governments encourage private planned-parenthood associations to carry out various phases of the programmes. In some countries as many as eight or 10 agencies and organisations may co-ordinate in this effort. Governments often integrate family planning in their maternal and child health services by emphasising birth spacing for health reasons. In the more prosperous African countries, such as Nigeria, the fertility rate is dropping very rapidly.

In addition to active family planning programmes, many African governments have taken legal measures to reduce fertility. For example, some countries have raised the legal age for marriage. Others have outlawed polygamy. Some countries also now limit child allowances for government officials to no more than three or four children and some limit the number of maternity leave periods (Tarver 1996). The effects of population changes on Japan are discussed in case study 7.1.

 JAPAN FACES CONTRACTION PAINS

CASE STUDY 7.1

Japan is getting old at an astonishing pace, a far cry from the position just after 1945. Then, the over-65s constituted around 5 per cent of the population, well below the figure for the other major economies. In 2007, the elderly account for 20 per cent of the population and average life spans have increased from 50 in 1947 to 82. By 2015, the proportion of the elderly will have risen to 25 per cent, thanks mainly to an unusually large post-war baby-boom generation who are now starting to retire at 60, the normal corporate retirement age.

The fertility rate fell below the 2.1 replacement level in 1970 and reached a low of 1.26 in 2005 before stabilising at 1.32 in 2007. In 2005, the actual population began to fall in absolute terms, with very little migration allowed to balance the picture. From 127 million in 2007, it is estimated that the population will drop to 95 million by 2050, with the elderly accounting for 40 per cent of the total.

As the proportion of elderly citizens increases, so the number of young people declines. Around 16 million are currently in their twenties but, in the next 10 years alone, this will drop to 13 million. Recent graduates are already reaping the benefit with more job offers than labour available, so pushing up the price of graduate jobs. However, the flipside is that today's young graduate must support an ever-larger proportion of retirees. By 2030, there will be two employees for each retiree; by 2050, the ratio will fall to 1.5 employee per retiree. Most commentators regard this as unworkable, as do most graduates, the majority of whom are not paying the fixed portion of their state pension scheme, which indicates that they expect the scheme to be closed before they retire.

The biggest falls in population are taking place in the countryside, where younger villagers have been migrating to the towns since the 1970s. The hugely inefficient agricultural sector has been subsidised equally generously for 50 years, backed by massive tariffs to keep out foreign rice and other products. While the economy grew, Japanese society went along with supporting traditional agricultural cultures and values, but the young voted with their feet and joined emerging, innovative industries and services. Now the over-65s make up 40 per cent of rural communities and 60 per cent of all farmers, so many communities have become unviable.

In response, one small isolated hamlet, down to nine villagers, all over 60, has contracted with an industrial waste company to sell its valley and all its farms so it will disappear under 150 feet of industrial ash. On a larger scale, Yubari, a former mining town on Hokkaido Island, has experienced a population fall from 100,000 to 13,000 since 1950 and has gone bankrupt through spending too much money trying to (unsuccessfully) promote the town's profile. Another town decided to actively shrink its physical environment, moving public institutions from the suburbs back into the centre of town and refusing permission for all additional dwellings outside a prescribed (and smaller) town boundary.

On the macro-conomic front, the government has taken radical decisions over state pensions. Eligibility for the fixed part of the pension will rise from 60 to 65 in stages by 2014 and eligibility for the flexible (and larger) part will rise to 65 by 2026. Most commentators regard this as

not fast enough. Businesses have a cultural problem with a higher retirement age. Pay is based very much on seniority so employees staying longer in the workplace would cost organisations much more money. However, because older employees are respected, it would be extremely difficult to impose pay cuts when employees stay on to a later retirement age.

If the retirement age is delayed until 65 or 70, it would go some way to solving the decline of the supply of labour. Japan already has one of the highest proportions of the elderly still in the workforce. This is not because the Japanese simply like to work or do not feel a useful part of society otherwise. For many it is that they have to work to survive. Most of these employment positions involve 'downshifting' into menial work such as repairs and night-watchman with wages that are mediocre.

However, a bigger influence would be to increase the participation rate of women, which was 63 per cent in 2007, compared to 68 per cent in UK or the US. Cultural problems are even greater in Japan, with male chauvinism dominating offices, a work culture of long hours and a shortage of childcare facilities. Japan still, apparently, does not have an expression for 'work–life balance'. Large numbers of women permanently drop out of the labour market when they have children. As the average Japanese father does not help in the home (partly due to the long hours culture), this engenders anxiety from the wife about extending the family. By the time their children have grown up, they then have caring responsibilities for their ageing parents, who are often living with them.

In 2002, the Japanese government announced that every Japanese woman who gives birth is to receive the equivalent of £1,700 plus up to £15,000 for help with childcare. The fact that this initiative is likely to cost around £5 billion indicates the degree of anxiety over the continuing decline in Japan's birth rate. So far, the effect seems to be marginal, even in the cities, as there is little attraction in bringing up families in tiny Japanese apartments, where beds are folded up during the day and the father is not present until late at night.

A rapidly ageing population, supported by fewer and fewer working people, could keep Japan in a state of semi-permanent recession. It is estimated that if current trends continue, young people in 2025 will have to pay around 25 per cent of their salary as a tax to simply keep pensions at their current level. It remains to be seen whether the financial inducements, the availability of 'baby shops' to help women with childcare, and 'grandmother networks' to support young families will make any difference or whether women will continue to wait until their aspirations in the workplace have been better satisfied.

(Sources: Norton 2002, *Economist* 2007, Woronoff 1996.)

Death rate

As measured by deaths per 1,000 of the population, the UK rate has fallen from 23 in 1851 to 11.7 in 2008. The advances of medicine, reduced infant mortality and generally improved health, clean water supply and sanitation facilities have allowed life expectancy to increase, as shown in table 7.5. The gap between male and female life expectancy was six years in 1971, but has narrowed since then to just over four years.

Table 7.5 UK life expectancy

	Male	Female
1901	48	52
1950	66	72
1990	72	78
2008*	77.4	81.6

(Source: ONS 2006a.) *Estimate

The UK life expectancy is around the European average but some developed countries such as Japan and Singapore exceed the UK rates. So, as people live longer, the death rate falls. The actual number of deaths, however, has not fallen by the same proportion because the population has substantially increased over this period. In 1900, the number of UK deaths was 624,000 and the figure for 2008 was 562,345.

The picture is not rosy throughout the world. Although life expectancy in Europe averages 74 and in Asia it is 67, 28 per cent of all countries have a life expectancy of less than 60. The average for Africa is 50 and there are still sub-Saharan African countries where societies live with the appalling situation of life expectancy being less than 50, with the worst example – Sierra Leone – currently only 41 for women and as low as 39 for men. On top of poor health, there are numerous outbreaks of war and disease (especially HIV/AIDS and SARS), while poor living conditions are very common.

In developed countries, the main feature of a dropping death rate is the rapid ageing of the population with a rapid growth in the numbers over retirement age.

Migration

The third factor determining population levels is the number of people migrating into or out of a country. Clearly, if more people enter a country than leave it, then the population will rise. International migration has always been substantial. Man's original ancestors migrated out of Africa to populate the world, and most of North and South America, Oceania and parts of southern Africa have been colonised by migrants who replaced the small indigenous populations.

It has been estimated that about 191 million people live outside their country of birth or citizenship (UNFPA 2006). Political, social, economic and environmental upheavals have been the spur to large-scale movements. Religious dissension encouraged Puritan migration to America in the seventeenth and eighteenth centuries, and persecution has forced Jewish populations to leave their homelands, be it Russia in the nineteenth century or Germany under the Nazis. Due to very poor economic and social prospects, the Irish migrated all over the world for 150 years, Chinese labour was used to build the American railroads, and much of Dubai's current building boom is being built by Nepalese and Indian skilled craftsmen. Britain eagerly recruited in the West Indies and the Indian sub-continent in the early post-war years to staff the health service and public transport when local labour was in short supply. At the same time, there was a substantial outflow of skilled labour to take up new lives in Australia, Canada, New Zealand and South Africa, often under 'assisted passages' incentives.

On a world scale, certain migration paths are especially important, as Dicken (2003, p521) explains:

> ... there are massive movements across the Mexico–United States border and from parts of Asia to the United States. Australia has become an important focus of migration from South East Asia ... and from countries around the Mediterranean to Germany.

In general terms, the twentieth century has seen far more restrictions placed upon migrants by governments fearful of the economic and social consequences of mass immigration. Although immigration was never easy (both America and Australia veered towards operating a 'whites only' policy for decades), the latter half of the twentieth century has seen severe restrictions imposed by countries all over the world, exacerbated by fears of terrorism in the twenty-first century.

In the case of the UK, the Commonwealth Immigration Act in the mid-1950s imposed severe limitations on free entry for mostly ethnic would-be migrants, and subsequent legislation tightened the regulations further. Commonwealth immigration dropped sharply from 150,000 per annum to less than 50,000 within a few years and continued at roughly this rate until the 2000s.

Since the mid-1990s, the net inflow of migrants has escalated substantially, as shown in table 7.6.

Table 7.6 UK net inflow of migrants (thousands)

1990	19
2001	190
2004	244
2006	200
2008	163

(Source: ONS 2009.)

For much of the 1980s and 1990s, there was a rough balance between emigration, mostly to the 'old' Commonwealth (Australia, Canada, etc) and America, and immigration (mostly from the 'new' Commonwealth-Indian subcontinent and Caribbean). During the 2000s, however, there was a substantial rise in migrants from the EU A8 accession countries, especially Poland, and an increase from the 'new' Commonwealth, with the numbers from Africa also rising. 2008 showed a sudden reverse of this situation with a large number of migrants returning home, including an estimated 50,000 Polish workers – applications for work permits from the A8 countries halved in the three months to December 2008 compared to 2007, a drop of 24,000 (*People Management* 2009). Additional barriers to immigration were introduced by the UK government in 2006, with a revised points system reducing the number of potential applicants for work permits.

Case study 7.2 illustrates the effect on the labour market of the rise in migration from eastern Europe.

CASE STUDY 7.2

MIGRATION FROM EASTERN EUROPE AND ITS EFFECT ON THE LABOUR MARKET

This case study examines the effects of the migration from the countries that acceded to the EU in 2004 and on whom no restrictions on movement and work were placed by the UK government. These are Poland, the Czech Republic, Estonia, Hungary, Latvia, Lithuania, Slovakia and Slovenia (the so-called A8 countries).

Level of migration

Nearly 580,000 migrants from the A8 countries registered for work between 2004 and 2006 (Home Office 2007), and a further 100,000 have been estimated to be working on a self-employed basis. Poland is the main source, totalling over 300,000 migrants, and the effect on the internal Polish labour market has been so great that Poland has had to ease its own restrictions on entry of labour from Ukraine, Belarus and Russia to fill skilled vacancies and gaps in the seasonal agricultural market (Polska 2006).

This is way in excess of the official UK government forecast figure in 2003 of around 10,000 per year. Expectations have been massively exceeded due to:

- a large number of migrants were already working unofficially in the UK and their registration allowed their work to be 'legal'

- most of the A8 countries have high unemployment figures (20 per cent in Poland, for example)

- earnings in A8 countries are typically *six times lower* than in the UK

- working conditions, including health and safety provision, are often at a lower standard than in the UK

- the arrival of cheap flights and coach travel has made the regular journeys cheaper and easier.

The degree to which agency intervention would apply was greatly underestimated, especially in the building, agriculture and hospitality sectors.

On top of that, the freedom of entry from these countries has meant that an unspecified number have been able to settle permanently without restriction in most cases. Of that number, it is estimated that 380,000 have stayed on a permanent basis. However, this is only an estimate as there is no register of A8 migrants leaving the UK.

Nature of migrants, chosen work and pay levels

Most migrants were young with 80 per cent under 35, while 80 per cent had some form of qualification (mostly technical), although only 5 per cent had degrees. Only 6 per cent had dependants arriving with them. Around 70 per cent worked in low-paid, unqualified work, such as process operation/packing and in warehousing (40 per cent), hospitality (18 per cent) and farming (4 per cent) while 6 per cent worked as care assistants and sales assistants. The average pay was between £4.50 and £5.99 an hour.

Good for the economy?

The government has spelt out the apparent benefits of this unprecedented migration. It identifies fewer unfilled jobs, less inflationary pressure (which could fuel higher pay increases) and faster economic growth. The Ernst & Young ITEM Club estimated that the activities of the migrants reduced interest rates by 0.5 per cent and increased GDP by around 0.2 per cent (ITEM Club 2006). The Bank of England concluded that the level of unemployment that could be sustained without raising inflation has been lowered as migrants take the low-paid jobs that often remain vacant (Blanchflower et al 2007). Moreover, responses by employers rated migrants higher than conventional employees in terms of productivity, reliability, attendance and quality of work (CIPD/KPMG 2005).

On the downside, however, there was some increased strain on the social infrastructure, notably housing, transport, hospitals and welfare. Overall, although the picture looked very positive, there was a contrary view from House of Lords Economic Affairs Committee in 2008, which found no evidence of large-scale economic benefits and that immigration had a negative impact on the low-paid and training for young UK workers, and contributed to higher house prices.

(Sources: Philpott 2007, McSmith 2007, Whitehead 2008.)

Note: Statistics for migrants are notoriously unreliable. Although records of those entering the UK are regarded as accurate, at least in terms of actual numbers, those leaving the UK are much less so, due to less arduous emigration procedures. Much of the estimates are made up of samples from the International Passenger Surveys and other surveys of migrants' intentions, which many commentators regard as suspect. Figures for illegal immigration are completely unknown, with the UK government refusing to even make an estimate. An example of the unreliability of the migration estimates arose when the Home Secretary, Jacqui Smith, had to apologise to Parliament in 2007 for underestimating by 300,000 the number of foreign workers entering the UK in the 10 years up to 2007 (Stewart 2007).

On another front, there was been a significant rise in asylum seekers to the UK in the early 2000s, which peaked at 103,000 in 2002 but fell to 26,000 in 2008 (ONS 2009). Government actions to speed up the system of dealing with applications have caused some reduction in applications but not eliminated the total. Only around 20 per cent of asylum seekers have their application accepted but many are able to stay in the UK while their appeal is heard, which can take many months.

The reasons for the increasing numbers of migrants include:

- Britain's economic performance since the mid-1990s has been very positive, better than most of Europe

- there is a strong culture of entrepreneurship, with open opportunities for small businesses to flourish, perhaps more so than other parts of Europe, although not so strong as in America

- there are in Britain established ethnic communities from all parts of the world, allowing greater ease of transition and community support

- the number of low-paid unskilled jobs available is very high, especially in the hospitality, caring and building industries. Some are in the black economy, encouraging asylum seekers and illegal immigrants

- in the education field, there has been a huge growth in undergraduate and postgraduate courses taken up by international students, who are able to help their financing through part-time work.

Europe has been faced with a similar situation. While the UK's number of asylum seekers represents 0.5 per cent of the population, Sweden's 333,000 represents nearly 4 per cent, while Austria's is 5 per cent. Asylum seekers to France and Germany are currently running around half the UK rate.

ETHNICITY OF POPULATION

An inevitable development of the increase in migration has been a growth in the ethnic variation in most developed countries. In the UK, of 6.3 million who were born outside the UK, around 8 per cent of the population, around five million are from ethnic minorities, nearly double the figure in the 1970s (Ellis 2009). The largest group – around 55 per cent of the total – is from the Indian subcontinent, while West Indians make up a further 15 per cent (actually a declining proportion as many retire back to their countries of origin), with the remainder from Africa, Asia and the Middle East.

They have generally settled over the years in urban localities, with large congregations in inner east London boroughs and towns in the Midlands and the north. As a whole, they have a lower age profile with a much smaller percentage over 65, chiefly because migrants tend to be in lower-age categories. Also, many migrants retire to their countries of origin. The effects of the increase in ethnic minority sectors is discussed later in this chapter.

Ethnicity of population is far greater in the US, as shown in case study 7.3.

LATINOS AS A MAJOR FORCE IN THE US ECONOMY

People of Hispanic origin (Latinos, as many prefer to be called), make up 12 per cent of the US workforce today, but this will become at least 25 per cent in 50 years' time due to their much larger families and current age profile. They originate from across Latin America but predominantly Mexico and their growth rate is 3 per cent per annum, compared to 0.8 per cent for the rest of America. As a group, they are a key catalyst for economic growth. In some of the larger cities, such as Los Angeles, they make up the majority of the under-18 age set. Their disposable income jumped 29 per cent from 2001 to 2004, double the pace of the rest of the population, and they have a growing influence on all consumer patterns, especially food, clothes and entertainment.

The Latino boom brings a welcome charge to the economy at a time when other countries' population growth has slowed to a crawl. Without a steady supply of new workers and consumers, a greying US might see a long-term slowdown along the lines of ageing Japan.

Yet this demographic change produces potential problems. One of the major issues relates to language. With a huge Spanish-speaking minority, there could be pressures for recognition of an official second language, much as French is in Canada today. This could harm assimilation and encourage a form of separatism in states such as California, just like it has been a major cause of conflict in Quebec.

Another issue is the perception that large numbers of poorly educated, non-English speakers undermine the US economy. Although the steady influx of low-skilled workers helps keep America's gardens tended and floors cleaned, those workers also exert downward pressure on wages, causing friction with other groups of workers in this sector.

A case in point is Harris County in Texas, which includes the city of Houston where the population increased by 21 per cent during the 1990s. The county is 42 per cent of Hispanic origin, and this ethnic group is responsible for 80 per cent of the growth. There are no zoning laws in the county so developers can build wherever they think there is a demand. At the new 28,000-acre community of Woodlands, a three-bedroom house costs around US $130,000 (£65,000) compared to an equivalent house in San Francisco costing US $700,000. The area is surrounded by woodland and crime is very low.

Rapid growth in this form may eventually cause environmental problems, but it greatly slows the pace at which America ages.

(Sources: *Business Week* 2004, *Economist* 2006.)

Migration is a very emotive subject, bringing to the mix a number of political, economic, social and psychological issues. Broadly speaking, there are a set of reasons for encouraging migration and another set for discouraging it, as follows.

Encouraging migration

- We live in a global economy and we need to make the best use of all talents from whatever the source.
- Migrants have energy and enthusiasm and a willingness to succeed. They have made a substantial effort to move from their home country, and practice indicates that they are motivated to work hard.

- Most migrants are in the age group 18–40 and, in an ageing population, it is important to have a good source of younger labour.

- Migrants make up such a large proportion of the labour force, estimated at 7 per cent (Salt 2006), that the labour market would tighten dramatically if this source was reduced or eliminated. In fact, 15 per cent of firms employ 10 per cent or more migrants in their workforce (Smedley 2008).

- Migrants can fill the low-skilled jobs that are currently difficult to fill – they prevent wage rates rising too high.

- It is not unusual for migrant entrepreneurs to offer ethnic goods and services which expand the marketplace to be benefit of the consumer. Thai food and ethnic textiles are obvious examples.

- It is arguable that it is more beneficial for the UK economy for migrants to carry out work in the UK rather than for that work to be outsourced to a migrant's home country.

- Why should migrants be prevented from benefiting from the UK's successful economy? After all, for 200 years, the UK benefited from running the economies of its colonies, so it is time for those benefits to be shared.

- Remittances from migrants back to their home country have been substantial and help to alleviate poverty. For some African countries, such as Kenya, they account for bigger flows of capital than aid or foreign investment (*Economist* 2009a).

Discouraging migration

- The UK is very densely populated and an inflow of immigrants leads to pressure on housing and jobs.

- Where there is a large source of low-skilled labour, it discourages employers from becoming more productive by automating production or showing innovation.

- Too much migration encourages the growth of the black economy, which reduces tax revenue and is associated with crime.

- The process of policing and administering prospective migrants is very expensive and difficult to carry out efficiently and fairly.

- Migrants can be socially marginalised, staying in their own communities, retaining their own cultures and religions and not integrating effectively. This can create social problems and difficulties with the next generation.

- Excessive migration can cause security problems, with international conspiracies leading to terrorist activity (Nichiporuk 2000).

OTHER DEMOGRAPHIC CHANGES

Working population

You will have seen in Chapter 3 an outline of changes in the UK employment structure. Table 7.7 shows the comparative statistics for 2006 and 2009.

Table 7.7 UK labour market 2006 and 2009

thousands

	Male		Female		Total	
	2006	2009	2006	2009	2006	2009
Employed	12,800	12,600	12,480	12,285	25,280	24,884
Self-employed	2,780	2,738	1,020	1,114	3,800	3,852
Total labour market	15,580	15,338	13,500	13,399	29,080	28,737
Part-time	1,600	2,056	5,700	5,608	7,300	7,664
Temporary	700	671	800	762	1,500	1,433
Unemployed					1,400	2,400
Economically active					31,160 (79%)	31,388 (79%)
Economically inactive					8,120 (21%)	8,040 (21%)

(Source: Social Trends 2009.)

Compared to the early 1990s, there has been a growth of around four million in the total working population, made up of a natural growth in the population (including the rise in migrant workers) and an increase in the participation level. The rate of employment for women has risen much more steeply than for men, with the women's total rising by more than two million over the last 10 years (see Chapter 3 for a discussion on the feminisation of work).

From 1992 to 2007, there was a steady reduction in unemployment, which halved over the period and led to a more confident labour market, so the number of temporary employees declined. However, the recession starting in 2008 substantially altered this picture, with a rise of one million in unemployed over the two-year period. In addition, the number of adults claiming incapacity benefit (a proportion of which can be regarded as hidden unemployed) rose to 2.6 million by 2008, an increase from 800,000 in 1983. The number of people self-employed has stayed steady in recent years, having increased substantially in the 1980s under the Thatcher period, when entrepreneurial activity was strongly encouraged.

The decline in the birth rate leading to an ageing population has already affected the size and nature of the potential working population, those within the age range 16 to 60 (female) or 65 (male). Table 7.8 shows this information starkly.

Table 7.8 UK population–age distribution 1901 to 2026

percentages

	Under 16	16–24	25–44	45–64	Over 65
MALES					
1901	34	20	28	15	4
1931	26	18	29	21	7
1961	25	14	27	25	9
1991	21	14	30	22	13
2001	21	11	31	23	13
2011*	19	12	27	27	15
2026*	18	10	26	26	19
FEMALES					
1901	31	20	28	15	6
1931	23	17	30	21	8
1961	22	13	25	26	14
1991	19	12	28	21	18
2001	20	10	29	23	18
2011*	18	11	26	26	18
2026*	17	10	25	26	22

*forecast

(Source: ONS.)

Table 7.8 shows that the younger male working population aged 16–44 has fallen from 48 per cent of the population in 1901 to 39 per cent in 2001 and is expected to decline further to 36 per cent by 2026, with a similar picture for women. The percentage in the age group 16–24 has actually halved. On the other hand, there

CASE STUDY 7.4

AGE STEREOTYPES AND DISCRIMINATORY ATTITUDES TOWARDS OLDER WORKERS: AN EAST–WEST COMPARISON

This study compared age stereotypes among 567 respondents sampled in the UK and Hong Kong and examined how these stereotypes were related to discriminatory attitudes at work. Compared to the Hong Kong sample, UK respondents saw older workers as more effective at work, but less adaptable to change. As expected, the respondents' own ages were predictive of positive age stereotypes, although for supervisors this relationship was moderated in the case of perceptions of work effectiveness. Stereotypical beliefs were found to significantly affect respondents' attitudes towards the training, promotion and retention of older workers, their willingness to work with older employees, and their support for positive discrimination. Findings also suggest that anti-age discrimination policies in the respondent's organisation had a positive impact on beliefs about the adaptability of older workers and possibly also on attitudes towards providing them with training. Implications of the findings were discussed in light of the existing socio-political environment in the UK and Hong Kong.

(Source: Chiu et al 2001.)

has been a considerable growth in the older employee groups. In fact, the number of employees aged 50 and over has increased by 1.3 million (about 26 per cent) in the 10 years up to 2004. Not all pensioners are an immediate drain on the economy as many chose to work after retirement age. There are around a million in this category, a figure that has risen by 34 per cent over the last 10 years. However, they do face a degree of discrimination, as shown in case study 7.4.

Given that far more young people go on to further and higher education, with the government target of 50 per cent attending some form of higher education, this reduces even further the younger working population.

 ## ACTIVITY 7.1 ATYPICAL EMPLOYMENT

A development in the working population in recent years has been the growth of what is known as 'atypical employment', which is not full-time 9 to 5 employment. It covers part-time, shift-work, teleworking and a host of variable working arrangements. What are the driving forces for this growth?

Participation rates

People used to work until they reached pensionable age (many, of course, did not last that long, worn out by heavy industrial work or poor diets). As late as 1975, 84 per cent of men aged 60–64 were 'economically active' in the UK, but this fell to 65 per cent by 1995. This was chiefly the result of the recession in the early 1990s where many older men lost their jobs and found it difficult to obtain alternative employment. Many were disabled and obtained disability benefits, which are more generous than unemployment benefits. Organisations also encouraged older employees to take early retirement, sometimes providing generous redundancy payments or enhanced pensions.

By the early 2000s, this position was changing. Participation rates for men 50 to 64 rose from 65 per cent to 79.5 per cent from 1995 to 2005 (ONS 2007), and for those over retirement age it has risen from 7.5 per cent in 2000 to 12 per cent in 2009 (ONS 2009). This can be explained partly by the prosperous economy where many part-time jobs are available, especially in the service sector, and partly by the decline in pension prospects arising from the two stock-market crashes in 2003 and 2008 where the value of personal pensions declined by as much as 50 per cent. It is an unusual feature of the late 2000s recession that the number of post-retirement age employees has continued to increase, both male and female.

For women, there has been a substantial increase in the participation rate, rising from 63 per cent in 1979 to 75 per cent in 2009. Women have developed their careers, continued at work while raising a family or returned to work more quickly than in previous decades. They have also taken up new careers and skills through obtaining qualifications, many through some form of government initiative. Other support has come through the strengthening of equal opportunity legislation, where the barriers to women's employment and development have been steadily removed.

The economically inactive can be regarded as a 'reserve army' that can be drawn on during periods of tight labour markets (Smallwood 2006). He explains that (p6):

> There are huge economic benefits associated with a growing workforce, mirrored by the severe problems that arise when a country's population starts to decline. After all, gross domestic product growth over the longer term is the sum of the growth in the employed workforce and the rise in productivity of that workforce, so the faster the working population goes up, the faster the economy grows. Over the past decade, the growth in the working population has added well in excess of £50 billion to GDP, and swelled the treasury's coffers by nearly half that.

The growth in European participation rates mirrors the UK situation, although the average rate is still lower at 78 per cent for men and 60 per cent for women in 2000. In France, for example, the male rate was 75 per cent and female 62 per cent while the Italian rate for women was as low as 46 per cent in the same year.

ACTIVITY 7.2 BUILDING UP THE PARTICIPATION RATE

Two organisations have just set up in an area of high unemployment and low participation, with the support of various government grants and loans. They are as follows:

Jones Supermarkets has set up a regional distribution centre to employ 450 staff in warehousing and logistics positions on 24/7 operations.

Williams Toys and Games has established a manufacturing and distributing centre to employ 200 staff. There is a seasonal element to the work so a number of staff will be working flexibly, including evening shifts and weekends for the busy autumn period. Most of the toys and games are imported finished or semi-finished so the work is essentially unskilled and semi-skilled and involves a high element of packing and distribution.

Given that setting up in the area will help reduce the unemployment rate, are there ways in which the organisations can help further improve the participation rate?

Sectoral employment

The number of people working in manufacturing has been declining since the 1950s, when it stood at over six million. Since 1993, however, there has been a particularly steep drop both in real terms and as a percentage of total employment, as shown in table 7.9.

Table 7.9 Sectoral employment 1993 to 2009

thousands

	1993	2009	Change
Manufacturing	3,952	2,885	– 1,067
Construction	966	1,269	+ 296
Service sector	17,419	25,263	+ 7,844
Sections of the service sector			
Warehousing/retailing, hotel and catering	5,266	6,816	+ 1,550
Post, telecommunications, transport	1,362	1,854	+ 408
Business and financial services	4,569	6,409	+ 1,840
Public administration	1,467	1,675	+ 208
Education	1,892	2,468	+ 576
Health	2,511	3,469	+ 958

(Source: *Labour Market Trends* 2009.)

Table 7.9 shows two further trends: firstly, a reflection in the changing pattern of consumer demand, where we spend much more money on consumer and leisure activities, eg holidays, eating out, shopping and at the hairdressers. (In fact hairdressing saw the highest rate of growth of any individual job from 1990 to 2005.) Secondly, there was increased expenditure by the Labour government on health and education, as promised in its election manifesto, which has led to an increase in jobs in both sectors.

But the biggest increase of all is the category involving computer-related jobs (although this category is a rather vague one and does include some non-computer activities), which has risen by 40 per cent. This will reinforce what you will read in Chapter 8 where IT developments (automation, communications) have replaced the need for skilled and unskilled labour in manufacturing. The major improvements in productivity have all taken place in this sector so output has risen, prices have come down and overall industrial employment has diminished. Also, much of the manufacturing has migrated to parts of the world where labour is cheaper and the products are then imported into the UK.

A further trend in this area is that the majority of jobs created in the 10 years since 1997 have been in the public sector, either directly or indirectly (Buchanan et al 2009), where 'para-state' jobs, which depended entirely on government funding, were included. Of 2.23 million jobs created, fewer than one million were true private sector jobs. In the West Midlands the total rise in employment was down to the public sector, with no new private sector jobs generated overall. An interesting finding here was that the financial sector appeared to have made a negligible contribution to employment. The researchers concluded that the business model was undisclosed and unsustainable.

ACTIVITY 7.3 CLOSING DOWN

Consider the scenario where the main manufacturing employer in a country town, employing 1,500 staff, announces it is closing down. What are the implications for the local economy? What are the overall implications for the UK of the decline in manufacturing employment?

Changes in geographical population location

A final aspect of demography is the internal movement of population within countries. For over 200 years, there has been a steady movement away from the land and into the cities around the world as agriculture has become mechanised and farms consolidated. In the last 100 years or so, this movement has extended in certain countries to widespread geographical patterns. In Italy, there has been a mass movement from the poor, rural south to the more prosperous urban north. In the UK, the movement is in the opposite direction with a general move from the industrial areas, especially in the north, to the more balanced economies of the south and east (Stilwell et al 1992). The population of the north-eastern counties of England actually dropped in the 1990s and population increases in Yorkshire and Lancashire were quite small. On the other hand, counties in the south-east, such as Cambridgeshire, increased by 10 per cent or more as an estimated 250,000 citizens moved from north to south (Brindle 1999).

TRENDS TO WATCH – THE FUTURE?

If the world's population continued to increase at its current rate, then all estimates show such a growth to be completely unsustainable. Food and energy would run out, leading to the Malthusian nightmares of war, pestilence and disease, which would eventually lead to a decline in population back to sustainable levels. Economists have been divided as to the scenario at 2050, with some estimates of population at 10 billion and still growing and others indicating a more conservative outcome. Happily, those with an optimistic viewpoint are becoming more plentiful. At a 2002 United Nations conference, the director of the population division, Joseph Chamie, confidently predicted a peak of eight billion at 2040 followed by a falling world population at 2050 for the first time since the Black Death. Subsequent forecasts have been a little less optimistic, due to the surprising resurgence in fertility rates in some western nations, but the consensus appears to identify around 2050 as the peak year of world population at around 9.2 billion.

The conference was called to discuss the implications of unexpectedly fast declines in fertility in dozens of countries, including some very large ones. Mexico, India and Brazil have all forecast a decline in their birth rate below replacement level within 20 years. The assumption that, as nations develop their economies, women settle down with 2.4 children, now appears erroneous.

Women in developing countries appear to be to striving for the freedoms achieved in the developed countries where the decisions open to them include not having a family at all or just having one child. Bangladeshi women today have 3.3 children while the Vietnamese have halved their fertility rate in 10 years to 2.3, just above the replacement level (*Economist* 2009b). So far, fewer births will automatically result in eliminating population growth.

There is also a question mark over increasing life expectancy. It is still likely that we can all expect to live a little longer every decade, but AIDS has had a serious effect in sub-Saharan Africa and is spreading its tentacles into other areas with rapid growth in HIV rates in eastern Europe, South America and the Far East. So the increase in life expectancy, although having in itself important consequences, will only marginally influence the long-term decline in population.

In the UK, the stabilisation of the fertility rate at around 1.9 will inevitably bring to an end the natural population growth, probably around 2035 or 2040, where it will peak at around 70 million, depending on migration assumptions, according to latest predictions. However, the Government Actuary's Department has reported that life expectancy is growing faster than previous predictions, and should rise to 81 for men and 85 for women by 2030 (Doward 2003). If this occurs, then the population will continue to grow for a little longer, although the average age of the population will rise.

However, there is no doubt that the population will become older. In 2030, 15 million Britons will be over current pensionable age, compared to 11 million now. By 2007, there were more pensioners than children. The average age is set to rise from 38.8 in 2000 to 42.6 in 2025.

To summarise, the world population will continue to grow rapidly for the next 20 years, but this growth will then start to taper off and will probably reverse by 2050. Populations in developed countries will become distinctly older and internationally diverse. Populations in developing countries will also age but from a very low base figure, and will become internationally mobile.

IMPLICATIONS OF DEMOGRAPHIC PREDICTIONS

As indicated at the start of this chapter, future demographic trends will impact substantially at local, national and international levels across the world. We will examine these implications in outline for the following groups:

- organisations, especially in the UK private sector
- governments, especially the UK government
- international society.

IMPLICATIONS FOR ORGANISATIONS

A slowdown in population growth and an ageing population have effects both on the nature of the marketplace and in the sources of labour. Adaptations to current business practices could take the following forms.

Sources of labour

With far fewer school leavers and younger people generally, organisations will have to look elsewhere for labour, particularly if the economy continues to grow steadily under the full employment conditions seen in the 16 years up to 2008. Alternative sources can involve moving away from the traditional full-time 9 to 5 job design to a more flexible model where much greater use is made of part-time jobs, job shares, flexible hours and working from home. These flexible modes can meet the working needs of those with caring responsibilities, principally (but not exclusively) women, and older people generally who are retired or semi-retired. Some retailers, such as B &Q and Tesco, have specifically sought to employ older staff, which has led not just to an easing of recruitment difficulties but to considerable customer satisfaction arising from the knowledge such staff bring to the job. As a spokesperson for Nationwide Building Society explained: 'Many customers prefer dealing with more maturity and experience and older workers tend to be more loyal and committed' (*Economist* 2004).

An example of a local authority following the same path is shown in case study 7.5.

'AGE POSITIVE' SUCCESS AT BRIDGEND COUNTY BOROUGH COUNCIL

CASE STUDY 7.5

In the late 1990s, Bridgend County Borough Council began to feel the impact of a changing demography as its employee average age had risen to 41 and the reduced number of school leavers were being snapped up by major competitors in the area such as Sony and Ford. Action was needed to ensure the continued maintenance of a skilled workforce and that suitable employment was available, irrespective of age.

Recent initiatives have included:

- the abolition of age limits in advertisements

- eliminating the date of birth on the application form

- employees who work beyond their normal retirement ages can continue to contribute towards their pension scheme up the maximum of 40 years' service.

- introducing a mentoring scheme that involves those who intend to retire coaching younger employees to ensure valuable skills are not lost

- ignoring an employee's age when considering training and development opportunities.

What has been more important is the changing culture where being 'age positive' is built into the way the council is run, where it is seen as open-minded, flexible and committed to people's development. For example, employees are encouraged to continue working as long as everybody is comfortable. This has worked well in areas such as social care where maturity can be a positive benefit, and with specialist positions, such as continuing to employ a fitness instructor (well into his 70s) on a part-time basis.

Success in this area has been recognised by a national award from Age Positive, the government body campaigning to tackle workplace ageism.

(Source: Persaud 2004.)

It is also unlikely that the offers of early retirement with enhanced pensions will be so generous in the future. The UK government has already moved away from funding such arrangements centrally, requiring each department or agency to bear the costs involved. This has already led to a substantial reduction in such offers, and employees choosing early retirement currently have to fund this out of their own pension schemes, in most cases.

Given these factors, it is not surprising that a greater proportion of those over retirement age choose to continue to work, enhancing the participation rates of pensioners, as detailed earlier.

However, as in the example of Japanese older workers in case study 7.1, there is the danger of 'Balkanisation' of labour markets, where employees at both ends of the demographic market have poor job security, menial work and low pay (Roberts 2006).

In the commercial sphere, many companies are changing their policies towards the employment of older employees. Retailer ASDA offers a variety of flexible working practices, including 'Benidorm leave', where employees can take up to three months' unpaid leave in the winter to take an extended holiday. They also offer grandparents' leave, and carers' leave together with a seasonal colleagues scheme which attracts older people to work 10 weeks a year at the peak times. Store managers are encouraged to visit older people's clubs and these policies have resulted in the number of 65+ employees rising to 3,500 in 2006 (CIPD 2007).

Change in markets

As the patterns of population change, their consumer needs alter accordingly. With an ageing population, there will be a decline in demand for products for the young, such as baby foods and prams and, eventually to products for teenagers and the age group 18–25. The brewing industry has seen a substantial decline in the demand for beer as the largest consumers have traditionally been those aged 18–25, a declining age group, although their drinking habits have also changed. Similarly, sales of teenage fashion goods – clothes, compact discs, jewellery – have become sluggish in recent years. Although the per capita spending has increased as the general level of prosperity has risen, it does not make up for the reduced population in those age brackets.

On the other hand, there are some sectors of industries which gain from an ageing population. The most dramatic is the travel and tourism industry as older people spend a higher proportion of their income on holidays than most other groups. For a number of cyclical reasons, they also have become a much wealthier segment of the community. Saga, floated on the stock market for close to £1 billion in 2004, is the clearest winner, providing a vast range of holidays – active and inactive – to a growing market, broadening its product range to insurance and other financial services.

On the financial front, it has been estimated that, worldwide, people over the age of 55 hold around 70 per cent of the planet's wealth, and there is a huge market here for service providers involved in investments, pensions and general financial security, as shown in case study 7.6.

 WEALTH ADVICE FOR THE ELDERLY IN THE US

CASE STUDY 7.6

Examples of some of the services provided especially for older US citizens include:

Reverse mortgages

In 2006, 76,000 US citizens took out mortgages where they receive a lump sum or a line of credit and do not pay any interest while the mortgage is running. All the fees and accumulated interest are paid off when the house is sold, usually (but not always) when the mortgagee dies. Currently, the federal government guarantees such mortgages, so that, if a homeowner's debts are greater than the value of his/her home at the time of death, the estate will not have to make up the shortfall. This partly explains why the number of reverse mortgages taken out increased by 77 per cent over the total for 2005. However, fees can be very high for this financial instrument (as much as 10 per cent) and the mortgagees' heirs are not always happy with the way that their inheritance is eroded by high fees and interest payments.

Elder Services

A product marketed by Wells Fargo and other providers to the banks' ageing and generally prosperous clientele, the bank will handle investments, pay regular bills, process insurance claims, arrange and monitor health care (including the high costs associated with surgery and treatment in the US) and provide regular reports on the client's financial situation. Some go further and give advice on funeral arrangements, nursing homes, organise taxi contracts when eyesight fails and even deal with regular logistics for pills and other pharmaceutical products.

Wealth management

An increasing number of providers are entering the market to handle investments for the elderly. Citigroup, for example, has built 17 regional 'planning centres' for its wealthy customers – mainly baby-boomers on the cusp of retirement with more than US $5 million in assets to invest. They bring together tax and trust lawyers, specialists in insurance, philanthropy and experts in small business sales so all the options are covered. Wachovia has developed a financial programme that allows it to focus on customers with a minimum of US $250,000.

Due to the complexity of this financial area and the declining faculties of some of the clients, the providers are increasingly attempting to avoid the 'hard-sell' approach. A number, including HSBC bank, are using older or even semi-retired, employees to carry out the sales negotiations so, hopefully, the claims for mis-selling are reduced.

(Source: *Economist* 2007.)

ACTIVITY 7.4 SERVICES FOR THE OLDER CONSUMER

Summarise the effects of an ageing population on the tourism, retailing and banking industries.

Housing presents an interesting reflection of demographic changes. Although the population is now growing only slowly, the price of houses has risen substantially due, mostly, to a somewhat unexpected higher demand. This has come about because, as the fertility rate drops and the population ages, there is no corresponding drop in the number of households. Whereas young children live with their parents, older people live mostly in their own housing unit. Many stay in their own homes looking after themselves to the end, or nearly the end, of their lives, assisted by a benefits system that encourages such behaviour. Add to this the increase in divorce, which often creates additional demand for housing, and the rise in students living away from home, and perhaps the rise in house prices is not so unexpected. Winners here have been the construction companies that provide retirement homes in the UK, such as McCarthy and Stone.

Other clear winners in the demographic stakes are those who market products specifically for the elderly. There will be growing markets for mobility products and those aimed at improving health care, from pharmaceutical products to private hospitals. These include:

- 'Nutraceuticals', including vitamins, nutrients, minerals and herbal extracts, a market estimated to be worth $8 billion in the US alone. Nutritional scientists are working on a new array of food products that are scientifically designed to improve your health and longevity and which will have specific appeal to the middle-aged and elderly.

- There are more than 100 US biotech companies actively researching age-related disorders (Wallace 2002), such as the role of telomeres in cell ageing that may keep skin young and elastic, and tissue engineering, which may offer the prospect of replacement parts for the body.

- Stannah Lifts has become another household name while magazines devoted to older readers (such as *Yours*) have substantially increased their circulations.

The same reasoning can be applied to the next age group down – the 'middle aged' – where their demands for financial services (savings products, pensions, etc) and some luxury products (Mercedes cars, boats and homes in the sun) have grown very strongly in recent years.

IMPLICATIONS FOR GOVERNMENTS, ESPECIALLY THE UK GOVERNMENT

For governments, the biggest potential difficulty arising from the ageing population is the increase in the dependency ratio. The dependency ratio is the ratio of working-age population to the dependent population. The dependent population are children under 16 and older people over retirement age.

As the proportion of the population over retirement age increases, it puts a much greater strain on the working population, who need to fund the services for older people. As detailed above, there has been much greater reliance on the state for looking after older people. There is no doubt this strain will be with us soon, as shown in figure 7.1.

Figure 7.1 UK dependency ratio (ratio of 16–64-year-olds to over-65s)

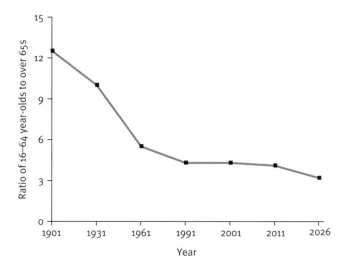

Figure 7.1 shows the startling change in dependency that has occurred already and will get worse in the future. Currently just over four employees provide earned income to support one pensioner. This will decline to just over three by 2026. The position is worse for other countries. For Germany and Japan, the ratio will be less than three by the same year, and it is estimated that the German rate will be around two by 2040.

The problem for governments is how to raise the increased revenue required from what could be a dwindling working population. It has been estimated that each pensioner costs the government around £10,000 per year, net of any tax receipts, through the old-age pension, a variety of benefits (housing, disability, etc) and the vast range of medical services (primary care, free prescriptions, hospital stays, etc). Older people are much more prone to illness and therefore impose much greater costs on the health service. It could be argued that some of the additional money required can be raised by savings on services to young people with reduced expenditure on maternity units and compulsory schooling, although any closure or reduction in services is generally met by solid resistance from the community. One research estimate is that the additional funding for health is about £1 billion a year, which can be saved by reducing school expenditure, but state pension provision will cost an additional £4 billion a year under existing arrangements (National Institute of Economic and Social Research, quoted in McCrone 1999). Because employees in their 40s and 50s earn more than employees in their 20s, it is expected that increased tax revenue will go some way towards filling this gap.

The problem is acute in the fire service and the police force. Their pension fund allows retirement after 30 years' service on two-thirds of annual salary and many others retire early on health grounds. This has given rise to the situation where Merseyside Fire and Rescue Service has 1,678 working staff but is paying the pensions of 1,691 retired staff, and a similar situation exists in police forces in Lincolnshire, Northern Ireland and the City of London, among others. Efforts have been made to reduce the huge costs involved, and police and fire crews who have joined the service since 2006 will have to work for 35 years (Watts 2008).

The pension implications are tough for the UK and America, but at least there is reasonable private pension provision that is located in properly funded systems. This, however, is the exception compared with the rest of the world. For most of Europe and other developed countries, the proportion of pensions paid by the state is very much higher and this is funded as transfer payments under a pay as you go (PAYG) basis, ie directly out of taxation income, rather than from an actual fund of money that has been invested. A major cause of the Greek government's financial crisis in 2010 was the over-generous unfunded state pensions.

Table 7.10 shows the implications for selected countries in terms of the huge government expenditure necessary to pay the pensions as a proportion of their GDP.

Table 7.10 Public pension expenditure as a percentage of GDP

	1995	2020	2040*
UK	4.5	5.2	7.1
America	4.1	5.2	7.2
Netherlands	6.0	8.4	12.1
France	10.6	11.6	14.3
Sweden	11.8	13.9	14.9
Spain	10.0	11.3	16.8
Germany	11.1	12.3	18.4
Italy	13.3	15.3	21.4

* estimate

(Source: Ecofin 2006.)

There are already substantial problems in France, Germany and Italy over the high levels of public sector borrowing. The EU attempted during 2002–04 to fine these countries as part of the stability pact arrangements made at the time of the establishment of the euro to prevent governments incurring excessive expenditure to buy themselves out of financial difficulties. Many commercial organisations are moving production out of these countries to the UK, eastern

Europe and the developing world to avoid existing high taxation rates. So how such pension liabilities can be met is sorely testing the economic advisers and central banks in these countries. This problem has been exacerbated by the greatly increased level of government debt incurred to bail the banks out of the 2007–09 financial crisis.

ACTIVITY 7.5 THE OPTIMIST

Not all writers regard the pension liabilities as insurmountable or see the necessity of huge increases in taxation or reductions in benefit to solve the pensions problem. What do you consider to be the basis for their optimism?

A further problem arises from irregular internal migration. Those parts of the country that attract population are faced by considerable pressures on housing, transport and infrastructure services. For example, the housing shortages in London and the south-east have produce continuous shortages in essential public services, particularly teachers and nurses who cannot find affordable housing, especially early on in their careers. Similar problems occur in the Milan and Turin areas of northern Italy. The governments are faced with planning dilemmas. If they allow housing on greenbelt land around London, it arouses massive opposition. If new roads are built to alleviate congestion, then the traffic merely increases within a short time to clog up the system (Champion 1993).

In some parts of the world, all these difficulties gel into a bleak prognosis. In California, for example, the State Department of Finance has forecast a 75 per cent increase in population to 60 million by 2050, making it a 'country masquerading as a state' (Kyser 2007). This will lead to a water and power catastrophe, decaying infrastructure, education funding gaps and huge state debt.

Finally, there are problems associated with the skills base. As Jackson (1998, p125) explains:

> One reason why the market has been unable to absorb the … unemployed has been the increasing demand for employees with appropriate skills and capabilities. Gaining entry to the labour market has become more difficult as manual occupations have declined and as employers have become more selective about recruits to jobs in the service and quaternary sectors. Britain needs a better trained workforce if it is to meet the challenge from its competitors in Europe and overseas and the current skills gap means that many find themselves excluded from the opportunities of employment.

OPTIONS FOR GOVERNMENTS

Governments will need to either raise taxes or reduce benefits. Some countries have already taken bold steps, such as New Zealand, which has abolished the universal right to an old-age pension, and the UK government is raising the age when women can claim the pension to 65 in the period 2010–20 and the state pension to 67 for both men and women by 2046. However, this can be very damaging politically and is not done lightly. Certainly people can be encouraged to increase their savings for the future by making a larger contribution to their pension schemes, which is done by most governments. In Japan, this has been very successful and the Japanese are the highest savers in the world. (Incidentally, this high saving and reduced consumption has contributed towards a prolonged recession in Japan through most of the 1990s and early 2000s.)

It is also likely that when the full effects of the higher dependency ratio reach the population as a whole, society will be much more affluent and willing to pay the additional costs as part of the understanding that a measure of the decency of a society is how it looks after vulnerable groups, such as the elderly. This will have the effect of placing a greater emphasis on community care for the elderly (Bartlett and Peel 2005).

An alternative approach is to attempt to reverse the demographic trends and to encourage bigger families. This can be done by providing greater financial incentives (tax reliefs and maternity/child benefits) and by encouraging organisations to be more family-friendly so that women are able to combine motherhood and a job more easily. The Chinese government is moving away from the 'one-child policy' instituted in 1979, as shown in case study 7.7.

    CHINA AND THE ONE-CHILD POLICY

CASE STUDY 7.7

By 2050, China will have more than 438 million people over 60, with 100 million aged over 80. There will be just 1.6 working-age adults to support every person over 60, compared with 7.7 in 1975. One of the unexpected outcomes of the one-child policy has been to encourage Chinese families to be great savers. This is because the one-child policy created a surplus of men and has driven up the cost of marriage, as more men compete with fewer women. To keep up, families with sons have been holding off spending to create wealth that boosts their son's marriage prospects. Economists have concluded that Chinese

marriage-price inflation could account for as much as half of the increase in the country's household saving since 1990.

The spectre of an ageing population hangs heavy over Shanghai where the proportion of working adults to retirees is low and threatens a major burden. Family-planning authorities in the city use extensive publicity and home visits to encourage families with one child to have a second, although financial incentives have not yet been introduced.

(Sources: Coonan 2009, Dubner and Levitt 2009.)

The problem is that such actions by governments, eg those shown by Japan in case study 7.1, appear to have only a marginal effect on the indigenous population. Despite actions in similar forms by many governments in developed countries, it has done little to reverse the flagging fertility rate.

A drastic action could be to open the doors wider to migrants from developing countries. This makes a great deal of long-term economic sense but has a number of political obstacles to overcome in terms of the perceptions of migrants 'taking jobs' and the additional pressures on housing and transport.

One response to overcrowding in some parts of a country has been to attempt to disperse government departments (as long ago as the early 1970s, the Department of National Savings was moved to Durham, for example) and to provide additional tax and benefit incentives to businesses to move to poorer regions. This is a major pillar in the EU's economic policy.

The most drastic governmental action seen so far has been in Ulyanovsk, in Russia, where 12 September has been declared Conception Day and couples that conceive under their 'Give Birth to a Patriot' scheme can win cars, fridges or cash prizes (*Sunday Times* 2007).

Not everybody, however, insists that an ageing population is so great a problem. Mullan (2002) argues that demographic ageing has no determinate relationship to national economic activity and that modest levels of economic growth will be more than sufficient to create the wealth required to sustain the costs brought on by greater numbers of elderly dependants.

IMPLICATIONS FOR INTERNATIONAL SOCIETY

The global economy

The most worrying aspect of the current demographic changes is that the mature and ageing population appears to lead directly to reduced economic growth. Europe and Japan have seen the fastest decline in fertility rates and have also seen the slowest economic growth in the early twentieth century. North America, on the other hand, has had a milder strain and has managed to maintain a faster growth rate over the period. In the 'Tiger' economies – China, South Korea, Taiwan – and on the Indian sub-continent, where fertility rates, although falling, still remain at or above replacement level, there is a much higher rate of economic growth.

The United Nations has projected that North America, with its higher fertility rate and greater migration, will catch up Europe's population by 2040 (currently it stands at 100 million less) and exceed it by 40 million by 2050. The economic implications are far-reaching. The working population of Europe will start to decline in 2010 but, for America, the current steady growth in its workforce will even start to accelerate in 2025. This will result in the US economy growing twice as fast as that of Europe for the next 50 years. In 2000, America accounted for 23 per cent of global GDP compared to Europe's 18 per cent. By 2050, the United Nations estimates America's share will be 26 per cent while Europe's will have shrunk to only 10 per cent. By 2050, the American economy will be two and a half times as big as Europe's with all the additional political clout that this implies (Smallwood 2003).

In reality, the only way this situation could be reversed would be by radically changing Europe's tight immigration controls, which is a very unlikely event, or if North America's fertility rate dropped sharply, as it becomes a mature economy.

International migration of work

In the early 2000s, Barclays Bank and other financial institutions announced that they would be cutting their workforces and transferring chunks of their customer service and 'back-office' administration work to other countries, particularly India. The costs of carrying out this work in developing countries is just a fraction compared to UK costs and the workforces are young, educated, English-speaking and flexible in their approach to working hours and the nature of work. These decisions were made because the demographic changes, and the responses made by governments (India has invested heavily in English-speaking education), have made such countries good substitutes for UK labour.

This situation has been replicated around the globe. In North America, work migration is an important political issue dividing the parties, while German unions have had to respond to threats to move industrial work in organisations like Volkswagen to eastern Europe by agreeing to reduce hourly wages (see case study 7.8).

EXAMPLES OF GERMAN JOBS EXODUS 2002–2004

CASE STUDY 7.8

- Lufthansa – European ticket sales based in Krakow, Poland. Aircraft engines serviced in Hungary, China and the Philippines.

- Motorola – 600 engineering jobs moved to China. Repair work moved to eastern Europe.

- Deutsche Bank – Deutsche Software subsidiary moved to India with 4,000 jobs.

- SAP (business software and systems) – Created 1,500 jobs in Bangalore, India and new 120-strong research and development centre in Shanghai.

- Continental Tyres – Three German factories closed and work transferred to three new factories in Romania, the Czech Republic and Slovakia.

(Source: Woodhead 2004.)

ACTIVITY 7.6 NURSES ON THE MOVE

In 2003, the South African government placed a prohibition on UK companies recruiting qualified nurses to work in the NHS, viewing the exodus of skilled workers such as nurses as a potential long-term disaster for the country. Do you agree with this viewpoint? Discuss the issue from both viewpoints.

World's resources

In the twentieth century, the inventiveness, organisational powers and application of technology from farmers, merchants, entrepreneurs and companies of all sizes allowed the tripling world population to be adequately provided for in terms of food, water and power. (Not completely of course, with intermittent famines and a growing imbalance between rich and poor countries.) However, it had been considered unlikely that such expansion of resources could continue at this breakneck pace for another 100 years.

The forecasts of a levelling-out of the population by mid-century must be regarded, therefore, as good news for everybody. The strains on space and exploitation of a limited land mass, especially where global warming appears to be reducing capacity, may now be much lessened, although these pressures are brought about not just by numbers of population but by their overall demands. A richer, more consuming population still has the capacity to wreak enormous damage on our planet's infrastructure.

SOCIAL TRENDS

INTRODUCTION

This section will analyse recent trends in demography, society and social structure in the UK as well as social mobility and inequality, and the continuing presence of poverty in the UK. This will be followed by an examination of diversity in the UK, its desirability, associated difficulties and implications for management.

SOCIAL MOBILITY

Social mobility is the movement of people up or down the social hierarchy, either within one generation (intra-generational mobility) or between generations (inter-generational mobility). Inter-generational mobility is easiest to measure, by taking the occupation of fathers and comparing this with the occupation of their offspring.

Another distinction is between absolute social mobility (the proportion of people who move from one social class to another) and relative social mobility (the probability of a member of a social class moving to another class). Opportunities for social mobility are one dimension of an individual's life chances, ie the opportunity to better their quality of life. Other dimensions are the absence of poverty, and access to decent standards of health and education. Quality of life varies with social class, ethnic group, gender and locality (Aldridge 2004).

Until the Second World War, there was considerable absolute social mobility in Britain, but downward mobility was nearly as common as upward. Since the Second World War, upward absolute social mobility has considerably outweighed downward mobility, with the trend increasing – it is much higher for men born in 1950–59 (the latest available figures) than for men born in 1920–29 (the first group to have reached maturity after 1945). The main reason for this upward mobility is that there is 'more room at the top'. In 1900, the middle class made up 18 per cent of the population, while the working class made up 62 per cent. By 2000, the middle class was 42 per cent of the population and the working class 38 per cent.

While the picture on absolute social mobility looks positive, the picture is very different when one looks at relative mobility. Because the middle class is bigger, this means that children of middle-class parents have less risk of moving down into the working class, ie downward social mobility has fallen. The result has been that the chances of a working-class child making it to the middle class have changed little – it is estimated that a working-class child is 15 times less likely to make it into the middle class than a middle-class child is to stay in the middle class.

Most worryingly, there is some evidence that social mobility, however it is measured, is slowing down. This is best shown by figures on income. Studies have been made of the correlation between fathers' earnings and offsprings' earnings. A correlation of zero would imply complete income mobility between generations (ie that a father's income has no influence on his offspring's income) while a correlation of one would imply total immobility, ie that an offspring's place in the income scale is exactly the same as his/her father's. For the UK correlations have been found of between 0.4 and 0.6 for sons' earnings, and between 0.45 and 0.7 for daughters' earnings. The higher the correlation, the less income mobility, and, by implication, the lower the level of social mobility.

Closer examination of the correlations shows two disturbing trends:

● correlations are much higher in the UK than in countries such as Canada, Sweden or Finland

● a comparison of those born in 1958 with those born in 1970 shows the correlations increasing, ie social mobility in the UK is falling.

One study compared two sons, both born in 1958 who left school in the 1970s. The parents of one earned twice as much as the parents of the other. By their early thirties, the son of the richer parents earned 17.5 per cent more than the poorer son. For two comparable boys born in 1970 who left school in the 1980s, the income gap had widened to 25 per cent (Blanden et al 2005).

In 2007, the educational charity the Sutton Trust researched the educational backgrounds of 500 leading figures in the law, politics, medicine, journalism and business. They found that over half had been educated in an independent school, although these only educate 7 per cent of the population, and that this figure had barely changed over the past 20 years. In addition, 47 per cent of the top 500 were Oxbridge-educated (Sutton Trust 2007).

In January 2009, the government published a White Paper on social mobility ('New Opportunities: Fair Chances for the Future'). This identified the crucial role of education in driving social mobility. Research has shown that children on free school meals (a useful proxy for poverty) have only half the average child's chance of getting five good GCSE passes (Toynbee 2009). This is crucial, as five good GCSEs is the entry requirement for A levels, and 95 per cent of those with A levels go on to higher education, and the increased life chances that follow from this. The government proposed paying bonuses of £10,000 to teachers working in the toughest schools, defined as the 500 'national challenge' schools,

CASE STUDY 7.9

SOCIAL MOBILITY: MANAGERS AND PROFESSIONALS

Both managers and professionals are clearly members of the middle class. However, as Fielding (1995) has shown, the two groups have different experiences of social mobility. Using the OPCS Longitudinal Study (a 1 per cent sample of the population), he tracked mobility over the period 1981–1991.

He found that managers were much less socially secure than professionals. Of those who were in professional positions in 1981, and were still in the labour market in 1991, 69 per cent remained in a professional position, but only 51 per cent of managers were still managers. One in three managers experienced downward social mobility over the decade, compared with one in six of professionals. The difference was even more marked for women. Of women managers in 1981, nearly half had experienced downward mobility by 1991, while this was true of only 30 per cent of male managers.

Why should there be this difference between managers and professionals? The most likely explanation is that most managers in the UK have received no specific management education. Their status depends on their position within a particular organisation, and is not easily transferable to another organisation. A professional, on the other hand, has a highly transferable educational qualification.

where less than 30 per cent achieve five good GCSE passes including maths and English, and a high proportion are eligible for free school meals (Sparrow 2009). The government also proposed to invest £57 million in an expanded nursery and childcare programme for 15 per cent of the most disadvantaged families.

The White Paper also announced plans to set up a cross-party panel chaired by the former health secretary, Alan Milburn, a leading Blairite, to identify ways to increase the number of people from low-income backgrounds entering professional jobs. Milburn's panel produced 'Fair Access to the Professions' in July 2009 (Milburn 2009a). He pointed to an increased opportunity for social mobility if entry to the professions could be widened, as 90 per cent of the jobs likely to be created by 2020 would be professional and managerial. He updated the Sutton Trust figures in entry to the professions quoted above, and found that if anything, the independent school bias was increasing. Only 7 per cent of children attended private schools, but they made up 75 per cent of judges, 70 per cent of finance directors, and a third of MPs. In nine out of 12 professions, including medicine and the law, the proportion coming from wealthy families was increasing (Jack 2009). Milburn also quoted evidence that of six (unnamed) European countries, the UK had the lowest rate of social mobility for men, and the second lowest for women.

The report saw the key to social mobility as being in education. Private schools (and the best state schools) not only produced better-qualified children, but they also developed the soft skills of confidence, teamwork and interview skills, through extra-curricular activities and mentoring. Later, privately educated children made full use of professional internship programmes, which were usually organised on the basis of 'who you know'. State school pupils had neither the aspirations, the skills nor the contacts to break into the charmed circle

Milburn made a number of recommendations, including (BBC 2009):

- university students to be recruited from wider social backgrounds
- no-fee degrees for students living at home
- professions to publish more details on the social background of their intakes
- better careers advice aimed at raising aspirations
- more extra-curricular activity for state school pupils.

Milburn also stressed that it was not just the working class that was blocked from the professions. Writing in the *Observer*, he said (Milburn 2009b), 'It will be more and more middle class kids, not just working class ones, who miss out,' and 'We need a new focus, unleashing aspirations, not just beating poverty.'

INEQUALITY

Inequality in society can be measured in a number of ways, but the easiest is distribution of wealth or income. Wealth is extremely unevenly distributed in the UK, although rather less unevenly than in the 1950s, and much less unevenly than in the 1920s, when the top 1 per cent owned over 60 per cent of marketable wealth (Abercrombie and Warde 2000).

Table 7.11 UK distribution of wealth (per cent)

	1954	1975	1981	1994	2002
Top 1 per cent	43.0	23.2	18.0	19.0	23.0
Top 10 per cent	79.0	62.4	50.0	51.0	56.0
Top 50 per cent	–	92.0	93.0	93.0	94.0

(Source: ONS 2004.)

Several points can be drawn from these figures:

- Inequality in wealth fell over the period 1954 to 1981. The main reason for this seems to have been the spread of home-ownership, from perhaps 20 per cent just after the war to around 75 per cent by 1994. For the first time this gave most of the middle class, and some sections of the working class, access to wealth.

- Wealth inequality has widened since 1981, in reality from the election of the Thatcher government in 1979. Drastic cuts in the higher rates of tax, privatisation and the long-term rise in the stock market have all contributed to this trend, which has not been reversed under New Labour. The top 1 per cent hold 75 per cent of privately held shares; the top 5 per cent own 90 per cent.

- The bottom half of the population has never enjoyed significant wealth, and this has not changed in recent years.

If we exclude the value of dwellings, wealth is even more unevenly held. In 2002, the top 1 per cent held 35 per cent of all marketable wealth less value of dwellings; the top 5 per cent held 62 per cent; and the top 50 per cent held 98 per cent (ONS 2004).

A slightly less pessimistic picture comes if we include the right to a state old-age pension as part of wealth. If we do this, the share of the top 50 per cent for 1994 falls from 93 to 83 per cent.

The same pattern emerges if one examines distribution of income, as shown in table 7.12.

Table 7.12 UK distribution of income before housing costs

	1961	1979	1997	2007
Top 10 per cent	22.0	21.0	26.0	30.0
Top 20 per cent	37.0	35.0	41.0	42.1
Top 50 per cent	70.6	68.0	72.0	72.6
Bottom 10 per cent	4.2	4.2	2.1	1.5

(Adapted from George and Wilding 1999, and Lansley 2009.)

Key points from this table are:

- income inequality narrowed marginally between 1961 and 1979, but has widened substantially in the last 30 years
- Margaret Thatcher's 'trickle-down' theory – that increasing the wealth and income of the rich would produce a trickle down of greater income and wealth lower down the scale – appears to be a myth
- even when inequality was lessening, this did not benefit the bottom 10 per cent.

In the early years of the Labour government, the share of the bottom 10 per cent improved slightly, largely as a result of Gordon Brown's use of tax credits targeted at the poorest, but inequality widened during the course of the 2000s. An increased emphasis on indirect rather than direct taxes, which started well before 1997, has tended to hit the bottom end of the distribution harder than the top. Since 1979, the proportion of income paid in tax by the lowest 20 per cent of taxpayers has risen from 31 to 42 per cent, while the proportion paid by the highest fifth has fallen from 37 to 34 per cent (Clark 2004). In fact, the poor pay a higher proportion of income in tax than the rich.

Inequality is still increasing. The highest 1 per cent of earners increased their share of national income by 3 per cent since Labour came to power in 1997; the share of the top 0.1 per cent in 2007 was the same as it was in 1937 (Milne 2007).

A method used by statisticians to measure inequality is the Gini coefficient. This expresses income distribution on a scale of 0 to 100, with 0 representing total equality. The higher the figure, the more uneven the distribution. The Gini coefficient figures have changed as follows:

Table 7.13 Gini coefficient (before housing costs)

1961	1970	1979	1991	1997	2002	2008
26	26	25	34	33	36	36

(Sources: George and Wilding 1999, Clark 2004 and IFS 2009.)

On the Gini figures, inequality was constant over the period 1961–79, widened greatly under the Thatcher governments, narrowed very slightly under the Major government, and widened under New Labour since 1997.

Inequality in the UK is significantly higher than in the rest of the EU. The Gini figure for the EU (15 members) was 31 in 2005. It was 32.7 in France (2008), 27 in Germany (2006), and 32 in Italy (2006). Inequality is much lower in Scandinavian countries: 23 in Sweden (2005), and 24 in Denmark (2005). However, on a world scale, the UK does not fare so badly. The Gini coefficient in the US was 45 (2007), in Japan 38 (2002), in China 47 (2007) and in India 36.8 (2004) (CIA 2009).

These trends towards a rising inequality in earnings were confirmed by the 2010 National Equality Report. The 90:10 ratio on net earnings has risen from 3:1 to 3.9 since 1970. (The 90:10 ratio shows how much larger an outcome is for someone nine-tenths of the way up the distribution than for somebody one-tenth of the way up. The larger this ratio, the greater the inequality.) The after-tax income share of the top one in 2,000 (0.05 per cent of the population) has risen from 0.5 per cent to 2.5 per cent over the same period.

CHANGES IN FAMILY STRUCTURE

The move to smaller families and a higher participation rate for women has led to changes in the structure of families and the role of family members. Working women (especially those in full-time work) spend less time on domestic routines, which has led to a considerable growth in industries devoted to convenience foods, eating out and hired-in domestic help. Information from the Family Expenditure Survey shows that the proportion of income spent on eating out has increased by 50 per cent over the period 1980 to 2009. The changes in the labour market have led to changes in the nature of society, as shown in case study 7.10.

ACTIVITY 7.7 DECLINING MANUFACTURING

What actions can the government take to mitigate the negative consequences of areas of declining manufacturing?

CHANGING SOCIETY IN SOUTH WALES

CASE STUDY 7.10

Doreen Massey (1984) carried out a survey of the implications of the massive closures of the steel and coal-mining industries in the early 1980s and identified the difference between the former labour market, which was heavily male-dominated with a high proportion of manual and semi-skilled labour, and a new labour market that had grown up with economic restructuring.

This was typified by new jobs in the electronics industries and high level of female employment. The previous labour market had created a patriarchal society that had remained relatively stable over many generations. The new market offered less stability and less security and led to changes in social patterns and family organisation.

Other changes have involved the caring responsibilities for children becoming more shared between spouses, while there are many examples of active grandparents taking a substantial responsibility for day-to-day care of younger children.

On the other hand, there is the challenge of looking after older relatives, with around half living into their 80s and many into their 90s and beyond. In the past, many have lived with their extended family, but in Europe this practice is declining, although it is still the norm in Japan. The need for a degree of personal privacy, the day-to-day medical and psychological challenges of coping with an elderly relative, and the widespread growth in sheltered accommodation have been reasons for this trend.

Another trend has been the decline in marriage, as shown by figure 7.2.

Figure 7.2 Marriages in the UK

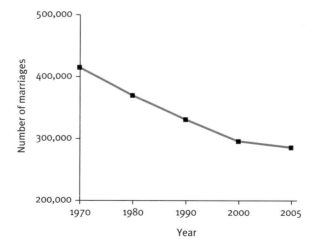

This is not just a UK phenomenon. In Scandinavia, over 50 per cent of children are now born out of wedlock (Kurtz 2004). The issue of declining marriages and rising divorces (157,000 in 2001) will be discussed later in this chapter, but the rising number of single-parent families and the dependence of many such families on the benefit system, which is especially strong in the UK, presents a further financial challenge to governments as well as implications for housing provision and, in certain areas, has an effect on crime (Haskey 1993).

POVERTY

Absolute poverty in the Ethiopian sense does not exist in the UK. A more useful definition is relative poverty, and this is inescapable in a society in which income is distributed unevenly. However, relative poverty can be defined in many different ways: assistance level; assistance level plus x per cent; half median earnings; 60 per cent of median earnings; before or after housing costs, etc. The definition standardised throughout the EU is household income below 60 per cent of median income (after housing costs) – approximately £12,000 a year in 2004. Using this definition, poverty rose steadily throughout the Thatcher and Major years, reaching a peak of 13.9 million people (nearly a quarter of the population) in 1997, falling to 12.4 million in 2004 (Clark 2004). Of 16 industrialised countries measured for poverty in 1995, the UK was 12th, with twice the level of poverty of Sweden or Finland, and slightly less than Ireland, Greece, Italy and the US (Aldridge 2004).

Poverty is particularly influenced by three factors:

- *Children*. The percentage of households with incomes below 60 per cent of the median was around 20 per cent of the whole population in 2000–01, but around 30 per cent for households with children. The proportion for single-parent households was even higher. When New Labour came to power, one of its main objectives was to eliminate child poverty, which had grown from one in seven in 1979 to one in three in 1997. By 2003, they had reduced it to one in four, but 72 per cent of children of lone parents were still classed as poor in 2007 (Toynbee 2007). One in four of all children (2.7 million) were in a lone-parent family in 2001 (Carvel 2003).

- *Gender*. Despite 30 years of equal pay legislation, average female hourly earnings are still only around 82 per cent of male earnings, and women on average work fewer hours than men. This particularly hits single-parent households headed by women (the vast majority).

- *Ethnicity*. Ethic minority groups are likely to have lower incomes than whites. The average weekly male pay in 2000 was £297 for whites, £264 for Chinese, £254 for Afro-Caribbeans, £222 for Pakistanis, and £142 for Bangladeshis. Only Indians, at £307, have a higher income than whites, at £307. However, after we take account of the fact that Indians on average have higher educational qualifications than whites, their 'like for like' earnings are lower. In 1995, more than a third of the ethnic minority population was in the poorest fifth of the population (George and Wilding 1999). In 1991, unemployment rates for all ethnic minority groups were twice those of the white population, and unemployment rates for Bangladeshis were three times as high for men and five times as high for women.

Poverty matters because it affects future life chances. Infant mortality rates are twice as high for unskilled manual groups as they are professionals. Life expectancy for male professionals in 1997–2009 was 79, and for female professionals 83, while for unskilled manual groups the corresponding figures were 75 and 77. The lower your income, the more likely you are to be a victim of burglary.

The percentage of children aged between five and 15 experiencing mental disorders is between two and three times higher for those living in households with an income of less than £100 a week than for those in households earning over £700 a week. Most poor children fail. Their depressed parents are unable to give them aspirations (Toynbee 2009).

Poverty persists across the generations. Of people whose families were poor when they were in their teens in the 1970s, 19 per cent were poor in their early thirties, while where families were not poor in the 1970s, 10 per cent were poor as adults. Dividing 19 per cent by 10 per cent shows that the odds of being poor as an adult were doubled if one's parents were poor. For teenagers in the 1980s, the odds of being poor were quadrupled when parents were poor (Blanden and Gibbons 2006).

Research in 2007 by the Joseph Rowntree Foundation examined public attitudes to poverty. More than half of the UK population felt that there was quite a lot of poverty in Britain, and 46 per cent thought poverty would increase over the next 10 years. Seventy-three per cent of the UK population in 2004 felt that the gap between high and low incomes was too large. While they did not necessarily think that those on low incomes were underpaid, they felt that those on high incomes were very overpaid. However, only half as many people supported redistributive measures to reduce poverty as felt that the income gap was too great (Orton and Rowlingson 2007).

How easy is it to move out of poverty? The answer seems to be not easy, but not impossible. Evidence from the British Household Panel Survey shows that just over half of the individuals who were in the bottom quintile (lowest 20 per cent) for income in 1991 were still there is 1996. In other words, half had escaped from dire poverty. Over a one-year time-span, 65 per cent stayed in the bottom quintile, and of those who escaped, most stayed in the bottom two quintiles (ie the bottom 40 per cent) (Giddens 2006). McKnight (2000) found that the unemployed are most likely to gain employment in the lowest-paid sectors when they do find work, and that the lower paid are more likely to become unemployed than the higher paid.

Even after recent falls in child poverty, the UK has the fourth worst figures among the EU 25. Only Italy, Portugal and the Slovak Republic have higher rates. Contributory factors include pay inequalities, a high proportion of lone parents, their low chance of working, and less generous welfare benefits (Hirsch 2006). Child poverty could be ended, but at a cost. It would involve a massive increase in child tax credits, estimated at £30 billion up to 2020. Barnard and Goulden point out that this only represents one year's economic growth. Money alone will not be enough. Considerable practical and emotional support in increasing the self-esteem of lone-parent families will also be needed, through the expansion of educational programmes such as Sure Start and employment programmes like New Deal.

ACTIVITY 7.8 POVERTY AND INEQUALITY

- In 2001, the average CEO in the UK earned £509,000, while the average manufacturing worker earned £20,475, a differential of around 25:1. German CEOs averaged £298,000, 11 times the earnings of a German manufacturing worker. The ratio in the US was 32:1. Executive pay in the UK had soared by 29 per cent between 1999 and 2001, and has risen relative to average wages since 2001 (Duncan 2001). What do you think the impact of these differentials is likely to be on the motivation of manufacturing workers in the UK?

- Why should social inequality matter to employers? What can they do about it?

- The Joseph Rowntree Foundation in 2007 identified five types of household:

  - core poor: income poor, materially deprived and subjectively poor

  - breadline poor: living below a relative poverty line

- exclusive wealthy: so much wealth that they are outside the norms of society

- asset wealthy: holding assets which reach the inheritance tax threshold

- average: everyone else.

The research also found that poor, rich and average households are less and less likely to live next door to each other in 2000 than in 1970. Both the poor and the wealthy have become more and more clustered in different areas (Dorling et al 2007).

Questions:

1. What do you think are the social consequences of the trends identified above?

2. What can the government do to increase social mobility and equality of opportunity, and to reduce poverty?

Figures for these groups in 1980 and 2000 were (per cent):

	1980	2000
core poor*	10	12
breadline poor	17	27
exclusive wealthy*	7	6
asset wealthy	17	23
average	66	50

*core poor is a subset of breadline poor; exclusive wealthy is a subset of asset wealthy. Exclusive wealthy declined sharply during the 1980s, then rose from 1990 to 2000.

HAS POVERTY INCREASED UNDER NEW LABOUR?

The evidence on this is mixed. As shown above, the Gini coefficient has risen over the period 1997–2008, which means that income inequality has increased under Labour. This would suggest that there has been an increase in relative poverty. However, the main reason for the rise in the Gini coefficient is the considerable increase in income at the very top of the income scale. This has the effect of pulling up average income, but not mean income (the income of the person in the middle of the income distribution). Mean income is considerably less than average income because of this skewed distribution of income. This would lessen relative poverty, except in the technical sense that 99 per cent of the population have got relatively poorer than the top 1 per cent.

Income after inflation has risen for every part of the population except for the bottom 3 per cent. As a result, absolute poverty has increased for those at the very bottom of the income scale. However, the Institute for Fiscal Studies (IFS 2009) points out that those with the lowest recorded incomes often have access to informal and unrecorded sources of income.

On child poverty, the record of Labour is positive, although it could not achieve its aim of halving child poverty by 2010. On the other hand, because resources have been directed towards families with children, there has been some increase in relative poverty among working-age adults without children.

As so often, the answer to the question must be – on the one hand, yes, but on the other hand, no. Unlike under Thatcher, the Labour government fiscal policy has attempted to reduce poverty and inequality, but to some extent these efforts have been stymied by other social forces: the effects of globalisation, the acceleration of the bonus culture, etc.

ACTIVITY 7.9 SOCIAL CLASS

- 'There is no such thing as society' (Margaret Thatcher)

- 'The classless society' (John Major)

- 'We are all middle class now' (anon).

Explain each of these statements. Do you agree with any of them?

EQUAL OPPORTUNITIES AND DIVERSITY

The UK is a very diverse society: diverse in terms of race, sex, sexual orientation, religion, age, disability and life experience. Equality of opportunity is based on legislation, and has as its main aim assimilation – that whatever a person's background, they should all have the opportunity to achieve the same outcomes. Diversity is much more about difference. The differences between the two are illustrated in table 7.14

Table 7.14 Differences between equal opportunities and diversity

Equal opportunities	Diversity
Externally imposed	Internally driven
Groups	Individuals
Assimilation	Diversification
Systems	Total culture
Responsibility of personnel/HR	Responsibility of all, permeates the culture

(Adapted from Ross and Schneider 1992.)

In 2005, the CIPD published three related Change Agenda documents on diversity, entitled *Managing Diversity; Measuring Success* (Tatli, Özbilgin, Worman and Mulholland 2005), *Managing Diversity: learning by doing* (Taylor, Piasecka and Worman 2005), and *Managing Diversity: linking theory and practice to business performance* (Mulholland, Özbilgin and Worman 2005). These are invaluable in an understanding of diversity.

The CIPD defines diversity as 'valuing everyone as an individual – valuing people as employees, customers and clients' (CIPD 2010, p1). This brings out three key elements:

● diversity is about individuals, not social groups

● it is about valuing, not meeting legal requirements

● it applies as much outside the organisation as inside.

However, in this section we will concentrate on diversity within the organisation.

Diversity is traditionally viewed as being concerned with categories of race, gender, ethnicity, age and disability, but true diversity is much wider than this. Anderson and Metcalfe (2003) identify three different types of workforce diversity:

● *Social category diversity*: differences in demographic characteristics such as race and sex (the traditional definition).

● *Informational diversity*: differences of knowledge, experience, functional background, etc.

● *Value diversity*: differences in personality and attitudes.

A need for diversity is being driven by economic and social change – a more culturally mixed society as a result of immigration, an ageing population, pressures of globalisation and the trend towards a 24/7 society. There are simply not enough white, English-born, young and middle-aged males to fill all the jobs.

There is clear evidence of a continuing inequality based on race and sex. The National Equality Panel (Hills 2010) found the following:

● White British pupils with GCSE results around or below the national median are less likely to go on to higher education than those from minority ethnic groups. Pakistani, Black African and Black Caribbean boys have results at the age of 16 well below the median in England.

- Compared with a white British Christian man with similar qualifications, age and occupation, Pakistani and Bangladeshi Muslim men and Black African Christian men have an income that is 13–21 per cent lower. Nearly half of Bangladeshi and Pakistani households are in poverty.

- Girls have better educational outcomes than boys at school and are more likely to enter higher education and achieve good degrees, but women's median hourly pay is 21 per cent less than men's, although this difference has narrowed since the 1970s. In fact, median earnings differ by around 12 per cent for full-time earners but the big difference is in part-time rates, where women form the large majority and are crowded into low-pay sectors, such as catering, caring and retailing.

THE BUSINESS CASE FOR DIVERSITY

Tatli et al (2005) identify three major benefits from diversity:

- it enhances customer relations and increases market share

- it enhances employee relations and reduces the cost of recruitment and retention

- it improves workforce quality and performance in terms of diverse skills, creativity, problem-solving and flexibility.

Jones (2006) has examined the business case in detail. She identifies a number of benefits:

- *Marketing*: Sales tend to increase when staffing reflects the organisation's customer base, eg Lloyds TSB reported a 30 per cent increase in sales in branches where staffing was changed to reflect the ethnicity of customers.

- *HR*: Rajan et al (2003) found that diversity led to higher staff motivation, higher retention and reduced recruitment costs. Diversity policies also made employees feel valued and respected, and this increased their sense of engagement.

- *Stakeholders*: Diversity policies improve the organisation's image with its stakeholders.

- *Creativity and decision-making*. Diverse organisations tend to be more creative. Diverse teams avoid the risk of groupthink and tended to make better decisions (Janis 1982). However, in some situations, homogeneous groups tended to perform better – where the main tasks were routine, and where the organisation was contracting rather than growing (Jones 2006, CIPD 2006).

ACTIVITY 7.10 BINNA KANDOLA AND THE BUSINESS CASE

The psychologist and diversity expert Binna Kandola (2009, p26) has said that, 'The search for the business case for diversity is an exercise in futility.' He argues that diversity is ultimately a moral issue, and that what prevents diversity from moving forward is the bias and stereotyping that we all carry.

Do you agree?

If you are a CIPD member, you can read Kandola's articles on the *People Management* website.

MANAGING DIVERSITY

It is important to note that these benefits of diversity do not just happen. Diversity has to be managed effectively. Mulholland et al (2005) liken it to managing change. They quote the example of the turkey producer Bernard Matthews, who was suffering from a shortage of labour in rural Norfolk. This was tackled by bringing in immigrant labour from Portugal, which increased the proportion of Portuguese employees from 3 to 30 per cent of the workforce. However, in order to make it work, Bernard Matthews developed local support networks, promoted local English language training, and created partnerships with the Home Office, Norfolk Police and HSBC to facilitate integration of the new workforce.

Diversity strategies can operate at three different levels, and achievement of all three is necessary for an effective diversity policy (Jones 2006):

- *Representational diversity*: ensuring that the workforce is more representative of the population as a whole. The key here is recruitment.

- *Inclusive processes*: underlying processes, eg retention, progression, development, etc, must support representational diversity. Bernard Matthews clearly did this.

- *Inclusive culture*: provide people with a culture where they feel respected. The attitudes of top management are critical here.

Kandola and Fullerton (1994) identify three key elements of diversity.

- diversity is a source of real value to the organisation

- diversity is not only about obvious visible differences, but is about all the ways in which people can differ

- the aim of diversity is to enrich the organisational culture and working environment.

All of these points are illustrated in the following case studies.

DIVERSITY

CASE STUDY 7.12

A. The war against crime

The Metropolitan Police has set up a Cultural and Communities Resource Unit, headed by a (black) detective chief inspector, Keith Fraser. The unit maintains a database of the range of backgrounds, lifestyles and specialisms in the Met and the City of London Police. The unit has 800 people on its books, and has located experts who have helped with 700 criminal enquiries all over the country.

Examples of the work of the unit include:

- The murder of an elderly Bengali woman, where white officers were getting no co-operation from the community. Bengali officers immediately got co-operation.

- A Chinese person had been missing in the north of England for two weeks. A Chinese policeman from London found him in a day and a half.

- Tamil officers are investigating violence between rival Tamil gangs.

- A voodoo expert helped interpret seemingly innocuous but actually sinister objects sent to a Bangladeshi man.

As detective chief inspector Fraser says, 'The unit highlights the true meaning of diversity and the fantastic opportunities and benefits it gives policing' (Cowan 2004).

B. Shariah mortgages

Islamic finance is regulated by shariah law. One of the main principles of shariah law is a prohibition on usury, the payment of interest. This makes a conventional western mortgage impossible under shariah law. The solution developed by Islamic banks is a version of sale and lease-back. The customer in effect sells their house to the bank, pays rent (not interest) on it, and then at a later stage buys the house back from the bank. Interestingly, exactly the same process had developed in late medieval England to get round Christian prohibitions of usury. Unfortunately, under UK law this represented two property sales, each of which was liable to stamp duty. In the 2006 Budget, Gordon Brown recognised this, and abolished the requirement for double stamp duty (Parker 2006).

C. Pearson

The publisher Pearson, which owns the *Financial Times*, came top of a 2009 survey of FTSE 350 companies which measured both the quality of equal opportunities and diversity policies, and the proportion of women on the board. The chief executive and the chief finance officer are both female. In 2003, 9 per cent of its staff were from ethnic minorities, and by 2009 this figure had increased to 15 per cent. This follows on from a five-year plan launched in 2002 to communicate diversity awareness to employees. Pearson holds annual outreach programmes for students which help produce candidates for its internship scheme. The *Financial Times* is part of a scheme in Tower Hamlets which acts as a matchmaker between firms and ethnic minority jobseekers (Sunderland 2009).

WOMEN ON THE BOARD

CASE STUDY 7.13

In 2009, The Co-operative Asset Management, a fund manager, carried out a survey of female representation on the boards of FTSE 350 companies, extensively reported in the *Observer*. They ranked companies on two measures:

- the sophistication of equal opportunities and diversity policies

- female representation on boards of directors.

Companies tended to score better on theory than on practice. Many had impressive-sounding policies, and 94 per cent said they had an equal opportunities policy, but then failed to have women on their boards. Typical was Barclays, which scored 7.8 out of 10 for its policies, but zero for its board, which contained no women. Royal Bank of Scotland was even less diverse, as its board was not only all men, but also predominantly Scottish. This may in part explain the banking crisis. A separate survey showed that 89 per cent of business executives thought that the banking culture encouraged excessive risk-raking, and 83 per cent thought that this was fuelled by male machismo. The only company with a perfect score for both policies and practice was Pearson (see case study 7.12).

Overall, women held only 34 executive board seats out of 970. Most female directors were non-executives, and 130 companies (nearly half of the 297 companies that responded) had no women on the board. Of a total of 2,472 directorships, women held just under 10 per cent.

Opinion is divided over whether diverse boards improve performance. One study suggests that women on the board do not improve financial performance, but could improve governance, while another study found that firms with more diverse boards had better financial performance. However, common sense suggests that companies which do not have female directors are missing out on an important source of talent.

Suggestions to improve the gender balance include:

- *Increasing the availability of flexible working*. At lower levels of management, where flexible working is generally available, the gender balance is relatively equal. However, higher up the organisation, flexible working is less likely to be available, and this discriminates against women.

- Overcoming a tendency for male bosses to recruit in their own image.

- Providing mentoring and networking opportunities for female executives.

- Using succession planning to identify and fast-track outstanding female candidates.

- *Shareholder pressure*. Co-operative Asset Management intends in future to consider diversity when it is assessing company governance.

(Source: Sunderland 2009.)

A fuller discussion of organisational strategy on flexible working is found in Chapter 10.

KEY LEARNING POINTS

- The major demographic trends across the world are a major decline in the birth rate, population ageing and increasing migration, both of people and jobs. These trends are strongest in the developed world, especially Europe.

- These trends are likely to continue to produce a reversal of world population expansion around 2050. Developed countries are likely to be faced by declining populations before that time unless they change policies and allow higher rates of migration.

- These demographic changes provide opportunities for organisations to move into new product and service areas. The reduction in the availability of younger labour means that organisations will need to reorganise work patterns to encourage greater participation from women, older people and other groups.

- Governments will increasingly be faced by the need for higher expenditure on pensions, benefits and health services as a result of demographic changes. At the same time, the higher dependency ratio is likely to necessitate higher levels of taxation to finance this expenditure. Initiatives to combat these difficulties can include encouraging larger families through incentives, reducing benefits and stimulating personal savings for pensions and health.

- It is likely that an ageing population will be a less poductive one, providing challenges for the world economy and wealth creation. There has been a rapid transferring of jobs and services around the world as an outcome of globalisation.

- Throughout most of the twentieth century, social mobility in the UK was high, as the absolute size of the middle class rose considerably at the expense of the working class, but these trends have slowed in recent years.

- There are considerable inequalities in both income and wealth in the UK, and these inequalities have been widening in recent years.

- Inequality is closely related to relative poverty, which has persisted in the UK, and which leads to an impairment of the life chances of the poor.

- Equal opportunities is about assimilation, while diversity is about celebrating difference.

- Diversity is of different types: social category diversity, informational diversity and value diversity: differences in personality and attitudes.

- In order to manage diversity, it is necessary to achieve representational diversity, inclusive processes and an inclusive culture. The attitudes of top management are critical.

QUESTIONS

1. What have been the main changes in sectoral employment in the UK since 1992?

2. Provide five reasons why migration can provide benefits for an economy and set out five problems that migration can bring.

3. How can the UK government handle the current crisis in pension provision due to the ageing population? What options does it have?

4. How is the participation ratio measured, and what has caused the rate to rise in the UK since the late 1990s?

5. What are the implications for organisations in terms of changing markets arising from demographic changes?

6. How can demographic changes affect HR activities and policies?

7. What is the difference between absolute and relative social mobility?

8. What is the Gini coefficient, and what does it tell us about inequality in the UK?

9. Identify three main differences between equal opportunities and diversity.

10. Why is representational diversity only one element of a successful diversity strategy?

EXPLORE FURTHER

Further Reading

The most readable and dynamic book source on demography remains Paul Wallace's *Agequake* (2001). A more statistical approach can be found in *Demography: measuring and modeling population Processes* by Preston, Heuveline and Guillot (2000), while regular reports on all areas of UK demography can be found on the ONS website. A wider perspective is given in a new book by the American writers Poston and Bouvier (2010), *Population and Society*.

Social class and social mobility are discussed in any good sociology textbook. Poverty and inequality are covered in Vic George and Paul Wilding, *British Society and Social Welfare: towards a sustainable society* (1999). Excellent overviews of the evidence on social trends are given in two papers by Stephen Aldridge, an economist in the Prime Minister's Strategy Unit (formerly the Performance and Innovation Unit), listed in the Bibliography. A series of CIPD 'Change Agendas' published in 2005 are valuable for diversity. You should read the excellent CIPD 'Factsheets' relevant to this chapter, which are regularly updated, including subjects such as the psychological contract, work–life balance and diversity, together with the regular legal updating the CIPD website provides.

Websites

The Work Foundation (www.theworkfoundation.com) publishes several research reports on social topics. The journal CentrePiece (www.cep.lse.ac.uk/centrepiece), published by the Centre for Economic Performance at the London School of Economics, has useful articles with social themes.

SEMINAR ACTIVITY

SOCIAL MOBILITY, EDUCATION AND THE MERITOCRACY

- After the Education Act 1944 it was thought that the 11-plus examination, which determined whether children would go to a grammar school (and receive an education leading to middle-class occupations) or to a secondary modern school (leading to working-class occupations) would increase social mobility, by selecting on the basis of intelligence rather than father's social class. By the 1970s, the theory behind this was discredited, and a switch was made to comprehensive education, whereby all children, whatever their intelligence or social background, would go to the same school. This does not seem to have been effective in increasing social mobility. Why do you think that changes in the education system have failed to increase social mobility?

- In 1958 the sociologist Michael Young published *The Rise of the Meritocracy*. In this book he examined the likely consequences of a society in which success was based solely on merit (ie on ability) rather than on social background, and in which there was total social mobility – in other words, something very like the aspirations of the 1944 Education Act. However, Young saw considerable downsides to this. What do you think these downsides could have been?

- The slowdown in social mobility is of increasing concern to Labour politicians. Typical is a speech made by Alan Milburn to the Institute of Public Policy Research in November 2004. Why do you think that New Labour would be concerned about a fall in social mobility?

Technology

INTRODUCTION

No one doubts that massive technological advances have changed the world, as set out in the causes of globalisation in Chapter 6. The developments in information and communication technologies, biotechnology, energy supply and transportation have altered the world beyond recognition over the last 50 years. To put it more accurately, technological change enables massive changes in organisation, communication, products, marketing and distribution together with associated ways of managing people. The uniqueness of technology is that, once it has been invented, it cannot be uninvented. Other resources can be used up (oil), suddenly disappear (chief executives), or be replaced (buildings) but technological knowledge will always survive. In fact, once one organisation uses that technology and gains competitive advantage, then it needs to be adopted in some form by all the competitors to ensure survival.

The speed of technological advance is increasing, prompting even speedier changes in society. In fact, writing about examples is quite difficult because, by the time this is printed, most of the examples will be out of date and the most influential changes of the next 10 years are only known about by small cliques of researchers in multinational research and development labs and their counterparts in leading universities.

PAUSE FOR THOUGHT

Recognising the importance of new technology can sometimes be tricky. In 1979, the medium-sized organisation I worked for as head of HR bought its first word processor, set up in its own specially designed room. I was tasked to recruit an operator internally and expected to have to fight off the wave of applicants. Surprisingly, nobody applied; they did not want to 'sidelined' into specialised work. They liked the routine and variety of being a secretary and the kudos of being accurate, including sending letters out with only the occasional mistake. At last, I was approached by one of the newest and youngest (and brightest) employees to take the job on. Within two years, she was working for the chief executive with a doubled salary and a guaranteed career. Her knowledge was unique in the organisation and she had to be adequately rewarded to prevent her leaving.

WHAT'S HAPPENING IN TECHNOLOGY

PATTERNS OF TECHNOLOGICAL DEVELOPMENT

The common differentiation made between man and other animals is the ability to design and use tools: primitive technologies have been utilised for many thousands of years. However, the beginnings of the Industrial Revolution in the mid-seventeenth century saw the early stages of fundamental technological growth where machines replaced hand operations.

Although technological invention appears to follow a continuous and unrelenting line, a pattern has been identified by, among others, Hall and Preston (1988). Named K-waves, after the Russian Kondratiev who first developed the concept in the 1920s, a 50-year cycle for each wave has been identified as follows:

K1	1770s to 1830s	Early mechanisation in textiles and water power with the construction of canals, which led to the first large-scale factories and companies.
K2	1830s to 1880s	Invention of steam power used in railways and machines, which lead to vastly improved communications and location independent of water sources.
K3	1880s to 1930s	Inventions of electricity, steel, chemicals and synthetics, creating new industries with reliable and powerful energy, leading to very large-scale production and control (trusts and cartels) and opening up of transportation and communication through cars and aircraft. Technologies were integrated to create assembly-line techniques.

| K4 | 1930s to 1980s | Explosion of development of cars and aircraft together with petrochemicals and consumer durables. Controlled through integrated manufacturing processes and by multinational organisations |
| K5 | 1980s to current | Information and communication technologies developments producing ability to source and manufacture flexibly across the world, creating global brands, communicated by television, radio and Internet technologies. Robotics allows complex manufacturing and medical processes. |

There can be much debate about the timing of these waves and the overlapping feature of new technologies, but an economic pattern emerges that shows four stages. Firstly, the invention and diffusion of the technology produces prosperity, especially for the organisations leading the way. However, after a period, demand slackens or competitors catch up, leading to a recession where new investment falls. After such a period, the third stage is that of outright depression arising from reduced activity and restructuring with mass unemployment before the final stage, recovery, appears when the economic conditions improve sufficiently for the next wave of technological development.

 ACTIVITY 8.1 THE DOWN PHASE

There is some evidence that the current technological cycle is swinging towards a down phase. Set out the reasons why this down phase might be occurring and also explain why the contrary may be true – that the current technological phase is gathering more steam.

TYPES OF TECHNOLOGICAL CHANGE

Freeman (1987) identified four different types of technological change:

- *Incremental innovations* – These are small-scale changes made at a local level. For example, a quality circle might come up with a new way to calibrate existing equipment in a factory.

- *Radical innovations* – These change the way things are done. For example, the development of semiconductors rather than valves in the 1960s changed the ways in which computers could operate.

- *Changes of technology systems* – These often involve linking together two existing technological systems to form a new system. For example, multimedia entertainment systems bring together computer and TV technologies.

- *Technology revolutions* – These occur about every 50 years or so and revolutionise our approach to technology. One was the development of the steam engine in the 1770s; another, the growth of the railways in the 1830s. The development of the computer in the 1940s and the creation of the World Wide Web/Internet have been the latest two.

INFORMATION TECHNOLOGY

In all technological developments, it is in the field of information technology (IT) that the speed of development has been the greatest, as has the subsequent effect upon society. A stream of inventions has followed the arrival of the first commercial computer in the 1950s. In hardware, the integrated circuits have become increasingly powerful through the invention of optical chips and biochips paralleled by the improvements in data storage systems. The price of PCs continues to decline while ever more powerful laptops allow work to be carried out at any location and on the move. In software, the ability to network information so it is available to multiple organisational users; to operate real-time systems so leisure activities, such as flights or theatre tickets can be booked electronically; in banking, money markets around the world are linked with instant access to information and market changes; programs can control tools to perform any task previously carried out by hand such as cut, weld or burn; and controls can be programmed into complex machinery which determines the output and the quality of the process.

All these developments have led to the computer being at the heart of business and, increasingly, private lives. Production, sales, distribution, finance and HR are all aided by computer systems which increase the speed of operation, while providing reliable operations, communications and storage. Recent developments, badged 'business intelligence' (BI), aim to transform large amount of data, often scattered across the organisation, into the key information that drives informed decision-taking, and delivering it in an easily read form through the computer screen to anybody where and when they need to know. So essential is this intelligence that the estimated worldwide market for BI systems in 2008 was around £20 billion.

COMMUNICATION TECHNOLOGIES

Supporting the development in IT have been two major technological developments in communication. Firstly, satellite communication, from the mid-1960s, has increased exponentially so that there are now over 100 geo-stationary satellites in orbit facilitating cheap and instantaneous communication and data transmission.

Secondly, the invention and development of optical fibre technology has provided a competitor in huge capacity handling at great speed. FLAG Europe-Asia, for example, is a 27,000 km system servicing half the world at lower and lower costs. An example (*Economist* 2000) is that the cost of transmitting the *Encyclopedia Britannica* electronically from New York to Los Angeles cost US $187 in 1970. By 2000, the entire contents of the Library of Congress could be sent the same distance for less than US $40.

Both these developments have led to the creation of mass markets, allowing consumers to be aware of the goods and services on offer. Even if incomes are low, the spread of multinational advertising and brand creation produces images that people can aspire to so that they become future consumers. Television has had the most dramatic effect because it makes no demands on a standard of literacy, unlike the printed word. The technological development improvements since its invention in the 1930s, which have consistently reduced the price and increased quality and reliability, have had two effects on the mass markets. The first effect is direct, in that most television channels are commercial so the products and services are directly communicated to the consumer. The second effect is more elliptical in that television programmes show styles of life that create aspiration. This was most pronounced in eastern Europe under communism where the nightly broadcasting of western shows indicated clearly how far behind the communist economic model was compared to the West and contributed to its eventual collapse.

The swiftness of communication improves the effectiveness of markets. Producers and consumers widely use mobile phones to aid their business choices. Jensen (2007) researched the rapid spread of mobile phones among the Kerala fishermen off the Indian coast and found that they were able to land their catch in the markets which provided the best return. This reduced the overall price for consumers, provided more consistency of supply and prevented the widespread wastage that occurred when fish could not be sold. Thus, a much more efficient market prevailed. The "smart phone" has intergrated information and communication with a portable package, available at increasingly affordable prices.

TRANSPORTATION TECHNOLOGIES

The 'shrinking world' is a simplistic but accurate description of the rapid technological change since the 1940s, heralded by the invention of the jet engine and its development into the commercial jetliner. The time difference in travel by air compared to boat and train has been so substantial that it has created two linked mass markets. Firstly, for the traveller, whether business or pleasure, for whom the swiftness and pleasure of the journey is associated with the activities it allows. Secondly, for the tourist where the travelling is a means to take holidays in other countries and where a vast supporting infrastructure has been built up – hotels, holiday complexes, leisure activities, etc. The break-up of the nationalised, non-competing flag-carrying airways has allowed the creation of a flood of low-cost carriers, bringing regular travel to the mass market. A weekend flight to Geneva can be cheaper than a taxi journey across London.

Another less publicised but considerably important development has been 'containerisation' for the movement of freight across land and sea. It is such a simple and obvious development that it tends to be overlooked that it only started in 1956 and, before that time, loading and unloading cargo could be a slow, hazardous and wasteful activity (Levinson 2006). It was also associated with strong union presence in the ports of most developed countries, threatening strike action against developments that may reduce labour costs or employment.

By the 1980s, the union power had been broken in both America and the UK and, today, the container can be 'stuffed' on the factory site, then loaded and unloaded quickly by crane and enjoys protection against weather and theft throughout its journeys.

THE INTERNET

There has been an astonishingly rapid development of Internet technology since its origins in the US Defense Department in the mid-1970s and its commercial usage since the mid-1990s. It now affects all aspects of work and leisure at a steadily reducing cost that now puts its utilisation within the grasp of most citizens in the developed world and many in the developing world. Society communicates through e-mails, while hard-copy communications (such as letters) are used only in specific situations. Some organisations, such as EasyJet, have attempted to become completely paper-free by scanning all incoming post and insisting on all correspondence (internal and external) being carried out via e-mail. The Internet provides a huge range of information that is relatively simple for anybody to access (although, surprisingly, has little effect on book sales). It facilitates buying and selling transactions to take place at the workstation.

 ACTIVITY 8.2 NET COMMERCE

Not all organisations have been enthusiastic to implement online buying and selling. What holds them back from gaining advantages in this area?

A more recent development is the 'cloud'. This is the concept that the electronic information the consumer wants is stored and processed on computers somewhere else (in the 'cloud') and delivered to the consumer when and how they need it. The Internet becomes the operating system; online software runs in the computer's browser to create the files that are needed; and these files are stored in remote data centres. Films can be streamed from the cloud directly onto net books; books streamed onto e-Readers; music onto iPods. Software for our own device will not need to be upgraded because the software we use will be tested and constantly 'sprinkled' into the cloud by operators. No longer will there be need to back up data or fear of losing our laptop because no important data will be stored on the devices (Arlidge 2009).

As Nicolas Carr (2008, p12) explains:

> A hundred years ago, companies stopped generating their own power with steam engines and dynamos and plugged into the newly built electric grid. The cheap power pumped out by electric utilities didn't just change how businesses operate. It set off a chain reaction of economic and social transformations that brought the modern world into existence. Today, a similar revolution is under way. Hooked up to the Internet's global computing grid, massive information-processing plants have begun pumping data and software code into our homes and businesses. This time, it's computing that's turning into a utility.

The difficulty faced by the communication industry is how to continue to obtain income from their services (books, newspapers, TV, music, etc) now they are not being sold in the traditional way. The transfer from individual consumer purchase to subscription services may not generate as much income.

The main concern for businesses and individuals is security. Signing up for cloud services inevitably means not only providing personal information but also surrendering all our data to the cloud provider. A hacker can obtain access simply by knowing a password, rather than having to get access to a computer system. A fire at a data storage unit could destroy vast amounts of data.

More distant worries include the fact that the individual consumer's data can be mined to provide a purchasing profile which will be profitable for advertisers who can target each consumer individually and that one company will emerge as the giant of the industry and, in effect, own all the data – every e-mail or document produced. Here, governments are currently discussing future regulatory environments to prevent monopolies emerging.

 SHOPSAVVY – IMPROVING COMPETITION

CASE STUDY 8.1

One of the cloud-based applications offered in 2009 by Google was Shopsavvy. The camera on one's phone is used as a barcode scanner for a product you want to buy in one shop and data will be directed to your phone giving you a list of shops (with their locations) where it can be bought cheaper.

(Source: Arlidge 2009.)

WEB 2.0

Coined by Tim O'Reilly in 2004, Web 2.0 is a term which refers to the sociable and interactive aspects of the Web which allow a user to discuss and share ideas. It is generally deemed a 'people-centric' Web as it stimulates networking and collaboration, including blogging and social networking. This has a series of benefits and difficulties for HR practitioners, as discussed later in the chapter.

BIOTECHNOLOGY AND MEDICAL TECHNOLOGIES

Biotechnology is the process of altering life forms, essentially through genetic modification. Arising from the fundamental discovery of the structure of DNA in 1953 by Crick and Watson, modification of biological processes allows such interventions as the introduction of new genes into organisms, breeding organisms to form new variants, or treating organisms with new compounds.

One example of biotechnology is in the creation of genetically modified organisms (GMOs). Here, plants, animals and micro-organisms (bacteria, viruses) have had their genetic characteristics modified artificially in order to give them new properties. This could include a plant's resistance to a disease or an insect; the improvement of a food's quality or nutritional value; or a plant's tolerance of a herbicide.

The implications for food production and medical advance are astounding. The biotechnology industry has promised a vast increase in food production that would be sufficient to eradicate all forms of under-nourishment worldwide. In medicine, applications promise the eventual eradication of genetic diseases, such as cystic fibrosis, as well as better understanding and treatment in common diseases and conditions, such as cancer and Alzheimer's disease. Governments around the world have co-operated in the massive genome project to map all human genes, which was successfully completed in 2004.

However, the outcomes in recent years have proved problematic. In food production, there has been considerable opposition to the acceptance of GM foods in many countries, especially the UK, to the extent that all UK trials of GM cereals were halted in 2004. Europe and Africa have followed the same path. There have also been very few signs of medical developments. In cystic fibrosis, for example, the discovery of the errant gene in 1984 has not led to any improved treatment due to technical problems of gene therapy processes, and similar problems have occurred in other treatments, as shown in case study 8.2.

 GENE THERAPY

CASE STUDY 8.2

In 1999, Jesse Gelsinger, a 19-year old with a rare liver disorder, participated in a voluntary clinical trial using gene therapy at the University of Pennsylvania. He died of complications from an inflammatory response shortly after receiving a dose of experimental adenovirus vector, a new device to direct the new gene to the appropriate location. His death dealt a blow to the confidence of scientists and halted all gene therapy trials in the US.

(Source: Subramanian 2004.)

ARTIFICIAL INTELLIGENCE AND ROBOTICS

Artificial intelligence (AI) is the science and engineering of creating intelligent machines, especially computer programs. It is related to the similar task of using computers to understand human intelligence. AI is studied in overlapping fields of computer science, psychology, philosophy, neuroscience and engineering dealing with intelligent behaviour, learning and adaptation.

Research in AI is concerned with producing machines to automate tasks requiring intelligent behaviour. These are synthesised in what are called expert systems. Examples include control, planning and scheduling; the ability to answer diagnostic and consumer questions; speech; and facial recognition. A recent development has been the extension into computer vision where tests have shown that computers can be trained to 'recognise' complex objects in photographs marginally better than humans can (*Economist* 2007).

As such, the study of AI has also become an engineering discipline, focused on providing solutions to real-life problems, knowledge mining and software applications, together with games. However, the world had to wait until 1977 for IBM's Deep Blue to beat the world chess champion, Garry Kasparov. One of the biggest difficulties with AI is that of 'comprehension'. Many devices have been created that can do amazing things, but critics of AI claim that the AI machine has never displayed comprehension.

From the early days of computers, attempts have been made to replicate human activity, with the first industrial robot used by General Motors in 1961. Robots are utilised in four main ways.

In place of humans

The most common use has been in manufacturing where robots have replaced humans in jobs that are dirty, dangerous and difficult. They work faster, to more reliable degrees of quality and can operate around the clock. The introduction of paint-spraying in car factories by robots reduced the labour force by 85 per cent and improved the quality standards by 90 per cent. They are now seen in all manufacturing environments, as shown in case study 8.3. Another example is unmanned surveillance planes, both in the military and increasingly in civil surveillance, such as that used in unauthorised migration watch on extended borders between the USA and Mexico, and Russia and its neighbours.

CASE STUDY 8.3

INDUSTRIAL ROBOTS ARE RESHAPING MANUFACTURING

It would be tough to find a company seemingly more evocative of twentieth-century, 'old economy' America than Allied-Locke Industries. The family-owned- and-run manufacturing firm is headquartered about 100 miles due west of Chicago in rural Dixon, Illinois. No one walking on to Allied-Locke's low-light, high-decibel factory floor is going to mistake the place for a clean room at a semiconductor manufacturing plant. Allied's operations appear about as unglamorous

and low tech as one might expect at a maker of chains and sprockets – except, that is, for a smattering of robots.

Although the pervasive grease and grime make these computerised machines with their articulated arms look like they originally came with the place, the robots – all adorned with user-friendly female names like Heidi – are relative newcomers at the 300-employee firm. In 2000, the company picked up four used robots (they formerly resided in a now-shuttered Caterpillar plant) for around US $40,000 each to assist in the heated hardening of pins that help form the links in its chains.

Those four robots – along with seven more purchased since then for various tasks such as welding and loading – have allowed Allied-Locke to get more production out of the same number of workers. And that has helped it avoid new hiring. That sort of situation represents the other face of the well-publicised issue of America's declining manufacturing employment. If American workers aren't losing jobs making Nike sneakers to Vietnamese workers, then they are losing out to machines as companies look to increase productivity.

As the saying goes in manufacturing, 'automate or evaporate'. And robots represent the cutting edge of automation technology in the US. While Japan is often thought of as most adept at the use of robots, America is now a top market for them. In 2003, North American manufacturing companies shelled out US $877 million for robots and the amount is rising by over 20 per cent per annum.

Materials handling has remained the largest application for robots, followed by spot welding. The automotive industry is still the biggest robot user, ordering nearly two-thirds of robots sold across the America.

(Source: Pethokoukis 2004.)

Doing jobs that humans find difficult

Robots can be miniaturised to work in very confined spaces where access for humans is difficult or impossible, such as drains. They have been designed to work in areas affected by earthquakes or tornados to help to identify the trapped and injured.

To help humans perform better

In the military, robots have been utilised for walking through minefields, deactivating unexploded bombs or clearing out hostile buildings.

Boston Dynamics has produced a legged robot which can travel at three miles per hour, climb steep terrains and carry up to 120 pounds in rough terrain impenetrable to wheeled or tracked vehicles. Robots designed to help soldiers on the battlefield have to be carried on to the battlefield by those soldiers. For that reason, robot builders try to design 'man-portable' designs. A man-portable robot can be carried by a single soldier, usually in a special backpack.

For civilians, robots are developing much more slowly in the field of household gadgets to cook, vacuum and clean buildings. Mitsubishi, for instance, has designed and marketed a one-metre-tall humanoid Wakamaru robot, costing around £7,000, to act as a mechanical house-sitter and secretary. It can recognise up to 10 faces and understands 10,000 words and can be utilised to watch over homes while owners are away, alerting them to possible burglaries, record notes and appointments, and remind their owners with well-timed announcements. It can even monitor the condition of a sick person.

Training for humans

Case study 8.4 demonstrates the benefits of using robots for simulation purposes.

CASE STUDY 8.4

MEDICAL SCHOOLS' USE OF ROBOT BIRTH SIMULATORS FOR TRAINING

The American Institute of Medicine, an arm of the National Academy of Sciences, estimates that as many as 98,000 US patients die annually from preventable medical errors. By using a robot and analysing in detail what went wrong, these errors can be engineered out. Noelle is a lifelike, pregnant robot used in increasing numbers of medical schools and hospital maternity wards.

The full-sized, blonde, pale mannequin is in demand because medicine is rapidly abandoning centuries-old training methods that use patients as guinea pigs, turning instead to high-tech simulations. It's better to make a mistake on a US $20,000 robot than a live patient. The robot mannequins range in price from Us $3,200 to US $20,000, the most expensive being the closest to approximating a live birth. She can be programmed for a variety of complications, can labour for hours and produce a breach baby or unexpectedly give birth in a matter of minutes.

She ultimately delivers a plastic doll that can change colour, from a healthy pink glow to the deadly blue of oxygen deficiency. The baby mannequin is wired to flash vital signs when hooked up to monitors. The computerised mannequins emit realistic pulse rates and can urinate and breathe.

A training session would involve a set of doctors and nurses tended to Noelle, who would be hooked up to standard delivery monitoring machines. However, in the corner would be an engineer from the manufacturer using his laptop to inflict all sorts of complications through wireless signals to the robot which would override any pre-programmed instructions. The medical team would learn through their role plays how to deal with all types of emergencies and the harm they inflict in making wrong decisions.

(Source: Elias 2006.)

IMPACT ON BUSINESS STRATEGY, GOODS AND SERVICES

The impact of new technology can be seen in two main developments: in business strategies and the method of operation on the one hand, and in new products and services on the other.

EFFECTS ON BUSINESS STRATEGIES AND OPERATIONS

The biggest effect is for organisations to have the ability to be flexible and to be eager to change. New developments put old technologies out of business very quickly. For example, in the 1990s, only luxury cars had air conditioning; in the twenty-first century, few cars, except those at the very cheapest end, will sell without it. Given the extended period of design and development, manufacturers need to build in the ability to alter the standard product quickly and effectively to within a very tight budget. In reality, the product must combine the extreme reliability that new technology has brought with design obsolescence to ensure the customer continues to purchase a company's new products.

Schumpeter (1976) identified the potential risks of not reacting quickly enough to major technological inventions as 'creative destruction' which can completely destroy the organisation. As an example, the arrival of digital technology in the early 2000s completely undermined Kodak's film and photographic paper operations. Although generally recognised as slow to react, it eventually produced its own digital equipment and provided innovations, such as self-service kiosks and an online printing service.

Associated with this trend is the need to mass-customise your products, perhaps something of a contradiction. Mass production is needed to produce the cost saving, but varieties are required to meet all the customers' varied needs. A good example in services is Compass PLC, which delivers thousands of catering contracts across the world, every one different but with some essential common sourcing, marketing and administration systems. The system becomes more complex, but IT systems allow control and monitoring of every detail. The customised feature has altered manufacturing approaches to assembly lines, many of which have been abandoned in favour of cell production systems, where groups of multi-skilled employees work in teams to meet the differing production contracts, taking responsibility for quality, waste reduction and innovation.

The vast improvements in efficiencies in production, brought about through robotics and other IT processes, and the ability to manufacture on a global basis, has led to a growing decline in manufacturing in developed countries as the technology has been transferred to developing countries (simultaneously using the sources of cheap capital and labour). Examples have been given in Chapter 7 of outsourcing manufacturing from Germany to eastern Europe and from UK call centres to India.

Technology has offered two additional marketing opportunities. Better knowledge of an organisation's customers through manipulation of a vast amount of purchasing data allows much closer targeting of its requirements, a process that retailers, such as Homebase and Tesco, have developed through loyalty cards (see case study 8.5). This quantity of information is only available to large organisations, but the second opportunity, the Web, can be used by any sized business. In fact, the Web has allowed many niche organisations to market, sell and distribute their products and services at low costs, many without the overheads of retail premises. Web-based business activity has expanded exponentially since the mid-1990s, especially business-to-business where sourcing can be fixed through Web-based tendering or even a quasi-auctioning system. Web-marketing opportunities allow small firms to access huge markets for specialised products.

TESCO'S CLUBCARD

In 1995, Tesco launched its Clubcard and, by 2009, it had 16 million members (50 per cent of households) providing complex information on each individual's shopping habits. Dunnhumby, its majority-owned marketing subsidiary, processes 100 baskets a second, equal to six million transactions per day. Each product carries 45 pieces of data; it is judged, for example, whether it is cheap or expensive, brand or own-brand, ethnic or traditional, exotic or basic. Non-food purchases have their own sets of classification. By their purchases, consumers are filtered by demographic, socio-economic and lifestyle characteristics. It is possible to generate a map of how the individual thinks, works and shops. They can be classified across 10 categories – wealth, travel, promotions, green, time-poor, credit, living style, creature of habit, charities – and into sophisticated sub-groups, such as whether they are pet owners and whether they cook for themselves often or not at all.

A personality build-up can define a 'Mrs Pumpkin' who makes pennies work when she shops, mostly uses cash, has a steady repertoire of products but experiments with new ones, has increased her spending on eco-friendly items, is involved in charity-giving, is rarely away and likes using the promotions offered.

This information is integrated with information in the public domain from electoral rolls, Land Registry and Office of National Statistics to generate a profile of the area.

This information helps Tesco to decide on major strategic moves, such as the launch of Express convenience stores and the 'Finest' range, and also in micro-strategies such as which products should go on to the shelves at what times and what personal communications and offers should be made to customers. For example, if customers have stopped buying bread for a period, they must be buying it elsewhere so special cut-price bread vouchers are sent to them to entice them back. It is invaluable in launching specialised Clubcard clubs, such as a wine club and a mother and toddler club, which provide more direct marketing opportunities.

This personal information is then sold on to major suppliers who can use it to research and develop their product range according to shoppers' taste and individual promotions. The information itself has been classed in such a way that it circumvents disclosure provisions in the Data Protection Act so it is difficult for individuals to know what Tesco's personal information on them contains.

(Sources: Tomlinson and Evans 2005, Davey 2009.)

ACTIVITY 8.3 COMPETITIVE ADVANTAGE

It is evident that some forms of technological development provide organisations with a competitive advantage. One example is the invention by the St Helens glassmaker Pilkingtons of the float glass process in the 1950s. This brought huge competitive advantages in both the quality of the sheet glass and the productivity levels. Apple's marketing of iTunes, where it is impossible for songs bought to be played on competitors' equipment, allowed Apple to capture 80 per cent of the US and UK market in the first two years and gave it huge bargaining power with the major record companies.

Think of a further three examples of this process and explain why such an advantage was gained in this way.

SPECIFIC PRODUCTS

The implications for the marketplace arising from the recent rapid developments in IT and communications are substantial. Here are just a few examples at the time of writing:

- Increasing offering by subscription of movies, music and television/radio programmes by operators such as Disney, Comcast and Rhapsody will mean that programming-on-demand will take the place of normal TV and radio schedules. It is likely that the BBC will eventually set up a subscription service for its huge archive of programmes. This will allow the viewer to choose exactly which episodes of, say, 'Allo 'Allo or a set of 1970s *Play for Today* they want to watch, when they want to watch them.

- Flat-screen, computerised TVs will consistently drop in price and become essential furniture within the networked home, with users demanding ever more bandwidth to fill the high-definition screens.

- Myriad websites compete with TV, music and video producers and distributors. Individuals can beam up their own productions on to the Web and become their own publishers.

EFFECTS ON LABOUR MARKETS AND HR

Technology both eliminates jobs and creates them. The introduction of railways in the nineteenth century eliminated most jobs in the canal transport industry but created a substantial net increase in jobs in total, both in the rail industry itself, in the suppliers to the industry and in the associated expansion of industry and commerce that fast rail transport provided.

The same is true in today's technological changes. The IT software industry has created a huge number of jobs around the world, while the outcomes of its labour have reduced jobs selectively in manufacturing, distribution and administration. As mentioned earlier, introducing robotics into paint-spraying operations in car production, for example, has reduced the labour requirements in this function by 85 per cent. On the other hand, this technological change, among others, has reduced the price of the finished car to the extent that it is affordable to a greater mass market and the number of employees in car manufacturing around the world continue to show a small overall increase.

It is the nature of the labour force that has changed with technological innovation. A polarisation has occurred, with an increased demand for highly trained professional and technical employees and, at the same time, a reduced demand for low-skilled assembly and production operatives on the other. An even bigger decline has occurred in the demand for semi-skilled employees or those with traditional apprentice-served skills, most of which have been replaced by automation. This is also reflected geographically with most of the employees in Silicon Valley and other high-tech clusters in America and Japan in the high-skills category, while the actual production of semiconductors, printers and other hardware is carried out in east Asian countries and Mexico by largely low-skilled employees.

The perceived need for a reservoir of highly skilled employees has been the driving force for advanced countries, including the UK, to lay greater stress on achieving an increased percentage of the population to be qualified through higher education (the current target is 50 per cent) or through educational programmes of skills 'achievements'.

INCREASE IN TEMPORARY LABOUR

IT can provide information in a more reliable form and at a much more rapid rate. This allows organisations to respond far quicker to variations in consumer demand which, in turn, requires the labour market to become far more flexible.

Employers have responded in their employment models by making much greater use of non-standard employment, such as part-time or temporary employees. Supermarkets, for example, use their sales data to forecast precisely the number of checkouts required every hour of the year, and use part-time employees to resource the varying needs. The need for temporary staff for Christmas and holiday periods can also be precisely pinpointed through the accurate data provided. This allows them to reach their business target of queues no greater than one or two people.

Case 8.6 shows a micro example of this process.

LETTUCE LEAVES AND THE LABOUR MARKET

CASE STUDY 8.6

It has become clear in recent years that consumers are steadily reducing their purchases of whole lettuces and increasingly selecting packages of prepared lettuce leaves in a variety of forms. For supermarkets, this has provided an excellent opportunity, with Tesco selling over £150 million-worth a year, with a very high mark-up (as applies to most ready-prepared foods). But such packs have a very short shelf life, despite the chemical methods employed during their preparation. In addition, the purchase of such packs (often on impulse) varies very much in line with the weather.

Supermarket responses to this scenario are to assemble incredibly accurate information on purchasing trends, adjust for forecast weather conditions and put in their orders with a very short delivery time – usually no more than a day in advance, sometimes shorter. The suppliers, who are dealing with large orders they cannot afford to lose, in turn need to adjust their labour requirements flexibly. Most cannot afford to operate a system of on-call labour so they turn to labour service providers. One pack house, for example, contracted in 2004 for 2.7 million hours of temporary labour for lettuce and other convenience salad packs. The providers, now known as 'gangmasters', have large groups of itinerant labour, mostly from overseas, whom they call on a daily basis to meet heavily fluctuating demand in preparing lettuce packs and other highly seasonal goods.

Estimates of the immigrants (legal and otherwise) engaged in such work vary greatly but it continues to rise by every report. Provista, a major player, recruits regularly from eastern Europe, which goes some way to explain the increase of 70,000 in reported work permits from that area since the accession of a group of such countries in 2004.

(Source: *Economist* 2004.)

The direct implications for HR practitioners of new technologies can be seen in the fields of recruitment and selection, teleworking and call centres, and in the way the HR operation is structured.

RECRUITMENT/SELECTION PROCESSES

Most organisations use the Web to post their current job vacancies and require applicants to complete their application online, saving considerable costs. Technology also enables telephone screening of applicants to take place, as shown in case study 8.7.

 TELEPHONE SCREENING AT STANDARD LIFE

CASE STUDY 8.7

Applicants for vacant positions advertised online called a dedicated telephone number and they then went through an automated telephone screening interview. The company sorted through 561 candidates before taking on 15 recruits and claimed that the screening system saved 143 work days. The phone lines were open 24 hours a day, seven days a week. The system, developed by Gallop, was tested on 100 existing staff and looked for six generic performance attributes: achiever, conscientiousness, responsibility, agreeableness, numeracy and stability.

(Source: *People Management* 1998.)

A further example of automated shortlisting is the use of equipment to electronically read CVs using optical character recognition (OCR) software. The system's AI reads the texts and, by using search criteria such as qualifications, job titles and companies where the applicant has worked, will produce a ranking list of applicants against the mandatory and optional aspects of the person specification.

This system is quicker and more consistent than if it were carried out manually but will only be as efficient as the search engine and will certainly miss many potential candidates. The difficulty the technology faces in trying to understand poor handwriting also creates limitations.

 ACTIVITY 8.4 APPLYING ONLINE

What are the advantages and disadvantages to employers and employees of online recruitment?

TELEWORKING

The development of the World Wide Web and associated technological innovations has facilitated the process of working at a distance to the employee or main contractor. The process allows a variety of models, ranging from the ability to work one or two days at home with a laptop to being a fully fledged teleworker hundreds of miles away, where physical contact with the office site is restricted to an annual conference visit. As phones merge with computers, video calls will become far more common, with far-flung teams working on shared documents in virtual meetings.

Advantages of teleworking:

- *Productivity gains* – Employees working from home are often more productive. They get away from the frequent interruptions and distractions that pepper the working day. It is also in their interests to show they are more productive so the teleworking arrangement can continue.

- Employees can work out a work–life balance much more easily where more time is spent at home. Caring responsibilities can be balanced with work to be completed, as long as the will and self-discipline are present.

- *Time saving* – For mobile teleworkers, the ability to complete tasks at remote locations, rather than returning to a central office, saves considerable time and expense. Time is saved on regular commuting to work.

- *Reduced accommodation costs* – Most organisations sell teleworking to their boards through setting out the huge savings in accommodation costs, especially where these are in central city locations.

Difficulties that could arise:

- Teleworking can be difficult to manage without the daily face-to-face contact. Managers often want quick answers to questions or a special task performed quickly. This is far more difficult with remote workers. Supervisors and managers need specialised training to manage the remote worker. Contact has to be regular but not too intrusive.

- Performance management systems need to be carefully devised and be based much more on outputs and outcomes rather than traditional measures such as attendance. Regular meetings need to be held to discuss the employees' performance.

- Employees may not have the work distractions but they may have the home ones instead – children, other family members, friends, callers, etc can all disrupt a steady workflow. Relationships with family members can suffer if the borders between work and home are not drawn tightly to everybody's satisfaction.

- Health and safety in the home needs to be carefully monitored.

- Dealing with confidential documents in the home setting has to be addressed.

- Some teleworkers feel too remote from the workplace. They miss the comradeship of the office and lose out on the regular gossip and social activities. There is also a general concern that teleworkers lose training and promotion opportunities because of their low visibility.

An example of the benefits of teleworking is shown in case study 8.8.

TELEWORKING AT BAXTER INTERNATIONAL

CASE STUDY 8.8

Baxter International is a leading US manufacturer and supplier of technology relating to the blood and circulatory systems, employing over 40,000 worldwide. In the late 1990s, as part of its close technological relationships with Nortel Networks, it implemented Nortel's HomeOffice 2 system, which connects remote workers to the corporate phone system and intranet as if they were still in the office. This system matched their need for increased flexibility because:

- The global and distributed nature of the business meant staff had to go to the office regularly in the early hours for audio conferences.

- Many of their offices, including the UK base at Compton in Berkshire, were in rural settings, requiring long drives for staff to get to and from work.

- The life-critical nature of the business meant that some staff needed to be available all hours for the hospitals and to be able to direct the action required through the organisation's system. This had previously meant 24-hour rotas in workplace, which was unpopular.

- Similarly, call centre staff at their dialysis-equipment-supplying subsidiary cover the period from 8.00 am to 10.00 pm with every patient having a named agent. Working early and late was, again, not very popular.

Introduced in 1999, the scheme has become so popular that around 20 per cent of non-manufacturing staff now work from home, working out with their manager how often and when they come into the office. Worldwide, over 3,500 employees use the teleworking system.

The set-up cost per employee was around £3,000, including the Nortel system installation, a fax, copier, printer and scanner, a desk and ergonomic chair, fire extinguisher and a smoke detector. There are also ongoing costs as the company paid for ISDN costs and personal calls. Most employees concerned had already been issued with laptops.

The organisation has gradually changed its culture in response to its distributed system of operation. Performance management is now almost totally related to outputs. Managers with homeworkers have needed to be trained in target-setting, measurement and relationships with their staff, for example.

A number of additional benefits have arisen since the scheme began. Retention of existing employees has improved but so has the ability to trawl through a relatively small pool of crucial specialists who no longer will necessarily have to relocate to the company's main centres. This ability to avoid family disruption can be crucial in the decision as to whether to accept a job opportunity, as well as saving a large amount of relocation costs.

In addition, the proportion of staff returning from maternity leave has risen as many have joined the teleworking loop and take part in audio-conferencing to keep themselves up to date.

Overall, the scheme has been considered very successful indeed, not just for the speed of take-up by staff but by the hard-nosed measures of increases in productivity – estimated at around 30 per cent on average. Alongside this has been the substantial saving in office space.

(Source: *Flexible Working* 2000.)

ACTIVITY 8.5 HOME ALONE

Research has shown that teleworkers often suffer from social isolation. Can you suggest ways that these effects can be mitigated?

CALL CENTRES

The invention and development of the automated call distribution (ACD) system, which both removed the need for a switchboard operator and also provided detailed call information, has promoted the introduction of a growing number of call centres. In 2007, it is estimated that over 600,000 employees were UK call-centre employees, a number that is increasing despite the dispersal of many such jobs to the Indian subcontinent where labour rates are cheaper (Peacock 2007).

Operators work with the required database to answer customer queries or process sales and service agreements, and most organisations build in an interactive instruction guide for the employee to follow, which reduces the time and cost for training. The technology also allows management to monitor calls to identify process glitches, training needs and earnings through any incentive scheme. Call centres can take a distributed form, allowing calls to be channelled to teleworkers at distant locations, with the technology allowing access to all necessary data.

The implications for HR practitioners are quite complex; there has been much debate about the high staff sickness and turnover, quality of job design and the ethical nature of the job requirements.

ACTIVITY 8.6 CALLING OFF

Call centres have some of the highest staff turnover rates (average over 40 per cent) and absenteeism rates (over 6 per cent) in any UK employment sector. Can you suggest why this has happened and what should be done about it?

EFFECT ON THE STRUCTURE OF HR OPERATIONS

Sparrow et al (2004) and Reddington et al (2005) have set out some of the opportunities that technology has provided in facilitating new and developing HR systems.

Shared services

The system adopted by many large organisations, such as Standard Chartered Bank (see case study 8.9), Whitbread and HSBC, allows them to extract the routine HR processes from operating units and place them in a central service, not necessarily anywhere near a head office. Activities include payroll, record keeping (attendance, starters and leavers, pensions, etc), the operation of recruitment, job advertising and shortlisting, together with advice on company HR systems and employment law. Technology allows the access to the databank of information held at the centre that can be drawn upon by local managers, and video-conferencing arrangements for wider discussion of action on, say, a difficult disciplinary situation. Many shared services have access to a network of experts for areas such as reward and benefits or selection testing.

The savings that are made by using this system involve the cutting back of duplication of HR support at each operating unit (averaging 20–40 per cent), moving the work to low-cost locations, saving on the purchasing of technology, and services at one point rather than many, and a near certainty that consistent decisions will be made, avoiding litigation in discrimination and other legal areas (Reilly 2000).

E-enablement of HR processes

The ability to get HR information to and from, and support on to, line managers' desks without a formal HR intervention allows far more time for the HR department to focus on more strategic areas. The early stage of developments here (eg access to policy documents and routine statistical processes) has moved on to empowering line managers to take greater control of their HR responsibilities. They can access external information on pay and benefits; authorise pay increases; select the appropriate standardised terms and conditions to be laid out in an offer letter; process key data on an individual's performance management; and manage their staff and training budgets. Norwich Union (Parry et al 2007) had four key drivers when they introduced an HRIS self-service functionality in 2006:

- *Enabling line management* – Encouraging managers to take more responsibility for managing their people through being able to access and maintain records.

- *Improving and simplifying core processes* – Providing real-time updates on core data, removing duplication and increasing online processing, increasing standandisation and economies of scale in administration.

- *Adding value through HR expertise* – Allowing HR to move from transactional activities to performance-enhancing activity, facilitating the introduction of new HR activities online, such as competencies and flexible benefits, thus encouraging individuals to take increased ownership of their own details and career management.

- *E-enablement of HR* – Mirroring business practice.

Outsourcing of HR

Service centres and e-empowerment can be organised in-house or may be outsourced to firms that have the technological expertise to offer such services at low cost. For example, Arinso has contracted with Shell to produce a shared services system utilised by over 100,000 employees across 45 countries (Glover 2004). HR departments may therefore be reduced in capacity, with interesting implications for career planning. The normal stepped climb up the organisation may instead become leaps between service providers and organisations, not unlike the current career path of senior management.

An example of shared services is shown in case study 8.9.

CASE STUDY 8.9

SHARED HR SERVICES AT STANDARD CHARTERED BANK

In the early 1990s, Standard Chartered Bank decentralised its decision-making processes to regional centres around the world. However, this led to a patchwork of different approaches, duplication of effort, myopia, constant reinvention of the wheel and a large increase in costs.

In 2001, the company decided to revert to centralising standard transactional processes and delivering them to its 32,000 employees in 56 countries through web technology from Chennai in India. This was picked because of its technology infrastructure, well-educated workforce and low costs. Here 45 staff would handle routine enquiries, supporting the standardised HR systems and processes available on the Web. Eighty-five local HR jobs were eliminated in the process, with substantial cost savings.

The local HR teams would lose much of their autonomy, with the driving force the concept of 'a single recruitment and reward process so that everybody does it the same way time and time again' (p36). The menu on offer includes development planning, scheduling of training courses, talent management tools and e-learning.

Routine calls would be handled by staff with a call-centre background. If they could not solve the query, it would be referred to a case analyst, who has postgraduate HR qualifications. The remaining HR structure consists of a 12-strong organisational effectiveness team based at head office responsible for formulating HR strategy and working with the business to improve its performance. The next level down consists of centres of excellence: small, geographically dispersed groups of specialists in resourcing, reward and organisational learning.

(Source: Arkin 2002.)

USING SOCIAL NETWORKING SITES IN HR

There are a number of ways that the popularity of social networking sites can be utilised to improve HR:

- In recruitment, organisations have transferred much of their recruitment profile onto an adapted social networking site (such as Facebook), which then enhances the brand to a younger audience.

- For induction and general employee communication, organisations such as Beds and Bars (see case study 8.10) have created a form of internal social networking.

- For knowledge management, organisations, such as InterContinental Hotels Group, have used social networking technology to allow employees throughout the world to connect with each other to share learning and develop skills. This process is estimated to cost only 5 per cent of the cost of a leadership workshop.

CASE STUDY 8.10

BEDS AND BARS EMPLOYEE CONSOLE

Beds and Bars operates a large number of hostels, pubs and bars across Europe and its workforce is primarily young. 'One of the key challenges we face in the youth travel industry is communication with our employees,' says Duane Vanner, UK people manager. 'Using a medium they are familiar with, can understand and respond to is essential when it comes to efficient and cost-effective on-the-job training.'

In early 2008, it was decided to create an interactive HRM tool based on social networking technology. Staff now log into the console as part of their introduction to the company and staff members are given a profile which they can update online. Through the console, employees can instantly communicate with each other across Europe, access custom-made training videos, apply for places on a variety of training courses and access internal job listings. The development challenges faced included the heavy security required for the site and ensuring it was fully functional across all platforms, including mobile phones. Vanner says that the project's goals – to increase employee involvement in company learning activities, provide accurate and accessible up-to-date training and increase product knowledge and awareness – have all been met.

(Source: *People Management* 2009.)

A number of employment issues have arisen, however, regarding social networking. Firstly, the question of whether employees should be disciplined for criticising their organisation on their personal networking site, which, in terms of the personal and temporary nature of such communications, is far from uncommon. On occasions, it can be close to the boundaries of libel or deformation. In October 2008, 13 Virgin Atlantic crew members were dismissed following their participation in a discussion on Facebook during which it was alleged they brought the company into disrepute and insulted passengers. They had apparently criticised their company's health and safety standards and also called their passengers 'chavs'.

Secondly, employees may engage in criticising other members of staff, including both colleagues and their own managers. This, in its extreme forms, can be regarded as bullying, and the question arises as to whether the company should step in to stop extended and painful personal campaigns, under its duty-of-care responsibilities. If the organisation does not take appropriate disciplinary action against the posting of such information, then it could be held vicariously liable for those comments and in breach of its duty of care owed to the employee about whom information was posted.

Thirdly, the issue of whether employers should investigate potential employees' social networking sites to obtain a more detailed personal profile, including such areas as their drinking habits. However, there are potential dangers here for the employer, apart from the obvious risk of information from this source being unreliable. There is also the potential for a discrimination claim. An unsuccessful job applicant could bring such a claim if they feel that they were not successful in their job application because of a discriminatory perception of them by the prospective employer. For example, if a job candidate has a social networking profile that reveals his/her age, religious belief or sexual orientation, and is invited to an interview and discovers that his/her profile was viewed by the prospective employer but he/she was not subsequently appointed (and they believed that they were the best candidate for the job), then there is a chance that they may consider bringing a claim for discrimination.

Fourthly, employees can spend a considerable time in the workplace on their social networking sites, generally referred to as 'cyberslacking'. In one study, employees admitted to at least one hour per week using the Internet and e-mail for non-work-related purposes, of which Facebook and Twitter were two of the most used sites (Foster 2010). Some employers have decided to block such sites, including Portsmouth City Council in 2009, but other organisations have taken the view that this is draconian and that employees should be trusted in this area, as they are generally trusted with private phone calls and occasional personal Web searches during working hours. Other organisations have become specific, including one which specifies allowing 'up to five brief e-mails a day' and another limiting employees to 'no more than 30 minutes a day use during break times'. In Foster's research, the views of employees are similarly broad. In response to the statement 'I should be allowed unlimited access to e-mail and Internet for personal use without restriction at work,' there was an almost symmetrical response from strongly agree through to strongly disagree.

An example of an integrated approach to using technology in developing the HR function is shown in case study 8.11.

 IMPACT ON THE CHANGING ROLE OF HR IN NORTEL

CASE STUDY 8.11

The company

Nortel is a recognised leader in delivering communications capabilities that enhance the human experience, ignite and power global commerce, and secure the protect the world's most critical information. The company's next-generation technologies, for both service providers and enterprises, span access and core networks, support multimedia and business-critical applications and help eliminate today's barriers to efficiency, speed and performance by simplifying networks and connecting people with information.

HR structure

Nortel has over 30,000 employees worldwide servicing customers in over 150 countries and about 6,500 employees in Europe. The HR structure is based on the Ulrich (1998) model, with HR shared-service centres (SSCs) in four global locations, six HR delivery teams, four core HR strategy groups and a number of HR business partners supporting different parts of the business. Due to the volatile nature of the markets for their main products, the businesses have been reorganised on a number of occasions – from centralisation to decentralisation and from a hands-off approach to a more management-controlled style. Underlying Nortel's ability to make these changes has been the significant investment in IT infrastructure and particularly HR information systems.

Changing the system

In 2005, an HR Evolution project was launched which included the deployment of SAP employee and manager self-service modules in 2006. Traditionally, HR had the responsibility for people transactions and processes, but by empowering the managers in HR functions through the self-service tools, HR has been able to focus on delivering added value to the business in other areas such as strategy and process design.

Nortel's HR SSCs became responsible for ensuring that the HR transactional services were delivered consistently across the company and that any change request approved by the line manager was within company policy and guidelines, a job previously carried out by HR managers wearing their 'policeman' hat.

In effect, the new system has empowered the line manager to take decisions as if they themselves owned the business. No longer are they involved in a multilayer, paper-based bureaucratic decision-making process – they are held accountable for the people changes they make that impact on their budget. Much more training has taken place to ensure that line managers are aware of HR policy and practice and the legislative context. It was well understood that, previously, there were too many HR staff touching every part of the transactional work. Under the new system, managers are expected to grasp the people action initiative and take responsibility for developing their own people skills, as well of those of their staff. One of the key skills is in clear objective-setting and communication of expectations, open discussion of issues that affect performance and honest feedback. No longer can they say, 'This is not in my hands, go and see HR.'

When it comes to obtaining advice and information, in the majority of cases line managers can find what they want on the intranet in areas such as recruitment, reward, termination, discipline and benefits.

Where they need more help, managers or employees can call the SSC, and trained team members will guide them on policy interpretation or action required when unusual events have occurred. Where answers are not forthcoming from this source, the question is referred to members of the HR delivery teams where a specialist in, say, compensation, will provide the definitive answer. Their main role, however, is for process design, improvement and delivery, where they work very closely with the SSC. As the processes evolve and new approaches and systems are defined, the delivery team will work out how best to translate the changes into workable end-to-end processes from the line managers, through the systems and on to the SSCs.

The technology is further utilised by constantly reviewing the SSC user metrics to identify the regular problems. The skills required to interpret the metrics and then translate them into process-improvement activities are a new experience to the more 'traditional' HR professional.

The final part of the HR structure is the core HR strategy group, which deals with employee relations, compensation and benefits, talent strategy and diversity. Here the designs for future people strategy are formulated, using data from all other HR groups, together with benchmarking and competitive intelligence exercises.

Technology is at the heart of all these changes. By automating as many processes as possible and devolving others to management through the use of manager self-service, HR has been able to reduce significantly the amount of time spent on routine administration tasks, which thereby facilitates other non-administrative tasks, such as learning, recruitment and strategic analysis. This should allow HR professionals to manage the HR function in a strategic manner and to become the real partners in the business.

(Source: Parry et al 2007.)

KNOWLEDGE MANAGEMENT

So great is the speed of technological innovation and so dominant in the changes that it brings in the form of new products, services or the way we live and work, that commentators have expressed the view that we now live in the 'knowledge economy'. Furthermore, as Prusack (1997, p ix) notes:

> A firm's competitive advantage depends more than anything on its knowledge, or, to be slightly more specific, on what it knows, how it uses what it knows and how fast it can know something new.

Having the knowledge can be regarded as even more important than possessing the other means of production – land, buildings, labour and capital – because all the other sources are readily available in an advanced global society while the right leading-edge knowledge is distinctly hard to obtain. Linked to this thinking is the concept of 'intellectual capital', which can be bought (and, if appropriate, stored securely) either through purchasing patents or intellectual property rights or through employing the highly skilled/intelligent employees or consultants who possess that capital (Stewart 2001).

This capital is not necessarily discoveries and processes that can be patented. Society is developing in such a way that services are becoming the dominant commodity over manufacturing. This means that skilled services in areas such as advertising, design, leisure and even sport can command very high fees – just look at the prices paid for the world's top 100 footballers, film stars or music performers. So wealth created in the economy is increasingly perceived as derived from knowledge and intangible assets (Storey and Quintas 2001).

 ACTIVITY 8.7 KNOWLEDGE VALUE

Do you see knowledge as a source of competitive advantage in the marketplace? If so, how?

Because it is such an important asset, organisations are starting to assess their own collection of knowledge bases and ensure they are available for use. This is not just about sorting patents but analysing the knowledge gained through the experiences of their skilled staff. In HSBC, for example, a senior manager has been appointed to identify banking expertise among staff and ensure this knowledge is not lost when they retire or leave the organisation and to organise ways that critical knowledge can be shared across the organisation. Part of the role is to develop tacit knowledge, such as the intuitive approaches to problem-solving in a particular work context or vague ideas about a new product or service, into explicit knowledge that can be written down and communicated (Stredwick and Ellis 2005).

Consideration must also be given to the development of what Hansen et al (1999) refer to as codification strategies, where knowledge is codified and stored in databases where it can be readily accessed and used by employees, and personalisation strategies, where knowledge is closely tied to the person who developed it and is shared mainly through direct person-to-person contact. How to ensure the balance between these two approaches is crucial to the success of knowledge management. For example, if greater emphasis is given to personalisation, then there needs to be formal encouragement of a highly developed process of social networking to allow informal opportunities to arise for knowledge-sharing outside of standard meetings. Many knowledge-based companies organise social events, and even organise company holiday weekends for this purpose.

In the HR field, how knowledge workers are recruited, trained and motivated has come under much scrutiny in recent years. As a group, research has shown that they can be distinguished by their demand for greater autonomy in their work, by their intrinsic motivation and greater sense of task satisfaction and by their emphasis on career-progressing projects rather than immediate financial gratification (Scarborough and Carter 2007). The implication is that recruitment pays as much attention to skills and potential as to actual knowledge and that the performance management process is crucial to retention success.

TECHNOLOGY — THE DARKER SIDE

Although technological developments generally lead to improvements in standards of living, not all are seen as universally benign. For every five citizens that welcome new products, job opportunities, improved quality and variety of services, better healthcare and ease of transportation, a sixth will see a darker side with bleaker effects. This can be examined firstly by looking at each of the three of the case studies illustrated in this chapter.

GENE THERAPY (SEE CASE STUDY 8.2)

In itself, this is a dispiriting case of unfulfilled expectations but there are further difficulties in this area. One of the success stories has been the development of devices to allow accurate screening for genetic disorders. This can be carried out at any age and even for unborn babies. The main benefit is that such disorders can be treated at an early stage so that the prognosis improves. However, this presents a number of problems. First of all, insurance companies (and employers who provide and pay for life insurance for their employees) are very interested in carrying out such tests before accepting insurance risk. For those citizens with no disorders and long life expectancy, life insurance costs would be cheap but pensions expensive. For those with a disorder, the opposite would apply, with life assurance virtually impossible to obtain. There is considerable debate currently as to whether such tests should be compulsory, the outcome of which would leave vulnerable citizens uninsurable and regarded as second-class. Alternatively, governments can attempt to force insurance companies to ignore the results of such tests and not apply prohibitive insurance costs. A second problem is the dilemma faced by the parents where pre-natal tests show up genetic disorders. It provides the opportunity for the birth to be aborted and some of the lifelong pain averted, but such an irreversible decision is a very hard one to take and most parents (except those who already have one disabled child) choose to avoid taking such tests.

LETTUCE LEAVES (SEE CASE STUDY 8.6)

There are a number of ethical and regulatory issues surrounding this topic. Firstly, it is becoming very difficult to challenge the power of the largest supermarkets in pressing such tight schedules upon suppliers and, subsequently, their employees. In America, Wal-Mart, with over 25 per cent of the huge US market, virtually writes the rules, with suppliers being unable to match their negotiating power. The situation in the UK is somewhat better with a competing group of supermarkets matched against, in certain product areas, a similar group of large producers, but the growing dominance of Tesco is creating some worries for regulators. This issue is discussed further in Chapter 5. The second issue is whether it is ethical for so much migratory labour, living in poor conditions, to provide fresh food for the community in the twenty-first century. It is hoped that they are protected by the National Minimum Wage Act, but many will slip through the net, and the rules concerning deductions for accommodation are very complex, with such situations being rarely investigated. Added to this are some safety issues, which were shown graphically by the death of 20 illegal Chinese immigrants working as cockle-pickers in Morecambe Bay in 2003. Consumers may demand fresh produce at affordable prices but these may come at indefensible cost.

SHARED SERVICES (SEE CASE STUDY 8.11)

There are experiences of 'one product fits all' which may not apply in fast-moving, customer-oriented businesses. The quality of the service provided by unqualified staff can be questionable, with a background in call-centre work rather than HR. Many opportunities for seriously effective HR interventions and innovations can occur through regular discussions about routine issues, often in informal settings, which are far less likely to happen under formalised shared services environments. Moreover, services that are shared across countries run the risk of cultural confusion.

THE DARKER SIDE OF EMPLOYMENT

Alongside the potential problems faced by employees in call centres, teleworking and social networking sites, there has been much research into the inherent problems that new technology brings to the workplace, demonstrating its dialectical nature, where advances in one direction produce problems of their own (Martin 2005). These can take various forms such as:

- Deskilling of manual work, especially in industries such as house-building where prefabrication, using computer-controlled design and machine tools, has replaced many traditional skills. A major consequence in the UK has been the near collapse of trade training by large house-builders which, in turn, has led to severe shortages of servicing and maintenance trades, such as plumbers and electricians where the market is dominated by small organisations. Even software work has been substantially automated and routinised.

- Call centres have been roundly criticised as the new 'industrial sweatshops' with automatons working in psychic prisons on prepared scripts to finely tuned bonus schemes, leading to poor employee morale and depressive illnesses (see case study 8.12).

- Internet misuse can take a number of forms. One that has proved costly is the spreading of false information via the Internet. Employers can be held vicariously liable for their employees' activities when using the Internet and are responsible if staff send e-mail messages that breach confidentiality or are defamatory. In the case of *Western Provident v Norwich Union*, Norwich Union was forced to shell out £450,000 in damages and costs for slander and libel after Western Provident discovered damaging and untrue rumours circulating on Norwich Union's internal e-mail system. They were about Western Provident being in financial difficulties, and being investigated by the Department of Trade and Industry (Hall 2004).

- The intrusion of surveillance technology has presented dilemmas for employers, who have the responsibility and opportunity to monitor employees to ensure no laws are being broken (such as downloading of pornography) but appreciate employees' fears and resentment at such a process taking place. Monitoring attendance (through card-swiping security systems) and performance (such as call-centre systems, detailed earlier) have become cheap and accurate, but present challenges to employment cultures where employees' trust and independence of action are highly valued. Surveillance may focus employees' attention on organisational and strategic targets but also have the tendency to discourage innovation (Taylor 2004).

- A special problem of e-business employment is the lack of contact with the customer and a poor level of social interaction. This has led to higher levels of staff turnover than in conventional businesses (PricewaterhouseCoopers 2000). There has also been some sense of alienation related to virtual meetings, where the growth of video-conferencing can be surprisingly slow, although most evidence would support the view that the correct usage of mobile phones and e-mails has generally enhanced employees' social contact.

- Some commentators picture ICT in a tyrannical frame in the sense that it provides more intensive work through the huge amount of data it provides and the options available, and it also demands longer hours at the work face through its additional ability to provide 24/7 coverage (Green 2002). However, not all research supports this view. In a CIPD-financed project, Nathan et al (2003) provided little evidence that ICT directly impacted on increased working hours. Employees were using more technology and were working longer hours, but the causal relationship was not proven.

- Although many of the accident-riven jobs in traditional industries have been eliminated by automation, new health problems have emerged, both physical (repetitive strain injury, eyesight deterioration) and psychological (stress-related illnesses).

- Many employees have shown considerable reluctance to share knowledge in a formalised system, with doubts expressed over the possible reduction in value of their personal human capital and expertise (Scarborough et al 1999).

 SUICIDES AT FRANCE TELECOM

CASE STUDY 8.12

Over an 18-month period during 2008–09, 24 employees at France Telecom committed suicide following the implementation of a wide-ranging restructuring plan called Time to Move. A sociologist, Monique Crinon, who interviewed a cross-section of staff, identified feelings of being undervalued and low self-esteem running through the company from top to bottom. One senior worker in her 50s was demoted to work in a call centre and reported that she had stepped back in time to an era where mainly young women staff were terrorised and controlled. Employees had to make several sales an hour from dictated scripts, ask permission to leave for toilet breaks and file a written explanation for going

one minute over a lunch break. The teams were repeatedly broken up with staff being moved to other centres at two days' notice, leaving workers feeling isolated and like failures in a bonus-driven system. In a similar case, a 51-year-old employee was moved from a back-office job to a call centre and eventually committed suicide by throwing himself off a motorway bridge in September 2009.

Less than a week later, the company suspended the restructuring and Louis-Pierre Wenes, deputy chief executive and the architect of the restructuring, resigned.

(Sources: Chrisafis 2009, *Investor Today* 2009.)

In labour market terms, a divide has developed between two major segments of employment: the knowledge-intensive organisations and the knowledge-routinised ones, called the 'hourglass' model by Coyle and Quah (2004). Knowledge-intensive jobs use advanced and complex ICT skills and require high human-capital levels. Employees work long and often unsociable hours but their jobs are often (but not always) associated with high pay, extensive training, career development and high personal and job satisfaction. Knowledge-routinised jobs, on the other hand, are low-paid, require much lower levels of human capital and the routine ICT work provides much less personal satisfaction.

TRENDS TO WATCH – WHAT OF THE FUTURE?

'THE HORSE IS HERE TO STAY!'

Forecasting the effects of new technology is very tricky and many serious and well-respected forecasters have got their forecasts very wrong. In an excellent article by Smith (2004), which details truly awful forecasts, he quotes pioneers in the IT industry from whom we would have expected a clearer vision.

For example, IBM forecast in 1952 that their worldwide sales of mainframe computers would be 52 in total for the year. Thirty years later, it had raised the estimate to 200,000, roughly what they now ship a week. Even Bill Gates made gaffes, such as stating in 1981 that '640K should be enough for anybody'. Going further back, the president of Michigan Savings Bank advised people in 1901 against investing in the Ford Motor Company, making the statement at the top of this section.

There was a better performance by Kahn in his 1967 book *The Year 2000* where he predicted computers, mobile phones, video recorders and satellite dishes. But he, like many forecasters since, seriously misjudged the effect of technology on working lives. Almost everybody forecast that we would all be working far fewer hours (30 a week at most, according to Kahn), have much more holiday and retire very early. This was because technology would take away jobs, which it clearly does. What almost all futurologists failed to grasp is that, while some jobs disappear, more arise in their place. Production jobs have disappeared either through automation and robotics or to developing countries with cheaper wages. In their place have risen industries that provide services – either business services, such as IT, financial services and all manner of consultancies, or those that provide personal services, such as leisure, health and beauty and personal finances. At the same time, services that used to operate for the few, such as hotels, eating out, travel and tourism, are now used by everybody in increasing numbers.

What is just as significant is that such new and developing industries are generally very labour-intensive (automated hairdressing is still not with us) so technology has released employees from the grind of heavy production but provided instead the more sociable but equally routine (and absolutely vital) activities involved in such activities as housekeeping in hotels and care working in hospitals and old peoples' homes. This explains why the average working week has decreased only marginally in the last 25 years and why unemployment in flexible societies, such as the UK and America, remains very low.

KEY LEARNING POINTS

- Technological development can occur through incremental innovation, radical innovation, change in technological systems or technological revolution (Freeman 1987).

- Business intelligence is a key concept where the aim is to transform large amounts of data, often scattered across the organisation, into the key information that drives informed decision-taking, and to deliver it in an easily read form through the computer screen to anybody where and when they need to know.

- Technological developments provide the capacity for organisations to be flexible and eager to change, in fields such as product design, advertising and marketing (especially on the Web), customer relations and quality development.

- Technology has had a profound effect upon labour markets through facilitating novel flexible working practices, such as annualised hours, complex shift systems and multi-skilling, together with the development of sophisticated recruitment and selection processes.

- HR systems have been affected by the technological changes that allow systems of shared services, outsourcing and e-enablement of HR processes.

- It has been recognised in recent years that knowledge management is a vital process to ensure that organisations can collect, store and distribute key areas of knowledge that help create competitive advantage.

- Technological progress produces its own ethical dilemmas in areas such as gene therapy, consumer choice and outsourcing.

QUESTIONS

1. In what ways does technology offer improved marketing opportunities?

2. Name five difficulties associated with the employment of teleworkers.

3. Provide four examples of how technology helps HR administration and management become more efficient.

4. What is the difference, according to Freeman, between a radical and an incremental innovation?

5. Give three examples of developments in communication technologies and their effect on markets.

6. Provide four examples of how technology can provide difficulties in the employment setting, as well as benefits.

7. What are the four main cycles of K-waves?

8. Give four examples of the use of technology in the recruitment and selection process.

9. What is the connection between technology and flexibility requirements?

10. What are shared services in the HR setting, how are they facilitated by technology, and what savings are made?

EXPLORE FURTHER

Further Reading

The best source of contemporary technology and its effects is the weekly *Economist*, which has a dedicated section on this subject. A useful learned journal in this area is *Work, Employment and Society*, which often deals with the effects of technology on working practices and HR. Other valuable sources include:

- Halil, W. (2008) *Technology's Promise: expert knowledge on the transformation of business and society*. London: Palgrave-Macmillan.
- Schmidt, S. (2008) *The Coming of Convergence*. New York: Prometheus Books.
- Spielberg, N. and Anderson, B. (1995) *Seven Ideas that Shook the Universe*. New York: Palgrave Wiley.

SEMINAR ACTIVITY

TELEWORKING – IMPLICATIONS FOR HR

Consider the operation of HR systems in case study 8.8 (Teleworking at Baxter International) and identify where difficulties could arise, for both line managers and HR staff.

Identify the likely overall impact of such a structure on:

- employee engagement
- communication systems
- skills of HR staff
- careers for HR staff.

CHAPTER 9

Ethics, Social Responsibility and Sustainability

LEARNING OUTCOMES

By the end of this chapter, you should be able to understand, explain and critically evaluate:

- different approaches to ethics and ethical principles
- the problems involved in resolving ethical dilemmas
- whistleblowing
- the nature of professional ethics
- how far business ethics exist as something separate from general ethics
- values and codes of business ethics
- approaches to corporate governance
- the principles of risk management
- the principles and issues underlying corporate social responsibility
- the principles and issues underlying sustainable development
- the role of HR in corporate social responsibility and sustainability
- the role of the government in corporate social responsibility and sustainability
- corporate social responsibility and profit.

INTRODUCTION

This chapter examines the nature of ethics, and different approaches which can be taken to ethical problems. It discusses professional and business ethics; stakeholder theory; values; and codes of ethics. The second half of the chapter analyses corporate governance; corporate social responsibility (CSR) and sustainability; the role of businesses, HR and the government in promoting CSR; and the extent of compatibility between CSR and profit.

ETHICS

The theory of ethics can be extremely complex, and in order to be of use in a day-to-day work situation, it must be made practical. Here we immediately run up against a problem. To philosophers, ethics is about the theory of right and wrong, not about the practical application of those principles. This is the area of morals. Ethics involves the values that a person seeks to express in a certain situation; morals the way he/she sets out to achieve this (Billington 2003).

A wider definition of ethics is given by Connock and Johns (1995). This includes three elements:

- fairness
- deciding what is right and wrong
- the practices and rules which underpin responsible conduct between individuals and groups.

Billington (2003, pp20–25) lists five distinctive features of ethics:

- Nobody can avoid ethical decisions. We all make ethical decisions every day.
- Other people are always involved in ethical decisions. There is no such thing as private morality.
- Ethical decisions matter – they affect the lives of others.
- Although ethics is about right and wrong, there are no definitive answers. The philosopher can put forward principles which should guide decisions, but the ultimate decision is always down to the individual.
- Ethics is always about choice – a decision where the individual has no choice cannot be unethical.

 ACTIVITY 9.1 ETHICAL CHOICE

Can you think of any situations where an individual has no choice about what action they should take – in a work environment, or any other situation?

ETHICAL PRINCIPLES

Billington (2003), identifies three different approaches to ethics:

- *Absolutism.* Ethics are underpinned by absolute values, which apply in all societies and to all situations – the Ten Commandments, for example. The problem here is that an absolutist might make decisions which could be seen as morally repugnant. For example, a pacifist who believes literally in the absolutist statement 'thou shalt not kill' would logically have found himself refusing to fight the evil of Nazism.
- *Relativism.* Ethics depend on the situation, and on the cultural mores prevalent at a particular time or place. Thus for example, racism in Victorian England,

or child labour in present-day Pakistan must be seen as reflecting the mores of those societies. This is the 'when in Rome' principle. This approach has been criticised on two grounds: that it freezes the status quo and is therefore inherently conservative, and that in practice every major religion (Buddhism, Christianity, Confucianism, Hinduism, Judaism, Islam and Sikhism) subscribes to the absolutist golden rule (see below) (Snell 1999).

- *Utilitarianism.* As Jeremy Bentham put it in the early nineteenth century, 'The good of the greatest number is the criterion of right or wrong' (Billington, 2003, pp35–40, 119). This begs the question what does 'good' mean?

Carroll (1990) widened out these principles into 11 ethical guidelines.

Table 9.1 Carroll's ethical guidelines

Name of principle	Description
Categorical imperative	You should not adopt principles of action unless they can be adopted by everyone else.
Conventionalist ethic	Individuals should act to further their self-interest as long as they do not violate the law.
Golden rule	Do unto others as you would have them do to you.
Hedonistic ethic	If it feels good, do it.
Disclosure rule	You should only take an action or decision if you are comfortable with it after asking yourself whether you would mind if all your associates, friends and family were aware of it.
Intuition ethic	You do what your 'gut feeling' tells you is right.
Means-end rule	You should act if the end justifies the means.
Might-equals-right ethic	You should take whatever advantage you are powerful enough to take.
Organisation ethic	Be loyal to your organisation.
Professional ethic	Do only that which can be justified to your professional peers.
Utilitarian principles	The greatest good of the greatest number.

The three most popular of these principles among managers were the golden rule, the disclosure rule and the intuition ethic.

THE ETHICS OF MPS' EXPENSES

CASE STUDY 9.1

The MPs' expenses scandal made headlines for weeks in the summer of 2009. The *Daily Telegraph* had obtained tip-offs from a whistleblower, which it drip-fed into the public arena. The result was to finish many political careers, and to throw the whole parliamentary system into disrepute.

Examples included Sir Peter Viggers' infamous duck island, Douglas Hogg's moat, Jacqui Smith's husband's 'adult' videos, Gordon Brown's cleaning bill and Cheryl Gillan's dog food.

Six different ethical categories can be identified:

- *The silly but petty*: the dog food and the adult films.

- *The silly but outrageous*: the duck island and the moat.

- *The retrospectively punished*: MPs were allowed to claim cleaning expenses, with their reasonableness assessed by the Parliamentary Fees Office. However, when Sir Thomas Legg, the Commons auditor, reported in October 2009, he retrospectively imposed a limit of £2,000 a year on cleaning, with the result that the prime minister, Gordon Brown, was required to repay over £10,000.

- *Playing the system*: In one case an MP repaid a relatively small mortgage on his London home, and took out an extremely large mortgage on his constituency home. The mortgage interest on this was claimed as an expense.

- *Tax avoidance*: The widespread practice of 'flipping' mortgages. Inland Revenue rules permit the proceeds of selling a designated first house to be free of capital gains tax (CGT), but the sale of a second house is liable to CGT. In one case, an MP designated her constituency home as her main residence for one month, so avoiding CGT.

- *Fraud*: In one case (an MEP rather than

an MP), the person involved claimed a secretarial allowance of £3,000 a month, but paid his assistant only £500. The result in this case was a prison sentence.

I feel that the ethical implications in these cases are different. In the first case, no real ethical principles are involved, although they could fall foul of the disclosure rule. The amount spent on dog food was petty, and Jacqui Smith claiming for the adult films was clearly a mistake. In the second case, the MPs involved should have thought of the disclosure rule. The sums of money involved in each case (over £1,000) were excessive, and the MPs should have considered what public opinion would be if these were made public.

Retrospective punishment raises more ethical issues for Sir Thomas Legg than for the MPs concerned. Retrospective punishment is generally viewed with disfavour by the UK legal system. As commentators pointed out at the time, £2,000 a year does not cover much cleaning in London if you pay the London living wage, National Insurance, holiday pay and so on.

Playing the system is, I feel, unethical, although it is not in any way illegal, and some would see it as acceptable. I think it falls foul of the golden rule, the disclosure rule and the professional ethics rule. Tax avoidance again is not illegal, but would generally be seen as unethical, and again is covered by the golden, disclosure and professional ethics rules. The final case (fraud) is clearly unethical as well as criminal.

Two problems with the expenses system were:

- An unclear distinction between expenses and allowances. In some cases MPs received allowances, for example for communications, which implies a right to claim up to the full amount of the allowance, while other spendings were designated as expenses, where the right is only to be reimbursed for actual spending. This distinction was not always clearly made in the press.

- The system of allowing MPs to take out mortgages on designated second homes, and allowing mortgage interest on these second homes as an expense. This was justified on the grounds that most MPs needed a base in London as well as their constituency home. This not only permitted flipping, but also meant that even where there was no sharp practice, the MP would almost certainly make a capital gain (whether taxed or not) at public expense. It also raised the issues of cleaning and gardening, neither of which would have applied if an MP had been renting a serviced flat.

Eventually in November 2009 Sir Christopher Kelly, the chairman of the Committee on Standards in Public Life, produced a blueprint for a reformed system.

- MPs within commuting distance of London would no longer be able to claim for a second home. If they have to work late in Westminster, they could claim for an overnight hotel stay, capped at £125.

- Other MPs could claim for a second home, but must rent not buy, with rent capped at £1,250 a month.

- No more claims for cleaning, gardening or furnishing.

- Any capital gain on a state-funded mortgage should be 'surrendered to the taxpayer'.

- No communications allowance.

- A ban on MPs employing relatives, to be phased in over five years.

(Sources: Watt et al 2009, Watt and Stratton 2009, Stratton 2009, Summers 2009.)

ETHICAL DILEMMAS

Managers face ethical dilemmas every day of their working lives. Some typical examples are examined in activity 9.2 below. On the basis of interviews with managers in Hong Kong, Snell (1999) identified a number of typical sources of dilemmas.

Table 9.2 Sources of dilemmas

Source of dilemma	Per cent incidence
Subordinates' perceived deceit, incompetence or disobedience	18
Policy, or request by superior, that is mistaken	25
Policy, or request by superior, that is ethically suspicious, exploitative or unfair	13
Improper, suspicious or unfair request from client, supplier or colleague	6
Conflicting instructions, decisions or directives from above	9
Caught in the middle of a direct conflict between other parties	5
Direct dispute with another party	6
Aware of another's misconduct, neglect or unfairness, but not directly responsible	8
Other	10

Snell's interviews also suggested four possible responses arising from requests by a superior to do something they knew to be wrong:

- 'little potato' obedience (quiet, fearful, humble, deferential conformity)
- token obedience (following orders half-heartedly and semi-incompetently)
- undercover disobedience (only pretending to obey, and keeping disobedience hidden)
- open disobedience (conscientious objection).

Carroll's ethical guidelines can be used as a template for resolving ethical dilemmas:

Stage 1 – Rank each of Carroll's guidelines from 11 (most important to you) to one (least important to you).
Stage 2 – Consider your ethical dilemma against each of the guidelines. If you can justify the action under a criterion, put + in the next column, if you cannot justify action, put –.
Stage 3 – Score each criterion by taking its ranking and putting + or – in front of it.
Stage 4 – Add up the scores. If the figure is positive, for you the action is ethically justified; if negative, it is unjustified.
Stage 5 – If the overall score comes to zero, change the rank for your most important criterion to 12, and redo the sums.

Remember that this method can only tell you whether or not a particular action is ethically justifiable, not exactly what you should do about it.

An example of the scoring is given below.

Table 9.3 Ethical scoring

	Rank	+/–	Score
You should not adopt principles of action unless they can be adopted by everyone else.	9	–	–9
Individuals should act to further their self-interest as long as they do not violate the law.	5	+	+5
Do unto others as you would have them do to you.	11	–	–11
If it feels good, do it.	2	–	–2
You should only take an action or decision if you are comfortable with it after asking yourself whether you would mind if all your associates, friends and family were aware of it.	10	–	–0
You do what your 'gut feeling' tells you is right.	6	–	–6
You should act if the end justifies the means.	1	+	+1
You should take whatever advantage you are powerful enough to take.	3	+	+3
Be loyal to your organisation.	4	+	+4
Do only that which can be justified to your professional peers.	8	–	–8
The greatest good of the greatest number.	7	+	+7
Overall score			**–26**

In this case, the conclusion is quite clear: according to your values, you find this course of action ethically unacceptable, and should not do it.

 ACTIVITY 9.2 ETHICAL DILEMMAS

Question 1

You are an HR manager for a medium-sized company, and you are faced with what you see as a series of ethical dilemmas. Consider how you would approach each scenario, and what ethical principles you would apply:

Scenario 1 – It is the custom in your industry for customers to be lavishly entertained. Your company gives each customer's sales manager a bottle of very good quality malt whisky on his/her birthday, his/her partner's birthday, and at Christmas. Your purchasing manager expects similar perks from his suppliers.

Scenario 2 – Your organisation is undertaking a number of redundancies. You decide who is to be made redundant. The production manager asks you to add a particular worker to the list. This worker does not meet any of your criteria for redundancy, but he is well known for not getting on with the production manager. You point out that if you sack this worker without justification, he will take you to an employment tribunal and will win a claim of unfair dismissal. The production manager's response is, 'Fine, it'll be worth it to get rid of him'.

Scenario 3 – You are responsible for training, and you have used an old friend of yours to run a recent training programme. Your friend met all your criteria, and had adequate if not glowing references. However, the feedback from the programme is strongly negative. You are about to repeat the programme, and your friend has asked you if he/she will be given a repeat contract.

Question 2

How far do you think Snell's identified responses to ethical dilemmas are likely to be universally valid, and how far do you think they reflect the culture of work in Hong Kong?

Question 3

You are export sales manager for a large company. You have been approached by an intermediary, who has asked for a large commission to obtain his influence to secure a large overseas deal. Such bribes are a long-established part of doing business with that country. Using the Carroll template, decide whether you should pay the commission.

WHISTLEBLOWING

Whistleblowing describes a situation where an individual is so concerned about the behaviour of an organisation or of individuals within it that he/she feels constrained to raise this with a third party, who may be inside the organisation, but is normally outside.

De George (1999) argued that six conditions must apply before whistleblowing can be morally justified:

1. a product or policy of the organisation needs to have the potential to do harm to members of society

2. the employee should report all the facts to their immediate supervisor

3. if the immediate supervisor does not act effectively, the concerned employee should take the matter higher in the company, exhausting all internal channels

4. the employee should hold documentary evidence to support their charges

5. the employee must believe that whistleblowing will lead to a change in the product or policy (ie don't sacrifice yourself pointlessly)

6. the employee must be acting in good faith without malice or vindictiveness.

THE PUBLIC INTEREST DISCLOSURE ACT 1998

The Public Interest Disclosure Act (PIDA) gives some protection to whistleblowers, although it does not give a right to whistleblow, as strict criteria are laid down which must be met. The act also places the burden of proof on the complainant.

The disclosure must relate to a specified set of malpractices:

- a criminal offence
- failure to comply with a legal obligation
- a miscarriage of justice
- danger to health and safety
- damage to the environment
- deliberate concealment of any of the above.

Internal procedures can only be sidestepped (De George's steps 2 and 3) if the employee:

- reasonably believes they would be penalised by the employer for making the disclosure
- is concerned that evidence would be concealed or destroyed
- has previously disclosed essentially the same information to the employer.

If the whistleblowing case falls within the definitions of the PIDA, the employee will be entitled to compensation if he/she has been victimised or dismissed as a result of the whistleblowing act (Fisher and Lovell 2006).

PROFESSIONAL ETHICS

The following words are often used to describe what it means to be a professional:

- qualified
- objective
- impartial
- honest

- competent
- accountable.

These words all imply ethical principles, and one main role of a profession is to set and maintain ethical standards for its members. Rosemary Harrison (2002) stresses two aspects:

- qualified advice
- standing by the integrity of that advice.

This implies two ethical responsibilities:

- to the organisation for which one works (organisational ethics)
- to impartial integrity (an absolutist ethic, which lies at the heart of professional ethics).

Most professions lay down ethical standards for their members to follow through a code of ethics, and the CIPD is no exception. Its 'Code of Professional Conduct and Disciplinary Procedures' (2003a) can be downloaded from www.cipd.co.uk.

Lawton (1998) suggests 10 functions for a code of professional ethics:

- to promote ethical, and deter unethical, behaviour
- to provide a set of standards against which to judge behaviour
- to act as guidance to decision-making
- to establish rights and responsibilities
- a statement indicating what the profession stands for
- to create a contract between professionals and clients
- to act as a statement of professional development
- to legitimise professional norms and justification for sanctions
- to enhance the status of the profession
- a statement of professional conduct.

 THE DISCIPLINARY POWERS OF THE CIPD

CASE STUDY 9.2

In an article in *Personnel Today* in October 2001, Paul Kearns argued that the CIPD should be prepared to 'strike off' negligent, incompetent or dishonest members, in the same way that the General Medical Council strikes off doctors, or the Law Society solicitors. He argued that this was essential for the CIPD to have credibility as a professional body, particularly given its new chartered status. The implication was that such a striking off should be public,

and that a person who had been struck off should be prevented from practising the profession.

In response, the secretary of the CIPD, Kristina Ingate, made three points. First, a comparison with professions such as medicine or the law is not appropriate. Personnel is not a statutory closed shop, unlike medicine or law, and CIPD membership is not a requirement to work in the personnel field. Secondly, the CIPD has a disciplinary procedure, and as a last resort, members in breach of its Code of Professional Conduct can be expelled from the Institute, although admittedly this is likely to be for misconduct rather than for incompetence. However, she urged caution. By its very nature personnel is about human relationships, frequently in stressful situations. As a result, a complaint about a personnel practitioner will frequently either be totally unwarranted, or in reality a complaint against the policies or practices of the employer, rather than the individual practitioner. Thirdly, CIPD members have high standards of both conduct and competence, and members are expected to keep their competence up to date through continuing professional development.

BUSINESS ETHICS

We have now moved some distance from our original concern with individual ethics. As we have seen, professions can impose ethics on their members. We now go one step further, and consider whether there is, or should be, a distinct field of study called business ethics – in other words, does a business, organisation or public body have any ethical responsibilities over and above the ethical responsibilities of the individuals who work for it?

Peter Drucker (1990) argues that ethics is by its very nature a code of individual behaviour. As a result, a business has no ethical responsibilities separate from those of every individual. An act which is not immoral or illegal if done by an individual cannot be immoral or illegal if done by a business. For example, if an individual pays money to an extortioner under threat of physical or material harm, that individual has in no way acted immorally or illegally. However, he quotes the case of the Lockheed aircraft company, which gave in to a Japanese airline which extorted money as a prerequisite for purchasing its L-1011 airliner, and was heavily criticised for doing so. He says (p236), 'There was very little difference between Lockheed's paying the Japanese and the pedestrian in Central Park handing over his wallet to a mugger.'

It seems to me that Drucker's example is a poor one. The mugger can do the pedestrian a great deal of physical harm if he does not hand over his wallet. On the other hand, the airline could not positively harm Lockheed by not buying its plane. I would regard the Lockheed case not as extortion by the airline, but as bribery by Lockheed, and a clear case of breach of business ethics.

In contrast, Michael Hoffman (1990) argues that companies can be held morally responsible. Companies can be morally good or bad according to the consequences of their actions. They espouse values, and individuals coming into the corporation are subject to those values. These values are maintained and reinforced by the culture of the organisation. As a result, it is quite legitimate to talk of business ethics as separate from individual ethics.

ACTIVITY 9.3 COCO DE MER

Coco de Mer is a sex shop or 'erotic emporium' in London's Covent Garden owned by Sam Roddick, daughter of Anita Roddick (founder of the Body Shop). Roddick insists that everything she sells is ethically sourced, including fair trade 'spanking paddles' and leather handcuffs, and a World Wildlife Fund endorsement for non-toxic sex toys. The business also supports sex-related human rights projects, including the Pleasure

Project, which educates women in developing countries on how to use contraception while at the same time enjoying sex, and the Belles of Shoreditch, which acts to protect the interests of strippers in East End pubs.

Is Coco de Mer an ethical business? How would your answer differ if we were talking about a manufacturer of cluster bombs rather than a sex shop?

ACTIVITY 9.4 THE CHILD LABOUR DILEMMA

You are HR manager for a UK clothing retailer. In addition to your personnel duties, you are also the company's ethics officer, responsible for implementing the code of ethics. One of your successful clothing lines is T-shirts, which are assembled in Pakistan and imported into the UK.

Checking your e-mails today, you find a report from one of your buyers of his recent visit to Pakistan. He reports that in a plant in Lahore he has seen girls who look no older than 10 sweeping the floor between the rows of sewing machines the other women work on. Your code of ethics does not specifically mention child labour, but it does contain a clause about treating all workers, both directly employed and employed by suppliers, with dignity and respect.

Your first action is to e-mail your agent in Lahore and to ask him to investigate. He reports back that working conditions aren't bad. The girls concerned are aged from 11 upwards, and are the daughters of female production workers. He also says that child labour below the age of 14 is illegal in Pakistan, but there is widespread evasion of the law, which is not generally enforced.

Your first reaction is to tell your purchasing department to insist that the supplier stops employing the children, or your contract with them will be cancelled. However, a friend then brings to your attention the view of the International Confederation of Free Trade Unions (ICFTU), which has called for clauses

on labour standards to be incorporated into World Trade Organisation (WTO) agreements, despite claims by developing countries that they could be used to prevent Third World goods competing against western products.

The ICFTU is concerned by employers that pay low wages, use child labour, ignore health and safety standards and deny staff union representation. Some argue that free trade is exacerbating exploitation by allowing companies to relocate to wherever production costs are lowest, regardless of local employment standards. But non-governmental organisations (NGOs) and developing countries argue that if Third World countries are to compete in the global economy, they cannot afford to pay the same levels as western employers, because their productivity levels are much lower. Developing countries should not be denied the competitive advantage they gain from cheaper wages.

You are now thoroughly confused. Do you have the right to impose western moral principles on the factory in Lahore, if there is a risk that as a result the girls and their mothers will lose their jobs?

You decide that the best way forward is use Archie Carroll's ethical principles.

Using in turn the golden rule, the disclosure rule, the intuition ethic and the utilitarian principle, think about what your response to this problem would be.

VALUES

Values underpin ethics, and the values of an organisation underpin its business ethics. Organisational values answer the question 'What do we stand for?' ie, 'What are the key principles that matter to us?' This is the second of three questions which organisations must ask themselves as they evolve their mission statement (BITC 2000):

- What are we here to do? (purpose)

- What do we stand for? (values)

- What would we like to see ourselves become? (vision)

Values, as long as they are shared, help to bring together the people in an organisation, and get them working for a common aim (purpose and vision). Successful companies place a high emphasis on values, and share three characteristics (Deal and Kennedy 1990, p108):

- they stand for something

- management fine-tunes their values to conform to the environment of the organisation

- the values are known and shared by everyone in the organisation, and are also known, understood and supported by key stakeholders.

A value-driven company is likely to be more consistent in its decision-making, to be single-minded, and not deflected from its long-term vision by short-term expediency. Its staff is also likely to be more committed and motivated, as long as it has ownership of the values. However, values can be counterproductive if top management behaviour is not consistent with their stated values. For example, one of the long-standing values of Marks & Spencer was support of suppliers, and the company lost a great deal of public sympathy when it axed long-standing suppliers in the UK in order to buy more cheaply abroad.

CODES OF ETHICS

One definition of a code of ethics is 'a written, distinct, formal document, which consists of moral standards which help guide employee or corporate behaviour' (Schwartz 2001, p27).

Codes can be of three different types (Brinkmann and Ims 2003):

- Educational – aimed at increasing moral awareness and behaviour within the organisation.

- Regulatory – detailed rules for behaviour, which recognise moral conflicts and help with resolving them.

- Aspirational – laying down general values, and communicating ideals to individuals within the organisation.

Poor codes of ethics tend to be inward-looking, and to ignore external stakeholders, and they tend to be regulatory and over-detailed. Many companies do not make their codes of ethics available to external stakeholders, and some do not even make them easily available to their own staff (which would seem to make them totally counterproductive).

Good codes of ethics recognise the importance of relationships with all major stakeholders, both internal and external, and involve stakeholders in their preparation. They are also clearly communicated to all stakeholders, and training is provided to stakeholders in order to ensure that they are understood and effective.

Even a good code of ethics is no guarantee of ethical behaviour. The existence of codes of ethics did not prevent the scandalous collapse of Enron and WorldCom in the US, or the deliberate over-statement of oil reserves by Shell. Just as with values, top management must live the code of ethics at all times. If they do not, all respect for the organisation is likely to collapse.

Finally, an American survey in 1987 measured opinions on codes of ethics among American business people. Respondents were asked to comment on a number of statements, with responses coded from 1 (strongly agree) to 4 (strongly disagree).

Table 9.4 Opinions on codes of ethics

	Mean response
Professionals consider codes as a useful aid when they want to refuse an unethical request impersonally.	1.8
Codes raise the ethical level of the industry.	2.1
A code helps managers in defining clearly the limits of acceptable conduct.	1.9
In cases of severe competition, a code reduces the use of sharp practices.	2.7
People violate codes whenever they think they can avoid detection.	2.5
Codes are easy to enforce.	3.3
Codes protect inefficient firms and retard the dynamic growth of the industry.	3.3

 ACTIVITY 9.5 MULTIGENOME AND ITS CODE OF ETHICS

Multigenome (a fictitious company) is a US-based multinational research company. Its code of ethics is reproduced below.

Critically evaluate this code of ethics.

Because we are separated – by many miles, by diversity of cultures and languages – we need a clear understanding of the basic

principles by which we will operate our company. These are:

- That the company is made up of individuals – each of whom has different capabilities and potentials – all of which are necessary to the success of the company.

- That we acknowledge that individuality by treating each other with dignity and respect.

- That we will recognise and reward the contributions and accomplishments of each individual.

- That we will continually plan for the future so that we can control our destiny instead of letting events overtake us.

- That we maintain our policy of providing work for all individuals, no matter what the prevailing business conditions may be.

- That we make all decisions in the light of what is right for the good of the whole company, rather than what is expedient.

- That our customers are the only reason for the existence of the company.

- That we must use the highest ethics to guide our business dealings to ensure that we are always proud to be a part of Multigenome.

- That we will discharge the responsibilities of corporate and individual citizenship to earn and maintain the respect of the community.

- As individuals and as a corporate body we must endeavour to uphold these standards so that we may be respected as persons and as an organisation.

CORPORATE GOVERNANCE

Corporate governance is concerned with:

- in whose interests should an organisation be run
- how should these purposes be determined.

CASE STUDY 9.3

CORPORATE GOVERNANCE IN THE VENETIAN REPUBLIC

The Venetian Republic dominated the Mediterranean for 1,000 years, from its founding in the ninth century as a group of poor fishing villages, to its abolition by Napoleon in the early 1800s. Much of its success was due to its elaborate system of corporate governance.

The head of the Venetian Republic was the doge, who was elected for life. However, his power was strictly limited. Each doge on election signed a contract (*promissione*), which set out and limited his powers, and against which his performance was monitored each year. Over the centuries, these *promissioni* were progressively tightened. Weak or ineffective doges were retired, and really bad ones ran the risk of assassination. Even after his death,

the doge was still subject to independent review. If he was found to have been a bad or ineffective ruler, his family could be fined.

Each doge was assisted by four ducal counsellors, who were independently appointed by the state, not by the doge himself. Their term of office was short (two or three years), which meant that they could not become too powerful. There were also a whole series of other state committees, which ensured that leadership experience was widely diffused, providing a wide pool of potential doges or ducal counsellors.

(Source: McKee 2003.)

The two key issues in corporate governance are conflict of interest and accountability. Conflict of interest comes back to the agency issue discussed above. Managers are the agents of shareholders, but because of their control over key resources, particularly information, their power is greater than that of shareholders. How should this power be managed, and how should managers be held accountable to shareholders (and other stakeholders)?

Company law in the UK and US (the Anglo-Saxon model) supports the shareholder approach – companies must be run in the interests of their shareholders – although UK corporations do have legal responsibilities to other stakeholders. Other countries take a different approach to corporate governance. In Germany, companies have two-tier boards, a supervisory board and a management board (the Rhine model). The management board runs the company on a day-to-day basis, but is answerable to the supervisory board, which has shareholder, employee and third-party representatives on it, and which represents the interests of stakeholders (Farnham 1999).

Big business in Japan is organised through large integrated corporations called *keiretsu* (Mitsui, Mitsubishi, etc). These are both vertical, where manufacturers, suppliers and sub-contractors are members of the same *keiretsu*, and horizontal, where the *keiretsu* companies operate in different markets. Mitsubishi, for example, is involved in gas, chemicals, plastics, steel, aluminium, cement, butter, brewing and paper (Charkham 1994).

Customers and suppliers are thus frequently within the same *keiretsu*, and relationships with them are therefore much closer than in the West. (As a corollary, customers and suppliers outside the *keiretsu* might find themselves much more harshly treated, leaving the system open to charges of cronyism.) Japanese society is also heavily based on the concepts of family, consensus and *wa* (harmony). This leads naturally to a heavy reliance on the stakeholder approach. The hierarchy of interests tends to be customers first, employees second, managers third, and shareholders last. The assumption was that managers and employees 'eat their rice out of the same pot', ie that differentials should be narrow. The controversy over excessive 'fat cat' rewards to top management which is so prevalent in the UK would have been impossible in Japan. However, because the stakeholder approach is supported by culture rather than law, it is vulnerable to changes in that culture, and has been shaken by the long recession in Japan over the last two decades.

In 1990, foreign institutional investors held 5 per cent of shares in Japanese companies. By 2006, this had increased to 26 per cent. These foreign investors want results now, not at some vague time in the future. Dore (2006) examined Japan's two most recent recoveries from recession, in 1986–1990, and 2001–2005. In the earlier period, wages rose by 19 per cent, salaries and bonuses of directors by 22 per cent, and dividends by only 2 per cent. In the later period, the balance was totally different. Wages were down by 6 per cent, directors' rewards up by 97 per cent, and dividends by 175 per cent.

Each system has its strengths and weaknesses, as summarised below.

Table 9.5 Corporate governance systems

	Strengths	Weaknesses
Anglo-Saxon model	Dynamic and innovative Fluid capital investment	Volatile and unstable Short-termism Weak governance
Rhine model	Long-term strategy Stable capital investment	Lack of flexibility Conservatism
Japanese model	Very long-term strategy Stable capital investment	Financial speculation Crony governance Weak accountability

The conflict of interest and accountability questions are also tackled in different ways. In the US, the approach is one of compliance, where corporate governance regulations are laid down by law, and must be followed. Typical is the Sarbanes-Oxley Act of 2002, which followed the scandals in Enron and WorldCom. This states that all companies listed in the US must introduce codes of conduct, ethics policies and whistleblower hotlines. This also applies to foreign companies seeking a listing on the New York Stock Exchange. However, the key weakness of the compliance approach is that it does not internalise corporate governance in the culture of the corporation. As with other law, determined managers will find ways to obeying its letter, but thwarting its spirit. Enron had a code of ethics, and on paper abided by all legal requirements (Crane and Matten 2007).

The UK approach is to use voluntary codes of practice, but to force firms to issue explanations if they choose not to abide by them. The key to the UK approach is separation of powers. In 1992 the Cadbury Report called for separation of the roles of chairman and CEO in listed companies. The CEO represented the executive managers, while the chairman acted in the interests of shareholders. The supermarket chain Morrisons had a combined chairman and CEO (Sir Ken Morrison, the founder) until it took over Safeway in 2003, but its explanation, that in effect it was a family business, was accepted by the Stock Exchange. Cadbury also called for the increased use of non-executive directors (NEDs) on boards, who again would represent the interests of shareholders. This was strengthened by the Higgs Report in 2003, which called for NEDs to be a majority on boards, and for them to be independently appointed, to avoid charges of cronyism if they were selected through the 'old boy network' from among friends of the chairman or CEO (Fisher and Lovell 2006). Again, the example of Enron illustrates the risk of cronyism. The vast majority of its directors were non-executive.

BSKYB

CASE STUDY 9.4

Three principles run through the UK's approach to corporate governance:

- the separation of the roles of chairman and chief executive (Cadbury Report)
- the independent role of the NED (Higgs Report)
- the active involvement of shareholders (shareholder activism).

All three came into play in the case of the BSkyB accession in 2003.

BSkyB was formed by a merger between Sky, owned by Rupert Murdoch's News Corporation, and British Satellite Broadcasting in 1990. It was listed in 1994, and is among the top 20 companies in the UK by market capitalisation. News Corporation owns 35 per cent of the shares, and Rupert Murdoch is chairman. No other shareholder owns more than 3 per cent.

In September 2003 the CEO, Tony Ball, left the company, and a committee headed by Lord St John, the senior independent non-executive director, was set up to find a successor. However, it produced only one candidate, James Murdoch, the 30-year-old son of Rupert. Considerable concern was expressed about this being a 'put-up job' and also because it seemed to flout the spirit, if not the letter, of the principle of separation of chairman and CEO.

Matters came to a head at the company's AGM, held in November 2003. Eighty per cent of non-Murdoch shareholders who voted opposed or abstained on the resolution to re-elect Lord St John as an independent director, and 72 per cent voted against or abstained on the remuneration report. However, with the News Corporation block vote on his side, Lord St John won the vote with 59 per cent in favour, although he stepped down as senior independent director to an ordinary non-executive position. The remuneration report received 61 per cent approval, and James Murdoch's appointment as CEO 77 per cent.

Rupert Murdoch was unrepentant. He told dissident shareholders who did not approve of the company's corporate governance to sell their shares and go away.

(Sources: Tassell 2003, Snoddy and Hopkins 2003.)

CORPORATE SOCIAL RESPONSIBILITY

Corporate social responsibility (CSR) is the way in which an organisation expresses its values in behaviour towards stakeholders. The European Commission (2001, p28) defines it as 'a concept whereby companies decide voluntarily to contribute to a better society and a cleaner environment', while the DTI (2002) defines it as an organisation which recognises that its activities have a wider impact on society; takes account of the economic, social, environmental and human rights impacts of its activities, and works in partnership with other groups and organisations.

Carroll (1991) puts forward a four-part model of CSR:

Economic responsibilities:	required by society
Legal responsibilities:	required by society
Ethical responsibilities:	expected by society
Philanthropic responsibilities:	desired by society

Several key points come out of these definitions:

- CSR is voluntary. Mere compliance with legal requirements is not CSR. An organisation's CSR behaviour must go beyond the law.

- CSR is active. It involves behaviour, not just good intentions.

- CSR involves environmental as well as social responsibilities.

- CSR is often carried out in partnership with others.

- Although the EC only mentions companies, CSR extends to all organisations, public and private, profit-making and not-for-profit.

CSR can take a number of forms. These include:

- Community involvement, frequently in partnership with other organisations. This can include sponsorship of worthy bodies, or direct involvement of the organisation's employees in community activities.

- Socially responsible investment, which can include ethical banking, and refusal by pension funds to invest in companies making, for example, armaments or cigarettes.

- Corporate governance, concerned with the behaviour of a company towards its shareholders, and including elements like the appointment and responsibilities of NEDs.

- Fair trade – buying goods produced by suppliers who are, for example, organic, or non-employers of children, or not based in human rights abusing-countries like Burma.

- Sustainability – acting in such as way as to assist the long-term survival of the planet.

Several of these are illustrated in case studies below, derived from winners of Business in the Community Awards for Excellence 2004.

 THE CO-OPERATIVE BANK

CASE STUDY 9.5

The Co-operative Bank launched its ethical policy in 1992, after consultation with customers. It launched its Partnership Approach in 1997, identifying seven groups of stakeholders, or partners, and pledging to deliver value to them in a socially responsible and ecologically sustainable manner. It published its first triple-bottom-line (profit, society, environment) independently verified Partnership Report in 1998. The 2002 Partnership Report sets out 77 targets, in each case giving the name of the individual in the organisation who is charged with its achievement.

It is the UK's biggest provider of financial services to the Credit Union Movement, which tackles financial exclusion. Its community investment, at 2.7 per cent of pre-tax profits, is among the best in the UK. Its campaigns mobilise its customers to protest on international human rights issues, for example, against the illicit trade in conflict diamonds – a source of finance which has fuelled civil wars and human rights abuses in Africa – and against the use of cluster bombs.

MARKS & SPENCER

CASE STUDY 9.6

Marks & Spencer has pulled together its wide range of community involvement programmes into a more focused approach called Marks & Start. This runs the biggest work experience programme in the UK, designed to help people who face the biggest barriers to obtain sustained employment.

It also takes responsibility for the total footprint of its business through the manufacture, use and disposal of its products. It is rated number one by

Greenpeace on avoiding GM food, and by Friends of the Earth on pesticide reduction. It is supporting an innovative approach to fisheries management called Invest in Fish, which brings together stakeholders (fishermen, fishing communities, NGOs and the fish trade) to develop a fishing industry which is successful economically, and socially and environmentally responsible. In 2007, it introduced its Plan A, designed to make the company carbon-neutral.

CSR has been criticised as often being little more than a PR stunt, designed to boost sales rather than to benefit society. This is particularly true of community involvement activities. This has been called 'cause-related marketing'. For example, Vodafone sponsors the England cricket team, but in return gets endless exposure of its logo on players' shirts during Test matches. Tesco runs its Computers for Schools project, which supplies computers to schools, but only after customers have collected vouchers to verify their spend in Tesco stores (for a spirited condemnation of cause-related marketing, see Monbiot 2001).

In March 1999, Industrial Relations Services carried out a survey of ethics in the workplace (*Employment Trends* 1999). The survey asked why organisations were involved in community activities. Respondents could choose any number of responses. The results were:

		Per cent
1	Enhancement of corporate image	82
2	Moral obligation	62
3	Employee satisfaction	59
4	Develop staff potential	51
5	Promote the business	46
6	Improve profitability	15

Short-term profits (6) were mentioned by only a small minority of respondents, while long-term profitability (1 and 5), employees (3 and 4) and moral obligation (2) were seen as much more important. Perhaps community involvement is a rare example of a true win–win situation (see also Kelly 1999).

ACTIVITY 9.6 IS YOUR OWN ORGANISATION INVOLVED IN THE COMMUNITY?

Find out what community activities (if any) your own organisation is involved in. If possible, also try to find out why the organisation chose these particular activities.

Was the primary motive short-term profit, long-term profit, employee benefit or moral obligation (or a mixture of several of these)?

  FAIRTRADE

CASE STUDY 9.7

Fairtrade is one of the retail successes of the 2000s. Sales of Fairtrade coffee grew from £15.5 million in 2000 to £65.8 million in 2006, when it commanded 18 per cent of the UK roast and ground coffee market. Similar rates of growth have been seen for tea, chocolate and cocoa, and bananas.

Fairtrade is a product-labelling scheme, which acts as an independent guarantee that disadvantaged producers in the Third World are getting a better deal. Its standards are set by an international certification body, Fair Trading Labelling Organizations International, and administered at a country level by national Fairtrade organisations. In the UK the administering body is the Fairtrade Foundation, a charity set up by Cafod, Oxfam, Christian Aid, Traidcraft Exchange and the World Development Movement.

The majority of coffee and cocoa is grown by small farmers, organised into co-operatives, while bananas and tea are usually produced on plantations. In the former case, it is the co-operative which is given Fairtrade certification; in the latter, it is the plantation, which guarantees minimum health and safety and environmental standards, and that no child or forced labour will be used.

In return, producers are guaranteed a price which is sufficient to cover sustainable production, plus a premium which is invested in community development.

For example, the minimum price paid for Fairtrade cocoa is US $1,600 a ton, plus US $150 per ton premium, as long as the world (New York) price is below US $1,600. If the New York price rises above US $1,600 a ton, the Fairtrade price will be the New York price plus US $150 premium. This means that producers are guaranteed a stable price, and they are insulated from market fluctuations, which in the case of primary products can be severe.

An example quoted on the Fairtrade website is the Juliana-Jaramillo group of banana farmers in the Dominican Republic. Until 1962, the Granada Food Company ran vast plantation estates in the area, providing housing, water supply and schools. In 1962, they pulled out of and the infrastructure collapsed. Granada even took the zinc roofs off the estate houses. The government divided 15 per cent of the estates among local farmers, giving each worker about 15 hectares each.

In 2000, Fairtrade introduced the local farmers to a UK-based company, Mack Multiples, and they worked together to improve the quality of their fruit and to develop sales to Sainsbury's. A local farmer, Alfredo Martinez, says that he is now guaranteed a minimum price, receives money weekly, and is making twice what he was before Fairtrade. Environmental standards have been improved, and education and health standards have been restored.

However, not everyone is so impressed with the Fairtrade achievement. Firstly, Fairtrade is not necessarily the same as ethical sourcing. For example, Marks & Spencer sells Fairtrade cotton clothing. This guarantees that the raw cotton was produced ethically, but not necessarily that the whole of the supply chain was ethical. In any case, Fairtrade cotton only makes up about 1 per cent of that purchased by Marks & Spencer each year.

Secondly, there is a feeling that Fairtrade is being exploited by large retailers. They see the Fairtrade label as a way to segment socially aware consumers, who are willing to pay a premium price for Fairtrade products. The result is that the main beneficiaries are the supermarket groups, rather than the Fairtrade producers.

Thirdly, major producers are also jumping on the Fairtrade bandwagon. The best known is Nestlé, whose Partner's Blend coffee has Fairtrade certification. This is seen as unacceptable by some ethical campaigners, who point to the long-standing claims that Nestlé unethically promotes its powdered milk compounds in Third World countries.

Fourthly, Fairtrade has been criticised by some economists, particularly Americans, because it is seen as biased towards co-operatives and because it guarantees a minimum price. The rival US-backed scheme, Rainforest Alliance, does not guarantee a price, and has been described as 'Fairtrade lite' by its critics. This became a bone of contention in the attempted takeover of Cadbury by the US food conglomerate Kraft in 2009. Cadbury has obtained Fairtrade certification for its Dairy Milk chocolate, while Kraft has Rainforest Alliance certification for its Kenco coffee. Kraft argued that it opposes Fairtrade because it provides a subsidy that distorts the workings of the open market.

Finally, building on Kraft's point, some economists claim that Fairtrade, by guaranteeing a price above the world price, is in effect encouraging over-production. Fairtrade counters by saying that for all commodities, Fairtrade is only a small percentage of world output, and that the Fairtrade price gives farmers surplus income which encourages them to diversify.

On balance, like me, you may well think that Fairtrade benefits the Third World and should be encouraged, but as with most things, the situation is not as simple as it appears at first sight.

(Sources: Fairtrade website (www.fairtrade.co.uk), Crane and Matten 2007, *Economist* 2006, Prosser 2007, Bowers 2009.)

SUSTAINABILITY

Sustainability is about our responsibility to the ultimate stakeholder: our own future, and the future of the planet. We are using up the resources of the Earth and degrading the planet at an increasing rate, and this can only be at the expense of future generations. Sustainable development is 'development that meets the needs of the present without compromising the ability of future generations to meet their own needs' (Fisher and Lovell 2006, p21). This definition stresses that sustainability must be based on needs, not on wants. DesJardins (2007) quotes the formula I = PAT. Environmental impact (I) is the product of population (P), consumption per head or affluence (A), and technology (T). A sustainable society will limit its population growth, avoid excessive consumerism and promote technology that reduces resource use. 'To operate sustainably, an organisation must ... [be] supportive of the survival of the physical environment and also the communities and economies in which it operates' (*Accountability Primer: Sustainability* (nd).

DesJardins quotes the example of Gold'n Plump in Minnesota, which processes four million pounds of chicken a week. Its waste-water treatment plant produces large amounts of solid waste. Each week it sends 100,000 pounds of solid waste to Mississipi Topsoils, where it is combined with residential waste and sawdust to produce saleable compost. An opposite example is the UK's trade in gingerbread. Every year the UK imports 465 tonnes of gingerbread, while at the same time exporting 460 tonnes. This results in excessive use of resources in transportation, and increases the UK's carbon footprint, for no obvious benefit (Simms 2009).

At the macro level, we have the problem of global warming and the associated climate change, the result of the excess of greenhouse gases, particularly carbon dioxide, in the atmosphere, caused at least in part by our excessive burning of fossil fuel. This can only be tackled at global level (global social responsibility). The Kyoto Treaty in 1999 committed industrialised countries to large reductions in carbon emissions, but this effort was frustrated by the refusal of the Bush Administration to ratify the treaty. The UK is fully committed to the Kyoto principles, and has introduced a climate change levy on polluting industries.

At a micro level, sustainability concerns us all, organisations and individuals alike. At an individual level, it is as basic as composting our garden waste, rather than sending it to landfill sites, and turning off our television sets at night, rather than leaving them on standby. At an organisational level, it can be about energy conservation, and also about the kind of activities highlighted in case study 9.8 and activity 9.7 below.

 PLASTIC BAGS — AN UNSUSTAINABLE OPTION?

CASE STUDY 9.8

Seventeen billion plastic carrier bags are used in the UK every year, 14 billion of which are given away by supermarkets. Only one in 200 of these are recycled. The rest go into landfill, weighing 100,000 tonnes, where they take up to 1,000 years to decompose. The vast majority of bags are made from oil derivatives. Most are non-degradable; a few are degradable – they break down when exposed to sunlight (but not in landfill) – and a very few are made of corn starch, so biodegradable, and do break down in landfill.

Several countries have taken action to control their use of plastic bags. In 2002, Bangladesh banned them outright, as they were causing flooding by blocking storm drainage channels during the monsoon. They are also banned in South Africa, and San Francisco is the first US city to impose a ban. Taiwan has banned plastic plates, cups and cutlery as well as plastic bags, leading to a 25 per cent cut in its landfill.

Ireland took a different route, introducing a tax of 15 cents (about 10p) a bag in 2002. This cut plastic bag usage by at least 90 per cent, although some small bags are exempt. Usage has slowly crept up again since 2002, leading to an increase in tax to 22 cents in July 2007.

In the UK there are no official restrictions on the use of plastic bags, although the Scottish Parliament considered and rejected a tax of 10p a bag in 2006, and a MORI poll suggested that throughout the UK 63 per cent would support a 10p tax. London is considering a ban, while the prime minister, Gordon Brown, has said that he would like to see a total ban on single-use plastic bags.

The small town of Modbury in Devon became the first town in Europe to ban plastic bags in April 2007. None of the town's 43 traders, including the Co-op supermarket, issues plastic bags.

Individual stores have taken unilateral action. IKEA charges 10p a bag, and has seen plastic bag use fall by 97 per cent. The discount stores Aldi and Lidl have always charged for bags.

Tesco, the heaviest bag user of all, with four billion bags issued each year, costing it £40 million at 1p per bag, introduced a scheme in 2006 whereby customers received one 'green' Clubcard point, worth 1p, for each bag which they reused, whether or not the reused bag originally came from Tesco. This is intended to cut Tesco's usage by 25 per cent, or one billion bags a year. Each bag saved saves Tesco 1p, so the only net cost to Tesco is when it pays out for other stores' bags. Tesco has also made all its bags degradable (but not biodegradable).

Tesco's move has been welcomed by the government, but criticised by Friends of the Earth as 'a very small step' and a 'greenwash', as it does nothing to cut the excessive amounts of food packaging used by Tesco and all other supermarkets, and because Tesco has chosen not to go biodegradable.

However, the plastic bag industry is fighting back. Barry Turner, the chairman of the UK Carrier Bag Consortium, claims that although plastic bags are made from oil, they use by-products such as naphtha, ethylene and propylene, which would otherwise have to be flared off. He also criticises the use of paper bags rather than plastic. Paper bags weigh more than plastic, are four times as expensive to produce, and most seriously, whereas plastic bags in landfill remain inert, paper bags decompose to release the greenhouse gases methane and CO_2.

Although the obvious response to Turner's claims is, 'He would say that, wouldn't he?', the situation is clearly more complex than at first sight. Perhaps the ideal solution is that advocated by Sainsbury's and Tesco – the more extensive use of 'bags for life', more heavy-duty bags which sell for 10p, can be reused many times, and which the store guarantees to replace for free when they wear out, whereupon Sainsbury's send the worn-out bag for recycling.

(Sources: Turner 2006, Finch and Allen 2006, Butler 2006, *Economist* 2007, Barkham 2007, Aldred 2007, Wintour 2007, Hickman 2009.)

ACTIVITY 9.7 TOBIN TAX AND GLOBAL WARMING

What is a Tobin tax?

It is a transaction tax, originally proposed by the US economist James Tobin in the 1970s. It would impose a small levy of all financial transactions throughout the world. Tobin originally proposed a 1 per cent tax, but what is now being suggested is much smaller – 0.05 or even 0.005 per cent.

How much money would it raise?

The sums involved are enormous. The volume of financial transactions in the global economy is estimated to be nearly 75 times as big as global GDP, most of it in speculation on the derivatives markets, which are seen as of dubious real value. Adair Turner, chairman of the Financial Services Authority, described some City activities as 'socially useless'. A 0.005 per cent levy on foreign exchange trades alone would raise US $30 billion, while a study by the Austrian government suggested that a 0.05 per cent levy on UK financial trades would raise US $100 billion a year (and US $420 billion worldwide), even if it led to a two-thirds fall in transactions.

Who would pay for the tax?

Like all output taxes, the cost would be shared between buyers and sellers – the financial speculators and the banks.

Who is in favour?

France and Germany have been in favour for some time, and Gordon Brown announced his conversion in November 2009. At present, the US and the IMF are opposed, although some economists close to the Obama administration are thought to be in favour

What has this got to do with global warming?

In order to combat global warming, all economies must invest huge sums in greener energy technologies. The West can afford this, but the developing world, and India and China, cannot. Coal is the primary energy source in both India and China. A clean coal-fired power station is 50 per cent more efficient (ie less polluting) than the average plant in India and China. Implementing clean coal technology would cost India up to US $8 billion a year. Gordon Brown has proposed that only half of the proceeds from a Tobin tax should be spent at home. The other half would finance economic development and climate change reduction in the developing world.

Question: What do you think would be the practical obstacles to the implementation of a Tobin tax?

(Sources: Elliott 2009, Mathiason and Treanor 2009.)

RISK MANAGEMENT

An important element of sustainability is risk management. Risk management is not necessarily about avoiding risk – it is about assessing risk, and ensuring that it is consistent with the strategy of the organisation, whether it is risk averse or risk seeking. On the whole, an organisation seeking sustainability will tend to be relatively risk averse.

Risk management is about answering several questions:

- What risks are we facing?
- What are the underlying causes of those risks?
- What is the likelihood of the risky event occurring?
- What is the outcome if the risky event does occur? Risk is measured by likelihood times outcome.
- What can be done about the risk? Possibilities include avoidance, reduction, retention or transfer (see below).
- What decision is taken about the risk?
- How can be decision be tracked, monitored and reviewed?

It is important to note that in identifying a risk, we must identify its causes rather than its symptoms. A technique for doing this is an Ishikawa, fishbone or cause–effect diagram (named after its inventor, Kaoru Ishikawa, a Japanese quality expert). This is frequently done in a group as a brainstorming exercise. An effect is identified, and then possible causes for this effect are brainstormed. These are then grouped into major categories, and the problem is further brainstormed to identify sub-causes, plotted as sub-bones on the skeleton diagram below. Categories commonly used for problems with a large HR element are the four Ps: place, procedure, people, policies.

Figure 9.2 An Ishikawa diagram

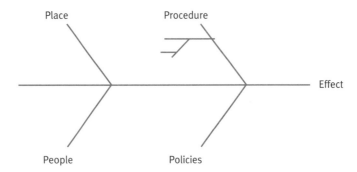

Quantitatively, two risks (likelihood x outcome) might appear identical, but one may have a high likelihood (eg 50 per cent) and a low financial cost (eg £10,000), and the other a low likelihood (eg 0.1 per cent) and a high financial cost (say £5 million). Each would represent a risk of £5,000, but how they are treated is likely to be very different. In the first case, the risk may be ignored (ie retained within the organisation), while in the second case, it is likely that the risk will be transferred (eg through insurance).

The possible strategies for dealing with risk include:

- *Avoidance.* Here a risky activity is not performed at all. For example, after the terrorist attacks in London in July 2005, many Americans avoided all travel to the UK. In a business context, avoiding risk usually means also giving up the opportunity of profit, so except in extreme cases it is unlikely to be a viable strategy.

- *Reduction.* This involves the use of methods which reduce the severity of the loss or the likelihood of it occurring. An example here is the prohibition on the use of hand-held mobile phones while driving.

- *Retention.* Here the risk is accepted when it occurs. This will frequently be done where the risk is small, or where a very large organisation finds it cheaper to self-insure rather than pay insurance premiums to another organisation.

- *Transfer.* Here the risk is transferred to someone else, usually through an insurance contract, but also sometimes through outsourcing. This is commonly used for risks which have a low likelihood of occurrence, but which would be catastrophic if they did happen – for example, the second scenario discussed above, where the likelihood of occurrence was very low (0.1 per cent), but the outcome very high (a loss of £5 million). Here the risk is only £5,000, but the organisation might be prepared to pay a higher insurance premium than this (say £10,000) to eliminate the risk.

Once a decision has been taken about how to manage a particular risk, this decision then has to be monitored and periodically reviewed, as the risk parameters may change over time.

EASTER ISLAND

CASE STUDY 9.9

Easter Island is a small isolated island in the South Pacific Ocean, 3,700 km from Chile to the east, and 2,000 kilometres from the Pitcairn Islands to the west. Its history over the last 500 years is a warning case study in the dangers of unsustainable development.

Easter Island is believed to have been settled by Polynesian people (related to the Maori of New Zealand) between the fifth and the twelfth centuries AD. Its population is thought to have peaked at about 10,000 in the mid-sixteenth century, and then to have collapsed. When the island was discovered by the Dutch in 1722, it was found to be barren, and to have a population of about 3,000 who were living in abject poverty. What had gone wrong?

Easter Island is mainly famous for its gigantic statues, known as *moai* (there is a striking example in the courtyard of the British Museum). There were some 600 of these, up to 20 feet high and weighing up to 80 tons. It seems that they were built as a part of competition between clans on the island, and the accepted opinion is that they helped to contribute to ecological disaster.

When Easter Island was first settled, it is thought that it was covered with a slow-growing type of palm tree, which constituted the main resource of the islanders. It provided them with nuts for food, timber for boats, fuel and building materials, and sledges for moving statues from the quarries to their final sites. The rate of statue-building seems to have increased in the sixteenth century, and this led to an almost total deforestation of the island. Normally in such a situation, Polynesians would have taken to the sea, and moved to another island, but in Easter Island's case, the distances were too great, and the wood for long-distance canoes was no longer available. The islanders descended into poverty, civil war and possibly cannibalism. Rival clans started toppling each other's *moai*, and the whole cultural basis of island society collapsed. In the 1860s the Chileans raided the islands for slaves, and the population fell to an all-time low of around 100 in the 1870s.

(Source: Foot 2004.)

THE RNLI

Sustainability is not just about efficient use of resources. At an organisational level, it is about managing the organisation in such a way as to maintain its long-term viability. Among many other things, this involves:

- taking a long-term rather than a short-term perspective

- prudent risk management

- developing and maintaining a culture that creates a shared sense of purpose and a shared value system which supports sustainability.

We can see the opposite of each of these in the way that many financial institutions were managed in the run-up to the credit crunch in 2007–09:

- almost total emphasis on short-term profit maximisation

- a willingness to take high financial risks, with little evidence of any risk management

- a bonus system based on huge rewards for short-term success, and a willingness to poach whole investment teams from each other.

An example of the opposite approach is the Royal National Lifeboat Institution (RNLI), one of Britain's oldest (founded in 1824) and most successful charities.

The RNLI has:

- a long-term planning horizon, which includes a 20-year strategic plan

- long-term financial planning, which recognises the risk that social and environmental changes may adversely affect the RNLI's income in the future

- a very strong sense of purpose that underpins the RNLI's core mission – 'the charity that saves lives at sea'.

(Source: CIPD 2009.)

CORPORATE SOCIAL RESPONSIBILITY, SUSTAINABILITY AND HR

Carroll (1979) identifies four philosophies of organisational responsiveness to CSR:

Reaction: The company denies all responsibility for social issues, claiming that they are the responsibility of government (the Friedman approach).

Defence: The company accepts responsibility but fights it, doing the least that seems to be required (the tobacco industry?).

Accommodation: The company accepts responsibility and does what is expected of it (most major companies in the UK).

Proaction: The company does more than is expected (Body Shop, Co-op Bank).

Who should be responsible for directing an organisation's policy on ethics and CSR? There are three leading contenders, each reflecting a particular perception of ethics and CSR:

- Marketing/PR, if CSR is primarily seen as a marketing tool, and the key relationship being that with customers (defence).

- The company secretary, if CSR is primarily seen as a matter of regulation, and the key relationship being the corporate governance one with shareholders (accommodation).

- HR, if CSR is primarily seen as a cultural issue and about human behaviour, and the key relationship being that with all stakeholders (proaction).

The theory on ethics and CSR would strongly suggest that the policy can only be meaningful if it permeates all the activities of the organisation, and if everyone in the organisation truly internalises the policy, rather than merely paying lip service to it. This would suggest that HR should be the lead department. However, of even greater importance is that, whichever department is in day-to-day charge, top management, in the form of the CEO, should at all times behave ethically him/herself. Just as quality has total quality management, so ethics/CSR requires total ethical management.

So what in detail should be the role of HR in ethics/CSR?

- *Helping to identify the values of the organisation.* HR should have experience with values, and is well placed to canvass opinions on values across a wide range of stakeholders. Here HR has a clear strategic contribution to make.

- *Drawing up a code of ethics.* HR should be used to drafting policies, many of which themselves have a clear ethical content.

- *Behaving ethically in its own relationships with a key stakeholder, the organisation's own staff.* Here the concept of the 'psychological contract' is important (CIPD 2003b). This defines the implicit deal between employer and employees, as distinct from the formal deal contained in the contract of employment. It is an understanding about what each side can expect from the other. This has two implications for HR in the context of ethics/CSR: the psychological contract should itself be an ethical one, and the concept of the psychological contract can be extended to relationships with other stakeholders.

- *Managing the culture of the organisation.* A culture which fully supports ethics does not just happen, it has to be nurtured, maintained and communicated.

- *Development.* If staff in an organisation are presented with a CSR policy and a code of ethics, it will mean nothing to them until they are thoroughly trained in what these mean and how they should be implemented. This presents HR with a crucial development role, at all levels of the organisation. Some help here is likely to come from the launch of the DTI's online CSR Academy in July 2004 (*Personnel Today* 2004).

- *Maintaining the 'employer brand'.* Increasingly companies want brand values to be reflected in everything that the organisation does. An ethical brand value has clear marketing advantages and recruitment/retention advantages (CIPD 2003b).

HR should also have a leading role in promoting and maintaining sustainability.

It could take part in setting up an environmental policy, and in the development, training and communication that supports such a policy.

The policy could include:

- *Energy minimisation* – turning off lights and computers overnight and at weekends, lowering central heating temperatures to 19°C, and use of video-conferencing rather than energy-hungry face-to-face meetings.

- *Transport policy* – choosing less polluting company cars, subsidised parking for staff who car-share, public transport loans or subsidies, loaning bicycles to staff, etc. Boots has reduced staff car journeys by 20 per cent through its green transport plan.

- *Flexible working and homeworking.* Flexible working can enable staff to avoid rush-hour congestion, so saving on energy, and also makes bicycle usage more attractive (Davies and Smith 2007).

The TUC has promoted a Green Workplaces Project, which helps to ensure trade union support for sustainability initiatives. A joint union–management environment group at Scottish Power found that a call-centre site had 200 old-fashioned VDU screens, with high energy usage. Half of these were left on at night and at weekends. Switching to low-energy screens and PCs, and development of a 'switch it off' culture could help to save a third of the site's emissions of CO_2. Actual savings in 2006–07 were 5 per cent (TUC 2007).

 ACTIVITY 9.8 INSTITUTIONAL RACISM

In 1999 the Macpherson Report on the murder of Stephen Lawrence identified the principle of institutional racism. The report defined this as 'The collective failure of an organisation to provide an appropriate and professional service to people because of their colour, culture or ethnic origin. It can be seen or detected in processes, attitudes and behaviour which amount to discrimination through unwitting prejudice, ignorance, thoughtlessness and racial stereotyping which disadvantages minority ethnic people' (Home Office 1999, p79). Macpherson argued that because of its ingrained culture (the so-called 'canteen culture'), the Metropolitan Police was institutionally racist. This does not mean that every Met officer is racist, nor that there is a deliberate policy of racism in the organisation, but that the organisation is unthinkingly racism in its attitudes and behaviour.

After the publication of the report, the Met pledged itself to eliminating institutional racism, as did other police forces.

What actions could the police take to eliminate institutional racism?

CORPORATE SOCIAL RESPONSIBILITY AND THE GOVERNMENT

The government has two main roles in CSR. Firstly, the government is itself a major employer and a major purchaser and supplier of services. In this role, it can and should behave ethically just like any other organisation.

However, the government also has a role in the promotion of CSR (Cowe 2004).

In March 2000, the first minister for CSR was appointed, within the Department for Trade and Industry (DTI), now the Department for Business, Innovation & Skills.

The main interest of the government has been in securing greater transparency. The Pensions Act 2000 requires pension-fund trustees to make a statement of investment principles, disclosing their policy on social, environmental and ethical issues. Its company law review has led to the introduction in 2005 of a requirement on all public companies to include an operating and financial review in their annual report to shareholders. In addition, the government set up a new CSR academy in 2004.

However, locating the responsibility for CSR within the DTI has inevitably led to an emphasis on the corporate governance aspects of CSR. Other departments clearly also have an involvement in CSR – the Department of Work and Pensions in pensions, the Department for International Development in trade and aid aspects of CSR, and the Department for the Environment, Food and Rural Affairs in issues of pollution, sustainability and climate change. The involvement of the government is likely to increase.

THE BOTTOM LINE

Do CSR and ethical behaviour increase a company's profits? A series of studies suggests that they do.

Firstly, CSR seems to benefit an organisation's reputation. In 2002, Business in the Community carried out a survey on what the public thought of corporate responsibility. Business leaders in general are not trusted. Only 25 per cent of respondents trusted them to tell the truth – only ahead of politicians and journalists, and well below doctors and teachers. This suggests that business has a lot of ground to make up. The public wants business to be responsible. Only 2 per cent think that companies should maximise their profits, regardless of society or the environment. Eight times as many thought companies should make a major contribution to society, regardless of cost.

Responsible behaviour also affects peoples' purchases. Eighty-six per cent in 2002 thought it very or fairly important that the organisation shows a high degree of social responsibility, up from 68 per cent in 1997. One in six people have actively boycotted a product on ethical grounds in previous years.

Is this evidence conclusive? No. It is suggestive, but little more. If you were interviewed by Business in the Community, you might have a shrewd idea of the kind of answers which the interviewer would like! It is also unfortunately true that there is often a gap between what people say they do, and what they actually do.

The second piece of evidence is a report written by the management consultants Arthur D Little in 2003, again for Business in the Community, 'The Business Case for Corporate Responsibility'. This identifies a number of benefits from CSR:

- It offers a means by which companies can build the trust of their stakeholders. This is supported by the American strategy guru Michael Porter, who is reported as saying that how a company is perceived by its stakeholders is becoming a source of competitive advantage (Golzen 2001).

- CSR offers more effective management of risk. CSR encourages firms to understand and empathise with society and the environment, and this makes it more likely that they will be proactive about social and environmental risk.

- CSR helps to attract and retain a talented and diverse workforce.

- CSR stimulates learning and innovation within organisations.

- CSR facilitates access to capital. Over half of analysts and two-thirds of investors believe that a company that emphasises CSR is attractive to investors.

- CSR improves competitiveness, market positioning and profitability. The report quotes from Collins and Porras' *Built to Last* (2000), a pioneering study in the 1990s, which compared successful companies that had been in business for at least 50 years, with a control group who had been less successful. They found that a key characteristic of the successful 'visionary' companies was that they had a core purpose beyond making money.

Is the Arthur D Little evidence conclusive? It is certainly very strong. Although some of the findings are based on opinion, others are based on hard evidence of changes in behaviour.

The third study was carried out by the Institute of Business Ethics in 2003. This examined a sample of FTSE 350 companies which were perceived as being ethical (they had had code of ethics in operation for at least five years, they scored highly on *Management Today*'s annual league table of 'most admired companies', and they were rated highly by the specialist ratings agency SERM on their 'socio-ethical risk management'). These ethical companies were compared with a control sample.

The ethical companies were found to score more highly on three measures of financial performance: market value added, economic value added and price/earning ratio. On a fourth measure, return on capital employed, they did less well until the stock market collapse of 2000, but have performed better since then, suggesting that their profits are more stable (Caulkin 2003 and Maitland 2003).

Is this evidence conclusive? Again, it is very strong, but unfortunately it is not conclusive. There is clearly a strong correlation between ethical behaviour and profits, but this does not prove that the ethical behaviour causes the profits. The link may be the other way round – profitable companies may be more likely to be ethical – or both may be the result of some unknown third factor.

A more theoretical approach was taken by Reitz, Wall and Love (1998). They concentrated on the relatively narrow area of business negotiation, and argued that taking an unethical stance in negotiation has four major costs:

- *Rigidity*. Unethical negotiators will tend to stick to the patterns of negotiation which have paid off in the past. They will thus trap themselves in a rigid bargaining position which can be matched and exploited by their opponents.

- *Damaged relationships.* If a bargaining partner feels that he/she has been manipulated through underhand tactics, he/she is likely to feel embittered and to seek revenge.

- *Sullied reputation.* Success in business frequently depends on reputation. If you develop a reputation for cheating or other unethical behaviour, this will harm your future business prospects.

- *Lost opportunities.* Negotiation is about finding a win–win situation, whereby both sides gain. A reputation for sharp dealing may lead potential partners to avoid making concessions to you, for fear that you will not make concessions back.

Their conclusion is that ethical negotiation is not only morally desirable; it is also good business.

ACTIVITY 9.9 CSR AND PROFITS – THE CONTRARY VIEW

A strong case against CSR has been made by David Henderson (2001). He makes the following points:

- CSR involves organisations in higher costs, and, in so far as it means that they may forgo some activities seen as non-responsible, lower revenue. The result will be lower profits (although Henderson concedes that in some cases, this could be offset by gains as a result of enhanced reputation). This argument is supported by evidence that in 2003, the Dutch insurance company Aetna spent 20 million euros in order to comply with the US Sarbanes-Oxley regulations, introduced after the Enron scandal (Targett 2004).

- Some of the leading CSR companies have gone through spectacular collapses in profits. He cites the US jeans manufacturer Levi Strauss, but the same point could be made about Body Shop and Ben & Jerry's ice cream.

- The CSR agenda is frequently set not by 'society', but non-governmental organisations (NGOs) like Greenpeace, which Henderson sees as anti-capitalist pressure groups, and as unrepresentative of society as a whole.

Critically evaluate these arguments.

KEY LEARNING POINTS

- Three main approaches can be taken to ethics, and these lead to a larger number of ethical guidelines. The most commonly used of these are the golden rule, the disclosure rule and the intuition ethic.

- All managers face ethical dilemmas on a daily basis in their work; professionals have an ethical responsibility both to their organisation and to impartial professional integrity.

- There is a considerable argument over whether a separate business ethic exists.

- Values underpin ethics, and an organisation's values underpin its business ethics. Codes of ethics, unless they are internalised in the organisation's culture, do not guarantee ethical behaviour.

- Corporate governance is concerned with issues of conflict of interest and accountability.

- CSR is the way in which an organisation expresses its values through its behaviour towards stakeholders.

- Sustainability or sustainable development is concerned with safeguarding the environment for future generations. Risk management is an important element of a sustainability strategy.

- HR and the government have key roles to play in promoting CSR and sustainability.

- Although the evidence is not totally conclusive, it appears extremely likely that there is a positive correlation between CSR and profit.

QUESTIONS

1. Distinguish between the absolutist, relativist and utilitarian approaches to ethics.

2. Describe the golden rule, the disclosure rule and the intuition ethic.

3. According to De George, what conditions must apply before whistleblowing is morally justified?

4. Does an organisation have any ethical responsibilities over and above those of the individuals within it?

5. Define purpose, values and vision.

6. How useful are codes of ethics?

7. What are the key features of CSR?

8. Define sustainable development.

9. In the context of risk management, what do you understand by risk avoidance, risk reduction, risk retention and risk transfer?

10. What is the role of HR in supporting CSR and sustainable development?

Further Reading

Connock and Johns' *Ethical Leadership*, published by the CIPD in 1995, is a useful summary of ethical issues from an HR standpoint. The CIPD also published a useful factsheet on 'Corporate Responsibility and HR's Role' in 2003 (revised in 2009 as factsheet 'Corporate Social Responsibility'), and has other useful factsheets on sustainable development and corporate governance. Excellent books on ethics are Fisher and Lovell's

Business Ethics and Values (2006), 2nd edition, although this is rather heavy-going, and Crane and Matten's *Business Ethics* (2007) 2nd edition.

Websites

A useful website is Business in the Community (www.bitc.org.uk), which contains a number of useful reports and case studies on ethics and CSR.

EXPLORE FURTHER

SEMINAR ACTIVITY

RESPONSIBLE TOURISM

Activity 1

Richards and Gladwin (1999) have put forward their definition of a socially sustainable enterprise:

> The characteristics of a socially sustainable enterprise are that it would:
>
> - return to communities where it operates – giving as much as it gains from them
>
> - meaningfully include stakeholders impacted by its activities in associated planning and decision-making processes
>
> - ensure no reduction in, and actively promote, the observance of political and civil rights in the domains where it operates
>
> - widely spread economic opportunities and help to reduce or eliminate unjustified inequalities
>
> - directly or indirectly ensure no net loss of human capital within its workforces and operating communities

> - cause no net loss of direct and indirect productive employment
>
> - adequately satisfy the vital needs of its employees and operating communities
>
> - work to ensure the fulfilment of the basic needs of humanity prior to serving luxury wants.

Explore Worldwide is a UK tour company, specialising in small group exploratory holidays. Its 2004–05 brochure stresses its commitment to sustainability:

Respecting our planet
Our commitment to Responsible Tourism

Explore's dedication to Responsible Tourism is the driving force behind our Environmental Policy. Far from being an abstract ideal for us, Responsible Tourism shapes all our major decisions – from the concept that 'Small Groups Leave Fewer Footprints' to the choice of local agents and suppliers.

Here are our guidelines in a nutshell:

- By operating in small groups, we minimise the impact on the local culture and resources, whilst blending in more easily.

- We issue our travellers with clear guidelines on responsible tourism. These cover a variety of issues from litter and waste disposal in remote areas, to begging and artefacts. We encourage customers to buy local crafts and support local skills, but never to buy products that exploit wildlife or harm the habitat.

- We use locally owned suppliers wherever viable to provide and run services. This ensures that the local economy benefits directly. We also expect local suppliers to meet our standards, with particular consideration for the environment.

- When recruiting Tour Leaders, we assess their environmental credentials and then train them to our own standards. They are also required to complete a Responsible Tourism Audit on each tour.

Throughout a tour, the Leader will encourage the education of our customers on the social workings of a region. And part of their role is to make sure that the local communities benefit from our visit, ensuring that we will always be welcome.

Explore's passion for travel goes beyond the yearning for discovery. Ours is a reasoned, tried and tested approach to the enjoyment of a truly amazing planet.

Question: Critically evaluate Explore's Responsible Tourism policy against Richards and Gladwin's principles.

Activity 2

Mark Ellingham, the founder of the *Rough Guide* series, has recently declared that 'binge flying' constitutes a threat to the global environment: 'If the travel industry [ignores] the effect that carbon emissions from flying are having on climate change, we are putting ourselves in a very similar position to the tobacco industry' (quoted in Hastings 2007).

Question: Is overseas tourism unsustainable?

Strategic Management

INTRODUCTION

This chapter will analyse the nature of strategic management, and identify different models of strategy. It will analyse the stages of strategic decision-making: analysis, choice and implementation. The last part of the chapter will concentrate on the nature and practice of change management.

WHAT IS STRATEGIC MANAGEMENT?

The origins of strategy are military, and concern the art of war. A *strategos* was a general in command of a Greek army. Quinn (1980) identifies three elements of strategy:

- Goals or objectives. What is to be achieved, and when it is to be achieved. Major goals that affect an organisation's overall direction are strategic goals.

- Policies are guidelines which set out the limits within which action should occur. Major policies are strategic policies.

- Programmes lay down the sequence of actions necessary to achieve objectives. They set out how objectives will be achieved within the limits set by policies.

In other words:

- Where do we want to get?

- What actions should we take to get there?

- How can we carry out these actions?

The essence of a strategy is to build a position so strong that the organisation will achieve its objectives no matter what unforeseeable forces attack it (ie how can we win whatever the enemy does?). Effective strategies should:

- contain clear and decisive objectives – sub-goals may change in the heat of battle but the overriding objective provides continuity over time

- maintain the initiative

- concentrate power at the right time and place

- have built-in flexibility so that one can use minimum resources to keep opponents at a disadvantage

- have committed and co-ordinated leadership

- involve correct timing and surprise

- make resources secure and prevent surprises from opponents.

Strategic decisions have a number of characteristics (Johnson et al 2004):

- They are concerned with the scope of an organisation's activities, ie the boundaries an organisation sets to its activities.

- They seek to match the activities of an organisation to its environment.

- They are concerned with matching the activities of an organisation to its resource capability.

- They often have resource implications for an organisation – if current resources do not permit a particular strategy, can the necessary resources be acquired?

- They affect operational decisions: a whole series of implementing sub-decisions must flow from the making of a strategic decision.

- They are affected by the values and expectations of those who have power in and around the organisation – its stakeholders.

- They affect the long-term direction of an organisation.

Strategy can be seen at several levels:

- Corporate level – concerned with the overall scope of the operation, its financial performance, and the allocation of resources to different operations.

- Competitive or business unit level – how to compete within a particular market at the level of a strategic business unit (SBU).

- Operational level – how the different functions of the organisation contribute to the overall strategy. This level is often seen as tactical rather than in any real sense strategic, but it can equally be seen as the implementation stage of strategy.

Strategic management is about doing the right things. It is:

- ambiguous
- complex
- non-routine
- organisation-wide
- fundamental
- involving significant change
- environment- or expectations-driven.

Operational or tactical management is about doing things right. It is:

- routinised
- operationally specific
- involving small-scale change
- resource-driven.

MODELS OF STRATEGY

CORPORATE PLANNING

This was a product of the 1950s and 1960s, a period with a largely placid environment. Detailed corporate plans covering the whole organisation were drawn up by a central planning team and then agreed by top management. The details of the plan were extremely complex, as were the models used, but the planning process itself was relatively simple because the corporate future was expected to be a continuation of the past. The role of line management was to implement the plan. The main exponent of corporate planning was Igor Ansoff. There are clear parallels with the system of central planning used to run the Soviet Union.

The strength of the corporate planning approach is its rigour, and the vital information which is collected in the course of drawing up the plan. However, it has a number of weaknesses. It is inflexible – the plan is too vast and complex to cope with rapid change in the environment. However, some of the best corporate planners – eg those at Shell – cope with this by developing a range of scenarios about the future environment. One of these forecast exactly the rise in oil prices in 1973, with the result that Shell could react very quickly to the new situation.

Centralised corporate planning is also demotivating. Nobody owns the plan except for the planners – the line managers who have to implement it have no commitment to it. At worst, corporate planning was an academic exercise, and the plan was put away in a drawer and quietly forgotten.

STRATEGIC MANAGEMENT

This model emphasises adaptability in the face of a turbulent environment. There is no rigid long-term plan, although there are long-term visions and values. Strategy becomes bottom-up, as line managers react to or anticipate changes in the environment. The organisation has to be very responsive to changes in the environment, which requires managers at all levels constantly to monitor the environment. The organisation becomes a learning organisation in the fullest sense of the term, as it is constantly scanning and learning from its environment.

Leading exponents of the strategic management concept are:

Tom Peters

In Search of Excellence (Peters and Waterman 1982) stressed the importance of a number of attributes for excellence, which emphasised values, simplicity, quick reactions and understanding the customer:

- stick to the knitting
- close to the customer
- productivity through people
- autonomy and entrepreneurship
- hands-on, value-driven
- bias for action
- simple form, lean staff
- simultaneous loose–tight properties.

Peters followed this up with *Thriving on Chaos* (1985), where he argued that the organisation should cope with chaos by becoming chaotic itself, ie being in a continual state of flux.

Michael Porter

Porter approached strategic management as an economist. He stressed the importance of the competitive position of an industry (the Five Forces) (1980), the nature of generic strategies, and the importance of the organisation's value chain in identifying its competitive advantage (1985).

Ralph Stacey

In *The Chaos Frontier* (1991) and *Strategic Management and Organisational Dynamics* (1993), Stacey developed the application of chaos theory to strategic management. The environment facing organisations is one of chaos, ie multiple and ultimately unpredictable reactions follow from a single event. The further the forecaster looks into the future, the more outcomes become possible. As a result, the organisation must be highly responsive and reactive. The role of top management is to develop and support creativity and innovation.

Gary Hamel and C K Prahalad

In *Competing for the Future* (1994), Hamel and Prahalad stressed that the key role of management is to manage the organisation in such a way that it is flexible and able to respond to a changed environment. This means identifying and developing the core competencies of the organisation. We will return to this later. Hamel later developed the '10 principles of revolutionary strategy' (1996):

1. *Strategic planning isn't strategic* – it assumes that the future will be more or less the same as the present.
2. *Strategy-making must be subversive* – strategy is about breaking rules and assumptions.
3. *The bottleneck is at the top of the bottle* – top managers are most resistant to change.
4. *Revolutionaries exist in every company.*
5. *Change is not the problem, engagement is* – senior managers fail to give people responsibility for managing change.
6. *Strategy-making must be democratic* – senior managers must recognise that creativity is spread throughout an organisation.
7. *Anyone can be a strategy activist* – senior managers must see activists as positive, not as anarchists.
8. *Perspective is worth 50 IQ points* – organisations have to use all their knowledge to identify unconventional ideas.
9. *Top-down and bottom-up are not alternatives* – both are necessary.
10. *You can't see the end from the beginning* – strategy can often throw up surprises.

James Quinn

In *Strategies for Change: logical incrementalism* (1980), Quinn developed the concept of logical incrementalism, ie that strategy does not consist of a big bang, but rather of a series of small steps.

HENRY MINTZBERG AND STRATEGIC MANAGEMENT

One of the most trenchant critics of corporate planning has been the Canadian guru Henry Mintzberg whose writings include *The Rise and Fall of Strategic Planning* (1994). He argues that old-style corporate planning was all about left-brain activity, ie numbers, linearity, analysis. Strategic management is right-brain, ie ideas, patterns, relationships, intuition. He talks of crafting strategy, rather than planning strategy.

Mintzberg is famous for his 'Five Ps of Strategy', with strategy as:

- *A plan for action.* Here the strategy is made in advance of the actions to which they apply, and it is applied consciously and purposefully. However, as we will see later, outcomes may not be as expected.

- *A ploy*, a manoeuvre to outwit opponents.

- *A pattern.* A pattern of behaviour becomes a strategy. If a particular course of action tends to lead to favourable results, a strategy emerges. The strategy is the result of events, rather than the cause of them.

- *Position.* Strategy here is about finding a niche in the market, a position that balances the pressures of the environment and the competition.

- *Perspective.* Here the strategy reflects how the organisation views the world and its place in it. A classic example is Hewlett-Packard's 'HP way', where the whole approach of the organisation is based on engineering excellence and innovation. The important thing here is consistency in behaviour.

Planned strategies often require modification as they are implemented because environmental or organisational factors change. It is very rare that a long-term strategic plan can be implemented over a period of years without modification. The intended strategy may not be realised in practice, and even if it is, it may not achieve the desired results.

THE ELEMENTS OF STRATEGIC MANAGEMENT

The analysis so far may seem extremely complex, but the important thing to remember is that the essence of strategic management is very simple. It consists of reaching answers to four questions:

- Where are we?

- Where do we want to get?

- How can we get there?

- What do we have to do to get there?

From this we can derive the three elements of strategic management:

- Strategic analysis –what is our current position and where to do we want to go?

- Strategic choice –how can we get there, ie what strategy should we choose?

- Strategic implementation – what do we have to do to implement our chosen strategy?

STRATEGIC ANALYSIS

Strategic analysis is concerned with the strategic position of the organisation. What are the key characteristics of the organisation, what changes are going on in the environment, and how will these affect the organisation and its activities? The aim is to form a view of the key influences on the present and future well-being of the organisation:

- Expectations of stakeholders, the culture of the organisation, and most important, the organisation's vision and values.
- The environment, as identified through a STEEPLE analysis. The main problem is to distil out of the complexity the key environmental impacts for the purposes of strategic choice.
- Resources. Strategic capability is about identifying strengths and weaknesses by considering the key resource areas of the business such as physical plant, management, finance, products, etc.

Classical corporate planning saw environmental analysis as the key element in strategic analysis, while strategic management sees culture and values as most crucial.

GAP ANALYSIS

The extent to which there is a mismatch (a gap) between current strategy and the future environment is a measure of the strategic problem facing the organisation. As figure 10.1 shows, over time the current strategy is likely to get more out of line with the environment, and a planning gap will grow.

Figure 10.1 Gap analysis

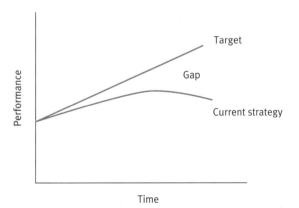

The organisation needs to choose a new strategy which will ensure that this gap is filled.

STRATEGIC CHOICE

Strategic choice involves three steps:

- *Generation of strategic options.* Three levels of analysis are involved here: what fundamental or generic strategy should be followed? Within this generic strategy, what strategic directions are needed? And then what methods of strategic direction are most appropriate?

- *Evaluation of strategic options.* This involves testing options for suitability (do they fit the generic strategy, and will they provide the desired results?); feasibility (are resources available or obtainable?); and acceptability (do they fit the values of the stakeholders?).

- *Selection of strategy.* Either logically, using some kind of weighting criteria; or politically.

STRATEGIC IMPLEMENTATION

Strategic implementation involves resource planning, organisational structure, systems, change management techniques, etc.

STRATEGIC ANALYSIS

VISION, MISSION, VALUES AND OBJECTIVES

Vision, mission, values and objectives are closely linked, and often confused. However, they are clearly distinguished by Peter Senge in *The Fifth Discipline* (1990).

- Vision is the *what?* – The picture of the future we want to create, or the desired future state of the organisation (where do we want to get?).

- Mission is the *why?* – The overriding purpose of the organisation, its scope and boundaries (what business are we in, why do we exist?).

- Values are the *how?* – The underlying beliefs and ethical stance which drives how the business behaves (how are we going to behave while we are getting there?).

- Objectives operationalise all the other three – A precise statement of where we want to be and when, which turns the vision, mission and values into concrete quantifiable terms. It is frequently said that objectives should be SMART:

  Stretching
  Measurable
  Achievable
  Relevant
  Time-limited

CADBURY AND A FAILURE OF VALUES

The chocolate manufacturer Cadbury was founded in Birmingham in 1824 by John Cadbury, a local Quaker. Like other nineteenth-century Quakers, Cadbury was a committed social reformer. He founded the Animals Friend Society, a forerunner of the RSPCA. The company remained true to its Quaker principles, and was a shining example of corporate social responsibility long before the term was invented. It took a leading role in promoting education in Birmingham, built the Bournville model village for its workers, was the first company in the country to introduce a half day on Saturday, and launched a pension fund as early as 1906 (Cadbury 2007).

The emphasis on Quaker values continued well into the twentieth century, as long as the company was directly controlled by the Cadbury family. It was a member of the family, Adrian Cadbury, who produced one of the first reports on corporate governance in the early 1990s.

It is clear from the Cadbury website that the company is still very proud of its Quaker heritage, and so it came as a great shock when the company was fined £1 million for a breach of safety regulations that led to a salmonella outbreak. What was worse was that the outbreak was a direct result of the company's own policy. In 2003, it had changed its policy on salmonella contamination from a 'zero tolerance' policy, where a product was destroyed automatically if any trace of salmonella was detected on test, to a policy allowing a 'tolerable level' of salmonella. This was despite scientific opinion that no level of salmonella could be regarded as safe.

In January and February 2006 there were 36 positive tests for salmonella, but the company did nothing until it was linked to an outbreak of salmonella poisoning in June 2006, in which at least 42 people were infected (Williams 2007). It then recalled all the products concerned. It is estimated that the recall and the resultant bad publicity cost the company £40 million (Tait and Wiggins 2007).

In the company's trial under food hygiene regulations, it was claimed by the prosecution that the change in policy was a deliberate and cynical act of cost-cutting. The judge said the company had fallen 'seriously short of its obligations', but accepted the company's defence that although it was negligent, it was not deliberately aiming to cut costs. Simon Baldry, the former managing director of Cadbury Trebor Bassett, was one of the casualties of a management shake-up which followed the product withdrawal (Elliott 2007).

What this case shows is that the higher an organisation's standards and values, the more serious are any shortcomings in failing to meet those standards.

The mission and objectives of the organisation are constrained by four main factors: (Johnson et al 2004):

Corporate governance — External constraints on the organisation, set by company law; reports of investigations such as the Cadbury Report on non-executive directors or the Greenbury Report on directors' pay; regulatory bodies such as the Financial Services Authority, and targets and controls. Imposed by the government on public bodies (ie best value for local authorities).

Stakeholders	Stakeholders can influence the organisation's strategic direction through their power and/or their interest.
Business ethics	Ethics can impact on an organisation at three levels: general ethical policy; how the organisation interprets its corporate social responsibility when it formulates its strategy; and the ethical behaviour of individuals within the organisation. Clearly ethics is all about values, particularly the values of top management.
Culture	Culture in organisations operates at three levels:

- Values, often written down as part of the mission statement, but often vague, like 'service to the community'.

- More specific beliefs, often expressed as policies.

- Taken-for-granted assumptions – the organisational paradigm – the 'way things are done here'. At grass-roots level, these may often be in conflict with the values and beliefs officially expressed at a higher level. For example, the police force in the UK is totally committed to eradicating institutional racism, but at the level of 'canteen culture' there are still racist PCs.

THE MISSION STATEMENT

This is the most generalised statement of organisational purpose. It sets the direction of the organisation, and provides a benchmark against which policies can be evaluated.

An effective mission statement should:

- be visionary and long-term. It is meant to inspire and drive the organisation

- clarify the main intentions and aspirations of the organisation and the reasons why the organisation exists

- describe the organisation's main activities and the position it wishes to attain in its industry

- contain a statement of the key values of the organisation in relation to its stakeholders

- be taken seriously within the organisation

- be a focus for activity, which can serve as a continual guide, rather than a closed aim which can be fully achieved.

However, there are two great dangers with mission statements. The first is a risk that they can appear grandiose, or even ridiculous. Too many overblown mission statements have tended in the past to lead to the whole concept being treated with ridicule. Typical is the *Dilbert* website (www.dilbert.com), which will produce randomly generated mission statements.

The other danger is that the mission statement may become set in concrete. The external environment may change in a way that renders the mission statement obsolete, and a hindrance rather than a help to strategy formulation.

ACTIVITY 10.1 THE WEA (NORTHERN IRELAND)

The Workers Educational Association (WEA) in Northern Ireland publishes its mission statement values on its website (www.wea-ni. com), as follows:

The WEA Mission Statement

We will make learning accessible to all men and women, especially those removed from the educational experience. As well as offering opportunities to individuals we will assist those who wish to work collectively for the benefit of their communities and for the good of society as a whole.

The Value Base of the WEA

The WEA has been a catalyst for social change since it began in Belfast in 1910. The following values underpin our commitment to social change:

- Social inclusion – we make special efforts to reach those most removed from the learning experience.

- Voluntarism – we provide opportunities for people to volunteer to work both individually and collectively for the betterment of our society.

- Active citizenship – we equip people to play a full role in the social, economic, cultural and political life of our society.

- Building alliances – we work closely with others to improve opportunities for learning.

- Sharing experience – we share good practice to promote mutual learning.

- Equality – we promote equality of opportunity through learning.

Evaluate the WEA mission statement against the six characteristics of an effective mission statement listed above.

RESOURCE ANALYSIS

Resource analysis is internal to the organisation. It is concerned with the strengths and weaknesses parts of SWOT analysis, and measures the efficiency and effectiveness of an organisation's resources, and their degree of fit with the external opportunities and threats also identified through SWOT. Ideally strengths should support opportunities, and be able to counteract threats. Resources should be seen in the widest sense, to include the organisation's competitive position, as identified through techniques such as Five Forces and portfolio analysis. However, SWOT analysis has severe limitations. The most important of these is that it is subjective – different analysts will identify totally different strengths and weaknesses. Stevenson (1989) found no consensus among the managers in the companies he studied on the strengths and weaknesses of their companies. Higher-level managers tended to be more optimistic about the balance of strengths and weaknesses than lower-level managers.

Prahalad and Hamel (1990) identified the concept of the core competences of the organisation, ie those factors that give the organisation its key competitive advantages. Unlike resources, which are tangible, tradeable and easily replicable, competences are based on the accumulated knowledge and skills of the organisation, are unique to it, and difficult to copy. They are based on people rather than things. Examples are the way in which Dell builds all its computers individually to order, or the reputation of Body Shop as an ethical crusader. Other analyses have suggested that the crucial competence needed by all organisations is the ability to be nimble, flexible and responsive to rapid and unpredictable changes in the external environment. The core competence model is very closely connected with the resource-based model of strategic HR.

Core competencies can be based on:

- *Cost efficiency*. Many advantages based on cost efficiency are not really core competencies, as they can relatively easily be copied by other organisations. One which may lead to a core competence is cost efficiency based on experience – the more experience an organisation has, the lower its costs tend to be.

- *Value added*. Is the organisation more effective than the competition? In the early stages of the quality movement in the 1970s and 1980s, quality could be a core competence. Now it is a given – it is expected of all organisations and it does not in itself give a competitive advantage. Value added is more likely to be experienced by the customer through service than through the product itself, eg Dell does not necessarily sell a better computer, but it gives the customer a flexible computer configured to his/her requirements.

- *Managing linkages*. Between different stages of production, or through alliances with other organisations. For example, the low-cost airlines like EasyJet and Ryanair pioneered the use of Internet-based ticket-booking systems and paperless tickets, giving them both a cost and an effectiveness advantage, as well as allowing a very flexible pricing system. They also offer web links to suppliers of hotels and car hire.

- *Robustness*. How easy is it to ensure that the competences are difficult to copied?

If it can develop a number of core competences, an organisation can greatly strengthen its strategic position. However, there is the danger that over time the core competences may no longer match the external environment. If computing becomes based on mobile phones rather than PCs and laptops, Dell's core competence may prove to be a weakness rather than a strength.

ACTIVITY 10.2 HARRY POTTER AND THE PORTENTS OF DOOM

Bloomsbury Publishing was founded in 1986 by Nigel Newton, who is still the company's chairman. His mission was to publish books of the highest quality, and to bring quality to the mass market (Bloomsbury 2007a). The company initially grew slowly, and by the early

1990s its turnover was barely £10 million. It then went public in 1994, raising £5.5 million, followed by a rights issue in 1998 which raised another £6.1 million.

By then Bloomsbury's fortunes had been transformed after it accepted a children's book from an unknown author, J K Rowling. This was published as *Harry Potter and the Philosopher's Stone* in 1997, and the rest is history. Bloomsbury owns the English language rights to Harry Potter throughout the world except the US (where the rights are owned by Scholastic). Worldwide sales of the first six *Harry Potter* books totalled 325 million (Jordan 2007).

As the sales of Harry Potter soared so did Bloomsbury's fortunes. Turnover rose from £20 million in 1999 to £109 million in 2005, while profit rose from £2.6 million in 1999 to £20.1 million in 2005 (Bloomsbury 2007b). However, events were then to show how dependent the company was on *Harry Potter*. The sixth book, *Harry Potter and the Half-Blood Prince*, was published in July 2005, and no Potter title appeared in 2006.

The result was that both sales and profits collapsed in 2006. 2006 turnover was £74 million, lower than 2003, while profits slumped to £5.2 million, the lowest figure since 2000. All the fall was due to a fall in turnover in the children's division (basically *Harry Potter*) (Shelley 2007).

Fortunately for Bloomsbury, the last book in the series, *Harry Potter and the Deathly Hallows*, was still in the pipeline, and was published in July 2007. In the first 24 hours 2.6 million copies were sold in the UK, plus another 400,000 English language copies in Germany (Bloomsbury 2007c).

Clearly the success of the seventh and final title generated healthy profits for Bloomsbury in 2007, but this boost was likely to be short-lived, because of the peculiar nature of the *Potter* market.

The major supermarkets all see *Harry Potter* as an ideal vehicle for a short-term price war. In a sense, the fact that retailers make no money out of the book does not matter to Bloomsbury, because they get their £9.89 a copy anyway. But in another sense it does matter. The typical pattern with a bestselling book is that it is initially published in hardback at a high price, with only moderate but very profitable sales. Then a year later, a paperback edition appears, at a lower price, but with greater volume. The publisher has two bites at the apple. This does not happen with *Harry Potter*. Because of the discounting and hype, people who might have waited for the paperback buy the hardback instead. As a result, sales of *Harry Potter* are minimal after the year in which the title is published.

Bloomsbury is a classic example of an organisation whose success is resource-driven. Its key asset is the intellectual property embedded in the *Harry Potter* titles. Like a pharmaceutical company with a blockbuster drug, it must ensure that a stream of new products is developed to replace the blockbuster. If this is not done, profits collapse.

Question: How can Bloomsbury escape from the portents of doom and ensure its long-term future?

STRATEGIC CHOICE

GENERIC STRATEGIES

The concept of generic strategy was introduced by Michael Porter (1985). He identified possible strategies as being:

- *Cost leadership*. An organisation will succeed if it can achieve lower costs than its competitors, but sell its products at or near the industry average price.

- *Differentiation.* An organisation will succeed if it can produce a differentiated product which commands a premium price, but at the same time keep its costs to the industry average.

- *Focus.* An organisation will succeed if it concentrates on a niche market, in which it can achieve either cost focus or differentiation focus.

Porter argued that depending on the circumstances, any of the three generic strategies could be viable, but that a mixed or hybrid strategy, combining two of the generic strategies, was highly unlikely to be viable.

Porter's model is now a quarter of a century old, and it was developed a long time before the rise of the Internet and e-commerce. However, a study by Kim et al (2004) found that at least in the case of business-to-consumer (B2C) e-commerce, Porter's model still held, with one important exception.

The characteristics of B2C seem to make cost leadership an attractive strategy. E-commerce has very low entry barriers, strategic initiatives and pricing are transparent and can easily be copied by competitors, and there are increasing returns to scale. It therefore makes sense to opt for low prices in order to build up market share quickly. However, although cost leadership was a good entry strategy, it was less effective in the medium term. Because of the ease of market entry, it was all too easy to get into a cost-cutting and ultimately unprofitable price war.

Differentiation was also an effective strategy. Although price was the most important factor for low-value items, for higher-value ones like computers, furniture and cars brand was more important, and so was the level of service. A superior level of service was some protection against the entry of low-cost competitors. Amazon was successful because of its enormous stock list, quick delivery and added-value services like personalised recommendations. Focus was also effective. A niche market was a cheap way to enter, and an easy way to develop and deliver value to the customer.

In their empirical research, Kim et al made two interesting findings. One was that despite Porter, the most effective strategy was a hybrid cost leadership–differentiation one, such as that pursued by Amazon. The second was that hybrid 'clicks and mortar' companies, with both a high street and an Internet presence, were more effective than 'pure play' e-commerce companies. Clicks and mortar companies often had an established brand reputation, and also could offer additional services, such as the ability to return goods bought online to a local store.

The next four case studies illustrate the application of Porter's generic strategies.

RYANAIR: A SUCCESSFUL FOCUSED COST LEADER

In 1991, Ryanair was a small, unsuccessful Irish airline, when its newly appointed CEO, Michael O'Leary, went to America to meet Herbert Kelleher, Southwest Airlines' founder. The low-cost carrier had transformed the economics of air travel in the US. From Kelleher, O'Leary learned the importance of cost control, through the use of one type of plane, point-to-point flights only, and elimination of all frills (*Business Week* 2006).

Since then, Ryanair has pushed the Southwest business model even further, and has become the biggest and most profitable low-cost airline in Europe. Its success is based on three pillars: cut costs to the minimum ('nail down costs'), 'give nothing, sell everything', and efficiency.

Cost cutting

- Ryanair flies only one type of plane – the Boeing 737-800. This enables economies of scale in pilot training and maintenance.

- Ryanair's seat density on the 737 is 189, 15 per cent greater than other airlines.

- Ryanair places its orders for aircraft in a counter-cyclical fashion, taking advantage of weak demand to wring better prices out of Boeing. For example, it placed a very big order in the immediate aftermath of 9/11. In 2007, it was rumoured by the *Financial Times* to be selling some of its planes second-hand for more than it had paid for them (Done 2007).

- The company's planes are stripped of all non-essentials – seats do not recline, there are no window blinds, and no seat-back pockets. This shaves several hundred thousand dollars off the cost of each plane.

- Like other low-cost airlines, Ryanair does not use travel agents, thus saving up to 15 per cent commission, but it has gone further than its rivals in promoting booking over the Internet, which minimises handling costs. By 2007, 98 per cent of bookings were made over the Internet.

- Ryanair does not use air bridges at airports – passengers must walk to the plane. This saves on airport charges.

- Ryanair is notorious for using secondary, but very cheap, airports. These are often some way from the city which they nominally serve. Copenhagen-Malmo is actually in Sweden, not Denmark, and Frankfurt-Hahn is 140 km from Frankfurt. As EasyJet repeatedly points out, this means that Ryanair's low fares are deceptive, as further transport costs are needed to reach the final destination. The secondary airports used are desperate for Ryanair's business, and are prepared to offer extremely good terms.

- Advertising on planes is widespread, as well as liveries, which attack other airlines.

- Extensive use is made of eastern European (particularly Polish) cabin crew.

- Aircrew are worked hard. Ryanair pilots fly 887 hours a year, close to the legal maximum of 900. EasyJet pilots fly 780 hours a year (Felsted 2003).

As a result of its rigorous cost-cutting programme, Ryanair's costs are two-thirds of those of EasyJet, 60 per cent of UK holiday charter airlines, and half those of full-service carriers (Thompson 2005).

Charges

- Ryanair is notorious for charging its staff for perks normally seen as free: crew must pay for their own uniforms, they must pay for water drunk on flights, and they are banned from recharging their mobiles on company power sockets.

- Like other low-cost airlines, passengers are charged for refreshments on flights.

- Ryanair was the first airline to introduce a charge for baggage. This has the effect of raising revenue, and also of cutting the number of bags carried, so lowering baggage handling costs by an estimated £20 million a year (*Air Transport World* 2006a). By 2009 the charge was £15 per bag per one-way flight.

- In September 2007 it introduced a charge for checking in at the airport, which could only be avoided by checking in online (Milmo 2007b). By 2009, it was also charging for checking in online. It also charges £5 per person per flight for payment using a credit or debit card.

- In 2002, Ryanair was heavily criticised when it refused to provide wheelchairs for disabled passengers at Stansted. A court ruling in 2004 judged that the responsibility for disabled passengers was shared between the airport and the airline. Ryanair's response was to place a 33p surcharge on all its ticket prices, which raised far more revenue for Ryanair than the costs which it claimed to cover (Starmer-Smith 2006).

In 2009, EasyJet made £511 million from baggage fees, insurance, early boarding and credit card fees – a fifth of its total revenue. Both the total and the proportion will be at least comparable for Ryanair (Milmo 2009).

Ryanair has made few friends. On the other hand, millions of travellers like its low fares. The airline is also unquestionably good at what it does.

Efficiency

As Ryanair gleefully points out on its website, the airline is extremely efficient. It claims:

- The best on-time record in Europe (91 per cent on time arrivals in 2003, compared with 83 per cent for British Airways and 82 per cent for EasyJet).

- The lowest level of cancellations.

- Fewest lost bags – 0.6 bags per 1,000 passengers in 2003, compared with BA's 14.2) (Ryanair 2003).

Results

Ryanair's model seems to be successful. In 2005, it had the fourth highest operating profit in Europe (behind BA, Air France-KLM and Lufthansa), and the 12th highest in the world, the 11th highest net profit in the world, and the 15th highest number of passengers carried (*Air Transport World* 2006b). In August 2005, for the first time it carried more passengers than the entire worldwide BA network (Ryanair 2007).

Conclusion

Ryanair seems to have got the focused cost leadership business model cracked. However, there are potential clouds on the horizon:

- In 2007, Ryanair operated 136 planes. However, it also had orders which would take its fleet size to 262 (Done 2007). Given Ryanair's flight pattern, it requires 250,000 passengers a year to operate a plane profitably. To fill all the planes on order, Ryanair would have to nearly double its present number of about 45 million passengers a year. Can the company's growth rate be maintained indefinitely?

- The full service carriers are fighting back. They have cut their fares, increased their online bookings, and heavily marketed their own selling features – meals, free drinks, seat allocations, more convenient airports, etc.

KWIK SAVE: A FAILED COST LEADER

Kwik Save was founded in Rhyl, North Wales in 1959, and floated on the Stock Exchange in 1970. At its peak in 1993, it had over 1,000 stores, made an annual profit of £135 million, was a member of the FTSE 100, and in volume terms was the third biggest food retailer in the UK, with a market share of over 10 per cent, more than Asda, and behind only Tesco and Sainsbury's.

Its success was due to its aggressive pursuit of a strategy of cost leadership. It aimed directly at the bottom of the market. Its stores were in secondary high-street sites, which were cheap to acquire. It sold only branded tinned and packaged goods, which were sold direct from cardboard boxes, so cutting costs to the bone. It stocked only 1,000 lines, exploiting the 80:20 rule. As it pointed out in 1993, 80 per cent of typical supermarket sales came from only 20 per cent of its lines. Kwik Save stocked only these fast-moving lines, ignoring the rest (Tempus 1993). As a result, its prices were more than 10 per cent lower than those of the major supermarkets (Gilchrist 1993a). In value-added terms, Kwik Save was the most successful retailer in the UK, with a value-added return of 25 per cent, compared with 10 per cent at Sainsbury's (Lord 1990).

However, even at the peak of Kwik Save's success, small clouds were appearing on the horizon. In the early 1990s, the Danish discount retailer Netto entered the UK market, followed by the German companies Aldi and Lidl. All three had long experience in cut-throat European markets, and had deeper pockets than Kwik Save. By 1993, Netto had a 2.5 per cent price advantage over Kwik Save, and Kwik Save was warning that a price war would hit its profits (Gilchrist 1993b).

The response of Kwik Save was twofold. It cut its prices further, and introduced a No Frills own brand, selling at or below cost.

Simultaneously, it tried to move upmarket by stocking fresh and chilled food. However, both proved to be mistakes. The low-price message was diluted; the price cuts provoked Tesco into retaliation; while Kwik Save found that although fresh and chilled food could be more profitable, they also required specialised retailing skills which Kwik Save did not possess (Sivell and Dolan 1995).

In 1994–95, profits were down from their peak, and like-for-like sales were down 2.5 per cent (Bagnall 1995). Kwik Save shoppers were voting with their wallets, and deserting the high street for the out-of-town superstore.

Kwik Save called in Andersen Consulting, whose solution was that Kwik Save should become more like Tesco – widen its range, and widen its margins. The advice was disastrous: Kwik Save shoppers had shopped at the chain because it was different from Tesco. If it became the same as Tesco, why not shop at Tesco? Kwik Save also accelerated its store-opening programme, spending money and lowering its return on capital. By 1996, Kwik Save's profits were still falling, Tesco had matched its 3p price for a tin of baked beans, and the continental retailers were taking 1.5 per cent of the market, soon expected to rise to 5 per cent (Stevenson 1996, Cope 1996).

In February 1998 Kwik Save merged with Somerfield in the hope that their greater combined size would enable them to overcome their trading problems. The merger was described with ironic understatement as 'not quite the deal of the century', while an analyst said, 'Both of them would have hit a brick wall at some stage. Now they will just hit a bigger one' (Hollinger 1998).

Although nominally a merger, it soon became clear that Somerfield held the whip hand. Plans were announced to rebrand all the Kwik Save stores as Somerfield.

This proved a disaster, and within 18 months some former Kwik Save stores were announcing falls in sales of up to 50 per cent (Cope 1999). The merger was described as 'one of the most disastrous in corporate history' (Finch 2000). Another U-turn saw the Kwik Save brand resurrected. A further blow came late in 1999, when Asda was taken over by Wal-mart. Asda was even more aggressive on price than Tesco, and now had the bottomless pockets of Wal-mart behind it.

Kwik Save–Somerfield sales continued to decline, and eventually in October 2005, the company was taken over by a private equity consortium headed by billionaire

Robert Tchenguiz (Finch 2005). The new owners quickly offloaded Kwik Save to another company, Back to the Future, in February 2006 (Rigby 2006). By the end of 2006, Kwik Save sales had collapsed to a market share of 0.2 per cent. By May 2007, the group was boycotted by its suppliers, by June it could not pay its staff, and in July it went into administration (Finch 2007).

What this case shows us is the very high risk associated with a cost leadership strategy. Caught in a vice between the continental discounters and Tesco and Asda, Kwik Save was slowly squeezed to death.

CASE STUDY 10.4

MARKS & SPENCER SIMPLY FOOD: A SUCCESSFUL FOCUSED DIFFERENTIATOR

In the late 1990s, Marks & Spencer's (M&S) inexorable growth seemed to hit the buffers. Its clothes ranges were tired and the company seemed to have run out of steam. However, this did not apply to its food ranges, which seemed to be exactly what the consumer wanted. Research showed that M&S was highly rated for the quality of its food, for offering more unusual items, for its high reputation and its ready meals. It scored low on value for money and on convenience (Hamson 2004).

M&S decided to capitalise on its food reputation, and in July 2001 opened the first Simply Food outlet in Surbiton, Surrey. The store was aimed at commuters, with a high footfall but low spend per customer, selling 4,000 food lines, plus newspapers and magazines. At 2,500 square feet, it qualified legally as a convenience store, and so was entitled to open extended hours on a Sunday (8am to 6pm) (Bruce 2001).

The format proved successful, and expansion was rapid. By the summer of 2003, 30 stores had opened, and there

were plans to develop a further 40 stores on railway stations in partnership with Compass (Bruce 2003). The first Simply Food store at a motorway service station followed in August 2003. The stores were also made more flexible. Some went above the 3,000 square feet convenience-store limit, while stores would now carry between 800 and 15,000 lines, depending on local demand (The Grocer 2003).

The stores which proved most successful were those which generated annual turnover in excess of £3 million, and were situated well away from other M&S stores (Watson 2004). At the railway stations, customers were in a hurry, and their spend was lower. The priority here was to have an adequate number of tills to cope with the high footfall. Motorway service station customers were prepared to spend longer in store, and also almost by definition had cars, so their average shop was higher (Hamson 2005).

Expansion accelerated in 2006, when M&S acquired 28 ex-Iceland stores. The stores were cherry-picked with great care, using a number of key success criteria (*The Grocer* 2006a):

- strong footfall from high-street shoppers
- high penetration of affluent shoppers
- strong comparable premium retailer offering
- proximity to public transport
- large local resident population
- Large work-based grocery expenditure.

A trial with BP on petrol station forecourts in late 2005 also proved successful (*The Grocer* 2006b).

Partly because of Simply Food, M&S has increased its share of UK food grocery sales to 4 per cent, with like-for-like sales in 2006 growing by up to 6 per cent (Durston 2006).

By November 2006, M&S was operating more than 200 Simply Food stores, with a further 100 planned for 2007, of which 60 would be on BP forecourts (*The Grocer* 2007).

Why has Simply Food been so successful?

- builds on M&S high reputation for food quality
- successfully extends the M&S brand
- avoids cannibalisation by developing new types of site, ie railway stations, motorway service stations, smaller towns, petrol station forecourts

- very careful site selection
- working with franchise partners (Compass and BP) lowers risk and level of investment, and also brings in outside expertise
- the goods on offer are carefully tailored to the type of outlet.

The result is that 50 per cent of Simply Food shoppers are in the 16–34 age band – a much younger demographic than for traditional M&S stores (Durston 2006).

By January 2009, Simply Food had 355 stores, but food sales across M&S were very poor over Christmas 2008, and the decision was taken to close 25 Simply Food outlets. The stores were seen as vulnerable in a time of recession, as they were priced very much at the premium end of the market (Leroux and Walsh 2009). In March, the investment company Credit Suisse went further, saying that M&S should close down or sell the whole of Simply Food (just-food 2009). However, the crisis soon passed. Although all the food retailers lost sales in the short term to the hard discounters Lidl and Aldi, this trend was short-lived, and growth at Simply Food was soon resumed. The chain moved into hospitals for the first time, with 20 stores planned (*Reading Post* 2009), and a move into Western Europe was also reported as being under consideration (O'Connor 2009).

NORTHERN ROCK: A FAILED FOCUSED DIFFERENTIATOR

CASE STUDY 10.5

Over a weekend in the middle of September 2007, the UK experienced the first serious run on a bank for a century. Hundreds of people queued for hours outside the branches of Northern Rock, desperate to withdraw their savings before the bank collapsed. How had a previously well-respected bank come to such a pass?

Northern Rock was a typical building society – taking in deposits from its members, and

lending these out as mortgages. It was safe, solid and respectable. It share of the national mortgage market was 2 per cent. It was also very popular in the north-east because it had been very sympathetic to miners with mortgage arrears during the mining strike of the early 1980s.

In 1997, it demutualised, forming Northern Rock plc, and its status changed from a building society to a bank. As a public company its priorities changed. Rather than providing a service for its members, its priority was now to make profits for its shareholders. Within months, it showed a new face when it was criticised by the Office of Fair Trading of being 'cavalier' for unilaterally changing the terms offered to its depositors (Hughes and Tighe 2007).

Unlike some of the other demutualised ex-building societies, Northern Rock did not attempt to develop general banking services, but continued to specialise in mortgages. However, it was faced with problems in expanding in this area. Firstly, it only had 79 branches, mainly concentrated in the relatively impoverished north-east. This limited its ability to raise funds from depositors (known as retail funds). By comparison, the leading building society, Nationwide, had over 700 branches, and the big high-street banks had thousands.

Northern Rock tackled this problem by raising funds through the inter-bank market, from other financial institutions (known as wholesale funds). As a building society, it would have been limited by law from raising more than 50 per cent of its funds from the wholesale market, but no such restrictions applied to banks (BBC2 2007). At its peak in the early autumn of 2007, Northern Rock raised more than three-quarters of its funds from the wholesale market, on terms ranging from overnight to three months.

Wholesale borrowing is generally regarded as more risky and volatile than retail borrowing. Although retail depositors can in theory withdraw many of their funds on demand, in practice they are highly unlikely to do so. On the other hand, other banks will move their money elsewhere if they think they can get a better return. Northern Rock's reliance on wholesale funds was described by one experienced banker as akin to overtaking a queue of traffic on the outside of a bend: 'Everyone knows it works (for a time), but only fools or the inexperienced would attempt it' (Croggon 2007).

Even when Northern Rock obtained more

funds, it still had to persuade people to take out more of its mortgages. It did this through aggressive lending policies. It became known as the bank which would lend even if you had a patchy credit record. It was also prepared to lend more than other banks or building societies. In 2002, it introduced its Together loan, which allowed a borrower to borrow up to 125 per cent of a property's valuation, or six times annual income. As other lenders were not prepared to lend more than four times income, borrowers flocked to Northern Rock.

Massive expansion continued throughout the first half of 2007, at a time when increasing warnings were being issued of the frothy state of the UK housing market, and of a worrying level of consumer debt. In the first half of 2007, Northern Rock took a 25 per cent share of the new mortgage market, making it the biggest mortgage provider (Collinson and Seager 2007).

With hindsight, it was clear that Northern Rock was over-trading and taking unacceptable risks. In June 2007 it was forced to issue a profits warning, and its shares started to fall. Its strategy was described by Professor Willem Buiter, one of the founder members of the Bank of England's Monetary Policy Committee, as 'an extremely aggressive and high-risk strategy' (Duncan and Webster 2007).

Northern Rock might still have got away with it had it not been caught up in the backlash from a separate but related financial crisis, the sub-prime crisis in the US. Here, US financial institutions had pursued a Northern Rock-style strategy of aggressive lending to poor credit risks (the sub-prime market), eventually leading to a collapse of the US housing market in the summer of 2007. One consequence of this was a freezing-up of the interbank lending market in the UK, as well as the US. This meant that Northern Rock, which continually needed to roll over its wholesale borrowing, faced a liquidity crisis.

The crisis for Northern Rock came to a head on 13 September 2007, when the bank applied to the Bank of England for emergency assistance (known as 'lender of last resort'). On 14 September the Bank of England agreed to lend virtually unlimited funds to Northern Rock, but at a penal rate of interest, believed to be 7 per cent.

This should have been the end of the crisis, but Northern Rock retail depositors interpreted this as a sign that the bank was about to fail, and a run on the bank's cash started and quickly accelerated. Bank deposits are guaranteed, but only up to a maximum of £35,000, and only up to 90 per cent. On the Friday and Saturday of that week, a sum estimated to be between £2 billion and £3 billion was withdrawn from Northern Rock branches. Eventually, to stop the run, the Chancellor, Alistair Darling, announced on 16 September that the government would guarantee all deposits in Northern Rock, without limit. The immediate crisis was over, but the troubles of Northern Rock then became part of the general financial crisis of 2008–10. Northern Rock was nationalised, and the deposit guarantee was raised to 100 per cent of £50,000.

This case illustrates several important points. One is that Northern Rock's strategy differentiated it from the rest of the mortgage industry, but only at the price of unacceptably high risk. Secondly, the case demonstrates the nature of moral hazard. The Bank of England was reluctant to intervene at an earlier stage in the crisis because of the risk of moral hazard – that in effect a rescue would reward Northern Rock for its reckless behaviour, and might encourage other institutions to be reckless in the future. Eventually, the Bank of England had no choice, and was forced to intervene to safeguard the stability of the whole banking system, as there was a risk that the panic might spread to other institutions. The bail-out safeguarded not only Northern Rock's depositors, who were innocent victims, but also the bank's management and shareholders, who should have known better (Davies 2007).

Porter's generic strategy concept has been further developed by Bowman and Faulkner (1996), who proposed the strategy clock, based on a combination of price and perceived added value. Eight possible strategies were identified:

- Low price/low added value – not likely to be feasible in the long term unless the organisation operates in a protected niche.
- Low price/standard added value – equates to Porter's cost leadership.
- Low price/high added value (hybrid) – the strategy pursued by Japanese companies in the 1970s and 1980s, when they were gaining a foothold in European markets.
- Standard price/high added value (differentiation) – this would be a sensible strategy as a progression from the hybrid strategy.
- High price/high added value (focused differentiation) – likely to be a niche strategy, similar to Porter's differentiation focus.
- High price/standard added value – not a long-term viable strategy; why should customers pay more if they are not gaining added value?
- High price/low added value – only feasible for a monopoly in a market which is not contestable.

- Standard price/low added value – not viable in the long term; what is in it for the customer?

SELECTION OF STRATEGIES

This is concerned not with what strategies should be chosen, but how they should be chosen. Johnson and Scholes propose four models:

Formal evaluation

Here the choice is based solely on analytical techniques. The decision process is impersonal and rational, and appears to be objective. This avoids the risk of taking decisions solely on gut feeling, but it should be remembered that a lot of the analytical techniques are themselves in practice subjective.

Enforced choice

Here choice is imposed on the organisation from outside. This may be because of the dominant influence of an external stakeholder; for example, a supplier to Marks & Spencer has very little control over its own strategy. However, in the long term, even a firm in this situation does have some strategic choice – to widen its customer base, for example.

Learning from experience

The emphasis here is on incremental change on a pilot basis with operating units, and then the application of the experience learned from this throughout the organisation. This method is increasingly used by government, which trials new policy initiatives through a pilot study before going for a national launch, and by many manufacturers, who test-market new products before attempting a national launch. It is similar to Quinn's concept of logical incrementalism, which we discussed earlier. The advantage is that it pushes responsibility for strategic development down the organisation, but there is the possible disadvantage that there is never a fundamental strategic rethink – the organisation can suffer from strategic drift.

Command

Here the dominant stakeholder (who may be the CEO, the biggest shareholder or a government department) selects the strategic direction, and imposes it on the organisation. This has been the experience of the National Health Service, which has had fundamental strategic change imposed on it by successive governments at regular intervals.

EVALUATION OF STRATEGIES

Possible strategies should be evaluated on three levels: suitability, acceptability and feasibility.

Suitability

Is this a strategy which will produce a sound fit between the organisation and its environment?

- Will it exploit opportunities in the environment and avoid or neutralise threats?
- Will it capitalise on the organisation's strengths and core competencies and avoid or neutralise weaknesses?

Various analytical techniques can be used to help answer these questions.

Life cycle analysis

The consultants Arthur D Little have identified the life cycle/portfolio matrix (see Johnson and Scholes). Here the strategies to be adopted depend on the stage of the product/industry life cycle (embryonic, growing, mature or ageing), and the competitive position of the organisation (dominant, strong, favourable, tenable or weak). For example, the prescribed strategies for a strong firm in a growing industry are: fast grow, catch-up, attain cost leadership or differentiation, while for a weak firm in an embryonic industry they are: find niche, catch-up or grow with industry. The model is open to criticism, as the definitions used are subjective (what is a favourable position in one environment may be a weak one in another), and because, like all models, it ignores all variables except those actually built into the model (stage of maturity and competitive position). For example, it ignores speed of technological development.

Portfolio analysis

We discussed the Boston Matrix in Chapter 3. Briefly, this categorises product lines on a matrix of market share and market growth rate, as:

Cash cows:	Low market growth, high market share
Stars:	High market growth, high market share
Question marks:	High market growth, low market share
Dogs:	Low market growth, low market share

Here the preferred strategic options would be to attempt to balance to the portfolio between stars and cash cows. Stars are profitable, but they do not generate much cash, while cash cows may be less profitable but are highly cash-generative. Hence cash cows can be used to finance stars. As with the life cycle model, this is superficially attractive, but again it ignores other variables.

Value chain analysis

Value chain analysis is yet another model developed by Michael Porter. He says that the activities of an organisation should be seen as a sequence of primary events:

- inbound logistics, deliveries, storage, etc

- operations
- outbound logistics (warehousing, wholesalers, deliveries, etc)
- marketing and sales
- service.

Underpinning all of these were support activities:

- the firm's infrastructure
- HR management
- technology
- procurement (purchasing, raising capital, recruitment).

All of these serve to add value for the organisation and form the value chain. The greater the synergies between the various elements, the greater the added value. Conversely, the whole value chain is only as strong as its weakest link. The aim of strategy should therefore be to strengthen the value chain as a whole, by building on existing strengths, or correcting weaknesses.

For example, the primary part of the chain might be strong, but the organisation may have problems caused by high turnover of staff. The strategic choice here would be to concentrate on improving staff turnover using HR techniques. Alternatively, the product might be strong, but its reputation is let down by poor after-sales service. After digging deeper, it might be discovered that the IT systems supporting service are inadequate.

The strength of the value chain technique is that it forces an analysis of how the organisation actually functions, and it avoids over-concentration on some of the more obvious strategic possibilities like merger or takeover. The weakness is that it is exclusively inward-looking. It should be combined with a rigorous analysis of fit with the environment.

Acceptability

Strategies have to be acceptable to internal and external stakeholders. This can be assessed in three ways: return, risk and stakeholder reaction.

Return can be assessed using a range of standard accounting techniques, including profitability analysis (discounted cash flow, etc), shareholder value analysis (looking at the overall increase in value for the shareholder, using techniques such as economic value added), or cost–benefit analysis (looking at non-financial as well as financial factors).

Risk can be assessed using techniques including:

- Break-even analysis – if the break-even point for the new strategy is a very high percentage of capacity, the project is highly risky.
- Ratio analysis – if the new strategy will result in very low levels of liquidity, as measured by standard ratios, it is high risk.

- Sensitivity analysis – how sensitive is the profit of the project to a shortfall in any of the key financial variables?

Stakeholder reactions can be assessed using techniques such as stakeholder modelling (discussed in Chapter 1). Stakeholders may well have strong views on risk, and these should be taken into account.

STAKEHOLDER ACCEPTABILITY

CASE STUDY 10.6

An acceptable strategy – Ben & Jerry's and Unilever

Ben & Jerry's ice cream was one of the leading lights of the ethical business movement. It was not only concerned to trade ethically, it also wanted to change the world. It donated heavily to radical causes, and was deeply involved in the anti-globalisation movement. These values were fully supported by its staff and customers, both key stakeholders.

In April 2000, Ben & Jerry's was taken over by the strait-laced Anglo-Dutch conglomerate Unilever, a classic representative of the globalisation that Ben & Jerry's had opposed. Although it had a good ethical reputation, Unilever was in no sense radical. Ben Cohen, the joint founder of Ben & Jerry's, forecast that the takeover would lead to the destruction of the company.

However, when Unilever appointed a 25-year Unilever man, Yves Couette, to run Ben & Jerry's, he was given the licence to be a 'grain of sand in the eye' of Unilever. He abandoned his suit and tie, and followed a deliberate policy of empowerment and delegation. Tough profit targets were set, but Couette pointed out to staff that this would mean that more money would be donated to charity through the Ben & Jerry's Foundation, which would continue to have a free hand to support any charity or movement which it chose.

An unacceptable strategy – Marconi

Throughout the 1980s and 1990s, GEC was seen as a safe, rather stolid company, dominated by the safety-first philosophy of its long-time chairman, Arnold (Lord) Weinstock. The company prospered in household electrical goods and defence electronics, and built up a bank balance of several billion pounds. It appealed to risk-averse shareholders.

In the late 1990s, new management, headed by George Simpson, decided on a radical new strategy. The defence electronics business was sold to British Aerospace, most of the domestic electric businesses (Hotpoint, etc) were sold, and the company, now renamed Marconi, began a dash for growth in the exciting new world of Internet electronics. The rationale was that Marconi would benefit from the dot-com boom which was raging at the time.

Unfortunately, the purchases were made right at the peak of the dot-com bubble, and when the bubble burst, many of the new acquisitions were effectively worthless. Marconi's share price plummeted, and when the company eventually went through a financial restructuring, shareholders effectively lost all their money.

Like all shareholders, the Marconi shareholders should have realised that any share investment is by its very nature risky, but they could legitimately argue that they had originally bought their shares in GEC precisely because it was seen as a low-risk company.

Feasibility

Strategies have to be feasible in terms of resource availability. Techniques to measure this include:

- Funds flow analysis – what is the implication for future cash flows? If sufficient cash is not currently available, can it be acquired on reasonable terms?

- Break even analysis – what is the break-even point given the present cost structure? If the break-even point is too high, can the cost structure be improved?

- Resource deployment analysis – what are the key resources and competencies required for each strategy, and does the organisation already possess them? If not, can it reasonably acquire them?

STRATEGIC OPTION SCREENING

Several methods can be used to screen options to see whether they meet criteria on suitability, acceptability and feasibility. These include:

Ranking

Here options are assessed against key factors in the environment, resources and stakeholder expectations, and a score (or ranking) established for each option. To take a very simple example, assume that a company has two strategic options, A and B, and two success criteria, profitability and stakeholder acceptability. It has established that it regards profitability as more important, and has given this a weighting of 70. Stakeholder acceptability has a weighting of 30 (producing a total weighting of 100).

Strategy A scores 50 out of 70 for profitability, but only 10 out of 30 for stakeholder acceptability. Strategy B scores less well on profitability, scoring 30 out of 70, but it scores 20 out of 30 for stakeholder acceptability.

This gives a total score for strategy A of 60/100 (50 + 10), and a total score for strategy B of 50/100 (30 + 20). Strategy A is thus the preferred option.

Decision trees

Here options are progressively eliminated by testing them against various criteria. For example, a company has two decision criteria: high growth (most important) and low cost (less important). It is considering four strategies:

Strategy W	high growth, high cost
Strategy X	high growth, low cost
Strategy Y	low growth, low cost
Strategy Z	low growth, high cost

The first decision step would eliminate strategies Y and Z, because they are low growth, leaving W and X. The next decision step would eliminate W, leaving X as the preferred strategy.

Scenario planning

Here the options are evaluated against various scenarios for the future. For example, if the organisation thinks that the most likely future for UK exchange rate is stability, this would favour a policy of manufacturing in the UK. If the most likely scenario is seen as a rising pound, this would favour manufacturing overseas.

ACTIVITY 10.3 STRATEGIC EVALUATION

A risk-averse firm with a strong current financial position, but little access to long-term capital, has decided that it must adopt a policy of unrelated diversification, in order to reduce its dependence on a declining industry. It has evaluated a number of areas for diversification, and decided on the appropriate industry to enter. It is now considering the best way to enter the new market.

Its options are:

A   Develop and manufacture a new product

B   Manufacture an existing product under licence

C   Set up a joint venture with a firm that already has expertise in this field

D   Buy out a firm already in the industry

E   Market under its brand name an existing

Taiwanese product not currently imported into the UK

It has established the following criteria, and weighted them as follows:

	Weighting
(a) Low risk	40
(b) Speedy entry into the market	20
(c) Low capital cost	20
(d) Profitability	15
(e) Short payback period	5

Questions:

1. Discuss the advantages and disadvantages of each method of entry.

2. Using your own judgement, assign scores to each strategy and rank them.

HR, STRATEGY AND PERFORMANCE

CAN HR INFLUENCE EVENTS?

Although there may be considerable doubt concerning the actual role HR should perform and how it should be done, HR professionals established a place at the senior management table by the early 1990s through their ability to identify and solve practical problems in fields such as recruitment, employee relations and training. HR professionals and researchers then turned their attention to interpreting and reinforcing the maxim that 'people make the difference'.

Researchers have attempted to identify whether adopting HR practices can make an observable difference in practice to organisational performance in measurable terms. If it can be proven that the adoption of HR systems, policies and procedures makes a difference, then this will reinforce the claim that HR has to a seat on the top table and a co-responsibility for strategic initiatives. This has often been referred to as 'opening the black box'.

In attempting to examine the impact of HR practices on organisational performance, a number of researchers have discovered some impressive and direct impacts and influences. This is referred to by Ramsey et al (2000) as the 'high road' approach to management, in which organisations choose to compete primarily on quality and rely especially on HR development and employee contributions to succeed in this.

Much of this research has been carried out in America, with the best-known being Mark Huselid (1995). He carried out in-depth surveys in top companies, matching the nature of the HR practices against performance measures, such as growth, productivity and profits. Using market value as the key indicator, he found that organisations with significantly above-average scores on using HR practices provided an extra market value per employee of between US \$10,000 to \$40,000. He also found that the introduction of such practices led to an immediate impact (Guest 1998).

In the UK, a CIPD-financed project by the University of Sheffield's Institute of Work Psychology (West and Patterson 1998) concluded that HR practices are not only critical to business performance but also have a greater importance than an emphasis on quality, technology and research and development in terms of influence on bottom-line profits. For example, effective HR practices were found to account for 19 per cent of the variation in profitability and 18 per cent in productivity, while research and development accounted for only 8 per cent. This led them to conclude that the most important area managers should emphasise is the management of people.

Some of these findings have arisen from broad surveys across sectors and others from selected industries. Thompson (2000), for example, investigated 400 UK aerospace companies and concluded that high-performing organisations, as measured by value added per employee, tend to use a wider range of innovative HR practices covering a higher proportion of employees. The greatest differentials between higher- and lower-performing organisations (as measured by value added per employee) was in the use of two-way communication systems, broader job gradings and employees being responsible for their own quality.

A more detailed survey of such studies can be found in Marchington and Wilkinson (2008).

THE ROLE OF HR IN RAISING PERFORMANCE

It appears evident from research detailed above that HR can make a sizeable contribution towards raising organisational performance. There are two major viewpoints as to how this can be done:

- Firstly, a number of projects have been set up to examine what makes up a truly exceptional collection of HR practices, often called 'bundles', that raises performance in the organisation.

- Secondly, there has been a considerable debate, one that is still very much alive, as to whether such a collection of practices (called 'best practices') will work in every situation, or whether the context and nature of the organisation puts different demands upon the practices to be operated (called 'best fit').

A third model is the resource-based model, which has close links to the core competence model discussed above.

BEST-PRACTICE APPROACH — BUNDLES OF HR PRACTICES

At the same time that researchers were attempting to prove conclusively that successful and effective HR practices improved the bottom-line performance, it became clear that a differentiation needed to be made between such practices: in effect, that some worked better than others and, more critically, that although individual practices may be relatively unsuccessful, when brought together in a bundle their combined outcome was much greater than their individual contribution. A number of writers have formulated these bundles into what they call a system of 'high performance' or 'high commitment', indicating that using the full set will inevitably lead to improved organisational improvement. It is emphasised by all the researchers that these bundles have to be coherent and integrated to have their full effect.

The level of commitment shown by employees is seen as key to high performance. Without such a commitment, employees will not be prepared to develop their skills and competencies, take on board the enhanced responsibilities for quality, work organisation and problem-solving and 'go the extra mile' to come up with improvements and innovations or improve the customer's experience. That is why a number of researchers use the level of commitment as a key reflection of organisational success from a people-management viewpoint.

For Purcell et al (2003), a committed employee will use discretionary behaviour in that the employee can give co-operation, effort and initiative because they want to, arising out of the fact that they like their job and feel motivated by the systems in place, especially the HR ones.

Researchers have found that a high level of commitment comes about from the implementation of the following HR practices:

Employee involvement

The thinking here is that it is impossible to gain the employees' trust if they do not both have the essential business information available to management and that they have at least the opportunity to be consulted on important issues that may affect their jobs and the way they are carried out. This passes the message that employees are treated as mature, intelligent beings, not just 'hands' or 'labour' who leave their brains in their lockers. The process of involvement can include briefing groups, staff surveys, focus groups or more sophisticated systems such as quality circles or recognition schemes. It can also extend to financial involvement through employee share-ownership. Marchington (2001) points out from his research that these practices are very popular with employees (80–85 per cent of employees involved in such practices want them to continue), although he adds the disillusioning caveat that some employees enjoy working with them because it is 'better than working' or 'gives me a half hour off work'.

Employee voice

Millward et al (2000), by using the data from the 1998 Workplace Employee Relations Survey (WERS), have shown the close association between positive responses in attitude surveys and direct voice arrangement. A 'voice' for the employees does not have to be through a formal trade union, and it is certainly not just ensuring there is a formal grievance procedure. The importance of this practice is that the employer recognises the importance of employee group viewpoints and suggestions and that the employee does not feel isolated so important issues can be raised in a formal (or informal) setting without the employee themselves having, in effect, to raise their heads above the parapet.

There has been a greater emphasis in recent years on the concept of employee engagement, which combines the better features of involvement and employee voice (see the seminar activity below).

Harmonisation of terms and conditions

'Everybody works for the same team' is a common form of encouragement from senior management but falls on deaf ears if there is a clear manifestation of differing benefits at varying levels in the organisation. When Japanese companies began setting up satellite operations in the UK in the late 1970s and early 1980s, one of the surprises to commentators was the degree of egalitarian symbols on display.

In Nissan in Sunderland, for example, there was one canteen serving everybody and it was frequented by all staff including senior management; everybody was on the same level of holiday entitlement and wore the same overalls. Employees respected the equality and it fed the belief in the 'one company' ethos leading in turn to effective teamworking at all levels (Wickens 1987).

Employment security

The 'jobs for life' culture evident some 30 to 40 years ago no longer exists. Rather, it never really existed in the first place, except in pockets of the public services, such as prisons and the post office. Employees may have had a clear, well-trodden career pathway set out, but the precise directions, both geographically and occupationally, may have worked out very differently from expectations and preferences. In the last 20 years, the global and business environmental changes have caused such changes in employment that the pathway has disintegrated.

So how can any business promise employment security? The theorists indicate that the security is of a different dimension. There may be short-term guarantees of employment, such as 12 months or of the life of a large-scale contract or, more usually, it is the cultural imperative of the organisation that redundancies will only take place as a very last resort. Internal transfers, skills retraining and short-time working are all alternatives to try to extend the employee's contract as long as possible to get over difficult times. It is, in effect, the opposite of the tough employer's 'high and fire' short-term employment policy. It keeps to the HRM thinking that the employee is a critical asset, not a cost to be reduced.

Alongside these practices to encourage commitment, there are a group of practices that integrate with the organisation's business strategy:

Sophisticated recruitment and selection

Sophistication is essentially the combination of recognising the importance of bringing into the organisation the right people with the right skills and personality (having a strategic approach to HR planning) and carrying out careful and detailed recruitment and selection procedures. These procedures especially refer to using psychological tests and structured interviews that match people effectively to the organisational culture, to the job and the team requirements.

Extensive training and development

It is clearly not enough to select the right people. In a swiftly changing world, employees need to constantly learn new jobs, which involves developing their skills and knowledge. They must also be prepared for enlargement of their jobs and to be ready for promotion opportunities. The emphasis switches in a subtle way from the organisation providing training courses to the organisation encouraging employees (individually or in groups) to undertake learning experiences, which can take many forms. The 'ideal' form of this item in the bundle is of employees undertaking self-directed lifelong learning within the framework of a 'learning organisation'.

Self-managed teams

The practice of allowing teams to have greater control over their work is a relatively recent one, although theorists, such as Mayo in the 1930s, have been advocating it throughout the twentieth century. It is linked closely to involvement and, in a fully fledged system, team members are involved in decisions concerning work rotas, breaks, changes in production processes, leave and sickness arrangements. Moreover, they are encouraged to think about and promote local improvements on an individual and team basis. It involves reducing the power and day-to-day authority of local management,

same time, retains their accountability. The research has shown that,
...rks well, it is closely associated with high productivity and overall
...e.

...systems of flexibility

If constant and rapid change is the norm, then successful organisations need a
workforce that is flexible enough to respond quickly to the required changes.
They need to be multiskilled, willing to work hours that suit the customer and
to switch jobs and locations when necessary. The organisation also needs to have
in place facilities to increase and reduce the employee numbers when required
through systems of annualised hours or use of temporary and short-term
contracts, or by outsourcing work.

Performance pay

The emphasis on high-performance outcomes inevitably has meant that pay
systems are geared to reflect the level of performance. Employees' pay at all levels
is contingent; in other words, it has an element that varies depending on the
success of the outcomes. Examples of these systems can include bonus schemes
for production employees and call-centre staff, incentive systems for sales
and service staff and executive bonuses for directors. Commitment should be
encouraged by aligning the pay of employees with organisational performance.

Given that a bundle of HR practices leads to improved performance, then it
follows that using this bundle is the best thing to do. In theory, it becomes a set of
'best practices' which can be universally applied.

BEST-FIT APPROACH

When reading the previous section it would have been easy to conclude that
there does not appear to be much consensus as to which HR practices make up
the full set. Each item of research comes up with a different set of best practices,
some of which overlap with other research, but each has a special leaning. In
America, Bosalie and Dietz (2003) have reviewed 10 years of research in this area
and have found little that recommends a common approach, with the practices
reported more extensively being training and development, participation and
empowerment, performance pay and information sharing through involvement.

Because the extensive research reveals such a varied set of bundles, considerable
doubt has been shed on whether the application of the set of bundles or best
practices will lead inevitably to improved performance. Many writers, therefore,
have taken an alternative view that there is no 'holy grail' of practices which
will magically improve organisational performance. What works well in one
organisation may fail dismally in another where the context may be totally
different. In a private sector organisation (a manufacturing company, for
example), you may well expect performance pay to be widespread and to form
the bulwark of performance management and motivation systems; however, in
the voluntary sector (a hospice charity, for example), it is highly unlikely that any

of the staff would work under a performance pay scheme. The context, the vision, the values – they are so different.

Huselid himself comes down firmly on the side of a range of possible bundles, based on the reasoning that sustained competitive advantage depends partly on being able to develop arrangements that are hard to imitate (the resource-based concept). If the 'holy grail' was quite distinctive, then every organisation would immediately adopt it and the competitive advantage would be lost.

Thompson (2000, p19), similarly, is reticent in recommending wholesale adoption of the innovative HR practices associated with high-performing aerospace companies: 'That is probably too simplistic a message.' Marchington and Grugulis (2000, p1121) adopt the same viewpoint: 'Best practice, it seems, is problematic … there are times when they appear to be contradictory messages.'

How do you know which HR practices an organisation should adopt? Only by a combination of knowing and understanding the true nature and strengths of the organisation, so you can eliminate those practices that have little chance of success, and then by experiment.

In the knowledge-intensive firms, the best fit of practices have been found to be the kind that develops intellectual and social capital needed in order to acquire business– and manager–customer relationships. Here, the crucial aspect is the development of knowledge-sharing processes, not just the knowledge and skills of the workforce (Swart et al 2003).

Purcell's (1999) distinct preference for 'best fit' (although not uncritical acceptance) has led him to urge a much greater emphasis on sharing employee knowledge throughout the organisation. If organisations have unique circumstances that require unique sets of HRM practices, then it is vital that the knowledge and understanding of both circumstances and practices are held in common by all employees. With Peter Boxall, he argued that best-practice HR is much more likely where the production system is capital-intensive or high-tech. Firms characterised by intense, cost-based competition, such as supermarkets, typically adopt a low-skill model of HR (Boxall and Purcell 2008). An example of a highly successful company whose HR practices could not be further from the best practice model is Ryanair, which was extensively discussed earlier in this chapter.

Although there appears to be extensive evidence of HR practices adding to organisational improvement, there are a number of critics who doubt the close association. The greatest is Legge (2001) whose scepticism has been consistent and vociferous for many years. She points out the vagueness of definition 'best practice' and the appropriateness of the measures used for organisational success. She also doubts whether the use of the practices actually influences the performance (the lack of causality).

There have also been studies that demonstrate that HRM practices can lead to a deterioration in working life. Danford et al (2004) researched the high-performance HR practices introduced in an aerospace company but found some major negative impacts on the employees, such as substantial downsizing, a superficial implementation of empowerment and a lack of trust between the parties.

STRATEGIC IMPLEMENTATION

The final stage in the strategy process is implementation – having decided on the chosen strategy, how is it put into practice? Frequently this will be the most difficult phase of the whole process. It involves a key competency of all managers: the ability to manage change.

INCREMENTAL AND TRANSFORMATIONAL CHANGE

Most of the writers on strategic implementation distinguish between incremental and transformational change, although their terminology varies. Johnson et al (2004) see strategic change on a two-by-two matrix: type of change and extent of change. A small change is incremental, a large change transformational. Each is of two types, dependent on whether the change is proactive or reactive. Proactive incremental change is tuning; reactive incremental change adaptation; while transformational change is divided into planned and forced change.

Walton (1999) defines transformational change as change which results in entirely new behaviour on the part of organisational members. He sees transformational change as in its very nature strategic. However, drawing on the work of Quinn on logical incrementalism, he sees incremental change as a possible route to strategic change. He also identifies transitional change, the process of carrying out change.

Porter (1999) concentrates on the outcome rather than the process. Changes such as the introduction of re-engineering or Total Quality Management are transformational, but they are not strategic. He sees them as improving operational effectiveness rather than changing the strategic position of the organisation. They are about doing better the same things as the competition are doing. Operational effectiveness is about running the same race faster; strategy is about running a different race.

MODELS OF CHANGE

The classic model of change was identified by Lewin in the 1950s and developed by Schein in the 1980s (Armstrong 1999, Walton 1999). They identified three stages in change management:

- Unfreezing – creating a readiness for change, through creation of a sense of anxiety about the present situation. The sequence here is to enable those involved to be convinced of the need for change.

- Movement – taking action that will encourage the desired new behaviour patterns. This involves doing things differently, based on access to new information, and identifying with new role models.

- Refreezing – embedding the new ways of working into the organisation.

Lewin (1943) also developed the concept of force field analysis – analysing the restraining and driving forces within the organisation which oppose or support the proposed change, and then taking steps to encourage the driving forces and decrease the restraining forces.

Beer (CIPD, 2004) took a different approach. He argued that the approach which tries to change attitudes in order to change behaviour is flawed. He argued that change should be approached in an opposite way – put people in new roles which require new behaviours, and this will change their attitudes. This is similar to the theory of cognitive dissonance which we discussed in the previous chapter in relation to ethics. Beer proposed a six-stage model of change:

- mobilise commitment to change through joint analysis of problems
- develop a shared vision
- foster consensus and commitment to the shared vision
- spread the word about the change
- institutionalise the change through formal policies
- monitor and adjust as needed.

The Lewin and Beer models both come out of relatively placid environments. They have been criticised for their assumption that it is possible to plan an orderly transition from one static state to another static state (Burnes 1996). In a more dynamic and chaotic environment like that experienced at present, a more continuous and open-ended change process is more appropriate. They also assume that a 'one size fits all' model of change is appropriate, whereas a more modern perspective would be to take a contingency approach and to argue that each organisation has a unique relationship with its environment. Its approach to change should reflect this.

The emergent approach to change as put forward by Beer and Shaw (CIPD 2004) stresses that change is not linear – it is not a movement from state A to state B: it is continuous and messy. Just like its environment, an organisation is in a continuous state of flux, and the forces for change emerge as the organisation engages with its environment. Change in this model is bottom-up rather than top-down, and it emerges through experimentation. What is important is to ensure that the organisation is responsive to change, and the best way of doing this is to ensure that the organisation is a learning organisation.

McCann (2004) relates change directly to the changing nature of the environment. In a placid environment, change is likely to be episodic, ie low-level and easily managed. Here the objective is to control change. Organisations cope with this by building some slack into their systems, which can act as a buffer in periods of change. As the environment grew more turbulent, change became continuous. Here the objective is to embrace change, by building agility into the organisation and removing barriers to change. Finally, in a very turbulent environment, shocks such as 9/11, the credit crunch or the swine flu pandemic will lead to disruptive change. To cope with this the organisation must prepare for change, by planning for contingencies and assuring a capacity for recovery and renewal.

OPEN SYSTEMS

The open systems school is primarily interested in seeing organisations in their entirety, and therefore takes a holistic view rather than a particular perspective. This is reflected in its approach to change. Burke (1980) suggested this is informed by three factors:

- Sub-systems are interdependent. Therefore account must be taken of the dependence of other parts of the organisation.

- Training, as a mechanism for change, is unlikely to succeed on its own. This is because it concentrates on the individual and not on the organisational level. Burke argues that 'there is scant evidence that attempting to change the individual will in turn change the organisation' (p27).

- For success, organisations need to tap into and direct the energy and talent of their workforce. This involves the removal of barriers and the promotion of positive reinforcement. Given that change is likely to require altering such things as norms, reward systems and work structures, the approach must therefore be at an organisational level, rather than an individual or group perspective.

Open systems approaches have attracted much research and interest but some shortcomings have been identified. Butler (1985) argued that social systems are so complex that sorting out all the cause-and-effect relationships may be impossible, while Beach (1980) argued that open systems theory runs the risk of being abstract rather than operationally useful.

MANAGING CHANGE

Kotter (1995) proposes an eight-step plan for transformation

- Establishing a sense of urgency – realising that change is needed.
- Forming a powerful guiding coalition – a powerful and influential group of change leaders is needed.
- Creating a vision – what will things be like after the change is achieved?
- Communicating the vision.
- Empowering others to act on the vision.
- Planning for and creating short-term wins – a long change process that appears to be getting nowhere can be demotivating. Building in some short-term wins can improve morale.
- Consolidating improvements and producing still more change.
- Institutionalising new approaches – similar to Lewin's refreezing process.

Bridges and Mitchell (2000) identify three stages in a change programme:

- Saying goodbye – letting go of the way that things used to be.
- Shifting into neutral – the in-between stage when nothing seems to be

happening, but everyone is in a stressful state of limbo. In the case of a major merger, this phase might take two years.

- Moving forward – when people have to behave in a new way.

They describe seven steps in managing transition:

- Describe the change and why it must happen – in one minute or less.

- Make sure that the details of the change are planned carefully and that someone is responsible for each detail.

- Understand who is going to have to let go of what.

- Make sure that people are helped to let go of the past.

- Help people through the neutral zone with communication, stressing the '4 Ps':
  - the purpose – why we have to do this
  - the picture – what it will look and feel like when we get there
  - the plan – how we will get there
  - the part – what each person needs to do.

- Create temporary solutions to the temporary problems found in the neutral zone.

- Help people launch the new beginning.

 MOSES IN THE WILDERNESS

CASE STUDY 10.7

Bridges and Mitchell (2000), discuss the change management techniques used by Moses on his way to the Promised Land.

- *Magnify the plagues.* Moses had to convince a key stakeholder (Pharaoh) that change was needed: that he had to let the Jews go. He did this through creating problems for Pharaoh – the seven plagues. The worse the current situation seems, the greater the impetus for change.

- *Mark the ending.* After the Jews crossed the Red Sea, there was (literally) no going back.

- *Deal with the 'murmuring'.* Don't be surprised when people lose confidence in the neutral zone. Moses faced lots of whingeing. He dealt with it by talking to people about their concerns.

- *Build up change champions.* Moses and his lieutenant Joshua appointed a new cadre of judges to champion the change.

- *Capitalise on creative opportunities.* It was in the wilderness, not in the Promised Land, that the Ten Commandments were handed down.

- *Resist the urge to rush ahead.* Not much seems to be happening in the neutral zone, but it is where the true transformation takes place. Moses was in the wilderness for 40 years!

- *Different stages need different leadership styles.* Moses was an ideal leader for the neutral zone, but the Promised Land required a new type of leadership, provided by the conqueror of Jericho, Joshua.

RESISTANCE TO CHANGE

Pugh (1978) sees organisational change as a paradox. Situations and problems which cry out most strongly for change are the very ones which resist change most stubbornly. Individuals perceive change as a threat and react like rabbits caught in the headlights of a car – they go rigid.

Resistance to change can be better understood if you view organisations as a coalition of interest groups in tension. The organisation is a particular balance of forces which has been hammered out over time. Any change which threatens the current balance will encounter resistance. Combine this with psychological resistance from rigid people under threat, and it is easy to see how managing change is difficult. Organisations are ultra-stable – they run like mad to stay in the same place.

As a consequence, real organisational change often:

- comes about much too late
- is a response to a threat posed by situations of considerable failure
- is with insufficient thought and little consideration of alternatives
- is in order to live to fight another day.

At a more immediate level, change is most likely to be accepted by individuals or departments who are basically successful in their tasks but who are currently experiencing difficulties. They will have the two basic ingredients of confidence in their ability and motivation to change. The next most likely to change are the successful; they will have the confidence but might not have the motivation. The least likely to understand and accept change are the unsuccessful.

An effective manager:

- anticipates the need for change
- diagnoses the nature of the change that is required and carefully considers alternatives
- manages the change process over a period of time so that it is effective and accepted.

Pugh (1978) has six rules for managing change effectively:

- Work hard at establishing the need for change.
- Don't only think about the change, think through it. This means thinking about the effects the change will have on individuals in terms of their jobs, status, prestige and so on.
- Initiate change through informal discussions to get feedback and participation.
- Positively encourage those concerned to give their objections.
- Be prepared to change yourself.
- Monitor the change and reinforce it.

Resistance to change can be of two types:

- Resistance to the content of change, ie opposition to the specific nature of the change.

- Resistance to the process of change, ie opposition to how to the change is introduced.

Each might be a perfectly rational response to change, however inconvenient to management.

Armstrong (1999) identifies eight reasons why individuals might resist change:

- The shock of the new – people tend to be conservative, and they do not want to move too far from their comfort zones. To this I would add regret for the passing of the old.

- Economic fears – threats to wages or job security.

- Inconvenience.

- Uncertainty.

- Symbolic fears – the loss of a symbol, like a car parking space, may suggest that bigger and more threatening changes are on the way.

- Threats to interpersonal relationships.

- Threat to status or skill – a change may be seen as deskilling.

- Competence fears – concern about the ability to cope or acquire new skills.

THE ROLE OF HR IN CHANGE MANAGEMENT

The crucial role of HR in change management can be clearly identified using Beer's model of change. HR intervention is crucial at each stage of the model, as follows:

- *Mobilise commitment to change through joint analysis of problems.* HR should play a leading role in benchmarking and other environment-scanning techniques, and so help to spot the need for change. HR staff are likely to be the organisers of the teams and workshops who are involved in problem identification and analysis. Underpinning this should be a learning organisation, in which HR should be a prime driver.

- *Develop a shared vision.* This involves an understanding of the culture of the organisation, and the ability to support and direct the visions which underpin the culture.

- *Foster consensus and commitment to the shared vision.* It is essential that those affected by the change should feel that they have ownership of it. Developing and supporting ownership is a key HR skill, as is the fostering and supporting of change champions.

- *Spread the word about the change.* Here, as noted by McCarthy (2004), communication is key. McCarthy stresses that this should involve communication *with*, rather than communication *at*, those involved. He suggests the concept of 'conversation' as being appropriate here.

- *Institutionalise the change through formal policies.* This may well include the development of new HR policies on recruitment, reward and development. It is crucial that the reward system supports the new ways of doing things, for example.

- *Monitor and adjust as needed.* HR policy will need to be proactive after the change process is apparently completed. Development policies should be responsive to the need for any new competencies which become apparent.

Armstrong (1999) identifies a number of guidelines for change management, in most of which the role of HR is key. These include:

- commitment and visionary leadership from the top
- understanding the culture
- development of temperament and leadership skills at all levels which support change
- an environment conducive to change – a learning organisation
- full participation of those involved, so that they can own the change
- the reward system should recognise success in achieving change
- a willingness to learn from failure – a support culture rather than a blame culture
- support for change agents
- protection of those adversely affected by change.

Ridgeway and Wallace (1994) discuss the role of HR in managing a common strategic change – a takeover. Here matching the culture of the predator and the target are key. They quote from Furnham and Gunter (1993) on how such a match should be identified. It would involve:

- identifying the culture of the acquiring company
- deciding on any changes needed to ensure that culture supports the proposed strategy
- identifying potential acquisitions and their cultures
- isolating likely changes to those cultures
- designing a format for assessing other cultures
- establishing criteria by which to identify suitable acquisitions.

Crucial here is establishing how the senior management of the target company will fit with the acquirer's culture, and what senior staff gaps will be exposed.

The HR department of the acquiring company will also be responsible for ensuring that the procedures and systems of the two companies are compatible, or can be made compatible, including any industrial relations implications. During the takeover process, the HR department also needs to manage communication. This will involve close liaison with PR, as employees of the target company will get a lot of their information about the takeover via the media.

ACTIVITY 10.4 PEARMOUNT COLLEGE

Pearmount College is a medium-sized further education (FE) college in the town of Hetherleigh (population 75,000). In many ways it is a typical FE college. In its Ofsted inspections, most aspects are rated as satisfactory (grade 3, the middle of the five grades available). A third of its courses are rated as above average, a third as below average. However, Pearmount is not typical in that it is a tertiary college. Unlike most FE colleges, it is responsible for all post-16 education in Hetherleigh. This gives the college a particular social responsibility. As the only post-16 provider, it cannot be selective in its recruitment policy. It is expected to provide educational opportunities for all of the post-16 population in the town.

There are four main types of post-16 providers, all of which compete to score highly in government league tables. These are school sixth forms, which are often selective; sixth-form colleges, which are almost always selective; tertiary colleges, which are normally non-selective; and ordinary FE colleges, which tend to offer mainly vocational courses rather than A levels. The main league table competition is between sixth forms, sixth-form colleges and tertiary colleges, and concentrates on A level results. Sixth-form colleges tend to score more highly than school sixth forms and tertiary colleges. A recent Ofsted inspection of Pearmount noted that its A level results were average, but below the average for sixth-form colleges. It also criticised teaching as unimaginative, although it said that some vocational provision was excellent.

Post-16 education is funded by the Learning and Skills Council under government guidance. Government funding policy concentrates on three main target areas: full-time 16–19 education, adult basic literacy and numeracy skills, and adult level 2 qualifications (broadly GCSE grade A–C level). FE and tertiary colleges have responded to this by withdrawing from adult education unless it fits into the funding priorities, or is fully funded by employers. Pearmount is typical in this. Over the last decade it has withdrawn from many advanced vocational and professional part-time programmes and concentrated much more on full-time 16–19 programmes. The other continuing pressure from the LSC is to drive up the quality of FE provision while under the threat of withdrawn funding from courses within the priority areas which are deemed to be of low quality.

Jim Merryweather was appointed as the new principal of Pearmount College in September 2006, following the retirement of his predecessor, who had taken an active role in the town. Within a month of taking up his post, he produced a new teaching and learning strategy for the college. This stressed individual daily targets for students, with daily assessment and measurement of achievement; all assignment work to be completed in college; and fortnightly reports to parents on progress and attendance. His aim was to make the college one of the best sixth forms in the country.

Although there was some concern that the new strategy seemed to focus solely on full-time 16–19 students, it was broadly welcomed by teaching staff, and rapid progress was made in its implementation.

However, Merryweather also faced the problem that many of his staff were ageing, while others, who mainly taught vocational programmes for adults, were seeing much of their workload disappearing. Clearly the college staffing needed to be restructured. One way to do this could have been an early retirement programme, but what often happens in these programmes is that the people opting to take early retirement are the very people who you do not want to lose. Another option could have been a programme of retraining and redeployment.

Merryweather's solution was to propose a radical restructuring, which was announced just before the Easter holidays in April 2007. A new staffing structure was proposed, with more higher-paid posts, but also some low-level posts with a salary ceiling well below that previously available to lecturers. All members of staff were expected to reapply for posts under the new structure, with the clear expectation that some would be unsuccessful.

In addition, holidays were reduced, and the normal working week was increased to 37 hours, all of which could in theory be spent teaching. The working week was also extended to five and a half days, and staff could be requested to work on Saturdays. Staff would no longer be entitled to overtime or time off in lieu.

The reaction of staff was one of horror, particularly as the new posts were advertised internally immediately, although the proposals came under the 90-day consultation period for major redundancies. Teaching staff held

a number of one-day strikes, were fully supported by their union and the students' union, and also attracted a lot of support within the town.

By the end of the summer term in 2007, half the teaching staff had been made redundant, had found new posts, or had taken early retirement. There was severe concern that college staffing would be inadequate to meet demand in 2007–08, and also that the adverse publicity would dissuade many potential students from attending the college.

Questions:

1. Critically evaluate Jim Merryweather's strategy for implementing change at Pearmount College.

2. What techniques do you think can be used to overcome resistance to change?

CHANGE LEADERSHIP

Ridgeway and Wallace (1994) identify a number of competencies required for effective change leadership. These are:

- Intellectual skills – intellectually curious and able to handle ambiguity.
- Influencing skills – assertive, proactive and energetic.
- Counselling and people skills – sensitive, flexible and adaptable, with a high tolerance of pressure.

While this list is solid, I think that it misses the true essence of change leadership. A good change leader must above all be driven by a vision of the future, and be able to inspire others with that vision. This involves a strong appreciation of values, exceptional communication abilities, a sense of inspiration and the ability to empower others with the vision. All of these qualities are illustrated in case study 10.8.

NELSON MANDELA

Nelson Mandela is almost universally recognised as the last, and one of the greatest, inspirational leaders of the twentieth century. His career illustrates the characteristics of a brilliant change leader.

Mandela was born in 1918, a member of a chiefly clan in the Xhosa tribe. He trained as a lawyer, and was drawn at an early age into the struggle against white domination through his membership of the African National Congress. The political struggle intensified in the 1950s after the election of the white supremacist National Party government, and the establishment of the apartheid system of racial segregation.

In the early 1960s, Mandela was on trial for his life. His statement from the dock in his trial put forward his vision: 'I have fought against white domination. I have fought against black domination. I have cherished the ideal of a democratic and free society in which all persons live together in harmony and with equal opportunities. It is an ideal which I hope to live for and to achieve. But, if needs be, it is an ideal for which I am prepared to die.'

Mandela was sentenced to life imprisonment on Robben Island, where he was to remain for 27 years. For much of this he was under a hard-labour regime. A telling incident from his imprisonment throws more light on his vision. A particularly tough prison governor imposed a brutal regime on the prisoners, but when he was transferred, he wished Mandela and the other ANC leaders the best for the future. To Mandela, this illustrated the possibility of redemption. The man was brutal not because he had a brutal nature, but because he was conditioned by a brutal system. Like the Catholic Church, Mandela distinguished between the sin and the sinner. From this came his concept of redemption and reconciliation, which was to be a driving force of his presidency.

By the mid-1980s, another key player had entered the scene – F W De Klerk, the new National Party leader. De Klerk recognised that the apartheid system must go, and that a settlement must be negotiated with the ANC. In Bridge's terms, this marked the end of the old system, and a move into the neutral transition zone. After lengthy negotiations, Mandela was released from prison in 1990. A new constitution was negotiated, leading to democratic elections in 1994, and the election of Mandela as the first democratic president of South Africa.

Mandela now faced his most severe test as a leader – how to hold the new South Africa together, and forge a new multiracial democratic state. He faced threats on all sides. A right-wing Afrikaner element was threatening civil war, and there was also an undeclared civil war between the ANC and the Zulu Inkatha Freedom Party. The Zulus were the largest tribe in South Africa, and resented the power hold by the Xhosa Mandela.

Mandela's approach was to use symbolic acts of reconciliation. He visited the widow of the architect of apartheid, Hendrik Verwoerd. He also presented the rugby world cup to the victorious South African team wearing a South African rugby shirt. Rugby is an Afrikaner sport in South Africa, with almost totally white support. This action helped to reconcile the Afrikaner community to the new South Africa. He also pursued reconciliation with the Zulus. The Inkatha Freedom Party leader, Mangosuthu Buthelezi, was made minister for home affairs, and number three in the government, after Mandela and the vice-president Thabo Mbeki.

Mandela also used the idea of redemption through the Truth and Reconciliation Commission, which he launched with Archbishop Desmond Tutu. The idea here was that perpetrators of political crime could confess their involvement, and receive public absolution. Mandela insisted that this should apply as much to members of the ANC as to the agents of the apartheid regime.

Mandela's last great act of leadership was to recognise that by the end of his term as president in 1999, the transition phase had ended, and that South Africa was into the new beginning. Even his greatest admirers would not call Mandela a great administrator, and he recognised that a new type of more structured leadership was now

needed. He therefore retired, leaving the way for Thabo Mbeki, a less charismatic but more structured politician, to succeed him.

When the sculptor Rodin was asked how he would sculpt an elephant, his reply was that he would start with a very large block of stone, and then remove everything which was not elephant. Mandela had a similar vision. Everything which was not part of his vision of a democratic, multicultural South Africa was irrelevant, including bitterness, revenge and recriminations.

KEY LEARNING POINTS

- Approaches to strategy are connected with the nature of the environment. In the 1950s and 1960s, a placid environment encouraged the rational, logical corporate planning approach, while a more turbulent environment since the 1970s encouraged the more contingent, experimental strategic management approach. The leading exponent of the corporate planning approach was Igor Ansoff, while the leading exponents of the strategic management approach are Tom Peters, Michael Porter, Ralph Stacey, Gary Hamel and C K Prahalad, James Quinn and Henry Mintzberg. It is important to distinguish between intended strategy and realised strategy.

- Strategic analysis is concerned with the strategic position of the organisation. What are the key characteristics of the organisation, what changes are going on in the environment, and how will these affect the organisation and its activities? This involves an analysis of the expectations of stakeholders, the culture of the organisation, the organisation's vision and values; the environment, as identified through a STEEPLE analysis; and the key resource areas of the business. The

extent to which there is a mismatch (a gap) between current strategy and the future environment is a measure of the strategic problem facing the organisation.

- Vision, mission, values and objectives are closely linked, and often confused. The mission and objectives of the organisation are constrained by corporate governance, stakeholders, business ethics and culture. The mission statement provides a benchmark against which policies can be evaluated.

- Resource analysis is internal to the organisation. It is concerned with the strengths and weaknesses parts of SWOT analysis, and measures the efficiency and effectiveness of an organisation's resources.

- Prahalad and Hamel identify the concept of the core competencies of the organisation, ie those factors which give the organisation its key competitive advantages.

- The concept of generic strategy was introduced by Michael Porter and developed by Cliff Bowman.

- Possible strategies should be evaluated on three levels, suitability, acceptability and feasibility.

- Transformational change is change which results in entirely new behaviour on the part of organisational members, and is in its very nature strategic.

- Bridges and Mitchell identify three stages in a change programme: saying goodbye, shifting into neutral and moving forward. Resistance

to change can be rational, and must be managed. This is one of the key functions of HR in change management. The critical role of a change leader is to be inspirational and visionary.

- There are three major models of strategic HR: the best-practice, best-fit and resource-based models.

QUESTIONS

1. Explain what Quinn means by his three elements of strategy.

2. Why is the corporate planning approach inappropriate for a turbulent environment?

3. What are the differences between vision, mission, values and objectives?

4. What do you understand by the expression 'core competence'?

5. Explain the concept of generic strategy as developed by Michael Porter.

6. What HR practices are normally identified as part of a high-performance workplace?

7. In what situations is the best-fit model more appropriate that the best-practice model?

8. What are Pugh's six rules for managing change?

9. Why might individuals resist change?

10. 'Best practice HR may be desirable, but it is not always feasible.' Do you agree?

EXPLORE FURTHER

Further Reading

The leading UK text on strategic management is Gerry Johnson, Kevan Scholes and Richard Whittington, *Exploring Corporate Strategy*, (2004), 7th edition. Other valuable strategic management texts are John Thompson with Frank Martin, *Strategic Management: awareness and change* (2005), 5th edition; Robert Clark, *Contemporary Strategy Analysis* (2005), 5th edition; and Bernard Burnes,

Managing Change: a strategic approach to organisational dynamics (2004), 4th edition. John Walton's *Strategic Human Resource Development* (1999) is useful for the HR contribution to strategic management, while Mick Marchington and Adrian Wilkinson's *Human Resource Management at Work* (2008), 4th edition is excellent on the best-practice, best-fit and resource-based models of HR.

SEMINAR ACTIVITY

MODELS OF HR

The three major models of HR: best practice, best fit and resource-based, have been extensively discussed in this chapter. Using the material in this chapter, in Chapters 3 and 4 of Marchington and Wilkinson's *Human Resource Management at Work*, and in the following case studies, critically examine the three models.

Case study 1 Japanese multinationals in the UK

Doeringer, Lorenz and Terkla (2003) discussed the extent to which Japanese high-performance work practices were used in Japanese-owned manufacturing plants in the UK, the US and France. In this case study we will look mainly at the evidence for the UK.

The authors investigated the extent to which Japanese manufacturing transplants used four practices which they saw as typical of high-performance work systems: job rotation, quality circles, self-managing teams and employee responsibility for quality control. They found that 66 per cent of plants surveyed in the UK used at least one of these practices, but only 2 per cent used all four. By far the most common of these practices in the UK was employee responsibility for quality control, used by 60 per cent of respondents. None of the other three practices was used by more than 20 per cent. Results were comparable in France, but the US made more use of quality circles and self-managed teams.

The typical pattern for a Japanese transplant is that senior management will be Japanese, with long experience of operating high-performance work systems in Japan. However, HR will usually be the responsibility of western managers, hired because of their familiarity with local industrial relations practices. Their role is to design hybrid HR systems that adapt Japanese practices to local conditions.

High adopters of Japanese practices (using three or more of the techniques) have made a significant move towards partnership arrangements, with employee involvement in decision-making, high investment in training, opportunities for the career advancement of shop-floor workers, and long-term employment guarantees.

The central obstacles to the greater adoption of high-performance practices were lack of skills and training, and status. Employees with formal technical qualifications were reluctant to work directly alongside production workers in the same team.

A producer of photocopiers and fax machines had used Japanese supervisors and team leaders as teachers and technical troubleshooters. When they were replaced by British supervisors, the company found that the new supervisors lacked the knowledge to teach and troubleshoot across the whole range of assembly jobs. Operators had little problem-solving experience or ability, and the new supervisors did not have the skills to train them. The result was that operators lacked the ability to take an effective part in quality circles and continuous improvement (*kaizen*), and these initiatives failed.

Case study 2 The Bosman case and the football transfer system

Before 1995, a professional footballer could only move to another club with the agreement of his current club, even if his contract with the current club had ended. The buying club had to purchase the player from his current club, through the payment of a transfer fee, unless a free transfer was agreed. The latter was only common in the case of a player nearing the end of his career. The current club could prevent a transfer, even if the player was out of contract.

Jean-Marc Bosman, a Belgian footballer with RFC Liège, wanted to be transferred to the French club Dunkerque. Liège refused without the payment of a transfer fee, which Dunkerque was unwilling to pay. Bosman claimed that as an EU citizen, he had the right of freedom of movement within the EU, and that the existing transfer system prevented him from exercising this right.

The European Court of Justice found in his favour in 1995. As a result, transfer fees for out-of-contract players were illegal where a player was moving between one EU country and another. In effect, an out-of-contract player would always move on a free transfer.

The implications of the case for the structure of the football industry have been far-reaching:

- Small clubs have been hard hit. Previously, they recruited young talent, with the hope that the player would develop, and could then be transferred to a bigger club for a large profit. After Bosman, they could only benefit from player development if they signed the young player on a long contract. This was very high risk, because if the player did not develop as hoped, they would be stuck with paying his wages until the end of the contract.

- To protect their investments in star players, bigger clubs also signed them on longer contracts. This meant that if a club were relegated, they would be forced to continue to pay star wages which they could no longer afford in a lower division.

- Player power was vastly increased. Star players either had the security of a long contract, or they could hold out for much higher wages when negotiating the renewal of a contract. Alternatively, when their contract ended, they could move elsewhere, and demand a high signing-on fee (often running into the millions) from their new club.

(Sources: Pearson (nd), Fordyce 2005.)

Case study 3 Engaging for success

In the summer of 2009, David MacLeod and Nita Clarke produced a report for the Department of Business, Innovation and Skills on employee engagement. Their brief was 'to take an in-depth look at employee engagement [one of the key components of the high-performance workplace], and to report on its potential benefits for companies, organisations and individual employees' (p3).

Employee engagement proved elusive to define. The report found more than 50 definitions, including the useful 'you know it when you see it'. Eventually, building on the work of David Guest, the report defined employee engagement as (p9):

> A workplace approach designed to ensure that employees are committed to their organisation's goals and values, motivated to contribute to organisational success, and at the same time to enhance their own sense of well-being. Engaged organisations have strong and authentic values, with clear evidence of trust and fairness based on mutual respect, where two-way promises and commitments – between employers and staff – are understood, and are fulfilled.

The report found a strong correlation between high levels of employee engagement and measures of performance:

- Highly engaged organisations averaged 18 per cent higher productivity and 12 per cent higher profitability than those with low engagement.

- Fifty-nine per cent of engaged employees said that their job brings out their most creative ideas compared with 3 per cent of disengaged employees.

- Engaged employees take an average of 2.69 sick days a year, the disengaged 6.19 days.

- Engaged employees are 87 per cent less likely to leave the organisation than the disengaged.

- Seventy-eight per cent of engaged employees would recommend their company's products or services, as against 13 per cent of the disengaged.

The flip side is that disengagement costs money. While 30 per cent of workers were engaged, 20 per cent were disengaged, and there is some evidence that this figure may be rising. Between 1992 and 2001, the proportion saying they had a great deal of discretion over how to do their job fell from 57 to 43 per cent.

Forty-two per cent would refuse to recommend their organisation as an employer to family or friends. Gallup suggested that in 2008 the cost of disengagement to the UK economy was between £59.4 and £64.7 billion.

The report quotes many case studies. One concerns the construction equipment company JCB, which was hard hit by the recession in the construction industry in 2008. In October 2008 it proposed a shorter working week to the union, GMB, in order to avoid over 300 redundancies. Running up to the ballot, JCB held face-to-face sessions with employees to explain the background to the business situation and the steps that were being taken in response to it. As a result, employees understood the rationale behind the company's proposals and decisions. The union ballot voted two-to-one in favour of the shorter working week, although this meant a pay cut.

CHAPTER 11

The National Health Service: Activities

This final chapter applies the themes explored earlier in this book to a series of activities based within one organisation, the National Health Service (NHS). The NHS has been chosen because it is large, complex, subject to a great number of pressures, and familiar – and important – to us all.

INTRODUCTION

The NHS employs more than 1.5 million people. It is the fourth largest employer in the world, after the Chinese People's Liberation Army, Walmart and Indian Railways. It deals with one million patients every 36 hours. When launched in 1948 it had a budget equivalent to £9 billion at current prices. In 2007–08 its budget was over £90 billion (NHS 2009a).

Health care in the UK before the Second World War had been a mix of private, municipal and charity provision, including the remnants of the Poor Law. In 1942 the Beveridge Report on post-war reconstruction recommended a national health service, and this was implemented in the National Health Service Act 1946, which came into force on 5 July 1948.

The act laid down the core principles of the NHS:

● that it meets the needs of everyone

● that it be free at the point of delivery

● that it be based on clinical need, not ability to pay.

In 2000, new principles were added: The NHS will:

● provide a comprehensive range of services

● shape its services around the needs and preferences of individual patients, their families and their carers

- respond to the different needs of different populations
- work to continuously improve the quality of services and minimise errors
- support and value its staff
- work with others to ensure a seamless service for patients
- help to keep people healthy and work to reduce health inequalities
- respond to the confidentiality of individual patients
- public funds for health care will be devoted solely to NHS patients.

Strict application of the free-at-the-point-of delivery-principle lasted only three years. In 1951, the Labour government, faced with escalating NHS costs, proposed the introduction of charges for prescriptions, dentures and spectacles. Nye Bevan, the architect of the NHS, resigned from the Cabinet in protest. The charges were actually introduced by the incoming Conservative government in 1952. Prescription charges were abolished in 1965, but reintroduced in 1968. With the introduction of devolved governments in the UK, the NHS became a devolved service. One of the major areas subject to national variation has been prescription charges. From April 2009, the prescription charge in England is £7.20, in Scotland £4, in Northern Ireland £3, and in Wales nothing.

The original hope was that demand for the new NHS would be at worst constant, and it was expected that once the backlog of ill health which had built up during the depression and the Second World War was dealt with, the cost of the NHS would fall. Many diseases had been wiped out in the nineteenth and early twentieth centuries through improved sanitisation and nutrition, and immunisation, and it was expected that this would continue. Indeed, infectious disease did continue to decline, with effective immunisations for tuberculosis and polio being developed, and antibiotics dealing with other infectious illnesses. However, degenerative diseases proved much more difficult and expensive to treat, and became more common as the population aged (Evans and Evans 2002). The growing sophistication and cost of medical equipment also put pressure on the budget.

By 1997, the UK was the lowest spender on health care among the members of the Organisation for Economic Co-operation and Development (OECD). Total expenditure on health care was 6.8 per cent of GDP (85 per cent of this being public expenditure, the highest percentage in the OECD). France spent 9.6 per cent, Germany 10.7 per cent, Canada 9.3 per cent and the US 13.9 per cent (Gage 2001a). At the same time, the level of satisfaction with the NHS was high. Eighty-one per cent rated care as good or excellent, compared with 84 per cent in Canada and 82 per cent in the US, with over-65s in the UK giving a higher rating than those in Canada or the US. Rating of hospital care as good or excellent in each country was equal to 82 per cent (Gage 2001b).

In January 2000 the prime minister, Tony Blair, announced that funding for the NHS would move towards the 'European average'. Apparently the Chancellor of the Exchequer, Gordon Brown, who would have to provide the money, was not consulted. In March 2000, the announcement was operationalised as a plan to increase the percentage of GDP spent on health care from 7 per cent in 1999 to 7.6 per cent in 2004 (Dixon 2001).

By 2007, after an enormous spending programme which increased spending on the NHS between 2000 and 2007 by 4.7 per cent a year in real terms, UK spending on health care was 8.4 per cent of GDP, with the number of doctors per 1,000 population up from 1.9 in 2000 to 2.5 in 2007, but still below the EU average. France's spend on health care was up to 11 per cent, Germany's down slightly to 10.4 per cent, Canda's up to 10.1 per cent and the US up to 16 per cent (OECD 2009).

The NHS as set up in 1948 was a typical nationalised industry: bureaucratic and based on command and control. The whole ethos was paternalist, based on 'doctor knows best'. Since 1948, many attempts have been made to introduce more choice into the system, and to make it more customer-responsive. In 1972, for the first time, patients were considered as consumers, while in 1989 an emphasis was placed on patient choice. In 2003, the White Paper 'Building on the Best: Choice, Responsiveness and Equity in the NHS' outlined plans to build more personal choice into the system and to empower patients by involving them in their own treatment, while in 2007 the launch of the NHS Choices website gave people the tools to make better, more informed choices about their health. The site gave up-to-date information about conditions and treatments, and the ability to check hospital profiles and performance online (NHS 2009b). Choice was also one of the main themes of the Darzi Report, which is covered in greater detail in activity 11.2 below.

Another theme running through the history of the NHS is the desire to ensure efficiency. The Thatcher government attempted to do this through the purchaser/ provider split and the internal market, whereby GPs (primary care) were given budgets to purchase hospital services for their patients (secondary care). The incoming Labour government in 1997 pledged to abolish the internal market, but have instead retained a modified version of it.

Primary care is organised through Primary Care Trusts, which are in charge of GPs and NHS dentists, provide community care services, and commission secondary care. Secondary care is provided by 175 acute NHS trusts and 60 mental health trusts, which run 1,600 hospitals and specialist care centres. Of the acute trusts, 115 are foundation trusts, which have greater financial autonomy. Cost-effectiveness is also ensured through the National Institute for Health and Clinical Excellence (NICE), which ensures that clinical treatments and pharmaceuticals used in the NHS are evidence-based and cost-effective. NICE is frequently criticised when it bans the use of a new drug within the NHS, but the motive here is often to put pressure on the pharmaceutical companies to lower their prices (NHS 2009a).

This chapter will examine a number of NHS-based case studies and activities. These include:

- the introduction of lean working in the NHS
- the Darzi Report and quality in the NHS

- clinical negligence
- human rights in the NHS
- the implementation of the Working Time Directive for junior doctors
- the swine flu pandemic and the NHS
- the recruitment of Filipino nurses.

ACTIVITY 11.1 THE LEAN NHS

In 2006, the NHS sent a team to visit Toyota's factory at Burnaston in Derby. The aim was to learn from the Toyota production system (TPS), and to develop ideas that could be used in the NHS.

The TPS is based on two main principles:

- innovation, creativity and problem-solving
- elimination of waste.

Toyota's philosophy is centred on continuous improvement (*kaizen*) and respect for people. It is a top-down philosophy, but everyone in Toyota is committed to it. All members (staff) are trained in the TPS, and commitment to the philosophy is a prerequisite for promotion. Attitude rather than skill is the main criterion for appointment. The desired attributes are: teamworking, problem identification, problem-solving, learning ability, numeracy and ability to innovate and develop improvement ideas (Westwood 2006).

The second Toyota principle is the elimination of waste (*muda*). Costs in any organisation are of two types:

- Costs that deliver value to customers. These costs should not be eliminated.
- Costs that do not deliver value. These are waste and should be eliminated.

There are seven types of waste:

- *Defects* – The need for rework because of quality processes. In an NHS context this could include readmission to hospital because of premature discharge.
- *Waiting* – Work cannot be processed because people are waiting for other people, equipment or information, eg in the

NHS, waiting for a doctor to be available to discharge a patient.

- *Transportation* – Unnecessary movement of materials, eg having to go to a central store to collect items in constant use.
- *Overprocessing* – Performing unnecessary steps that do not add value, eg asking for patients' details several times.
- *Inventory* – Too much stock or work in progress, eg in the NHS excess stock or waiting lists.
- *Motion* – Things not within reach or not readily accessible – this is clearly applicable to the NHS.
- *Overproduction* – Producing more than is needed – requesting unnecessary pathology tests 'just in case'.

One type of waste particularly important to Toyota is inventory. This has led to the development of the just-in-time or *kanban* principle. Stock is delivered to the production areas as it is needed, not held in reserve. This is controlled by *kanban* cards. As an item is used, the *kanban* card will become visible, which indicates that a replacement must be procured.

The NHS Institute for Innovation and Warwick University worked on ways of implementing lean working in the NHS.

The first step was to identify value to the patient. This is any activity which improves the patient's health, well-being and experience. Patients value no delays, a high standard of service, and being treated in the right place at the right time by the right person. They do not value processes which cause delay, ie cancelled outpatient appointments or operations.

The second step involves identifying the patient journey or value stream. This will identify the components of the patient journey which add value, and those which do not.

Thirdly, manage the value flow. This involves an understanding of the demand for services and the need to avoid batching and queueing. As an example, do not send all patients attending an outpatients' clinic the same appointment time. Patients with similar types of needs require similar processes. For example, the NHS is increasingly attempting to discourage patients with minor injuries from attending A & E departments, but instead is directing them to specialist minor injuries units. A & E then concentrates on major injuries and resuscitation processes. Both types of unit can then operate more efficiently, increasing value to patients.

Fourthly, base the system on customer pull, rather than system push. In the NHS traditionally the patient fits into the system rather than the other way round. For example, traditionally A & E patients who need a bed are pushed to a ward – it is A & E staff's responsibility to find a bed. In a pull system, admitting wards notify A & E when beds are available, and they pull patients from A & E.

The final step in the process is continuous improvement. Every process can be further improved. Continuous improvement is infinite, not finite.

Bolton Hospital applied the lean principles in 2005 to its non-elective trauma patients, ie patients usually admitted after a serious accident. After a year it had achieved:

- 50 per cent reduction in mortality for older patients with fractures of the neck or femur

- 37 per cent reduction in overall mortality for adult trauma patients

- 32 per cent reduction in hospital length of stay.

The HR implications of going lean are clear:

- involve all staff

- going lean is a strong motivator for staff

- top management support is essential

- training is essential, and lean teams need ongoing support.

The lean process can often be extremely simple and produce very quick payoffs. For example, at Heart of England Foundation NHS Trust, over 100 prescriptions per day are written in the A & E department. On average it took two to three minutes to find the prescription pad in order to write each prescription. Now each doctor has a prescription pad taped to the desk in their office. It is no longer possible for a doctor to 'lose' his or her pad. Result: 200–300 minutes saved each day (Westwood et al 2007).

Questions:

1. Do you feel that lean working is appropriate for a 'caring' organisation like the NHS?

2. Were the change management techniques used appropriate?

 ACTIVITY 11.2 THE DARZI REPORT: 'HIGH QUALITY CARE FOR ALL'

In 2007, the incoming prime minister, Gordon Brown, appointed the eminent surgeon Lord Darzi as a junior health minister. This was part of a general move to bring non-politicians into government, known colloquially as the GOATS – government of all the talents. Darzi's brief was to lead the NHS Next Stage Review, to develop a vision of the NHS fit for the twenty-first century. Darzi's report, 'High Quality Care for All', was published in June 2008 (Department of Health 2008d).

The central theme of 'High Quality Care for All' was putting the patient first. This involved:

Better access to primary care. The report recommended 152 new GP-led health centres (polyclinics), open 12 hours a day, seven days a week, providing a range of services under one roof, including many previously only available in hospitals, such as blood tests, X-rays and ultrasound. This proposal was controversial, because it was felt that patients would lose contact with an individual GP, and might have to travel further to a GP, but the advantages of local access to specialist services was thought to outweigh this. By the summer of 2009, 50 polyclinics were open. Other recommendations included 100 new GP practices in under-doctored areas, of which 65 were open in 2009, and extended opening hours at GPs. By 2009, three-quarters of GP practices were open either in the evening or early morning and/or at weekends, ahead of the target of 50 per cent.

Faster access to drugs and treatment. More resources were put into NICE, enabling it to assess new drugs more quickly. New out-of-hours services, run by nurses, were also set up, and measures were taken to ensure that where people wished to die at home, they were given support to enable this.

Empowering patients. Personal health budgets are being developed, giving patients with chronic conditions more say in their treatment. Over nine million people now have an individual health plan. To improve patient privacy, mixed-sex wards are to be phased out by 2010.

Making the NHS safer. Investment has been made to combat hospital-transmitted infections. Rates of both *C. difficile* and MRSA infections have fallen by more than target. From April 2009, all elective admissions are screened for MRSA.

Preventing ill health. One long-running criticism of the NHS is that it is really a National Illness Service, treating illness rather than preventing it. Measures are being taken to identify those at risk of heart disease, and to prevent obesity, and NHS health checks are to be offered to everyone aged 40 to 74.

Improving quality. NICE will publish quality standards setting out what quality care will look like in various specialties, and every NHS organisation will be required to publish annual quality accounts. The Care Quality Commission (CQC) was set up in April 2009, with tough enforcement powers to ensure high-quality care.

Like many other organisations, the NHS is having difficulty in internalising the drive to higher quality. NHS trusts initially self-assess for quality through a tick-box exercise, which is usually accepted by the CQC. Basildon and Thurrock University Hospitals Foundation NHS Trust received a 'good' performance rating, and 13 marks out of 14 on 'safety and cleanliness' in 2009 on the basis of its self-assessment. However, when the CQC examined death rates for the trust, it found them a third higher than expected: 350 excess deaths a year. It then carried out two on-site inspections and found blood-splattered floors and equipment, and mould growing in medical machines (Bowcott 2009b, Asthana and Campbell 2009).

Darzi recognised that although the initiative to improve quality must come from the centre, actually internalising a quality culture can only be done locally. Clinicians should be empowered to lead change locally, being given ownership of budgets and accountability for the quality of their services and freedom to set their own clinical priorities within national targets. This would encourage creativity and innovation. Progress in quality should be recognised through accreditation schemes.

Darzi recognised that his vision had a 10–15-year time span, and some progress has been made in the first year. The director of policy at the NHS Confederation, Nigel Edwards, thinks he can see changes already taking place 'at the coalface – people are taking about the quality agenda', but Chris Ham, professor of health policy and management at Birmingham University, fears that the recession will lead to financial belt-tightening in the NHS, and a possible resurgence of command and control rather than empowering leadership (Carlisle 2009). Time will tell.

Question: How far do you feel that the High Quality Care for All strategy is consistent with the values of key stakeholders within the NHS?

ACTIVITY 11.3 CLINICAL NEGLIGENCE

Like any other organisation, the NHS is subject to human error. However, unlike many other organisations, mistakes in the NHS can have fatal consequences. Eight per cent of prescriptions written by junior doctors contain errors, and so do 5 per cent of those written by consultants. Two per cent of these are potentially lethal, and a further 5 per cent potentially serious (Boseley 2009).

In 2008–09 the total cost of clinical negligence claims to the NHS was a staggering £454 million, made up of £306 million damages paid, £46 million defence costs and £101 million claimant costs (Medical Negligence Online 2009). However, this must be put in perspective, given the millions of procedures carried out each year in the NHS. One study in Oxfordshire Health Authority in the 1990s found that the rate of claims per 1,000 completed consultant episodes (courses of treatment) was less than one (Rickman and Fenn 2001).

Clinical negligence in the NHS is managed by the NHS Litigation Authority (NHSLA), set up in 1995. This is not an insurance company, but part of the NHS which pools risk – in effect providing in-house insurance. Its main vehicle is the Clinical Negligence Scheme for Trusts (CNST). Although membership is technically voluntary, all foundation trusts, NHS trusts and primary care trusts are members. Contributions from trusts are based on a range of factors, including the type of trust, the size of the trust and the specialties offered. Discounts are available to trusts with a good claims history (no claims discount) and who comply with the CNST's risk management standards as assessed after a two-day visit from the NHSLA (NHSLA 2009).

The risk management standards are divided into three levels. Generally speaking, level one is concerned with documentation, ie demonstrating that the process for managing risks has been clearly described and documented; level two is concerned with implementation, ie demonstration of the processes for managing risk; while level three is concerned with monitoring performance, ie

the process for managing risk working across the entire organisation (NHSLA 2008).

Compliance with the standards is worth money. Success at level 1 leads to a 10 per cent discount, level two to 20 per cent, and level three to 30 per cent. In December 2009, Princess Alexandra Hospital in Harlow improved its rating from level one to level two for its maternity unit. The result was an annual decrease of £500,000 in payments to the NHSLA (*Harlow Star* 2009).

If a clinical negligence claim is made against an NHS trust, the case will then be defended through the courts by the NHSLA, and the procedure will be the same as for any other claim made under the tort of negligence. In order to win a case, the patient must prove that he/she was owed a duty of care which was breached, that the breach led to the damages claimed, and that the damages claimed are accurate. The system is based on the proof of fault. This means that if someone is injured by a medical procedure where negligence cannot be proved they will receive no compensation, although their financial needs will be as great as if fault had been proved.

One consequence of the fault system is that it could lead to the practice of 'defensive' medicine – where doctors opt for simple treatments, and avoid the more complex, but possibly more effective, ones where the risk of something going wrong is greater.

Questions:

1. An alternative to the fault system of dealing with clinical negligence claims is a 'no fault' system as used in New Zealand. Here the determining factor for compensation will be the extent and nature of the injury, not the existence or non-existence of negligence. What do you think would be the advantages and disadvantages of a change to a no-fault system?

2. You are the HR director of an NHS hospital trust. At present, your trust is at level one on the NHSLA risk criteria. How would you set about moving up to level two?

ACTIVITY 11.4 HUMAN RIGHTS AND THE NHS

The Human Rights Act 1998 (HRA) incorporated into UK law most of the rights defined in the European Convention of Human Rights of 1950. The act applied to all public bodies in the UK, including the NHS, and meant that people could now take their human rights cases through the UK court system, rather than having to take complaints to the European Court of Human Rights in Strasbourg.

The HRA is based on what are known as the FREDA principles:

- **F**airness
- **R**espect
- **E**quality
- **D**ignity
- **A**utonomy

These principles are expressed in 15 basic rights:

- to life
- not to be tortured or treated in an inhuman or degrading way
- to be free from slavery or forced labour
- to liberty and security
- to a fair trial
- to no punishment without law
- to respect for private and family life, home and correspondence
- to freedom of thought, conscience and religion
- to freedom of expression
- to freedom of assembly and association
- to marry and found a family
- not to be discriminated against in relation to the enjoyment of any of the rights contained in the European Convention
- to peaceful enjoyment of possessions
- to education
- free elections.

Three main types of right are defined in the HRA. These are:

- Absolute rights, which cannot be limited in any way, eg the right not to be tortured.
- Limited rights, which can be limited in specific and finite circumstances. For example, the right to liberty is limited in the cases of convicted criminals and people compulsorily detained under the Mental Health Act.
- Qualified rights, where one person's right can conflict with someone else's, for example the right to respect for private life. Any interference with a qualified right must be:
  - in pursuit of a legitimate aim which is set out in the Act
  - prescribed by law
  - necessary
  - proportionate.

An example relevant to health care would be a care home which has a blanket policy of installing CCTV in the bedrooms of all residents for safety reasons. This is a breach of the HRA because it interferes with the right to respect for private life. In order to conform with the act, it was decided that only residents who are a risk to themselves or others would have CCTV installed.

The Department of Health recommends that all organisations within the NHS should take a human rights-based approach. This involves five key principles:

- putting human rights principles and standards at the heart of policy and planning
- ensuring accountability
- empowerment
- participation and involvement
- non-discrimination and attention to vulnerable groups.

Activity:

Six rights are seen as particularly relevant to the NHS. Three of these are:

- *The right for respect for private and family life*. Relevance to the NHS includes the use of mixed wards in hospitals, and the separation of families in residential care settings.

- *The right to a fair trial*. Relevance to the NHS includes staff disciplinary proceedings, and the working of the Mental Health Review Tribunal.

- *The right not to be discriminated against*. Relevance to the NHS includes refusal of medical treatment solely on the basis of age, or non-English-speakers being presented with health options without an interpreter being available.

Questions:

1. Identify examples of practices in the NHS

which could breach each of the following rights:

- the right to life

- the right to liberty

- the right not to be tortured or treated in an inhumane or degrading way.

2. The HRA applies only to public authorities, which include any person or organisation 'whose functions are of a public nature'. This would include private organisations such as companies or charities when they are carrying out a public function. Does your own organisation qualify under this definition? Whether or not your organisation is covered, how could an application of the values embodied in the HRA benefit your organisation?

(Sources: Department of Health 2008a, 2008b, 2008c.)

ACTIVITY 11.5 THE WORKING TIME DIRECTIVE AND JUNIOR DOCTORS

The European Working Time Directive was enacted into UK law as the Working Time Regulations from 1 October 1998. The regulations call for:

- an average of 48 hours' working time each week, measured over a reference period of 26 weeks

- 11 hours' continuous rest in 24 hours, ie no shift can exceed 13 hours

- 24 hours' continuous rest in seven days, or 48 hours' in two weeks, ie the maximum number of consecutive days of duty is 12

- a 20-minute break in work periods of over six hours

- 5.6 weeks' annual leave, pro rata for part-time staff.

Individuals have the right to opt out of the 48-hour week provision, but cannot be forced

to do so, and have the right to opt back in at any time. There is no opt-out from the rest and leave provisions.

Initially junior doctors in training were exempt from the regulations, although they applied to all other doctors and NHS workers. Junior doctors were notorious for working up to 100 hours a week, and often being on duty for 24 hours or more continuously. The regulations were extended to junior doctors in 2004, with a maximum average working week of 58 hours, reduced to 56 hours a week by August 2007, and to 48 hours a week from August 2009.

Until 2002, it was thought that when the regulations were extended to junior doctors, their impact would be less serious because of the on-call system. On-call time was not normally regarded as working time, unless the doctor was actually called on. This was changed by the European Court of Justice in 2002 in the *Jaeger* judgment. The ECJ ruled that on-call time where the doctor is required to be on the premises counted as working time, even if the doctor was actually asleep for part of this time. For doctors on call but not required to be on the premises, working time only started when the doctor responded to a call (NHS Employers 2009).

The NHS has recognised that there are particular problems with the 48-hour regulations in some hospitals, and a postponement of implementation (a derogation) was obtained from the EU covering specialities such as paediatrics and obstetrics in 38 trusts, permitting an average 52 hours a week until 2011 (Hope 2009).

Opinion within the medical profession was divided. The strongest opposition came from the Royal College of Surgeons (RSC). A survey found that 64 per cent of surgeons felt that implementation had worsened the quality of care given to patients, while 44 per cent said that patient safety had been compromised (Brockett 2009). The RCS has called for the government to ask the EU for an exemption permitting a 65-hour week for surgeons (House 2009).

The surgeons put forward two main arguments against implementation of the 48-hour week:

- Continuity of care would be disrupted, as patients would be seen by more different junior doctors, which would make it more difficult to detect subtle changes in a patient's condition.

- More seriously, training would be disrupted. Surgeon training is still very much based on 'sitting by Nellie', ie observing consultants at work. A shorter working week would considerably cut the opportunities for this.

The NHS response to the surgeons' concerns on training is that medical education has changed. Greater use is being made of e-learning, simulation and skills labs, leading to less need for the 'sitting by Nellie' approach (NHS Employers 2009).

The Royal College of Physicians called for postponement of implementation, but is less solidly opposed than the RCS. It called for the recruitment of more consultants. The British Medical Association (BMA), the doctors' trade union, supported the introduction of the 48-hour week, but recognised that there would be problems (House 2009).

Nurses were much more favourable towards the regulations. When interviewed by the *Nursing Times*, Wendy Reid, the national clinical lead for the European Working Time Directive, said that it was important not just to tackle the problems of implementation by juggling the rotas of junior doctors. What was needed was a fundamental rethink of skills mix and a reduction of artificial barriers between roles. Many of the jobs carried out by junior doctors could be done as well, if not better, by nurses. She cited the Hospital at Night programme, whereby multidisciplinary teams were used to provide out-of-hours clinical cover. Many of these teams were led by nurses. 'Patients no longer care what your badge says,' she said (Ford 2009).

The main lessons to be drawn from this case are, firstly that it is essential to think holistically and outside the box when introducing a change as radical as this one. Merely reducing junior doctors' working hours is not enough. Working practices, training practices and skills mix all have to change as well. Secondly, it is important to seek and accommodate the views of key stakeholders, but sometimes it not possible to satisfy them all. This is when management earns its wages. It is perhaps significant that when researching this case, I found plenty of material on the views of medical stakeholders, but there was not the same wealth of material on the views of patients!

Question: Critically evaluate the arguments put forward by the consultants against full implementation of the Working Time Directive.

ACTIVITY 11.6 SWINE FLU

Throughout the last decade, the world has been expecting an outbreak of a lethal influenza-type pandemic, with the potential to kill millions of people worldwide. There were two outbreaks which turned out to be false alarms: severe acute respiratory syndrome (SARS) and bird flu. Both originated in south-east Asia and had a high mortality rate, but both quickly burnt themselves out with limited fatalities.

Then the outbreak of a new strain of influenza, H1N1, known as swine flu, was identified in Mexico in March 2009. It quickly spread to the southern US, and the first cases in the UK were diagnosed in April. By June, it was declared as a pandemic by the World Health Organisation, meaning that the virus had now spread worldwide, the first pandemic since 1968. Figures were announced of a worst-case scenario of 65,000 deaths in the UK. Fortunately, the early expectation of a high mortality rate proved to be unfounded, but the death rate was still significant, concentrated among children and young adults, rather than the elderly, who are the main casualties of normal seasonal flu. Sixty per cent of deaths in the UK occurred among under-44s, compared with around 1 per cent of seasonal flu deaths (Bowcott 2009a). By November 2009, the death level in the UK was around 300, with an expected maximum of 1,000.

The UK had already taken steps to ensure readiness for a pandemic before the outbreaks of swine flu. Stockpiles of anti-viral drugs (Tamiflu and Relenza) had been built up, sufficient to enable treatment of 50 per cent of the population; advance purchase agreements had been placed to purchase up to 132 million doses of pandemic-specific vaccine as it became available; and a network of anti-viral collection points had been planned (House of Lords 2009, House of Lords Science and Technology Committee 2009).

In addition, two major planning exercises had been held to test UK readiness. These were Exercise Common Ground in 2005, an EU-wide exercise aimed at testing member states' national pandemic plans, and Exercise Winter Willow in January and February 2007, aimed at testing all levels of the planned UK response to an influenza pandemic. The WHO recognised the UK as being one of the best-prepared countries in the world.

UK reaction to the pandemic followed several phases. The first phase – containment – involved isolating victims, confirmation of diagnosis through laboratory analysis, and tracing and treatment of contacts with anti-virals. It was always recognised that containment would ultimately fail, but that it would buy time, which was critical given the length of time needed to develop an effective vaccine.

In May, the government distributed a leaflet, 'Important information about swine flu', which was distributed to every household in the UK. This gave information about the outbreak, and everyday measures that people could take to protect themselves and reduce the spread of infection. The message was 'Catch It. Bin It, Kill It.'

In July, the response moved to the next phase – mitigation – or the treatment phase. This involved the setting-up of the National Pandemic Flu Service, an online and call centre diagnosis and information service. People who thought they had swine flu were told to contact the service, where they were taken through a diagnostic checklist. If as a result of this they were thought to have swine flu, they were given a reference number, which a 'flu friend' could then use to collect anti-virals (Tamiflu) from a distribution centre. (These were meant to be convenient for all, but although I live only 30 miles from London, the nearest collection points were at least 10 miles away, and involved at least two bus journeys.) The government published details of numbers of new cases each week, but it was recognised that these figures were approximate, and only really useful to identify a rising or falling trend. Many people with mild swine flu recovered without diagnosis or treatment, while others distantly diagnosed did not have swine flu at all, but some other illness like a heavy cold. Flu patients were strongly discouraged from visiting their GPs, unless they were pregnant or had an underlying condition like diabetes or asthma.

The mitigation phase also involved planning for a doubling of the number of available critical-care beds in hospitals. This involved contingency plans for postponing elective operations, and re-employing and retraining currently non-employed healthcare workers. It was recognised that the virus might develop resistance to Tamiflu, so the decision was taken to hold the alternative antiviral (Relenza) in reserve in case this happened.

The expected pattern for the progress of the pandemic was that cases would continue to escalate rapidly until the start of the school holidays in late July (children were the main vector for spread of the virus). There would then be a lull, with a second wave coming in the autumn, and peaking some time during the winter. This duly happened, but it appeared by early December that the second wave had already peaked. However, overconfidence about the end of the pandemic could be premature – the Spanish flu pandemic in 1918–19, the biggest ever experienced, had a third wave.

The third phase of the government response was the launch of a vaccination programme, as vaccines developed by GlaxoSmithKline

and Baxter became available. This was started in November 2009. The first priority was to vaccinate frontline health and social care workers (about two million people), as they would be vital in keeping the health service operating if the situation became critical. Other priority groups were:

- people aged over six months and under 65 in the current seasonal flu vaccine clinical at-risk groups (five million people)
- all pregnant women (500,00 people)
- household contacts of people with compromised immune systems (500,000 people)
- people aged 65 and over in the current seasonal flu vaccine clinical at-risk groups (3.5 million people).

Otherwise healthy over-65s were not a priority, as they appeared to have some natural immunity, as a result of having lived through previous pandemics.

At the end of November, the vaccination programme was extended to all children.

(Source: Stationery Office 2009.)

Questions:

1. Given the generally mild nature of swine flu, did the UK government overreact in its planning?

2. What forward planning, if any, did your own organisation carry out in planning for swine flu?

 ACTIVITY 11.7 FILIPINO NURSES

In February 2010 a team left Princess Alexandra Hospital in Harlow with the objective of recruiting 50 qualified nurses in the Philippines, working with a leading Filipino recruitment agency.

The recruitment drive follows a similar exercise in 2000, when 72 Filipino nurses were recruited. Of these, around 40 still work

at the hospital, an excellent retention rate for nursing. The hospital's director of nursing rates the Filipino nurses very highly, saying that they are thoughtful, considerate in patient care and holistic in their approach.

Terri-Gel Lopez, one of the 2000 intake, who is now a ward manager, stresses the support provided by the hospital and the local community, and says that the Filipino nurses were made to feel very welcome.

(Source: Holland 2010.)

Questions:

1. What steps can be taken to ensure that the 2010 intake of Filipino nurses settle successfully into their new home?

2. What ethical issues are involved in an overseas recruitment exercise like this?

Bibliography

Chapter 1

Ansoff, I. (1987) *Corporate Strategy*. London: Penguin

Argenti, J. (1993) *Your Organisation, What Is It For? Challenging traditional organisational aims*. Maidenhead: McGraw-Hill

Arndt, M. (2006) '3M's Seven Pillars of Innovation', *BusinessWeek*, 10 May

BBC2 (2007) 'Independent cost' on 'Working Lunch', 18 June

Boxall, P. and Purcell, J. (2008) *Strategy and Human Resource Management*, 2nd edition. Basingstoke: Palgrave-Macmillan

Chakrabortty, A. (2009) 'What's bad for General Motors is good for the world', *Guardian*, 2 June

Chandler, A. E. (1962) *Strategy and Structure: chapters in the history of the American enterprise*. Cambridge MA: MIT Press

Child, J. (2005) *Organization: contemporary principles and practice*. Oxford: Blackwell

CIPD (2003) *Corporate responsibility and HR's role*. London: CIPD

CIPD (2009) *HR outsourcing and the HR function: threat or opportunity?* London: CIPD

Clark, A. (2009a) 'General Motors declares bankruptcy – the biggest manufacturing collapse in US history', *Guardian*, 2 June

Clark, A. (2009b) 'General Motors emerges from bankruptcy after 40 days', *Guardian*, 10 July

Clegg, S., Kornberger, M. and Pitsis, T. (2008) *Managing and Organizations*, 2nd edition. London: Sage

Clover, C. (2003) 'Members "suspect voting system in National Trust"', *Daily Telegraph*, 24 April

Collins, C. and Porras, J. (2000) *Built to Last: successful habits of visionary companies*, 3rd edition, London: Random House

Contractor, F. and Lorange, P. (1998) 'Why should firms cooperate? The strategy and economics basis for cooperative ventures', in Contractor and Lorange (eds) *Cooperative Strategies in International Business*. New York: Lexington Books

Curtis, P. (2004) 'Market graders', *Guardian*, 17 August

Daily Telegraph (2006) '2600 travel jobs axed as consumers book flights on Internet', 16 December

Delery, J. and Doty, H, (1996) 'Modes of theorizing in strategic human resource management: tests of universalistic contingency, and configurational performance predictions', *Academy of Management Journal*, Vol.39 No.4

DesJardins, J. (2007) *Business, Ethics and the Environment*. New Jersey: Pearson/Prentice Hall

Dussauge, P. and Garrette, B. (1999) *Cooperative Strategy: competing successfully through strategic alliances*. Chichester: John Wiley.

Dyer, J., Kale, P. and Singh, H. (2004) 'When to ally and when to acquire', *Harvard Business Review*, Vol.82 Issue 7/8, July/August

Fayol, H. (1916/1949) *General and Industrial Management*. Pitman: London.

First Choice (2007) www.firstchoiceholidaysplc.com [accessed 3 August 1997]

Fisher, L. (2005) 'Ricardo Semler won't take control', *strategy + business*, Winter

Gillespie, A. (2000) 'Dell Computers', *Business Review*, September

Gimenez, F. (1999) 'Miles and Snow's strategy model in the context of small firms'. www.baer.uca.edu/research/icbs/1999 [accessed 7 September 2007]

Grant, R. (2008) *Contemporary Strategy Analysis,* 6th edition. Oxford: Blackwell

Hales, C. (2001) *Managing through Organization*, 2nd edition. London: Business Press/Thomson Learning.

Hansen, M. and Von Oetinger, B. (2001) 'Introducing T-shaped managers', *Harvard Business Review*, Vol.79 Issue 3, March

HF Holidays www.hfholidays.co.uk [accessed 14 July 2007]

Hindo, B. (2007) 'At 3M, a struggle between efficiency and creativity', *BusinessWeek*, 11 June

Holidaybreak (2007) www.holidaybreak.co.uk [accessed 14 July 2007]

Houlder, V. (2003) 'Dark cloud of suspicion hangs over National Trust', *Financial Times,* 26 April

Inkpen, A. and Ross, J. (2001) 'Why do some strategic alliances persist beyond their useful life?', *California Management Review*, Fall

Johnson, G. and Scholes, K. (1997) *Exploring Corporate Strategy*, 4th edition. Hemel Hempstead: Prentice Hall.

Johnson, G., Scholes, K. and Whittington, R. (2004) *Exploring Corporate Strategy*, 7th edition. Harlow: FT/Prentice Hall

Jowit, J. (2001) 'Why an accident like Hatfield was waiting to happen', *Financial Times*, 22 February

Kafka, F. (1964) *The Trial*. London: Secker & Wasburg

Keynote (2006) 'Activity holidays', February

Legg, R. (2005) 'Breach of Trust', *Guardian,* 14 September

Lewis, J. (2002) 'Testing time', *Personnel Today*, 9 April

Marchington, M. and Wilkinson, A. (2008) *Human Resource Management at Work*, 4th edition. London: CIPD

Marketing (2004) 'Trouble strikes the travel agent', *Marketing*, 23 June

McCurry, J. (2009) 'Deflation stalks Japan as jobless figure hits peak', *Guardian*, 29 August

Miles, R. E. and Snow, C. C. (1978) *Organizational Strategy, Structure and Process*. Maidenhead: McGraw-Hill

Mintzberg, H. (1998) 'The structuring of organisations', in Mintzberg, H., Quinn, J. B. and Ghoshal, S., *The Strategy Process*. Hemel Hempstead: Prentice Hall Europe

Nathan, M. (2000) 'The paradoxical nature of crisis', *Review of Business*, Vol.21 Issue 3.4

National Trust (2006) 'Annual Report and Financial Statements 2005–6'

Norman, P. (2001) 'Are your secrets safe?: knowledge protection in strategic alliances', *Business Horizons*, Vol.44 Issue 6, November–December

Noyes, T. (2009) 'Building a new General Motors', *Guardian*, 1 June

Oxfam (2009) 'Turning the tide: how best to protect workers employed by gangmasters, five years after Morecambe Bay'

Page, R. (2005) 'The sorry tale of Peter Rabbit', *Daily Mail,* 14 October

Parkhe, A. (2001) 'Interfirm diversity in global alliances', *Business Horizons*, Vol.44 Issue 6, November–December

Payne, S. (2005) 'Dog owners savage the National Trust', *Daily Telegraph*, 5 December

Peng, M. W., Tan, J. and Tong, T. W. (2004) 'Ownership types and strategic groups in emerging economies', *Journal of Management Studies*, Vol.41 Issue 7, November

Pickard, J. (2006) 'Cable & Wireless calls time on outsourced HR', *People Management*, 26 October

Pickard, J. (2009) 'BP and Hewittt renew HR outsourcing deal', *People Management*, 12 February

Porter, M. E. (1980) *Competitive Strategy*. New York: Free Press

Porter, M. E. (1985) *Competitive Advantage: creating and sustaining superior performance*. New York: Free Press

Proby, W. (2005) 'Out of the country house and into the back to back', *Guardian,* 15 September

Ruigrok, W. (2004) 'A tale of strategic and governance errors', *European Business Forum,* Issue 17, Spring

Schuler, R. and Jackson, S. (1987) 'Linking competitive strategies with human resource management practices', *Academy of Management Executive,* Vol.1 No.3

Schwartz, P. (2003) *Inevitable Surprises: think ahead in times of turbulence.* New York: Gotham Books

Semler, R. (1993) *Maverick!* London: Arrow Books

Shortell, S. M. and Zajac, E. (1990) 'Perceptual and archival measures of Miles and Snow's strategic types: the role of strategic orientation', *Academy of Management Journal,* Vol.33 Issue 4, December

Slywotsky, A. and Nadler, D. (2004) 'The strategy is the structure', *Harvard Business Review,* Vol.82 Issue 2, February

Sull, D. (2005) 'Dynamic partners', *Business Strategy Review,* Summer

Taylor, F. W. (1947) *Scientific Management.* New York: Harper & Row

Thompson, J. with Martin, F. (2005) *Strategic Management: awareness and change.* London: Thomson

Travel Weekly (2004) 'Waymark still clients' choice', 3 January

Vidal, J. (2007) 'Broader horizons', *Guardian,* 25 July

Warner, M. and Witzel, M. (2003) *Managing in Virtual Organizations.* London: Routledge

Waters, R. and Menn, J. (2009) 'Microsoft and Yahoo on defensive', *Financial Times,* 31 July

Wearden, G. (2009) 'General Motors – countdown to collapse', *Guardian,* 1 June

Weber, M. (1964) *The Theory of Economic and Social Organisation.* New York: Free Press

Weihrich, H. (1982) 'The TOWS matrix: a tool for situational analysis', *Journal of Long Range Planning,* Vol.15 Issue 2

Whittington, R. and Mayer, M. (2000) *The European Corporation: strategy, structure and social science.* Oxford: Oxford University Press

Worthington, I. and Britton, C. (2006) *The Business Environment,* 5th edition. Harlow: FT/Prentice Hall

Chapter 2

Bion, W. R. (1961) *Experiences in Groups: and other papers.* London: Tavistock

Blake, R. and Mouton, J. (1964) *The Managerial Grid: the key to leadership excellence.* Houston: Gulf Publishing Co

Boxall, P. and Purcell, J. (2003) *Strategy and Human Resource Management.* London: Palgrave

Brown, D. (2003) 'A capital idea', *People Management,* 26 June, pp42–46

Conway, N. and Briner, R. (2005) *Understanding the Psychological Contract at Work.* Oxford: Oxford University Press

Deming, W. (1986) *Out of Crisis: quality, productivity and competitive position.* Cambridge: Cambridge University Press

Dixon, M. (1978) *Financial Times,* 2 November, p38

Drucker, P. (1981) *Managing in Turbulent Times.* London: Pan Books

Enterprise (2009) 'Case Study: Customer Contact Centre with the MoD Housing Contract'. www.enterprise.plc.com [accessed 19 April 2010]

Fayol, H. (1947a) *General and Industrial Management.* London: Pitman

Fayol, H. (1947b) *General and Industrial Administration.* London: Pitman

Fielder, F. (1967) *A Theory of Leadership Effectiveness.* New York: McGraw-Hill

Fraterman, E. (2009) 'The case for customer satisfaction'. http://www.customerfocusconsult.com/articles/articles_template.asp?ID=30 [accessed 19 April 2010]

French, W. L. and Bell, C. H. (1984) *Organization Development.* Englewood Cliffs NJ: Prentice Hall

Griffin, E., Finney, L., Hennessy, J. and Boury, D. (2009) *Maximising the Value of HR Business Partnering*. Horsham: Roffey Park Institute

Guest, D. and Conway, N. (2002) *Pressure at Work and the Psychological Contract*. London: CIPD

Hall, C. and Lindzey, G. (1978) *Theories of Personality*. New York: Wiley

Hammer, M. and Champy, J. (1993) *Re-engineering the Corporation*. London: Nicholas Brealey

Hennessy, J. (2009) 'Take your partners and advance', *People Management*, 29, 26 January.

Herriot, P. (1998) 'The role of the HR function in building a new proposition for staff', in Sparrow, P. and Marchington, M. (eds) *Human Resource Management: the new agenda*. London: FT/Pitman

Hill, T. (1991) *Production and Operations Management: text and cases*. London: Prentice Hall

Hunt, J. (1979) *Managing People at Work*. London: Pan Books

IDS (2004) 'The Royal Bank of Scotland group', *HR Studies*, Update 769, 14–17 March

Infoquest (2002) 'Annual business survey', Los Angeles

IRS (2003) 'Rewarding performance: Sainsbury's new bonus scheme', *IRS Employment Review*, 784, 19 September, pp33–36

IRS (2004) *IRS Employment Review*, 792, 23 January, pp33–34

Johnson, G. and Scholes, K. (1988) *Exploring Corporate Strategy*. London: Prentice Hall

Juran, J. (1988) *Quality Control Handbook*. New York: McGraw-Hill

Kübler-Ross, E. (1969) *On Death and Dying*. New York: Macmillan

Legge, K. (1978) *Power, Innovation and Problem-Solving in Personnel Management*. London: McGraw-Hill

Lewin, K. (1958) 'Group decisions and social changes', in Swanson, G. E., Newcomb, T. M. and Hartley, E. L. (eds) *Readings in Social Psychology*. New York: Holt, Rinehart & Winston

MacMillan, I. (1978) *Strategy Formulation: political concepts*. St Paul: West Publishing Company

Maslow, A. H. (1943) 'A theory of human motivation', *Psychology Review*, 50, pp370–396

Mayo, E. (1933) *Human Problems of an Industrialised Society*. New York: Harpers

Morgan, G. (1986) *Images of Organisations*. Beverley Hills CA: Sage Publications

Mullins, L. (1989) *Management and Organizational Behaviour*. London: Pitman

National Audit Office (2009) 'Ministry of Defence: Service Families Accommodation'. http://www.nao.org.uk/publications/0809/service_families_accommodation.aspx [accessed 19 April 2010]

Needle, D. (2004) *Business in Context*. London: Thomson

Peters, T. (1987) *Thriving on Chaos*. New York: Knopf

Pfeffer, J. (1981) *Power and Organisations*. Boston: Pitman

Pickard, J. (2004) 'One step beyond'. *People Management*, 30 June, pp27–31.

Porter, M. (1985) *Competitive Advantage: creating and sustaining superior performance*. New York: Free Press

Pugh, D., Hickson, D. and Hinings, C. (1971) *Writers on Organisations*. London: Harmondsworth

Purcell, J. and Ahlstrand, B. (1994) *Human Resource Management in the Multi-Divisional Company*. Oxford: Oxford University Press

Rucci, A. (1997) 'Should HR survive? A profession at the crossroads.' *Human Resource Management*, Vol. 36 No. 1, 169–173

Schein, E. (1980) *Organisational Psychology*. Englewood Cliffs NJ: Prentice Hall

Schutz, W. (1966) *The Interpersonal Underworld: FIRO — a three dimensional theory of interpersonal behavior*. Palo Alto CA: Science and Behavior Books

Shafer, R., Dyer, L., Kilty, J., Amos, J. and Ericksen, J. (2001) 'Crafting a human resource strategy to foster organisational agility' Vol. 36 No. 3, *Human Resource Management* pp197–211

Slack, N., Chambers, L. and Johnston, R. (2007) *Operations Management*, 5th edition. London: FT Prentice Hall

Storey, J. (1992) *Developments in the Management of Human Resources*. London: Blackwell

Storr, F. (2009) 'Humberside TEC, a Learning Company'. www.trojanmice.com/articles/becoming/htm [accessed 19 April 2010]

Stredwick, J. (1997) *Cases in Reward Management*. London: Kogan Page

Swart, J., Kinnie, N. and Purcell, J. (2003) *People and Performance in Knowledge-intensive Firms*. London: CIPD

Taylor, F. (1947) *Scientific Management*. New York: Harper & Row

Taylor, S. (2008) *People Resourcing*, 4th edition. London: CIPD

Thomas, K. (1976) 'Conflict and conflict management', in Dunette, M. D. (ed) *Handbook of Industrial and Organisational Psychology*. Chicago: Rand McNally

Townely, B. (1996) *Reframing Human Resource Management: power, ethics and the subject at work*. London: Sage

Tuckman, B. (1965) 'Developmental sequence in small groups', *Psychological Bulletin*, 63, pp384–99

Ulrich, D. (1998) *Human Resource Champions: the Next Agenda for adding value and delivering results*. Boston, MA: Harvard Business School Press

Ulrich, D. and Brockbank, W. (2005) *The HR Value Proposition*. Boston, MA: Harvard Business School Press

University of Hull Business School (2007) 'Case Study: Humberside Training and Enterprise Council'. Itsy.co.uk/sisn/orange/humber.doc [accessed 19 April 2010]

Weber, M. (1925) *Economy and Society*. Oxford: Oxford University Press

Wickens, P. (1987) *The Road to Nissan: flexibility, quality, teamwork*. Basingstoke: Palgrave-Macmillan

Wood, P. (1995) 'The four pillars of human resource management: are they connected?' *Human Resource Management Journal*, vol. 5 No. 5, pp49–59

Chapter 3

Akerlof, G. (1970) 'The market for lemons: quality uncertainty and the market mechanism', *Quarterly Journal of Economics*, Vol.84, August

Atkinson (1984), 'Manpower strategies for the flexible organisation' *Personnel Management* August

Bailey, D. (2009) 'How to plan for economic restructuring, redundancies and/or closure', Centre for Urban and Regional Studies, University of Birmingham

Barber, B. (1998) Speech to the New Labour and the Labour Movement Conference, 19/20 June

Briner, R. and Conway, N. (2001) *Understanding Psychological Contracts at Work: a critical evaluation of theory and research*. Oxford: Oxford University Press

Capelli, P. (2008) *Talent on Demand: managing talent in an age of uncertainty*. Cambridge, MA: Harvard Business School Press

Cascio, W. F. and Wynn, P. (2004) 'Managing a downsizing process', *Human Resource Management*, Vol.43

Central Statistical Office (1992) 'Business Monitor PA 1002: Report on the Census of Production 1990'. London: HMSO

Churchard, C. (2009a) '"Survivor syndrome" hits UK workforce', *People Management*, 7 August

Churchard, C. (2009b) 'CBI proposes alternative to redundancy scheme', *People Management*, 6 July

Churchard, C. (2009c) 'Honda staff vote for 3 per cent pay cut to save jobs', *People Management*, 16 June

Churchard, C. (2009d) 'Voluntary measures will secure BA's future, says HR chief', *People Management*, 17 July

CIPD (2003) *Work–Life Balance*, Factsheet. London: CIPD

CIPD (2004) *Frequently Asked Questions: parental rights and other family-friendly provisions*. London: CIPD

CIPD (2005) *Managing the Psychological Contract*, Factsheet. London: CIPD

CIPD (2009a) *Labour Market Outlook*, Spring. London: CIPD

CIPD (2009b) *Labour Market Outlook*, Summer. London: CIPD

CIPD (2009c) *Employee Outlook: job seeking in a recession*. London: CIPD

CIPD (2009d) *Work–Life Balance*, Factsheet. London: CIPD

CIPD (2009e) *Talent Management: an overview*, Factsheet. London: CIPD

Clancy, C. (2009) 'The labour market and the economy', *Economic and Labour Market Review*, February

Competition Commission (2007) *Groceries Market Investigation: emerging thinking*, 23 January

Connecting Industry (2009) 'CBI outlines new employment measures to help business through critical recovery period', 13 July

DirectGov (2010), 'Statutory guarantee pay', www.direct.gov.uk/en/Employment/Understandingyourworkstatus/Temporarylayoff/DG_177591 [accessed 12 April 2010]

Downes, L. (1997) 'Technosynthesis: beyond Porter', *Context*, www.contextmag.com/archives/199712/technosynthesis.asp?process=print [accessed 19 April 2010]

Draca, M. and Dickens, R. (2005) 'The employment effects of the October 2003 increase in the National Minimum Wage', CEP Discussion Paper, June

EasyJet (2007) EasyJet website www.easyjet.com [accessed June–July 2007]

Finch, J. (2009a) 'Morrisons beats rivals with bumper Christmas sales', *Guardian*, 23 January

Finch, J. (2009b) 'Supermarkets: big four fight back in discount food feud', *Guardian*, 25 July

Gallie, D. (2000) 'The labour force'. in Halsey, A. H. and Webb, J. (eds), *Twentieth Century British Social Trends*. Basingstoke: Macmillan

Ghoshal, S. (2000) 'Value creation', *Executive Excellence*, November, Vol.17 Issue 11

Giddens, A. (2006) *Sociology*, 5th edition. Cambridge: Polity Press

Girma, S., Goyt, A., Strobl, E. and Walsh, F. (2007) *Creating Jobs through Public Subsidies: an empirical analysis*, IZA Discussion Paper 3168

Grimshaw, D., Ward, K., Rubery, J. and Beynon, H. (2001) 'Organisations and the transformation of the internal labour market', *Work, Employment and Society*, Vol.15 Issue 1

Guest, D. E. and Conway, N. (2002) *Pressure at Work and the Psychological Contract*. London: CIPD

Handy, C. (1991) *Inside Organizations*. London: BBC

Hiscott, G. (2004) 'Big chains strengthen hold on Britain's shoppers', *Independent*, 10 August

Hodgkin, P. (2007) 'Gift rap', *Guardian*, 5 September

Hoyos, C. (2006) 'Opec vows to defend minimum $60 for oil', *Financial Times*, 20 October

Hyman, R. (1987) 'Strategy or structure: capital, labour and control', *Work, Employment and Society*, Vol.1 Issue 1, p30

Joyce, P. and Woods, A. (1996) *Essential Strategic Management: from modernism to pragmatism*. Oxford: Butterworth-Heinemann

Kay, J. (2003) *The Truth about Markets*. London: Allen Lane/The Penguin Press

Kent, K. (2009) 'Employment changes over 30 years', *Economics and Labour Market Review*, Vol.3 No.2

Kim, C. and Mauborgne, R. (2001) 'How to earn commitment', *Financial Times*, 22 October

Kimberly, J. and Craig, E. (2001) 'Work as a life experience', *Financial Times*, 5 November

Lipsey, R. and Chrystal, A. (1999) *Principles of Economics*, 9th edition. Oxford: Oxford University Press

Lynch, R. (2006) *Corporate Strategy*, 4th edition. Harlow: FT-Prentice Hall

McAfee, R. and te Velde, V. (2005) 'Dynamic pricing in the airline industry', California Institute of Technology, www.caltech.edu/mcafee [accessed 11 July 2007]

McCarthy, T. (2009) 'BA staff shows blitz spirit', *People Management*, 30 July

McCartney, C. (2009) *Fighting Back through Talent Innovation*. London: CIPD

Manning, A. (2003) *Monopsony in Motion: imperfect competition in labor markets*, Princeton, NJ: Princeton University Press

Manning, A. and Petrolongo, B. (2005) 'The part time pay penalty', *Centrepiece*, December

Marchington, M. and Wilkinson, A. (2008) *Human Resource Management at Work*, 4th edition. London: CIPD

Metcalf, D. (2007) 'Why has the British National Minimum Wage had little or no impact on employment?', CEP Discussion Paper, April

Moynach, M. and Worsley, R. (2001) 'Prophet sharing', *People Management*, 27 December

People Management (2009a) 'CIPD calls for subsidy for young jobseekers', 24 August

People Management (2009b) 'British Airways staff asked to work for free', 16 June

Philpott, J. (2002) 'HRH – a work audit', *CIPD Perspectives*, Summer

Philpott, J. (2009a) 'The cost to employers of redundancy', *Impact* 26, February

Philpott, J. (2009b) 'Labour cost savings from alternatives to redundancy', *Impact* 27, May

Pidd, H. (2009), 'Honda's Swindon factory reopens', *Guardian*, 1 June

Porter, M. (1980) *Competitive Strategy: techniques for analyzing industries and competition*. London: Macmillan

Professional Manager (2001) 'Focused females forge ahead', November

Purvis, A. (2004) 'Why supermarkets are getting richer and richer', *Observer*, 25 June

Retail Week (2009) 'Co-op reports record full-year results', 6 May

Social Trends (2004) 'Chapter 13: Lifestyles and social participation', Vol.34. London: HMSO

Rousseau, D. (2004) 'Psychological contracts in the workplace: understanding the ties that motivate', *Academy of Management Executive*, Vol.18 No.1, February

Schumpeter, J. (1950) *Capitalism, Socialism and Democracy*, 3rd edition. New York: Harper & Row

Stewart, H. (2009) 'Union says yes to Honda pay cut', *Guardian*, 22 June

Thomas, T. (2009) 'Tesco eyes loyalty value with Clubcard relaunch', *Marketing*, 13 May

Walker, R. (1990) 'Analysing the business portfolio in Black and Decker Europe', in Taylor, B. and Harrison, J., *The Manager's Casebook of Business Strategy*. Oxford: Butterworth-Heinemann

Walsh, J. (2001) 'A happy reunion', *People Management*, 8 November

Weiss, R. and Mehrotra, A. (2001) 'Dynamic pricing and the future of e-commerce: an economic and legal analysis', *Virginia Journal of Law and Technology*, Vol.11, Summer

Wheatcroft, P. (2004) 'Supermarkets take a convenient route', *Times*, 17 August

Chapter 4

Article 13 and CBI (2007) 'Dwr Cymru Welsh Water', *CBI–CSR Case Studies*, September

Bank of England (2003) 'Remit for the Monetary Policy Committee of the Bank of England and the New Inflation Target'. www.bankofengland.co.uk [accessed 30 October 2004]

Bank of England (2004a) 'The Labour Market'. www.bankofengland.co.uk/targettwopointzero [accessed 30 October 2004]

Bank of England (2004b) 'How do interest rates affect inflation?' www.bankof england.co.uk/ targettwopointzero [accessed 30 October 2004]

Batty, D. (2009) 'Timeline: the Baby P case', *Guardian*, 22 May

Batty, D. and Weaver, M. (2006) 'Q&A: private finance initiative', *Guardian*, 3 May

Blake, R. and Mouton, J. (1964) *The Managerial Grid: the key to leadership excellence*. Houston: Gulf Publishing Co

Booth, R. (2009a) 'Welcome to Barnet, the Tory test-pilot of no-frills government', *Guardian*, 27 August

Booth, R. (2009b) 'Tory-controlled borough of Barnet adopts budget airline model', *Guardian*, 27 August

Booth, R. (2009c) 'The Ryanair pricing model that could be a route to budget care in Barnet', *Guardian*, 27 August

Bowcott, O. (2004) 'Transcript reveals doctor's pleas for dying teenager', *Guardian*, 18 October

Bowcott, O. (2009a) 'Social work vacancies as high as 39 per cent', *Guardian*, 17 June

Bowcott, O. (2009b) 'Baby P council looks to US for social workers', *Guardian*, 3 October

Brindle, D. (2009) 'Ministers back plan for a national social work college', *Guardian*, 29 July

Briner, R. (2001) 'Why family-friendly practices can also be performance-friendly', *People Management*, 8 November

Brown, K. (2001) 'Standard that has delivered', *Financial Times*, 30 October

Burgess, J. (2009) 'The budget airline model won't work for councils', *Guardian*, 2 September

Cable, V. (2009) *The Storm: the world economic crisis and what it means*. London: Atlantic Books

Carvel, J. (2003) 'Blair puts NHS out to tender', *Guardian*, 14 May

Carvel, J. (2009) 'Government pledges £58m to recruiting top quality social workers following Baby P case', *Guardian*, 6 May

Caulkin, S. (2003) 'Wanted: one kick in the pants', *Observer*, 18 May

CBI (2005) *CBI response to Leitch Review of Skills*.

CIPD (2008) *The Skills Agenda in the UK*, Factsheet. London: CIPD

CIPD (Ireland) (2009) *Social Partnership and the National Economic Recovery Plan*, December

Conservative Party (2008) 'Building skills, transforming lives: a training and apprenticeships revolution'

Daneshkhu, S. (2007a) 'The quest for improved productivity', *Financial Times*, 22 May

Daneshkhu, S. (2007b) 'Output still trails other large countries', *Financial Times*, 26 June

De Grauwe, P. (2001) 'Competitiveness and compassion', *Financial Times*, 8 November

Department of Trade and Industry (1998) 'Building the Knowledge Driven Economy'. www.dti.gov.uk/ competitive [accessed 29 August 2004]

Department of Trade and Industry (2001) 'Opportunity for All in a World of Change'. www.dti.gov.uk/ opportunityfor all [accessed 29 August 2004]

De Vita, E. (2009) 'Fast track India', *Management Today*, August

DIUS (2007) *World Class Skills: implementing the Leitch Review of Skills in England*, Cm 7181

Dolton, P. (2005) *The Labour Market for Teachers: a policy perspective*. Office of Manpower Economics

ECB (2004) 'Objective of monetary policy'. www.ecb.int [accessed 18 September 2004]

Economist (2005) 'From Lisbon to Brussels', 19 March

Elliott, L. (2010) 'Soaring jobless, plunging benefits ... is Ireland a glimpse of Tory-led UK?', *Guardian*, 8 February

European Union (2004) 'European Performance in Competitiveness and Innovation'. www.europa. eu.int [accessed 18 September 2004]

Farnham, D. (1999) *Managing in a Business Context*. London: CIPD

Federal Reserve (2004) 'Frequently Asked Questions: monetary policy'.
www.federalreserve.gov [accessed 18 September 2004]

Forman, F. N. and Baldwin, N. D. J. (1999) *Mastering British Politics*, 4th edition. Basingstoke:
Macmillan

Giles, C. (2007) 'Productivity loses steam under Labour', *Financial Times*, 23 January

Goyal, A. and Jha, A. (2004) 'Dictatorship, democracy and institutions: macro policy in China and
India', *Economic and Political Weekly (India)*, 16 October

Guardian (2003a) 'Duisenberg decorated but still dithering', 10 May

Guardian (2003b) 'Accountability vacuum', 3 May

Harding, R. (2004) 'Social enterprise: the new economic engine', *Business Strategy Review*, Winter

Hellowell, M. (2006) 'Alive and kicking', *Public Finance*, 17 November

Hencke, D. (2004) 'Big players lobbying for piece of the action', *Guardian*, 27 October

Hilton, I. (2004) 'A rampaging market, but a long way from global power', *Guardian*, 13 November

Hirst, J. (2005) 'The awkward age', *Public Finance*, 14 January

House, J. D. and McGrath, K. (2004) 'Innovative governance and development in the new Ireland:
Social Partnership and the integrated approach', *Governance*, Vol.17 No.1

Hudson, B. (2009) 'Captives of bureaucracy', *Community Care*, 9 April

Hutton, W. (2004) 'We must dare to be dynamic', *Observer*, 7 November

Hutton, W. (2007) *The Writing on the Wall*. London: Little Brown

IPPR (2001) *Building Better Partnerships*, June

Jacques, M. (2009) *When China Rules the World*. London: Allen Lane

Kay, J. (2002) 'The balance sheet', *Prospect*, July

Kay, J. (2003) *The Truth about Markets – their genius, their limits, their follies*. London: Allen Lane

Keegan, W. (2004a) 'Erm, there's a danger in paradise', *Observer*, 17 October

Keegan, W. (2004b) 'Keeping an eye on the competition', *Observer*, 31 October

Kirkpatrick, I. and Ackroyd, S. (2003) 'Transforming the professional archetype?: the new
managerialism in UK social services', *Public Management Review*, Vol.5 Issue 4

Lawton, A. and Rose, A. (1994) *Organisation and Management in the Public Sector*. Harlow: FT/
Prentice Hall

Leitch, S. (2006) *Leitch Review of Skills: prosperity for all in the global economy – world class skills*.
London: HM Treasury

Lennan, D. (2001) 'Cartel crooks belong in jail', *Financial Times*, 2 November

Lipsey, R. G. and Chrystal, K. A. (1999) *Principles of Economics*, 9th edition. Oxford: Oxford University
Press

LSC (2008) *National Employers Skills Survey 2007: key findings*.

Lucas, E. (2009) 'Businesses that "put back" are bucking the trend', *Professional Manager*, September

Mac Cormaic, R. (2008) 'Twenty years of social partnership agreements', *Irish Times*, 4 August

Maltby, P. (2003) *Public Interest Companies: fad or permanent fixture?* Institute for Public Policy
Research

Mathiason, N. (2004) 'Casino bill derailed by bitter split in Cabinet', *Observer*, 24 October

Meredith, R. (2007) *The Elephant and the Dragon: the rise of India and China and what it means for all
of us*. New York: Norton

Merrick, N. (2001) 'Minority interest', *People Management*, 8 November

Moreton, S. (2006) 'Are "professional" HR practices compatible with volunteer management?'. Attend

Mulholland, H. (2009) 'We will follow example of efficient Tory councils, says Osborne', *Guardian*, 10 September

Mulvey, S. (2003) 'The EU law that rules our lives'. *BBC News Online*. news.bbc.co.uk [accessed 18 October 2004]

Nelson, P. (2001) 'Does IIP still make the grade?', *Personnel Today*, 13 November

Newman, M. (2009) 'Social work degrees difficult to fail, MPs told', *Times Higher Education*, 6 August

Osborn, A. (2003) 'State's golden share in BAA is illegal', *Guardian*, 14 May

Palmås, K. (2005) *the UK Public Interest Company: the idea, its origins, and its relevance for Sweden* (CbiS Discussion Paper 1). Göteborg University, Sweden

Phillips, A. W. H. (1958) 'The relationship between unemployment and the rate of change of money wage rates in the UK 1861–1957', *Economica*, Vol.25 No.2

Philpott, J. (2002) 'Productivity and people management', *Perspectives*, Spring

Philpott, J. (2003) 'Europe', *Perspectives*, Summer

Porter, M. and Ketels, C. (2003) *UK Competitiveness: moving to the next stage* (DTI Economics Paper No. 3). DTI/ESRC

Rudiger, K. (2008) 'The UK and India: the other "special relationship"?' The Work Foundation Provocation Series, Vol.4 No.3

Samuel, M. (2009) 'Celebrities back social work in government recruitment push', *Community Care*, 1 September.

Sawford. A. (2009) 'How Whitehall betrayed social workers', *Guardian*, 12 March

Smith, D. (2007a) 'We still have a grip on inflation, says Bank', *Sunday Times*, 22 April

Smith, D. (2007b) *The Dragon and the Elephant: China, India and the new world order*. London: Profile

Steele, J. (2001) 'Food for thought: Amartya Sen', *Guardian*, 31 March

Stratton, A. (2010) 'Labour's plan for first "John Lewis" council', *Guardian*, 18 February

Tomlinson, M. (2004) *14–19 Curriculum and Qualifications Reform (the Tomlinson Report)*. London: DES (now DCSF)

TUC (2008) 'After Leitch: Implementing Skills and Training Policies: TUC submission to the Innovation, Universities and Skills Committee Inquiry'

Travers, T. (2009) 'Osborne shows he is a true blue', *Guardian*, 10 September

Treasury (2006) *PFI: strengthening long-term partnerships*. London: HM Treasury

Ward, L. (2000) 'Parties in key battle over families cash', *Guardian*, 22 February

Ward, S. (2000) 'Brown to gamble on "spend more" call', *Guardian*, 10 November

Warner, J. (2003) 'Network Rail spends away, but is it really value for money?', *Independent*, 8 May

Warner, J. (2007) 'Governor's letter should not be seen as a non-event. Rather, it highlights policy failings', *Independent*, 18 April

Wileman A. (2007) 'India rising', *Management Today*, July

Woodward, W. (2003) 'School firms' forte is "lobbying for work"', *Guardian*, 5 May

World Bank (2000) *Beyond Economic Growth: meeting the challenges of global development*. www.worldbank/depweb/beyond/global./chapter4 [accessed 24 April 2007]

Wright, R. (2007a) 'Cost rises in the first three years', *Financial Times*, 16 July

Wright, R. (2007b) 'Working relationship proved dear', *Financial Times*, 18 July

Chapter 5

Brooks, I. and Weatherston, J. (2004) *The Business Environment*, 3rd edition. London: FT-Prentice Hall

Cartwright, S. and Cooper, S. (1997) *Managing Workplace Stress*. London: Sage

Competition Commission (2003) 'Extended warranties on domestic electrical goods: A report on the supply of extended warranties on domestic electrical goods within the UK'. www.competition-commission.org.uk/rep_pub/reports/2003/485xwars.htm#full [accessed 22 April 2010]

Curwen, P. (1997) *Restructuring Telecommunications: a study of Europe in a global context.* Basingstoke: Palgrave-Macmillan

Dey, I. and Smith, D. (2009) 'Mr Darling's exceedingly poor fudge', *Sunday Times Business*, 12 July, p7.

Earnshaw, J. and Cooper, C. (1996) *Stress and Employer Liability.* London: IPD

Electricity Association (1998) 'Electricity Industry review'. London: HMSO

Friedman, M. (1970) *The Counter-Revolution in Monetary Theory.* London: Institute of Economic Affairs

HSE (2006) '2005/6 Survey of self-reported work-related illnesses'. London: Health and Safety Executive

IRS (2002) 'Court of Appeal guidelines for stress at work cases'. *Employment Law Review* 748, 25 March

Martin, S. and Parker, D. (1997) *The Impact of Privatisation: ownership and corporate performance in the UK.* London: Routledge

Mathiason, N. (2009) 'Recruitment firm Hays to appeal against £30million price-fixing fine', *Guardian*, 30 September, p12

Miller, S. (1999) 'Council pays £67,000 for stress injury', *Guardian*, 6 July, p4

Ofcom (2010) www.ofcom.org/consumeradvice/guide [accessed 19 April 2010]

Palmer, B. and Quinn, P. (2004) 'Protracted agony', *People Management*, 6 May, p17

Pollack, C. (1997) 'European Union policies', in Lewington, I. (ed) *Utility Regulation.* London: Centre for the Study of Regulated Industries and Privatisation International

Rick, J., Hillage, S., Honey, S. and Perryman, S. (1997) *Stress: big Issue, but what are the problems?* Institute of Employment Studies Report 311, July

Scott. A. (2009) 'HSE raps health trust for "failing" on stress. *People Management*, 26 February, p9

Tehrani, N. (2002) *Managing Organisational Stress: a CIPD guide to improving and maintaining well-being.* London: CIPD

Waples, J. (2009) 'Water feature', *Sunday Times Business*, 4 October, p4

Watkins, J. (2003) 'Wellness beats output slump', *People Management*, 18 December, p12

Yarker, J. and Lewis, R. (2007) 'Management competencies for preventing and reducing stress at work'. London: HSE

Chapter 6

Aisbett, E. (2003) 'Globalization, poverty and inequality: are the criticisms vague, vested or valid?' NBER Pre-conference on Globalization, Poverty and Inequality

Akcapar, B. and Chaibi, D. (2006) 'Turkey EU accession: the long road from Ankara to Brussels', *Yale Journal of International Affairs*, Winter–Spring

Aragon, B. (2008) 'The hidden costs of a "maquiladora"', *New Mexico Independent*, 23 July

Bartlett, C. and Ghoshal, S. (1991) *Managing across Borders.* Boston, MA: Harvard Business School Press

BBC (nd) 'Born abroad, immigration map of the UK'. news.bbc.co.uk [accessed 17 April 2007]

BBC (2005a) BBC news website. news.bbc.co.uk [accessed 24 April 2007]

BBC (2007) 'At-a-glance: EU treaty proposals'. news.bbc.co.uk [accessed 24 June 2007]

Bergin, P., Feenstra, R. and Hanson, G. (2008) 'Offshoring and volatility: evidence from Mexico's *maquiladora* industry' (NBER Working Paper)

Boone, P. (2005) 'Effective intervention: making aid work', *CentrePiece*, Winter

Branzei, O. and Nadkarni, A. (2008),' The Tata Way: evolving and executing sustainable business strategies', *Ivey Business Journal*, March–April

Church, C. and Phinnemore, D. (2006) 'The rise and fall of the Constitutional Treaty', in Cini, M. (ed) *European Union Politics*, 2nd edition. Oxford: Oxford University Press

CIA (2007) *CIA World Factbook*. Online version at https://www.cia.gov/library/publications/the-world-factbook [accessed 18 April 2007]

CIPD (2006) *Offshoring and the Role of HR*, Survey report. London: CIPD

CIPD (2009) *EU employment policy* Worksheet. London: CIPD

Clark, R. (2005) *Contemporary Strategy Analysis,* 5th edition. Oxford: Blackwell

Clennell, A. (2004) 'Call centre switches jobs back from India to Britain', *Independent*, 23 January

Cohen, R. and Kennedy, P. (2007) *Global Sociology*, 2nd edition. Basingstoke: Palgrave-Macmillan

Crainer, S. and Dearlove, D. (2005) 'Indian think', *Business Strategy Review*, Winter

Datamonitor (2006) *Tesco plc Company Profile*, May

De Jonquieres, H. (2003) 'How enlightened international co-operation turned into a show case for indecision', *Financial Times*, 31 March

Doward, J. (2009), 'Banana price war in supermarkets brings fear to the developing world', *Observer*, 11 October

Doward, J. and McKenna, H. (2007) 'Immigration figures "are false"', *Observer*, 29 April

Economist (2003) 'The Doha squabble', *The Economist* (US), 29 March

Economist (2006a) 'In the twilight of Doha', *The Economist* (US), 29 July

Economist (2006b) 'Trouble at till', *The Economist* (US), 4 November

Economist (2007a) 'Rebranding Thaksinomics', *The Economist* (US), 13 January

Economist (2007b) 'Home and abroad', *The Economist* (US), 10 February

Elliott, L. (2004) 'What the WTO needs is a new Reformation', *Guardian*, 2 August

Elliott, L. and Connolly, K. (2007) 'In 2005, G8 pledged $50bn for Africa. Now the reality', *Guardian*, 25 April

Emmott, B., Crook, C. and Micklethwait, J. (2002) *Globalisation: making sense of an integrating world*. London: The Economist/Profile Books

Finch, J. (2003) 'In India, it's service with a compulsory smile', *Guardian*, 17 November

Fischler, F. and Lamy, P. (2003) 'Free farm trade means an unfair advantage', *Financial Times*, 1 April

Fletcher, R. (2006) 'Thailand junta warns Tesco over expansion', *Daily Telegraph*, 28 September

Fortune (2006) 'Fortune Global 500 2006'. www.money.cnn.com/magazines/fortune/global500 [accessed 8 May 2007]

Fukuyama, F. (2004) 'Bring back the state', *Observer*, 4 July

Gamble, J. (2003) 'Transferring human resource practices from the United Kingdom to China: the limits and potential for convergence', *International Journal of Human Resource Management*, Vol.14 Issue 3

GAO (2003) 'Mexico's maquiladora decline affects US–Mexican border communities and trade recovery depends in part on Mexico's actions' (GAO-03-891), Washington DC: General Accounting Office

Ghemawat, P. (2003) 'The forgotten strategy', *Harvard Business Review*, Vol.81 No.11, November

Gray, J. (1995). *False Dawn*. London: Granta

Hales, C. (2001) *Managing through Organization*. London: Thomson Learning

Hofstede, G. (2009) 'Geert Hofstede Cultural Dimensions'. www.geert-hofstede.com/hofstede [accessed 14 October 2009]

House of Lords (2008) *The Economic Impact of Immigration: Vol I: Report* (HL Paper 82-I). London: House of Lords Select Committee on Economic Affairs

Iglicka, K.(2005) 'The impact of the EU enlargement on migratory movements in Poland'. Warsaw: Centrum Stosunkow Miedzynarodowych (Centre for International Relations). www.csm.org.pl [accessed 30 May 2007]

Interbrand (2006) 'Interbrand Best Global Brands 2006'. www.interbrand.com [accessed 18 June 2007]

International Labour Review (2006) 'The internationalization of employment: a challenge to fair globalisation?', *International Labour Review*, Spring–Summer

Jacobs, M. (2001) 'Bridging the global divide', *Observer,* 11 November

Jacques, M. (2009) *When China Rules the World*. London: Allen Lane

Jitpleecheep, S. (2001) 'Boots expansion is on hold in Thailand; to sell its wares in Tops supermarkets', *Bangkok Post*, 2 August

Jitpleecheep, S. (2002a) 'Less is more for Boots in Asia', *Bangkok Post*, 8 December

Jitpleecheep, S. (2002b) 'Boots slimming down', *Bangkok Post*, 6 March

Jitpleecheep, S. (2002c) 'Superstore: saturation foreseen in big-store sector', *Bangkok Post*, 12 June

Kirisci, K. (2007) 'Turkey in the EU: a win–win scenario', in Fraser, M. (ed) *European Union: the next 50 years*. London: FT Business

Legrain, P. (2003) *Open World: the truth about globalization*. London: Abacus

Lucas, C. (2001) 'Doha spells disaster for development', *Observer*, 18 November

Lungesen, D. (2004) 'Turkey's unrequited EU love'. BBC news website news.bbc.co.uk [accessed 30 June 2007]

MacShane, D. (2006) 'Immigration: don't close our borders', *The Economist* (US), 30 October

Madeley, J. (2001) 'No end to shackles', *Observer*, 21 January

Mangaliso, M. (2001) 'Building competitive advantage from *ubuntu:* management lessons from South Africa', *Academy of Management Executive*, August

Marchington, M. and Wilkinson, A. (2008) *Human Resource Management at Work*, 4th edition. London: CIPD

Mathiason, N. (2003) 'Debt duties', *Observer*, 20 April 2003

Micklethwait, J. and Wooldridge, A. (2000) *A Future Perfect: the challenge and hidden promise of globalization*. London: Heinemann

Migration Watch (2007) 'Outline of the problem', 2 January. www.migrationwatch.org.uk [accessed 27 May 2007]

Morris, H. and Willey, B. (1996). *The Corporate Environment*. London: Pitman

Nugent, N. (2006) *The Government and Politics of the European Union*, 6th edition. Basingstoke: Palgrave-Macmillan

Ohmae, K. (1990) *The Borderless World*. Glasgow: Collins

Perlmutter, H. V. (1969) 'The tortuous evolution of the multinational corporation', *Columbia Journal of World Business* 4

Philips (2007) www.philips.com [accessed 4 June 2007]

Pucik, V. (2007) 'Reframing global mindset', in Schuler, R. and Jackson, S., *Strategic Human Resource Management,* 2nd edition. Oxford: Blackwell

Rollinson, D. (2008) *Organisational Behaviour and Analysis*, 4th edition. Harlow: Pearson

Ryle, S. (2002) 'Banana war leaves the Caribbean a casualty', *Observer*, 24 November

Scholte, J. A. (2000) *Globalization: a critical introduction*. Basingstoke: Palgrave

Segal-Horn, S. (2002) 'Global firms – heroes or villains? How and why companies globalise', *European Business Journal*, Vol.14 Issue 1

Shah, S. (2004) 'India "losing ground to UK" in battle of the call centres', *Independent*, 10 April

Sharma, A. K. and Talwar, B. (2004) 'Business excellence enshrined in Vedic (Hindu) philosophy', *Singapore Management Review*, Vol.26 Issue 1

Simpson, D. and Woodley, T. (2007) 'Organisation and solidarity across frontiers are the future', *Guardian*, 1 May

Spencer, S., Ruhs, M., Anderson, B. and Rogaly, B. (2007) *Migrants' Lives Beyond the Workplace: the experiences of Central and East Europeans in the UK*. Joseph Rowntree Foundation

Stiglitz, J. (2003) *Globalization and its Discontents*. London: Penguin

Swann, C. (2004) 'Sixty years on, and still contentious', *Financial Times*, 29 May

Swyngedouw, E. (2004) 'Globalisation or glocalisation? Networks, territories and rescaling', *Cambridge Review of International Affairs*, Vol.17 No.1, April

Tesco Lotus (2007) 'Tesco Lotus Key Facts', February 2007. www.tescolotus.net/company/keyfacts.asp [accessed 27 April 2007]

Thurow, L. (1999) *Creating Wealth*. London: Nicholas Brealey

Tisdall, S. (2007) 'Confident Turkey looks east, not west', *Guardian*, 26 March

Vanhonacker, W. (2004) 'When good *guanxi* turns bad', *Harvard Business Review*, Vol.82 Issue 4

Venables, T. (2005) 'Multinationals: heroes or villains of the global economy?', *CentrePiece*, Spring

Warren, E. (2007) 'Stars of India', *People Management*, 22 February

Watt, N. (2009) 'Tory leader ditches referendum and backs away from EU "bust-up"', *Guardian*, 5 November

Williams, F. (2007) 'Global foreign investment flows "set to fall to 40%"', *Financial Times*, 19 September

Chapter 7

Abercrombie, N. and Warde, A. (2000) *Contemporary British Society*, 3rd edition. Cambridge: Polity Press

Aldridge, S. (2001) 'Social Mobility: a discussion paper'. London: Cabinet Office, Performance and Innovation Unit

Aldridge, S. (2004) 'Life Chances & Social Mobility: an overview of the evidence'. London: Cabinet Office, Prime Minister's Strategy Unit

Anderson, T. and Metcalfe, H. (2003) *Diversity: stacking up the evidence*. London: CIPD

Bartlett, H. and Peel, N. (2005) 'Healthy ageing in the community', in Andrews, G. and Phillips, D. (eds) *Ageing and Place*. London: Routledge

BBC (2009) 'Glass ceiling blocking top jobs', July. news.bbc.co.uk/1/hi/education/8160052.stm [accessed 22 April 2010]

Blanchflower, D., Saleheen, J. and Shadforth, C. (2007) 'The impact of the recent migration from Eastern Europe on the UK Economy'. Bank of England Working Paper

Blanden, J., Gregg, P. and Machin, S. (2005) 'Social mobility in Britain: low and falling', *CentrePiece*, Spring

Blanden, J. and Gibbons, S. (2006) 'Cycles of disadvantage', *CentrePiece*, Summer

Brindle, D. (1999) 'Northerners heed south's siren call', *Guardian*, 27 August, p3

Business Week (2004) 'America's Bebe Boom', 15 March, pp50–52

Carvel, J. (2003) 'Marriage and family divorced as 41% of children reared in alternative ways', *Guardian*, 8 May

Champion, A. (1993) *Population Matters: the local dimension*. London: Paul Chapman Publishing

Chiu, W., Chan, A., Snape, E. and Redman, T. (2001) 'Age stereotypes and discriminatory attitudes towards older workers: An East–West comparison', *Human Relations*, Vol. 54, No. 5, pp629–661

CIPD (2003a) *Managing the Psychological Contract*, Factsheet (May). London: CIPD

CIPD (2003b) '*Work–Life Balance*', Factsheet (April). London: CIPD

CIPD (2006) *Managing Diversity, Measuring Success*, Change Agenda. London: CIPD

CIPD (2007) *Age and Recruitment*. London: CIPD

CIPD (2010) *Diversity: An overview*, Factsheet (November). London: CIPD

CIPD/KPMG (2005) *Quarterly Labour Market Outlook*, Summer/Autumn survey

Clark, D. (2004) 'Unto him that hath', *Guardian*, 6 August

Coonan, C. (2009) 'China relaxes one-child rule to beat pension crisis', *Independent*, 25 July, p18

Cowan, R. (2004) 'Met harnesses its diversity in the war against crime', *Guardian*, 2 December

Dicken, P. (2003) *Global Shift*. London: Sage

Dorling, D., Rigby, J., Wheeler, B., Ballas, D., Thomas, B., Fahmy, E., Gordon, D. and Lupton, R. (2007) *Poverty, Wealth and Place in Britain 1968 to 2005*. Bristol: Policy Press for the Joseph Rowntree Foundation

Doward, J. (2003) 'Future imperfect as longer lifespan looms', *Observer*, 28 December, p9

Dubner, S. and Levitt, S. (2009) http://freakonomics.blogs.nytimes.com/ [accessed 22 April 2010]

Duncan, G. (2001) 'Pay of business chiefs soars', *Times*, 26 July

Ecofin (2006) 'The impact of ageing on public expenditure: projections for the EU25 member states on pension, health care, long-term care, education and unemployment, 2004–2050'. Brussels: Ecofin

Economist (2004) 'Return of the wrinklies', 17 January, p24

Economist (2006) 'Now we are 300,000,000', 14 October, pp57–58

Economist (2007) 'From cheque books to checking pulses', 14 April, p85

Economist (2009a) 'The people crunch', 17 January, pp56–57

Economist (2009b) 'Go forth and multiply a lot less', 31 October, pp35–38

Ellis, A. (2009) 'UK resident population by country of birth', *Population Trends* 135, Spring 2009, ONS

Fielding, T. (1995) 'Migration and middle class formation in England and Wales 1981–91', in Butler, T. and Savage, M. (eds), *Social Change and the Middle Classes*. London: UCL Press

George, V. and Wilding, P. (1999) *British Society and Social Welfare: towards a sustainable society*. Basingstoke: Macmillan

Giddens, A. (2006) *Sociology*, 5th edition. Cambridge: Polity Press

Goldthorpe, J. (1968–1969) *The Affluent Worker in the Class Structure*, 3 volumes. Cambridge: Cambridge University Press

Haskey, J. (1993) 'Trends in the number of one-parent families in Great Britain', *Population Trends*, 71, pp26–33

Hills, J. (2010) 'Report of the National Equality Panel'. London: Government Equality Office

Hirsh, D. (2006) *What Will it Take to End Child Poverty? Firing on all cylinders*. York: Joseph Rowntree Foundation

Home Office (2007) 'Accession monitoring report' (February)

IFS (2009) 'Have the poor got poorer under Labour?', *IFS Observations*, October. Institute for Fiscal Studies

ITEM Club (2006) 'Spring forecast', Ernst and Young

Jack, I. (2009) 'Onwards and endlessly upwards', *Guardian*, 25 July

Jackson, S. (1998) *Britain's Population*. London: Routledge

Janis, I. (1982) *Groupthink*, 2nd edition. Boston. MA: Houghton Mifflin

Jones, A. (2006) 'Rising to the challenge of diversity'. Work Foundation (January)

Kandola, B. (2009) 'Under the skin', *People Management*, 30 July

Kandola, R. and Fullerton, J. (1994) *Managing the Mosaic*. London: IPD

Kurtz, S. (2004) 'The end of marriage in Scandinavia', *Weekly Standard*, 9, p20

Kyser, J. (2007) '60 million Californians by mid-century', *Los Angeles Times*, 10 July

Labour Market Trends (2009) December, p.42

Lansley, S. (2009) *Life in the Middle*. London: TUC

Lucas, E. (2006) 'Red fades to grey', *Economist*, 27 May, p46

Massey, D. (1984) *Spatial Divisions of labour: Social Structures and the Geography of Production*. Basingstoke: Macmillan

McCrone, A. (1999) 'The pounds and pence of an ageing Britain', *Business Day*, 21 September

McKnight, A. (2000) *Earnings Inequality and Earnings Mobility 1977–1996: the impact of mobility on long term inequality*, Employment Relations Research Series No 8. London: DTI

McSmith, A. (2007) 'Figures show number of eastern Europeans in Britain exaggerated', *Independent*, 20 January, p24

Milburn, A. (2009a) *Fair Success to the Professions*. London: HMSO

Milburn, A. (2009b) 'The UK is an unequal society in which class background too often determines life chances', *Observer*, 19 July

Mulholland, G., Özbilgin, M. and Worman, D. (2005) *Managing Diversity: linking theory and practice to business performance*. London: CIPD

Mullan, P. (2002) *The Imaginary Time Bomb*. London: Tauris

National Statistical Office (2009) www.statistics.gov.uk

Nichiporuk, B. (2000) *The Security Dynamics of Demographic Factors*. Santa Monica, CA: Rand Publishing

Norton, C. (2002) 'Japan bribes mothers in bid for baby boom', *Sunday Times*, 15 September

ONS (2004) 'Distribution of wealth in the UK, Social Trends'. *Table s.26* London ONS

ONS (2006) 'Life Expectancy continues to rise'. www.statistics.gov.uk/cci/nugget.asp?id=168 [accessed 22 April 2010]

ONS (2007) '16% of UK population are over the age of 65'. www.statistics.gov.uk/cci/nugget.asp?ID=949

ONS (2009) 'Migration reaches record high in 2008'. www.statistics.gov.uk/cci

Orton, M. and Rowlingson, K. (2007) *Public Attitudes to Economic Inequality*. York: Joseph Rowntree Foundation

Persaud, J. (2004) 'Carry on working', *People Management*, 29 July, pp36–37

People Management (2009) 'A8 requests down', 12 March, p14

Philpott, J. (2007) 'Britain's eastern European migrant workforce', *Impact*, 19 (May), pp24–27

Polska (2006) Economic Ministry, Poland. www.poland.gov.pl [accessed 12 November 2006]

Poston, D. L. and Bouvier, L. F. (2010) *Population and Society*. Cambridge: Cambridge University Press

Preston, S. H., Heuveline, P. and Guillot, M. (2000) *Demography: measuring and modeling population processes*. Oxford: Blackwell

Rajan, A., Martin, B. and Latham, J. (2003) *Harnessing Workforce Diversity to Raise the Bottom Line*. London: London Resource Group Centre

Roberts, I. (2006) 'Taking age out of the workforce', *Work, Employment and Society*, vol. 20 No. 1, pp67–86

Ross, R. and Schneider, R. (1992) *From Equality to Diversity – a business case for equal opportunities*. London: Pitman

Salt, J. (2006) 'Current trends in Internal Migration in Europe', Migrant Research Unit, University College London

Smallwood, C. (2003) 'People power rings changes', *Sunday Times*, 10 August

Smallwood, C. (2006) '"Reserve army"' can defuse demographic time bomb', *Sunday Times*, 20 August

Smedley, T. (2008) 'And now for the good news', *People Management*, 6 March, pp25–30

Social Trends (2004)

Social Trends (2009)

Sparrow, A. (2009) 'Gordon Brown launches package of measures to boost social mobility', *Guardian*, 13 January

Stewart, E. (2007) 'Apology over wrong migration statistics from Home Secretary', *Guardian*, 30 October

Stilwell, J., Rees, P. and Boden, P. (1992) *Migration Processes and Patterns, Vol. 2: Population Redistribution in the UK*. London: Belhaven

Sunday Times (2007) 'Russians told: have a baby and win a fridge', 19 August, p23

Sunderland, R. (2009) 'Women still face a steep climb to the top table', *Observer*, 23 August

Sutton Trust (2007) *The Educational Backgrounds of 500 Leading Figures*

Tatli, A., Özbilgin, M., Worman, D. and Mulholland, G. (2005) *Managing Diversity; Measuring Success*. London: CIPD

Tarver, J. (1996) *The Demography of Africa*. Praeger Publishing

Taylor, W., Piasecka. A. and Worman, D. (2005) *Managing Diversity: learning by doing*. London: CIPD

Toynbee, P. (2009) 'Harman's law is Labour's biggest idea for 11 years', *Guardian*, 13 January

UNFPA (United Nations Population Fund) (2006) *State of World Population* unfpa.org/swp/2006 [accessed 22 April 2010]

United Nations (2005) *Report on World Fertility Rates at 2003*. New York: United Nations

United Nations (2009) *World Population Prospects*. Department of Economics and Social Affairs

Wallace, P. (2001) *Agequake*. London: Nicholas Brealey

Watts, R. (2008) 'Retired staff outstrip serving firemen', *Sunday Times*, 26 October, p12

Whitehead, T. (2008) 'Benefits of migrant labour "overstated"', *Telegraph*, 1 April, p14

Woodhead, M. (2004) 'Exodus heralds end of Schoder's IT dream', *Sunday Times*, 17 November

Woronoff, T. (1996) *Japan as Anything but Number 1*. New York: Macmillan

Young, M. (1958) *The Rise of the Meritocracy*. Harmondsworth: Penguin

Chapter 8

Arkin, A. (2002) 'The package to India', *People Management*, 24 January, pp34–36

Arlidge, J. (2009) 'Are our heads in the cloud?' *Sunday Times Magazine*, 9 August, pp42–45

Carr, N. (2008) *The Big Switch – rewiring the world from Edison to Google*. New York: Norton

Chrisafis, A. (2009) 'Stress and worker suicides mean the future's not bright at Orange', *Guardian*, 19 September, p9

Coyle, D. and Quah, D. (2004) *Getting the Measure of the New Economy*. London: The Work Foundation

Davey, J. (2009) 'Every little bit of data helps Tesco rule detail'. *Sunday Times Business*, 4 October, p7

Economist (2000) 'Communication advances', 23 September

Economist (2004) 'Salad days', 6 November, pp38–39

Economist (2007) 'Easy on the eyes', 7 April, pp85–86

Elias, P. (2006) 'Robot birth simulator used in med schools', Associated Press. www.Livescience.com/robots

Flexible Working (2000) 'Case: Baxter International', October, pp11–14

Foster, S. (2010) 'In light of the increasingly integral role of the internet in the workplace, how do HR professionals best approach the monitoring and policing of its usage?' Unpublished master's dissertation, University of Bedfordshire

Freeman, C. (1987) *Technology Policy and Economic Performance: lessons from Japan*. London: Pinter Publishers

Glover, C. (2004) 'Tomorrow's world', *People Management*, 26 February, pp40–41

Green, F. (2002) 'Why has work effort become more intense? Conjectures and evidence about effort-based technical change and other stories'. University of Kent Discussion Papers in Economics (July)

Hall, L. (2004) 'Where to draw the line', *Personnel Today*, 1 June

Hall, P. and Preston, P. (1988) *The Carrier Wave: new information technology and the geography of innovation, 1846–2003*. London: Unwin Hyman

Hansen, N., Nohria, N. and Tierney, T. (1999) 'What's your strategy for managing knowledge?', *Harvard Business Review*, March–April, pp106–116

Investor Today (2009) 'Boss at suicide firm France Telecom asks to go', 5 October

Jensen, R. (2007) 'The Digital Provide: information technology, market performance and welfare in the south Indian fisheries sector', *Quarterly Journal of Economics*, August

Kahn, H. (1967) *The Year 2000*. London: Macmillan

Levinson, M. (2006) *The Box: how the shipping container made the world smaller and the world economy bigger*. Princeton, NJ: Princeton University Press

Martin, G. (2005) *Technology and People Management*. London: CIPD

Nathan, M., Carpenter, G., Roberts, S. (2003) *Getting By, Not Getting On: technology in UK workplaces*. London: The Work Foundation

Parry, E., Tyson, S., Selbie, D. and Leighton, R. (2007) *HR and Technology: impact and advantages*. London: CIPD

Peacock, L. (2007) 'Location beats pay as a top factor in attracting people to work in UK call centres', *Personnel Today*, 14 May

People Management (1998) 'Telephone screening at Standard Life', 28 May, p11

People Management (2009) 'Beds and Bars Employee Console', 24 September, p26

Pethokoukis, J. (2004) 'Meet your new co-worker', *Money and Business*, 3 July

PricewaterhouseCoopers (2000) 'HR in e-commerce survey' London: Pricewaterhouse Coopers

Prusack, L. (1997) *Knowledge in Organisations*. Boston, MA: Butterworth-Heinemann

Reddington, M., Williamson, M. and Withers, M. (2005) *Transforming HR: creating value through people*. Oxford: Elsevier

Reilly, P. (2000) *HR Shared Services and the Realignment of HR*, Institute of Employment Studies Report 368

Scarborough, H. and Carter, C. (2007) *Investigating Knowledge Management*. London: CIPD

Scarborough, H., Swan, J. and Preston, J. (1999) *Knowledge Management and the Learning Organisation: a review of the literature*. London: CIPD

Schumpeter, J. (1976) *Capitalism, Socialism and Democracy*. London: Routledge

Smith, D. (2004) 'Prophet warning', *People Management*, 23 December, pp24–29

Sparrow, P., Brewster, C. and Harris, H. (2004) *Globalizing Human Resource Management*. London: Routledge

Stewart, T. (2001) *The Wealth of Knowledge: intellectual capital in the 21st century organisation*. London: Nicholas Brealey

Storey, J. and Quintas, P. (2001) 'Knowledge management and HRM', in Storey, J. (ed) *Human Resource Management: a critical text*. London: Thomson Learning

Stredwick, J. and Ellis, S. (2005) *Flexible Working Practices*. London: CIPD

Subramanian, S. (2004) 'Biotechnology and society', chennaionline [accessed 24 November]

Taylor, R. (2004) 'Skills and innovation in modern Britain'. Economic and Social Research Council. Future of Work Programme seminar series

Tomlinson, H. and Evans, R. (2005) 'Tesco stocks up on inside knowledge of shoppers lives', *Guardian*, 20 September, p12

Ulrich, D. (1998) *Human Resource Champions*. Boston, MA: Harvard Business School Press

Chapter 9

Accountability Primer: Sustainability (nd). www.progressio.org.uk/shared_asp_files [accessed 23 April 2010]

Aldred, J. (2007) 'Q&A: Plastic bags', *Guardian*, 13 November

Argenti, J. (1993) *Your Organisation, What Is It For? Challenging traditional organisational aims.* Maidenhead: McGraw-Hill

Barkham, P. (2007) 'World asks town that banned the plastic bag: how can we do it too?', *Guardian*, 12 May

Billington, R. (2003) *Living Philosophy: an introduction to moral thought*, 3rd edition. London: Routledge

BITC (2000) 'Putting your heart into it: purpose and values' (Report of the Business Impact Task Force 2000). www.bitc.org.uk

Bowers, S. (2009) 'Kraft chews on a sweeter deal for Cadbury', *Observer*, 8 November

Brinkmann, J. and Ims, K. (2003) 'Good intentions aside: drafting a functionalist look at codes of ethics', *Business Ethics: A European Review*, Vol.12 No.3

Butler, S. (2006) 'Would you like a bag with that, Madam?', *Times,* 7 October

Carroll, A. B. (1979) 'A three-dimensional model of corporate social performance', *Academy of Management Review*, 4

Carroll, A. B. (1990) 'Principles of business ethics: their role in decision making and an initial consensus', *Management Review*, Vol.28 No.8

Carroll, A. B. (1991) 'The pyramid of corporate social responsibility: towards the moral management of organizational stakeholders', *Business Horizons*, July–August

Caulkin, S (2003) 'Ethics and profits do mix', *Observer*, 20 April

Charkham, J. (1994) *Keeping Good Company: a study of corporate governance in five countries.* Oxford: Oxford University Press

CIPD (2003a) *Code of Professional Conduct and Disciplinary Procedures*. London: CIPD

CIPD (2003b) *Corporate Responsibility and HR's Role*. London: CIPD

CIPD (2009) *Corporate Social Responsibility*. London: CIPD

CIPD Research Insight (2009) *Shared Purpose and Sustainable Organisational Performance*. London: CIPD

Collins, C. and Porras, J. (2000) *Built to Last: successful habits of visionary companies*, 3rd edition. London: Random House

Connock, S. and Johns, T. (1995) *Ethical Leadership*. London: CIPD

Cowe, R. (2004) 'Commanding heights', *Guardian*, 8 November

Crane, A. and Matten, D. (2007) *Business Ethics: managing corporate citizenship and sustainability in the age of globalisation*, 2nd edition. Oxford: Oxford University Press

Davies, G. and Smith, H. (2007) 'Natural resources', *People Management*, 8 March

Deal, T. and Kennedy, A. (1990) 'Values: the core of the culture', in Campbell, A. and Tawadey, K., *Mission and Business Philosophy*. Oxford: Butterworth-Heinemann

De George, R. T. (1999) *Business Ethics*, 5th edition. New Jersey: Prentice Hall

DesJardins, J (2007) *Business, Ethics and the Environment*. New Jersey: Pearson/Prentice Hall

Dore, R. (2006) 'Japan's shareholder revolution', *CentrePiece*, Winter 2006/07

Drucker, P. (1990) 'What is "business ethics?"', in Campbell, A. and Tawady, K., *Mission and Business Philosophy*. Oxford: Butterworth-Heinemann

DTI (2002) *Business and Society: corporate social responsibility*

Economist (2006) 'Voting with your trolley', 9 December

Economist (2007) 'Plastics of evil', *Economist* (US), 31 March

Elliott, L. (2009) 'Brown is right: rich western banks must pay for developing nations to go green', *Guardian*, 9 November

European Commission (2001) *Promoting a European Framework for Corporate Social Responsibility*'

Explore Worldwide (2004) 2004–2005 brochure

Farnham, D. (1999) *Managing in a Business Context*. London: CIPD

Finch, J. and Allen, K. (2006) 'Tesco offers carrot to reduce use of plastic carrier bags', *Guardian*, 5 August

Fisher, C. and Lovell, A. (2006) *Business Ethics and Values: individual, corporate and international perspectives*, 2nd edition. Harlow: FT/Prentice Hall

Foot, D. (2004) 'Easter Island: a case study in non-sustainability', *Greener Management International*, Vol.48, Winter 2004–5

Friedman, M. (1962) *Capitalism and Freedom*. Chicago: Chicago University Press

Friedman, M. (1970) 'The social responsibility of business is to increase its profits', *New York Times Magazine*, 13 September

Golzen, G. (2001) 'What's the big idea?', *Global HR*, September

Harrison, R. (2002) *Learning and Development*, 3rd edition. London: CIPD

Hastings, M. (2007) 'Binge flying is just the beginning. The only way to stop this is a severe tax', *Guardian*, 7 May

Henderson, D. (2001) 'Misguided virtue: false notions of corporate social responsibility', Institute of Economic Affairs. www.iea.org.uk [accessed 24 August 2007]

Hickman, L. (2009) 'Do we really need to ban the bag?', *Guardian*, 11 August

Hoffman, M. (1990) 'What is necessary for corporate moral excellence?', in Campbell, A. and Tawady, K., *Mission and Business Philosophy*. Oxford: Butterworth-Heinemann

Home Office (1999) *The Stephen Lawrence Inquiry: report of an inquiry by Sir William Macpherson of Cluny*. London: The Stationery Office

Industrial Relations Services (1999) *IRS Employment Trends 675*, March

Johnson, G. and Scholes, K. (1997) *Exploring Corporate Strategy*, 4th edition. Hemel Hempstead: Prentice Hall

Johnson, G., Scholes, K. and Whittington, R. (2004) *Exploring Corporate Strategy*, 7th edition. Harlow: Pearson

Kearns, P. and Ingate, K. (2001) 'Should the CIPD strike off poor practitioners?', *Personnel Today*, 23 October

Kelly, E. (1999) 'Corporate citizenship costs more than cash', *Professional Manager*, January

Lawton, A. (1998). *Ethical Management for the Public Services*. Buckingham: OUP

Lewis, J. (2002) 'Testing time', *Personnel Today*, 9 April

Maitland, A. (2003) 'Profits from the righteous path', *Financial Times*, 3 April

Mathiason, N. and Treanor, J. (2009) 'Brown in secret push to sell "Tobin tax" to City', *Guardian*, 10 November

McKee, G. (2003) 'Managing human nature: leadership lessons from Venice', *Leader to Leader*, April

Milner, M. (2007) 'Private equity is the workers' friend, CBI told', *Guardian*, 27 November

Monbiot, G. (2001) 'Superstores brand us to ensure we belong to them', *Guardian*, 31 July

Personnel Today (2004) 'CSR help is at hand', 27 July

Reitz, J., Wall, J. and Love, M. S. (1998) 'Ethics in negotiation: oil and water or good lubrication? *Business Horizons*, May–June

Richards, D. and Gladwin, T. (1999) 'Sustainability metrics for the Business Enterprise', *Environmental Quality Management*, Spring

Schwartz, M. S. (2001) 'A code of ethics for corporate codes of ethics', *Journal of Business Ethics* 41

Simms, A. (2009) 'Questions for a new world', *Guardian*, 17 November

Snell, R. (1999) 'Managing ethically', in Fulop, L. and Linstead, S., *Management: a critical text*. Basingstoke: Macmillan

Snoddy, R. and Hopkins, N. (2003) 'BSkyB responds to investors' disquiet', *Times*, 15 November

Stratton, A. (2009) 'MPs' expenses: Christopher Kelly outlines reforms'. www.guardian.co.uk [accessed 11 November 2009]

Summers, D. (2009) 'British ex-MEP Tom Wise faces jail after £36,000 expenses scam'. www.guardian.co.uk [accessed 11 November 2009]

Targett, S. (2004). 'Is good governance good value?', *Financial Times*, 17 April

Tassell, T. (2003) 'Keeping BSkyB firmly in the family', *Financial Times*, 8 November

TUC (2007) 'GreenWorkplaces Project 2006–7: objectives and outcomes report'. London: TUC

Turner, B. (2006) 'Plastic bags are much the lesser evil', *The Grocer*, 11 February

Watt, N. and Stratton, A. (2009) 'Anger and anarchy among MPs at extent of Legg's demands'. www.guardian.co.uk, 14 October [accessed 11 November 2009]

Watt, N., Taylor, M., McVeigh, K., Topping, A., Siddique, H. and Sturcke, J. (2009) 'MPs' expenses: what the latest information reveals about key figures'. www.guardian.co.uk, 18 June [accessed 11 November 2009]

Wintour, P. (2007) 'Brown sets tough targets for reducing carbon', *Guardian*, 20 November

Chapter 10

Air Transport World (2006a) 'Ryanair: ryanair.com', July

Air Transport World (2006b) 'The world's top 25 airlines', July

Ansoff, H. I. (1965) *Corporate Strategy*. Harmondsworth: Penguin

Armstrong, M. (1999) *Managing Activities*. London: CIPD

Bagnall, S. (1995) 'Kwik Save slips as price war bites', *Times*, 3 November

BBC2 (2007) 'Working Lunch', 19 September

Beach, S. (1980) *Personnel*. London: Macmillan

Bloomsbury (2007a) 'Summary of corporate milestones'. www.bloomsbury-ir.co.uk [accessed 8 August 2007]

Bloomsbury (2007b) 'Financial results'. www.bloomsbury-ir.co.uk [accessed 8 August 2007]

Bloomsbury (2007c), 'Press release – record breaking first 24 hours of *Harry Potter and the Deathly Hallows*', 23 July. www.bloomsbury-ir.co.uk [accessed 8 August 2007]

Bosalie, P. and Dietz, G. (2003) 'Commonalities and contradictions in research on HRM and performance', *Academy of Management Conference*, August

Bowman, C. and Faulkner, D. (1996) *Competitive and Corporate Strategy*. Homewood, IL: Irwin

Boxall, P. and Purcell, J. (2008) *Strategic Human Resource Management*. Basingstoke: Palgrave-Macmillan

Bridges, W. and Mitchell, S. (2000) 'Leading transition: a new model for change', *Leader to Leader* 16, Spring

Bruce, A. (2001) 'This M&S is Simply Food', *The Grocer*, 21 July

Bruce, A. (2003) 'Simply Food set to grow fast', *The Grocer*, 24 May

Burke, W. (1980) *Organisation Development*. Toronto: Little Brown

Burnes, B. (2004) *Managing Change: a strategic approach to organisational dynamics*, 4th edition. London: Pitman

Business Week (2006) 'Walmart with wings', 27 November

Butler, V. (1985) *Organisation and Management*. London: Prentice Hall

Cadbury website (2007) www.cadbury.co.uk [accessed 18 June 2007]

CIPD (2004) *Change Management*, Factsheet. www.cipd.co.uk [accessed 28 August 2007]

Collinson, P. and Seager, A. (2007) 'Northern Rock crisis: call to City grandees that threw lifeline to drowning bank', *Guardian*, 15 September

Cope, N. (1996) 'Pile 'em high, sell 'em cheap, take £1bn', *Independent* 19 August

Cope, N. (1999) 'Somerfield back on the discount shelf', *Independent*, 26 July

Crainer, S. and Dearlove, D. (2003) 'Windfall economics', *Business Strategy Review*, Vol.14 Issue 4, Winter

Croggon, P. (2007) 'Letter to the editor', *Times*, 17 September

Danford, A., Richardson, M., Stewart, P., Tailby, S. and Upchurch, M. (2004) 'High performance work systems and workplace partnership: a case study of aerospace workers', *New Technology, Work and Employment*, Vol. 19 No. 1, pp14–29.

Davies, G. (2007) 'The roots of moral hazard', *Guardian*, 15 September

Doeringer, P., Lorenz, E. and Terkla, D. (2003) 'The adoption and diffusion of high performance management: lessons from Japanese multinationals in the West', *Cambridge Journal of Economics*, Vol. 27

Done, K. (2007) 'Ryanair orders 27 Boeing jets', *Financial Times*, 31 May

Duncan, G. and Webster, P. (2007) 'MPC founding member comes out swinging against Bank's bailout decision', *Times,* 15 September

Durston, J. (2006) 'Food sales drive group recovery at upbeat M&S', *The Grocer*, 27 May

Elliott, V. (2007) 'Cadbury fined £1m for selling contaminated chocolate bars', *Times*, 17 July

Felsted, A. (2003) 'The Dublin-based airline has become a leading force in European aviation', *Financial Times*, 4 November

Finch, J. (2000) 'No one wants to buy Kwik Save', *Guardian,* 19 April

Finch, J. (2005) '£1.1bn Somerfield takeover agreed', *Guardian*, 15 October

Finch, J. (2007) 'Integration hasn't gone as well as we'd have hoped', *Guardian*, 6 July

Fordyce, T. (2005) '10 years since Bosman', BBC Sport. news.bbc.co.uk/sport1/hi/football [accessed 14 October 2009]

Furnham, A. and Gunter, B. (1993) *Corporate Assessment*. London: Routledge

Gilchrist, S. (1993a) 'Supermarkets face cut-price threats', *Times*, 26 January

Gilchrist, S. (1993b) 'Kwik Save warns price war will hit profit growth', *Times*, 25 November

Guest, D. (1998) 'Combine harvest', *People Management*, 29 October

Hamel, G. (1996) 'Strategy as revolution', *Harvard Business Review*, July–August

Hamel, G. and Prahalad, C. K. (1994) *Competing for the Future*. Boston, MA: Harvard Business School Press

Hamson, L. (2004) 'Marks's quality is its key advantage', *The Grocer*, 6 November

Hamson, L. (2005) 'Simply ideal food for UK travel hubs', *The Grocer*, 30 April

Hollinger, P. (1998) 'Somerfield, Kwik Save hope that size will matter', *Financial Times*, 17 February

Hughes, C. and Tighe, C. (2007) 'Impregnable self-belief takes a battering', *Financial Times*, 15 September

Huselid, M. (1995) 'The impact of human resource management practices on turnover, productivity and corporate financial performance', *Academy of Management Journal*, 38, pp400–422

Johnson, G., Scholes, K. and Whittington, R. (2004) *Exploring Corporate Strategy*, 7th edition. Harlow: Pearson

Jordan, D. (2007) 'Time comes for Harry to fly to the rescue', *Times*, 4 April

Just-food (2009) 'UK: M&S needs to offload Simply Food – analyst'. www.justfood.com/article.aspx?id=105667, 3 March [accessed 22 November 2009]

Kim, K., Nam, D. and Stimpert, J. (2004) 'Testing the applicability of Porter's generic strategies in the digital age: a study of Korean cyber malls', *Journal of Business Strategies*, Vol.21 No.1

Kotter, J. (1995) 'Leading change – why transformation efforts fail', *Harvard Business Review*, March–April

Legge, K. (2001) 'Silver bullet or spent round? Assessing the meaning of the "high commitment management/performance relationship"', in Storey, J. (ed) *Human Resource Management: a critical text*. London: Thomson Learning

Leroux, M. and Walsh, D. (2009) 'Marks & Spencer to close 27 stores and cut 1000 jobs', *Times*, 8 January

Lewin, K. (1943) 'Defining the "Field at a Given Time"', *Psychological Review*, Vol.50

Lord, R. (1990) 'A measure of corporate success', *Times,* 30 July

MacLeod, D. and Clarke, N.(2009) *Engaging for Success, Enhancing Performance through Employee Engagement*, Department of Business, Innovation and Skills, Crown Copyright

McCann, J. (2004) 'Organizational effectiveness: changing concepts for changing environments', *Human Resource Planning*, Vol.27 Issue 1

McCarthy, B. (2004) 'How to manage organisational change', *People Management*, 9 December

Marchington, M. (2001) 'Employee involvement at work', in Storey, J. (ed), *Human Resource Management: a critical text*. London: Thomson

Marchington, M. and Grugulis, I. (2000) '"Best Practice" human resource management: perfect opportunity or dangerous illusion?', *International Journal of Human Resource management*, Vol. 11 No. 6, pp1104–1124

Marchington, M. and Wilkinson, A. (2008) *Human Resource Management at Work*, 4th edition. London: CIPD

Millward. N., Bryson, A. and Forth, J. (2000) *All Change at Work: British industrial relations, 1980 to 1998 as portrayed by the Workplace Industrial Relations Survey Series*. London: Routledge

Milmo, D. (2007b) 'Ryanair introduces £4 check in fee as latest surcharge to slash costs', *Guardian*, 25 August

Milmo, D. (2009) 'EasyJet warns of tough winter ahead after profits decline by £80m', *Guardian*, 18 November

Mintzberg, H. (1994) *The Rise and Fall of Strategic Planning*. Hemel Hempstead: Prentice Hall

O'Connor, R. (2009) 'Marks & Spencer may add Simply Food to the menu of continental expansion', *Times*, 12 November

Pearson, G. (nd) 'University of Liverpool FIH Factsheet: the Bosman case, EU law and the transfer system'. www.liv.ac.uk/footballindustry/bosman.html [accessed 14 October 2009]

Peters, T. (1985) *Thriving on Chaos*. New York: Macmillan

Peters, T. and Waterman, R. (1982) *In Search of Excellence*. New York: Harper & Row

Porter, M. (1980) *Competitive Strategy: techniques for analysing industries and competition*. New York: The Free Press

Porter, M. (1985) *Competitive Advantage: creating and sustaining superior performance*. New York: The Free Press

Prahalad, C. K. and Hamel, G. (1990) 'The core competence of the corporation', *Harvard Business Review*, May–June

Pugh, D. S. (1978) 'Understanding and managing organisational change', *London Business School Journal*, Vol.3 No. 2

Purcell, J. (1999) 'Best Practice and Best Fit: chimera or cul-de-sac?', *Human Resource Management Journal*, Vol. 9 No. 3 pp26–41

Purcell, J., Kinnie, N. and Hutchinson, S. (2003) 'Open minded', *People Management*, 15 May, pp30–33

Quinn, J. (1980) *Strategies for Change: logical incrementalism*. Homewood, IL: Irwin

Ramsey, H., Scholarios, D. and Harley, B. (2000) 'Employees and high performance work systems: testing inside the Black Box', *British Journal of Industrial Relations*, Vol. 38 No. 4, pp501–531

Reading Post (2009) 'M&S Simply Food to open at the Royal Berkshire Hospital', 18 November

Ridgeway, C. and Wallace, B. (1994) *Empowering Change: the role of people management*. London: IPD

Rigby, E. (2006) 'Somerfield makes a Kwik sale', *Financial Times*, 25 February

Ryanair (2003) 'Economy and Mobility: the Ryanair Business Model'. www.ryanair.com

Ryanair (2007) www.ryanair.com/site/EN/about [accessed 18 July 2007]

Senge, P. (1990) *The Fifth Discipline*. London: Century Business

Shelley, T. (2007) 'Bloomsbury looks for magic after Potter', *Financial Times*, 4 April

Sivell, G. and Dolan, L. (1995) 'Supermarkets shape up food price fighters', *Times*, 10 January

Stacey, R. (1991) *The Chaos Frontier: creative strategic control for business*. Oxford: Butterworth-Heinemann

Stacey, R. (1993) *Strategic Management and Organisational Dynamics*. Harlow: Pearson Education

Starmer-Smith, C. (2006) 'Disabled groups attack 33p Ryanair levy', *Daily Telegraph*, 13 May

Stevenson, H. H. (1989) 'Defining corporate strengths and weaknesses', in Bowman, C. and Asch, D. (eds), *Readings in Strategic Management*. Basingstoke: Macmillan

Stevenson, T. (1996) 'Kwik Save losing the bean war', *Independent*, 3 May

Swart, J., Kinnie, N. and Purcell, J. (2003) *People and Performance in Knowledge-intensive Firms*. London: CIPD

Tait, N. and Wiggins, J. (2007) 'Cadbury in record £1m fine for unsafe chocolate', *Financial Times*, 17 July

Tempus (1993) 'Kwik Save', *Times*, 30 April

The Grocer (2003) 'Flexible ranging for Simply Food', 8 November 2003

The Grocer (2006a) 'Fitting right in to the locality', 11 February

The Grocer (2006b) 'BP trial with M&S said to be driving spend footfall', 1 April

The Grocer (2007) 'Simply Food roars in forecourt drive', 26 May

Thompson, M. (2000) *The Competitive Challenge: Final Report; The bottom line benefits of strategic human resource management*. Society of British Aerospace Companies

Thompson, M. and Martin, F. (2005) *Strategic Management: awareness and change*, 5th edition. London: Thomson

Tomlinson, H. (2001) 'Stop me and buy a Ben & Jerry's', *Independent on Sunday*, 9 December

Walton, J. (1999) *Strategic Human Resource Development*. London: FT/Prentice Hall

Watson, E. (2004) 'Food standalones will continue', *The Grocer*, 17 July

West, M. and Patterson, M. (1998) 'Profitable personnel', *People Management*, 8 January, pp28–31

Wickens, P. (1987) *The Road to Nissan: flexibility, quality, teamwork.* Basingstoke: Palgrave-Macmillan

Williams, R. (2007) 'Cadbury fined £1m for salmonella offences', *Guardian*, 17 July

Wood, P. (1995) 'The four pillars of human resource management: are they connected?' *Human Resource Management Journal*, Vol. 5 No. 5, pp49–59

Wood, W. and Finch, J. (2009) 'Borders failed as Friends moved on', *Guardian*, 27 November

Workers' Educational Association (WEA) in Northern Ireland (nd) 'Mission Statement and WEA Values'. www.wea-ni.com

Wray, R. (2006) 'Bloomsbury's profits drop without Potter's magic this year', *Guardian*, 12 December

Chapter 11

Asthana, A. and Campbell, D. (2009) 'The worst NHS wards ... where safety is a lottery', *Observer*, 29 November

Boseley, S. (2009) 'Junior doctors make errors in 8% of prescriptions', *Guardian*, 3 December

Bowcott, O. (2009a) 'Hospital condemned over cleanliness gave itself top marks', *Guardian*, 28 November

Bowcott, O. (2009b) 'Swine flu surge in children may cause critical care bed crisis', *Guardian*, 19 November

Brockett, J. (2009) 'Working time rules are harming patients, say surgeons', *People Management Online*, 12 October

Carlisle, D. (2009) 'One year on: Darzi's long and winding road', *Health Service Journal*, 25 June

Department of Health (2008a) *High Quality Care for All*

Department of Health (2008b) *Human Rights in Healthcare: a short introduction*

Department of Health (2008c) *Human Rights in Healthcare: a framework for local action*, 2nd edition

Department of Health (2009) *High Quality Care for All: our journey so far*

Dixon, J. (2001) 'Transforming the NHS: what chance for the new government?', *Economic Affairs*, December

Evans, T. and Evans, H. (2002) 'Back to the future: towards a better state of healthcare', *Economic Affairs*, March

Ford, S. (2009) 'Working Time Directive tsar says the 48-hour week is good for nursing', *Nursing Times*, 2 June

Gage, H. (2001a) 'NHS malaise: diagnosis and treatment options', *Economic Affairs*, December

Gage, H. (2001b) 'Editorial: healthcare reform', *Economic Affairs*, December

Harlow Star (2009) 'Clean bill of health for maternity unit', 3 December

Holland, S. (2010) 'Hospital's Filipino operation', *Herts and Essex Observer*, 4 February

Hope, J. (2009) 'EU ban limiting junior doctors to 48 hour working week lifted over public health concerns', *Mail Online*, 16 October [accessed 7 December 2009]

House, J. (2009) 'Calling time on doctors' working hours', *The Lancet*, 13 June

Medical Negligence Online (2009) 'NHS: Negligence – 16 November 2009'. http://www.medneg.com/News/NewsDetail.aspx?Month=11&Year=2009#News1647 [accessed 22 April 2010]

NHS (2009a) 'About the NHS'. www.nhs.uk/NHSEngland/aboutnhs [accessed 20 November 2009]

NHS (2009b) 'History of choice'. http://www.nhs.uk/Tools/Documents/The%20history%20of%20 choice.htm [accessed 20 November 2009]

NHS Employers (2009) 'Working Time Directive: frequently asked questions for Employer implementation Teams' (September)

NHS Litigation Authority (2008) 'Delegate workbook; Preparing for an Assessment'

NHS Litigation Authority (2009) 'The NHS Litigation Authority Factsheet 1: background information'

OECD (2009) 'OCED Health Data 2009 – Frequently Requested Data'. http://www.oecd.org/document/16/0,3343,en_2649_34631_2085200_1_1_1_1,00.html [accessed 26 April 2010]

Rickman, N. and Fenn, P. (2001) 'Clinical negligence in the UK: throwing the baby out with the bathwater?', *Economic Affairs*, December

Stationery Office (2009) 'Government Response to the House of Lords Science and Technology Committee Report on Pandemic Influenza – 3rd Report of Session 2008–09'

Westwood, N. (2006) 'What can the NHS learn from "the lean machine"? Toyota visit, 2nd May 2006', NHS Institute for Innovation and Improvement

Westwood, N., James-Moore, M. and Cooke, M. (2007) 'Going lean in the NHS', NHS Institute for Innovation and Improvement

Index